Timber Construction Manual

HERZOG
NATTERER
SCHWEITZER
VOLZ
WINTER

Birkhäuser
Basel · Boston · Berlin

Edition Detail
Munich

The original German edition of this book was conceived and developed by **DETAIL**, Review of Architecture.

Authors:
Thomas Herzog, Prof., Dr. (Univ. Rome), Dipl.-Ing., architect
Munich Technical University, D (Chapter 1, 2, 3, 6)

Julius Natterer, Prof., Dipl.-Ing., structural engineer
Swiss Federal Institute of Technology, Lausanne, CH (Chapter 4, 5)

Roland Schweitzer, Prof., architect
Ecole d'Architecture de Paris-Tolbiac, F (Chapter 1, 6)

Michael Volz, Prof., Dipl.-Ing., architect
Frankfurt Technical College, D (Chapter 1, 2, 3, 6)

Wolfgang Winter, Prof., DDI, structural engineer
Vienna Technical University, A (Chapter 4, 5)

Editorial services:
Friedemann Zeitler

Drawings:
Kathrin Draeger

Translators (German/English):
Gerd Söffker, Philip Thrift; Hannover

A CIP catalogue record for this book is available from the Library of Congress, Washington, D.C., USA

Bibliographic information published by Die Deutsche Bibliothek
Die Deutsche Bibliothek lists this publication in the Deutsche Nationalbibliografie; detailed bibliographic data is available on the Internet at http://dnb.ddb.de.

This book is also available in a German language edition (ISBN 978-3-7643-6984-2).

First, corrected reprint 2008

© 2004, English translation of the fourth revised German edition
Birkhäuser Verlag AG
Basel · Boston · Berlin
P.O. Box 133, CH-4010 Basel, Switzerland
Part of Springer Science+Business Media

Printed on acid-free paper produced from chlorine-free pulp. TCF ∞

Layout and production: Peter Gensmantel, Cornelia Kohn, Andrea Linke, Roswitha Siegler

Printed in Germany

ISBN 978-3-7643-7025-1

9 8 7 6 5 4 3 2 1   www.birkhauser.ch

With contributions by:

Gerd Hauser, Prof. Dr.-Ing.
Kassel University, D

Gerhard Wagner, Dipl.-Ing.
Wiesbaden, D

Gerd Wegener, Prof. Dr. Dr. habil. Dr. h.c.
Munich Technical University, D

Tobias Wiegand, Dipl.-Ing.
Studiengemeinschaft Holzleimbau e.V.,
Wuppertal, D

Helmut Zeitter, Dipl.-Ing.
Wiesbaden, D

Bernhard Zimmer, Dr. Dipl.-Fw.
Holztechnikum Kuchl/Salzburg, A

Assistants:
Inga von Campenhausen,
Yann Benoit, Johannes Natterer, Denis Pflug
Plates: Verena Herzog-Loibl

Editorial assistance:
Susanne Bender-Grotzeck, Manuel Zoller

CAD assistants:
Bettina Brecht, Norbert Graeser, Marion Griese, Peter Lingenfelser,
Emese Köszegi, Nicola Kollmann, Elisabeth Krammer, Andrea Saiko

Assistants on previous German editions:
Arbeitsgemeinschaft Holz e. V., Dusseldorf, D,
Efrain Alonso Marbán, Markus Becker, Roland Czernawski, Michael Flach,
Elisabeth Kröhn, Burkhardt Niepelt, Ronald Faust, Hansi Hommel, Ute
Meierhöfer, Konrad Merz, Martin Pampus, Thomas Portmann, Katrin
Zwerch, Gerolf Geisler, Jürgen Graser, Christiane Niepelt, Claudia
Ostermeier, Anton Pittlinger, Oliver Schmidt, Claudia Schüßler-Volz,
students from Biel

Timber Construction Manual

Part 1 Cultural dimensions

- The material
  Tradition and diversity
- Wood as a building material –
  from the beginnings
  to the 19th century

Part 2 Fundamentals

- The anatomy of wood
- Species of wood
- Solid wood and solid
  wood products
- Wood-based products
- Building with wood is
  building for the future
- Development of building
  components
- Construction principles

Part 3 Basis for planning

- Grading and improvement
  of solid timber products
- Protecting wood
- Thermal performance of buildings
- Sound insulation
- Fire protection
- Prefabrication and erection

Part 4 Timber engineering

- The tasks of the architect
- The tasks of the structural
  engineer
- Material variations and cross-
  section forms for components
- Connectors and methods
  of connection
- Stability elements

Part 5 Built examples: structures

Part 6 Built examples: facades

- The diversity of the modern age
- Facades – built examples in detail

Contents

Part 1 Cultural dimensions

Thomas Herzog
The material   8

Tradition and diversity   9
Plates   9

Roland Schweitzer
**Wood as a building material –
from the beginnings
to the 19th century**   24
Prehistory/Greece/Rome   25
Africa/Indonesia   26
Japan/China   27
Europe   28

Part 2 Fundamentals

Michael Volz
The material   31
The tree   31
The trunk   31
Substances   31
Structure   32
Structure of cell walls   32
Anisotropy   32
Oven-dry density   32
Other constituents   32
Thermal aspects   32
Moisture   33

Species of wood   34
Softwoods   34
Hardwoods   36

**Solid wood and
solid wood products**   38
Protecting the wood   38
Building permission, standards and
approvals   38
Behaviour in fire   38
Round sections   38
Sawn solid timber made from
hardwood (LH) and softwood (NH)   38
Solid structural timber (KVH®)   39
Solid timber (MH®)   39
Four-piece beams   39
Duo/Trio beams   40
Glued laminated timber (glulam)   40
Profiled boards   41

Wood-based products   41
Three- and five-ply core plywood   42
Laminated veneer lumber (LVL)
and structural veneer lumber (SVL)   42
Plywood, blockboard, laminboard   43
Oriented strand board (OSB)   44
Particleboards   44
Wood-wool slabs   45
Wood fibreboards   45
Wood fibre insulating boards   46
Plasterboards   46
Cement fibreboards   46

Gerd Wegener, Bernhard Zimmer
**Building with wood
is building for the future**   47
Wood, the renewable raw
material from the Earth's forests   47
Wood, the intelligent material   47
Using wood to protect the climate   48
Building for the future   48
Life cycle assessments   48
Potential for saving energy and
carbon dioxide   49
Utilising timber products at the end of
their life cycle   49
Summary   49

Michael Volz
**Development of building
components**   50

Construction principles   51

Part 3 Basis of planning

Tobias Wiegand
**Grading and improvement
of solid timber products**   55
Conversion   55
Moisture content and drying   55
Machining   55
Grading   55
Fissures   56
Glued joints   56
Timber for carpentry work,
grading conditions to DIN 68365   56
Features of wood according
to DIN EN 942, Jun 1996   57
Grading and allocation of
characteristic values for design   57
Grading features for visual grading
according to the future edition
of DIN 4074 part 1   58

Michael Volz
Protecting wood   60
Risks and risk classes   60
Constructional measures   60
Planning and production   60
Transport, storage and installation   61
Precipitation and moisture
resulting from usage   61
Condensation   61
Chemical wood preservatives   62
Timber components, applications
and risk classes to DIN 68800 pt. 3   62
Wood-based product classes
required according to
DIN 68800 part 2   63
Protecting timber: interactive
actions on timber due to
mechanical, physical, bio-
logical and chemical actions   63

Gerd Hauser
Thermal performance of buildings   64
Weighting individual parameters   64
Requirements of statutory
instruments and standards   64
Energy Economy Act   65
Low-energy buildings   65
The influences of various
parameters using the example
of a low-energy building   66
New air-conditioning systems for
timber structures   67

Gerhard Wagner, Helmut Zeitter
Sound insulation   68
Sound insulation in timber structures   68
Fundamentals, definitions   68
Sound insulation requirements   69
Acoustic behaviour of building
components   69
Methods of analysis for sound
insulation   70

Fire protection   71
Building materials classes   71
Fire resistance   71
Fire protection concepts   72
Building classes   72
Design advice   72
The behaviour of wood in fire   73

Wolfgang Winter
Prefabrication and erection   74
Advantages of prefabrication   74
Rationalisation measures   74
Architects, contractors   74
Planning   74
Transport   74
Prefabrication in multistorey
timber-frame construction   75
Dimensions and joints   75
Connections between elements   75
Erection   75

Part 4 Timber engineering

Julius Natterer
The tasks of the structural engineer 76

Structural engineering **77**
Overview 77
The brief 78
Project planning and draft design 79
Preparing submissions for approval,
  planning of projects 86
Production of tender documents 90
Special services 91
Restoration and refurbishment
  methods 94

Material variations and
  cross-section forms for
  components **96**
Round sections 96
Logs and the resulting
  compound sections 96
Squared logs and the resulting
  compound sections 98
Glued laminated timber (glulam) 100
Outlook 105

Connectors and methods of
  connection **106**
Criteria for designing details 106
Craftsman-type connections
  and connectors 108
Engineered connections 110

Stability elements **124**
Vertical loadbearing systems 124
Vertical loadbearing systems
  at 90° to the primary
  loadbearing system 126
Horizontal and diagonal
  structural systems 130
Stability created by form and
  geometry 136
Stability due to three-dimensional
  structural behaviour 139
Outlook 139

Part 5 Built examples: structures

Julius Natterer, Wolfgang Winter
Structures **140**
Overview 140
Columns 142
Single and multiple linear members 148
Simply-supported beams 154
Continuous beams 176
Beams with pinned splices 184
Cantilevers 186
Articulated linear members 188
Single-pin frames 196
Two-pin frames 198
Three-pin frames 200
Frames 207
Two-pin arches 208
Three-pin frames 212
Suspended structures 218
Plates and slabs 222
Beam grids 232
Lattice beam grids 236
Space frames 241
Folded plates 242
Barrel vaults 244
Lattice barrel vaults 245
Lattice domes 247
Barrel-vault meshes 248
Lattice domes 250
Saddle shells 258
Suspended shells 262
Towers 266
Heavy-duty structures 270
Lightweight structures 271

Part 6 Built examples: facades

Thomas Herzog
The diversity of the modern age **273**
Plates 273

Thomas Herzog, Michael Volz
Facades – built examples in detail **290**
Overview 290
"Gucklhupf", Innerschwand,
  Mondsee, A [6] 292
Sea Ranch, California, USA, [1] 293
Private house, Brasilia, BR [6] 294
Holiday home, Chino, J [1] 295
Temporary café, FIN [2] 296
Temporary arts centre,
  Munich-Neuperlach, D [2] 297
Private house, Hohen Neundorf, D [6] 298
School hall, St Peter, CH [6] 299
"Silo house", Lukasöd, D [1] 300
Holiday home, Vallemaggia, CH [5] 301
Private house Darien,
  Connecticut, USA [4] 302
Detached house, Bernsberg, D [4] 303
Housing and studios, Paris, F [4] 304
House and studio, Deisslingen, D [4] 305
Media centre, Küsnacht, CH [4] 306
Laboratories and offices,
  Würzburg, D [4] 307
Offices, Munich, D [6] 308
Holiday home, Breitbrunn, D [4] 309
Private house, Sumvitg, CH [4] 310
Radio transmission station,
  Brauneck, D [6] 311
Semi-detached houses,
  Ebenhausen, D [6] 312
Youth conference centre,
  Michelrieth, D [6] 313
Garden retreat, Meckenbeuren, D [6] 314
Three houses on hillside,
  Brugg, CH [4] 315
Parish hall, Ebersberg, D [6] 316
Private house, Stuttgart, D [4] 317
Cemetery, Eching, D [6] 318
Terrace houses, Eching, D [6] 319
Semi-detached houses,
  Munich-Solln, D [6] 320
Studio house, Darmstadt, D [7] 321
Private house, Aachen, D [6] 322
Private house, Brest, F [6] 323
"Green" houses, Berlin, D [6] 324
School, Dischingen, D [6] 325
Private house, Regensburg-
  Kumpfmühl, D [6] 326
Youth education centre,
  Windberg, D [7] [8] 327
Private house, Waldmohr, D [6] 329
Semi-detached houses, Pullach, D [6] 331
Clubhouse and equestrian
  sports facility, Ecublens, CH [6] 332
Pavilion, Langenberg Animal Park,
  Langnau am Albis, CH [6] 333
Private house, Cambridge, UK [6] 334
Residential complex,
  Munich-Perlach, D [6] 335
Further education academy,
  Herne, D [6] 336
Youth village, Cieux,
  Haute Vienne, F [6] 337
Holiday home, Fuji-Yoshida, J [6] 338

Private house, Brunswick, D [6] 339
Modular house, Bad Iburg, D [7][8] 340
House and studio, Tsukuba, J [6] 341
Private house, Gmund am
  Tegernsee, D [9] 342
Private house, Glonn-Haslach, D [9] 343
Private house, Allensbach, D [8] 344
Forestry station, Turbenthal, CH [8] 345
Local government offices,
  Starnberg, D [8] 346
Home for the elderly,
  Neuenbürg, D [8] 347
Gallery, Munich, D [8] 348
University building, Wiesbaden, D [8] 349
Multi-storey building, Innsbruck, A [8] 350
Training school for forestry
  workers, Lyss, CH [8] 351
Residential complex,
  Regensburg, D [8] 352
Multi-storey car park, Heilbronn, D [8] 353
Mixed office and residential
  block, Kassel, D [8] 354
High-rise block, Hannover, D [8] 355
Factory building, Gelting, D [8] 356
Sports centre, Brétigny, F [9] 357
Factory building, Reuthe, A [6] 358
Factory building, Bad Münder, D [9] 359
Exhibition pavilion,
  various locations [10] 360
Sports stadium, Odate, J [10] 361
Holiday home, Göd, H [10] 362
Forest culture house, Visegrad, H [10] 363
Administration building,
  observation tower and
  museum, Miskolc, H [10] 364

Structures:
[1] Solid timber sections
[2] Edge-glued elements
[3] Cross-laminated timber
[4] Box-frame and panel construction
[5] Post-and-beam construction
[6] Timber-frame construction
Wood plus other materials:
[7] with masonry
[8] with concrete/reinforced concrete
[9] with steel
[10] Roof constructions

Appendix
Bibliography 366
Subject index 370
Index of architects and engineers 373
Picture credits 375

Part 1   Cultural dimensions

The material

Thomas Herzog

The colour plates on the following pages are the author's subjective selection. Their intention is to give the reader an insight into the universal applicability of wood for artistic and everyday uses, for structures and buildings, all of which are designed and built by humans. The applications in building, otherwise the focal point of this book, have been deliberately broadened here in order to illustrate forms specific to the material. The aim of this is to stimulate new design and structural concepts with a view to solving specific tasks.

Textures and frameworks, calmness and tension become apparent in the details. Surfaces are flat or curved, toroidal or faceted, small- or large-format. The sculpted artistic forms, the body of the rider and the richly differentiated marquetry works, which take their form from their artists' imaginations and can be accepted as artefacts in their own right, juxtaposed with the objects determined to a great extent by function alone, show great exactitude and individuality. The independent large-scale form of the transmission mast with its supreme elegance and lightness is a sharp contrast to the small knife, which in its finely detailed, gently rounded sheath of burr wood fits snugly into the hand. Especially charming are those objects with concave-convex forms that seem to form a unity with our hands, arms and shoulders – like a backrest, a yoke, a rifle. Function and engineering common sense bring a figurative type of charm to the foreground. When corners, transitions and junctions, the transfer and redirection of forces become expressive forms of detail and expose the constructional grammar at the point of maximum concentration.

Contact with the body and fully developed, tried-and-tested purposefulness characterise certain objects. Their plastic quality infuses them with life. Alongside them are architectural jewels that express great skills and have a long tradition in Europe and Central Asia in particular. Commodities, furniture and implements made from wood exploit ideal features typical to the material through their ease of formability and the sympathetic impression that awakens in us the need to touch them.

The scientific qualities important to building design, the ergonomic properties of the objects, the charismatic ageing of this organic material, robustness and elegance are characteristics that represent the perfect complement to the geometrical-architectural rules and principles from the classical, peerless perfection of the Katsura Palace to the possibilities of simple do-it-yourself construction. And in the presence of a superior design allow this part of the material world to become a stimulating but also familiar encounter with wood.

Plate 1 (facing page)

1   St Matthew of Raisio (Master of Lieto), 125 cm high, c. 1340
2, 3   Marquetry on the choir stalls of Bergamo Cathedral, Italy

1
2 3

Plate 2
1   Parasol of bamboo and oiled paper, Japan
2, 3 Violin by Jacob Stainer, Absam, Austria,
     17th c. (Musical Instruments Dept of Munich
     City Museum)

Plate 3

1   Yoke, 88 cm wide, Finland
2   Competition rifle, 118 x 7.4 cm, Finland, 1959
3   Penknife, 14 cm (design: Johannes Lauri), post-1950
4   Box for cloths, 15.5 x 38 x 20.5 cm, USA, 19th c.
5   Chest of drawers, 135 x 67 x 34 cm
    (design: Tapio Wirkkala), Finland, 1981

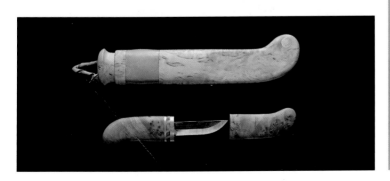

Plate 4

1   Corner detail on a stool
    (design: Alvar Aalto), Finland, 1954
2   Rocking chair, detail of armrest,
    19th c.
3   Chair (design: Josef Hoffmann),
    Austria, 1905
4   Chair (design: Richard Riemer-
    schmid), Germany, 1899/1900

Plate 5 (facing page)

5   Pedal-driven tricycle with rear-wheel
    steering, 1869
6   Dog sled, (design: Risto Kamunen),
    Finland, 1982
7   Building kit for small, motorised model
    aircraft
8   Inside the hull of a wooden ship
9   Timber transmission mast, 165 m
    high, Ismaning, Germany, 1932/1946
    (demolished in 1983)
10 Hay drying shed, Carinthia, Austria

Plate 6

1, 2, 3 Main building of the Katsura Palace in
        Kyoto, Japan, mid-17th c.

Plate 7

1   Eaves, Todai-ji in Nara, Japan, 733,
    restored in 1709
2, 4, 5 Imperial Palace (formerly the
    Forbidden City) in Beijing, China
3   Ceiling decoration, Temple of
    Heaven (Tiantun), Beijing, China, 15th c.

Plate 8

1   Stave church in Heddal, Telemark,
    Norway, mid-13th c
2   Roof to the Church of the Transfiguration
    in Khizi, Karelia, 1714
3   Kojumdschiolu House in Plovdiv,
    Bulgaria, mid-19th c.
4, 5 Decorated ceilings in noblemen's houses,
    Plovdiv, Bulgaria, mid-19th c.
6   Country house in Normandy, France

1		4
2		
3	5	6	7

Plate 9

1　House in Emmental, Switzerland
2, 5, 6　Town houses in the old quarter of Plovdiv, Bulgaria
3　Timber-frame house in southern England
4　Farmhouses in the Franconian Open-Air Museum, Bad Windsheim, Germany
7　Town house in Osnabrück, Germany

1	4	7
2	5	8
3	6	9

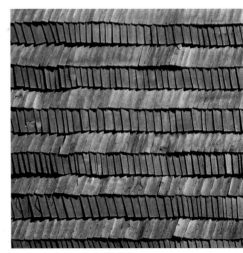

		3
1		4
2		

Plates 10 and 11 (previous double page)

1 Shingles as wall cladding, Sweden
2 Timber-frame walkway in Rouen, France
3 Stairs in Bygdøy near Oslo, Norway
4 Shingles as wall cladding, Switzerland
5 Timber-frame facade in Rouen, France
6 Stairs in the Seurasaari Open-Air Museum, Finland
7 Shingles as wall cladding, Switzerland
8 Barn in Bokrijk, Belgium
9 Steps in Petajävesi, Finland, 18th c.
10 Beam support detail, farmhouse in Schalkendorf, Alsace
11 Todai-ji Shosoin treasure storehouse, Nara, Japan, 8th c.
12 Temple column base detail, Japan
13 Vogtsbauernhof Open-Air Museum, Gutach, Black Forest, Germany
14 Alpine grain store, detail of base
15 Barn, northern Japan
16 House facade near Rovereto, Italy
17 Bridge pier, Kintai-Bashi, Japan

5	8
6	9
7	10

Plate 12 (facing page)

1 Purlin supported in fork of branches from the Bronze Age, 1800–1500 BC
2 Farmhouse Museum, Takayama, Japan
3 Bamboo pavilion for Expo 2000, Hannover, Germany (architect: Simon Velez, Colombia)
4 Cloister in Montvillier, France, 16th c.

Plate 13

5, 6 Farmhouse Museum, Amerang, Germany
7 Barn near Ljubliana, Slovenia
8, 9 Lattice gable for roof void ventilation, Tyrol, Austria, 17th c.
10 Gable wall, Bern, Switzerland

Plate 14

1 Bridge over River Brenta in
Bassano del Grappa, Italy, 1569
(architect: Andrea Palladio)
2, 3, 5 Bridge in Kintai-Bashi, southern
Japan, 1673
4 Bridge near Bulle, Switzerland

Plate 15 (facing page)

6, 9 Traversina Steg bridge, Viamala,
Switzerland, 1996 (design: Branger,
Conzett und Partner)
7 Bridge in Tajimi, Japan
8, 10 Bridge near Essing, Germany, 1986
(architect: Richard Dietrich)

6 | 9
7 | 10
8

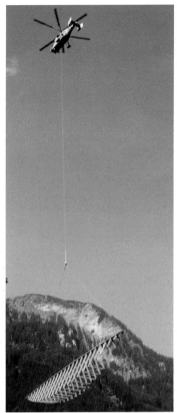

Wood as a building material –
from the beginnings to the 19th century

Roland Schweitzer

From prehistoric times to the start of the industrial age, wood always played an important role in our relationship with the environment. The use of wood, the oldest of all building materials, saw the inauguration of a form of construction from which all later forms took their lead. Over millennia, the knowledge about construction with wood and the associated architectural language spread throughout the world. It developed without regard to cultural, civilisational or geographical boundaries. Thus, the first methods of construction evolved and the necessary knowledge and skills for dealing with wood as a building material were

gradually amassed. At first this was in connection with simple housing, but later came to be used for more complex internal layouts. Witnesses to this rich store of knowledge are still around today. Despite their limited architectural vocabulary, prehistoric peoples were amazingly good at adapting their structures to suit the most diverse conditions. This unity in variety created the foundation for the development of a consistent, regional architectural language. When used as a building material, wood could respond to all requirements, seemingly as a matter of course. No other material could be employed in such diverse ways.

The following brief history of wood as a building material in Europe and Asia from prehistoric times to the 19th century illustrates the spread of cultural and technical influences. In the knowledge of this cultural development it is our duty today, by way of designing contemporary architecture, to continue the creative process that has been evolving since the very dawn of humankind. This architecture rekindles the omnipresent relationship between people and wood and contributes to a respectful handling of the natural world that surrounds us.

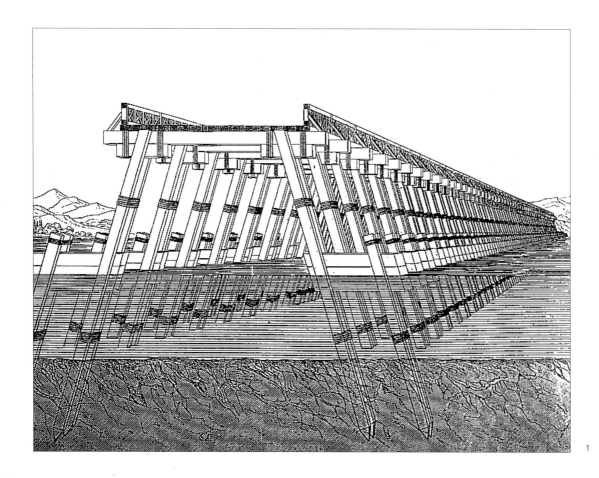

1

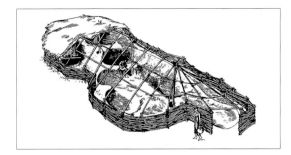

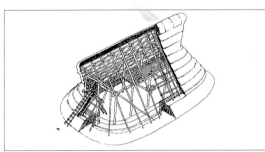

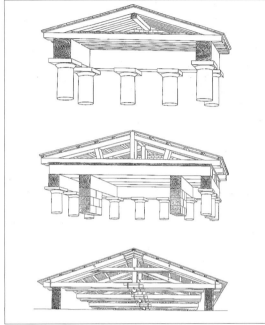

From prehistoric times to the first centuries of our era we find identical forms of housing throughout the world, sometimes lasting for periods of up to 1000 years. These range from indeterminate forms to the square house, which has existed for about 7000 years – from the Neolithic period.
The structures of the ancient Greeks date as far back as the 2nd century BC (Bouleuterion – Council House – of Priene, with a span of 15 m). The basilicas of St Peter and St Paul outside the city walls of Rome (4th century AD) had a span of 24 m, Emperor Constantine's basilica in Trier, Germany, 27.5 m. The Palace of the Roman Emperor Domitian had already spanned about 30 m at the end of the 1st century AD.

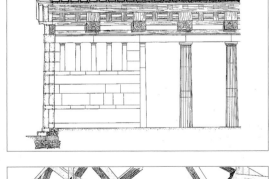

$\frac{2\ |\ 3}{4\ |\ 5}$
$6\ |\frac{7}{8}$

(facing page)

1 Bridge over the Rhine for Caesar's legions, after Alberti, length: 600 m

(this page)

2 House from the Neolithic period, Cologne

3 Typical house form from the Jomon Period, Utsunomiya, Japan, 3500 BC

4 Bouleuterion (Council House) of Priene, 2nd c. BC, span: 15 m

5 Three types of loadbearing structure for short, medium and long spans, after Vitruvius

6 Basilica of St Paul outside the city walls of Rome, Italy, 4th c. AD

7 Portico of Philipus, Delos, Greece, 2nd c. BC, lintel beam: 500 x 900 mm

8 Basilica of Fano, Italy, 1st c. BC, Vitruvius, span: 18 m

In Africa and Indonesia the nomadic tribes constructed countless different forms of tents. However, during the same period the sedentary tribes constructed simple, sometimes complex, forms of housing from wood and bamboo. All the structures were adapted to meet the functional needs of their users in the respective regions and used materials available locally.

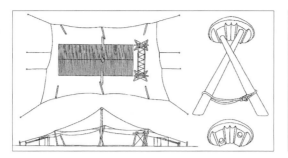

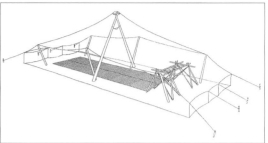

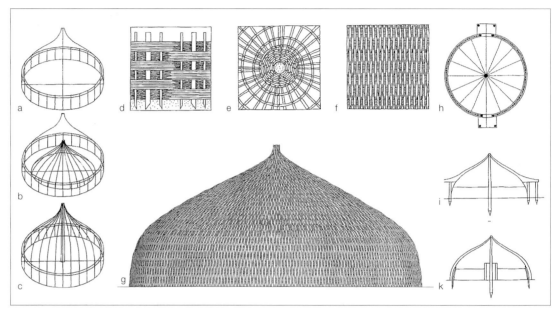

1	2
3	
4	5
6	7

1   Tecna tent, Morocco, linen, 5 x 8 m, wooden posts, detail of apex
2   Perspective view
3   Sidamo house, Hagara Salam, Ethiopia: (a) cylindrical construction, (b) roof built on the ground, (c) roof placed on cylinder and sealed with leaves from bamboo plants, (d) detail of cylinder, (e) roof detail, (f) detail of covering, (g) elevation, (h) plan, (i, k) sections
4, 5   Detached house in Lingga, Bata-Sumatra; transverse section, longitudinal section
6, 7   Grain store in Tobaz, Samosir-Sumatra; transverse section, longitudinal section

(facing page)
8   Inner shrine (Naiku) of Ise Grand Shrine, Japan, 692 AD, side elevation
9   End elevation
10   Horyu-ji Buddist Temple in Nara, Japan, 7th c. AD
11   Holy storehouse (Kofuzo), Horyu-ji Temple, Japan, 8th c. AD
12   Todai-ji Temple in Nara, Japan, AD 747–51, destroyed in 12th and 16th c., rebuilt in 1708 with three-fifths of the original parts, height to ridge: 48.50 m, span in central section: 22 m
13   Temple of Heaven in Beijing, China, 1420, Ming dynasty, diameter: 30 m, height: 38 m
14   Himeji Castle, Japan, late 16th c., section through seven-storey keep
15   Pagoda of the Toji Temple in Kyoto, Japan, AD 796, rebuilt in 1644, height: 55 m
16   Horyu-ji Pagoda, Kyoto, Japan, 1178
17   Yoshijima house in Takayama, Japan, rebuilt after two fires in 1862 and 1905, axonometric view of structure
18   Grain store on stilts, Amami, Oshima prefecture of Kagoshima, Kyushu

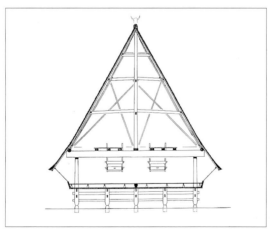

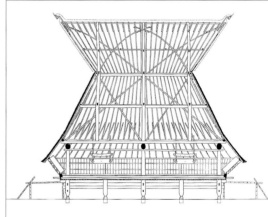

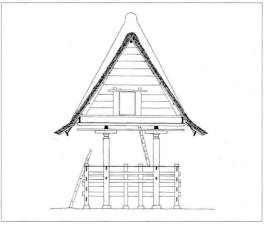

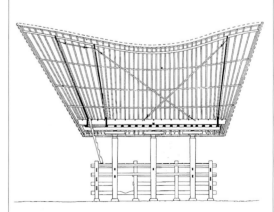

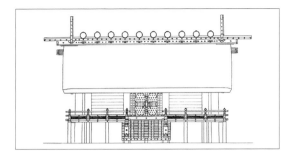

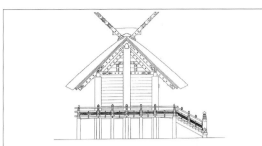

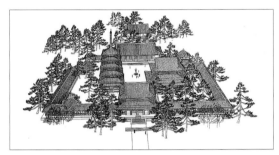

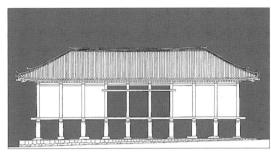

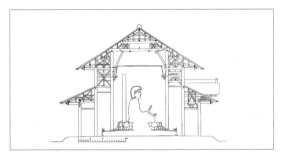

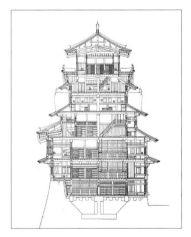

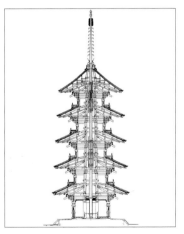

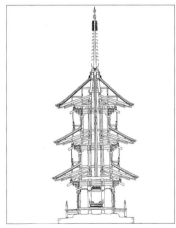

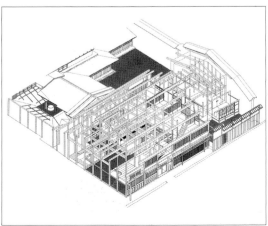

Wood has been used as the primary building material in Japan since the Jomon period (3500–300 BC). The knowledge that the seafarers from the provinces in Polynesia and Indonesia brought with them influenced the type of construction and gave rise to Shinto architecture. The discoveries made in Toro, near Shizuoka, are from the Yayoi period (300 BC to 300 AD). The structures were the archetypes of the Ise Grand Shrine, which was first built in 692 AD and since then has been re-erected every 20 years. Chinese and Korean influences brought about a second architectural form (Horyu-ji Temple in Nara) that evolved parallel with Buddhism, which was introduced into Japan in the 6th century. In the following period this style was repeatedly modified and adapted. In the 14th century the Japanese monks introduced Zen Buddhism and organic architecture. The adaptability of the modular system on which this was based was intended to create a dialogue between the natural and the built environment.

China is of special significance in the history of timber engineering. Only a few of the old monuments remain today because, traditionally, every new dynasty, with rare exceptions, destroyed the palaces and villas of the previous one. The most famous examples still standing include the Imperial Palace, the Temple of Heaven (38 m high) from the Ming dynasty (1420 AD), the Summer Palace (Yiheynan) in Beijing and the pagoda at Yingxian, which was built in 1056 AD and reaches a height of 67.31 m.

The selection of European structures is limited to all those in which timber plays the primary role in the architectural concept.

The Norwegians probably copied methods of construction from Western Europe, absorbed by the Vikings during their invasions. Hand in hand with their conversion to Christianity they developed their timber stave churches and log constructions, which can also be found in northern Russia.

In the Alpine region the geographical conditions led to the development of a heavyweight form of timber construction employing logs and planks. In contrast to this, the inhabitants of the plains of Central Europe preferred timber-frame construction, primarily of oak, with the panels filled with straw, cob or clay bricks.

Shipbuilding, from the longships of the Vikings right up to the warships of the 18th century, whose compound masts were up to 50 m high and yards up to 30 m long, helped in the development of timber frames in particular.

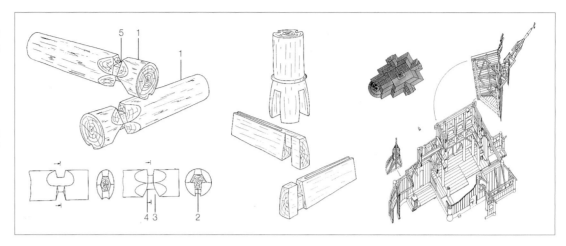

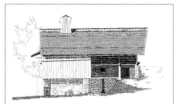

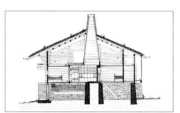

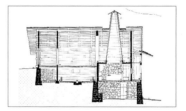

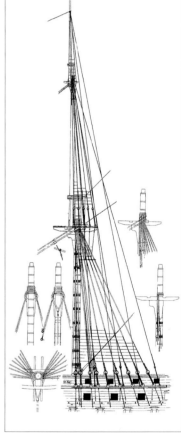

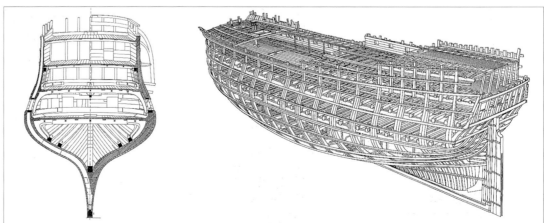

1　Norwegian log joints: 1 head, 2 neck, 3 shoulder, 4 throat, 5 notch

2　Norwegian timber stave construction, 11th c., connection between two sill beams and column

3　Borgund Church, Norway, 1150, exploded view

4　Church, Hermitage of Kiji, Lake Onega, Russia, log construction, height: 36 m, longitudinal section

5　Grain store in Boenigen, Switzerland, 1740

6　Schmidt house in Buelisacker, Switzerland, 1669

7–10　Mountain farm in Cuillery, Grand Bornand, French Alps

11　French warship, 18th c., height of mast: 50 m

12　Section through French ship with 74 cannons, 18th c.

13　Perspective view of ship's structure

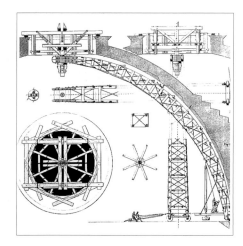

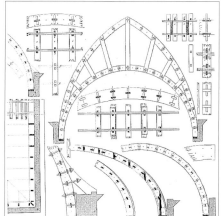

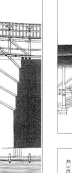

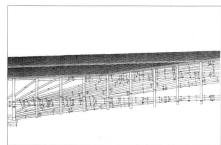

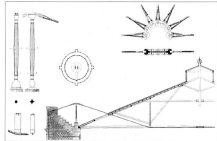

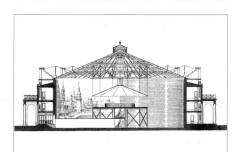

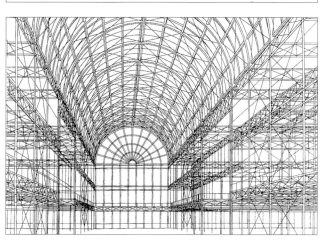

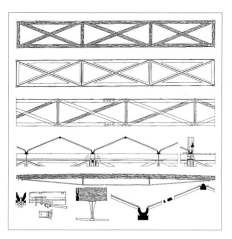

Since ancient times timber scaffolding has contributed greatly to the development of carpentry techniques. The rotating timber scaffolds for the Pantheon in Rome were specially designed by Campanarino for the restoration of the dome in 1756. Philibert Delorme presented a new load-bearing system for the Palace de la Muette near Saint Germain en Laye in 1548. This consisted of boards with a uniform length of 1.20 m, connected together with hardwood dovetail joints. The carpenter's imagination is revealed very clearly in bridge-building. Switzerland provides plenty of good examples: the bridge over the River Kandel (1757) and the first design by the brothers Jean and Hans Ulrich Grubenmann for the Rhine bridge at Schaffhausen (1758, destroyed in 1799), with a span of 119 m. The first half of the 19th century saw the following new construction systems:

- timber arches of curved boards (1825),
- wood-metal composites (1839), in which the timber tie was replaced by a steel cable in tension,
- three-dimensional timber frames, in which the timber parts are trussed with a mesh of steel cables.

In Konrad Wachsmann's opinion the 1851 Crystal Palace in London (architect: Joseph Paxton) is the decisive turning-point in construction. This building covering 70 000 m² was built from prefabricated elements of steel, cast iron, timber and glass. A total of 17 000 m³ of timber was used, principally for the construction of the central barrel vault.

1 Rotating scaffolding for the dome of the Pantheon in Rome, Italy, 1756
2 Philibert Delorme's system, France, 1548, loadbearing structure of compound sections
3 Bridge over River Kandel, Switzerland, 1757
4 Bridge over River Rhine near Schaffhausen, Switzerland, first design by the Grubenmann brothers, after C. von Mechel (1803)
5, 6 Rotunda for the exhibition of panoramas on the Champs Elysées, Paris, France, 1839, diameter: 40 m, architect: J.J. Hittorf, wood-metal construction
7 Foundry in Romilly, France, 1837; timber carries the compression, iron the tension, A.R. Emy
8, 9 Crystal Palace in London, England, 1851, perspective view of timber central vault, and details

Part 2   Fundamentals

The material	**31**
The tree	31
The trunk	31
Substances	31
Structure	32
Structure of cell walls	32
Anisotropy	32
Oven-dry density	32
Other constituents	32
Thermal aspects	32
Moisture	33
Species of wood	**34**
Softwoods	34
Hardwoods	36
Solid wood and solid wood products	**38**
Protecting the wood	38
Building permission, standards and approvals	38
Behaviour in fire	38
Round sections	38
Sawn solid timber made from hardwood (LH) and softwood (NH)	38
Solid structural timber (KVH®), Solid timber (MH®)	39
Four-piece beams	39
Duo/Trio beams	40
Glued laminated timber (glulam)	40
Profiled boards	41
Wood-based products	**41**
Three- and five-ply core plywood	42
Laminated veneer lumber (LVL) and structural veneer lumber (SVL)	42
Plywood, blockboard, laminboard	43
Oriented strand board (OSB)	44
Particleboards	44
Wood fibreboards	45
Wood-wool slabs	45
Wood fibre insulating boards	46
Plasterboards	46
Cement fibreboards	46

Building with wood is building for the future	**47**
Wood, the renewable raw material from the Earth's forests	47
Wood, the intelligent material	47
Using wood to protect the climate	48
Building for the future	48
Life cycle assessments	48
Potential for saving energy and carbon dioxide	49
Utilising timber products at the end of their life cycle	49
Summary	49
Development of building components	**50**
Construction principles	**52**

Some of the following sections deal with technical subjects whose treatment is closely tied to the relevant standards. As such standards can differ considerably between countries, the German standards quoted here should be replaced by the equivalent standards of other countries as appropriate.

The Material

Michael Volz

The tree

That living organism we call the tree forms the solid and load-supporting structure known as wood with its multitude of advantageous engineering properties. Trees are characterised by the great variety of species with their different characteristics. They live to considerably different ages and grow to considerably different sizes. The eucalyptus trees of Australia can reach 135 m. The largest trunk diameters known are those of the cypresses at 12 m and the large-leaved lime at 9 m. Spruces and firs grow to 50 m, when they have a trunk diameter of about 1.5 m. The oldest trees are the 5000-year-old bristlecone pines of California. Spruces and pines can live for up to 200 years, oaks and lime trees 1000 years and even longer. By contrast, the wood we use in the building industry originates from much younger trees, e.g. spruces or firs 60 to 120 years old, and oaks or beeches 80 to 140 years old.

Of the 30 000 known species of wood, between 1500 and 3000 are used for commercial or engineering purposes worldwide. About 500 are traded on international markets. The forests of Central Europe contain about 25 different species, 15 of which play a significant role in the building industry. This last group is described in more detail on the following pages.

The trunk

Trees have three organs: roots, stems (trunk, branches) and leaves or needles. In the building industry it is primarily wood from the trunk that we use. In the majority of species a cross-section through the trunk consists of pith, heartwood, sapwood, cambium, inner bark and outer bark. The longitudinal growth of trunk and branches takes place at their tips, the increase in diameter within the

cambium. The bark protects the cambium and the wood of the trunk from mechanical damage and excessive drying.

Trunks of different species have different structures. We distinguish between sapwood, ripewood and heartwood trees, according to the allocation of functions within the trunk of a living tree. In sapwood trees water and nutrients are transported throughout the entire cross-section. Limes and birches are in this group. The ripewood trees, e.g. spruce, fir, beech, transport water and nutrients primarily in the outer growth rings. In both types, ripewood and sapwood trees, there are normally no colour variations or other differences within the cross-section of the trunk. Conversely, heartwood trees exhibit a distinct, noticeable difference in colour between heartwood and sapwood due to the storage of substances in the heartwood. Oak, pine, larch and robinia trees fall into this group.

Trees in geographical regions with pronounced seasons have growth rings consisting of early wood laid down in the first part of the annual growth period and the subsequent late wood. In some species, e.g. larch, the difference in colour between early and late wood is characteristic of its appearance. This difference is not visible in other trees, e.g. beech, (see figures 1, 2 and 3).

Substances

We find the following elements in the wood of all species of tree:

~ 50% carbon
~ 44% oxygen
~ 6% hydrogen

The molecular components are:
40–50% cellulose
20–30% hemicellulose
20–30% lignin
Other substances found in wood include pigments, oils, tanning

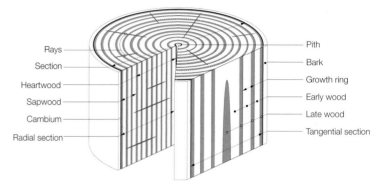

Fig. 1: Section through tree trunk

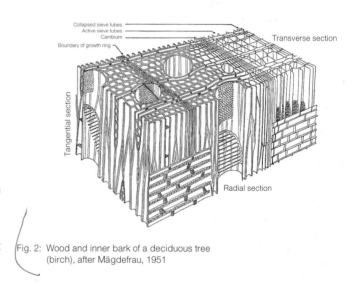

Fig. 2: Wood and inner bark of a deciduous tree (birch), after Mägdefrau, 1951

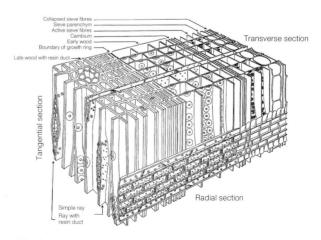

Fig. 3: Wood and inner bark of a coniferous tree (larch), after Mägdefrau, 1951

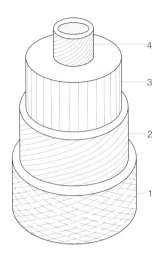

Fig. 4: Cell wall structure
Arrangement of microfibrils in different directions:
1   mesh-like
2+4 shallow angle
3   steep angle

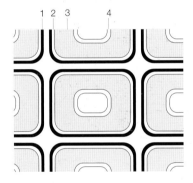

Fig. 5: Section through cell wall layers

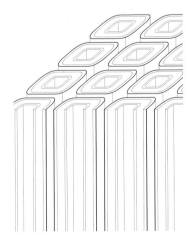

Fig. 6: Longitudinal section through cell wall structure

agents and resins. These determine the smell, colour and degree of resistance in the sense of preservation of wood, and may account for up to 10%.

Structure

The basic building block of wood is the cell, the smallest structure in the living organism. We distinguish between different types of cell according to their functions within the living tree, e.g. support, conduction and storage.

Most of the cells have an elongated form. They are therefore also known as fibres and lie almost exclusively in the longitudinal direction within the trunk cross-section. The exceptions are the rays, whose cells lie in the radial direction. The older – in evolutionary terms – coniferous wood has a simpler structure. It consists mainly of one type of cell, which transports water and nutrients while providing support. In the younger – in terms of evolution – deciduous wood the cells are more specialised, and vessels form. The position and direction of the cells and vessels with respect to each other, together with the growth rings, are responsible for giving the wood its grain structure, that important characterising, distinctive feature of each species of wood.

Structure of cell walls

The elementary structure of the cell walls is instrumental in determining the strength and elasticity of the wood. The walls have four layers (see figures 4, 5 and 6). Essentially, the layers consist of lignin for withstanding compressive forces and microfibrils for withstanding tensile forces. The latter are chain-like cellulose and hemicellulose molecules which, like tension reinforcement, lie in different directions – like a mesh in the outer layer (No. 1 in the figures), and at steeper and shallower angles in the other layers 2–4. Together with the lignin these form a fascinating composite structure.

Anisotropy

Wood consists of millions of such cells with their walls and cavities (pores). For simplicity we can consider wood as a bundle of tubes offset from each other in the longitudinal direction. This gives wood

its distinctly different properties in different directions, especially parallel or perpendicular to the grain. The ability of the cells to accommodate different directions of growth under the same conditions is known as anisotropy. The consequence of anisotropy is the completely different appearance of the various sections (transverse, tangential, radial) and the equally diverse behaviour of the wood parallel or perpendicular to the grain. This affects, for example, permissible stresses.
The permissible stresses for spruce parallel to the grain are:
· compression   up to 11 N/mm^2
· tension   up to 9 N/mm^2

but perpendicular to the grain only:
· compression   up to 2.5 N/mm^2
· tension   up to 0.05 N/mm^2

Directly related to this is the very high abrasion resistance of the wood on the surface of a transverse section compared to that on the surfaces of radial and tangential sections. This fact enables end grain blocks to be used for very heavily used floors. Another consequence of anisotropy is the different swelling and shrinkage in the three sectional planes parallel to the grain, and perpendicular to the grain in radial or tangential directions. In spruce the degree of swelling and shrinkage for every 1% change in the moisture content of the wood is:
· longitudinally < 0.01%
· transversely in the radial direction 0.15–0.19%
· transversely in the tangential direction 0.27–0.36%

Thermal conductivity also exhibits different values in the aforementioned directions. However, this difference is essentially ignored during design and construction.

Oven-dry density

The density of the pure cell wall substance is about 1.5 g/cm^3 for all species of wood. In contrast, the thickness of the cell wall and the size of the cell cavity varies from species to species, and also within a species. Furthermore, the cells of the early wood generally have larger cavities than those of the late wood (see figures 2 and 3). The ratio of cell wall to cell cavity

determines the oven-dry density and ranges from over 90% cell cavities in balsa wood with an oven-dry density of 0.1 g/cm^3 to about 10% in lignum vitae with an oven-dry density of 1.3 g/cm^3. The volume of cell cavities in spruce is 70%, the average oven-dry density 0,45 g/cm^3; that of oak is less than 60%, its oven-dry density correspondingly > 0,6 g/cm^3. Density has a considerable influence on the load-carrying capacity of the wood. It is established during machine grading.

Other constituents

According to the species of wood and the growing conditions of the individual tree, wood will have other constituents and features in different concentrations: knots, sloping grain, pith, width of growth rings, fissures, bark pockets, resin pockets, crookedness, discoloration, compression wood and insect damage. These features lead to a very wide scatter in the grades of solid timber and they play a decisive role in the questions of where and how an individual piece of timber can be used in a structure. The properties of wood are recorded during the grading process, as is described in detail in "Grading and improvement of solid timber products" (p. 55).

Thermal aspects

Owing to its porous structure, Central European building timber with its average density exhibits very good thermal insulation properties. The change in volume of the wood under the action of heat is extremely small and in practice only plays a role in very exceptional circumstances. The coefficients of thermal expansion depend on the species of wood. These are:
· parallel to the grain
  2.55 to 5 x 10^{-6} K^{-1}
· in the radial direction
  15 to 45 x 10^{-6} K^{-1}
· in the tangential direction
  30 to 60 x 10^{-6} K^{-1}

However, the increase in volume does not usually occur because as the temperature rises the wood starts to dry out, causing shrinkage and hence a decrease in volume. The strength of the wood diminishes as the temperature climbs. In certain cases, e.g. designing the fire protection, this must be taken into account, but otherwise it can be ignored in buildings with a normal range of ambient temperatures.

Moisture

The living tree contains water in its cell walls (bound moisture) and cell cavities (free moisture). The moisture content of the wood can amount to around 70% of the mass. At the maximum moisture absorption exclusively in the cell walls we talk of fibre saturation; this is in the range 22–35%. The symbol for moisture content is u, the associated definition as follows:

$$u = (m_u - m_o/m_o) \cdot 100 \ [\%]$$

m_u = mass of moist wood
m_o = mass of kiln-dried wood (cell walls and cell cavities without water)

We distinguish between the following terms and average moisture contents (u_m) when grading the timber:
- green
  area of section ≤ 200 cm^2
  $u_m > 30\%$
  area of section >200 cm^2
  $u_m > 35\%$
- semi-dry
  area of section ≤ 200 cm^2
  $20\% < u_m \leq 30\%$
  area of section > 200 cm^2
  $20\% < u_m < 35\%$
- dry
  $u_m \leq 20\%$

Regardless of its use, wood remains hygroscopic, i.e. it absorbs water and releases it again, depending on ambient humidity (see figure 7). The following equilibrium moisture contents tend to become established in timber in use:
- heated structures enclosed on all sides 9±3%
- unheated structures enclosed on all sides 12±3%
- roofed structures open on all sides 15±3%
- constructions exposed to the weather on all sides 18±3%

Inside the building, wood's ability to absorb and release moisture can have a favourable influence on the interior climate. However, during design and construction this moisture absorption property must be carefully considered owing to its possible consequences. The absorption and release of moisture leads to swelling and shrinkage of the wood respectively, i.e. to dimensional changes (see figure 8). The load-carrying capacity of wood decreases as its moisture content increases; the risk of damage by fungi and insects increases too. The disadvantages can be ruled out by installing the timber with a moisture content matching that expected in the long-term at a particular location. The wood must be dried in order to achieve the correct moisture content for processing and later use. This can be achieved partly through natural means. However, short drying times and low moisture contents are only possible by using drying plant, and this involves energy.

All timber building components in which an alternating moisture content is to be expected, e.g. components exposed to the weather, must allow for the inevitable associated dimensional changes. This applies, for example, to the timber outer leaves of facades exposed to the changing effects of sunshine and rain.

Rapid changes in moisture content bring a great risk of splitting. The dimensional changes associated with changing moisture content and deformation behaviour are shown in figures 8 and 9.

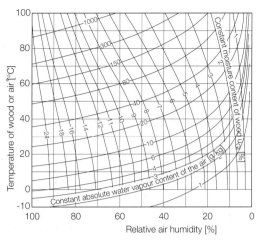

Fig. 7: Equilibrium moisture content

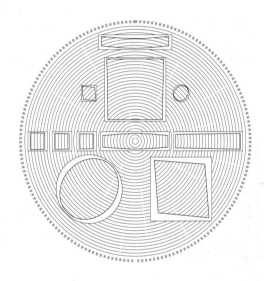

Fig. 8: Deformations of solid timber sections

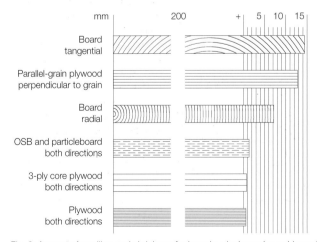

Fig. 9: Amount of swelling and shrinkage for boards, planks and wood-based products for a moisture difference of 20%

Sources:
DIN 1052, DIN 4074
Sell, J.: *Eigenschaften und Kenngrössen von Holzarten*, Zurich-Dietikon, 1987; *Holz-Lexikon*, Stuttgart, 1993

Softwoods

Common name, botanical name, DIN 4076 abbreviation

Douglas fir	Spruce	Scots pine (European redwood)	European larch
Pseudotsuga menziesii	*Picea abies*	*Pinus sylvestris*	*Larix decidua*
DGA	FI	KI	LA
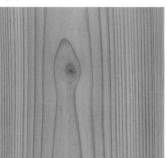		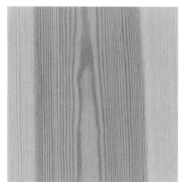	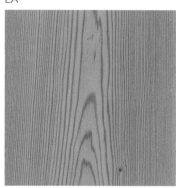

Applications

| Highly stressed internal uses, timber preservative required externally, floor coverings, shipbuilding, veneer for plywood, staves | Important European building timber, internal uses, timber preservative required externally, frames, core and veneer for plywood, poles, crates, industrial uses | Important European building timber, internal uses, timber preservative required externally, windows, furniture (solid and veneered), linings, mining uses, industrial uses, floor coverings | Highly stressed internal and external uses, furniture, linings, fittings |

Colour of wood, sapwood/heartwood

| yellowish white/reddish brown, darkening, late wood dark | early wood yellowish white, late wood reddish yellow, sapwood and heartwood not distinct | light yellowish white/reddish white, turning to brown, late wood darker | yellowish/reddish brown, darkening, late wood very dark brown |

Macroscopic-anatomical features: distribution of late and early wood, resin ducts

| wide late wood, distinct cut-off, resin ducts | narrow but distinct late wood, resin ducts | distinct late wood, many resin ducts | wide, distinct late wood, resin ducts |

Macroscopic-anatomical features: grain orientation, texture, appearance

| plain to decorative (plain sawn section) | plain to decorative (plain sawn section) | plain to decorative (plain sawn section) | plain to decorative (plain sawn section) |

Average density rN [g/cm³] for a moisture content of 12–15%

| 0.51...0.58 | 0.43...0.47 | 0.51...0.55 | 0.54...0.62 |

Theoretical amount of differential shrinkage in % per 1% moisture change, radial

| 0.15...0.19 | 0.15...0.19 | 0.15...0.19 | 0.14...0.18 |

Theoretical amount of differential shrinkage in % per 1% moisture change, tangential

| 0.24...0.31 | 0.27...0.36 | 0.25...0.36 | 0.28...0.36 |

Dimensional and form stability

| good | good | moderate to good | good |

Resistance (of heartwood) to fungal attack

| moderate, sapwood vulnerable to blue stain | low, vulnerable to blue stain | low to moderate, sapwood highly vulnerable blue stain | moderate to low |

Resistance (of heartwood) to insect attack

| moderate | low | low | moderate to high |

Growing regions

| west coast of North America, cultivated in Europe | Europe | Europe, northwest Asia | central Europe |

Sources: Sell, J.: *Eigenschaften und Kenngrössen von Holzarten*, Zurich-Dietikon, 1987; *Holz-Lexikon*, Stuttgart, 1993; Info-Dienst Holz, 04/2000

Softwoods

Pine *Pinus palustris, P. rigida, P. taeda* and 3 other *Pinus* spieces PIP	Fir *Abies alba* TA	Western hemlock *Tsuga heterophylla* HEM	Western red cedar *Thuja plicata Donn* RCW
As pitch pine (heartwood) for highly stressed internal and (with preservative) external uses, internal floor coverings, plywood; as red pine (sapwood) for internal uses	As for spruce: internal uses, timber preservative required externally, fittings, linings, inner plies of plywood, crates, poles, industrial uses	Moderately stressed internal uses, windows, linings, saunas, core and veneer for plywood	Low-stressed internal and external uses with good dimensional stability, linings, shakes and shingles
yellowish/reddish yellow to reddish brown/late wood dark	early wood almost white late wood pale reddish sapwood and heartwood not distinct	early wood light brownish grey occasionally lighter streaks, late wood darkening slightly, sapwood and heartwood not distinct	white/red-brown, darkening, late wood darker
late wood mostly very wide, many resin ducts	late wood distinct, no resin ducts	late wood less distinct, no resin ducts	narrow late wood,- no resin ducts
conspicuously large proportion of late wood determining the appearance, plain to decorative	plain to decorative (plain sawn section)	plain	plain to decorative (plain sawn section)
0.51...0.69	0.43...0.48	0.46...0.50	0.36...0.39
0.18	0.12...0.16	0.11...0.13	0.07...0.09
0.29...0.33	0.28...0.35	0.24...0.25	0.20...0.24
moderate to good	good	good	very good
sapwood low, heartwood moderate	low, vulnerable to blue stain	low to moderate	very high
low to moderate	low	low	high
southern and southeastern North America, Central America	central and southern Europe	northwestern North America, cultivated in Europe	northwestern North America

Hardwoods

Common name, botanical name, DIN 4076 abbreviation

Maple *Acer pseudoplatanus/platanoides L.* AH	Ekki (azobé) *Lophira alata* AZO	Beech (European beech) *Fagus sylvatica* BU	Oak *Quercus robur, Q.petraea* EI

Applications

For fittings and wood turning, especially decorative with wavy grain, furniture, kitchen equipment, musical instruments, parquet flooring	Highly stressed uses in agriculture and hydraulic engineering, e.g. bridges, locks, ramps, underground railway sleepers, parquet flooring	Moderate to highly stressed internal uses, parquet flooring, sleepers (impregnated), for wood turning, veneer for plywood, industrial uses	Highly stressed, internal and external uses, parquet flooring, storage barrels; narrow-ringed quality: high-quality veneers

Colour of wood, sapwood/heartwood

yellowish white, tendency to yellow, satin shine, sapwood and heartwood barely distinguishable	light red-brown/very dark red-brown with pale violet shade	light yellowish to reddish grey, often speckled, cloudy red-brown heartwood, sapwood and heartwood barely distinguishable	grey/grey-yellow, darkening to light to dark brown

Macroscopic-anatomical features: distribution of late and early wood, resin ducts

scattered, small	scattered, large	scattered, small, rays sometimes very wide and distinct	ring-porous, large

Macroscopic-anatomical features: grain orientation, texture, appearance

decorative wavy grain common, boundaries of growth rings distinct, decorative	spiral grain, growth zones indistinct, plain to decorative	growth rings moderately distinct, plain	growth rings very distinct, decorative

Average density rN [g/cm³] for a moisture content of 12–15%

0.61...0.66	1.02...1.12	0.70...0.79	0.65...0.76

Theoretical amount of differential shrinkage in % per 1% moisture change, radial

0.10...0.20	0.30...0.32	0.19...0.22	0.18...0.22

Theoretical amount of differential shrinkage in % per 1% moisture change, tangential

0.22...0.30	0.4	0.38...0.44	0.28...0.35

Dimensional and form stability

moderate to good	low to moderate	low	moderate

Resistance (of heartwood) to fungal attack

very low, also with respect to blue stain	high	very low	high

Resistance (of heartwood) to insect attack

very low to common furniture beetle and other insects	very high (also against termites and marine borer, except in tropical waters)	low	high

Growing regions

Europe to Asia minor	west Africa	Europe	Europe

Sources: Sell, J.: *Eigenschaften und Kenngrössen von Holzarten*, Zurich-Dietikon, 1987; *Holz-Lexikon*, Stuttgart, 1993; Info-Dienst Holz, 04/2000

Hardwoods

Dark red meranti, *Shorea spp.* esp. *S. pauciflora King* MER	Merbau *Intsia bijuga* etc. MEB	Robinia *Robinia pseudoacacia L.* ROB	Teak *Tectona grandis* TEK
Its wide variation in properties makes it suitable for highly stressed internal and external uses, especially windows, doors, shipbuilding, park benches; light red meranti is suitable for linings, furniture and lightweight constructions	Highly stressed uses with good dimensional stability, floor coverings, laboratory and work benches, shipbuilding	Structural timber for highly stressed internal and external uses, stairs, floor coverings, piles (also without chemical timber preservative like the heartwood of oak)	In solid and veneered forms for furniture, floor coverings, linings, internal and external uses with high dimensional accuracy, not permitted for loadbearing constructions, shipbuilding, laboratory fittings
yellowish grey to pink-grey/reddish brown	yellowish white/light brown to reddish brown, darkening (similar to afzelia)	light yellow to greenish yellow/greenish yellow to olive yellow, later shiny gold-brown	grey/gold-yellow, later medium to dark brown, often narrow black streaks, shiny
scattered, large, vertical resin ducts in tangential rings	scattered, large	ring-porous, large	loose ring-porous, large in early wood
slightly spiral grain, growth zones not distinguishable, plain to decorative	light to medium spiral grain, growth zones distinguishable, decorative	boundaries of growth rings distinct, mostly only short, straight-grain segments possible, often severely speckled, decorative	Growth zones distinct, no spiral grain, streaked or variegated due to ring-porosity and figure, highly decorative
0.54...0.76	0.81...0.90	0.74...0.80	0.59...0.70
0.14...0.18	0.13	0.20...0.26	0.13...0.15
0.29...0.34	0.26	0.32...0.38	0.24...0.29
good	very good	moderate	very good
high to moderate	very high	very high	very high
moderate to high	high to very high	high	very high (termite-resistant)
southeast Asia	southeast Asia, Madagascar, Papua New Guinea	southeastern North America, cultivated in Europe and elsewhere	southeast Asia, cultivated in other tropical regions

Log

Solid softwood section

Solid hardwood section

Solid wood and solid wood products

A host of new solid wood products have been developed in recent years for modern timber engineering. In terms of linear members, the spectrum ranges from round poles to glued laminated timber. The particular feature is the provision of as natural as possible solid wood products of reliable quality. The relevant standards and more stringent requirements provide the foundation for this quality assurance. This target is achieved, first and foremost, by grading, but also by conversion methods, drying, partial resawing of the trunks, the removal of pieces with defects, and bonding together pieces to form larger cross-sections and longer lengths. All the products are suitable for structures with demanding engineering and architectural needs.

Protecting the wood

If solid wood products are to fulfil loadbearing and bracing functions, the requirements of DIN 68800 part 2 "Protection of timber – preventive constructional measures in buildings" and DIN 68800 part 3 "Protection of timber – preventive chemical protection" must be observed. These define risk categories to which individual timber components (in the as-built condition) are assigned. These risk categories are in turn assigned constructional measures and resistance classes according to DIN 68364 "Characteristic values for wood species; strength, elasticity, resistance". Furthermore, preventive chemical wood preservative measures are specified for cases in which no other option is possible. The majority of solid wood products are available in various species of wood and guaranteed moisture contents. Correspondingly, this allows chemical wood preservatives to DIN 68800 to be dispensed with even in higher risk categories (see also "Protecting wood", p. 60).

Building permission, standards and approval

Solid wood products used for loadbearing or bracing purposes must be covered by a standard (DIN, DIN EN) applied by a building authority or an approval granted by the German Institute for Building Technology (DIBt) (e.g. Z-9.1-1000). If neither applies, there is the possibility of obtaining individual approval for a particular project, granted by the appropriate building authority. The relevant standards containing requirements for wood as a building material are listed below:

- DIN 1052: Structural use of timber; design and construction
- DIN 1052 part 2/A1: Timber structures – Mechanical joints; Amendment 1
- DIN 4074 part 1: Strength grading of coniferous wood; coniferous sawn timber
- DIN 4074 part 2: Building timber for wood building components; quality conditions for building logs (softwood)
- DIN 1074: Wooden bridges
- DIN 18203 part 3: Tolerances for building; building components of timber and wood-based panel products
- ATV DIN 18334: Contract procedures for building works – Part C: General technical specifications for building works; Carpentry and timber construction works
- DIN EN 350 part 2: Durability of wood and wood based products – Natural durability of solid wood – Guide to the natural durability and treatability of selected wood species of importance in Europe
- DIN 68140 part 1: Wood finger-jointing – Finger jointing of softwood for loadbearing structures
- DIN 4072: Boards tongued and grooved made of coniferous timber
- DIN 68122: Chamfered boards tongued and grooved made of coniferous timber
- DIN 68123: Weatherboards made of coniferous timber
- DIN 68126 parts 1 and 3: Profile boards with chamfer and broad root

Behaviour in fire

All the solid wood products described below belong to building materials class B 2, flammable, to DIN 4102 part 4.

Round sections

Description and manufacture
Round sections consist of trunks or trunk segments.
- Debarking
- If required, machining the cross-section to size over the length of the trunk
- If required, cutting of relieving grooves in larger cross-sections
- Air drying, if necessary with subsequent kiln drying
- Visual strength grading

Species of wood
Spruce, fir, pine, larch, Douglas fir, other species of wood according to DIN 1052 part 1/A1, tab. 1.

Surface finish
Three methods of manufacture are commonly used:
- manual debarking retaining the original trunk form
- machine debarking with minimum scraping of the surface
- machining to size, resulting in a constant diameter and smooth surface

Applications
- Solid timber walls and floors
- Loadbearing sections in timber-frame construction
- Agriculture and horticulture
- Scaffolding
- Bridges
- Foundations

Dimensions
- Lengths up to approx. 20 m and diameters at the top end of the trunk up to approx. 300 mm
- Larger dimensions are possible in spruce, fir and Douglas fir

Information required by tenderers
- Round section
- Species of wood
- Grade
- Diameter at top end of trunk, length
- Moisture content
- Machining to size
- Surface finish
- Wood preservative measures
- Payment based on m/m³

Sawn solid timber made from hardwood (LH) and softwood (NH)

Description and manufacture
Sawn timber is obtained from round sections by sawing or profiling.
- Conversion, e.g. using frame saws or bandsaws
- Air and/or kiln drying
- Visual strength grading
- If required, finger jointing and gluing sections together
- If required, planing and chamfering
- If required, further profiling (e.g. cutting rebates, grooves and tongues)

Species of wood
Spruce, fir, pine, larch, Douglas fir and other softwoods according to DIN 1052.
Beech (species group A), oak (species group A), ekki (species group C), teak (species group A) and other hardwoods according to DIN 1052 part 1/A1, tab. 1.

Surface finish
- Rough sawn; if required, planed and chamfered
- Further criteria to DIN 4074 and DIN 68365

Visual grading distinguishes grades according to wane, knots, growth ring width, slope of grain, fissures, discoloration, compression wood, insect damage, mistletoe infestation and distortion.

Applications
Squared sections:
- loadbearing sections in floors, walls, roofs
- formwork and civil engineering
- timber-frame construction
- oak squared sections for frame refurbishment and bridges
- ekki squared sections for bridges and hydraulic engineering
Planks:
- scaffold boards, walkways, bridge decks, balconies and terraces, and as a covering over ceiling beams
- Punched metal plate fasteners
Boards:
- formwork
- external cladding
- roof decking, for supporting the roof covering or for bracing the roof
- terrace decks and coverings

- diagonal boarding in bridge-building or space frames
- edge-glued floors and walls
- cross-laminated timber
- board system floors and walls
Battens:
- supporting constructions for roof decking, facades, wall and ceiling linings

Dimensions
We distinguish between the different sections according to the ratio of width to thickness/depth as follows:

	thickness d or depth h	width b
batten	d ≤ 40 mm	b < 80 mm
board	d ≤ 40 mm	b ≥ 80 mm
plank	d > 40 mm	b > 3 d
squared	b ≤ h ≤ 3 b	b > 40 mm

- Squared sections:
  6 x 6/8/12 cm
  8 x 10/12/16 cm
  10 x 10/12/20/22 cm
  12 x 12/14/16/20/24 cm
  14 x 14/16 cm
  16 x 16/18/20 cm
  18 x 22 cm
  20 x 20/24 cm
  length up to 16 m
- Planks, boards and battens:
  unplaned:
  16, 18, 22, 24, 28, 38, 44, 48, 50, 63, 70, 75 mm thick
  planed:
  13.5, 15.5, 19.5, 25.5, 35.5, 41.5, 45.5 mm thick
  planed Scandinavian timbers:
  9.5, 11, 12.5, 14, 16, 22.5, 25.5, 28.5, 40, 45 mm thick
  75, 80, 100, 115, 120, 125, 140, 150, 160, 175 mm wide
  1500–6000 mm long in 250 and 300 mm increments

Information required by tenderers
- Type of conversion
- Standards
- Grade
- Surface finish
- Species of wood
- Sawn timber class
- Moisture content
- Cross-section, length
- Payment based on m/m³

Solid structural timber (KVH®)
Solid timber (MH®)

Description and manufacture
Better quality sawn softwood timber products in terms of dimensional stability, form stability, reduced splitting and better surface finish.
- Heart-free or heart-split conversion in the sawmill or chipper canter plant
- Drying to a moisture content of 15±3%
- Visual strength grading to DIN 4074 part 1 and additional grading rules, stricter requirements regarding knots, fissures, discoloration, resin pockets etc.
- If required, finger jointing of sections (KVH®only)
- Planing and chamfering (KVH-Si® members), or scraping and chamfering (KVH-Nsi® members)
- Solid timber (MH®) is not finger-jointed, and remains free from adhesives
- Right-angled cross-cutting of ends

Species of wood
Spruce, fir, pine, larch
MH® also Douglas fir

Surface finish
- KVH®: two classes of finish are available – KVH-Nsi® for non-exposed members, and KVH-Si® for exposed members; both satisfy requirements stricter than those of grade S 10 to DIN 4074 part 1.
- KVH-Nsi®: at least scraped and chamfered
- KVH-Si®: planed on four sides and chamfered
- MH®: according to the charter and the instructions of the manufacturers' association (Herstellergemeinschaft MH® MassivHolz e.V.)
- MH-Plus®: planed on four sides and chamfered
- MH-Fix®: scraped and chamfered
- MH-Natur®: rough sawn

Applications
- Loadbearing sections in floors, walls, roofs
- The controlled moisture content means they are particularly suitable for creating fully insulated constructions without chemical wood preservative

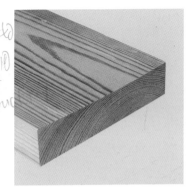

Board

Solid structural timber KVH®

Four-piece beam

Trio beam (duo beam similar)

Glued laminated timber (glulam)

Profiled boards

Dimensions
- KVH®:
  thicknesses up to 120 mm
  widths up to 240 mm
  cross-sections:
  60 x 120/140/160/180/200/240 mm
  80 x 120/140/160/200/240 mm
  100 x 120/200 mm
  120 x 120/200/240 mm
  lengths:
  non-finger-jointed sections up
  to 5 m, finger-jointed sections in
  any length up to 14 m
- MH®:
  squared sections as for sawn
  softwood available in lengths
  up to 13 m

Information for tenderers
- Solid structural timber with/
  without finger joints, or
- Solid timber
- Designation
- Species of wood
- Cross-section, length
- Surface finish
- Payment based on m/m³

Four-piece beams

Description and manufacture
The four-piece beam consists of
four softwood squared sections
glued together with the grain parallel and the wane placed on the
inside. This creates an irregular
void in the centre of the rectangular section running the full length
of the member.
- Sawing low-strength wood into
  halved logs
- Drying to a moisture content
  < 15%
- Profiling of quartered logs
- Visual strength grading of quartered logs as for squared sections to DIN 4074 part 1 and
  with additional grading criteria
  as given in the approval
- Applying adhesive, positioning
  and bonding the quartered logs
- Curing under pressure
- Strength grading of complete
  cross-section to DIN 4074 part 1
  and with additional grading criteria as given in the approval
- If required, finger jointing of pre-
  planed complete cross-section
  to form longer members
- If required, planing, chamfering
- Cutting to length

Species of wood
Spruce, fir, pine, larch, Douglas fir

and other softwoods according to
DIN 1052 part 1/A1, tab. 1.

Surface finish
- Rough sawn, or
- Planed and chamfered

Applications
- As for sawn softwood timber
- Particularly suitable for timber
  houses owing to its good form
  stability and low moisture content

Dimensions
Cross-sections from 80 x 100 mm
to 200 x 260 mm
Ratio of depth to width ≤ 2
Length up to 12 m

Approvals
Z-9.1-314, Z-9.1-415, Z-9.1-425,
Z-9.1-444

Information for tenders
- Four-piece beam
- Approval
- Grade
- Species of wood
- Cross-section
- Length
- Surface finish
- Wood preservative measures
- Payment based on m/m³

Duo/Trio beams

Description and manufacture
Duo and trio beams are made
from two or three flat-sided planks,
respectively, or squared sections
bonded together with the grain
parallel.
- Kiln drying of softwood boards,
  planks or squared sections to
  reach a moisture content ≤ 15%
- Visual strength grading
- Finger jointing of boards or
  planks to form laminations
- Planing of laminations and cutting to length
- Even application of adhesive to
  the wide face of the laminations
- Bonding of two or three laminations to form one section in a
  straight press
- Curing under pressure
- Normally, planing, chamfering
  and cutting to length after curing

Species of wood
Spruce, fir, pine, larch, Douglas fir
and other softwoods according to
DIN 1052 part 1/A1, tab. 1.

Surface finish
- Scraped, or
- Planed and chamfered

Applications
- As for sawn softwood timber
- Particularly suitable for timber
  houses owing to its good form
  stability and low moisture content

Dimensions
Width of individual lamination
≤ 280 mm
Thickness of individual lamination
≤ 80 mm
Supplied in lengths of up to 18 m
- Duo beams:
  80, 100, 120, (140, 160) mm wide
  100, 120, 140, 160, 180, 200,
  220, 240 mm deep
- Trio beams:
  180, 200, 240 mm wide
  100, 120, 140, 160, 180, 200,
  (220, 240) mm deep

Approval
Z-9.1-440

Information for tenderers
- Duo beam or trio beam
- Approval
- Grade
- Species of wood
- Cross-section, length
- Surface finish
- Wood preservative measures
- Payment based on m/m³

Glued laminated timber (glulam)

Description and manufacture
Glued laminated timber is an
improved form of solid timber in
which the growth-related defects
in the wood that tend to reduce
the strength have been partly elim-
inated. Glued laminated timber
consists of at least three dried
softwood boards or laminations
glued together with the grain parallel. Besides simple, straight
components, forms with a variable
cross-section and/or in single or
double curvature or twist about the
longitudinal axis are also possible.
- Kiln drying of softwood boards
  to attain a moisture content of
  about 12%
- Visual or machine strength grading, if necessary with removal of
  larger defects
- Planing the laminations and
  cutting to length
- Even application of adhesive to

the wide face of the lamination
- Bonding the laminations in a straight or curved press
- Boards of different grades can be arranged within the depth of the cross-section
- Curing under pressure
- Normally, planing, chamfering and cutting to length after curing

Species of wood
Spruce, fir, pine, larch, Douglas fir, possibly also western hemlock, southern pine, yellow cedar; see also DIN 1052 part 1/A1, tab. 1.

Laying up the cross-section
Laminations of different grades can be arranged over the depth of the cross-section. The grade of boards in the tension zone determines the overall grade of the glued laminated timber section. Components subjected mainly to tension must have a homogeneous lay-up.

Surface finish
- Planed and chamfered
We distinguish between three classes of finish: industrial, exposed and selected. The exposed finish complies with the requirements of ATV DIN 18334.

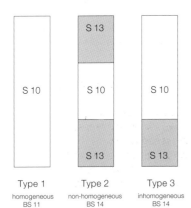

Type 1
homogeneous
BS 11

Type 2
non-homogeneous
BS 14
(symmetric
lay-up)

Type 3
inhomogeneous
BS 14
(asymmetric
lay-up)

Applications
- Heavily loaded and long-span components
- Components with particularly high demands on form stability and appearance

Dimensions and forms
60–220 mm (max. 300 mm) wide
100–2000 mm (max. 3000 mm) deep
Slenderness ratio B/H ≤ 1/10
(more slender sections are possible)
Length up to 30 m (max. 60 m)
Radius of curvature up to at least

150 x lamination thickness, but then with reduced permissible stresses

Information for tenderers
- Species of wood
- Glued laminated timber grade
- Adhesive joints
- Width, depth, length
- Surface finish
- Wood preservative measures
- Payment based on m/m³

Profiled boards

Description and manufacture
Planed and profiled sections are sawn from round sections, planed and routed.

- Tongue and groove board

- Tongue and groove board with close V-joint

- Tongue and groove weatherboard

- Tongue and groove board with open V-joint

Besides the forms and dimensions given in the DIN standard, numerous modified profiles with different dimensions are possible, depending on the tools available. These

profiled boards are manufactured to order in the planing shop and can be purchased from builders' merchants.

Species of wood
Spruce, fir, pine, larch, Douglas fir

Surface finish
- Scraped, or
- Planed

Applications
- Loadbearing and non-loadbearing leaves indoors and outdoors

Dimensions
- Tongue and groove board
  15.5, 19.5, 22.5, 35.5 mm thick
  95, 115, 135, 155 mm wide
  19.5, 22.5, 25.5 mm thick
  (Scandinavian timbers)
  96, 111, 121 mm wide
- Tongue and groove board with close V-joint
  15.5, 19.5 mm thick
  95, 115 mm wide
  12.5 mm thick (Scandinavian timbers)
  96, 111 mm wide
- Tongue and groove weatherboard
  19.5 mm thick
  115, 135, 155 mm wide
  19.5 mm wide (Scandinavian timbers)
  111, 121, 146 mm wide
- Tongue and groove board with open V-joint
  12.5, 15.5, 19.5 mm thick
  96, 115 mm wide
  12.5, 14, 19.5 mm thick
  (Scandinavian timbers)
  71, 96, 146 mm wide
  Lengths
  1500–4500 mm (in 250 mm increments)
  4500–6000 mm (in 500 mm increments)
  Lengths (Scandinavian timbers)
  1800–6000 mm (in 300 mm increments)

Information for tenderers
- Designation
- Standards
- Grade
- Species of wood
- Thickness, width, length
- Payment based on m²

Wood-based products

Wood-based products are boards or linear members made from small pieces of wood pressed together. The methods for generating the small pieces include the well-known methods such as sawing (boards), slicing and peeling (veneers), chipping and pulverising. The materials used are wood and wood products from the trunk to waste products free from impurities obtained through recycling. The industry supplies a large number of wood-based products, mainly in the form of boards. They are optimised for their particular use in building, exploiting the properties of the wood to best advantage. The main optimisation approaches are:
- size, in terms of length, width and thickness, for manufacturing larger components and for covering larger areas,
- strength, with the aim of achieving greater load-carrying capacity, and
- surface finish, with the aim of achieving maximum compatibility, e.g. in terms of appearance (surfaces of components) or weathering (facades). In doing so, the wood-based products made from boards or veneers usually achieve much higher strengths than a solid piece of timber of the same species.

Constituents and methods and manufacture
Wood-based products contain most of the species of wood that are also used in solid timber form in building. They also contain those that, in solid timber form, exhibit only limited suitability or are totally unsuitable, e.g. beech. The wet process makes use of a natural wood product – lignin – as a binding agent. The lignin is made to "flow" by means of very high pressure and thus, together with the felting (interlocking) of the wood constituents, forms the binding agent in fibreboards. The dry method requires a binding agent. Organic adhesives, usually synthetic resins, and also inorganic mineral binders, well-known in the field of mortar technology, are used. Adhesives tested and approved for the particular application are used for bonding.

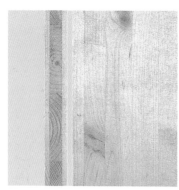
3-ply core plywood

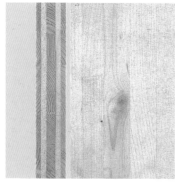
5-ply core plywood

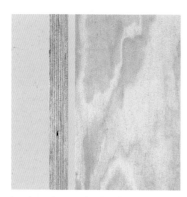
Laminated veneer lumber (LVL)

Gypsum and cement are the main products used for manufacturing mineral-bonded wood-based products. Further constituents may be included to protect against pests and fire.

Behaviour in fire
Wood-based products are available in building materials classes
- A, incombustible
- B, combustible

according to DIN 4102 part 1 "Building materials; concepts, requirements and tests". The binding agent has a decisive influence on the flammability and the behaviour in fire:
Adhesive-bonded wood-based products fall mostly into class:
- B 2, flammable

Cement-bonded wood-based products fall either into class:
- B 1, not readily flammable, or
- A 2, incombustible

Gypsum-bonded wood-based products fall into class:
- A 2, incombustible

Flame-retardant treatments (in impregnated or coating form) can help to improve the fire resistance. The classification according to a DIN 4102 part 1 building materials class can be ascertained from the aforementioned standard, from the relevant materials standard or from the general building authority approval.

Wood preservative and wood-based products (HWS) classes
If wood-based products are to be used for loadbearing or bracing functions, DIN 68800 part 2 "Protection of timber – preventive constructional measures in buildings", and part 3 "Preventive chemical protection" must be observed. They distinguish between HWS classes 20, 100 and 100 G, which are assigned maximum moisture contents that the wood-based products may not exceed in the respective ambient conditions. These moisture contents are as follows:

HWS class	max. moisture content
20	15% (fibreboards 12%)
100	18%
100 G	21%

The moisture contents are assigned to known usage situations, e.g. 15% for the internal lining of an external wall, 18% for voids and the external cladding to external walls, and 21% for loadbearing layers below the sealing layers of flat roofs, or horizontal boards in roof voids. The specific applications are given in DIN 68800 part 2, tab. 3. The said HWS classes can be achieved by using veneers made from wood species of a particular resistance category according to DIN 68364 "Characteristic values for wood species; strength, elasticity, resistance" or by chemical measures in the form of certain adhesives or the addition of a wood preservative. In some wood-based products made from laminated veneer lumber it is possible to pressure-impregnate an effective preventive chemical wood preservative according to DIN 68800 part 3. Products treated in this way can be used in situations up to risk category 4 "Timber components in permanent contact with the soil or freshwater".

Three- and five-ply core plywood

Description and manufacture
These boards consist of a stack of three or five plies glued together, with adjoining plies always at an angle of 90° to each other. The boards of the outer plies are parallel to each other. The strength properties cover a very wide range. They can be controlled through the quality of the wood used and the relationships between the thicknesses of the individual plies.

Constituents
- Softwoods, first and foremost spruce and Douglas fir
- Synthetic resins
- If required, wood preservative

Applications
- Non-loadbearing, load-sharing and bracing planking to walls, floors and roofs
- Outdoors with weather protection

Dimensions
3-ply: 16–75 mm thick
formats: 1000–3000 x 5000/6000 mm
5-ply: 33–80 mm
formats: 1000–3000 x 5000/6000 mm

Wood preservative
HWS classes 20, 100, 100 G to DIN 68800 part 2

Behaviour in fire
Building materials class B 2, flammable, to DIN 4102 part 4

Building authority approvals
Z-9.1-242, Z-9.1-258, Z-9.1-376, Z-9.1-404, Z-9.1-477

Information for tenderers
- Type of board
- Approval
- Species of wood
- If required, wood preservative measures
- Thickness, width, length
- Surface finish
- Payment based on m^2

Laminated veneer lumber (LVL) and structural veneer lumber (SVL)

Description and manufacture
Laminated veneer lumber (LVL) is produced by bonding together dried softwood veneers about 3 mm thick. We distinguish between two types:
Type S: the grain of all plies runs in the same direction, parallel to the direction of production, for primarily linear components and linear stresses.
Type Q: the grain of most plies runs in the same direction but some in the transverse direction, for planar components and in-plane stresses.
Type T is the same as type S in terms of grain direction but is made from lighter veneers (lower densities) with correspondingly lower load-carrying capacities. The veneers of each ply are generally joined together by a scarf joint or simple overlap.
Structural veneer lumber (SVL) is for essentially linear-type components and consists of the outer plies of LVL laminations glued together. The laminations are made from 2.5 mm thick veneer plies with the direction of grain parallel to the longitudinal direction of the board. Finger joints are employed for the longitudinal joints of the laminations.

Constituents
LVL:
- veneers, primarily spruce, pine (Kerto brand), Douglas fir, southern pine (Microlam brand)
- synthetic resins

SVL:
- Oregon pine, Douglas fir, to DIN 68705 part 3

Applications
LVL:
- beams, columns, chords, diagonals and verticals of plane and space frames, I-beams and related sections
- stressed-skin structures, e.g. stiffening diaphragms, loadbearing roof and floor decking
- high strengths and favourable deformation behaviour parallel to the grain, therefore highly suitable for more highly stressed parts of structures and for reinforcing loadbearing timber components

LVL type Q:
- beams and columns subject to transverse tension

SVL:
- beams, columns
- arcade constructions
- timber housing
- interior fitting-out
- high-strength stair treads
- floor coverings (parquet flooring)

Dimensions
- LVL type S: 21, 24, 27–75 mm thick (in 6 mm increments)
  formats
  up to 1820 x 23 000 mm or 2500 x 20 000 mm
- LVL type Q: 21, 24, 27–69 mm thick (in 6 mm increments)
  formats
  up to 1820 x 23 000 mm or 2500 x 20 000 mm
- LVL type T: 39–75 mm thick (in 6 mm increments)
  formats up to 200 x 23 000 mm
- SVL: width 50 mm
  depth 100–356 mm
  length up to 48 000 mm

Wood preservative
HWS class 100 because phenolic resin only is used for bonding. HWS class 100 G can be achieved by treating with an approved wood preservative.

Behaviour in fire
Building materials class B2, flammable, to DIN 4102 part 4

Building authority approvals
LVL: Z-9.1-100, Z-9.1-291, Z-9.1-245, Z-9.1-377
SVL: Z-9.1-539

Information for tenderers
- Type of board
- Manufacturer
- Approval
- Species of wood
- Thickness, width, length
- Wood preservative measures
- Payment based on m² or m³

Plywood
Blockboard
Laminboard

Description and manufacture
Plywood is made by gluing together dried veneers at right angles to each other. The veneers must be arranged symmetrically about the middle of the board. The majority of plywoods have an odd number of plies (at least three), but with an even number the two inner plies are bonded together with their grain parallel. In Germany these are known as "Multiplex" boards when the number of plies exceeds five and their thickness 12 mm. Plywood made from beech to DIN 68705 part 5 is made from between three and nine plies of beech veneer 1.5–3.2 mm thick. Blockboard and laminboard have a central core made from strips of wood. These measure approx. 24–30 mm wide in blockboard and 6–8 mm wide in laminboard (in each case measured in the plane of the board). One (3-ply) or two (5-ply) veneer plies are bonded to both sides of the central core. There is an unlimited number of possibilities for building up this type of board, particularly with respect to the quality and thickness of the veneer. This means that very diverse elastomechanical properties and strengths can be achieved.

Constituents
- Veneers, primarily spruce, pine, maritime pine, Douglas fir, hemlock, southern pine, mahogany, makoré, beech
- Strips, primarily spruce, pine, fir
- Synthetic resins
- If required, wood preservative to protect against pests, and flame-retardant treatment

Applications
Plywood:
- load-sharing and bracing planking to walls, floors and roofs
- beech plywood is particularly suitable for highly stressed components (static loads), e.g. strengthening around openings and notches in glued laminated timber beams.
- high-strength, fungi-protected boards of HWS class 100 G are used in scaffolding

Blockboard, laminboard:
- fitting-out
- no loadbearing functions

Dimensions
- Plywood
  8–40 mm thick, in 1–2 mm increments up to about 25 mm, thereafter in larger increments
  formats
  2500/3000 x 1250/1500 mm
  2400/3050 x 1200/1525 mm
- Blockboard, laminboard: 13–38 mm thick, in 2–3 mm increments up to about 30 mm, thereafter larger increments
  formats
  1220–4100 x 2440–5400 mm

Wood preservative
HWS classes 20, 100, 100 G
The use of species of wood complying with resistance class 2 to DIN 68364 or the addition of an approved wood preservative to the adhesive can achieve a board meeting the requirements of HWS class 100 G.
- Not suitable for direct exposure to the weather
- Hardly any risk of insect attack

Behaviour in fire
- Building materials class B 1, not readily flammable, and
- Building materials class B 2, flammable, to DIN 4102 part 4

Standards
- DIN 68705 part 3: Plywood; building veneer plywood
- DIN 68705 part 4: Plywood; core plywood for building purposes
- DIN 68705 part 5: Plywood; veneer plywood of beech for building
- DIN 68364 (1979-91): Characteristic values for wood species; strength, elasticity, resistance
- DIN EN 350: Durability of wood and wood-based products

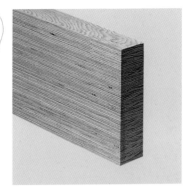

Structural veneer lumber (SVL)

Plywood

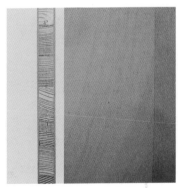

Blockboard

Oriented strand board (OSB)

Particleboard

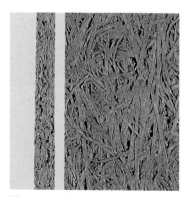

Wood-wool slab

Building authority approvals
Z-9.1-43, Z-9.1-6, Z-9.1-7,
Z-9.1-430, Z-9.1-431, Z-9.1-455

Information for tenderers
- Type of board
- Standards
- Approval
- Emissions class
- Thickness, width, length
- Surface finish
- Payment based on m²

Oriented strand board (OSB)

Description and manufacture
The manufacture of oriented strand board is achieved by bonding together larger particles (strands). The long, flat strands are approx. 0.6 mm thick, 75–130 mm long and approx. 35 mm wide. In the outer layers they lie primarily parallel with the length of the board (direction of production) and transverse to this in the middle layer. Oriented strand boards exhibit distinctly different strength properties depending on the direction of the strands; very high strength values are attained parallel to the primary direction of the strands.

Constituents
- Longitudinal strands, primarily: pine, maritime pine, Douglas fir, Oregon pine, alder, poplar
- Synthetic resins
- If required, wood preservative

Applications
- Load-sharing and bracing planking to floors, walls, ceilings and roofs (with weather protection outdoors)
- Webs of I-beams

Dimensions
6–40 mm thick, in 1–2 mm increments up to approx. 25 mm, thereafter in larger increments
formats
2440–5000 x 1220–2620 mm
Wood preservative
HWS class 100
- not suitable for direct exposure to the weather
- low risk of insect attack

Behaviour in fire
Building materials class B 2, flammable, to DIN 4102 part 4

Standards
DIN EN 300: Oriented Strand Boards (OSB) – Definitions, classification and specifications

Building authority approvals
Z-9.1-275, Z-9.1-326, Z-9.1-424, Z-9.1-387, Z-9.1-414, Z-9.1-503, Z-9.1-504

Information for tenderers
- Type of board
- Approval
- Emissions class
- Thickness, width, length
- Surface finish
- Payment based on m²

Particleboards, adhesive-(synthetic resin-), cement- and gypsum-bonded

Description and manufacture
Particleboards are produced by pressing small timber particles together with adhesives or mineral binders. The particles preferably lie parallel to the surface of the board and are generally arranged in several layers or with a gradual transition within the structure. In this way, virtually identical tension, compression and flexural strengths are achieved in both directions in the plane of the board. The tensile strengths for stresses perpendicular to the plane of the board are low as a result of the relatively loose structure in the middle layer. The strength can be influenced by using different cross-sectional structures (position and properties of the particles, type of adhesive, degree of compaction). The flexural strengths of multi-layer particleboards are generally higher than those of single-layer boards due to the higher proportion of binder in the outer layers.

Constituents
Adhesive-bonded particleboards:
- wood particles, primarily: pine, spruce, beech, birch, alder, ash, oak, poplar, chestnut
- woody fibres made from annual plants, flax and hemp shives
- binder: synthetic resins
Cement-bonded particleboards:
- highly compacted mixture of about 25% by weight wood particles (spruce or fir) acting as reinforcement
- approx. 65% mineral binder:

Portland cement, magnesia cement, water, additives
Gypsum-bonded particleboards:
- wood particles (spruce)
- binder: calcined gypsum

Applications
Adhesive-bonded particleboards:
- universal non-loadbearing, load-sharing and bracing planking and coverings to floors, walls, ceilings and roofs
- webs of I-beams
- webs of timber formwork beams
Cement-bonded particleboards:
- especially suitable for external planking of external walls and facades
Gypsum-bonded particleboards:
- load-sharing and bracing planking to wall panels for timber houses in panel construction

Dimensions
- Adhesive-bonded particleboards: 2–38 mm thick, in 1–2 mm increments; formats: 1250 x 2500/5000, 4100 x 1850, 2710 x 2080, 2750/5300 x 2050 mm lengths up to 14 000 mm
- Cement-bonded particleboards: 8–28 mm thick, in 1–2 mm increments, 32-40 mm thick, in 2 mm increments formats 1250 x 2600/3100/3200/3350, 3000 x 6500 mm
- Gypsum-bonded particleboards: 10, 12, 15, 18 mm thick formats 1200/1220/1250 x 2400/2600/3000 mm

Wood preservative
All HWS classes are possible. The adhesive- and gypsum-bonded particleboards are not suitable for use externally without protection. The cement-bonded particleboards have a high weathering resistance and a high resistance to pests.

Behaviour in fire
Adhesive-bonded particleboards:
- building materials class B 2, flammable, to DIN 4102 part 4
Cement-bonded particleboards:
- building materials class B 1, not readily flammable, or building materials class A 2, incombustible
Gypsum-bonded particleboards:
- building materials class A 2, incombustible

Standards
Adhesive-bonded particleboards:
· DIN 68763:
Cement-bonded particleboards:
· DIN EN 633: Cement-bonded
  particleboards; definition and
  classification
· DIN EN 634: Cement-bonded
  particleboards – specifications

Building authority approvals
Adhesive-bonded particleboards:
Z-9.1-129, Z-9.1-133, Z-9.1-134,
Z-9.1-156, Z-9.1-176, Z-9.1-182,
Z-9.1-202, Z-9.1-215, Z-9.1-224,
Z-9.1-303, Z-9.1-365, Z-9.1-398,
Z-9.1-405, Z-9.1-421, Z-9.1-456,
Z-9.1-463
Cement-bonded particleboards:
Z-9.1-89, Z-9.1-120, Z-9.1-173,
Z-9.1-267, Z-9.1-285, Z-9.1-325,
Z-9.1-328, Z-9.1-340, Z-9.1-384,
Z-9.1-486, Z-9.1-490
Gypsum-bonded particleboards:
Z-9.1-336, Z-9.1-187, Z-PA-III 4.864

Information for tenderers
· Type of board
· Standards
· HWS Class
· Type of binding agent
· Emissions class
· Thickness, width, length
· Surface finish
· Payment based on m²

Wood-wool slabs

Description and manufacture
Wood-wool slabs are produced
from wood shavings and mineral
binders such as cement or caustic-
burnt magnesite.

Applications
· Thermal insulation and sound
  insulation (attenuation and
  absorption)
· Fire protection
· Wood-wool slabs to DIN 1101
  are divided into the following
  applications types:
  W   unsuitable for compression
  WD suitable for compression
  WV suitable for transverse
      tension
  WB suitable for bending
  WS enhanced permissible
      stresses for special
      purposes
  ML multi-layer slab
· Multi-layer slabs (ML) in conjunc-
  tion with insulating materials
  made from rigid foam or mineral

wool are suitable for thermal
insulation purposes.

Dimensions
15, 25, 35, 50, 75, 100 mm thick
format: 500 x 2000 mm

Behaviour in fire
· Building materials class B 1, not
  readily flammable, to DIN 4102

Standards
DIN 1101: Wood-wool slabs and
multi-layered slabs as insulating
materials in building – requirements,
testing

Information for tenderers
· Type
· Standards
· Thickness, width, length
· Payment based on m²

Wood fibreboards
Hardboards
Medium boards
Medium density fibreboards (MDF)

Description and manufacture
Medium density fibreboards are
pressed with binders in the dry process. Medium boards are pressed
without binders in the wet process.
Hardboards can be manufactured
using either method. The bond is
based on the felting (interlocking)
of the fibres as well as their own
adhesive properties. When used
for load-sharing and bracing purposes hardboards must exhibit a
minimum density of 950 kg/m³,
medium boards and medium density fibreboards a minimum density
of 650 kg/m³. Hardboards have
virtually identical behaviour in both
directions in the plane of the board.
The properties can be altered by
changing pressure, temperature
and binder.

Constituents
· Wood fibres, primarily spruce,
  fir, pine, beech, birch, poplar,
  eucalyptus
· Woody fibres from annual plants
· With or without the addition of
  binder: synthetic and natural
  resins
· Other possible constituents are
  water-repellents such as wax
  (paraffin) and pest-repellent and
  fire-retardant treatments

Applications
· Limited to load-sharing and
  bracing planking and for the
  construction of wall, floor and
  roof panels for timber houses in
  panel construction to DIN 68754
  part 1

Dimensions
· Hardboards:
  density 800–1100 kg/m³
  thickness 5–16 mm
  formats
  max. 2100 x max. 5500 mm
· Medium boards and medium
  density fibreboards:
  density 330–650 kg/m³:
  thickness 12–40 mm
  formats 1250 x 2500 mm
  density > 650 kg/m³:
  thickness 6–25 mm
  formats 1250 x 2500 mm

Wood preservative
Hardboards: in HSW classes 20
and 100

Behaviour in fire
All wood fibreboards conform to
building materials class B 2, flammable, to DIN 4102 part 4; better
qualities are possible and, if necessary, must be validated by
approvals or test certificates.

Standards
DIN 68754 part 1: Technical building regulations; wood fibre boards

Approvals
Hardboards: Z-9.1-122
Medium boards and medium den-
sity fibreboards:
Z-9.1-234, Z-9.1-382, Z-9.1-442,
Z-9.1-443, Z-9.1-454, Z-9.1-500,
Z-9.1-505, Z-9.1-513

Information for tenderers
· Type of board
· Standards
· Approval
· If applicable, adhesives
· Emissions class
· Thickness, width, length
· Payment based on m²

Wood fibre insulating boards
Porous wood fibre insulating boards
Bitumen-impregnated wood fibre insulating boards

Description and manufacture
Wood fibre insulating boards are

Hardboard
(front and rear faces)

Medium board
Medium density fibreboard (MDF)

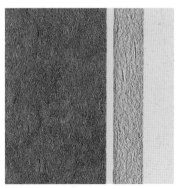
Porous wood fibreboard

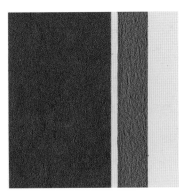

Bitumen-impregnated wood fibreboard

Plasterboard

Cement fibreboard

produced from wood fibres (ligno-cellulose fibres) using the wet process. The bond is based on the felting (interlocking) of the fibres as well as their own adhesive properties. The density is max. 400 kg/m³.

Constituents
- Wood fibres, primarily spruce, fir, pine, beech, birch, poplar, eucalyptus
- Woody fibres from annual plants
- Other possible constituents are water-repellents such as wax (paraffin) and pest-repellent and fire-retardant treatments

Applications
Porous wood fibre insulating boards:
- are used primarily for sound and thermal insulation purposes; we make the following distinctions: Boards to DIN 68755 part 1 for thermal insulation:
  W   unsuitable for compression
  WD   suitable for compression
  WDT suitable for compressive and thermal loads
  WV   suitable for pull-off and shear loads
  PT   high pull-off strength and enhanced requirements regarding dimensional stability

The following suffixes can be added to the main board codes:
  h   treated with water repellent throughout the thickness
  w   also suitable for use as attenuating material in voids
  s   also suitable for use as a facing leaf that can be taken into account in the calculations

Boards to DIN 68755 part 2 for impact sound insulation:
  T   suitable for use in floors, with normal compressibility
  TK   suitable for use in floors, with low compressibility

Bitumen-impregnated wood fibre insulating boards:
- BPH: thermal insulation in walls, roofs, floors
- BPH (PT): plaster backing board with high pull-off strength and dimensional stability
- thermal insulation composite systems (water-repellent PT board)
- BPH (w): attenuation in voids
- BPH (s): sound-insulating facing leaf

Wood preservative
Bitumen-impregnated wood fibre insulating boards: the bitumen constituent makes these boards insensitive to moisture, rotproof and resistant to pests and fungi.

Dimensions
density 150–450 kg/m³
thickness 6–100 mm
formats 400–1250 x 1200–2500 mm

Behaviour in fire
All wood fibreboards conform to building materials class B 2, flammable, to DIN 4102 part 4; better qualities are possible and, if necessary, must be validated by approvals or test certificates.

Standards
- DIN 68750:
- DIN 68752:
- DIN 68755: Wood fibre products for insulation of buildings
- DIN EN 316: Wood fibreboards – definition, classification and symbols

Information for tenderers
- Type of board
- Standards
- Thermal conductivity class
- Thickness, width, length
- Payment based on m²

Plasterboards

Description and manufacture
Plasterboards are produced from gypsum and paper fibres. The paper fibres are obtained through recycling and act as reinforcement. A homogeneous mixture of both raw materials is obtained by adding water – no further binders are necessary. The mixture is then pressed to form boards, dried and then cut to the respective formats.

Applications
- Non-loadbearing, load-sharing and bracing planking to floors, ceilings and walls. The permissible stresses are given in the respective general building authority approval.
- In designs to DIN 1052 plasterboards can be used as a component in floor and roof plates.
- Fire protection

Dimensions
10, 12.5, 15, 18 mm thick formats
1245/1250 x 2500/3000/3500 mm,
1000/1500/6000 x 2540 mm,
1245 x 2000/2540/2750 mm

Wood preservative
Plasterboards may be used wherever the use of HWS classes 20 and 100 is permitted.

Behaviour in fire
Building materials class A 2, incombustible, to DIN 4102

Building authority approvals
Z-9.1-187, Z-9.1-434, Z-9.1-339, Z-PA III 4.6

Information for tenderers
- Type of board
- Approval
- Thickness, width, length
- Payment based on m²

Cement fibreboards

Description and manufacture
These calcium silicate boards reinforced with cellulose consist of Portland cement, silica aggregates and cellulose fibres.

Applications
- Load-sharing and bracing planking to wall panels for houses in wood panel construction
- Outer planking to external walls, provided permanent effective weather protection is guaranteed. Validation by an authorised testing institute is required.

Dimensions
6–20 mm thick, in 2–3 mm increments
formats: 1250 x 2600/3000 mm

Wood preservative
Cement fibreboards may be used wherever the use of HWS classes 20 and 100 is permitted.

Building authority approvals
Z-9.1-358, Z-9.1-451, Z-9.1-452, Z-9.1-510

Information for tenderers
- Type of board
- Approval
- Thickness, width, length
- Payment based on m²

Building with wood is building for the future

Gerd Wegener, Bernhard Zimmer

Since the UN Conference on Environment and Development ("Earth Summit") in Rio de Janeiro in 1992 the nations of the world have committed themselves to a programme of sustainable development. This means that the binding criterion for local, regional and global action for people and businesses is sustainability because that is the only viable approach for the future. So our society has taken up the old forest management principle of sustainability and incorporated it in an expanded form in Agenda 21 as a motif and programme of action for the 21st century.

Besides purely economic action, ecological criteria and needs plus social aspects and responsibility must determine the lives and the economic activities of an ever-growing world population. In all this it is no longer just economic growth that is the key but a whole host of other aspects, including the preservation of the natural resources on this planet, the raising of living standards in the sense of quality of life, and the development of intelligent technologies that fulfil ecological criteria. Specific challenges of economic management for the future are, for example, conserving finite reserves of fossil resources through the increased use of renewable raw materials or sources of energy. That would reduce emissions of greenhouse gases and hence contribute to sustainable climate protection. However, low-energy materials flows and a consistent cradle-to-grave economy would achieve the same goals. Forests, forest management and the use of wood are mentioned in many chapters of Agenda 21 because they can make major contributions to a viable future through sustainable development interacting with the economy, ecology and society (see figure 1).

Sustainable, semi-natural forest management and the diverse, efficient use of wood can be regarded as a model case for the viable use of land in the future, and a long-term, practicable resources policy. In the tense relationship between sustainability and ecological, economic and social aspects, the importance of using wood has rarely been considered up to now, and has been undervalued in climate policy discussions. Not only extractive operations but also every form of technical production to satisfy our needs and desires in the end removes resources from the natural environment, and hence affects and changes it: for example, our space requirements, and the solid, liquid and gaseous wastes and emissions from countless production plants. Furthermore, production residues and the waste generated after we have used the products also lead to emissions, and if we think of landfill sites, also to space requirements.

Wood, the renewable raw material from the Earth's forests

Today, forests account for about 3.9 billion ha worldwide, i.e. about 30% of land is covered with trees. Some 57% of these forests are located in developing and newly industrialised countries in tropical and subtropical regions, and about 43% in the industrialised world. Despite various conservation activities, between 12 and 15 million ha of forest are lost every year in the southern hemisphere. This loss of tree-growing land and potential for wood cannot be compensated for by establishing forest plantations, even though in 2000 they exceeded 140 million ha and continue to increase. A total of 3.4 billion m³ of wood (logs) was felled in 2000 worldwide. Of this, approx. 55% was used for generating energy and approx. 45% used as a material

and improved (converted timber). Figure 2 shows these proportions in comparison with other important raw and building materials. In 2000 the most important semi-finished products made from the 1.5 billion m³ of converted timber were 420 million m³ of sawn timber, 180 million m³ of wood-based products (particleboards, fibreboards, OSB etc.) and 320 million tonnes of paper. So wood is not only a source of energy (approx. 6% of the global primary energy requirement is met by wood) but also an irreplaceable building material and feedstock.

Wood, the intelligent material

Wood is stored solar energy
Photosynthesis converts solar energy into wood. About 50% of its mass is carbon, which is fixed through absorption of the greenhouse gas carbon dioxide.

Wood is a global carbon store
Forests and wood products make an effective contribution to protecting the climate. The use of wood reduces the consumption of non-renewable fuels and products made from non-renewable resources.

Wood is a building material
Wood is a high-strength building material with low weight. It consists of cells whose cavities provide thermal insulation and whose cell walls absorb and release moisture. One of the benefits of that is to ensure a healthy interior climate.

Wood is a feedstock
Diverse wood-based products for structural and non-structural purposes in building are made from wood particles of various sizes in combination with efficient adhesives.

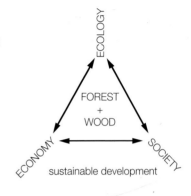

Fig. 1: The contribution to sustainable development made by forests and wood

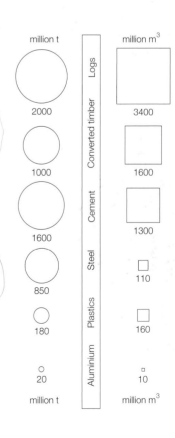

Fig. 2: Annual production (2000) or felling of wood compared to other important raw and building materials.

Fig. 3: Total life cycle of timber, which corresponds to the carbon dioxide cycle

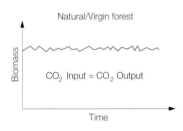

Fig. 4: Biomass development in primary and virgin forest, in a phase of dynamic equilibrium during which the same amount of biomass is produced as is decomposed. The carbon store is full, no additional carbon dioxide can be extracted from the atmosphere.

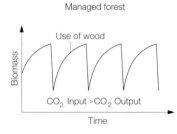

Fig. 5: Biomass development in a managed forest whose carbon store is emptied again and again by using the wood, so that the forest can then extract additional carbon dioxide from the atmosphere.

Wood is the raw material of paper
Wood fibres are converted into new paper in modern and environmentally friendly processes.

Wood is a raw material for the chemicals industry
Synthetic materials can also be produced from wood.

Wood is a source of energy
Wood is an ideal fuel, either in its natural form or after being used as a product.

Using wood to protect the climate
Taking the Earth Summit in Rio de Janeiro in 1992 as its basis, legislation passed by the German Bundestag on 27 September 1991 aims to reduce the energy-related carbon dioxide emissions in Germany by 25–30% by 2005 (reference year: 1987). The closed carbon dioxide life cycle of wood use is very important in terms of climate protection (see figure 3). The amount of carbon stored in living organisms (plants, animals, people) today is roughly equal to the current level of carbon occurring as carbon dioxide in the atmosphere. More than 80% of it, is fixed in the Earth's forests. In an ideal situation, natural forests, also known as virgin forests, are in a state of equilibrium. There is a balance between the absorption and release of carbon in the form of carbon dioxide. Once the carbon store is filled, no additional carbon dioxide can be extracted from the atmosphere (see figure 4).
Only by managing these forests and using the wood is the stored carbon removed from the forest, and only then is the forest in a position to extract further carbon dioxide from the atmosphere (see figure 5). The use of wood and its application in large quantities and in a wide range of products therefore leads to a reduction in the anthropogenic carbon dioxide emissions and thus to a slower rise in the carbon dioxide content of the atmosphere. After the wood products have been used, the chemical elements of the wood can be used to produce energy, or fed back into the natural life cycle by way of biological decomposition. The carbon dioxide that was removed from the atmosphere through photosynthesis is there-

fore released back into the atmosphere. While biological de-composition, e.g. in the composting process, does not exploit the solar energy stored in wood, energy generation produces a greater reduction in the carbon dioxide because the wood replaces other fossil fuels. Without doubt, the building industry holds the greatest potential for using more wood because it can be used for a host of applications. This starts with roof structures, where wood has a long tradition and is very important, but of course includes walls, floors, windows and doors, and many interior fittings (stairs, floor coverings, etc.). So the amount of wood used in a building can be matched to the ecological aims. Thermal insulation can also be made from wood-based materials. There is great scope here for using wood and wood-based products to a greater extent.

Building for the future
Building has a major and long-term impact on the cultural, social and economic aspects of our society, as well as the appearance of our urban and rural environments. Building has always reflected the cultural and spiritual values of society. But now besides the architecture, the building forms, the engineering criteria of materials and structures, building must also consider the ecological characteristics with a growing environmental awareness and so question and validate a structure's viability for the future. New criteria for building materials must therefore be developed and implemented, for example, in the:
· extraction and provision of raw materials (Where do they come from?)
· manufacture of products (What sort of technologies are we using?)
· product properties (What ecological advantages does a product have during its use and at the end of its life?)
In the light of this, building and the future role of wood in our buildings and lifestyles must be re-examined. Building is always coupled with environmental impact, and over the last 50 years in particular the relationships between building and its effects on the environment

have not been addressed adequately by architects, engineers and developers. Fast, cheap construction with "modern" building materials was all too often the priority, with environmental aspects ignored or misunderstood. All the building materials that developers, architects, planners, engineers and authorities consider, select or approve should in future be subjected to a fully comprehensive evaluation of the pros and cons. As the technical and technological data for the majority of building materials has been recorded better than their ecological properties, the future will provide plenty of work for those drawing up life cycle assessments.

Life cycle assessments
A life cycle assessment is one method in environmental management within a management system or a comprehensive ecological certification. Other methods in environmental management include risk assessment, product line analyses, environmental compatibility verification and location-related environmental studies. The aim of a product-related life cycle assessment is to examine the complete life cycle of a product, from extraction of the raw materials, through its manufacture and use, right up to disposal or returning it to the cycle. The effects on the environment are determined and evaluated throughout the product's entire life cycle. Product-related life cycle assessments must be drawn up when products manufactured from different materials or with different production processes have to be compared. Only product-related life cycle assessments supply the facts and figures necessary to equate the relevant environmental effects throughout the entire life cycles of products and hence enable comparisons to be made. One crucial requirement for a comparative study of products is a transparent and comprehensible method.
The following four international standards provide the basis for drawing up product-related life cycle assessments:
· ISO 14.040: Environmental management – Life cycle assessment – Principles and framework

- ISO 14.041: Environmental management – Life cycle assessment – Goal and scope definition and life cycle inventory analysis
- ISO 14.042: Environmental management – Life cycle assessment – Life cycle impact assessment
- ISO 14.043: Environmental management – Life cycle assessment – Life cycle interpretation

Accordingly, a life cycle assessment is divided into four sections:
- Establishing the objective and scope of the investigation
Important here is the description and stipulation of the assessment period (Which part of the life cycle is to be analysed?) and the functional unit (e.g. 1 m³ timber, 1 m² wood flooring, one window).
- Inventory
Here we quantify the materials and energy flows relevant to the environment as input and output variables.
- Impact assessment
The data established are allocated to impact categories, e.g. greenhouse potential, energy consumption, resource consumption, acidification etc.
- Interpretation
The data from the impact assessment are evaluated, e.g. the primary energy consumption during production, the quantity of carbon dioxide released etc.

Potential for saving energy and carbon dioxide

Example: forest management and manufacture of sawn timber

In the structure of 1000 kg of absolutely dry timber, photosynthesis extracts 1851 kg of carbon dioxide from the atmosphere and fixes 19 300 kJ of solar energy (calorific value H_u). About 15% of the energy content of this softwood sawn timber is consumed by the energy requirements of forest management, transporting the timber, conversion in the sawmill and kiln drying (see figure 6).
If this dried, sawn spruce wood is processed in some way, the energy balance improves. The production of 1 m³ of glued laminated timber requires approx. 2.4 m³ of spruce tree trunk, meaning that approx. 1.4 m³ of waste wood is generated

in the production of the glued laminated timber. If this is used properly in modern plants with a high degree of efficiency (co-generation), we can balance the equation because the production of our highly efficient glued laminated timber takes, in total, less energy than is contained in the product as the calorific value (glulam abs. dry = 8300 kJ). If at the end of this life cycle this energy content is again used efficiently, it becomes clear how thrifty wood products are in energy terms, from the raw material to the end of the life cycle, and what energy and hence carbon dioxide substitution potential they possess compared to building materials made from non-renewable resources. Similar assessments are available for particleboard, medium density fibreboard, oriented strand board and laminated veneer lumber.

Using timber products at the end of their life cycle

When timber products or components are no longer required, they become waste wood or used wood. This waste wood occurs in various forms, various mixtures and after different service lives, according to how the material has been used. Examples are timber from demolition works (roof trusses, windows, doors, floors etc.), old furniture and packagings. This wood can be used in three ways:
- biological decomposition
- material recycling
- energy generation

Germany's cradle-to-grave and waste legislation, Renewable Energy Act, Biomass Act and Waste Wood Act together regulate the handling of waste wood and the ways in which it can be used according to the degree of contamination with other materials (e.g. preservatives, adhesives, coatings, paints, plastics, fittings). The quantity of waste wood in Germany is about 8 million tonnes, and is on the increase. The aforementioned legislation and the associated financial subsidies mean energy generation is by far the most popular route at present. The ecological assessment has shown that in addition to the economic advantages, the use of waste wood in energy generation

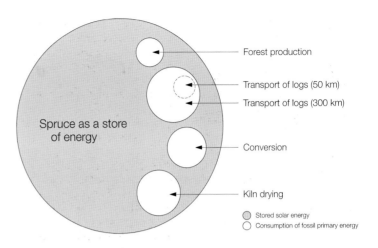

Fig. 6: Energy balance for the production of dried softwood sawn timber (white circles: fossil energy requirement in comparison to the energy stored in the wood).

has distinct advantages, primarily in terms of the impact categories greenhouse effect, land consumption and ozone potential.
On the whole we can see that the legal and economic frameworks enable us to take advantage of timber products at the end of their life cycle, which is a qualified success in technical terms and positive one in ecological terms.

Summary
Building with wood is building for the future because:
- wood is a renewable building material,
- wood is produced in the forest, the environment's and society's friendliest factory,
- forests and wood products store carbon dioxide,
- wood products save energy and carbon dioxide (low-energy production, energy gains from byproducts and residues, energy-saving insulation function, energy uses at the end of the life cycle),
- every use of wood instead of fossil or non-renewable materials relieves the environment and contributes to protecting the climate.

Development of building components

Progress in woodworking has led to a large variety of technical possibilities for building with wood. Below, we give the main steps in the most important lines of development from logs to semi-finished products to building components by way of selected examples. The linear members range from simply debarked logs to curved and twisted glulam sections. Walls, floors and roofs can be formed using edge-sawn logs or halved logs. If higher demands are placed on the geometry of the component or its load-carrying capacity, or components larger than the trunk sizes available are required, then

Compound column made from planar members and quartered log

Log column with relieving and connection grooves

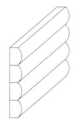

Wall made from halved logs

Wall made from edge-sawn logs

Solid web beam with flanges made from a quartered log

Log beam with relieving and connection grooves

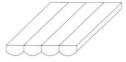

Floor/roof made from halved logs

Floor/roof made from edge-sawn logs

Quartered log

Log beam with relieving and connection grooves

Halved log, edge-sawn, with relieving grooves

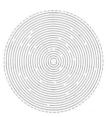

Log, edge-sawn, with relieving groove

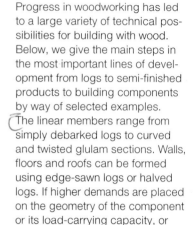

Log

Logs, squared logs

Quartered squared log

Log beam with relieving and connection grooves

Squared section with relieving and connection grooves

Split-heart squared log, boxed heart section

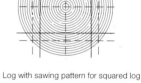

Log with sawing pattern for squared log

ribbed, box and solid sections made from boards and planks are possible solutions.

Structures employing logs are characterised by their low processing requirement. They are often relegated to "low-value" structures. However, the EXPO roof in Hannover, Germany (p. 260), the office building at Chalons-sur-Marne, France (p. 142), and the forestry station at Turbenthal/Rheinau, Switzerland (p. 345), demonstrate the potential of logs in highly demanding projects.

Squared sections have been able to enlarge their range of applications recently thanks to structural solid timber (KVH) and related

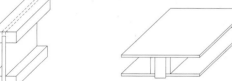

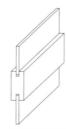
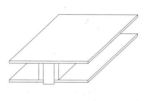

Solid web beam with flanges made from squared sections

Floor/roof made from squared sections exposed on the underside plus planking, boarding or wood-based panels

Squared-section beam with relieving and connection grooves

Floor/roof made from concealed squared sections plus planking, boarding or wood-based panels

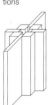

Compound column made from planar members and quartered squared log

Wall made from squared sections exposed on both sides plus planking

Squared-section column with relieving and connection grooves

Wall made from concealed squared sections plus planking

timber products. These are universal sections that can be used in any orthogonal system and especially in platform, balloon-frame and timber-frame construction.

Components made from planks and boards are available today in a very wide range, using different techniques and attaining different levels of quality. Still as important as ever and extremely diverse are boarding and planking. The cross-sections suitable for this range from boards with plain or profiled edges to strips or mouldings, and from overlapping arrangements to those with open joints.

The use of edge-glued and cross-laminated timber has resulted in solid wood constructions with

Edge-glued timber wall

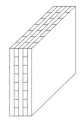
Cross-laminated timber wall

Board system wall

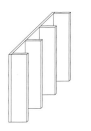
Ribbed wall

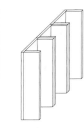
Channel-section wall

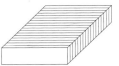
Edge-glued timber floor or roof

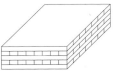
Cross-laminated timber floor or roof

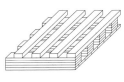
Board system floor

Box-section floor or roof

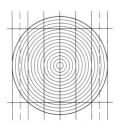
Log with sawing pattern for planks

Plank

Boards

Tongue and groove board

Tongue and groove board with close V-joint

Tongue and groove board with open V- joint

Tongue and groove weather-board

Batten Strip Moulding

Logs, squared logs

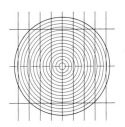
Log with sawing pattern for boards

simple component geometries and correspondingly favourable jointing conditions in terms of both economics and building science. The use of large quantities of timber while using the tree trunk effectively makes these constructions interesting from the ecological viewpoint.

Glued laminated timber is now an advanced product ideal for a broad range of applications. It has been optimised and has a highly remarkable potential. The main development and optimisation criteria have been dimensions, load-carrying capacity, form stability and quality of surface finish. Curvature and twisting have expanded the possibilities, especially for geometrically demanding tasks.

"Endless board" with finger joint

Glued laminated timber, rectangular section

Glued laminated timber, square and round sections

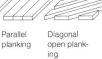
Parallel open planking

Parallel planking

Diagonal open planking

Diagonal planking

"Endless boards" in single curvature

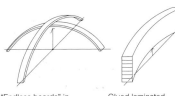
Glued laminated timber with upward camber

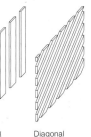
Glued laminated timber, plane and space frames

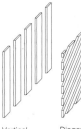
Vertical parallel open planking

Diagonal open planking

Vertical planking with profiled boards

Overlapping planking

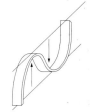
"Endless boards" in double curvature

Glued laminated timber with downward camber

Glued laminated timber in single curvature and with twist

Horizontal parallel open planking

Horizontal planking with profiled boards

Diagonal planking

Weather-boarding

Continuous beams

Continuous columns, primary and secondary beams; primary and secondary beams in pairs

Continuous columns, primary and secondary beams; columns and secondary beams in pairs

Continuous columns, primary and secondary beams at same level

- Primary beams on columns
- Secondary beams on primary beams
- Single-storey structures

- Primary beams attached to column sides
- Secondary beams laid on top
- Two- or multi-storey structures

- Primary beams attached to column sides
- Secondary beams laid on top
- Columns in pairs

- Primary beam fixed to side of column
- Secondary beam fixed to side of main beam

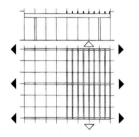

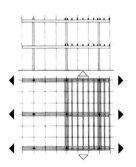

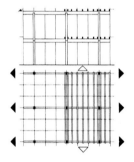

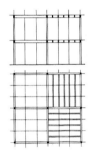

- Cantilevers possible in both beam directions

- Cantilevers possible in both directions

- Cantilevers possible in both directions

- Cantilevers not possible
- Uniform loading on primary beams by alternating direction of secondary beams

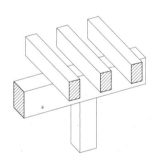

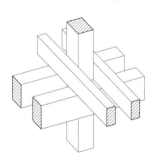

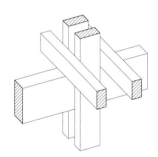

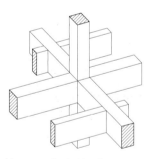

- Loadbearing junction requiring minimal connectors as beams are laid on top
- Simple geometry for facade and fitting-out
- Different structural depths and details at facade junctions and fitting-out around primary and secondary beams

- Primary and secondary beams in pairs
- Junction between main beam and column more complicated
- Complex geometry for facade and fitting-out

- Columns and secondary beams in pairs
- Junction between main beam and column more complicated
- Complex geometry for facade and fitting-out

- More complicated junctions between primary beam and column, secondary beam and primary beam
- Simple geometry for fitting-out and facade

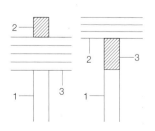

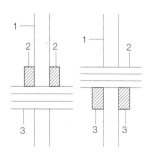

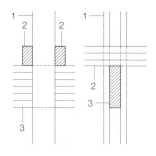

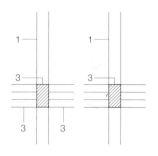

1 column, 2 secondary beam, 3 primary beam

| **Panel construction (timber-frame construction, platform construction)** | **Timber-frame construction (platform construction, balloon-frame construction)** | **Edge-glued timber** | **Cross-laminated timber** |

 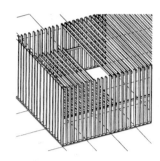 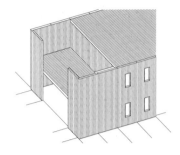 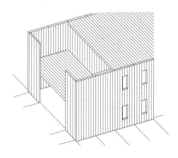

· Bracing by means of planking to post-and-rail construction
· Floors laid on top, storey-height posts

· Bracing by means of planking to post-and-rail construction
· Floor joists connected to sides, posts > storey height

· Self-bracing plate effect
· Wall equal to height of building: floor suspended; storey-height wall: floor laid on top

· Self-bracing plate effect
· Wall equal to height of building: floor suspended; storey-height wall: floor laid on top

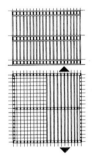 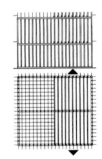 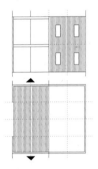 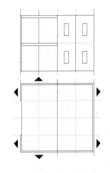

· Cantilevers possible in direction of beam

· Cantilevers possible in direction of beam

· Cantilevers possible in one direction

· Cantilevers possible in both directions

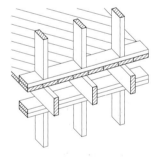 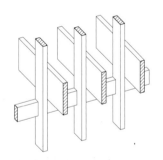 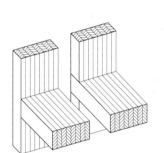 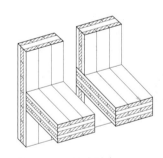

· Finely structured arrangement, normally with nailed connections
· Simple geometry for fitting-out and facade

· Finely structured arrangement, normally with nailed connections
· Simple geometry for fitting-out and facade

· Simple geometry for fitting-out and facade
· Standard mechanical connectors
a Floor suspended
b Floor laid on top

· Simple geometry for fitting-out and facade
· Standard mechanical connectors
a Floor suspended
b Floor laid on top

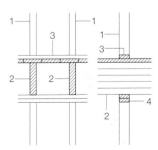  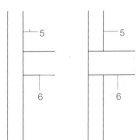 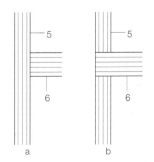

1 column, 2 beam, 3 sole plate, 4 header, 5 wall, 6 floor

Part 3   Basis for planning

**Grading and improvement
of solid timber products**   **55**
Conversion   55
Moisture content and drying   55
Machining   55
Grading   55
Fissures   56
Glued joints   56

Protecting wood   **60**
Risks and risk classes   60
Constructional measures   60
Planning and production   60
Transport, storage and installation   61
Precipitation and moisture
   resulting from usage   61
Condensation   61
Chemical wood preservatives   61

Thermal performance of buildings   **64**
Weighting individual parameters   64
Requirements of statutory
   instruments and standards   65
Energy Economy Act   65
Low-energy buildings   65
The influences of various
   parameters using the example
   of a low-energy building   65
The influences of various
   parameters using the example
   of a low-energy building   66
New air-conditioning systems
   for timber structures   67

Sound insulation   **68**
Fundamentals, definitions   68
Sound insulation requirements   69
Acoustic behaviour of building
   components   69
Methods of analysis for sound
   insulation   70

Fire protection   **71**
Building materials classes   71
Fire resistance   71
Fire protection concepts   72
Building classes   72
Design advice   72
The behaviour of wood in fire   73

Prefabrication and erection   **74**
Planning   74
Transport   74
Erection   75

Some of the following sections deal with
technical subjects whose treatment is
closely tied to the relevant standards.
As such standards can differ considerably
between countries, the German standards
quoted here should be replaced by the
equivalent standards of other countries as
appropriate.

Grading and improvement of solid timber products

Tobias Wiegand

The grade, i.e. quality, of structural solid timber products (softwood logs or sawn timber, finger-jointed solid timber, duo/trio beams, four-piece beams and glued laminated timber) can be influenced at various stages of production.

Conversion

If the cross-section of the trunk is divided up lengthwise so that the pith is cut through (split-heart conversion) or a heart plank containing the pith is removed (boxed-heart conversion), the drying stresses and hence the tendency to split or distort is considerably reduced. In the case of more demanding requirements concerning the appearance, split-heart or even boxed-heart conversion should therefore be specified. Owing to its make-up, the type of conversion of the individual laminations for glued laminated timber is less significant.

Moisture content and drying

The smaller the difference between the moisture content of the wood upon installation and the equilibrium moisture content of the structure, the lower the risk of splitting and distortion. The moisture content of the wood also affects its elastomechanical properties: as the moisture content decreases, so the strength and the moduli of elasticity and shear of the timber increase.

Generally applicable figures regarding the moisture content to be maintained upon installation can be found in, for example, ATV DIN 18334 "Contract procedures for building works - Part C: General technical specifications for building works; Carpentry and timber construction works" and the design standards (e.g. DIN 1052 "Design of timber structures – General rules and rules for buildings"), and details of ways of protecting the wood in DIN 68800

parts 2 and 3 (Protection of timber). Such moisture contents can only be achieved quickly by means of kiln drying. The required moisture content of solid timber should be specified in the tender documents. The technical codes for bonded solid timber products include advice on the moisture contents to be maintained during gluing, which correspond roughly to the moisture contents upon delivery. ATV DIN 18355 contains details of moisture contents to be maintained for joinery work.

Machining

Squared sections, boards and blanks can be supplied rough sawn. For other requirements concerning the surface finish and the accuracy of fit, e.g. for timber houses, planed surfaces and chamfered arrises are usually specified. Chamfers are a good way of preventing right-angled arrises from being damaged by lifting equipment. As the relevant standard for strength grading (DIN 4074 "Strength grading of coniferous wood; coniferous sawn timber", see table on p. 59) permits wane in squared sections, right-angled arrises must be specially agreed. In such cases, reference is usually made to cutting class S to DIN 68365 in addition to DIN 4074. Bonded structural solid timber products are usually planed and chamfered, but for non-exposed applications may be supplied merely scraped. Glued laminated timber and duo/trio beams for applications requiring a better surface finish may include the plugging of knotholes and patching over other growth irregularities. The minimum requirements for surface finishes for joinery work are again given in ATV DIN 18355.

Grading

In grading we must distinguish between grading according to

strength for loadbearing/bracing members as prescribed by the building authorities, and grading according to appearance.
In grading according to strength we further distinguish between visual grading and machine grading:

Visual strength grading relies solely on estimating the strength according to externally visible features, e.g. knots, width of annual rings. In machine strength grading, on the other hand, the modulus of elasticity, density, moisture content and proportion of knots are measured. The greater accuracy with which the material properties can be estimated with these measurements enables higher grades to be achieved. Machine strength grading is currently only customary for grading the laminations to be used in glued laminated timber and is therefore not included in the table on p. 60.
Visual strength grading takes into account a whole series of properties which are also relevant for grading according to appearance. For instance, a visually graded board of grade S 13 normally has much smaller knots than one of grade S 7. However, this is not the case in machine grading. A machine-graded high-strength board may well contain large knots that are aesthetically undesirable. Neither visual nor machine strength grading assesses, for example, the condition of the knots; any knots may be black or may even have fallen out completely. The choice of a higher grade or strength class therefore does not automatically result in a better appearance. The individual sections for bonded solid timber products for loadbearing purposes are always graded according to strength prior to gluing.

Grading by appearance is carried out according to the application and product, normally for non-

loadbearing components but also as an additional requirement for loadbearing components. Some of the grading features are identical with those for visual strength grading, but other limits are specified. Besides the general grading rules for "Structural timber for carpentry; quality conditions" (DIN 68365) and "Timber in joinery – General classification of timber quality" (DIN EN 942) referred to in the VOB (Standard Terms of Contract for Building Works) and partly reproduced here, there is a series of product-related grading rules, e.g. "Sawn timber of broadleaved species for stairs; quality requirements" (DIN 68368). Moreover, there are more detailed quality definitions for various solid timber products which have to be specially agreed. For example, there is an agreement for structural finger-jointed solid timber. This agreement specifies the moisture content and the surface finish and also more detailed requirements concerning conversion, dimensional accuracy and tighter tolerances for various grading features such as wane, condition of knots, width of fissures, discoloration, insect damage and resin pockets. Three surface finish qualities are defined for glued laminated timber ("BS-Holz-Merkblatt"). Special requirements concerning the surface finish can also be agreed individually with the manufacturer. When specifying individual criteria, however, in should be remembered that, for example, knots and shrinkage splits in solid timber products are intrinsic to the material.

Fissures

Fissures in structural solid timber products cannot be ruled out even with careful production and erection. The effects of normal shrinkage splits on the load-carrying capacity of bonded solid timber products have been allowed for when specifying the permissible stress or characteristic strength. Details of the permissible depth of fissures in squared sections are included in the strength grading rules for solid timber. These apply at the time of grading. Fissures with a depth of up to 1/6 of the width of the component from any side can be regarded as harmless according to the "BS-Holz-Merkblatt" for the case of glulam members subjected to unintended tension perpendicular to the grain.

In terms of the appearance, it is primarily the width of the fissure that is important. DIN 68365, however, only contains information regarding the permissible length of fissures. On the other hand, the aforementioned agreement for structural finger-jointed solid timber only includes recommendations concerning the width of fissures. No recommendations regarding fissure length or width are available for other structural solid timber products.

In contrast to these, DIN EN 942, which covers joinery work, gives the permissible width, length and depth of fissures.

Glued joints

Glued joints must be produced with extra care because adhesive defects are very difficult to establish later. Manufacturers of bonded products must therefore possess a "gluing licence" (proof of suitability for loadbearing timber members to DIN 1052 part 1,12.1 and appendix A) and the quality of their products must be constantly monitored (by both the manufacturer and outside institutes). Only tested adhesives may be used for gluing loadbearing solid timber products. Urea-formaldehyde resins, modified melamine resins and phenolresorcinol resins all contain formaldehyde. As the proportion of joints in the structural solid timber products shown here is very small and adhesives with a particularly low formaldehyde content are employed, the concentrations to be expected in the interior air are well below the limits of the formaldehyde directive.

Conversely, polyurethane adhesives do not contain any formaldehyde. However, as formaldehyde is a natural constituent of solid timber, even solid timber products bonded with formaldehyde-free adhesives still contain minimal amounts. The base of the finger joint for a loadbearing component does not have to be closed as it does for a window frame. However, with the light-coloured or transparent adhesives normally used, the finger joints remain inconspicuous. Bonded surfaces, which are necessary for producing duo/trio beams, four-piece beams and glued laminated timber, exhibit joint thicknesses of about 0.1 mm and, when using light-coloured or transparent adhesives, are barely perceptible. However, adhesive joints can be deliberately highlighted by using dark-coloured adhesives.

Timber for carpentry work, grading conditions to DIN 68365

1	2	3	4	5	6	7	8	9	10	11	12	13
	Softwood sq. sections SK = special class NK = standard class		Rough-sawn square-edged softwood boards and planks Grade			Rough-sawn softwood battens and strips Grade		Planed softwood boards and planks Grade			Planed softwood battens and strips Grade	
	SK	NK	0	I	III	I	II	I	II	III	I	II
Wane e.g. 1/4	Cutting class S np, Cutting class A 1/8, Cutting class B 1/3, Cutting class C yes, but each side at least edge-sawn over full length		np	p max. 1/4 thickness over 1/4 length	p max. equal to thickness over 1/2 length	p as col. 5	p	p on unplaned side, max. 1/4 thicknesse over 1/4 length			p as col. 9–11	p as col. 6
Discoloration of spruce, fir, Douglas fir	np	p brown/red streaks resisting fingernail pr.	np	p isolated spots of light shading	p up to 40% discoloration on surface	p up to 10% discoloration on surface	p	np	p as col. 7	p as col. 6	np	p as col. 7
of pine (also Weymouth pine in col. 9 & 10)	np	p blue	np	p isolated blue stain	p blue	p isolated blue stain	p blue	np	p surface up to 10% blue	p blue	np	p as col. 10
Knots W = width, L = length, D = diameter	np unsound & loose	np unsound	p sound per m 1 knot W ≤ 2 cm L ≤ 5 cm np in pine	p W ≤ 2 cm L ≤ 5 cm	p sound, isolated W ≤ 4 cm	p D ≤ 2 cm from ≤ 1/3 of associated side of section	p D ≤ 1/2 of associated side of section	p sound W ≤ 2 cm L ≤ 5 cm	p sound W ≤ 4 cm L ≤ 8 cm	p sound occasionally loose D ≤ 2 cm	p sound D ≤ 2 cm from ≤ 1/3 of associated side of section	p sound D ≤ 2 cm from ≤ 1/2 of associated side of section
Fissures	np	p to limited extent	p isolated L ≤ board or plank width, not passing through or sloping		p L ≤ 1.5 board or plank width	p L ≤ batten or strip width	p L ≤ 1.5 batten or strip width	p as col. 4 & 5		p as	p as col. 7	p col. 8
Worm & beetle damage	np	p insect damage on surface	np	np	p as col. 3	np	p as col. 3	np	np	np	np	np
Ring shake	np	p to limited extent				np	p to limited extent					
Planing flaws & plugged areas								np	p small	p	np	p small

Red or white rot, mistletoe infestation, heart shakes, outer and inner bark are not permissible. Distortion is not permissible in SK squared timber, in NK squared timber, 0.4 cm per m. Interlocked grain is not permissible in SK squared timber, only to a limited extent in NK squared timber.   p = permissible, np = not permissible

Features of wood according to DIN EN 942, Jun 1996

Feature		Exposed surfaces class J2	class J10	class J30	class J40	class J50	Concealed surfaces
Knots		max. 2 mm	30% max. 10 mm	30% max. 30 mm	40% max. 40 mm	50% max. 50 mm	All features listed are permissible on concealed surfaces provided they do not impair the mechanical properties of the timber product or the application
Fissures	max. width	not permissible	0.5 mm		1.5 mm, if made good		
	max. depth [1]		1/8 thickness of part		1/4 thickness of part		
	max. length		100 mm	200 mm	300 mm		
	max. total length per surface		10%	25%	50%		
Resin pockets & bark pockets		not permissible	permissible up to 75 mm long if made good and an opaque coating is to be provided [2]	permissible if made good			
Discoloured sapwood (incl. blue stain)		not permissible	permissible when invisible after decorative treatment or desired as a feature				
Exposed heart		not permissible			permissible if made good		
Damage by Ambrosia beetles		not permissible	permissible if made good				

[1] Measured with a 0.2 mm feeler gauge.
[2] Unless stated otherwise, improvement work in class J10 is not permissible.

Grading and allocation of characteristic values for design

Softwood

Grading specification			Allocation for determining permissible stresses/characteristic strengths	
currently		in future	currently	in future
sawn softwood timber DIN 4074 pt 1, Sept 1989	softwood logs DIN 4074 pt 1, Dec 1958	sawn softwood timber in future DIN 4074 pt 1	DIN 1052 pt 1/A1, Oct 1996 grading classes	in future DIN 1052 strength classes
S 7 [1]	GK III = S 7	S 7 [1][4]	S 7, GK III	C 16
S 10	GK II = S 10	S 10 [4]	S 10, GK II	C 24
S 13 [1]	GK I = S 13	S 13 [1][4]	S 13, GK I	C 30
MS 7 [2]	–	C 16 M [2][3]	MS 7	C 16
MS 10 [2]	–	C 24 M [2][3]	MS 10	C 24
MS 13 [2]	–	C 35 M [2][3]	MS 13	C 35
MS 17 [2]	–	C 40 M [2][3]	MS 17	C 40

Hardwood

Grading specification		Allocation for determining permissible stresses/characteristic strengths		
currently	in future	currently	in future	
applying the sense of DIN 4074 pt 1, Sept 1989	hardwood sawn timber in future DIN 4074 pt 5	DIN 1052 pt 1/A1, Oct 1996 grading classes	in future DIN 1052 strength classes	
			oak	beech
S 10	LS 10 [4]	average grade [5]	D 30	D 35
–	LS 13 [1][4]	–	–	D 40
–	D 30 M [3][6]	–	D 30	D 30
–	D 35 M [3][6]	–	D 35	D 35
–	D 40 M [3][6]	–	D 40	D 40

S xx = visual grading
MS xx = machine grading
LS xx = visual grading for hardwood numerical value
xx = permissible bending stress [N/mm²]
C yy = softwood strength class
C yy M = softwood, machine-graded
D yy = hardwood strength class
D yy M = hardwood, machine-graded
numerical value yy = characteristic bending strength [N/mm²]
GK = grade

[1] Only on request, currently not standard.
[2] Currently only available for laminations for glued laminated timber.
[3] The forthcoming revised edition of DIN 4074 due for publication shortly permits many more grading classes. However, it is anticipated that the correlation of the machine-graded classes customary up to now will become established.
[4] A "K" should be appended to the numerical value for boards, and planks primarily loaded on edge.
[5] Various permissible stresses are then specified for the various species of wood.
[6] Not available at present.

The standards covering strength grading and the design of timber structures are currently being revised at national and European level. The allocation of grading classes to characteristic values for design purposes can be seen in the table. When choosing material during the planning phase, the DIN 1052 grading/strength class designations are the most helpful because strength relationships are immediately obvious.

Visual grading for sawn softwood timber according to load-carrying capacity according to the future edition of DIN 4074 part 1[7])

Grading feature	Squared timber[1])			Boards/planks			Battens	
	S7, S7K	S10, S10K	S13, S13K	S7	S10	S13	S10	S13
Knots • single knot, gen. • single knot, pine • group of knots • knot on edge	up to 3/5 up to 3/5 – –	up to 2/5 up to 2/5 – –	up to 1/5 up to 1/5 – –	up to 1/2 up to 1/2 up to 2/3 –	up to 1/3 up to 1/3 up to 1/2 up to 2/3 [4])	up to 1/5 up to 1/5 up to 1/3 up to 1/3 [4])	up to 1/2 [6]) up to 2/5 [6]) – –	up to 1/3 up to 1/5 – –
Slope of grain	up to 16%	up to 12%	up to 7%	up to 16%	up to 12%	up to 7%	up to 12%	up to 7%
Pith	permissible	permissible	not permissible [2])	permissible	permissible	not permissible	not permissible [5])	not permissible
Width of annual rings • generally • Douglas fir	up to 6 mm up to 8 mm	up to 6 mm up to 8 mm	up to 4 mm up to 6 mm	up to 6 mm up to 8 mm	up to 6 mm up to 8 mm	up to 4 mm up to 6 mm	up to 6 mm up to 8 mm	up to 6 mm up to 8 mm
Fissures • shrinkage splits [3]) • Lightning/ring shakes	up to 3/5 not permissible	up to 1/2 not permissible	up to 2/5 not permissible	permissible not permissible	permissible not permissible	permissible not permissible	permissible not permissible	permissible not permissible
Wane	up to 1/3	up to 1/3	up to 1/4	up to 1/3	up to 1/3	up to 1/4	up to 1/3	up to 1/4
Distortion [3]) • bow • twist • cup	up to 12 mm 2 mm/25 mm width –	up to 8 mm 1 mm/25 mm width –	up to 8mm 1 mm/25 mm width –	up to 12 mm 2 mm/25 mm width up to 1/20	up to 8 mm 1 mm/25 mm width up to 1/30	up to 8 mm 1 mm/25 mm width up to 1/50	up to 12 mm 1 mm/25 mm width –	up to 8 mm 1mm/25 mm width –
Discoloration/Rot • blue stain • brown/red streaks resisting fingernail pressure • brown/white rot	permissible up to 3/5 not permissible	permissible up to 2/5 not permissible	permissible up to 1/5 not permissible	permissible up to 3/5 not permissible	permissible up to 2/5 not permissible	permissible up to 1/5 not permissible	permissible up to 3/5 not permissible	permissible up to 2/5 not permissible
Compression wood	up to 3/5	up to 2/5	up to 1/5	up to 3/5	up to 2/5	up to 1/5	up to 3/5	up to 2/5
Insect damage caused by green wood insects	boreholes ≤ 2 mm dia. are permissible							

[1]) Also applies to boards and planks primarily loaded on edge.
[2]) Permissible for squared sections with a width > 120 mm.
[3]) This grading feature is not assessed for timber graded before drying.
[4]) This grading feature does not apply to laminations for glued laminated timber.
[5]) Permissible in spruce.
[6]) Edge and arris knots that pass right through the section are not permissible.
[7]) The grading criteria are based on a measured reference moisture content of 20%.

Grading features for visual grading according to the future edition of DIN 4074 part 1

		Grading feature
Knotholes are equivalent to knots. • *Knots in squared sections* The smallest knot diameter d governs. In the case of arris knots the dimension d_1 applies if this is smaller than the diameter. The proportion of knots A is calculated from the diameter d divided by the associated side of the section. • *Knots in boards and planks* Knots are measured parallel to the arris. That part of an arris knot (a_1 in diagram) visible on the inside facing the pith need not be taken into account if the knot dimension (a_2) on the edge, related to the edge, does not exceed the permissible values for a single knot. Edge knots must be checked to see how far they extend across the width of the board Three features have to be checked for grading purposes: • *Single knot:* The proportion of knots A is calculated from the total of knot dimensions a_i on all cut surfaces on which the knot appears divided by two times the width b. • *Group of knots:* The proportion of knots A is calculated from the total of knot dimensions a_i for all cut knot surfaces located within a length of 150 mm divided by two times the width b. Knot dimensions that overlap are considered only once. Knot dimensions < 5 mm are ignored. • *Edge knot:* The relationship E of the total of knot lengths e_i projected onto the side of the board to the board width b must be considered. • *Knots in battens* Knots are measured only on the wide side and then parallel to the arris. The proportion of knots A is calculated from the total of knot dimensions a_i on one wide side within a length of 50 mm divided by the width b.	$A = \max\left(\dfrac{d_1}{b}; \dfrac{d_2}{h}; \dfrac{d_3}{b}; \dfrac{d_4}{h}\right)$ Single knot: $A = \dfrac{a_2 + a_4}{2b}$ Group of knots: $A = \dfrac{a_2 + a_4 + \dots a_7}{2b}$ $A = \max\left(\dfrac{a_1 + a_2}{b}; \dfrac{a_3 + a_4}{b}\right)$	**Knots**
The slope of the grain is the deviation of the direction of the fibres from the longitudinal axis of the sawn timber. The slope of the grain F is given as a percentage. Local deviations caused by knots are ignored.	$F = \dfrac{x}{y} \cdot 100$	**Slope of grain**
The pith is the central core of a trunk within the first annual ring. The pith is considered to be present even if only partly present in the sawn timber.		**Pith**
The width of the annual rings is measured in the radial direction in mm. It is calculated from the total of the measured width divided by the number of annual rings. In sawn timber containing heart, a zone 25 mm wide beginning at the pith is ignored.		**Width of annual rings**
• Lightning and frost shakes are radial fissures created while the tree is still standing. • Shrinkage splits are radial fissures that result from drying. • Ring shakes are fissures that follow the annual rings. The grading criterion here is the projections of the fissures onto the sides of the section. The depths of the fissures t_1, t_2, t_3 should be measured at the three quarter-points with a 0.1 mm feeler gauge. The fissure depth r is taken to be the average value of the three measurements t_1, t_2, t_3. Fissures with a length up to 1/4 of the length of the sawn timber, max. 1 m, are ignored. The grading criterion R is calculated from the total of the fissure depths r in a section divided by the dimension of the side affected. Projected fissure dimensions that overlap are considered only once.	$r = \dfrac{t_1 + t_2 + t_3}{3}$ $R = \dfrac{r_1}{b}$ $R = \dfrac{r_1 + r_2}{b}$	**Fissures**
The width of wane $h - h_1$ or $b - b_1$ is measured projected onto the respective side of the section and specified as a fraction K of the associated side.	$K = \max\left(\dfrac{h - h_1}{b}; \dfrac{b - b_1}{b}; \dfrac{b - b_2}{b}\right)$	**Wane**
• Twist, bow and spring are calculated as the rise h at the point of maximum distortion related to a length of 2000 mm. • Cup is calculated as the rise h at the point of maximum distortion related to the width of the sawn timber. Distortion is not usually visible when grading green timber and reaches its greatest extent when the wood is dry.		**Distortion**
• Blue stain is caused by infestation by blue stain fungus. This infestation has no influence on the strength properties of the timber. • Brown or red streaks are also caused by fungi. This is not usually associated with a reduction in strength, provided the streaks are resistant to fingernail pressure. In dry wood it is not possible for the problem to spread. • Brown and white rot represent an advanced stage of fungal infestation. The discoloration is measured on the surface of the sawn timber at the point of maximum extent at 90° to the longitudinal axis. The total of the widths v_i of all discolouring streaks is specified as a fraction V related to the periphery of the section.	$V = \dfrac{v_1 + v_2 + v_3}{2\,(b + h)}$	**Discoloration/ rot**
Compression wood is formed in the living tree as a reaction to external actions. When present to a moderate extent compression wood does not have any significant effect on the strength properties. However, compression wood can cause considerable distortion in sawn timber owing to its distinctive longitudinal shrinkage behaviour. The maximum extent of the compression wood is determined similarly to the extent of discoloration.	see Discoloration/rot	**Compression wood**
The infestation can be recognised on the surface of the wood by the boreholes. The infestation cannot spread in dry timber.		**Insect damage caused by green wood insects**

Protecting wood

Michael Volz

Weather protection for facades

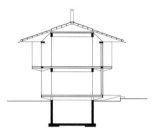

Overhanging eaves, jettied upper storeys

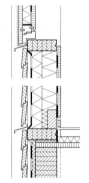

Overlapping profiled boards

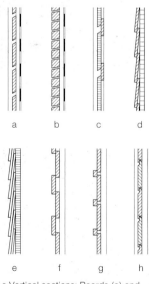

a-e Vertical sections: Boards (a) and
  strips (b) with open joints, planking of
  wood-based products (c), weatherboarding (d), shingling (e)
f-g Horizontal sections: staggered planks
  (f), with cover strips (g)
h Horizontal or vertical section:
  profiled boards

Risks and risk classes

Fungi and insects are hazards for which reliable protection must and can be provided. Fungi that destroy or discolour wood can grow when free moisture is available in the cell cavities, e.g. from condensation or precipitation. The maximum value is taken to be a moisture content of 20% (measured locally). Accordingly, protecting the wood against fungi in the first place relies on limiting the moisture content through the type of construction. Where it is not possible to limit the moisture content, e.g. roof coverings of wood shingles, outdoor floor coverings, resistant species of wood can ensure a durable construction. Only in places where neither the detailing nor a resistant species of wood can be used to provide protection is it necessary to use chemicals.

Insects can attack and destroy wood. The best ways of dealing with this are to leave the timber exposed so that it is easily inspected, e.g. exposed columns and beams in timber-frame construction, or to enclose the timber so that it is inaccessible to insects, e.g. behind walls and in floors. Chemicals should only be used to combat insects when the inaccessibility of the timber and its inspection cannot be guaranteed in the long term.

The regulations prescribe protection for loadbearing timber components and recommend it for non-loadbearing timber components. We distinguish between risk classes allocated to applications, actions and protective measures (see table 1). The table shows that simple measures can provide adequate protection for the wood. Even in the case of severe problems and risks, it is possible to achieve a durable construction without

chemicals, solely by employing a resistant species of wood. Table 2 specifies the applications and the corresponding wood-based product classes required.

Constructional measures

These include all measures that prevent a problematic change in the moisture content of timber components or prevent insects that attack timber from gaining access to concealed components. Problematic changes in moisture content lead to damaging deformations through swelling and shrinkage, or create the right conditions for fungi that destroy timber. Accordingly, the aim of building with wood must be to achieve the lowest possible risk class by means of constructional measures. Furthermore, constructional measures must aim to use appropriate resistant species of wood in those cases where a higher risk class is unavoidable.

Planning and production

The subject of protecting wood must be included at the start of the planning process. Essential conditions arise out of the geometry of the building envelope. Overhanging eaves and jettied upper storeys are among the most effective forms of protection and are equivalent to canopies and roofs made from weather-resistant or easily replaced materials. The plinths and bottom edges of raised structures and components are among the most critical zones. Problems caused by splashing water or snowdrifts are avoided by providing adequate clearance between the timber components and adjoining surfaces.

It is important to choose a species of wood that is resistant to the particular action and a wood-based product class to suit the respective application (see table 2). In

Sloping edge beams

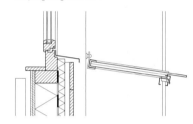

Easily interchangeable lamella

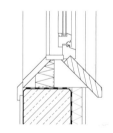

Protection provided by clearance and slope

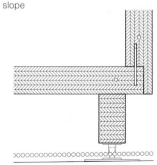

Protection provided by clearance and overhang

Weather protection measures for exposed constructions

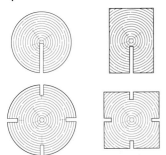

Provision of relieving grooves to prevent splitting

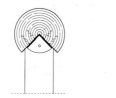

Protection provided by water run-off detail

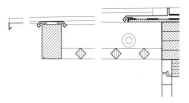

Protection by means of covering and fall

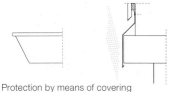

Protection by means of covering

Protection to end grain of beams by means of slope or covering

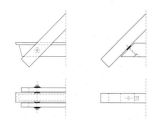

Column-beam junction   drip!

terms of detailing, protection for the wood begins with cutting relieving grooves in logs or squared logs to avoid uncontrolled splitting; and fissures are always an entry point for insects or water. Glued laminated timber and wood-based products are less at risk because they have a lower tendency to split. The sections below describe the geometry of the details that determines the protection against damaging influences. To ensure that the effects of shrinkage and swelling do not cause any damage, small material cross-sections and small surfaces are preferred for components exposed to the weather in particular.

Transport, storage and installation
The constructional measures also include transport. They likewise apply to the storage and installation of the timber components. Even at these earlier stages of the construction process it is important to rule out unfavourable influences: damp ground and precipitation, or excessive drying out as a result of being stored in direct sunlight for a long time. At the start of fabrication the moisture content of the wood and the wood-based products should be equal to the average value expected at the place of installation. The moisture content figures given in DIN 1052 can be taken as a guide:
· heated structures enclosed on all sides 9±3%
· unheated structures enclosed on all sides 12±3%
· roofed structures open on all sides 15±3%
· constructions exposed to the weather on all sides 18±3%

If this is not possible and the timber is therefore installed with a moisture content > 20%, it must be ensured that it is well ventilated. If damp timber is built in and concealed, the covering must allow the moisture to escape by diffusion such that the moisture content (measured locally) drops to a value ≤ 20% within a few months. The drying process may not cause any unfavourable effects on the construction as a result of timber shrinkage and the associated distortion. Water inherent in construction processes must be taken into account. Problematic

levels of moisture can occur in hybrid constructions with monolithic components. Such moisture levels can be dealt with by way of ventilation and maybe even heating in order to prevent an excessive rise in the moisture content of the timber.

Precipitation and moisture resulting from usage
The most effective protection against precipitation (rain or snow) and moisture due to the type of usage (e.g. bathrooms) is to keep the water away from wood and wood-based products by covering the entire construction, or at least the horizontal and sloping surfaces of components. Vertical surfaces such as external walls are protected by profiled or overlapping boards. If the outer leaves of facades are constructed with open joints, moisture protection must be ensured by layers of wood-based products or suitable plastic films positioned behind the outer leaf. Here, too, providing ventilation to the leaf is very important so that penetrating moisture can be carried away again during periods of evaporation.

The timber components that are exposed to the weather must be designed so that the water drains away as quickly as possible, e.g. a wood shingle roof with an adequate pitch. Just as important as a fast water run-off is the rapid drying out of the water absorbed by the wood through effective ventilation of the respective component.

Condensation
Condensation collecting on the surfaces of components cannot be completely avoided. The most important thing here is to limit the condensation to harmless quantities and generally avoid a gradual increase. Effective ventilation achieves this with exposed components.

The greatest danger in enclosed, and particularly in thermally insulated, components is due to the convection of warm air during the cold months of the year, especially at the edges of the component and around penetrations. Convection should therefore be prevented within the sections of thermally

Glued laminated timber beams with sloping, interchangeable boards as protection against moisture

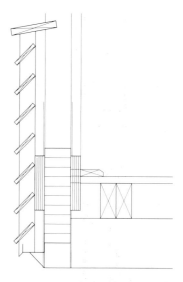

Protection to loadbearing construction of bridge by means of roof and timber lamella in spandrel panels

Protection to loadbearing construction of bridge by means of lamella cladding and sealed road deck

insulated components by providing an airtight barrier on the warm side. On the cold side it is important to guarantee airtightness in order to avoid convection of the external air and associated heat losses.

Residential buildings and those with similar uses may employ walls, floors and roofs open to diffusion. The diffusion resistance of the layers in these components must decrease from the inside to the outside. An analysis to DIN 4108 part 3 or EN ISO 13788 may be necessary in these cases to

prove that moisture diffusing into the structure during the cold months can dry out again during warmer seasons.

Vapour barriers and vapour checks on the warm side of thermally insulated constructions react to higher moisture developments by limiting the diffusion of moisture into the respective component to a harmless level or by preventing this altogether. These vapour barriers and vapour checks can also form a completely sealed component layer and also act as a barrier to convection.

Chemical wood preservatives

Preventive protection for the wood can be achieved by chemicals containing pesticides. These must be tested and carry appropriate test certificates in order to obtain approval from the German Building Technology Institute (DIBt) in Berlin. We distinguish between four test certificates allocated to the respective risk classes (see table 1). DIN 68800 part 3 contains detailed information concerning the method of application and quantities to be used plus other advice.

Table 1: Timber components, applications and risk classes to DIN 68800 part 3

Risk class	Risk due to				Applications	Actions	Measures
	insects	fungi	leaching	soft rot			
					Timber components not subjected to precipitation, splashing water or similar		
0	no	no	no	no	Internal components in heated and unheated interiors with effective ventilation to the room and the construction (average relative humidity ≤ 70%) or components subjected to similar conditions a) inaccessible to insects due to covering on all sides, or b) open to inspection from inside	Permanently dry, long-term moisture content of timber ≤ 20% (measured locally)	none
1	yes	no	no	no	As for risk class 0, but not covered on all sides and therefore accessible to insects with no chance of inspection	As for risk class 0	Use of dark-coloured heartwood with a sapwood proportion < 10% or treatment with wood preservative with test certificate Iv[1]
2	yes	yes	no	no	Internal components in interiors with limited ventilation to the room and the construction (average relative humidity > 70%) or components subjected to similar conditions Internal components in wet zones, with water-repellent covering External components not directly exposed to the weather	Timber not exposed to the weather and not in contact with the soil, but temporary wetting possible	Use of dark-coloured heartwood without sapwood of resistance class 1, 2 or 3 to DIN 68364, e.g. afzelia, ekki, Douglas fir, oak, greenheart, larch, keruing, mahogony, makoré, meranti, red cedar, wood preservative with test certificate Iv, P[1]
					Timber components subjected to precipitation, splashing water or similar		
3	yes	yes	yes	no	External components subjected to the weather but not in permanent contact with the soil and/or water Internal components in wet zones	Timber subjected to the weather or condensation	Use of dark-coloured heartwood without sapwood of resistance class 1 or 2 to DIN 68364, e.g. afzelia, ekki, oak, greenheart, keruing, makoré, meranti, red cedar, teak, or treatment with wood preservative with test certificate Iv, P, W[1]
4	yes	yes	yes	yes	Timber components in permanent contact with the soil and/or freshwater, e.g. in hydraulic engineering, or due to dirty deposits in fissures	Timber permanently subjected to severe wetting	Use of dark-coloured heartwood without sapwood of resistance-class 1 to DIN 68364, e.g. afzelia, ekki, greenheart, keruing, makoré, robinia, teak, or treatment with wood preservative with test certificate Iv, P, W, E[1]

[1] Test certificates according to the DIBt, Berlin: Iv = prevents insect attack, P = repels fungi, W = weather-resistant, E = repels soft rot

Table 2: Wood-based product classes required according to DIN 68800 part 2

Line	Product class	Applications
1 1.1 1.2	 20	Inner linings to walls, floors and roofs in residential buildings and buildings with similar usage [1)] General Upper planking plus loadbearing or bracing decking to floors below unused roof storeys
	20	a) ventilated floors [2)] b) non-ventilated floors
	100	• no or inadequate insulation layer [3)]
	20	• with adequate insulation layer (1/Λ ≥ 0.75 m²K/W) [4)]
2 2.1 2.2 2.3 2.4	 100 100 100 100	Outer planking to external walls Ventilated cavity between outer planking and facing leaf (weather protection) Curtain wall as weather protection, cavity inadequately ventilated, water run-off covering (open to diffusion) to planking Thermal insulation composite system laid directly on planking Masonry facing leaf, cavity inadequately ventilated, covering to planking with: a) water run-off layer with s_d ≥ 1 m b) rigid foam board, min. 30 mm thick
3 3.1 3.1.1 3.1.2 3.2 3.2.1 3.2.2 3.3 3.3.1 3.3.2	 20 100 G 100 100 G 100 G 100	Upper planking to roofs, loadbearing or bracing roof decking Planking or decking linked to interior air with covering layer of thermal insulation (e.g. in residential buildings, heated single-storey sheds) without covering layer of thermal insulation (e.g. flat roofs over unheated single-storey sheds) Ventilated roof cross-section below planking or decking Pitched roof with roof covering Flat roof with roof waterproofing [3)] Non-ventilated roof cross-section below planking or decking Ventilated cavity above planking or decking, wood-based product with water-repellent foil or similar covering to top side [3)] No vapour-check layers (e.g. foil) below the planking or decking, thermal insulation mostly above planking or decking

[1)] This also includes unused roof voids in residential buildings.
[2)] Cavities are considered to be adequately ventilated under this standard if the size of the air inlets and outlets are each at least 2‰ of the area to be ventilated,
    or, for floors below unused roof storeys, at least 200 cm² per m width of floor.
[3)] You are generally advised against the use of such constructions owing to the possibility of unintended moisture occurring, e.g. due to the formation of condensation,
    as a result of water vapour convection.
[4)] Thermal resistance 1/Λ; calculated according to DIN 4108-5

Table 3: Protecting timber: interactive actions on timber due to mechanical, physical, biological and chemical actions

Action	Effects	Possible consequences	Possible damage
Insects	• boreholes in surface • boreholes in cross-section	• reduction in woody fibres	• loss of strength and load-carrying capacity
Sunshine short-wave UV radiation	• photochemical attack • decomposition of woody fibres near surface due to photolysis (depolymerisation of cellulose)	• discoloration: yellowing, browning • possible increase in water absorption at the surface • infestation with fungi and lichens that discolour the wood: discoloration, greying	
Sunshine long-wave UV radiation Temperature changes	• fluctuations in the temperature and moisture content of the wood • drying out due to removal of moisture • stresses, dimensional changes due to swelling and shrinkage • mechanical stresses in the component	• leaks, fissures and gaps, damage to coatings • possible increase in moisture content • infestation by fungi that discolour and destroy the wood if moisture content is also high • possible infestation by insects in the fissures of unprotected timber surfaces	• rot • destruction of the wood
Wind	• erosion of woody fibres • ageing of sealing compounds	• leaks	
Rain	• washing out of constituents and decomposition production of photolysis	• weathering near the surface, discoloration: bleaching, efflorescence • mechanical weakening • increase in water absorption at the surface	
Damp soil Damp air Splashing water Meltwater/condensation	• increase in moisture content, stresses • dimensional changes due to swelling and shrinkage	• infestation by fungi that discolour and destroy the wood	• rot, destruction of the wood
Metal (e.g. connectors)	• extreme thermal conduction in metals • chemical reaction with metals because of constituents of wood (pH value)	• formation of condensation and hoar-frost • discoloration of the wood (e.g. iron-tanning agent reactions)	• rot, destruction of the wood • corrosion of metals
Chemicals	• chemical reaction of wood preservative with adhesives and connector materials	• adverse effect on adhesives and coatings • corrosion of plastics and metals	• destruction of the surface • destruction of connectors

Thermal performance of buildings

Gerd Hauser

The thermal performance of a building describes the interaction between the building envelope and the building services, taking into account the behaviour of users and the prevailing meteorological conditions at the location. The goal in doing this must be to secure the maximum level of comfort with the minimum amount of energy. The construction of low-energy buildings, a form of construction still dominated by timber, calls for the design team to deal intensively with the many building design parameters relevant to the thermal performance. The different factors and the extent to which they influence the energy requirements of a building are outlined below.

In Germany we make a distinction between summer and winter conditions. During the cold part of the year it is generally necessary to provide heating by way of appropriate systems, while during the summer thermal insulation measures can ensure an adequate level of comfort. The essential aspects of thermal insulation are therefore the thermal performance in summer and heating systems with a high degree of efficiency, taking into account hygiene aspects such as, above all, the prevention of mould.

This book does not cover those buildings that require no heating systems owing to their high level of thermal insulation, high passive solar energy gains and efficient ventilation systems, or those that require energy to dissipate heat in summer.

Weighting individual parameters

To be able to identify the importance of the different parameters, we use a detached family house as an example. We shall investigate what effect the various different building, plant and use-related influences have on the level of the

annual primary energy requirement. Table 1 shows variations of the different parameters. We consider the standard case of a building with a primary energy requirement of 125 kWh/m²a, and which complies with the current edition of Germany's Energy Economy Act in terms of the boundary conditions.

Building influences
If the thermal insulation is improved corresponding to the figures in table 1, the energy requirement can be reduced by about 12 kWh/m²a. Thermal transmittance values (U-values) that correspond roughly to the level of requirements in the 1995 Thermal Insulation Act lead to an increase in the primary energy requirement of around 12 kWh/m²a.
The inclusion of optimised details can cut losses at thermal bridges. A value of $\triangle U_{WB}$ = 0 W/m²K results in an annual primary energy requirement of approx. 115 kWh/m²a. Poor detailing around potential thermal bridges ($\triangle U_{WB}$ = 0.1 W/m²K) increases this latter value by about 21 kWh/m²a.
If adequate airtightness of the building, as required by DIN 4108 part 7, is not achieved, an air change rate of n = 0.7 h⁻¹ results in an annual primary energy requirement of 131.6 kWh/m²a. The influence of the type of construction (heavy/light) expressed in terms of the heat capacity is around 2%. This means that timber construction, in comparison with concrete or masonry construction, is hardly at a disadvantage.

Plant influences
Owing to the plant cost index, the use of low-temperature heating systems results in an increase of about 7 kWh/m²a in the annual primary energy requirement compared to the standard case, which is fitted with a condensing boiler

system. If the pipework is routed through unheated areas instead of heated areas as in the standard case, the annual primary energy requirement is 130 kWh/m²a. The primary energy requirement can be reduced by about 14 kWh/m²a if a ventilation system with heat recovery (degree of heat recovery 80%) is provided.

Use-related influences
The Energy Economy Act specifies a value of 19°C as the average interior air temperature. This takes into account partial heating of the interior, i.e. it is assumed that not

all the rooms in a building are heated to the standard interior air temperature. If we use an average interior air temperature of 17°C in our calculations, the annual primary energy requirement will be 108 kWh/m²a. Increasing the interior air temperature by 2 K to 21°C raises the energy requirement by around 18 kWh/m²a.

If compared with the standard case there is no night-time shutdown, approx. 5% extra energy is required. Taking into account climatic data specific to the location leads to a reduction in the annual

Parameters affecting the annual primary annual energy requirement of buildings

	Standard case		
Detached family home in Würzburg with central heating (condensing boiler system) U_{AW} = 0.35 W/m²K U_D = 0.22 W/m²K U_G = 0.36 W/m²K	100 %		
	Building influences		
Improvements to the thermal insulation: U_{AW} = 0.21 W/m²K U_D = 0.18 W/m²K U_G = 0.28 W/m²K	90 %		
Impairment of the thermal insulation: U_{AW} = 0.53 W/m²K U_D = 0.24 W/m²K U_G = 0.50 W/m²K	110 %		
Thermal bridges standard U_{WB} = 0.00 W/m²K	92 %		
Thermal bridges standard U_{WB} = 0.10 W/m²K	109 %		
Air change rate n = 0.7h⁻¹ (no leakage test carried out)	106 %		
light construction C_{eff}=15 kWh/(m³·K) · V_e	102 %		
	Plant influences		
Low-temperature system with central hot water provision distribution in heated areas	106 %		
Condensing boiler system with central heating, distribution in unheated areas	104 %		
Ventilation system with heat recovery	90 %		
	Use-related influences		
average temperature 17°C	86 %		
average temperature 21°C	114 %		
without night-time shutdown	105 %		
Location: Freiburg (region 12)	84 %		
Location: Hof (region 10)	115 %		

Table 1

primary energy requirement of around 20 kWh/m²a for Freiburg in south-west Germany (reference location for region 12 to DIN 4108 part 6). Using the climatic data of the reference location for region 10 (Hof on the Czech border), the requirement climbs to 144 kWh/m²a.

Requirements of statutory instruments and standards

Building code requirements regarding energy-saving construction are included in the Energy Economy Act. Furthermore, requirements covering components, connections between components and the building envelope, for reasons of hygiene and the prevention of damage, are included in various standards.

Energy Economy Act

The heating energy requirement, taking into account the hot water heating requirements and the inclusion of systems for providing heating and hot water, is specified for residential buildings. This parameter can be compared with the actual energy consumption. It therefore represents a characteristic value for the quality of the building in terms of energy requirements. In addition to this figure , which is very interesting for the user, there is also a provision in the Act concerning the permissible primary energy requirement. It also takes into account the losses that ensue during the production and transport of an energy medium.

Besides requirements concerning the primary energy requirement, conditions are also placed on
• the airtightness of the building,
• the minimum air change rate,
• the minimum thermal performance,
• thermal bridges,
• measures in existing buildings, and
• building services.

Level of requirements

The annual primary energy requirement for non-residential buildings in relation to the A/V_e ratio of the building may not exceed approx. 15–35 kWh/m³a for the building heating. If hot water provision is included in the equation (this approach is generally preferred for residential-type

buildings), this results in a maximum annual primary energy requirement measured in kWh/m²a depending on the type of system. We make a distinction here between central and non-central hot water provision.

Method of analysis

The annual heating requirement, calculated according to the method given in pre-standard DIN V 4108 part 6 "Thermal insulation and energy economy in buildings – calculation of annual energy use for building", represents the starting point for calculating the annual primary energy requirement. Besides the monthly balance, which requires a computer, the heating period balance method can also be used for simple applications. The annual heating requirement is the total of the heating energy requirement, the hot water heating requirement and the losses in the systems.

A fixed value of $Q_W = 12.5$ kWh/m²a should be taken for the hot water heating requirement in residential buildings. A hot water heating requirement is not considered for non-residential buildings.

The calculations in DIN 4701 part 10 "Energy efficiency of heating and ventilation systems in buildings – heating, domestic hot water, ventilation" specify that the description of the energy efficiency of the total system be carried out by means of plant cost indices.

The plant cost index represents the relationship between expenditure and benefits and is therefore the inverse of the degree of use, which was mainly used in the past. Taking into account primary energy factors, a primary energy plant index e_p is formed according to the systems and the energy medium used. This is multiplied by the total heating and hot water heating requirements to give the target annual primary energy requirement Q_P:

$$Q_P = (Q_h + Q_W) \cdot e_P$$

In addition to these requirements, a maximum specific transmission heat loss is incorporated. This is intended to guarantee that a minimum thermal performance is upheld in accordance with the 1995 Thermal Insulation Act. We distinguish between non-residential buildings with a window area

≤ 30% and residential buildings

$$H_{T,max}' = 0.3 + 0.15 / (A/V_e)$$

and non-residential buildings with a window area > 30%

$$H_{T,max}' = 0.35 + 0.24 / (A/V_e)$$

Consequences

The essential practical consequences of the new regulations are that designers responsible for thermal insulation and building services must coordinate their work at an early stage. "Bonus incentives", which reward good detailing and, of course, good workmanship, lead to better quality construction. The method of analysis given also clearly identifies the efficiency of good plant, and creates incentives for employing optimised heating and hot water systems.

Thermal bridges

Losses at thermal bridges become more significant as the level of thermal insulation increases. In accordance with the high standards set by the Energy Economy Act, their influence will therefore be taken into account in future when determining transmission heat losses. DIN 4108 part 6 describes two methods: a less favourable global allowance and a more favourable detailed consideration. It is assumed that the details are optimised in terms of their energy efficiency. The global specific thermal bridge surcharge $\triangle U_{WB}$ takes into account the thermal bridges effect without considering the type of construction.

In a detailed analysis the thermal bridges effect can be recorded accurately. However, this approach requires the linear thermal bridge loss coefficients for the main details to be known.

Airtightness

The airtightness of a building is generally specified with the help of the n_{50} value, which relates to the air change rate at 50 Pa pressure difference. The requirements for the airtightness of the building envelope are given in DIN 4108 part 7:
• building with natural ventilation: $n_{50} \leq 3.0$ h⁻¹
• building with mechanical ventilation: $n_{50} \leq 1.5$ h⁻¹

The Energy Economy Act prescribes that a leakage test must be carried out where a mechanical ventilation system is installed. If a leakage test is carried out in a building with natural ventilation (the form of ventilation that will soon be commonly encountered in practice) and the specified value is achieved, a bonus may be included in the analysis. The comparatively low cost of employing the blower-door method of measurement means that ensuring that the airtightness requirements are upheld is, in economic terms, a highly favourable option for improving the thermal performance. We can therefore assume that the leakage test will be employed for the majority of construction projects in the coming years, not only to help assess energy aspects but also to prove the quality of the construction, which is then less vulnerable to damage and does not lead to draughts.

Timber structures can achieve identical airtightness values as masonry structures. This has been verified by measurements carried out on numerous buildings.

Low-energy buildings

A much lower energy consumption than that given in the Energy Economy Act can be achieved with a multitude of individual measures. Specialist publications contain comprehensive information on the effects of such measures. Essentially, these can be assigned to the following categories:

Loss-reducing elements

These include all measures for reducing the transmission and ventilation heat losses, as well as losses in heat generation during conversion, distribution and steady-state conditions. The main elements here are external components with low thermal transmittance values, junctions between components with low thermal bridge loss values, an essentially airtight building envelope, demand-based ventilation with heat recovery, and plant with a maximum annual degree of usage.

Gain-increasing elements
Measures for increasing the thermal gains include those that increase the absorption of solar energy, as well as those that enable increased use of this solar energy and internal heat sources. Systems for preheating the incoming air can also be included in this category. In particular, the size, distribution and arrangement of windows, and the integration of unheated conservatories or glass annexes, atria etc., play a role here. In addition, special wall and facade arrangements with translucent outer skins, transparent thermal insulation and a throughflow of air (for preheating the incoming air) can also increase solar energy gains quite dramatically. Preheating the incoming air for mechanical ventilation systems by means of such facades or upstream geothermal heat exchangers will become more and more significant due to the unavoidable use of ventilation systems in low-energy buildings.

In cases of conflict – especially when considering the economic aspects – loss-reducing elements should be preferred to gain-increasing elements when planning a low-energy building. The first step in the planning procedure should always be to minimise losses, and subsequently to maximise gains. Likewise, the requirements for a low-energy building should first be met by means of constructional measures, and the plant then adapted to suit them.

The influences of various parameters using the example of a low-energy building

In the past, important aspects were commonly treated in a merely intuitive fashion when planning low-energy buildings. This led to disappointments among developers when the hoped-for energy consumption figures were well exceeded. In order to help the designers of such buildings, the influence of individual parameters on the energy behaviour of a building is outlined here (see also table 2).

Draft design
The calculation of the increased or reduced consumption is carried out for a detached family home (floor area 150 m²), a mid-terrace

house (110 m²) and an end terrace house (125 m²) to compare the effects of the different parameters on different building forms. The following parameters are considered:

Location
Although the choice of a building's location is unlikely to be made with respect to energy aspects, the bandwidth for locations within Germany serves for general orientation. Compared to the "average location Würzburg" (southern Germany), we see fluctuations from +13 (Hof) to -8 kWh/m²a (Freiburg).

Building type
Family homes can be built detached or joined to other buildings. Compared to a detached house, a mid-terrace house consumes 12 kWh/m²a less energy.

Building geometry
In conjunction with special measures for using solar energy, e.g. transparent thermal insulation, "exotic building forms" may be optimum solutions. Without these special measures, such forms, e.g. a segmental plan shape, can lead to extra consumption, which reached up to 19 kWh/m²a in one case. An increase in the surface area of the building envelope of up to 10% due to bays or projections increases the annual heating requirement by approx. 6%.

Building orientation
With a customary distribution of the windows on the individual facades – window proportions in standard case: south 33%, west 10%, north 6%, east 15% – the influence of the building orientation lies in the region of 6 kWh/m²a. The long side of a rectangular plan shape should face south.

Shading
Partial or even complete shading to all windows, external walls and roof surfaces can raise the heating requirement by up to 31 kWh/m²a.

Conservatory
A spacious, unheated, north-facing conservatory leads to a reduction of 7 kWh/m²a, a south-facing one 4 kWh/m²a. However, the effects of orientation on the possible uses

of the conservatory must be considered.

Detailed design
To compare the effect of different parameters within the scope of the detailed design, the calculation of the increased or reduced consumption is carried out for a single-storey detached family home measuring 9.50 x 10.75 m on plan and with the space under the duopitch roof converted into living quarters. The floor area is about 150 m². The heating requirement is affected by the following parameters:

Thermal performance
The thermal performance of the heat-exchanging building envelope is determined by the U-values of the individual components or one U_m-value and the design of the details with regard to thermal bridge effects and leaks. An increase in the U_m-value of 0.12 W/m²K corresponds to a rise in the heating requirement of 20 kWh/m²a.

Airtightness
The inclusion of more and more insulation in the external components increases the proportion of ventilation heat losses in the annual heating requirement. Ventilation concepts based on airflows through joints or manual surge ventilation (i.e. opening the windows) are unsuitable for low-energy buildings owing to the uncontrolled and wide variability of the air change rate. Furthermore, the necessary average air change rate of about 0.5 h⁻¹ cannot be guaranteed in less favourable areas. A central ventilation system is therefore included in the standard house. It should be remembered that as the leakage rate (infiltration) of the building increases, so the effectiveness of the ventilation system quickly decreases. In comparison with the standard case with its n_i-value of 0.10 h⁻¹, the heating requirement reduces by 4 kWh/m²a for $n_i = 0.05$ h⁻¹. With a less airtight envelope where $n_i = 0.20$ h⁻¹, the heating requirement rises by 9 kWh/m²a. High airtightness requires special care during planning and construction of the airtight barrier and its connections to other components.

Transparent thermal insulation
The use of transparent thermal insulating materials enables the incident solar radiation to be better used for reducing the annual heating requirement. The element considered here consists of a glass panel made from 4 mm glass panes and thin-walled, translucent glass or plastic tubes positioned perpendicular to the surface in the 122 mm cavity. The thermal resistance of the system is 1.37 m²K/W. The dependence of the radiation transmission of the element on the angle of incidence is taken into account according to the manufacturer's data. To absorb solar radiation behind the transparent thermal insulation we assume a 200 mm thick, matt black-painted concrete wall with an absorptance of 0.96. A wall area of approx. 14 m² is available in the ground-floor south-facing facade for the transparent thermal insulation and its concrete wall. In the most favourable case the annual heating requirement is reduced to approx. 40 kWh/m²a. However, it must be pointed out that such systems require really effective sunshading because otherwise excessive internal surface temperatures in the living quarters and unacceptably high temperatures in the absorption layer can occur.

Temporary thermal insulation
During periods without incident solar radiation, the window represents, compared to the plain external wall, a component with high thermal losses. One possibility for improving the behaviour of windows in terms of energy is to provide some form of temporary thermal insulation. This entails a movable insulating element, which can be positioned in front or behind the window opening at night. Many forms of such insulation are available. We assume an ideal situation in our simulation calculations, i.e. that the temporary thermal insulation closes tightly, there is no airflow in the cavity and no additional thermal losses at the junctions. In our study of the parameters the temporary thermal insulation is varied by way of an additional thermal resistance of 2.0 m²K/W externally at the window elements. The use of the temporary

thermal insulation is limited to the period without solar radiation. Conventional wood or plastic roller shutters achieve values of 0.15–0.30 m²K/W. Here, we assume a tight-fitting shutter. In a less well-fitting system the values drop to about 0.05 m²K/W. The annual heating requirement decreases by about 12% when using temporary thermal insulation with a thermal resistance of 2.0 m²K/W.

Heat capacity
Heat capacity is less important than the thermal insulation. Between the types of construction with the lowest and highest heat capacities there is a potential saving of 4 kWh/m²a.

Proportion of windows
Between 0% and 100% the window area on the south-facing facade affects the heating requirement by 5 kWh/m²a. However, if we include, as recommended, the electricity required for artificial lighting – weighted with a factor of 2.5 – in the equation, this relationship is reversed.

Colour of external components
The colour scheme of the external components influences the absorption a_s of the incident solar radiation. This heat source resulting from the absorption of radiation raises the temperature of the external surface and hence reduces the heat losses through the component. However, this effect decreases as the level of insulation of the external components increases.
A light colour (a_s = 0.3) for the external wall, window frames and roof produces an 8.2% increase in the annual heating requirement compared to a dark envelope with a_s = 0.9.

New air-conditioning systems for timber structures

As a rule, timber structures have a lower heat capacity than concrete and masonry structures, and therefore, under summertime conditions, lead to higher temperatures. However, this disadvantage can be compensated for by activating the heat capacity of the soil. To do this, water flows through components in the living quarters and the ground floor slab, thereby enabling heat to be removed from the interior and transferred to the soil. The advantage that might be expected from water flowing through layers near the ceiling does not actually occur in practice because the primary radiation energy strikes the floor and, when this too has water flowing through it, is immediately removed. As figure 3 shows, a favourable relationship is set up when using the well-known underfloor heating system so that no new types of construction are necessary, merely the coupling of the underfloor heating to a ground floor slab with water flowing through it.
The temperatures shown in figure 3 apply to a detached family home with relatively large windows, which are fitted with effective sunshading. These characterise the high efficiency of the system described.

Annual heating energy requirement

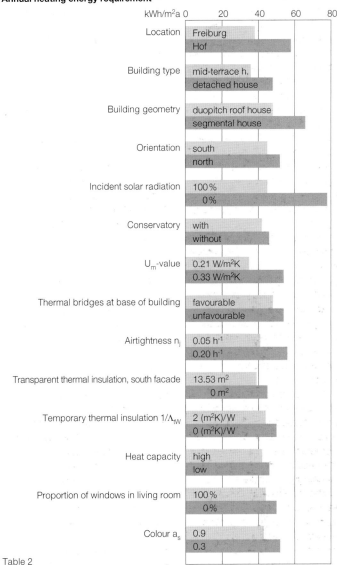

Table 2

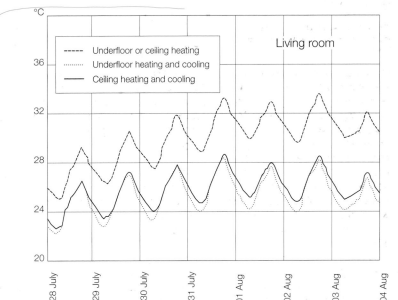

Fig. 3: Graph of the interior temperatures in the living room of a detached family home under summertime conditions, with and without cooling system

Sound insulation

Gerhard Wagner, Helmut Zeitter

Sound insulation is becoming increasingly important for our lifestyles and standard of living. Owing to its high priority, effective sound insulation – irrespective of the type of construction – must be carefully planned and properly implemented.

The point of sound insulation requirements is to protect people from unacceptable noise levels. Sound insulation measures are required to prevent the ingress of noise from outside and the transmission of noise from one room to another (e.g. between living and working areas with different occupants), or to the outside. In timber structures, good sound insulation values can be achieved with multi-skin arrangements and with a correct combination of layers within the component. Today's roof, wall and floor components can achieve the sound insulation requirements of DIN 4109 without the need for additional measures.

Only minor modifications are necessary to raise the airborne sound insulation margins and impact sound levels of timber structures to meet the enhanced sound insulation requirements of DIN 4109 supplement 2. Even with a higher external noise level, as is the case adjacent to busy roads or beneath airport approach corridors, effective sound insulation can be achieved in buildings with timber-frame external walls.

While the respective federal state building codes give requirements to protect against external noise and noise between areas with different occupants, there are no statutory provisions for private living and working areas. However, it is advisable to guarantee adequate sound insulation for "noisy" areas, e.g. children's rooms, music rooms. The level of sound insulation required by the developer should be discussed and agreed with the designers and contrac-

tors. Existing standards and guidelines (DIN 4109, DIN 4109 supp. 2, VDI directive 4100) can of course be very helpful here.

Sound insulation in timber structures

In terms of acoustics we distinguish between single-, double- and multiple-skin components. In single-skin components such as masonry or reinforced concrete walls, the sound insulation depends mainly on the mass per unit area – the heavier, the better. However, this often goes hand in hand with poorer thermal insulation characteristics. Lightweight, single-skin components cause problems for sound insulation. Timber structures cannot compete with masonry and concrete in terms of providing large masses of material. Instead, good sound insulation in timber structures is achieved with the proper arrangement of different layers.

Fundamentals, definitions

Sound transmission

There are two forms of sound transmission: airborne and structure-borne.

Airborne sound uses the surrounding air as the transmission medium. Sound sources, e.g. conversation, radios and televisions, cause the air to vibrate.

Structure-borne sound requires solid or liquid media to transmit it. Walking, flushing the toilet or operating a light switch causes walls and floors to be set in vibration, and these in turn excite the air of adjacent rooms to vibrate as well. In buildings, providing impact sound insulation is the most common way of dealing with structure-borne sound.

Sound and sound level

The term "sound" is the range of frequencies that can be perceived

by the human ear; in adults this ranges from 16 to 16 000 Hz. A frequency range of 100 to 3150 Hz is usually relevant for building acoustics.

The "sound pressure level" is the logarithmic measure of the relationship between a current sound event with amplitude p and the threshold of hearing p_0, and is measured in decibels (dB).

A-weighted sound level

Our perception of volume is determined by the frequency. Weighting filters to simulate the characteristics of the human ear are integrated into the measuring instruments. The A-filter is common, specified with the unit of measurement dB(A). The A-weighted sound level is employed to evaluate a noise, e.g. traffic, building services, over the entire prescribed frequency range. The individual frequency ranges corresponding to the sensitivity of the human ear are included in the evaluation with different weightings. Example: sound with a frequency of 31.5 Hz is not perceived until a sound level of approx. 53 dB has been reached; sound with a frequency of 2000 Hz is heard at 0 dB (threshold of hearing).

Sound reduction indexes for airborne sound, airborne sound insulation

The airborne sound reduction index (R) specifies how well a component attenuates the sound of a source of noise propagated in the form of airborne sound. It is the difference between the volume measured at the source of the noise and that measured in an adjacent room.

The higher this figure (R), the better the attenuating property of the component is.

Sources of noise
- Road traffic
- Railway
- Aircraft
- Machines, plant
- Impact sound caused by persons
- Music
- Conversation
- Events
- ...

Forms of sound transmission

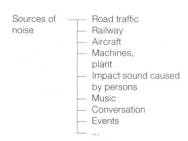

Airborne sound transmission

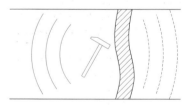

Structure-borne sound transmission

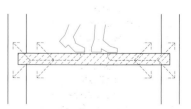

Impact sound transmission (structure-borne)

The actual way in which the component is incorporated into the structure is decisive for good airborne sound insulation. Sound is transmitted not only through the component separating one room from another (see figure 1), but also through all adjoining components, e.g. ceiling, floor, wall (see figure 2), which we call flanking transmissions. The characteristic value for airborne sound insulation between two rooms is the resultant sound reduction index (R') (see figure 3). To establish the airborne sound insulation index we must therefore decide whether the adjoining (flanking) components have been taken into account (R'_w) or only the component itself (R_w). The R'_w value is the one usually required for verifying the necessary sound insulation as it already allows for flanking transmissions via adjoining components. In timber structures flanking transmissions play a major, sometimes a decisive, role.

Sound reduction indexes for impact sound, impact sound insulation

Impact sound is caused, for example, by walking on upper floors and stairs, household appliances (e.g. washing machine), or the noise of impacts, which then generate vibrations. Building components excited in this way transfer the vibrations in turn to the air of the neighbouring rooms. The sound level L_n measured in an adjoining room (generated by a defined standard hammer) is designated the standard impact sound level. In contrast to airborne sound, it is not the attenuating effect of the component that is specified but rather the resulting volume in an adjoining area. The characteristic value is the standard impact sound level index L_{nw} or L'_{nw}.

The lower the value of the impact sound level index L_{nw}, the better is the construction of an upper floor in acoustic terms.

As with the sound reduction index for airborne sound, we must distinguish whether the actual situation within the structure has been considered (L'_{nw}) or only the separating component itself (L_{nw}) when determining the standard impact sound level index. We should take care with timber floors to make sure that the structure-borne sound

excitation for the structural elements due to the type of usage is "attenuated" as far as possible. If a timber floor construction satisfies the impact sound insulation requirements, it will generally fulfil the airborne sound insulation requirements as well.

Acoustic bridges

Acoustic bridges exist wherever there are air or non-decoupled layers to transmit vibrations. The example of the open window shows that wherever air can pass, so can sound. Components and their junctions with adjoining components must be airtight in order to avoid acoustic bridges for airborne sound. It is therefore particularly important to ensure careful workmanship or sealing measures at cable or pipe penetrations, power sockets etc. Typical acoustic bridges for structure-borne sound ensue at the joint between a floating screed and the wall or structural floor slab. These are due, for example, to cables passing between structural slab and screed, or the lack of a strip of insulation between the edge of the screed and the adjacent wall. Acoustic bridges between structural slab and screed lower the impact sound insulation further than those between screed and wall.

Sound insulation requirements

Sound insulation aspects covered in the building regulations

Requirements for sound insulation are prescribed in the federal state building codes. These make a distinction between standards relevant to legislative requirements and other standards. The latter can include provisions included in contracts between private persons, and, above all, can include sound insulation requirements within a building because these are not covered by any legislation. The relevant statutory instruments covering sound insulation requirements are:
• DIN 4109 "Sound insulation in buildings; requirements and testing"
• DIN 4109 supp. 1 "Sound insulation in buildings; construction examples and calculation methods"

Standards and directives not included in the statutory requirements and therefore to be agreed in the contract are, for example:
• DIN 4109 supp. 2 "Sound insulation in buildings; guidelines for planning and execution; proposals for increased sound insulation; recommendations for sound insulation in personal living and working areas"
• VDI directive 4100 "Noise control in housing – criteria for planning and assessment"

Sound insulation requirements (statutory provisions)

DIN 4109 lays down sound insulation requirements for external components and those between the residential units of different occupiers or between different types of use. These requirements are usually mandatory and must be observed.

DIN 4109 supplement 1 contains working examples for components that comply with the requirements of DIN 4109 without the need for acoustic tests. The specified sound insulation is achieved when a reasonable standard of workmanship is employed. This standard also gives methods of calculation for verifying airborne and impact sound insulation.

Acoustic behaviour of building components

Single-skin components

The acoustic insulation of single-skin components, e.g. masonry or concrete walls, and solid timber walls, depends mainly on the mass per unit area – the heavier the component, the better its sound insulation value. However, this effect does have its limits when high sound reduction indices are required. Sound reduction indices > 55 dB can generally be reliably achieved only by using double-skin components.

Double- and multiple-skin components

Due to their construction, timber structures mainly employ double- or multiple-skin components. The sound insulation of such components depends on the properties of the individual layers, their interconnection and the "attenuation" of the cavities between individual

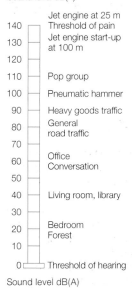

Sound level dB(A)

140	Jet engine at 25 m — Threshold of pain
130	Jet engine start-up at 100 m
120	
110	Pop group
100	Pneumatic hammer
90	Heavy goods traffic
80	General road traffic
70	
60	Office Conversation
50	
40	Living room, library
30	
20	Bedroom Forest
10	
0	Threshold of hearing

Sound level dB(A)

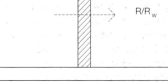

Fig. 1: Sound reduction index of building component

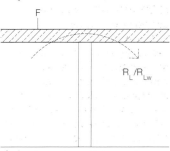

Fig. 2: Sound reduction index of adjoining component (flanking transmissions)

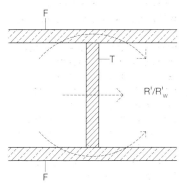

Fig. 3: Sound reduction index taking into account flanking transmissions

Party wall requirements to DIN 4109

Component	DIN 4109 reqd. R'$_w$ [dB]	DIN 4109 supp. 2 rec. R'$_w$ [dB]
Party walls between apartments	53	≥ 55
Walls to staircases	52	≥ 55
Party walls between buildings	57	≥ 67

Party wall requirements to VDI directive 4100

Component	Draft DIN 4109 pt. 10 (VDI 4100) SSt 2 rec. R'$_w$ [dB]	VDI 4100 SSt 3 rec. R'$_w$ [dB]
Party walls between apartments	≥ 56	≥ 59
Walls to staircases	–	–
Party walls between buildings	≥ 63	≥ 68

Ways of improving the flanking sound reduction index

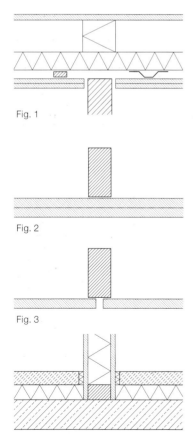

Fig. 1

Fig. 2

Fig. 3

Fig. 4

Sources: www.infoholz.de,
Holzabsatzfonds (public body), Bonn

layers. The following principles must be observed here:
• the use of non-rigid layers (e.g. plasterboard and wood-based boards)
• the decoupling of layers by using elastic fixings (e.g. for suspended ceilings)
• the provision of insulating materials to attenuate cavities
• the inclusion of non-rigid masses in floors (fillings of sand and chippings)
• ensuring the airtightness
• the avoidance of acoustic bridges

In timber housing the way in which components are connected is especially important. Assuming that the building has been designed and built correctly, hardly any sound energy will be transmitted via flanking components. The flanking sound transmission is low, the flanking sound insulation correspondingly high. Transmission of structure-borne sound via acoustic bridges must be avoided. Strips of insulation at junctions between components or special fixing collars for building services enable the respective component to be decoupled from a possible source of noise.

Flanking transmissions at party walls
Party walls should prevent disturbing noise being transmitted from neighbouring premises and also guarantee privacy within one occupancy. Party walls separating residential units must therefore comply with airborne sound insulation requirements. We distinguish between walls separating different residential units, walls to staircases and walls between buildings. DIN 4109 specifies the minimum requirements for these different types of party wall. Rigid connections can act as acoustic bridges. A compromise is often required between connections required for structural purposes and transmission points unfavourable in acoustic terms.

Ways of improving flanking transmission sound reduction indices
The following measures help to improve the sound reduction indexes for flanking transmissions:
• A "bulkhead" of mineral wall or another suitable material in the

cavity (e.g. in the floor) of the flanking component improves the value by about 3–4 dB (figure 1).
• Doubling the boarding to the ceiling improves the value by about 3 dB when it is fitted to battens (figure 1, left), and by up to 5 dB when an elastic fixing is provided (figure 1, right).
• Doubling the wall boarding can improve the sound insulation index by up to 4 dB (figure 2).
• Separating the boarding (e.g. with a gap) brings about an improvement of approx. 4 dB even when the planking is fixed to the same frame (figure 3).
• Screeds that are continuous between lightweight partitions are particularly problematic in acoustic terms. A floating screed should be interrupted by the partition (fixed to the structural slab) (figure 4). Wet screeds achieve better acoustic values than dry screeds.

Methods of analysis for sound insulation

There are five approaches to analysing the sound insulation, four of them covered by standards. Their advantages and disadvantages are briefly outlined below.

On-site measurements
The most reliable (standardised) method with regard to the actual sound reduction index. However, this method does not allow any preliminary measurement and the outcome cannot be planned beforehand. It is costly and time-consuming, and only limited improvements are possible.

Laboratory measurements
Special test rigs suitable for timber structures are not available in large numbers (at short notice). Some manufacturers of plasterboard or wood-based products do carry out measurements using their own test installations.

Simplified method of analysis
The simplified method of analysis to DIN 4109 makes use of a surcharge 5 dB higher than the required resultant sound reduction index. This surcharge applies to separating and flanking components:

Party wall:
$R_{wR} ≥$ reqd R'_w + 5 dB
Flanking component:
$R_{L,w,R,i} ≥$ reqd R'_w + 5 dB
This method presumes that the flanking sound reduction index is known beforehand, which is not always the case. Apart from that, this method is not particularly reliable because the "allowance" of 5 dB is inadequate in many instances.

Theoretical analysis
The most reliable approach during planning is to calculate the resultant airborne sound reduction index $R'_{w,R}$ using DIN 4109 supp. 1, eq. (7). The analysis is based on the laboratory values for separating and flanking components. However, these laboratory values must be determined through a one-off, reliable measurement in a test setup.

Verification using test certificates
The fifth (but not standardised) way makes use of the laboratory values provided by manufacturers and approved in the form of certificates issued by the German Building Technology Institute (DIBt). This approach allows designers and contractors to assess the necessary values for contemporary forms of construction at relatively short notice.

Fire protection

Gerhard Wagner, Helmut Zeitter

Fires in buildings and their effects on their surroundings are a risk to life and a health hazard. To prevent the outbreak and spread of fire the federal state building codes include fire protection requirements, which are virtually identical throughout Germany. According to these codes, structures must be built in such a way that
- they prevent the outbreak of fire,
- they prevent the spread of fire, smoke and fumes,
- they guarantee the escape and rescue of people and animals, and
- they enable effective firefighting measures to be employed.

Only for fire protection do the federal state building codes contain detailed requirements. Thermal insulation, moisture control measures, sound insulation and wood preservation are all covered by standards referred to in the codes.

Building materials classes
To achieve the aims of protection, requirements are placed primarily on the combustibility of the building materials and the fire resistance of the building components – in addition to the design criteria of preventive structural fire protection. The federal state building codes (based on the standard building code) essentially make use of the classification system used in DIN 4102 "Fire behaviour of building materials and building components". Furthermore, the latest standard building code defines a building component class "highly fire-retardant", which limits the temperature within a loadbearing component for a specified period of time. Wood and wood-based products are permissible as loadbearing components within this class (F 60-AB). Combustibility is a property of the building material. Solid timber and

the majority of wood-based products fall into building materials class B2, flammable. Building materials classes play a major role during the outbreak of a fire. For this reason, highly flammable materials (class B3) may not be used. Non-combustible building materials on the surfaces of components slow down the fire propagation rate. Linings to walls and ceilings along escape routes must therefore be non-combustible.

Fire resistance
The combustibility or non-combustibility of building materials does not allow conclusions to be made about the fire resistance of the building components constructed from those materials. Components are constructions that must fulfil certain functions within a structure. They may be built from several different materials, and in timber buildings in particular, multiple-skin components are customary. Fire resistance is a property of the building component. It designates the minimum number of minutes for which the component remains functional when exposed to a fire (e.g. F30 = 30 minutes fire resistance). Function implies both loadbearing functions and separating functions that prevent the transmission of smoke and heat. Components, as referred to by the standards, include columns, beams, internal and external walls, floors, roofs, doors and windows. DIN 4102 specifies the fire resistance of components using a letter for the components, e.g. F for loadbearing walls, columns and beams, T for doors, G for glazing elements etc. This letter is followed by the duration of resistance in the standard fire test, specified in minutes. The designation is concluded by specifying the building materials class or classes to be used. Unfortunately, not all Germany's building codes employ the same

Examples of building materials and their combustibility, and European classes		
Building material	Building materials class to DIN 4102 part 1	European class
Incombustible material (e.g. steel lattice girder)	A1	A1
Incombustible material with combustible components (e.g. plasterboard as interior finish to timber construction)	A2	A2
Not readily flammable material (e.g. oak parquet flooring on screed)	B1	B
Low contribution to fire		C
Flammable material (e.g. glued laminated timber joist)	B2	D
Acceptable behaviour in fire		E
Highly flammable material (e.g. untreated coconut fibre mat)	B3[1]	F
[1] not permitted in buildings		

Fire resistance classes to DIN 4102 part 2				
Fire resistance class	Building materials class to DIN 4102 part 1 for materials used in components tested		Designation[1]	Building-authority designation[1]
	main parts[1]	other parts not included in col. 2		
F30	B	B	F30-B	fh = fire-retardant
	A	B	F30-AB	fh, and the main parts made from incombustible materials
	A	A	F30-A	fh, and made from incombustible materials
F60	B	B	F60-B	–
F90	B	B	F90-B	–
	A	B	F90-AB	fb = fire-resistant
	A	A	F90-A	fb, and made from incombustible materials
[1] for explanations see DIN 4102 part 2				

designations as those in the standard building code; the terms "fire-retardant" and "fire-resistant" are more usual.

The loadbearing components of detached and semi-detached houses do not normally have to satisfy any requirements, or at best "fire-retardant", e.g. F30-B. This requires fire resistance of 30 minutes, and the loadbearing construction can be made from a combustible material, e.g. timber. Party or compartment walls, as required between terrace and semi-detached houses, must exhibit a higher fire resistance. This is also possible in timber structures.

Fire protection concepts
The standard building code and the federal state building codes prescribe a fire protection concept for buildings, with precise requirements laid down for the materials used on the surfaces of loadbearing components, floors, roofs, walls etc. and the fire resistances of components. The great majority of residential and office buildings can be properly designed and built using the fire protection provisions of the federal state building codes. Owing to the complexity of the relationships, deviating from the regulations very quickly leads to the need to involve the fire brigade. For special types of construction or special types of usage, employing the standard fire protection measures according to the provisions of the respective federal

state building code could well mean the actual aims of the fire protection are not achieved. Preventive fire protection in such cases can be achieved in another way. This applies especially to buildings for special purposes, e.g. places of assembly, restaurants, or public buildings such as schools, nurseries etc.
The use of a fire protection concept that guarantees the protective aims of the federal state building code allows, in principle, non-standard situations. Intrinsic to such a concept is not solely the fire resistance of a component but the overall project-related system of fire protection measures. These include:
• the use of (non-mains powered) fire and smoke detectors,
• minimum distances between buildings,
• escape route and rescue concepts (e.g. self-closing doors, incombustible surfaces),
• access for the fire brigade and their ladders,
• the use of sprinkler systems, and
• the connection of fire detection systems directly to the fire brigade headquarters.

Fire protection concepts are not usually necessary for detached family homes because the applicable requirements are usually satisfied by the type of construction itself.

Building classes
We make a basic distinction between buildings of normal construction for normal usage (e.g. residential and office buildings) and those of special construction for special usage. This latter group is covered by additional directives or regulations that apply in addition to the local building code:
• regulations covering the construction and operation of restaurants,
• regulations covering the construction and operation of hospitals,
• building authority standard directives for schools,
• regulations covering the construction and operation of sales premises,
• regulations covering places of assembly etc.

We make a further basic distinction between low- and high-rise multistorey residential and office buildings. Low-rise buildings are those in which the floor level of the topmost storey suitable for permanent occupation is < 7 m above the surrounding ground level. This corresponds to a window sill level of 8 m from which rescue could take place. This figure was based on the availability of rescue ladders. The scaling ladders available to all fire brigades throughout Germany are about 8.3 m long and so a window sill more than 8 m above the ground cannot be reached without further means. In normal cases only fire-retardant (F30-B)

construction is called for in low-rise buildings. This means that residential and office buildings with up to three storeys can be built in many federal states without having to apply special measures. Only in a few places in Germany, e.g. Hamburg, Rhineland Palatinate, Mecklenburg-Western Pomerania, Brandenburg and Berlin, are there exceptions when more than two residential units are involved.
Every building in which the floor level of the topmost storey exceeds 7 m currently requires a special fire protection concept and the approval of the local fire brigade and building authority. However, individual, economic solutions are possible if a fire protection consultant joins the design team.

Design advice
One important design, construction and control criterion is the intended fire compartmentation. Due to the nature of its construction, timber-frame construction, for example, includes cavities in which a fire can spread unnoticed if the following conditions are not fulfilled:
• Filling all cavities completely with insulating material wherever possible. This also helps sound and thermal insulation.
• All cavities in components should be encapsulated, i.e. they must be fully enclosed to provide fire protection on all sides.

Fire protection criteria

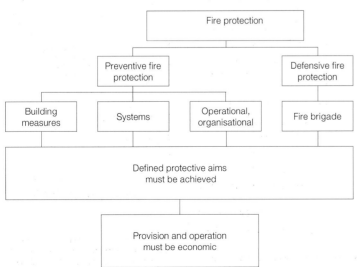

Development of a fire protection concept

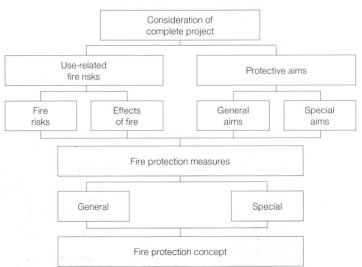

- Service shafts and ducts must be carefully planned and sub-divided into compartments.
- Facades and wooden windows/shutters should be examined to assess how they may contribute to spread of fire.

We can sum up the subject of fire protection as follows:
- The use of timber construction methods in normal buildings for normal usage is generally possible up to three storeys, although in some federal states there are restrictions regarding the number of permissible residential units.
- Special buildings for special usage with one or two storeys are normally possible, but taller buildings require individual fire protection concepts worked out with the help of a fire protection consultant.
- Deviations from the standard cases covered by federal state building codes are possible if fire protection concepts are worked out to guarantee the protective aims.
- Current research projects and the ongoing updating of the federal state building codes attempt to extend timber applications in multistorey constructions by taking into account BA components. We can expect that it will soon be possible to erect timber structures with a topmost storey having a floor level up to 14 m above the surrounding ground level. However, such

buildings will always require a fire protection concept.
- The clearance between adjacent buildings (3 or 5 m depending on location) must be considered for facades with a timber cladding.
- Generally, only incombustible materials should be used for the walls and ceilings of escape routes within buildings, especially the necessary corridors and staircases. Floor coverings of not readily flammable materials are possible.
- Besides the pure fire protection requirements, smoke protection concepts should also be considered, especially when controlled ventilation is being used.
- The provision of individual fire and smoke detectors is generally not mandatory but does lead to a significant reduction in risk and can constitute a valuable voluntary contribution.

The behaviour of wood in fire
No one disputes that wood is a combustible building material, providing any fire with a good source of "fodder". The use of wood therefore has both economic and technical limits in terms of fire protection. Many fires in which wood has been involved show that it is usually the wrong application and an unfavourable combination with other building materials that has led to the fast spread of a fire and hence to greater damage.

Statistically, timber buildings do not catch fire more often than buildings made of other materials because the causes of fire are almost always unrelated to the type of construction. In the first place it is mainly the fire load (combustible furniture, fittings, documents etc.) that determines the rate at which a fire spreads. The further course of the fire is, however, determined by the presence of efficient fire compartmentation functioning for a sufficiently long period of time. This fire compartmentation must be able – independently or with the help of firefighters – to limit a fire within a building to a certain area and thus prevent it spreading further. Modern timber buildings satisfy requirements concerning the correct combination of building component layers and building materials (combustible/incombustible), and the fire resistance of the components. The loadbearing wall elements comply with the customary F30-B fire resistance requirements without special measures as they are covered on both sides with plasterboard or other wood-based boards, and are filled with an insulating material. Additional covering with fire-performance or fibre-reinforced plasterboard enables adequate fire resistances to be achieved for the party walls in residential and other buildings, even multistorey timber structures. Where timber components are left exposed and at the same time

provide loadbearing functions, it is often sufficient to choose a larger cross-section to comply with the necessary fire protection requirements. Although wood burns, it exhibits a favourable behaviour during fire because the charcoal produced forms a natural layer of insulation that prevents a temperature rise in the wood underneath and hence a loss of strength. This is one of the great advantages of timber structures compared to steel, particularly in long-span single-storey sheds. However, all steel fixings must be protected from direct exposure to the fire by means of a sufficiently thick timber covering or concrete casing.

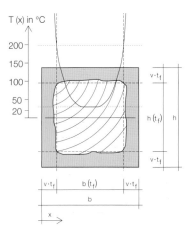

Temperature gradient for timber cross-section exposed to fire on all four sides

Sources: www.infoholz.de, Holzabsatz-fonds (public body), Bonn; Informations-dienst Holz, Feuerhemmende Holzbau-teile (F30-B), 07/2001

Rate of charring v in mm/min [$v_{\text{DIN 4102 pt 4 (Mar 94)}}$ = $v_{\text{ENV 1995-1-2}}$]

Type of timber[1]		Rate of charring [1] v in mm/min
Generally	Boundary conditions	$v_{top} = v_{side} = v_{btm}$ $v_{beam} = v_{col} = v_{ten\ mem}$
Glued laminated timber	Softwood, including beech	0.7
Solid timber		0.8
Solid timber	Hardwood with $\rho > 600$ kg/m³ except beech	$0.56 = 0.7 \times 0.8$ [1]

[1] There are the following differences between the DIN standard and ENV 1995-1-2:

a) Softwood according to the ENV has a density $\rho \geq 290$ kg/m³ and a min. dimension of 35 mm (not specified in the DIN standard) *

b) The limit for hardwood in the ENV is $\rho > 450$ kg/m³ ($\rho > 600$ kg/m³ in the DIN standard).

c) v-hardwood $_{\text{(solid timber or glulam ENV)}}$ = 0.5 mm/min instead of 0.56 mm/min in the DIN standard

* ρ means the characteristic value for the species of wood (5% fractile, oven-dry density)

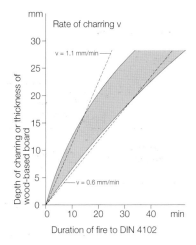

Depth of charring or thickness of wood-based board product with $\rho > 600$ kg/m³ (chipboard, wood fibreboard, plywood)

Prefabrication and erection

Wolfgang Winter

Prefabricated elements in timber engineering have many advantages over traditional types of construction. Traditional approaches to construction are expensive to design and implement, slow and complicated. About a quarter of the material consumed in a structure is simply waste. Prefabrication permits a rational form of building achieving a high standard of quality while saving resources and simplifying the collection and recycling of waste.

Advantages of prefabrication:
- High quality because the work is carried out under good conditions.
- Optimisation of costs.
- Less waste because less adaptation and adjustment is necessary.
- The waste generated in the prefabrication plant can be recycled.
- Lower erection costs on site.
- No construction moisture during erection.

Rationalisation measures
- Repetition: The repetition of elements presupposes their applicability for structures of different sizes and different purposes, and at different locations. Large-scale production is possible when elements have a particular form (standardisation). Buildings are divided into elements.
- Demarcation of work: The construction process is subdivided into distinct individual activities. This requires strict organisation of operations compared to manual trades.
- Organisation of processes: Exact organisation of the design, production and erection processes results in higher productivity at the expense of flexibility.
- Specialisation: Organising the subdivision of the work calls for specialists.

- Mechanisation: Increasing use of machinery results in enormous productivity gains. One disadvantage is the high overheads (upkeep of machinery) during slack periods in the construction industry.

Architects, contractors
As the degree of prefabrication increases, so the interface between the design and construction phases shifts forwards.

The system manufacturers sometimes take over as general contractors and may offer, for example, turnkey completion based on a given building application, including design work, for a lump sum. An architect active in this field will need to be familiar with the special requirements and characteristics of the systems, i.e. general knowledge, not related to any particular company's products, is required, as well as cooperation with the specialists at an early stage of the work.

Planning
The planning of prefabricated timber buildings demands close cooperation between architect, engineer and timber fabricator. The planning time increases, but erection time decreases. In the interest of optimising costs, more and more carpentry shops are prefabricating ever larger elements, right up to complete room modules. Alternatively, factory-made semi-finished fabrications, e.g. small-format, compact modules, may be employed. Team-based planning is the prerequisite for realising this construction process, which is changing the nature of timber design. Here, the coordinated sum of the individual services is no longer important, but rather the integrated overall performance of completely different specialisms. This is the only way to meet, for example, requirements

concerning ecological, energy-efficient structures and inexpensive construction and operation.

Transport
The options and costs of transport are important criteria in the planning of prefabricated elements. Erection times and costs partly depend on the weights and sizes of components. Decisions regarding transport routes and the choice of means of transport must therefore be made well in advance.

Comparison of various transport options

Means of transport	Dimensions for transport				Description	Cost estimate
By road	Max. dimensions for vehicle with load					
	Length 12–18.25 m	Width 2.55 m	Height 4.00 m	Weight 40 t	Volume of load: 2.50 m x 2.60 m x 12.00 m	Depends on approval requirements and escort vehicle requirements
without approval						
with approval	25 m	3.5 m	4.2 m	60 t	No escort vehicle up to 3 m	
Special transport vehicles	Dimensions > 3.50 m or height 4.20 m				Approval for route selected and escort vehicle requirements	
By rail						
Large container	Differences according to standards applied (ISO, EN) according to length (in feet) and type, e.g. Isobox container 40 x 8 ft (12.129 x 2.438 x 2.438 m), Eurobox container 254 (6.058 x 2.5 x 2.6 m)				Containers up to a load volume of 70 m³, handled with cranes or fork-lift trucks	Transport by rail is more economic for very long distances. However, the last leg of the journey to the building site is almost always by road.
Interchangeable bodies	HGV bodies without wheels				Transported on flat wagons	
Trailer (without tractor)					Transported on hopper wagons, handled at terminals or with cranes	
Direct transport of vehicles					Transported on low-platform wagons, handled at terminals or on mobile ramps	
By ship						
	Handled using containers (see above)				The container can be loaded directly at the factory or taken to the port by road or by rail.	The costs fluctuate depending on the route and the workload of the shipping company; distance, duration and fuel costs are also relevant.
By helicopter						
Depends on payload	up to 900 kg, up to 1500 kg, and up to 2500 kg				Helicopters are primarily used for sites with difficult access, for bulky loads and when quick delivery is critical.	Critical here are type of helicopter, rotation time (pure flying time) and difference in altitudes.

Production plant for large-format wall elements: fabrication table

Assembly table

Storage

Transport of wall elements

Erection of wall elements

Erection of floor elements

Prefabrication in multistorey timber-frame construction

In this form of construction the loadbearing structure and the wall elements are prefabricated separately. The interfaces are the structural connections and the joints, which must satisfy building science requirements.

Dimensions and joints

Dimensional deviations in the elements must be allowed for owing to manufacturing tolerances. Dimensional tolerances should compensate for inaccuracies in the construction and guarantee the simple installation of the elements during erection. Adhering to these dimensional tolerances is particularly important at the interfaces between different types of construction (concrete, steel, timber). The use of just one manufacturer may mean that smaller tolerances can be specified.

Connections between elements

The necessary joints between the loadbearing structure and non-loadbearing elements can be achieved in various ways:
- Butt joints or open (drained) joints: these require a high degree of accuracy because non-parallel edges and faces can impair the appearance ("gaping joints").
- Single rebates: the shadow of the joint is not readily apparent; inaccuracies at the joint between the individual components do not usually present any major problems.
- Double rebates: used with multi-skin constructions.

Joint widths in timber structures vary between 5 and 20 mm depending on the width of the elements.

Erection

Elements are delivered to site according to an erection schedule so that the time-savings from prefabrication are not wasted through coordination problems. The elements require lifting points, and guying until the bracing construction has been erected.

Erection sequences

for multistorey structures consisting of plates, panels, trusses and frames.

Individual elements
- Prefabricated columns and beams, wind and stability bracing, floor and wall elements

+ Flexible for complicated loadbearing structures, low transport volume, little space needed on site

- High cost of temporary supports, time-consuming, considerable labour requirements

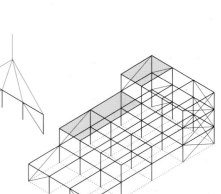

Storey-height frames
- Prefabricated trusses or frames with wind and stability bracing
- Prefabricated floor and wall elements

+ High degree of prefabrication, time-savings through pre-assembly, primarily for complicated, but standard connections
- Large transport volume, average space requirements on site (storage, handling), erection loading cases must be considered!

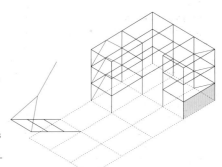

Multistorey frame
- Prefabricated trusses or frames with wind and stability bracing
- Prefabricated plates and panels

+ High degree of prefabrication, time-savings through pre-assembly, primarily for complicated, but standard connections
- Large transport volume, large space requirements on site (storage, handling), erection loading cases must be considered!

Multistorey, multibay frames
- Prefabricated trusses or frames with wind and stability bracing
- Prefabricated storey-height panel elements
- Prefabricated solid timber elements

+ Fast erection
- Trusses and girders must be erected on site because they cannot be transported already pre-assembled, and that requires large flat surfaces and heavy lifting plant

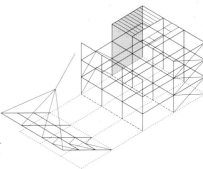

Part 4　Timber engineering

Julius Natterer

The forest is considerably important as a space for leisure and recreation, and a significant asset within the environment. Planned forest management and efficient use of wood are necessary to preserve and care for our forests. The added-value use of wood, e.g. as a building material, can help recoup the high cost of maintaining our forests. The use of wood as a loadbearing building material offers a host of design options. The demands of modern building methods can be fulfilled using the latest engineering approaches. However, this is not possible without new technological developments, which must be underpinned by scientific and theoretical models. The fundamentals for this lie in greater efforts in research and teaching.

Quality assurance

Architects, structural engineers and other specialist engineers are independent designers who, besides their pure planning activities, take on the important task of assuring the quality of a whole project. They are responsible, first and foremost, to their client. They act as trustees for the developer, and must guarantee the economic construction of a structure free from defects by the appointed building contractors. But their specialist knowledge places these independent designers in a position of responsibility with regard to the general public and the environment. They have to make sure that the balance between use of the resources required and the benefits to be obtained is reasonable, that the structure does not bring any risks for people or the environment, and that it also satisfies aesthetic demands.

The aim of structural engineering

Timber structures are complex assemblies participating, as a whole, in load-carrying functions. They have a wide range of applications, e.g. houses, roofs, single-storey sheds, bridges, towers, even machines and means of transport such as boats and aircraft. However, this section of the book will restrict itself to the design of roofs, single-storey sheds, bridges and multi-storey structures where the carrying of dead, imposed, snow, wind and other loads are important for the overall stability.

Quality criteria for timber structures

The choice of material, the method of jointing and the concept of the structural systems, forms of loadbearing system and details are especially relevant for the quality of a timber structure. This calls for collaboration between architect and structural engineer at an early stage of the work. It is the foundation for economic construction with wood, with the consumption of material placed in an equation with the architectural aims plus the functional and structural requirements on one side, and the costs on the other.

The economic efficiency of the structure can be defined thus:

$$\text{economic efficiency} \ = \ \frac{\text{requirements}}{\text{costs}}$$

The architect will see the realisation of his artistic concept for a structure as the prime quality criterion. An exposed timber structure can act as an important design element in this respect. The engineer will view a timber structure as a multitude of structural systems, which in conjunction with the form, type of material, type of jointing and method of fabrication, produce an almost infinite number of variations. The timber structure – acting as a three-dimensional loadbearing construction – must carry all the loads expected to occur with a certain probability. Thus, scatter within the characteristic values for materials and the loading assumptions can be compensated for safely, and the long-term reliability and serviceability are assured.

For the engineer, a primary quality criterion of the structural design is legibility of the flow of forces, i.e. the transfer of loads. And the consumption of material for the type of construction chosen is important when assessing a timber structure.

Some of the following sections deal with technical subjects whose treatment is closely tied to the relevant standards. As such standards can differ considerably between countries, the German standards quoted here should be replaced by the equivalent standards of other countries as appropriate.

The tasks of the architect | 78
The tasks of the structural engineer | 78

A   Timber engineering

1   The brief | 78

2   Project planning and draft design | 79
2.1   The development of the structural form | 79
2.2   Structural development of building
       envelope forms | 79
2.3   How structural systems carry the load | 80
2.4   Modelling the stiffness of structural systems | 81
2.5   Choice of material and modelling
       the cross-section | 82
2.6   Connectors and details | 83
2.7   Presentation | 84
2.7.1 Isometric and axonometric views | 84
2.7.2 CAD | 84
2.7.3 Structural models | 84
2.8.   Design variations | 84

3   Preparing submissions for approval,
       planning of projects | 86
3.1   The tasks of the engineer | 86
3.2   Engineering services | 86
3.3   Basic services for a timber
       engineering project | 86
3.3.1 Structural calculations | 86
3.3.2 Analysis of load-carrying capacity | 86
3.4.   Drawings for timber engineering projects | 87
3.4.1 Design sketches, proposals | 87
3.4.2 Fabrication and working drawings | 88

4   Production of tender documents | 90
4.1   Administrative details | 90
4.2   General conditions | 90
4.3   Project-related provisions | 90
4.4   Bill of quantities | 90
4.5   Special technical directives for
       timber engineering | 90
4.6   Terms of payment | 90

5   Special services | 91
5.1   Planning fire protection | 91
5.2   Planning sound insulation | 91
5.2   Planning thermal insulation | 91
5.4   Checking the working drawings | 91
5.5   Erection, temporary works and
       scaffolding drawings | 91
5.6   Progress charts and timetables | 91
5.7   As-built drawings and records | 91
5.8   Planning timber construction | 91
5.9   Quality control of production and deliveries | 92
5.9.1 Material quality | 92
5.9.2 Strength of timber | 92
5.9.3 Non-destructive testing | 92
5.9.4 Eurocode 5 | 93
5.9.5 Quality of workmanship | 93

6   Restoration and refurbishment methods | 94
6.1   Recording the residual strength | 94
6.2   Restoration and strengthening methods | 95
6.2.1 Repair of fissures | 95
6.2.2 Repair of damage to timber structures | 95
6.2.3 Strengthening of existing timber structures | 95

**B   Material variations and cross-section
       forms for components**

1   Logs | 96
1.1   Logs and the resulting compound sections | 96
1.2   Compound sections | 97

2   Sawn timber | 98
2.1   Squared logs and the resulting
       compound sections | 98
2.2   Profiled and composite sections made
       from sawn timber | 99

3   Glued laminated timber (glulam) | 100
3.1   Cross-sectional shapes | 101
3.2   Elevational forms | 101
3.3   Beam forms | 102
3.4   Special forms | 102

4   Wood-based elements und semi-products | 104
4.1   Beams with solid webs | 104
4.2   Cross-laminated timber | 104
4.3   Laminated veneer lumber | 104
4.4   Plywood | 105
4.5   Particleboard and chipboard | 105

5   Outlook | 105

**C   Connectors and methods of
       connection**

1   Criteria for designing details | 106
1.1   Deformation behaviour | 106
1.2   Transfer of forces | 106
1.3   From the connector to the detail | 107
1.4.   Design of the detail | 107

2   Craftsman-type connections and connectors | 108
2.1   Halving joints | 108
2.2   Supports | 108
2.3   Oblique dado joints | 109
2.4   Contact faces | 109

3   Engineered connections | 110
3.1   Nails in timber engineering | 111
3.1.1 Design and calculation of nailed connections | 111
3.1.2 Nailed forms of construction, examples | 112
3.1.3 Punched metal plate fasteners, examples | 113
3.1.4 Sheet metal connectors | 114
3.2   Bolts, close tolerance bolts | 116
3.2.1 Design and calculation | 116
3.2.2 Bolted construction, examples | 117
3.3   Dowels in timber engineering | 117
3.3.1 Design and calculation | 118
3.3.2 Dowelled construction, examples | 119
3.4   Glued construction | 120
3.4.1 Glued joints | 120
3.4.2 Factory-glued components | 121
3.4.3 Timber panel elements | 121
3.5   Special connectors and jointing techniques | 122
3.5.1 Cramped connections | 122
3.5.2 Building and scaffold cramps | 122
3.5.3 Bonded-in threaded rods for strengthening
       at supports | 122
3.5.4 Turnbuckles | 122
3.6   Special connections | 123

3.6.1 Bonded-in rods | 123
3.6.2 Cast-in channels | 123
3.6.3 Tensioning elements | 123
3.6.4 Anchor bolts | 123
3.6.5 Cast parts | 123
3.6.6 Elastomeric or sliding bearings | 123

D   Stability elements

1   Vertical loadbearing systems | 124
1.1   Restrained members | 124
1.2   Propped compressive members | 125
1.3   Guyed compressive members | 125

2   Vertical loadbearing systems at 90°
       to the primary loadbearing system | 126
2.1   Stability by means of frames | 126
2.2   Stability by means of trusses | 126
2.3   Stability by means of plates | 127
2.4   Stability by means of secondary
       loadbearing systems | 128
2.4.1 Purlin frames | 128
2.4.2 Kneebraces | 128
2.4.3 Lattice-type purlins | 129
2.4.4 Stressed-skin systems | 129

3   Horizontal and diagonal structural systems | 130
3.1   Girders | 130
3.1.1 Longitudinal girders | 130
3.1.2 Transverse girders | 131
3.1.3 Cantilever girders | 132
3.1.4 Cranked systems | 133
3.1   Roof and floor plates | 134
3.2   Roof and floor plates made from
       one layer of boards and planks | 134
3.2.2. Roof plates made from wood-based
       products | 135
3.2.3. Roof and floor plates made from composite
       materials | 135

4   Stability created by form and geometry | 136
4.1   due to the inherent stiffness of the primary
       loadbearing system in section | 136
4.2   due to the inherent stiffness of the primary
       loadbearing system in elevation | 137
4.3   due to the inherent stiffness of the primary
       loadbearing system on plan | 138
4.4   due to the inherent stiffness of the primary
       loadbearing system in three dimensions | 138

5   Stability due to three-dimensional structural
       behaviour | 139
5.1   Plane and space frames | 139
5.2   Vibration behaviour, ductility and
       seismic resistance | 139

6   Outlook | 139

Handling a large volume by breaking it down into several small units

Structure left exposed internally

Integration of structural geometry and natural lighting

Integration of loadbearing structure, natural lighting and building services

Extreme snow loads with cantilever

A timber structure requires close cooperation between architect and engineer because the possibilities of leaving the structure exposed, the form and the choice of material depend to a great extent on the structural design. Leaving the elements of the structure, interior fitting-out and services exposed, making them attractive and comprehensible, is a "voluntary exercise" in building. The result is measured in terms of quality of utilisation, durability, economy and beauty.

The tasks of the architect

- Clarifying the terms of reference (interior layout, boundary conditions resulting from functions and building codes relevant to the project)

- Drawing up a concept with particular reference to function, energy, form
- Coordinating the other specialists involved in the planning and incorporating their specialist contributions
- Estimating the costs

- Optimising the concept
- Proposing and establishing the geometry of the building
- Integrating the specialist contributions
- Specifying the project and calculating the costs according to DIN 276
- Clarifying the suitability for approval

- Producing the documentation required for approval according to the legal guidelines that apply to the project

- Presentation of the project with all the information necessary for its construction
- Disseminating instructions for the work of the other specialists involved and incorporating their specialist contributions

- Determining the quantities
- Producing a specification
- Agreeing the specification with the other specialists involved
- Assembling the contractual documents and specifications
- Obtaining quotations
- Checking and evaluating the quotations
- Negotiating with suppliers and assisting in the appointment of suppliers
- Providing an estimate of costs according to DIN 276

The tasks of the structural engineer

- Clarifying the terms of reference (boundary conditions for the structure, loading assumptions, foundation conditions)

- Drawing up a utilisation plan with details of loads and other actions on the structure
- Producing a concept for the loadbearing structure
- Producing a safety concept in agreement with the building codes applicable to the project
- Producing alternative concepts
- Providing advice regarding the loadbearing structure
- Supplying proposals for the geometry of the building
- Supplying proposals for the choice of material
- Estimating the cost of the loadbearing structure according to DIN 276

- Producing a structural solution
- Producing relevant engineering calculations
- Specifying the principal dimensions of the structure and parts thereof
- Supplying proposals for the details
- Specifying the loadbearing structure and calculating the costs according to DIN 276
- Assisting in negotiations

- Possibly calling for tenders for the structure early in the project

- Producing verifiable structural calculations
- Producing line drawings of the structure
- Negotiating with checking authorities and engineers

- Producing working drawings for the loadbearing structure and its details
- Producing general arrangement and reinforcement drawings
- Producing lists of materials

- Determining the quantities for the loadbearing structure, including jointing materials
- Producing a specification for the loadbearing structure

The brief

For architects and engineers the brief provides a framework for specifying the terms of reference for the design of a timber structure. This will include a description of the current situation, the production of interior layouts, analyses of locations, schematic diagrams of functions and utilisation drawings. The compatibility with the surroundings and neighbouring buildings must also be weighed up. For the engineer the conditions prevailing at the location, the use and the resulting loads are key factors that can have a decisive influence on the design. Relevant criteria should be recorded in writing and clarified with the developer and building authorities. The checklist below may need to be considerably expanded in individual cases.

Checklist

Stipulations	fire protection
	sound insulation
	rights of owners
	floor space index
	cubic extent index
	boundaries
	building lines
	building materials
	ecology
	...
Location	building plot
	infrastructure
	orientation
	topography
	exposure
	surroundings
	subsoil conditions
	...
Utilisation	clear space
	lighting
	fire protection
	plan layout
	functions
	vertical access
	...
Building services	ventilation
	heating
	artificial lighting
	acoustics
	water
	waste water
	escalators, lifts
	...
Loading	dead loads
	wind loads
	snow loads
	imposed loads
	lifting loads
	stored goods
	crane loads
	impact loads
	seismic loads
	thermal loads
	...

Part of structure left exposed externally

Access zone with glazed duopitch roof

Floor construction with regular beam grid

Primary structure trussed in two directions

Diamond-shaped bracing to a suspended shell

Section

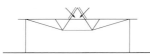

Trussed beam with continuous clerestory windows

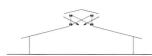

Primary loadbearing members and windows in longitudinal direction

Primary loadbearing members longitudinal, secondary loadbearing members transverse

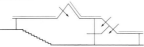

Primary loadbearing members with grandstand, suspended

Trussed, bottom chords raised

Trussed, maximum structural depth

Longitudinal system with natural lighting

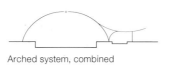

Arched system, combined

Arched system to match tipped materials

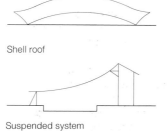

Shell roof

Suspended system

Project planning and draft design

The evolution of the form of a building envelope is essentially determined by the urban planning and landscaping framework. The playing area of a sports hall or the diving board of a swimming pool are, together with the lighting and ventilation arrangements, are examples of starting points for the clear interior space and the form of the loadbearing systems.

The development of the structural form

The architect specifies a motif and the desired character of the structure in the preliminary and draft design phases. The engineer develops alternative structural systems that both help to realise the concept and achieve the numerous technical and economic requirements. At the start of a project as many variations as possible should be drawn up in order to ensure the quality and economic efficiency of the design by comparing the different approaches.

Structural development of building envelope forms

The possibility of leaving the loadbearing system exposed, i.e. not having to clad the building for visual or thermal insulation requirements, for instance, is an artistic but, above all, an important economic aspect. In this respect wood is superior to other building materials.

The primary structural systems delineate the load-carrying paths and the points of support. Their design in conjunction with the wind and stability bracing lends the building its characteristic form. It is at this stage of the planning that decisions are made concerning how to ensure the stability of the building. Shear walls, bracing, fixed-base columns, frames or arches may be chosen, and the cost and complexity of the foundations must always be taken into account.

Elevation

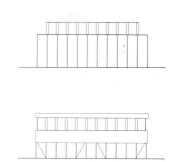

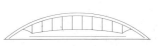

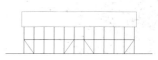

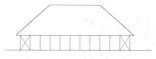

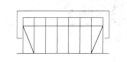

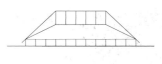

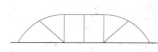

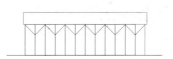

Plan views of primary structural systems

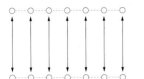

Linear – cumulative in longitudinal direction

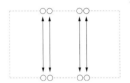

Linear – concentrated

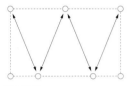

Diagonal

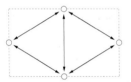

Linear and diagonal – combined

Linear in longitudinal direction – cumulative in transverse direction

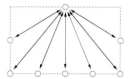

Radial

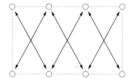

Crossing diagonals

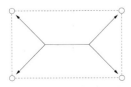

Diagonal and branched

Plan views of secondary structural systems

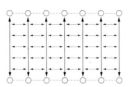

Linear between primary loadbearing members – cumulative

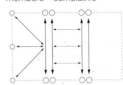

Radial and linear, combined

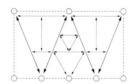

Orthogonal and diagonal – combined

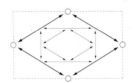

Diagonal

Cumulative linear or diagonal

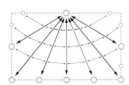

Cumulative radial

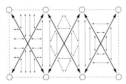

Linear-diagonal

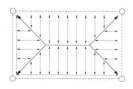

Linear

How structural systems carry the loads

Primary structural systems
The number of primary structural systems, their spacing and the positions of supports are governed by the plan layout. The design of the grid depends on the utilisation conditions, e.g. movable partitions, lighting.
Certain subsoil conditions may also justify loads being carried in the longitudinal direction. Circular or polygonal plan layouts give radial or three-dimensional arrangements for the primary structural members. Sculpted roof forms can often be realised economically with branched systems.

Secondary structural systems
Secondary structural systems give form to the roof and also the interior layout. The loadbearing arrangement is determined by the number and nature of the supports, the number and interconnection of independent loadbearing elements, and the form of the loadbearing members.
The span and clear space requirements are less critical for secondary loadbearing members than for primary ones. Skilfully selected secondary structural systems with a short span lend visual depth to a roof, fulfil stability requirements and make a major impact on the appearance of the interior.
Arranged as struts and ties, they provide numerous solutions that are both structurally beneficial and architecturally appealing. These include kneebraces and multiple struts, which in a three-dimensional arrangement can create umbrella- or mushroom-type structures.

Tertiary structural systems
For the selection of suitable supports for the roof decking, e.g. sheeting, wooden panels, solid timber elements, even trapezoidal metal sheeting, acoustic, thermal insulation and fire protection criteria are important. However, aesthetic and structural design aspects should also be considered.

Cumulative linear primary structural system

Cumulative linear primary structural system + orthog. secondary loadbearing members

Diagonal secondary loadbearing members

Central long. main loadbearing members

Longitudinal loadbearing system with space frame secondary structural system

Shell with a radial arrangement of curved primary ribs and an annular arrangement of secondary ribs

Strutting arrangements

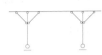

Straight kneebraces

Curved kneebraces

V-form

Multiple struts

Propped beam

Strut frame

Kneebraced strut frame

Trussed beams

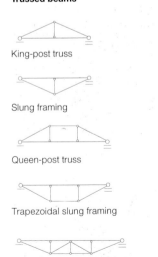

King-post truss

Slung framing

Queen-post truss

Trapezoidal slung framing

Extended trapezoidal slung framing

Fish-belly arrangement

Modelling the stiffness of structural systems

Essentially, the form of the primary and secondary loadbearing members can be created in line with the effective moment of inertia. The cube of the effective depth of the loadbearing member is used in the equation, whereas the width of the loadbearing member and the loaded area have only a linear effect.

$$J = \frac{b \cdot h^3}{12}$$

where:
J = moment of inertia
b = width of loadbearing member
h = depth of loadbearing member

h^3 is used in the stiffness equation

As a result, the stiffness depends essentially on the depth of the loadbearing member.
The efficiency of the form of a structural system can be modified by the shape of the cross-section, ties, struts, truss arrangements, joints and cantilevers. High bending and lateral (overturning) actions should be avoided to reduce the amount of material. The three-dimensional arrangement of the structural system is very important for the stability in particular and for the overall safety.
All structural systems can be optimised through stiffness modelling, i.e. matched to the bending moments diagram by adjusting the depth of the construction or by altering supports, joints and spans. The space available for the structure determines the type of loadbearing elements. A low structural depth means that only solid-wall loadbearing systems can be considered. However, greater depths enable the use of trusses and frames in which the load-carrying mechanism is by way of compression and/or tension.
Cantilevers, struts and truss arrangements are simple ways of modelling the stiffness. Structurally favourable continuous systems and the transition to three-pin trusses and frames can be varied in many ways. However, these generate horizontal loads, which must be resisted at the supports. Space and plane frames that simultaneously provide enclosing, loadbearing and stability functions create an impression of lightness and spacious interiors.
When optimising the details, the use and complexity of steel connectors should be in relation to the aesthetic and engineering requirements.
In the course of developing the structure, all structural systems can be shaped to match the requirements by way of stiffness modelling.

Continuous beams

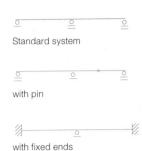

Standard system

with pin

with fixed ends

coupled

reinforced

with double kneebraces
spans up to 20 m

as truss

trussed above and below

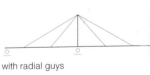

as triangular truss
spans up to 50 m

with radial guys

with parallel guys (harp arrangement)
spans up to 80 m

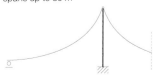

as suspended loadbearing member
spans up to 150 m

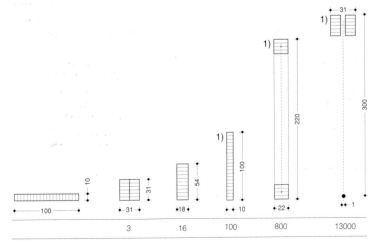

Comparison of various moments of inertia with the same cross-sectional area but different overall depths
1) protection against overturning necessary

Cross-section stiffnesses, logs

I_1

Single moment of inertia

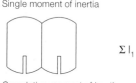

ΣI_1

Cumulative moment of inertia

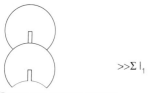

$>>\Sigma I_1$

Exponential moment of inertia
with nails or dowels

Cross-section stiffnesses, squared sect.

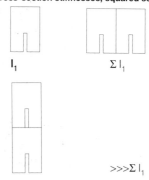

I_1 ΣI_1

$>>>\Sigma I_1$

Exponential moment of inertia
with nails or dowels

$>>\Sigma I_1$

Cross-section stiffnesses, planks

I_1 ΣI_1

$>>\Sigma I_1$

T-section

$>>>\Sigma I_1$

Double-tee section

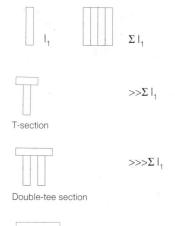

Box section

Choice of material and modelling the cross-section

The material for primary, secondary and subsidiary loadbearing systems should be chosen at the earliest possible stage in order to coordinate spans and loadbearing systems. There are many different products, e.g. logs, halved logs, edge-sawn logs, squared or profiled sections in compound forms, plus planks, boards and battens. A well-thought-out cross-sectional geometry can satisfy not only structural but also fire protection, acoustic and thermal performance requirements. In addition, glued laminated timber (glulam) forms allow almost any shape to be modelled. The architect can choose from a wide range of surface finishes: natural, rough sawn, planed or sanded. In terms of the colouring and the nuances of various types of wood, the design possibilities are infinite.
Wood-based products include laminated veneer lumber (LVL) boards, plywood, particleboards, fibreboards and various types of sandwich boards, which satisfy the requirements of weather resistance and fire protection.
Architects and engineers can still choose between different types of wood and grades with higher visual grading criteria; from spruce, pine, larch, oak and beech to more exotic species.
These materials are described in detail in "Fundamentals" (p. 30).

Cross-section stiffnesses, glued laminated timber

h I_1

Beam

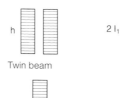

h $2 I_1$

Twin beam

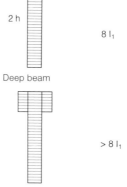

$2 h$

$8 I_1$

Deep beam

$> 8 I_1$

Reinforced deep beam

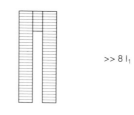

$>> 8 I_1$

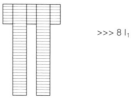

$>>> 8 I_1$

Reinforced twin-web beams

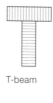

T-beam

I-beam

Bridge made from logs, dowelled

Bridge made from squared sections, dowelled

T-section beams

Truss members made from compound glulam sections

Beam grid made from compound glulam sections

Connectors and details

The type of connector and method of jointing should be discussed with the architect as early as possible. The appearance of a timber structure is influenced quite decisively by the detailing at the joints. The connections may be true wood joints, dowelled, nailed, screwed or bolted, with steel gussets let into the timber, or exposed steel connections. The choice depends on the materials used, e.g. round, squared or glulam sections. The fire protection requirements are critical when using steel connectors, the protection of the timber in the case of elements exposed to the weather. Concealed connectors have the advantage that the steel parts are protected from direct exposure to fire. Connections in multiple shear result, which means that the number of connectors can be reduced. However, this is offset by the increased work required to slit the wood and the fact that the cross-section is weakened.

Nail plates with hinge pin

Curved primary loadbearing member made from glued laminated timber

Geometry

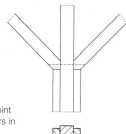

Direct-contact
oblique dado joint
$\alpha = 0-90°$
pinned joint

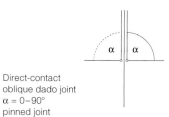

Circle of dowels
$\alpha = 0-180°$
partially rigid joint

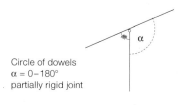

Metal plate let into timber
with dowels
$\alpha_1 \geq 90° \geq \alpha_2$
partially pinned joint

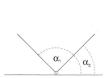

Hinge pin connection
$\alpha_1 \geq 90° \leq \alpha_2$
perfect pin joint

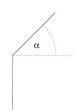

Finger joint
$0 < \alpha > 90°$
perfect rigid joint

Connectors and details, with details of possible spans

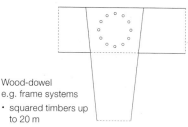

Wood-wood joint
linear members in
compression
· squared timbers up
  to 12 m
· glulam members up
  to 20 m

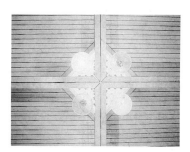

Wood-dowel
e.g. frame systems
· squared timbers up
  to 20 m

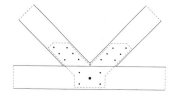

Wood-dowel
e.g. truss systems
· squared timbers up to
  40 m
· glulam members up to
  60 m

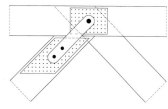

Wood-steel plate
e.g. frame systems
· squared timbers up to
  60 m
· glulam members up to
  80 m

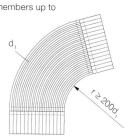

Wood-glulam construction
e.g. curved frame with finger-jointed corners
· glulam members up to 140 m

Examples of the arrangement of load-bearing joints and structural systems

Axonometric view

Ice rink in Schaffhausen

Perspective view

Salt store in Lausanne

Model

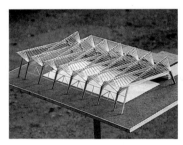

Ice rink in Burgkirchen

Photo collage

Project for a bridge

Presentation

Isometric and axonometric views
One vital quality criterion of the timber structure is the effect of the interior space. It is advisable to provide a three-dimensional presentation in the form of an isometric view at the preliminary design stage, because this allows even a layperson to appreciate the features of the timber structure. An isometric view is likewise advantageous at the tendering stage and for helping suppliers to optimise their fabrication methods. The desired quality of the details is therefore comprehensible at an early stage.

CAD
There is a great deal of freedom in arranging the geometry of the structure. The use of computer-aided design (CAD) is therefore advisable from an early stage. Three-dimensional drawings are essential in timber engineering, for both the architect and engineer. These require 3D programs, which are not simply drawing tools but rather aids to the structural engineer. Such programs permit variations and can be coupled with structural design programs; they even allow simulations of the interior and colour schemes. In timber engineering the processing of graphic data simplifies the compilation and modelling of geometric structures for strength analyses as well as design calculations. Above all, the variation of the structural systems in a graphic dialogue speeds up the optimisation process quite considerably. The aim of CAD is to define the entire structure in three dimensions and to generate the structural drawings on the basis of the data developed from this. The package of data can subsequently be sent to the fabricator for the production of fabrication drawings and for controlling automated fabrication plant.

Structural models
A model is an important tool for portraying the structure of the interior space. It enables the quality of the design to be conveyed to decision-makers such as building departments, local authorities and, above all, the developer in an understandable fashion. Details of

the construction – fundamental problems in particular – become readily apparent in a model; the discussions between architect and engineer are simplified. Models to a scale of 1:20 or 1:50 are adequate for assessing the design.

Design variations

The design criteria laid down and the boundary conditions dealt with in the previous paragraphs enable the development of variations on the form of the building envelope, loadbearing structures and cross-sectional models. Creativity, intuition and, above all, experience are required in order to concentrate on the best variations and present them in the form of sketches. They are subsequently given the relevant preliminary dimensions and checked against a list containing various criteria. Both the architect and the engineer have to provide planning services and prepare comprehensible documentation in order to assess the quality-related economic efficiency of a timber structure. The methodical procedure for assuring the quality of a timber structure calls for complete records of the planning procedure. Assumptions regarding the design criteria, specific boundary conditions and building authority stipulations all have to be presented in a verifiable format capable of comparison. The relationships and weighting of individual criteria can be illustrated in a critical comparative analysis and their influence on costs described. This planning work should be carried out during the preliminary project and draft design phases to ensure a transparent decision-making process. The avoidance of changes or even duplicated planning work when preparing approval submissions and the execution of the project itself, usually after the contract has been awarded, is the most effective approach to rationalising the planning and design workload.

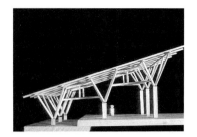

Optimisation process for a structural design by means of models

Optimisation and decision-making processes illustrated by way of an evaluation matrix for a proposed form of construction

Evaluation criteria	3	2	1	0	W	Σ
Division into separate rooms		x			2	4
Exploitation of height and structural space		x			1	2
Clarity and transparency	x				3	9
Adaptability of plan – layout		x			2	4
Cantilever – protection of timber		x			1	2
Materials consumed	x				3	9
Connectors required	x				3	9
Feasibility		x			2	4
Economy	x				3	9
Interior fitting-out – complexity	x				3	9
Clear space and spans	x				2	6
Appearance and serviceability	x				3	9
Freedom from competition (for construction)		x			2	4
Total weighting of construction proposal by the engineer						80

3 = very good, 2 = good, 1 = average
0 = poor, W = weighting,
Σ = total

Design process	CAD-assisted design procedure
Investigation of boundary conditions	
Plan dimensions Openings Clear space Roof pitch Loading assumptions	

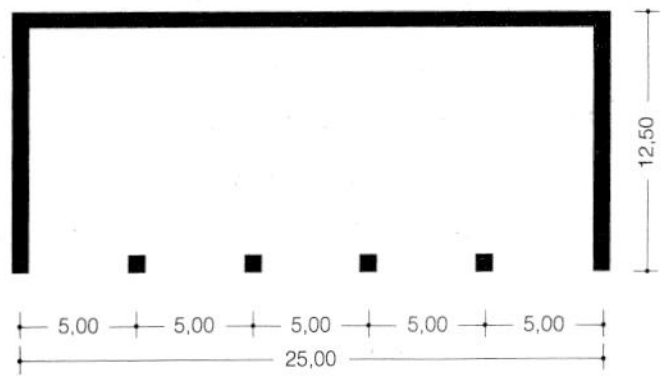

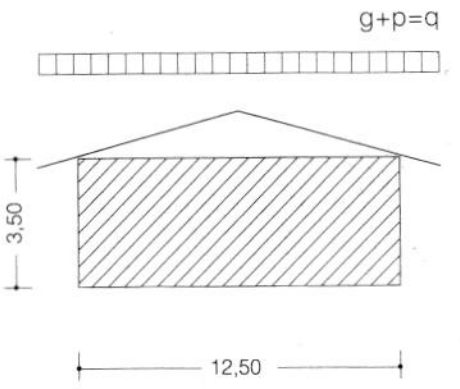

Variation 1   Variation 2

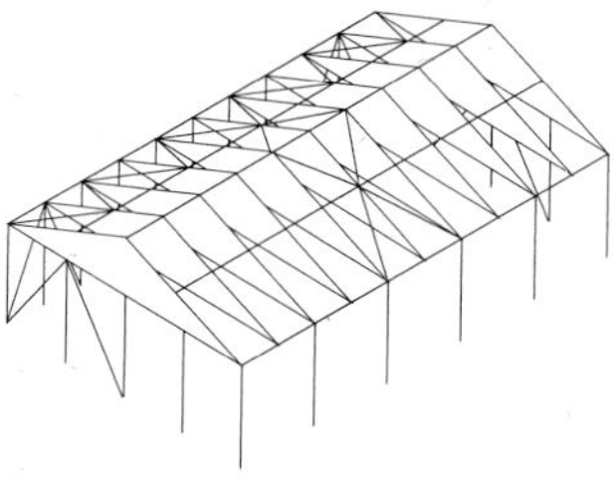

Investigation of variations using isometric drawings for:
columns
primary structural system
secondary structural system
bracing system
building envelope (roof, wall)

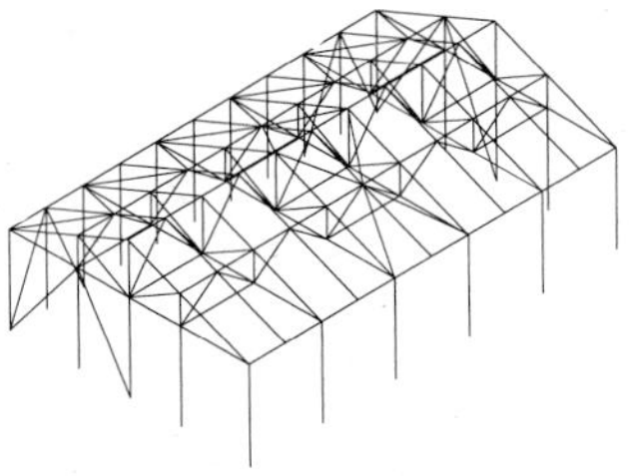

Preliminary dimensions and realisation of spatial concept in:
squared timber
glued laminated timber

structural system variation 1   structural system variation 2

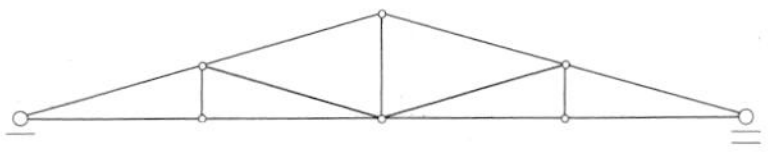

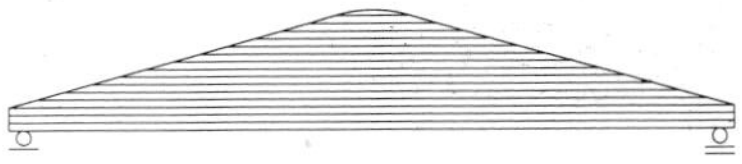

Decision   based on various comparisons   design
material costs
economic efficiency

Detailed design of project

structural calculations
structural drawings
detailed concept
tender documentation

Realisation of chosen variation

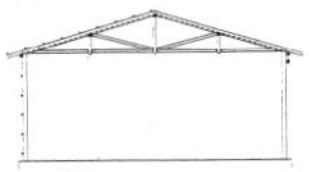

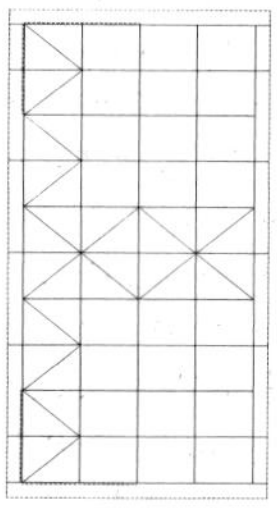

← Line drawings of structure

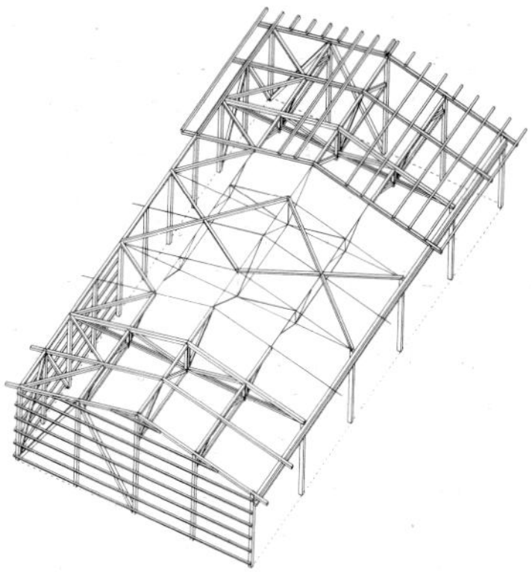

Detail drawings →

↓ Timber fabrication drawing

construction
line drawings of structure
timber fabrication drawings
other fabrication drawings
parts lists

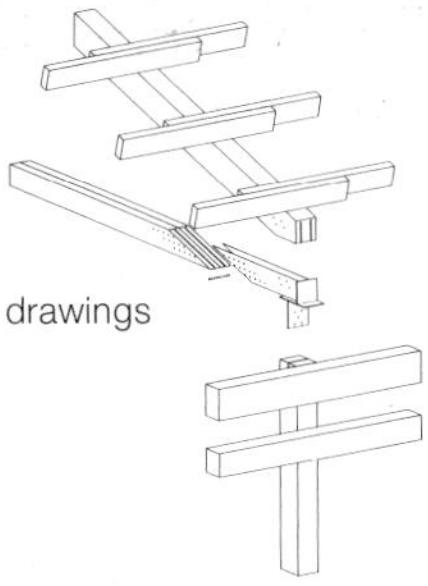

↓ parts list sawmill

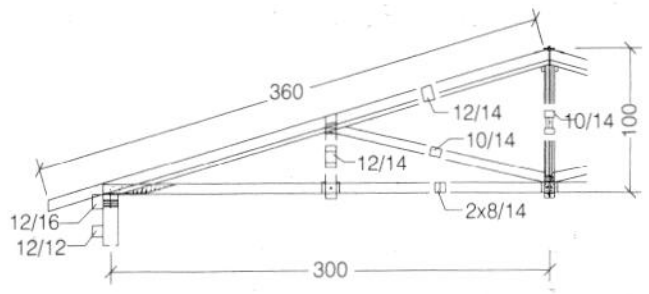

carpentry shop direct control of fabrication plant

Construction inspection   checking fabrication drawings, inspections during fabrication, inspections on site

Invoicing   by means of parts lists and quantities produced by CAD program

Symbols for depicting structural systems

○ Pinned support

○ Sliding support

Fixed support

○ Spring support

Rigid joint

Pinned joint

Example: three-pin frame

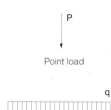

Symbols for depicting loads

P

Point load

q

Uniformly distributed load

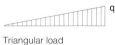 q

Triangular load

 M

Moment

Preparing submissions for approval, planning of projects

The tasks of the engineer
One prime task for the structural engineer is to develop and work out the details of a structure taking into account all the possible or probable actions affecting that structure. It begins with the construction phase and continues right to the end of the structure's expected service life.
The engineer must be familiar with the application of the standards that apply to the calculations and be able to describe the behaviour of the structure within foreseeable time periods. He should also be familiar with the reliability of the materials and details employed, without losing sight of the economic framework. The analysis and confirmation of assumptions should be provided by using mathematical models and recognised methods of design.

Engineering services
Once the timber structure has been determined and its construction confirmed by means of preliminary calculations and the results of the tendering procedure, the engineer must provide all the analyses required for safety and serviceability in a verifiable format. This is carried out according to the following scheme:
• Listing and taking into account the building codes, standards and special approvals on which the structural design was based.
• Determining the characteristic values for the subsoil and permissible soil pressure, if necessary taking into account a site survey and suggestions for suitable foundations provided by a specialist engineer.
• Establishing the loading assumptions and actions to be taken as the starting points for calculating internal forces.
• Specifying the characteristic values of the materials and the grading criteria on which the calculations are based; these must be clearly indicated on all documents.
• Preparing verifiable structural calculations for all components taking into account the information provided by other specialists during the draft design phase.

• Providing specifications plus structural and line drawings; these include all details of fabrication conditions, quality requirements, connectors, wood preservation measures and precautions to be taken during transport and erection.
• Assembling all the documentation, surveys, reports and the necessary building authority approvals.
• Negotiating with building authorities, checking authorities and checking engineers.
• Taking changes into account; a special task of the structural engineer that often occurs involves subsequent changes to the design, whether this reflects the wishes of the developer, the failure to observe building authority stipulations, or improvements to the quality of the planning.
• Checking the working drawings.
• Assisting in the award of contracts.
• On-site supervision or engineering inspections during construction.

Basic services for a timber engineering project

Structural calculations
The internal forces are determined using computer programs or special finite element methods (FEM). Suitable programs are available for the actual detailed design work.

Analyses of load-carrying capacity
As timber structures normally include the roof construction, the structural analysis begins with the roof covering. It is mainly the deflection case that governs for the roof covering, rafters, purlins and secondary loadbearing members. However, high snow loads mean that special attention must be paid to shear stresses. Analyses of various loading combinations are carried out for primary loadbearing members or primary structural systems. Calculations are required for single-person loads, dead loads, snow and wind, whereby wind forces govern in the case of structural systems with a tie. The superimposition of bracing forces should not be forgotten in the loading combinations.

Diagrams of internal forces

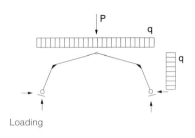

Loading

Deformation

Shear forces

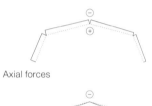

Axial forces

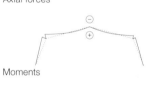

Moments

Stresses

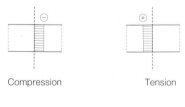

Compression   Tension

Bending   Compression plus bending

Shear

Structural analysis and design

Components primarily subjected to compression
(columns, struts, arches)
- Analysis of maximum slenderness ratio
- Simplified buckling analysis (w-method)
- Analysis of load-carrying capacity according to 2nd order theory
Allowance for unintended eccentricities, crookedness and weakened cross-sections. Eccentric load application and hence associated secondary stresses.

Components primarily subjected to bending (beams, frames)
Determination of internal forces
- Asymmetric loading cases, e.g. snow and wind loads from one side, uplift, e.g. due to wind suction.
- Analysis of bending stresses: weakened cross-section due to drilled holes or cut-outs on the tension side.
The increased bending stresses should be analysed in the bent zone and for an edge with excessively sloping grain.
- Analysis of shear stresses: reduction in internal forces around supports; take into account notches and openings.
- Analysis of torsion stresses: eccentric loads on edge beams.
- Analysis of transverse bending: bending stresses perpendicular to the grain occur in cranked, bent and notched beams, and at openings and suspended loads.
- Analysis of deflection: effects of yielding supports and shrinkage, and the elasticity of connectors.
- Analysis of overturning: for deep beams subjected to wind suction loads, and the corners of frames.
- Analysis of supports and connections.
Take into account the effects of displaced supports on the building envelope.

Anchorage detail for uplift forces
- Analysis of compression stresses perpendicular to the grain; twist at the supports may need to be considered.

Components primarily subjected to axial forces (trusses, lattice girders)
The internal forces are determined using computer models for plane frames. The chords are generally considered to be continuous and the diagonals as linear members with pinned or partially restrained ends. Eccentricity, partial restraint and transverse loads from linear members must be taken into account.
The following analyses are required for linear members:
- Analyses of tension, compression or combined stresses acting on the net cross-section.
- Stability check for struts that may be subjected to bending.
The superimposition of forces from horizontal bracing should not be forgotten.
Joints should be analysed as follows:
- Analysis of connectors.
- Analysis of stresses in the vicinity of connections, taking into account weakened cross-sections and eccentricities.
- Analysis of shear in the case of eccentricity or sloping contact faces.

The entire truss should be examined for the following cases:
- A deflection analysis should be carried out, taking into account the elasticity of connectors and possible partial restraint at the joints.
Precambering is recommended in all cases.
- The analysis of the overall stability is carried out including secondary loadbearing members and stiffening bracing for large spans.
Shrinkage phenomena as a result of transverse loads must be taken into account.

Drawings for timber engineering projects

Drawings of construction projects are the most important means of communication between all members of the construction team. Well-drawn drawings protect developer, architect, engineer and contractors from misunderstandings regarding the engineering and architectural nature, and quality of a timber construction.
For the contractors, the drawings form the basis for calculating costs and quantities of materials, and planning fabrication, assembly and erection. DIN 1356 regulates the production of drawings in the building industry, particularly in timber engineering.
In Germany the scope and content of the drawings to be produced by the architect and the engineer as part of their basic or special services are specified in the HOAI (Scale of Fees for Architects and Engineers). The developer may appoint the architect, the structural engineer or the contractor to carry out individual planning services. The production of working drawings is not included in the price of a timber structure (see VOB – Standard Terms of Contract for Building Works).

Design sketches
During the preliminary planning stage the different variations are presented for discussion in the form of sketches. These may well be freehand drawings produced during meetings between the architect and the engineer.

Design proposals
Various design proposals are then presented in the form of more elaborate scale drawings (1:200, 1:100, 1:50, details 1:10) and compared for optimisation. The structural system, bracing options, various materials and details should be clear from the drawings.

The engineer's sketches for a bridge

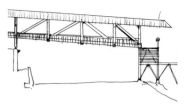

Lattice girder with roof

Frame with partial roof

Canopy with suspended construction and partial roof

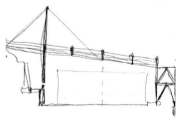

Diagonal cable construction with vertical pylon

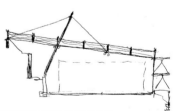

Diagonal cable construction with raking pylon

Photo of the finished project

Reactions and pockets drawings

Reactions drawings show the loads transferred from the timber construction to the supports. As a rule such drawings are required when the timber construction and the adjoining monolithic construction are the responsibility of different engineers. In addition, reactions drawings are necessary for preparing a foundation report.
Pockets drawings show the positions and sizes of recesses for anchoring the timber structure in monolithic components. Here, special attention should be paid to the required tolerances when choosing the size of the pocket. These tolerances depend on the size of the components to be anchored.

Reactions and pockets can also be combined on one drawing to provide the engineer responsible for the monolithic construction with all the necessary information in a compact form.
The usual scales for such drawings are 1:200, 1:100 and 1:50.

Tender drawings

If an early call for tenders is intended, it is advisable to show the timber structure on tender drawings containing details of the structural system, dimensions and principal details. Such drawings should help the tenderer to understand fully the type of construction involved and the degree of difficulty involved in fabrication, transport

and erection. There should be a note on the drawings stating that the dimensions at this stage of the planning have not yet been finalised. The usual scales for such drawings are 1:200, 1:100 and 1:50; in exceptional cases principal details may be shown at 1:10 or 1:5.

Line and general arrangement drawings

These drawings serve to locate components and details within the scope of the cooperation between architect and engineer. They are also used for fabrication and erection purposes. Line drawings are based on the grid of the structure with finalised dimensions. When included as an appendix to verifi-

able structural calculations, they should refer to the components in the calculations, the dimensions of the structure, the imposed loads, and the type and grade of building materials.

Structural drawings

The structural drawings show all the loadbearing components in plans, sections and elevations, with the necessary dimensions and information for producing the timber structure. It is important to note on the drawings that the dimensions given must be checked to ensure that they agree with the components already erected on site. The material grades on which the structural analysis was based,

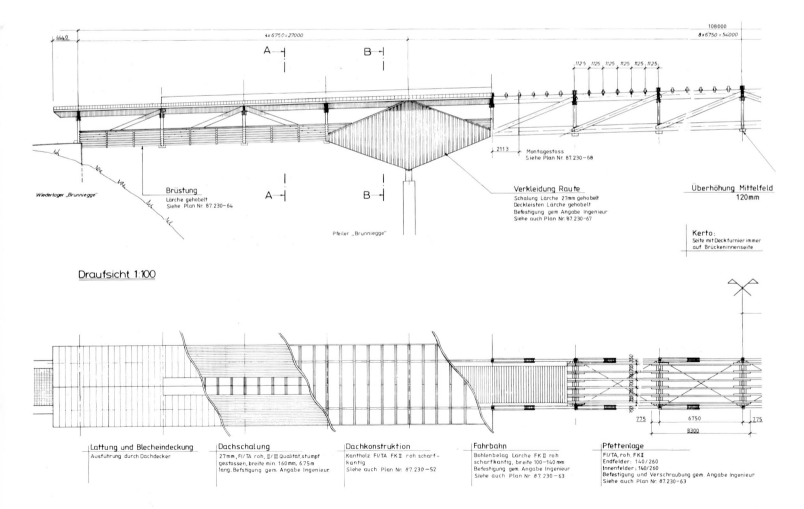

Example of a structural drawing (extract, German original)

the dimensions calculated and the size, number and arrangement of connectors must be given on the drawings. Only the principal details and those subjected to the maximum loads need be shown; those subjected to lower loads will be drawn as part of the fabricator's work. If agreed with the architect, the structural drawings can also supplement the working drawings. The structural drawings serve as the basis for fabrication drawings; the usual scales for such drawings are 1:50, 1:20 and 1:10.

Fabrication and working drawings

The fabrication drawings form the binding contractual basis for the construction of the entire timber structure. As a rule they are produced by the contractor, who thus gains a full appreciation of the construction of the project. If the contractor does not supply these drawings, they can also be produced by the engineer or the architect as a special service under HOAI cl. 64.

Timber fabrication drawings

These show the individual timber members with their exact geometry, cut-outs, drilled holes, etc. and all the dimensions necessary for their manufacture, including any precambering or other special requirements. These drawings enable the carpenter to build up the elements, or maybe produce templates if larger quantities are involved. The architect's working drawings and the engineer's structural drawings form the basis for the timber fabrication drawings. As a rule these are checked by the architect or the engineer prior to fabrication work beginning. Whoever produces the timber fabrication drawings is responsible for the correctness of the dimensions given there.

The usual scales for such drawings are 1:50, 1:10 and 1:5.

Steel fabrication drawings

These drawings are covered by DIN 5261. They should include the exact geometry and dimensions of each individual steel component together with details of all drilling, milling and welding requirements. Nails, screws, bolts and pins must also be specified in terms of type and number, even the exact thread length.

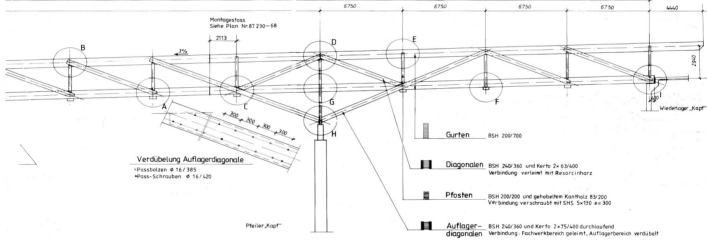

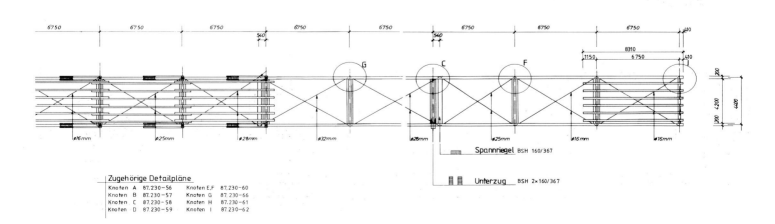

This table is intended to act as an aid when tendering.

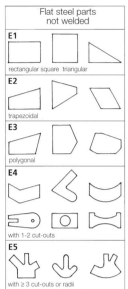

Flat steel parts
not welded

E1
rectangular square triangular

E2
trapezoidal

E3
polygonal

E4
with 1-2 cut-outs

E5
with ≥ 3 cut-outs or radii

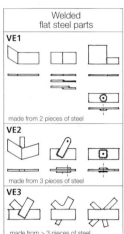

Welded
flat steel parts

VE1
made from 2 pieces of steel

VE2
made from 3 pieces of steel

VE3
made from > 3 pieces of steel

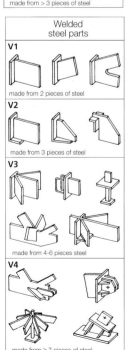

Welded
steel parts

V1
made from 2 pieces of steel

V2
made from 3 pieces of steel

V3
made from 4-6 pieces steel

V4
made from ≥ 7 pieces of steel

Production of tender documents

The complex structures of modern timber engineering call for accurate descriptions of the services to be provided by all parties. On the other hand, at the tender stage the design of a timber structure has not usually advanced to such a stage that all the information can be presented in full. Often, the principles of the construction are specified as far is possible. The individual details and means of connection are shown schematically so that the tenderer can assess the degree of difficulty and the fabrication work properly. This "open" type of specification must be drawn up in line with the relevant directives and standards (VOB parts A and B, DIN 1960 and 1961, Dec 2000 edition, and ATV DIN 18334). The possibility of using a standard specification for timber structures, which usually require customised structural geometries and means of connection, should be checked very carefully in advance. In any case, references to additional technical services and the provision of special specification texts will be required.
A tender for a timber structure consists of the following parts (this list does not claim to be exhaustive):

Administrative details
This part includes the following information:
- the persons involved (developer, architect, engineer, site manager, etc.)
- the timetable (tender due date, start date, completion date)

General conditions
These are the same for all building work and cover, for example:
- the approval of subcontractors
- the formation of consortiums
- invoicing and payment terms
- management operations
- relevant standards

Project-related provisions
These contain specific information related to the structure and vary from project to project:
- general specification of the construction work
- planning of the works
- quality control
- access to the site
- notes on transport and erection

Bill of quantities
This consists of individual items to which the corresponding quantities are added.
- Site facilities:
  This lists the work required for enclosing the site, scaffolding, hoist and cranes, electrical supplies etc.
- Manufacture and supply of all timber components, broken down into logs, halved logs, squared and glued laminated sections, planks, plywood boards and LVL boards.
- Supply of steel components and connectors, broken down into non-machined steel sections, machined steel sections, welded parts, threaded reinforcing bars, customary sheet metal parts, special assemblies, nails, bolts, screws, pins, holding-down bolts.
- Degrees of difficulty of steel parts have to be defined outside the scope of the standard specification and given in the right-hand column. We distinguish between flat non-welded, flat welded and welded steel parts.

This part contains all the services to be provided in order to produce the finished structure using the materials in the tender documents:
- manufacture and erection of the structure
- fabrication and assembly
- integration of connectors and steel parts

Special technical directives for timber engineering
- Requirements concerning fire protection, sound and thermal insulation
- Requirements concerning ventilation and interior climate conditions
- Timber preservatives in living accommodation, storage facilities, stalls or outdoors
- Moisture control during transport and erection (plastic film packaging or impregnation with preservative)
- Corrosion protection
- Requirements concerning the moisture content of formwork, squared sections, glued laminated timber, etc. upon installation
- Requirements covering glued laminated timber, glue approval, position of finger joints

- Surface finishes, including the edges of exposed components
- Details of the precambering necessary to meet structural or other criteria
- Steel parts: if applicable, welding documentation to DIN 18800

Terms of payment
The appropriate standards (section 5 of ATV DIN 18334) must be observed for determining services in timber engineering.
Cubic size (m^3) is calculated based on, for example,
- maximum lengths, including tendons and other wood joints,
- full cross-section without reductions for notches, cut-outs, reductions in the cross-section, etc.

Payment for structural steel parts is determined according to the appropriate standards (section 5 of ATV DIN 18360, metalworking, fitter's work). Payment is based on the total number of kilograms.
- Invoices based on length (m) use the maximum length, even for sections cut at an angle and notched. The outer developed length is used for bent sections.
- Invoices for individual components based on surface area (m^2) use the dimensions of the smallest circumscribing rectangle.

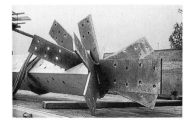

Welded steel component
for a 3D joint

Special services

Generally, a range of special services is required when planning a timber structure. All those not listed as basic services in the applicable scale of fees are defined as "special services".

During the preliminary planning stage the extra work involved in designing an exposed structure must be paid for, especially if optimisation or weighting is required. If the engineer applies form-finding methods, this represents a special service. During the approval and detailed design phases the determination of special loads and the production of a utilisation plan are also special services. Special loads include the imposed loads of, for example, fork-lift trucks, fire engines and refuse collection vehicles. The evaluation of dynamic loads to take into account impact surcharges and vibration factors are also classed as special services, as are the evaluation of erection and transport conditions.

The same is true for explosion loads, debris loads or the inclusion of the necessary seismic safety factors during the detailed design phase. Considerable extra work is involved when tender documentation has to include a reactions drawing to enable the subsoil conditions to be assessed. Timber engineering is usually associated with an above-average design workload. Often, new or novel details are developed and have to be paid for as a special service. The development of details on components exposed to the weather demands special attention and care. Other special services must be taken into account for preparatory work and assistance prior to awarding the contract. Appraisal of the economic efficiency of the construction in relation to various building science parameters is also regarded as a special service. They include fire protection, sound insulation and thermal performance analyses.

Planning fire protection

One very important special service in timber engineering is the assessment and analysis of the necessary fire resistance classes F30, F60 – and even F90 – in consultation with the authorities. Further analyses are unnecessary when approved components are being used, provided the timber construction complies with the specified fire resistance classes. The analysis of the fire resistance classes required can lead to larger cross-sections and more complex connections than those called for by the structural analysis. Compliance with the fire protection requirements must be observed at all stages of the planning work because not all types of construction attain the required standard of fire resistance. The analysis according to the applicable standards and approvals can be carried out using design charts or computer programs.

Planning sound insulation

The requirements for sound insulation should be defined in consultation with the developer, building authorities and project design team, in accordance with the applicable standards and approvals.

Sound insulation measures may be necessary to reduce the level of noise from outside or inside the building. In both cases appropriate maximum values, e.g. for airborne and impact sound, are defined in the relevant standards. The requirements affect the choice of construction, loading assumptions and the dimensions of components.

Planning thermal insulation

The thermal insulation requirements are laid down in relevant standards. The requirements concerning thermal performance in summer are particularly important for timber engineering to avoid mechanical air-conditioning. Thermal bridges must be avoided when developing the details. Great care is required during design and construction to ensure that the airtightness of the external envelope is maintained. Penetrations through components and the building envelope must be carefully detailed and built in order to prevent losses through open fissures caused by the shrinkage and swelling behaviour of wood.

Checking the working drawings

Checking the working drawings produced by the contractor is also classed as a special service. Their compliance must be carefully checked because incorrect interpretations, misunderstandings and negligence often lead to defects in the construction. In this respect, checking the grades of the building materials used is particularly important in timber engineering.

Erection, temporary works and scaffolding drawings

The erection of large-span structures such as single-storey sheds and bridges must be planned precisely. Erection drawings containing details of component loads, crane capacities and crane reaches are very helpful here. Attention should be paid to identifying and preparing the lifting points for timber components, and the (temporary) bracing of slender beams or trusses during erection.

Further important topics are the provision – during erection – of guy ropes and anchors to prevent wind uplift until the bracing members have been installed and the facade built. Even such temporary constructions must be defined on the drawings with all the necessary details and specifications.

Progress charts and timetables

These are required in order to guarantee the trouble-free progression of the building works and completion on time. They are prepared by the architect or the contractors depending on the project; on large projects by a specialist. The commonest forms are the bar chart and the network diagram. In addition to the actual building works, which they show schematically, progress charts show the necessary temporary works such as scaffolds and site facilities, with details of the plot boundaries, access routes, crane positions and crane slewing zones, and the location of electricity and water supplies.

As-built drawings and records

The compilation of a logbook with project notes and the production of as-built drawings should be considered, particularly for large spans or new types of loadbearing construction with special details. Such work falls under the remit of special services.

Accurate as-built drawings are essential for carrying out proper repairs or modifications once the building is in use. If such documents are not available, a costly and time-consuming survey, involving much awkward research work, is required.

As-built drawings are especially important in the case of frequent changes of use or where it is necessary to monitor the stability constantly. The drawings should include the main dimensions, details of materials used and loading assumptions. They are very similar to the structural drawings but with far fewer dimensions.

Planning timber protection

Extra care should be devoted to planning measures to protect the timber.

The most important rules to be observed in order to increase the service life of timber structures and decrease the maintenance costs are:

- Timber components, even inside a building, should be protected against moisture; moisture contents > 18% should be avoided.
- Protection against splashing water – the bases of columns should be raised ≥ 150 mm above the ground.
- Protective measures are required for end grain exposed to the weather.
- Horizontal surfaces exposed to the weather should be avoided as far as possible.
- Contact faces in which water can become trapped must be avoided at all costs.
- The inclusion of relieving grooves in order to prevent uncontrolled splitting of timber sections and, above all, to prevent water becoming trapped in such fissures.
- Galvanised steel, stainless steel or brass parts should be used outdoors.

Quality control of production and deliveries

Material quality

The construction of the structure must be checked by the structural engineer, the checking engineer or authority to ensure conformity with the verified structural documentation. In timber engineering, the grade of timber to be used must also be checked. Where monitoring to DIN 18200 is not possible, the quality control measures must be performed by a specialist institute. The taking of samples and also non-destructive testing are both possible methods for quality control.

Strength of timber

The strength of solid timber, glued laminated timber, laminated veneer lumber and wood-based products essentially depends on the oven-dry density. Knots, sloping grain and fissures, and finger or scarf joints produce local weaknesses. The relevant building codes give the permissible strength values for the various grades. Reliable non-destructive tests validate the use of non-standard values for highly stressed components.

Non-destructive testing (NDT)

This is an improvement on the results of visual grading according to the physical-mechanical characteristics of sawn timber. Recommended NDT methods include Pilodyn, ultrasound, impact tests, laser beams and stress grading. The latter is suitable for distinguishing more accurately between the different grades and particularly for testing timber destined for heavily loaded components. Such tests enable characteristic values, such as the modulus of elasticity for deflection analysis, or density variables, which are directly related to ultimate bending strengths, to be determined.

Of these various methods, ultrasound measurement is the most economic and most accurate way of producing meaningful results. This technology measures the velocity and maximum amplitude of a low-frequency ultrasonic wave (20 kHz) which propagates within a piece of wood. The transit velocity correlates with the modulus of elasticity (E_y) and the permissible bending stress (σ_{perm}), the measured maximum amplitude with the occurrence of local defects. Measurements are carried out with appropriate instruments in the two primary directions of the wood. Perpendicular to the grain this detects flaws within the microstructure of the wood, e.g. voids or rot in tree trunks, and delamination within a glulam section. Parallel to the grain we can determine the modulus of elasticity and the permissible bending stress of a timber component, taking into account, for example, a weakness in the cross-section caused by knots or an inaccurate finger joint. Based on the given safety concept a deterministic model of the permissible loads – similar to foundation engineering – can be determined and approved.

Non-destructive testing to grade timber with suitable equipment enables high-strength squared timbers to be selected and used for highly stressed diagonals, verticals, etc. The grading can be carried out in advance at the sawmill, which enables specific, high-strength sections to be ordered and delivered. Alternatively, the strongest members can be selected from a large number of identical pieces (e.g. continuous purlins) prior to fabrication, and used in the end bays. In addition, the reliability of the structure can be verified deterministically by discrete strength-testing of the timber around significant cross-sectional weaknesses at heavily loaded connections.

Random testing of the finger joints in glued laminated timber is recommended in certain cases. In particularly heavily loaded structures components can be tested on site prior to erection. Attention should be paid to the position and spacing of finger joints.

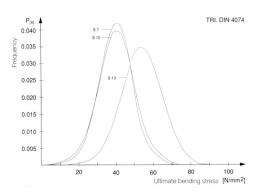

Scatter of quality of sawn timber according to grade

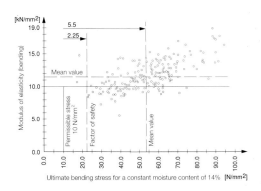

Relationship between modulus of elasticity and ultimate stress of 200 spruce beams with a moisture content of 16%

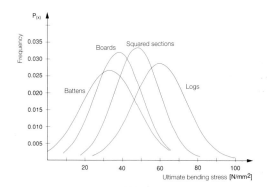

Scatter of quality of sawn timber according to type of section

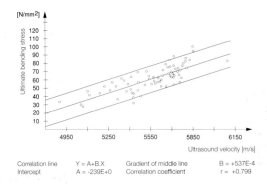

| Correlation line | Y = A+B.X | Gradient of middle line | B = +537E-4 |
| Intercept | A = -239E+0 | Correlation coefficient | r = +0.799 |

Correlation between ultimate bending stress and measurement of ultrasound velocity

Eurocode 5

Eurocode 5 is based on a probabilistic safety concept. Instead of working with permissible stresses, the limit states of load-carrying capacity and serviceability are employed. The design values for load-carrying capacity are compared with the design values of the actions. The design values are obtained through multiplying the characteristic values by partial safety factors. Eurocode 5 provides for grading – by means of visual inspection or machine – according to strength classes C1 to C10 in the future. Further distinctions are made between oven-dry density classes D300 to D800 in kg/m^3 as characteristic and NDT-verifiable values, moduli of elasticity and permissible stresses. Special grades for timber used for glued laminated members, taking into account the strength of the timber and type of finger jointing, are intended to provide the engineer with an improved basis for the reliable design of timber components. It should then be possible to distinguish more accurately between different grades than is presently the case.

Quality of workmanship

In view of the liberalisation of the European market, the quality control in the factory and on the building site will in future take on a special significance for the competitiveness of timber engineering.

In the factory

Visual inspection of timber quality	Knots, width of growth rings, slope of grain, resin pockets, reaction wood, callusing, fungal attack, insect attack
Machine inspection of timber quality	Modulus of elasticity, density, leading to conclusions regarding the probability of failure (by means of trials, Pilodyn, ultrasound, etc.)
Moisture content of timber	with measuring instrument, oven-dry method
Supply, fabrication	Dimensions of sections, tolerances, fissures, drilling, joints
Connections, connectors	Conformity with the fabrication drawings, number, size, arrangement, accuracy of fit, grade of steel, quality of welded seams, corrosion protection
Protective measures	Impregnation, paint, protection against moisture and impurities during transport and erection, protection to arrises and corners
Gluing conditions	Ambient temperature, ambient humidity, quality of glue, application of glue, open storage time prior to bonding, magnitude and duration of pressure, curing time
Production of glued laminated timber	Dimensions of laminations, lamination grades within the cross-section, moisture content, temperature and surface finish of laminations, finger joints, laying-up of laminations within the cross-section
Fabrication of frames and trusses	Dimensional accuracy, fissures, make-up, position of finger joints, repairs, appearance of surface (planed, scraped, sanded)

Ultrasound measuring instrument

Automatic factory grading with ultrasound

On the building site

	Quality of material, fabrication, etc. as described above
Intermediate storage	Protection against moisture, stacking on timbers
During erection	No holes drilled or slits cut without first consulting the engineer, stability against buckling, overturning, wind and storm actions, accurate alignment of columns and frames prior to erection of wind and stability bracing; in special cases: checking the stability of temporary works
Upon completion	Immediate closure and sealing of the external wall surface, slow rise in temperature to avoid shrinkage splits

Restoration and refurbishment methods

Regular inspections are recommended for assessing the condition of existing, particularly old, buildings in order to initiate the necessary maintenance measures in good time. If such inspections are not carried out, very often major and expensive repairs will be needed. We begin by analysing the condition of the building. Various methods can be employed to establish the cause and extent of the damage. These methods include thermography, the removal of cores of material and the use of endoscopes in less accessible places around the structure. Ultrasound can be used to discover decayed beam ends in masonry pockets – a common problem in old buildings. The results of the analysis are summarised in the form of a documentary report. This includes information on the condition of individual components, the current or planned use, measures that are considered necessary to guarantee the continued use of the building, and the cost of the proposed measures. The refurbishment of a timber-frame structure is summarised below:

Basis for decisions
- current and future usage
- outline survey
- structural and normal value
- estimate of costs

Planning phases
- survey
- documentation
- catalogue of damage
- description
- formulation of objectives
- planning
- refurbishment measures: draining, dismantling, additions, renewals – structure, roof, infill panels

Modernisation measures
- new utilisation
- structural calculations
- thermal insulation, sound insulation
- protection of timber
- building services
- fitting out
The sequence of work (planning and execution) takes place roughly in the following order:

Basis for decisions
- original use
- current use
- value to user, historical value
- compilation of site measurements
- outline survey
- formal and structural value
- significance for the location
- utilisation and objectives
- profitability ensuing from renewal
- public funding required
- preliminary discussions with building authority and historic buildings authority

Documentation
- photographs, including the surroundings
- dismantling of the structure
- measurements, survey
- determination of damage
- description and history of the building

Refurbishment of the structure
- reconstruction drawings
- reconstruction specification
- catalogue of damaged parts
- restoration plan
- coordination with building authority and historic buildings authority
- coordination with specialist engineers
- bill of quantities
- cost of refurbishment
- funding plan

Modernisation plan
- setting objectives
- planning utilisation
- specification
- cost of modernisation
- funding plan
- profitability calculations
- construction timetable, phased plan
- execution
- execution according to the phased plan
- invoicing
- performance review

The removal and experimental examination of full-scale samples is recommended in order to calibrate non-destructive testing methods. After that it is possible to examine every element individually by way of NDT measurements and to take decisions about replacing unreliable components or strengthening them with composite systems, e.g. with wooden panels or timber-concrete composite elements.

Recording the residual strength
Estimating the available residual strength is a significant problem for the engineer. Various tools and NDT methods, e.g. Pilodyn, impact tests or ultrasound devices, can be employed for this. They allow the existing moduli of elasticity and failure probabilities to be determined with far greater accuracy than is possible with estimates of the strength of a timber based on visual inspections. Such methods provide a very sound foundation for assessing the necessary refurbishment and restoration work.

Measuring the extent of rot in a tree trunk using ultrasound

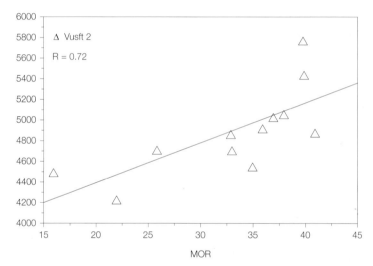

Correlation between ultrasound velocity and bending strength of beams in an old timber structure

In situ measurement of the residual strength of loadbearing components using ultrasound

Glue escaping from poorly drilled dowel holes at the base of a column

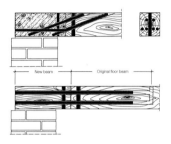

Butt-jointed new beam end made from reaction resin concrete reinforced with glass fibre-reinforced plastic

Example of a wood-wood addition to rafters

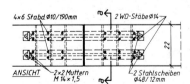

Detail of a butt joint with bonded-in rods

Example of a wood-wood addition with bonded-in rods

Repair of fissures

Splits, shakes and checks can occur in timber beams. They can be caused by the weather, thermal or moisture influences, design errors or lack of care during manufacture, fabrication and erection. Pressure-injection of the defects with epoxy resin is recommended. The adhesion and the strength of the resin allows fissures up to 5 mm wide to be sealed. Care should be taken to ensure that the resin is mixed with suitable fillers according to the building authority approval in order to achieve a fully interlocked mechanical connection.

Repair of damage to timber structures

If it proves too difficult to replace a structure or parts thereof, damaged areas can be repaired using the approved Beta method. Here, a two-part epoxy resin mortar reinforced with glass fibre is used to make good damaged areas. If a complete piece of a timber component has to be replaced, a fully interlocked mechanical connection can be created between the old and new timber sections using bonded-in rods.

Strengthening of existing timber structures

Old timber structures undergoing restoration often need to be strengthened, usually because of new uses with higher loads and more stringent requirements. One of the primary methods of strengthening consists of adding timber sections to increase the bending and shear strength as well as load-carrying capacity.

Wood-wood compound sections
Existing beams and new, additional sections made from solid timber, laminated veneer lumber or plywood can be connected together to form a common loadbearing element using nail-pressure gluing. More recent developments provide for the production of T-beam type compound sections. In this way existing floor joists can be strengthened by the addition of plywood or LVL board.

Timber-concrete composite sections
Deflection of floor joists that cannot be corrected can be compensated for by adding a concrete topping. Anchors are provided to create a mechanical bond between the new concrete and the existing timber. This achieves the maximum possible combined stiffness. The composite action of the ribs, or T-beam sections, and the structural concrete topping acting as the compression zone produces an economic cross-section. The resulting T-beam satisfies several requirements simultaneously:
• high stiffness, also to withstand vibration as well as
• good acoustic performance, up to 60 dB
• high fire resistance: F30, F60, F90

Timber and wood-based products are employed as loadbearing elements and permanent formwork. In comparison with a solid concrete slab, self-weight is also greatly reduced. The problem of the timber-concrete composite plate lies in the economic efficiency of the connectors, or the mechanical interlock between the timber ribs subjected to bending and the concrete topping in compression. Conventional means of connection such as split-ring connectors, screws, etc. are possible but lead to severe deformations, particularly under long-term loading as a result of shrinkage and creep of the concrete, creep of the timber connection and creep of the timber sections. In addition, in the timber-concrete composite sections common these days the transfer of shear forces into the concrete topping is not ideal structurally.
The other advantages of timber-concrete composite construction lie in the relatively good sound insulation and fire protection values that can be attained, plus the resistance to water damage.

Lamination of sections
The retrofitting of glass fibre or even carbon fibre fabrics allow higher load-carrying capacities to be achieved in timber engineering as well.

Strengthening the beams of a historical timber structure by using laminated veneer lumber boards

Various options for the connection in a timber-concrete composite construction

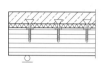

Embedded anchors

Inclined anchors

Prestressed anchors in notch

Timber-concrete connection anchor

Prestressed anchor in notch

Loading test on a timber-concrete composite floor construction

Forms of shrinkage

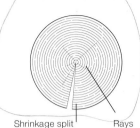

Shrinkage split   Rays

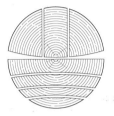

Column sections

Log with four relieving grooves arranged radially

edge-sawn log with relieving groove extending to the heart

Tubular section, with the heartwood bored or sawn out

Three-quarter log

Log with wedge

Material variations and cross-section forms for components

Logs and the resulting compound sections

Logs and profiled sections made from logs, as the natural form of this building material, can be employed economically in the most diverse structures. In agricultural buildings (pole construction), bridges and towers, children's playgrounds, noise control barriers, retaining walls, telephone masts and electricity pylons, logs are a cheap building material that can readily be pressure-impregnated.

One significant advantage of using logs is their higher strength. This is because the natural course of the fibres is not interrupted. The great disadvantage lies in the uncontrolled splitting. However, this can be reduced by providing relieving grooves and through profiling. This promotes faster drying and better impregnation.

The use of edge-sawn logs in the form of profiled sections can compensate for the inconvenient taper. In addition, such sections have flat faces ready for connectors.

The taper can also be dealt with highly economically by the cylindrical stripping of tree trunks, especially those of low-strength wood, which would otherwise be used as firewood. Cylindrical sections can be profiled in one operation and provided with relieving grooves. Profiled sections can be combined to form compound sections in order to act as columns or beams with a higher moment of inertia.

Nails and dowels are used as connectors. Numerous advantageous applications ensue for compound column sections or multiple components loaded in compression. Even heavily loaded components such as multistorey columns are suitable for this treatment.

Compound sections for columns and walls made from logs and profiled sections

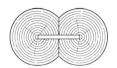

Made from two edge-sawn logs

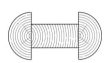

Made from two halved logs and one squared section, e.g. for fixed-end columns

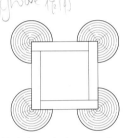

Made from planks or panels and three-quarter logs

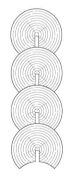

Wall made from dowelled log segments with relieving groove

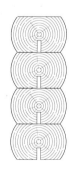

Wall made from dowelled edge-sawn logs with relieving groove

Pergola made from round sections

Pair of edge-sawn logs with relieving groove

Stave wall made from edge-sawn logs

Log construction employing horizontal edge-sawn logs

Log construction employing horizontal edge-sawn logs, view of interior

Retaining wall made from edge-sawn logs

Log struts in a trussed system

Factory production of dowelled beams

Dowelled cross-beams

Timber-concrete composite floor made from logs for an arch-shaped grandstand

Compound sections for beams and floors made from log and profiled sections

Beams with relieving groove extending to the heart

Three-quarter log   Segmental log

Split-heart halved log

in the form of a pair of ties

Roof or floor made from edge-sawn split-heart halved logs with relieving groove

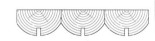

Solid timber roof or floor made from edge-sawn logs with relieving groove

The use of cylindrical sections is limited to spans of 12 m owing to the maximum sizes of material available.

Dowelled compound sections with a precamber and narrow profiles result in economic sections. The precambering counteracts the initial slip of the connectors and thus achieves a higher effective moment of inertia. Notched supports are particularly easy to fabricate with compound sections.

The manufacture of dowelled beams with precamber

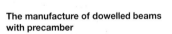

Dowelled beam:
Underside during assembly is topside after erection; to provide protection for the timber, the holes for the dowels are not drilled right through.

Dowelled beam:
The holes for the dowels are not drilled right through and thus not visible on the underside.

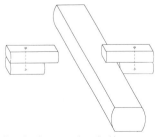

Junction between dowelled beams and purlin

Compound sections for beams in timber-concrete composite construction

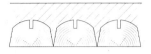

Traditional dowelled beam floor

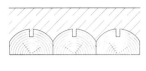

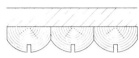

Edge-sawn split-heart halved logs with relieving groove acting as tension zone and permanent formwork for a timber-concrete composite floor

Various forms of dowelled beam

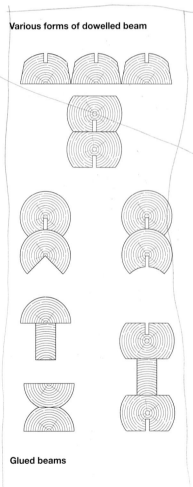

Glued beams

Column & Wall

Columns made from squared logs

Square with relieving grooves

relieving Grooves 4:10

Cruciform

Cruciform (split-heart with relieving groove)

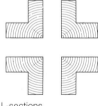

L-sections

Thick L-section

Squared logs and the resulting compound sections

One of most common sections in timber engineering is the squared log.

Its use is limited to lengths of up to 8 m owing to the sizes of material available. Relieving grooves and profiling can help to reduce significantly the disadvantages of splitting and twisting due to natural shrinkage, especially with large sections containing heart. Grooves and profiling following the line of natural growth have the advantage that the slope of the grain is interrupted, so the risk of twisting and splitting is avoided, and the final drying is speeded up. A great variety of compound sections for columns and beams can be produced from the various profiled sections: from cruciform and L-sections to appropriate compound sections for columns in timber-frame and single-storey shed construction; and thanks to the profiling there are good connection options for façades, doors and windows too. Squared logs with relieving grooves can be used with heart, which results in larger sections. A relieving groove also reduces the risk of the timber section tearing at a joint subjected to shear. It is recommended to take into account the structure of the annual rings in the case of pairs of ties with relieving grooves.

Beam bearing detail on a compound column

Compound sections for columns made from squared sections

Made from split-heart squared log (reversed), with internal relieving groove

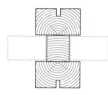

I-section made from split-heart squared log (flanges) and one squared section (web)

Cruciform section made from three squared sections

Rectangular section made from one plank and one quartered log

Compound sections for walls made from sawn timber

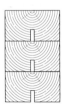

Made from boards or planks, nailed and dowelled, screwed or glued together

Made from split-heart sections with relieving groove

Three-part column in a frame

Corner treatment with cruciform column

Cruciform columns made from L-sections offer good connection options

Manual production of edge-glued timber element

Machine production of edge-glued timber element

Beam & floor

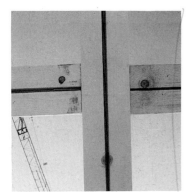
Beams made from squared sections with relieving groove

Beams made from boards on edge, two, three or four boards per beam depending on the span

Edge-glued timber floor in a house

Edge-glued timber floor undergoing testing

Stave wall of vertical squared sections

Beam sections made from sawn timber

Rectangular section with relieving groove extending to the heart

Split-heart sections with relieving groove

Quarter-sawn sections

Compound beam sections made from sawn timber

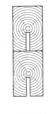

Profiled and composite sections made from sawn timber

Like logs, squared logs and planks can also be combined to form a great variety of profiled sections such as T- and I-beams or continuous plates. The recommended connectors are nails and screws, nails with nail-pressure gluing. However, care should be taken with the moisture content when processing; it should not exceed 16–18%, 15% for glued joints. Profiled sections in conjunction with concrete are useful for heavily loaded floor constructions. Various species of wood and grades can be combined, details and supports solved economically. The use of profiled sections provides timber engineering with further variations and applications for economic construction.

Compound floor sections made from sawn timber

made from boards or planks, nailed and dowelled, screwed or glued together

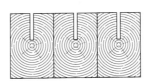

made from rectangular sections with relieving groove extending to the heart

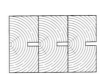

made from split-heart sections with relieving groove

Profiled sections made from boards and planks

with relieving grooves

as a tongue and groove element, glued

with various shapes to suit the adjoining construction

as a support for secondary beams

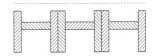

for timber-concrete composite floors

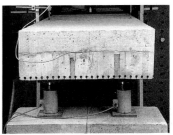
Timber-concrete composite floor undergoing testing

Fabrication

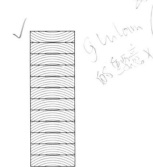

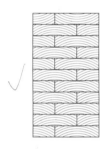

Beam with a width b ≤ 220 mm

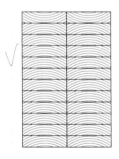

Beam section with two-part staggered laminations, narrow edges not glued, b > 220 mm

Two-part beam section, laid up in blocks, b > 220 mm

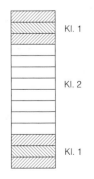

Kl. 1

Kl. 2

Kl. 1

Improved beam section with better-quality grades for the outer laminations

Glued laminated timber (glulam)
The development of this technology has enabled engineers to employ larger sections with better structural properties. This means that loadbearing capacities and the spans of timber structures are now much greater.

Species of wood and adhesives
As a rule, glued laminated timber is manufactured from softwood because it is easy to machine and satisfies the requirements of strength and durability. Spruce is the most common species in use, but occasionally pine, larch or Douglas fir may be used if special demands regarding impregnation and weathering resistance have to be met. Hardwoods are difficult to deal with and involve uncertainties regarding the strength of the glued joint.
The adhesives employed are urea-formaldehyde, resorcinol-formaldehyde and epoxy resins. A urea-formaldehyde resin is perfectly adequate for a normal interior climate. It is waterproof and its light colour makes it virtually indistinguishable from the wood itself. Components that are frequently exposed to the weather, high temperatures and severely alternating climatic conditions require adhesives based on resorcinol-formaldehyde resin. These can be recognised by the dark brown colour of the glued joint.

Production conditions
The manufacturers of glued laminated timber must adhere to exact stipulations and quality directives to guarantee the high reliability of heavily loaded glulam members. One important condition is the use of dry boards for glulam members; the moisture content at the time of processing may not deviate from the expected equilibrium moisture content by more than 3%. The boards are therefore kiln-dried prior to gluing, graded according to visual criteria and butt-jointed with finger joints. Continuous monitoring of temperature and humidity during production is essential. Quality control is carried out by the manufacturer and also by outside institutes. Adherence to the appropriate criteria must be explicitly referred to in the tender documents.

Grade of timber
Grading according to load-carrying capacity and the evaluation of knots is covered in DIN 4074 part 1 "Strength grading of coniferous wood; coniferous sawn timber"; suitability for use in glued laminated timber is dealt with in DIN 1052 part 1 "Structural use of timber; design and construction". The checks and shakes that appear on the surface as a consequence of shrinkage are intrinsic to the material; the standardised permissible stresses allow for flaws that penetrate up to a depth of about 1/6 times the width of the component. Special requirements regarding the appearance of the surface must always be agreed separately. During the design care must be taken to ensure that permissible stresses perpendicular to the grain and minimum curvature radii are adhered to.

Dimensions of glulam components
The maximum widths and depths of glued laminated timber sections are limited by the size of the planing machines available. The maximum length of a glulam member is governed by transport restrictions. With a favourable road network between factory and building site, straight members up to 60 m long can be transported. For curved members the maximum rise is governed by the width of the roads and/or overhead clearance. In Germany this is limited to 4.2 m for standard vehicles and 4.8–6.0 m for special transport vehicles. The depth of a member should be limited to 2.0 m in order to avoid high stress peaks in the tension zone. The slenderness should not exceed b/h = 1:10.

Protective coating
According to present knowledge components made from glued laminated timber that are to remain exposed within the building do not require any chemical timber preservative. However, if they are directly exposed to the weather, which should be avoided if at all possible, then a carefully applied chemical timber preservative is necessary, further application of which is necessary after the appearance of the unavoidable shrinkage splitting.

Finger joints

Right-angled notch without strengthening

Right-angled notch with strengthening

Tapered beam end

1:14

Strengthening in the form of bonded-in threaded or reinforcing bars

Right-angled notch

Taper to DIN 1052 part 1, section 8.2.2

Junction between glulam round column
and glulam beam

Kneebraced cruciform columns

Branched glulam column

Sections through various columns

Round, dia. > 220 mm

Square, b > 220 mm

Cruciform

Cross-sectional shapes

Round, square and rectangular
sections are the simplest and most
common sections.
Profiled sections can be produced
by nail-pressure gluing or by bonding together individual sections.
However, such sections require
special monitoring and care during the gluing process, and the
removal of beads of adhesive.
Profiled sections can also be produced as compound columns with
mechanical connectors. However,
the slip considerably reduces the
effective moment of inertia and
hence the radius of gyration for
the buckling analysis. It is possible
to produce round glulam columns
on a lathe in special cases.

Elevational forms

Columns can be produced with
various shapes on elevation, which
can be varied over their height in
order to match the structural requirements. Great care is required during production, i.e. in gluing and
assembly. Cut wood fibres should
be avoided or protected with covering laminations.

Elevations of various columns

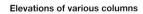

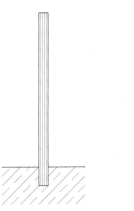

Fixed-based column in concrete

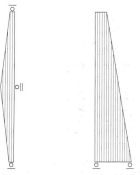

Fixed-based columns

Fixed-based column – wind bracing

I-section

Triform

Specially shaped cruciform raking column

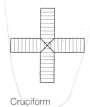

Cruciform

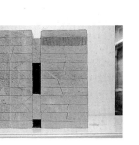

Custom I-section column

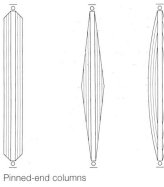

Pinned-end columns

Special forms

Sections through glued laminated beams

$h \leq 200$

$6 \leq b \leq 20$ cm

$h \leq 220$

$b \leq 20$ cm

$h \leq 240$

$20 \leq b \leq 22$ cm

$h \leq 280$

$22 \leq b \leq 28$ cm

Laying up in vertical blocks   Laying up in horizontal blocks

Beam forms
The longitudinal shape of beams made from glued laminated timber is particularly readily matched to the bending moment diagram; they can be shaped to match the structural requirements. The tensile stresses perpendicular to the grain due to the form must be taken into account in curved beams. The radius of curvature is limited, but can be influenced by the thickness of the laminations.
The diversity of possible longitudinal shapes enables the construction of loadbearing systems as frames, articulated systems or suspended members.

Special forms
Twisted and double-curvature glued sections can be produced for the edge members of hyperbolic paraboloid shells, the ribs of double-curvature stressed skin structures and stair stringers. The complex gluing process requires a three-dimensional jig in the pressing shop.

Compound sections
Glued profiled sections are produced by applying glue to the flanges/chords with nail-pressure gluing, or by applying adhesive on a gluing bed. Great care and good quality control is required when gluing large cross-sections. Today, laying up in blocks is the most common method of producing wide (b > 220 mm) glulam trusses and girders because it is more economic. Compound sections, I-beams in particular, are economic when certain conditions are taken into account. Further possible combinations are beams with glulam flanges and wood panel webs, or glulam webs and wood panel flanges, right up to T-beam geometries.

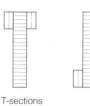

Compound sections

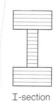
T-sections

Double-tee section, box section

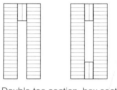
I-section

Two-part frame columns and beams with single diagonals in between

Main beams between two-part columns

T-section rafter
I-section column

I-sections, glued laminated timber

Channel section

Longitudinal beam forms

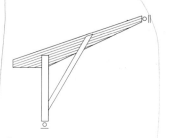

One-part beam, two-part column and strut

One-part beam, two- or three-part column, with tie

Glued laminated timber beam with precamber

Duopitch beam

Rectangular beam divided to form two monopitch beams

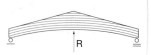

Duopitch beam with curved underside

Beam with compression perpendicular to the grain

Beam in double curvature

Building forms using glued laminated timber members
The wide variety of forms that can be produced using glued laminated timber using adjustable presses is a major economic criterion. Straight, cranked, cambered and curved forms can be produced with very little extra work.
DIN 1052 contains framework conditions regarding radii of curvature and reduction factors for finger joints. Superimposition of stresses at sloping edges, especially tensile stresses perpendicular to the grain at sloping edges in tension, should be avoided.
The maximum dimensions for transport should be taken into account during planning. The longitudinal forms of beams can be combined to form frames, or three-pin arrangements, continuous systems, frames and arches. Suspended systems are worth considering for particularly long spans.

Glulam frame supporting a folded plate structure

Glulam beams in single curvature as the primary structural system

Suspended shell made up of a radial arrangement of suspended beams with annular members in compression

Components for linear members, frames, arches, etc.

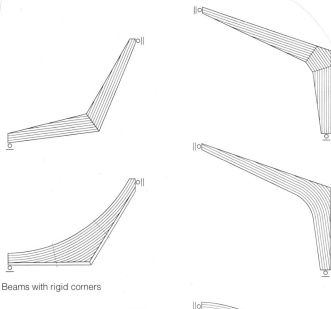

Beams with rigid corners

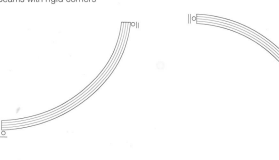

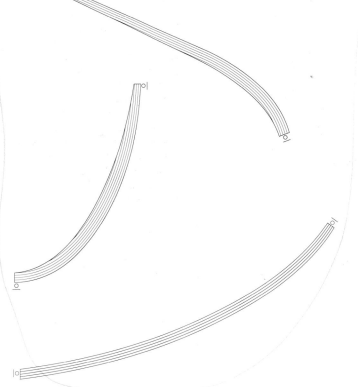

Beams in single curvature and suspended beams

Beam forms

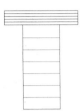

Glued laminated timber beam reinforced with laminated veneer lumber in the compression zone

I-beam with web made from laminated veneer lumber and flanges from squared or glulam sections

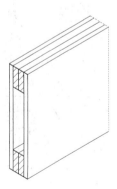

Nailed or glued box section

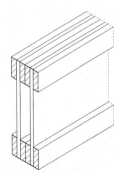

Twin-web section

Beams with solid webs
Webs consisting of several layers of boards glued together crosswise have been used for producing profiled beam sections. However, this form of construction is no longer employed owing to the high labour costs; glued laminated timber members are used instead. Kämpf, Wolf and Poppensieker beams have been essentially forced out of the market by TJI beams and joists, which originally came from America.
A thin web made from oriented strand board (OSB) is glued under high pressure into slots in the top and bottom flanges made from parallel strand lumber (PSL). Calculations, details and production are subject to building authority approvals.

Cross-laminated timber
Boards made from several plies glued together where the grain of adjacent plies forms an angle of 90° are now being manufactured in intensive industrial production. These boards are useful for roofs and walls.
The long lengths produced without finger joints are advantageous.

Laminated veneer lumber (LVL)
Gluing together veneers up to 3 mm thick results in boards with a high strength. The sheets of veneer are glued together with the grain in the same direction. Joints are merely overlapped. Single transverse plies for stability and to increase the transverse stiffness are possible.
LVL boards such as the Kerto brand are covered in Germany by building authority approvals and can be employed in conjunction with glued laminated timber or squared timber in linear members, beams or slabs. The economic efficiency of this method lies, above all, in the higher permissible stresses, and the possibility of producing elements up to 32 m long without finger joints in the form of compound profiled sections. Webs for beams and frames can be easily and economically employed owing to the adequate space for connections.

See also "Fundamentals" (p. 30)

Planar elements

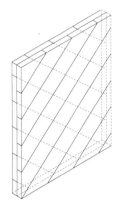

Two or more layers of boards glued together cross-wise

Plywood, grain of outer plies horizontal, central ply vertical

Plywood, grain of outer plies turned through 45°, central ply through 90°

Particleboard with tongue and groove

Junction between box beam and column

Box beams as rafters

Folded plate structure formed by wood-based panel webs

Dome formed by wood-based panel webs

Particleboards as roofing elements

Dome made from Kämpf beams

Curved kneebraces made from laminated veneer lumber

Folded plate structure made from reinforced Kämpf ribbed panels

Cellular beam made from LVL

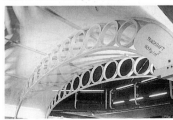

Curved cellular beam made from laminated veneer lumber

Curved panels made from laminated veneer lumber

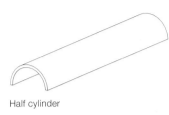

Half cylinder

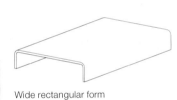

Narrow rectangular form

Wide rectangular form

Multiple-curvature shell

Chair shape

Plywood

Plywood has long been popular in the building industry. Its advantages lie in its use as a slab element with a high shear strength where a stiffening function is necessary, e.g. in roof plates, in conjunction with ribs as ribbed slabs. Plywood in conjunction with squared sections can also be made into panels for use in house-building. The consumption of material is low in I-beams, T-beams and box beams, but labour costs are high. The permissible stresses and design parameters for calculations are given in DIN 1052.

See also "Fundamentals" (p. 30)

Particleboard and chipboard

Chipboard is frequently used in roofs, walls and ceilings. The thickness ranges from 5 to 100 mm, tubular particleboards can be up to 120 mm thick. Chipboard can be employed as a permanently loaded structural material if the creep behaviour is allowed for in the design. It must be protected against moisture on the building site. The assumptions for calculations are given in the corresponding approvals in DIN 1052.

See also "Fundamentals" (p. 30)

Outlook

The efficiency of using untreated timber resources with regard to their load-carrying capacity is unsatisfactory in comparison to factory-processed materials. This situation is essentially a result of limited manufacturing methods, which hitherto have concentrated on cutting, sawing, planing, etc. The porous structure of wood and its plastic mouldability under the application of heat are leading to a new understanding of the material, where wood is no longer seen as a brittle material but instead as a mouldable, cellular solid. Compaction methods bring about a homogenisation of the growth-related irregularities in the fibres. The possibility of moulding the material allows the natural anisotropy of the wood to the exploited precisely for structural engineering purposes.

Squared section compressed to 45% of its original depth (photos from research work undertaken at Dresden Technical University, P. Haller)

Tubular section made from compressed half-round sections. The shape is the result of relieving the previously compacted microstructure at the outer edge.

Tubular sections made from solid fibreboards, rolled

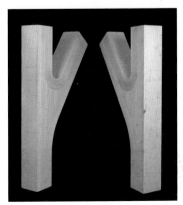

Strut junction with steam-bent wood in the gusset

Connectors and methods of connection

Criteria for designing details

Timber structures consist of components that are prefabricated in the factory and assembled on the building site. In this process the connectors are responsible for a significant share of the costs in timber engineering. But these costs can be reduced by rationalising the production and off-site fabrication. The amount of work on site should be kept to a minimum. Excessive transport and erection costs can be avoided by choosing the size of elements sensibly.

Deformation behaviour
In structural engineering we distinguish between elastic, mechanical connectors and woodworking joints. These can transfer tension, compression or shear forces or bending moments. As the forces are transferred an elastic connector exhibits a certain degree of slip, which is taken into account by the slip modulus. The stiffness of structural systems and compound sections depend to a great extent on this characteristic. DIN 1052 therefore requires that the deformation behaviour of the connectors be taken into account when assessing deflection and for compound sections. Weak points in the cross-section may well govern the size of members and the analysis of the force that can be transferred. Different means of connection with different elasticity, e.g. glued, mechanical, may not be combined. When designing the shape of the cross-section, the area required for the connections governs. On the other hand, the elasticity in the connections leads to a ductile failure behaviour, where advance warning of failure is an advantage over brittle failure of the wood. The associated load redistribution possibilities at the ultimate limit state in statically indeterminate systems increase the reserves of safety significantly. Consequently, it is no longer the failure loads but instead the deformations that govern the design. An optimum connection should be elastic so that it just reaches the permissible deformation under serviceability loads but still has a high factor of safety against failure of the timber.

It is recommended to include intermediate pads of hardwood, plywood or laminated veneer lumber at joints that transfer compression by direct contact in order to compensate for local weaknesses in the cross-section. Eccentricities that produce large moments and shear forces should be avoided wherever possible. The moisture content of the wood should be at a minimum when assembling the joint. Wood that is too wet leads to uncontrollable shrinkage splitting around the joint, thus decreasing its load-carrying capacity and increasing its elasticity. Shear sections are reduced in the case of continuous splits along a row of connectors. If a row of connectors is necessary, the theoretical load-carrying capacity according to DIN 1052 must be reduced. Short connecting faces at joints are therefore desirable.

Special attention should be given to avoiding eccentricities when designing connection details. The lines of action of the forces applied or the axes of the members should always intersect at one point. Undesirable tensile stresses perpendicular to the grain ensue with loads applied near an edge and perpendicular to the direction of the grain, or as a result of shrinkage. Pinned joints should be designed as pins according to the structural model so that secondary stresses do not occur as a result of unintended restraint and twisting of the member. The distances between the edges of adjacent components must be planned.

Transfer of forces
In timber structures compressive forces should always be transferred via direct contact. If tensile forces are involved, an overlapping of the components is necessary. To overcome eccentricity in single shear connections, forces can also be transferred through additional components, but in this case the arrangement must be duplicated.
In order to avoid eccentricities in the conception of connections, the lines of action of the incoming forces should all intersect at one point. The connectors should be arranged so that their centre of gravity coincides with the axis of

the member. Considerable additional stresses can arise if this is not the case. In structural systems resolved into individual members it is the performance of the connections and not the load-carrying capacity that determines the design of the diagonals and/or verticals. The economic efficiency of a joint is directly reflected in the number

and size of connectors, and indirectly in the consumption of timber in the members to be connected.

📖 Holzbau-Taschenbuch, Berlin 1986

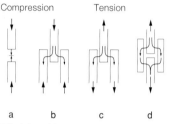

Principles of force transfer
a direct contact
b via shear in the case of compressive forces
c single overlap
d double overlap

eccentric system geometry

intersecting system axes (except for torsion)

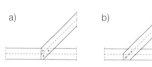

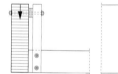

a) connectors eccentric to axes
b) connectors positioned on axes

Load transfer to upper chord

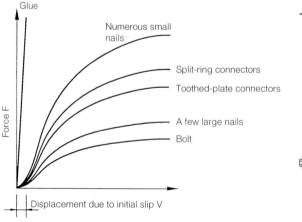

Glue

Numerous small nails

Split-ring connectors

Toothed-plate connectors

A few large nails

Bolt

Force F

Displacement due to initial slip V

Deformation behaviour of various connectors

From the connector to the detail

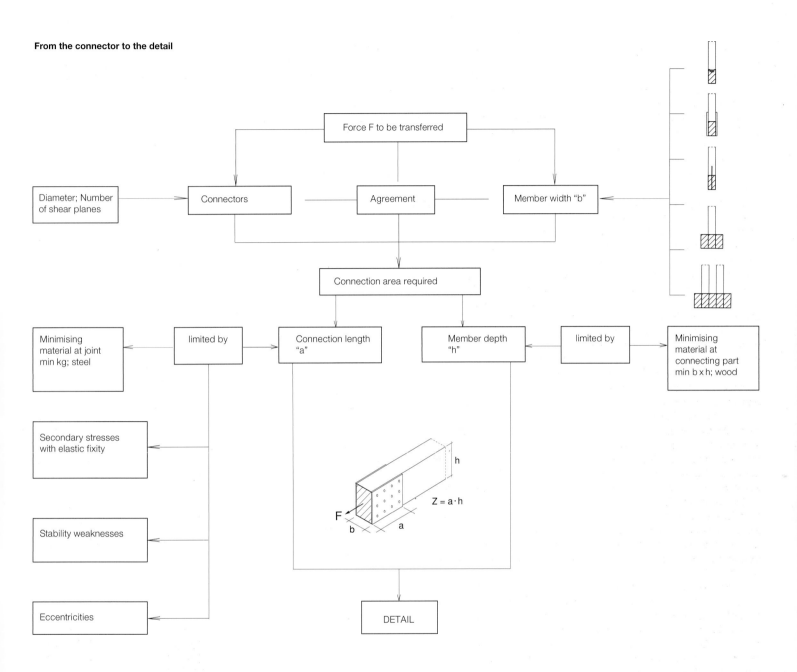

From the connector to the detail
Once a certain type of connection system has been chosen, the following factors must be considered:
· Selecting the diameter of bar-type connectors
· Selecting the grade of steel for the connector
· The possible increase in the depth of the connector due to a connection in multiple shear
· Establishing the timber cross-sections and the lengths of the connections

· Two areas must be considered in order to minimise the amount of material:
The component to be connected: the possibility of good utilisation of the weakened cross-section without oversizing the timber, i.e. the permissible force in the member corresponds to the permissible capacity of the connectors.
The joint: minimum materials for joint and connectors.
· Establishing the timber cross-sections

The choice of the width of the diagonals/verticals is primarily governed by the type of structural member selected, with gussets positioned inside or outside, single or multiple member sections. When gussets are fitted to the outside, the width of the diagonals/verticals clearly has to match that of the chords. But with gussets let into a slit in the material, or with multiple chords, the advantage is that the width of the diagonals/verticals does not need to match

that of the chords. There is a possibility here of distinguishing the diagonals/verticals from the chords. In this case the struts can provide a starting point for choosing a sensible width because economic use of material calls for a square or nearly square section.

Securing position with shear connector

Group of members on hardwood block, position secured with shear connectors

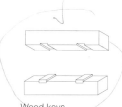

Shear connectors

Wood keys

Edge halved and tabled scarf joint with folding wedges

Forged nail and cramp

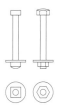

Pins with washer and cotter pin

Screws with washer and nut

Craftsman-type connections and connectors

Wood joints made by carpenters (e.g. tenons, halving joints, oblique dado joints) can now be produced with modern machinery, accurately and economically. Above all, these traditional joints are often a sensible alternative to customary connections using sheet metal parts for fabrication in large, computer-controlled plants. The forces are transferred mostly via contact faces that demand a high level of accuracy. The utmost care should be taken to ensure a low moisture content in the wood. The disadvantages of craftsman-type wood joints are considerable weakening of the members and the (usually) indistinct stress relationships. Theoretically, only relatively low loads can be carried due to the severe shearing and eccentricity effects.

Halving joints

The various halving joint variations are, first and foremost, structural connections with a low load-carrying capacity involving a considerable weakening of the cross-section. However, they are useful in, for example, roofs and frames. The use of traditional wood joints is still relevant in the exposed constructions of the historical buildings of past centuries and in the reconstruction of historical structures. Beams bearing on masonry, concrete etc. must always include a separating pad of material to prevent the saturation of the end of the timber.

Supports

Beams supported on secondary members in pockets, in mortices or on planted battens must include fish-plates to allow for the continuity effect. Such connections are easy to produce. This arrangement avoids bearing pressure on the edges and considerably increases the fire resistance.
In order not to exceed the permissible bearing perpendicular to the grain, beams supported on columns should include hardwood bearing pads or treated or glued veneer plywood.

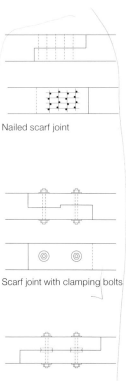

Nailed scarf joint

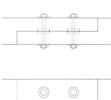

Scarf joint with clamping bolts

Dowelled scarf joint

Halving joint at the ridge

Halving joint at an intersection

Traditional tenon with cramps to provide tension resistance

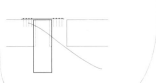

Pocket with nailed fishplate to provide tension resistance

Three-dimensional kneebraces and branched arrangement

Historical roof structure consisting of a queen post truss with upper king post

Double propped arrangement

Support to ridge purlin

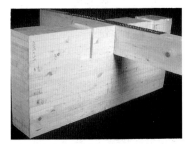

Secondary beam supported in pocket in main beam

Oblique dado connection with hardwood block

Cruciform column with widened supports for incoming beams

Joint with hardwood block in propped arrangement

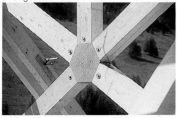

Plywood block joint

Cast frame corner

Oblique dados – examples

Approximation:

$$t_v \approx \frac{D}{0.70\,b}$$

Depth required:

$$t_v = \frac{D}{b} \cdot \frac{\cos \alpha}{\text{perm } \tau_a}$$

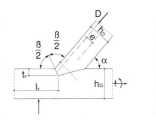

Oblique dado with thrust taken on the face

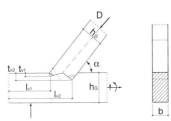

Stepped oblique dado with right-angled face and heel

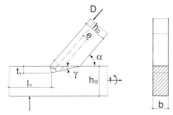

Thrust taken on right-angled face (hardwood)

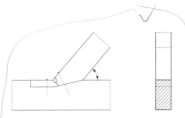

Oblique dado with thrust resisted by hardwood block

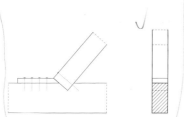

Oblique dado with thrust taken by planted hardwood block

Oblique dado joints

These days, the oblique dado joint is the most popular type of connection for joints in compression, and requires little steel. We distinguish between the oblique dado where the thrust is taken on the face, the version where the thrust is taken on the heel, and the stepped oblique dado. Relatively high forces can be transferred when the joint includes a hardwood block. However, the accuracy of the workmanship is the principal condition for transferring the forces ideally and without significant deformations. Large-scale oblique dados can also be used for glulam members. The position of the joint should be secured with bolts or screws. Here again, the suitability of the moisture content should not be ignored; it has a crucial effect on the deformation behaviour.

Contact faces

In order to exploit the timber cross-section to the full, additional joint elements generally have to be provided. These intermediate pieces are usually made from materials with a higher quality than the members themselves, e.g. steel, hardwood or treated wood-based products. They transfer the forces between the members. The full cross-sectional area of a strut can only be utilised when the surfaces in contact are perpendicular to the grain. Sloping contact faces require the compressive stresses to be severely reduced. Intermediate pads made from hardwood or veneer can be positioned corresponding to the direction of the grain so that all incoming members have compression faces perpendicular to the grain.

Ideal contact faces can be obtained by injecting the joint with high-strength, non-shrink cement or synthetic resin dispersions. Provided steel is not used for the intermediate pads, highly fire-resistant joints can be produced.

Direct contact joints

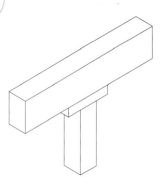

Support enlarged with hardwood bearing block

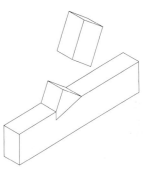

Cast block forming an oblique dado

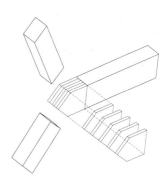

Joint in compression with shaped piece made from laminated veneer lumber

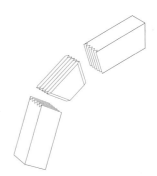

Finger-jointed frame corner with plywood block

Calculation of a nailed connection

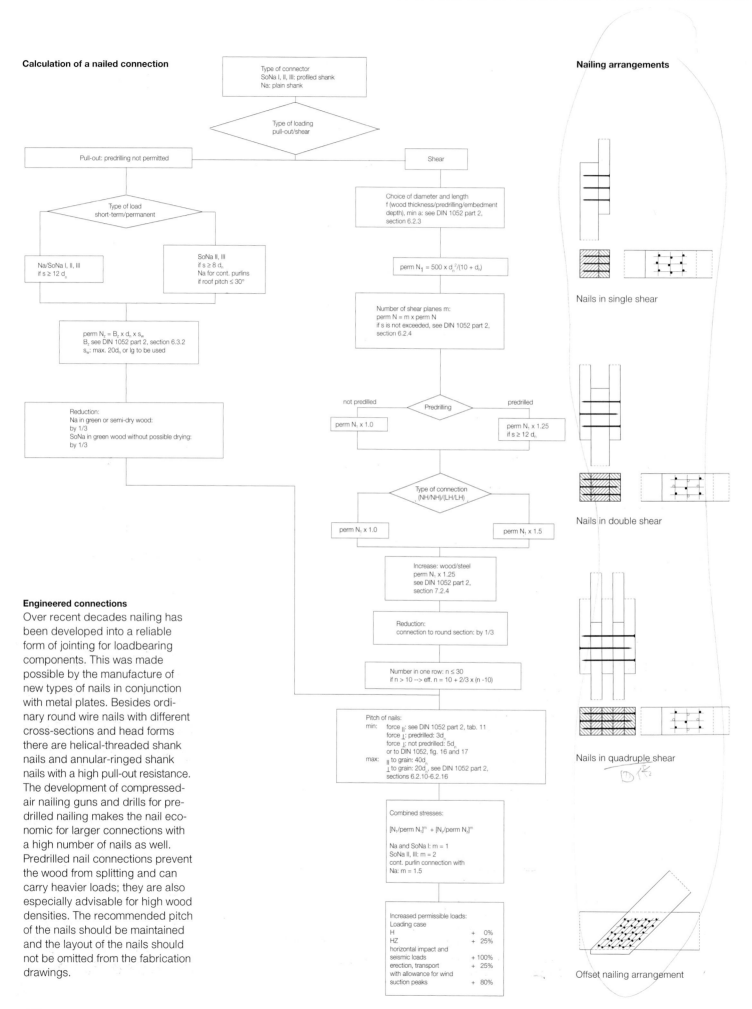

Type of connector
SoNa I, II, III: profiled shank
Na: plain shank

Type of loading
pull-out/shear

Pull-out: predrilling not permitted

Shear

Pull-out branch:

Type of load
short-term/permanent

Na/SoNa I, II, III
if $s \geq 12\,d_n$

SoNa II, III
if $s \geq 8\,d_n$
Na for cont. purlins
if roof pitch $\leq 30°$

perm $N_z = B_z \times d_n \times s_w$
B_z see DIN 1052 part 2, section 6.3.2
s_w: max. $20 d_n$ or lg to be used

Reduction:
Na in green or semi-dry wood:
by 1/3
SoNa in green wood without possible drying:
by 1/3

Shear branch:

Choice of diameter and length
f (wood thickness/predrilling/embedment depth), min a: see DIN 1052 part 2, section 6.2.3

perm $N_1 = 500 \times d_n^2/(10 + d_n)$

Number of shear planes m:
perm $N = m \times$ perm N
if s is not exceeded, see DIN 1052 part 2, section 6.2.4

Predrilling

not predilled — perm $N_1 \times 1.0$

predrilled — perm $N_1 \times 1.25$
if $s \geq 12\,d_n$

Type of connection
(NH/NH)/(LH/LH)

perm $N_1 \times 1.0$

perm $N_1 \times 1.5$

Increase: wood/steel
perm $N_1 \times 1.25$
see DIN 1052 part 2, section 7.2.4

Reduction:
connection to round section: by 1/3

Number in one row: $n \leq 30$
if $n > 10 \longrightarrow$ eff. $n = 10 + 2/3 \times (n\,{-}10)$

Pitch of nails:
min: force $\parallel$: see DIN 1052 part 2, tab. 11
      force $\perp$: predrilled: $3 d_n$
      force $\perp$: not predrilled: $5 d_n$
      or to DIN 1052, fig. 16 and 17
max: $\parallel$ to grain: $40 d_n$
      $\perp$ to grain: $20 d_n$, see DIN 1052 part 2, sections 6.2.10-6.2.16

Combined stresses:

$[N_1/\text{perm } N_1]^m + [N_z/\text{perm } N_z]^m$

Na and SoNa I: m = 1
SoNa II, III: m = 2
cont. purlin connection with
Na: m = 1.5

Increased permissible loads:

Loading case	
H	+ 0%
HZ	+ 25%
horizontal impact and seismic loads	+ 100%
erection, transport with allowance for wind	+ 25%
suction peaks	+ 80%

Engineered connections

Over recent decades nailing has been developed into a reliable form of jointing for loadbearing components. This was made possible by the manufacture of new types of nails in conjunction with metal plates. Besides ordinary round wire nails with different cross-sections and head forms there are helical-threaded shank nails and annular-ringed shank nails with a high pull-out resistance. The development of compressed-air nailing guns and drills for pre-drilled nailing makes the nail economic for larger connections with a high number of nails as well. Predrilled nail connections prevent the wood from splitting and can carry heavier loads; they are also especially advisable for high wood densities. The recommended pitch of the nails should be maintained and the layout of the nails should not be omitted from the fabrication drawings.

Nailing arrangements

Nails in single shear

Nails in double shear

Nails in quadruple shear

Offset nailing arrangement

Nails and screws

Ordinary round wire nails

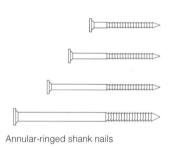

Annular-ringed shank nails

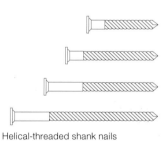

Helical-threaded shank nails

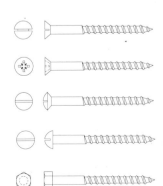

Wood screws

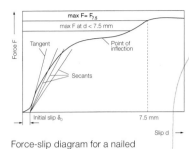

Force-slip diagram for a nailed connection (schematic)

Forms of construction using nailed boards

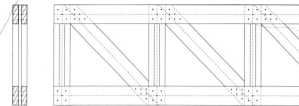

Nailed lattice girder with nailed connections in double shear

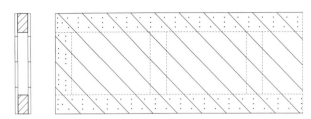

Box beam with webs of nailed boards

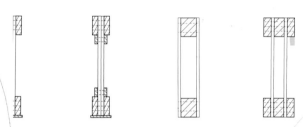

Sections through solid web beams, with webs of nailed boards

The ongoing development of nailed connections has also resulted in loadbearing systems made from nailed boards. Factory-produced nailed lattice girders are now highly economic propositions for short spans. Boarded beams or frames are commonly used for agricultural buildings. Larger spans are possible thanks to the use of new nailing techniques and pre-drilling in conjunction with thicker planks, and sections in multiple shear – interesting as economic alternatives for Third World projects. The shape of the nail head and the layout of the nails should not be neglected for situations with high aesthetic demands.

In shear wood screws behave just like nails, but their pull-out loads are higher and the appearance of the head is an improvement over nails.

The development of self-tapping connectors that can be installed with hand-held plant without needing to drill a pilot hole has made the use of these wood screws very economical and hence successful. In many instances components can be fixed in position with a tension-resistant connector by choosing a suitable size of screw. And the recently launched double-thread screws do not just join together several timber sections to form a compound member, but also enable butt joints between main and secondary members to be achieved without any further means of connection.

Self-drilling dowels render possible multiple-shear dowelled connections without having to drill the timber and sheet metal components first. The short thread just below the head of the dowel serves to secure the position of the member once installed.

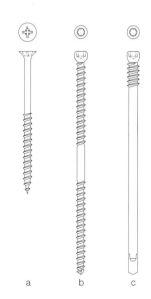

Self-tapping connectors:
a Spax self-tapping screw
b Double-thread screw
c Self-drilling dowel

Typical connections and joints

Nailed forms of construction

Nailing with metal gussets let into the timber
Fitting metal plates 1.0–2.0 mm thick into slits sawn in the timber and nailing through these without predrilling produces economic, multiple-shear connections. Metal plates subjected to compression must be checked for buckling. Building authority approvals determine the permissible loads. Careful workmanship is essential because the metal plates must fit tightly into the slits, especially in the vicinity of the mating faces. Examples of approved systems are the Greim system and the VB system.

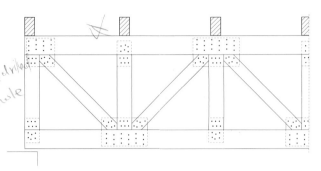

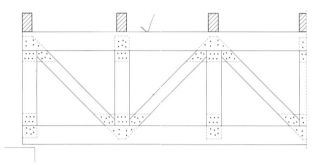

Lattice girder with gusset plates fitted into slits, nail holes predrilled in wood, nailed through metal plates

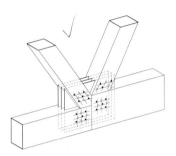

Greim system:
plates d < 2 mm, fitted into slits,
nail holes not predrilled

Truss joint in the Greim system

Lattice girder with vertical posts, diagonal struts and ties, Greim system connections

Predrilled holes are necessary when using steel plates > 2 mm thick. The holes are drilled through timber and steel in one operation, so nails can be driven through one or more plates without any problems. The diameter of the hole should be equal to the diameter of the nail. Again, this method calls for a tight fit between the metal plate and the sides of the slit, and the risk of buckling must also be checked. The spacing of the nails may be reduced when using predrilled holes, which means the metal gussets can be kept smaller. The use of drilling templates allows the arrangement of the nails to be maintained accurately.

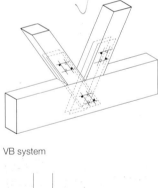

VB system

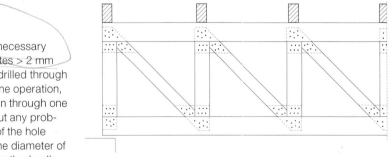

Greim system lattice girder, with verticals in compression, diagonals in tension

Steel plates d > 2 mm,
nail holes drilled simultaneously with
metal plate

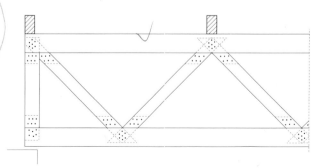

VB system lattice girder

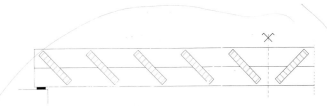

Compound beam with punched metal plate fasteners pressed on

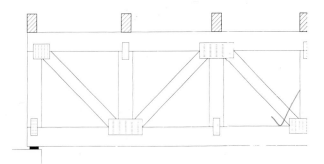

Lattice girder with punched metal plate fasteners pressed on

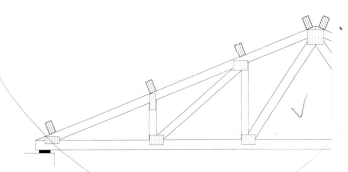

Truss with punched metal plate fasteners pressed on at joints

Butt joint in tension zone

Butt joint in bending zone

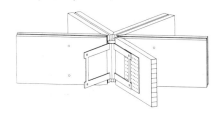

Three-dimensional butt joint in bending zone of twin girder

Punched metal plate fasteners
Machine-made punched metal plate fasteners enable the industrial fabrication of nailed roof trusses. These punched metal plates greatly reduce the workload compared to conventional forms of nailing. Both tension- and compression-resistant connections between single timber sections are possible. The punched metal plates are made from 1 to 2 mm thick steel sheet. The nail- or claw-shape punchings are pressed into the surface of the wood. It is not necessary for the timber members to overlap at the joint, and this saves on material. Related to the size of the joint faces, the force that can be transferred is, owing to the multitude of "nails", much higher than with conventional nailed connections. Forms of construction with punched metal plate fasteners, e.g. BAT-Multin, BF, Gang-Nail, Hydron, TTS Twinaplate, etc., are all covered by building authority approvals (DIN 1052 part 2).

Nailed and bolted pinned joints
It is advisable to employ multiple chords and diagonals with trusses carrying loads exceeding 300 kN. These are then connected with 4–6 mm thick nail plates in the factory and a bolt on the building site. As the transfer of forces is concentrated on one axis, a perfect pin is the result. The steel parts in this connection remain concealed and thus protected against fire. The nailing can be carried out in the factory without any extensive machinery. In this type of connection the transfer of forces is from the timber via the nails into the steel plate. From there, the forces are transferred through the welded edge strengthening by way of bearing pressure to the axis of the pin, which in turn transfers the forces via shear to the other steel plate. Predrilled nail holes enable the pitch of the nails to be reduced, and hence the overall size of the connection.

Gang-Nail punched metal plate fastener

Twinaplate punched metal plate fastener

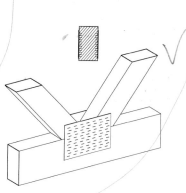

Gang-Nail in use

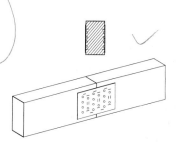

Twinaplate in use

Perforated plates nailed on, with hinge pin

Perforated plates fitted inside joint, with hinge pin

**Perforated sheet metal plates, straps
and angles**

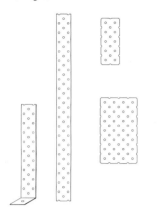

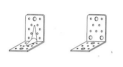

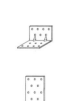

*Sheet metal timber connectors
for nailing*

Joints between members, supports and restraints are easy to produce using a wide variety of sheet steel connectors. Flat and shaped metal connectors are available in 2–4 mm thick zinc-coated, galvanised steel or stainless steel, cold-formed and drilled ready for receiving nails. They are fixed using helical-threaded or, better, annular-ringed shank nails, with a compressed-air nailing gun or by hand. The timber should be dry and the risk of buckling should not be ignored.

The multitude of applications in the form of plates, straps, angles, brackets, anchors, hangers, etc. has increased considerably in recent years. Load-carrying capacities of hangers, angles etc. are covered by building authority approvals and can be found in the corresponding manufacturer's literature or the approval documents, e.g. Barth, Bira, GH etc. Shown on this page are angles with and without stiffening for joints between timber members, between timber and masonry/concrete, and anchors and hangers for connecting joists to main beams or masonry/concrete.

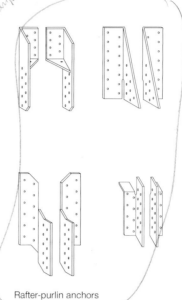

Rafter-purlin anchors

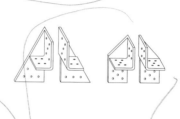

Joist hangers

Beam connectors

Cleat

Trigon multi-purpose connector

Joist hangers

Rafter-purlin anchor for lighter loads

Pinned joint at end of cantilever

Rafter-purlin anchor for heavier loads

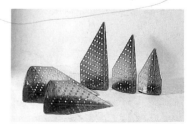

Trigon connectors

Star-shaped welded steel node

Welded steel connector for strut-bottom chord or kneebrace-column junction

Base of column fixed sideways into masonry, height-adjustable

Column dowelled into concrete plinth, height-adjustable

Pinned joint for frame or arch in glued laminated timber

Prefabricated column bases

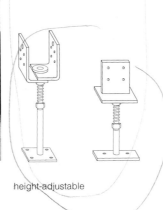

cast in

dowelled

height-adjustable

Welded steel connectors
Welded connectors nailed or dowelled to the timber as well as nailed-on steel parts for supports or pinned joints can be made from 3–10 mm thick material in accordance with DIN 1050 and DIN 18800. Such connectors are made up by welding and provided with appropriate certificates. Accurate fabrication and assembly of the timber members is especially important in order to avoid bearing stresses at the edges. If fire protection regulations require, all steel parts should be protected against direct exposure to fire, i.e. should be covered with timber or a mineral building material to attain the necessary fire resistance. In some cases a coating of intumescent paint will be adequate. Protection against corrosion for loadbearing steel connectors and fixings in timber structures is covered by DIN 1052 part 2, which distinguishes between low, moderate and high corrosion loads. Corrosion protection is particularly important in swimming pools, saline baths, fertiliser plants and salt storage sheds. In exceptional cases analyses of the interior climate and air should be carried out. Hot-dip galvanised or zinc-sprayed parts are recommended, but stainless steel or special alloys can be considered for special applications.

Welded steel connector for tension loads

Pinned joints and ridge joints

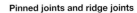

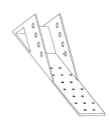

Oblique dado anchor

Rafter support

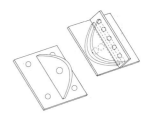

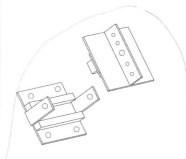

Pinned joints for heavily loaded structural connections at eaves and ridge

Dowels, bolts, close tolerance bolts

Dowels are cylindrical rods that are driven into predrilled holes. High loads and stiffnesses can be achieved because there is no play through shrinkage or the need for an oversized hole. According to recent studies it is not necessary to stagger the dowels with respect to the line of splitting (DIN 1052 part 2, E 5.7).

In contrast to dowels, bolts require an oversized hole to be predrilled. However, bolts can only be employed for locating purposes, or for carry-ing considerably lower loads than dowels when the deformation behaviour has only a small influence on the overall deformation of the structure.

The close tolerance bolt is driven into a predrilled hole and, as with a dowel, there is no play. When fitted with nut and washer, the short thread at the end of the bolt serves to locate the bolt and the component. Loads and stiffnesses are identical to those of dowels of the same size.

Arrangement of fixings

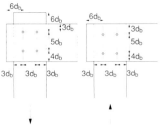

Minimum spacings for dowels and close tolerance bolts

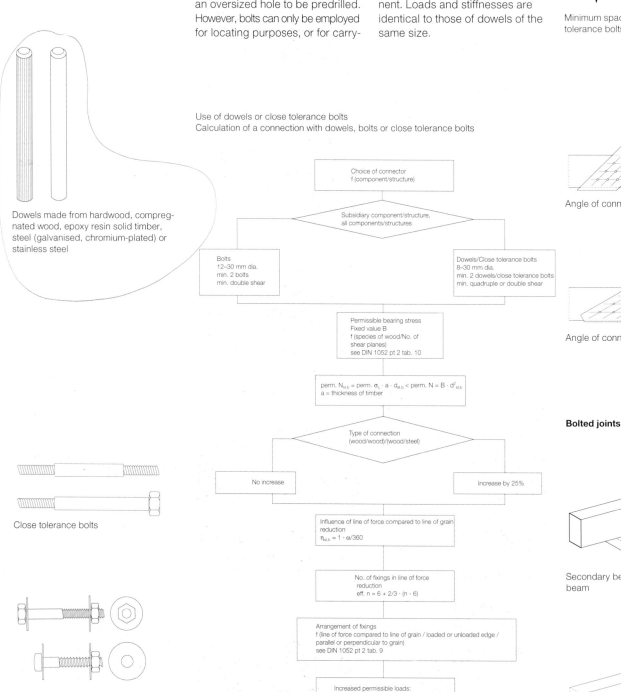

Use of dowels or close tolerance bolts
Calculation of a connection with dowels, bolts or close tolerance bolts

Dowels made from hardwood, compreg-nated wood, epoxy resin solid timber, steel (galvanised, chromium-plated) or stainless steel

Close tolerance bolts

Bolts with nuts and various washers

Choice of connector
f (component/structure)

Subsidiary component/structure, all components/structures

Bolts
12–30 mm dia.
min. 2 bolts
min. double shear

Dowels/Close tolerance bolts
8–30 mm dia.
min. 2 dowels/close tolerance bolts
min. quadruple or double shear

Permissible bearing stress
Fixed value B
f (species of wood/No. of shear planes)
see DIN 1052 pt 2 tab. 10

perm. $N_{st,b}$ = perm. $\sigma_L \cdot a \cdot d_{st,b}$ < perm. $N = B \cdot d^2_{st,b}$
a = thickness of timber

Type of connection
(wood/wood)/(wood/steel)

No increase

Increase by 25%

Influence of line of force compared to line of grain
reduction
$\eta_{st,b} = 1 \cdot \alpha/360$

No. of fixings in line of force
reduction
eff. n = 6 + 2/3 · (n - 6)

Arrangement of fixings
f (line of force compared to line of grain / loaded or unloaded edge / parallel or perpendicular to grain)
see DIN 1052 pt 2 tab. 9

Increased permissible loads:
Loading case
H   + 0%
HZ   + 25%
horizontal impact and
seismic loads   + 100%
erection, transport   + 25%
with allowance for wind
suction peaks   + 80%

Angle of connection $\alpha \geq 37°$

Angle of connection $\alpha < 37°$

Bolted joints

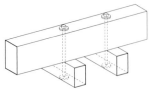

Secondary beams suspended from main beam

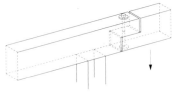

Pinned beam splice

Wood-wood connections

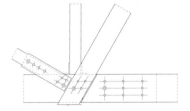

Rigid splice with plywood gusset, dowels not staggered

Dowelled construction

Dowels can be used to join timber members together directly, or combined with steel plates. Analyses must be carried out for the weakened cross-sections in the timber and the steel. A dowelled connection consists of at least two dowels. When using a large number of dowels it is recommended to provide one dowel with a thread, washer and nut, in other words one close tolerance bolt, to provide lateral restraint. A smaller thread helps when driving the bolt into the tightly fitting, predrilled hole. When using close tolerance bolts combined with steel plates care should be taken during fabrication to ensure that the plates do not coincide with the threads.

Template and finished welded part

Marking out holes for dowels using a template

Assembling a truss in the factory

A joint on a trussed beam, timber members connected with dowels and close tolerance bolts

Steel gusset-wood connections

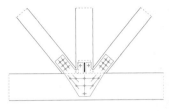

Joint with steel plate let into slits and fixed with dowels

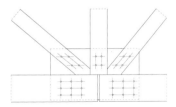

Joint at splice in bottom chord, with steel plate let into slits and fixed with dowels

Truss joint with splice in bottom chord

Compression joint with nailed or dowelled steel framing anchor

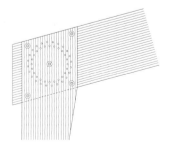

Corner of frame with ring of dowels and clamping bolts

Corner of frame with ring of dowels

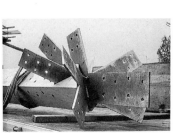

Welded steel connector for three-dimensional joint.

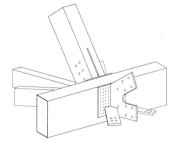

Joint with welded steel connector nailed on, diagonals fixed with dowels

Split-ring and shear-plate connectors

Type A (shear plate)

Made from hardwood, steel and cast aluminium/steel

Type B (split ring)

Toothed-plate connectors

Single-sided
d ≤ 75 mm

Single-sided
d = 95 or 117 mm

Type C

Double-sided round

Type C

Single-sided   Double-sided

Type D

Calculating a connection with split-ring, shear-plate or toothed-plate connectors

Species of wood
hardwood/softwood

Connector type A, B

Connector type C, D, E
Connector type A, B

Type of connection
end grain / other

perm.
type A

perm.
type A, B, C, D, E

Choice of diameter
f (timber cross-section)

Choice of diameter
f (timber cross-section)

perm. load
f (connector dia. / No. in row)
DIN 1052 pt 2 tab. 5

perm. load
f (connector dia. / angle between
line of force and line of grain)
type A see DIN 1052 pt 2 tab. 4
type B see DIN 1052 pt 2 tab. 4
type C see DIN 1052 pt 2 tab. 6
type D see DIN 1052 pt 2 tab. 7
type E see DIN 1052 pt 2 tab. 7

No. of connectors in row
n ≤ 10
if n > 2
eff. n = 2 + (1 · n/20) · (n - 2)

Connector spacing
edge distance V_d = b/2
DIN 1052 pt 2 tab. 5

Connector spacing
f (1 row / > 1 row)
1 row: see DIN 1052 pt 2 tab. 4, 6, 7
> 1 row: see DIN 1052 pt 2 tab. 8

Increased permissible loads:
Loading case
H   +   0%
HZ   +   25%
horizontal impact and
seismic loads   + 100%
erection, transport   + 25%
with allowance for wind
suction peaks   + 80%

Connector spacings

Non-staggered arrangement

Staggered arrangement

Tension connection with shear-plate and toothed-plate connectors

Connections using split-ring, shear-plate and toothed-plate connectors to DIN 1052 part 2 are divided into types A, B, C, D and E. Permissible loads parallel, diagonal and perpendicular to the grain plus minimum sizes of members and connector spacings are given in the tables. The maximum number of connectors that can be positioned in one row represents the limit to this type of connection. The permissible tension loads must be reduced when there are more than two connectors, and more than 10 connectors in a row is not permitted. All connectors must be secured with bolts, nuts and washers in accordance with DIN 1052. These connections result in a significant weakening of the cross-section, which must be taken into account when analysing the stresses. From that we can deduce the member sizes required at the joint.

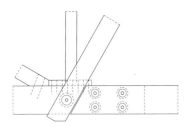

Joint in truss at splice in bottom chord

End grain connections, perpendicular and diagonal, with split-ring connectors

2 x single-sided connectors with box section at beam

Squared section with toothed-plate connector for end grain connection

End grain connectors

Single- and double-sided toothed-plate connectors

Split-ring connectors

Squared sections with routed circles ready for split-ring connectors

Wood-wood dowelled joints
Split-ring connectors can also be used for end grain connections. The clamping effect is achieved by way of M12 bolts in conjunction with round bars 24–40 mm dia., appropriately shaped pieces, or nuts with washers (DIN 1052 part 2, 4.3.2). The end grain connection is permitted only in glued laminated timber. This type of connection is mainly advantageous for multiple connections in trusses with low member forces, but also wood-wood connections in glued laminated timber frames with large joint faces. However, there are limits to using these connectors at the corners of frames with respect to shear stresses and the beam depth owing to the possible tension stresses perpendicular to the grain caused by shrinkage.

Connector-metal plate joints
Single-sided connectors in conjunction with sheet metal plates are useful for tension connections and points of fixity. The connectors are fitted into their routed cut-outs in the factory, and only the necessary bolts need to be added on site.

Wood-steel connections

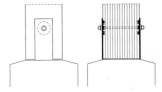

Column base connection with single-sided connectors

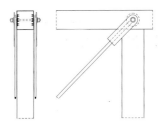

Tie connection with single-sided connectors

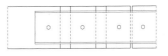

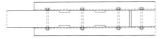

Rigid beam connection with channel section and flat steel connectors welded on

119

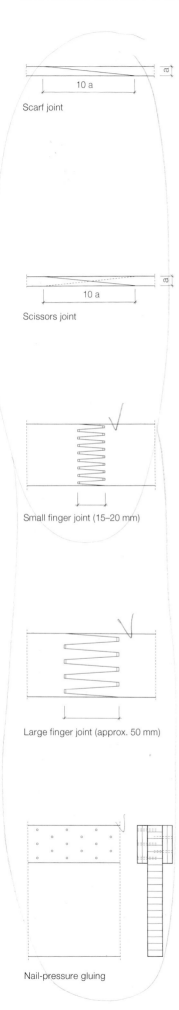

Scarf joint

Scissors joint

Small finger joint (15–20 mm)

Large finger joint (approx. 50 mm)

Nail-pressure gluing

Glued construction

Glues and glued joints were developed in conjunction with glued laminated timber. Only approved glues may be used for loadbearing components in timber engineering. The working conditions for gluing are very carefully monitored and must be adhered to. Only synthetic resin glues may be used for components exposed directly to the weather when in service. Such glues are also required for components in buildings in which the interior climate means that an equilibrium moisture content of 20% is exceeded, or the component is at a temperature of 50°C either frequently or permanently. These glues (e.g. resorcinol or melamine resin glues) must be tested to assess their resistance to all climatic influences. Epoxy resins are particularly suitable for bonding thick joints and wood-steel connections. The mixing ratios and suitability tests are specified in the relevant standards. As a rule, there is no problem with the compatibility of glues and wood preservatives. However, this may need to be checked in special cases.

Glued joints
Loadbearing glued joints may only be produced by companies with a "gluing licence". Such companies require appropriate facilities and trained personnel, monitored by the building authority. Practically immovable joints are possible with this technology, thus enabling structures with optimum cross-sections to be built. The laminations are first joined together in the longitudinal direction, for example, by glued finger joints. Then the laminations are glued together, and care must be taken to ensure that moisture content, quantity of glue and bonding pressure are all correct. In the production of profiled sections the additional pieces can be subsequently bonded, for example, using nail-pressure gluing. This method, in which the bonding pressure is assured by the nails, is particularly suitable for local strengthening with wood-based products.

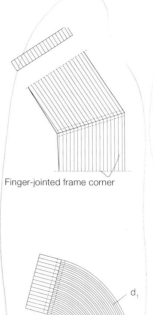

Finger-jointed frame corner

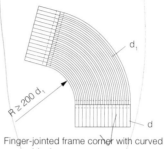

Finger-jointed frame corner with curved corner block

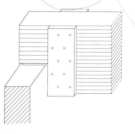

Nail-pressure gluing for withstanding tension perpendicular to the grain

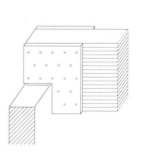

Nail-pressure gluing for strengthening at the support

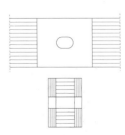

Hole reinforced with plywood and nail-pressure gluing

Finger joints

Finger-jointed hardwood block for frame corner

Three-pin frame made from glued laminated timber with finger-jointed frame corner

Finger-jointed splice in bottom chord

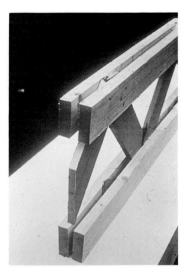

Section through Trigonit lattice beam

Trigonit lattice beams

Sine-wave web joists

Panel elements prefabricated in the factory

Panel elements for roofs, walls and floors

Beams

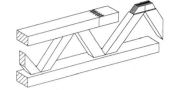

Lattice beam (e.g. DSB)

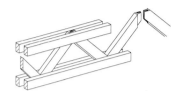

Trigonit lattice beam

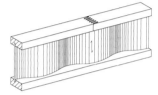

Sine-wave web joist (e.g. Wellsteg)

I-beam (e.g. TJI)

Solid timber system elements

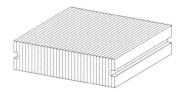

Factory-glued components
The production of trusses, lattice beams and solid-web beams with glued joints using rationalised methods of production is a tried-and-tested technology. Compound and glued cross-sections are particularly economic for secondary beams spanning 8–14 m, where squared sections alone are no longer adequate. Even primary beams spanning 20 m are possible. The structural depths of parallel-flange members are limited by the building authority approvals. Trigonit, DSB, Wellsteg and TJI are among the best-known brand-names.

Timber panel elements
These are produced by gluing together squared sections and veneer plywood or laminated veneer lumber (LVL) boards. They can also be connected with nails, with or without glue. The panel elements are usually in the form of hollow sections or I-beams, and can be used for building houses and single-storey sheds with minimum materials. In the form of load-bearing roof elements they can span up to 15 m, and as wall elements can help to stiffen a structure. They are covered by building authority approvals and may only be manufactured by companies with a "gluing licence".

Timber panel details

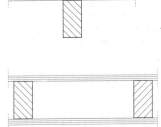

Profiled system elements

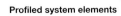

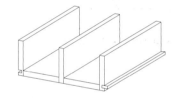

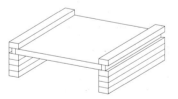

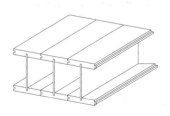

Cramps

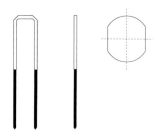

round section

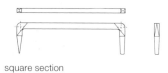

square section

rectangular section

Building or scaffold cramps to DIN 7961

Hardwood ties with bonded-in threaded steel rods

Special connectors and jointing techniques

A multitude of connectors and fittings are available to the structural engineer for successful detailing in timber structures. Only a brief selection is dealt with here:

Cramped connections
- Wood cramps
  These are made from galvanised or painted wire, 1.2–2.0 mm dia., driven in with a special gun. They function like two thin nails subjected to shear. Wood cramps are used for fixing boarding, battens and wall panel elements. Cramped connections are covered by chapter 8 of DIN 1052.

- Building and scaffold cramps
  These are among the traditional forms of wood connectors and are suitable for transferring low forces and securing items in position. Today, they are primarily used in scaffolding and temporary works. The permissible loads are given in DIN 1052.

- Bonded-in threaded rods for strengthening at supports
  These threaded metal rods or beech wood dowels are glued in to enhance the permissible compressive stresses perpendicular to the grain at supports. A high load transfer in a small space is possible when they are combined with nail plates.

- Turnbuckles
  Turnbuckles or sockets with opposing threads permit round bars in wind girders and trussed arrangements to be adjusted precisely. They enable subsequent adjustment to compensate for erection tolerances and temperature effects. Welded-on clamping bars are added in certain cases.

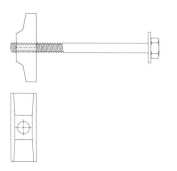

Simplex connector, elevation and section

Bonded-in threaded bars

Turnbuckles, also suitable for pre-stressing tendons

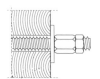

Connection with threaded bar

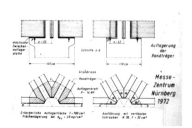

Detail of support with bonded-in screw

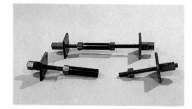

Special connectors

Section through end grain connection with split-ring connector and special connector

Turnbuckles

Turnbuckles for wind X-bracing

Bonded-in threaded bar after loading test

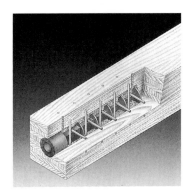
Bonded-in rod

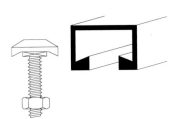
Cast-in channel

Hexagonal nut   Domed nut

Square and circular washers

Spring washers

Hilti heavy-duty expansion anchors

Special connections

· Bonded-in rods

These are suitable for carrying heavy loads. The rods are inserted into predrilled holes and subsequently grouted in. Compressive, tensile and shear stresses can be accommodated and rigid connections are therefore possible without enlarging the cross-section. The use of bonded-in rods to strengthen members at supports allows heavy, concentrated loads to be transferred. End grain connections can be loaded up to 192 kN. Pressure-grouting achieves a very accurate fit, thus maintaining the geometry of the structure.

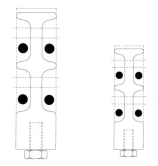
Connection with bonded-in rods

· Cast-in channels

The channels made by the Halfen company and others are useful for connecting timber constructions to concrete. Here again, building tolerances can be easily accommodated.

· Tensioning elements

Washers should always be of an adequate size. To ensure the clamping effect of bolts or a constant prestress for overcoming tension perpendicular to the grain, even after shrinkage spring washers are advisable. Disc spring washers have a significant degree of travel for keeping a prestress constant.

· Anchor bolts

Common anchor systems such as those from Hilti, Fischer and Upat are suitable for transferring heavy loads from timber members to concrete. As the holes in the concrete ground slab or ring beam are drilled on site, inaccuracies in the substructure can be compensated for. The permissible loads can be found in the approval documents. The edge distances in concrete must be observed.

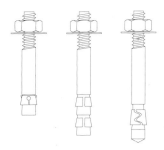
Heavy-duty expansion anchors for connecting to concrete

· Cast parts

Cast parts are suitable for larger numbers of individually designed connections.

· Elastomeric or sliding bearings

These bearings common in bridge-building are also suitable for timber structures where high loads have to be accommodated at supports. Twist is therefore able to develop without causing high edge bearing pressures. Sliding bearings require a Teflon coating. Elastomeric pads are recommended for heavily loaded columns in order to centre the load and avoid stress peaks. During the design, permissible stresses should be analysed as well as permissible deformations, e.g. twist or displacement.

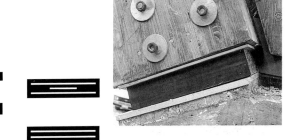
Elastomeric bearings

Pinned column base made from cast metal

Trussed arrangement with cast parts

Elastomeric pads for pivot, rocker and sliding bearings

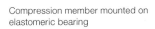
Compression member mounted on elastomeric bearing

123

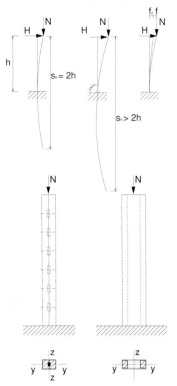

Solid, compound and box sections

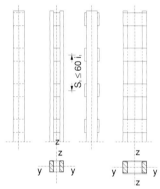

Battened columns

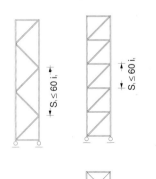

Laced columns

Stability elements

The permissible loads that can be carried by a primary structural system depend essentially on stability elements and can be influenced by many constructional measures. The greatest influences are those of material quality and accuracy during fabrication and erection. "Theoretically", the top flange of a beam can be restrained with a "little finger" – provided the beam is perfectly straight! However, in reality we must always reckon with deviations from the ideal geometry, tolerances, eccentricities, partial restraint, poor workmanship etc.

Vertical loadbearing systems
Stability elements for accommodating forces from out-of-plumb effects and eccentricities in compressive members, plates or frames must be adequately stiff. Their task is to prevent buckling, overturning or punching problems. The resulting internal forces are not transferred to the subsoil. Bracing is also designed to withstand horizontal loads such as wind, asymmetric snow loads, imposed loads, impacts, loose materials, braking forces and seismic loads, which must be transferred into the subsoil.

Restrained members
These are subjected to internal and external loads. Two methods of calculation are available to the designer: the equivalent member method and second order elastic analysis; the choice of the most suitable method is made by the engineer. The elasticity of the connection is taken into account by way of rotational stiffnesses. An individual analysis is replaced by a second order elastic analysis in complex systems. Restrained members are made from solid cross-sections consisting of squared timber or glued laminated timber, or from multiple sections.

Battened and laced columns
Columns made up of several members are divided into those joined continuously and those held apart with transverse members in which buckling must be assessed for the whole system and the flanges individually. The reduction

Maypole as fixed-base column

Four-part fixed-base column

in the effective moment of inertia as a result of the elasticity of the fixings is carried out according to DIN 1052.
Buckling of the overall system is checked using equivalent member lengths or a second order elastic analysis, with moments due to out-of-plumb effects and transverse loads possible.

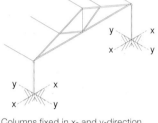

Column fixed in x- and y-direction

Columns fixed in x- and y-direction

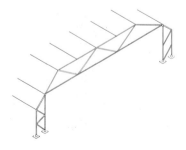

Columns fixed in x-direction

Laced columns fixed in x-direction

External propping to a single-storey shed

Props positioned in the wall

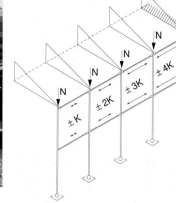

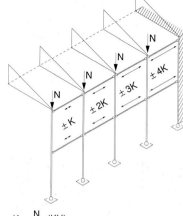

X-bracing positioned in front of the wall

X-bracing at the supports

$$K = \frac{N}{50} \quad (KH)$$

$$K = \frac{N}{100} \quad (BSH)$$

Structural system for bracing columns
KH = solid timber
BSH = glulam timber

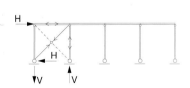

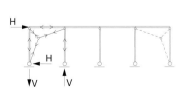

Guyed post-and-beam construction; the
steel must be analysed for deformations
due to temperature changes

Propped compressive members
Intermediate props are suitable for
reducing the buckling length and
hence the moments on compressive members. Unwanted out-of-
plumb effects or those that occur
in service are taken into account in
the calculations by resultant loads,
which are taken to be N/50 for
solid timber and N/100 for glued
laminated timber, where N is the
resultant maximum compressive
load.

Staircase tower acting as prop to timber-
frame building

Guyed compressive members
Compressive members can be
advantageously braced against
buckling by tension guy arrangements. The tension members are
made of steel and can subsequently be retensioned using
threaded bars and sockets. This
enables the member to be aligned
exactly. Dimensional tolerances
can be compensated for and facade
elements fitted in accurately.
Cyclic loads and temperature
changes should be taken into
account during the design and the
deformations checked. Pretensioning should be considered for
steel X-bracing.

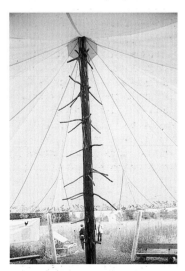

Pylon with membrane acting as guying
system

Propped arrangements

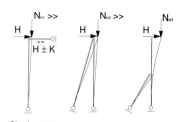

Single prop

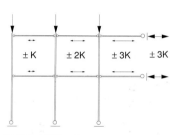

Multiple props

Guyed arrangements

Guyed mast

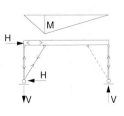

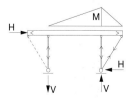

Guyed columns and beam

Rigid frame with finger-jointed corners

Vertical loadbearing systems at 90° to the primary loadbearing system

Stability by means of frames
Buildings requiring large door and window openings can have frames with larger clear openings where otherwise there would be awkward diagonal members. The frame positioned in the wall – at 90° to the direction of the primary load-bearing system – has to withstand wind loads from the wind bracing and the resultant loads from the out-of-plumb columns of neigh-bouring trusses. Special care should be taken to ensure ade-quate stiffness, especially with large areas of glazing. The frame can be fabricated from squared timber sections, glued laminated timber, laminated veneer lumber or, in extreme cases, steel sec-tions.

Multistorey frame

Open frame corners with laminated veneer lumber arches

Rigid frame with elastic fixings

Frames with open corners

Triangulated girders

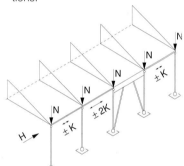

Kneebraced frame

Stability by means of trusses
Partly enclosed buildings often include bracing trusses within the walls. Compared to frames, the quantity of material required is considerably less, but the connec-tions are more complicated. The diagonals between posts and beams can be used as a frame-work for the wall construction. The ensuing loads, particularly those perpendicular to the wall, e.g. wind or silo loads, must be included in the design.

Continuous triangulated structure in the wall

X-bracing

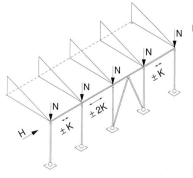

K-braced girders

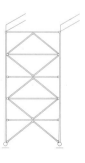

K-braced girders

V-shaped bracing

Multistorey residential block in log construction

Wall plate effect provided by diagonal planking

Wall plates made from timber panels

Sports centre with precast concrete walls

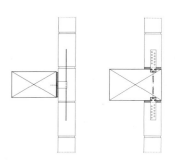

Multistorey office building in timber-frame construction

Plate

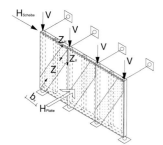

Loads on a wall consisting of three panels

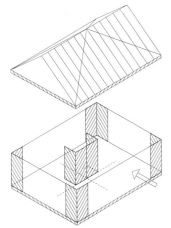

Symmetrical arrangement of shear walls

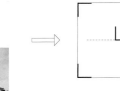

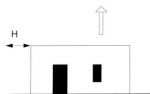

Shear wall with openings

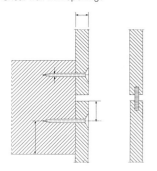

Joint detail for wood-based planks

Stability by means of plates

Wall plates (shear walls) can be formed from logs, squared sections or planking. Even planks or boards made of wood-based products and positioned diagonally can be used to brace or stabilise a structure, also plates comprising trapezoidal profile metal sheeting, concrete, clay or calcium-silicate brickwork. It is possible to create a shear-resistant wall plate with plain walls or those with openings (windows, doors etc.) < 25%. Large openings must be dealt with separately. Forces acting perpendicular to the plate must be treated as separate actions. The arrangement of the shear walls within the building must be planned so that no more than three lines of action coincide at one point. A favourable arrangement of the shear wall allows the ensuing wind and bracing loads to be handled corresponding to the lengths of the walls.

$$H_{xi} = \frac{b_{xi}}{\Sigma b_{xi}} \, W_x$$

$$H_{yi} = \frac{b_{yi}}{\Sigma b_{yi}} \, W_y$$

The position of joints must be planned carefully. All connectors must be designed to carry the loads in the plates. In particular, in transferring the loads from columns, floors and loadbearing systems to the wood panel elements or concrete/masonry components proper allowance must be made for construction moisture, shrinkage and creep.

Construction of shear walls

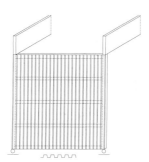

Logs   Diagonal planks

Wood-based boards

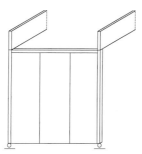

Trapezoidal profile metal sheeting

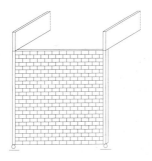

Precast concrete panels

Joint between timber column and masonry/concrete wall

Masonry

Purlin frames

Structural system

with plywood or particleboard

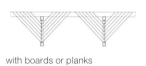

with boards or planks

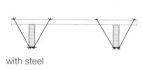

with steel

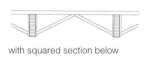

with squared section below

with squared section above

Stability by means of secondary load-bearing systems

Purlin frames
Structurally effective purlin frames are suitable for providing lateral restraint to beams in bending in solid-web or box-type construction, and to prevent buckling of truss chords. The clear opening between primary loadbearing members and the roof is used and given special treatment. Structural continuity of the secondary load-bearing system is achieved in a simple way and used to advantage. Asymmetric snow and wind loads must be taken into account in profiled roof forms.

Kneebraces
Probably the oldest and most common way of bracing a structure is to use kneebraces, which can take on a wide variety of forms. Pretensioning is recommended when using ties exclusively to provide lateral restraint and prevent buckling. The load transfer in the bottom chord must be checked carefully if purlins have to be additionally restrained at mid-span. It is especially important to verify the equilibrium of the horizontal forces in the end bays.

Purlin frames

with continuous squared timbers for services and lighting

with squared section

with squared section and truss left open on one side for lighting purposes

with laminated veneer lumber arch

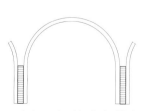

made from glued laminated timber

Curved kneebraces made from laminated veneer lumber

Purlin frame to stabilise a bridge beam

Kneebraces in all directions in a historical building

Kneebraces in all directions in a new building

Three-dimensional kneebraced construction

Trussed purlins

for bracing a truss

for bracing a solid-web continuous beam

for bracing a truss

for bracing the chords of a truss

Stressed-skin structures

for bracing solid-web beams

for stiffening a three-dimensional ribbed structure

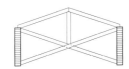

Trussed purlins for pitched roofs

Folded plate

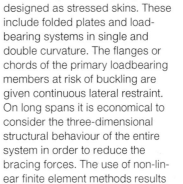

Hyperbolic-paraboloid shell

Lattice-type purlins
It is advisable to provide secondary loadbearing systems in the form of lattice beams or trusses for large spans or large truss spacings and deep structural systems. Roof form, interior design and position of services are all easily coordinated with the bracing tasks of the secondary loadbearing systems. These secondary loadbearing systems may have a great variety of forms.

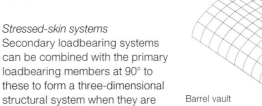

Lattice-beam secondary members spanning 30 m for bracing the lattice-beam primary members spanning 60 m

Stressed-skin systems
Secondary loadbearing systems can be combined with the primary loadbearing members at 90° to these to form a three-dimensional structural system when they are designed as stressed skins. These include folded plates and loadbearing systems in single and double curvature. The flanges or chords of the primary loadbearing members at risk of buckling are given continuous lateral restraint. On long spans it is economical to consider the three-dimensional structural behaviour of the entire system in order to reduce the bracing forces. The use of non-linear finite element methods results in a considerably better deformation behaviour.

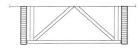

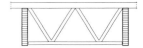

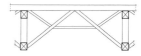

Trussed purlins for flat roofs

Barrel vault

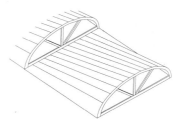

Conoid shell roof with glazed panels

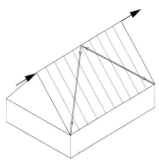

Bracing acting in tension only

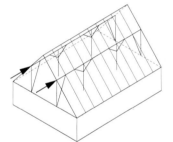

Bracing acting in tension and compression

Horizontal and diagonal structural systems

Longitudinal girders

Simple house roofs consisting of rafters or trussed rafters can be braced with diagonal steel straps, timber battens or planks fixed with nails.

Care should be taken to ensure that the wind loads are properly transferred to the underlying construction. If the gable walls are braced, the span of the rafters may be reduced by using a longitudinal girder. The longitudinal structural effect of kneebraced beams should be checked using DIN 1052.

Longitudinal girders in the form of trusses or parabolic trusses are economical for systems with poor foundation conditions, in which fixed-based columns or horizontal thrusts cannot be avoided, in order to guarantee the overall stability. Asymmetric snow and wind loads must be transferred to the subsoil.

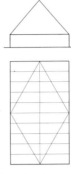

Bracing acting in tension and compression

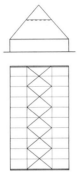

Wind girder in the longitudinal direction

Bracing acting in compression below continuous purlins

X-bracing in the plane of the roof

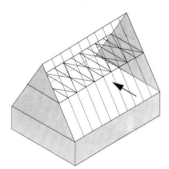

Kneebraces with frame action in the longitudinal direction

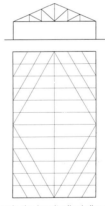

Propping in the longitudinal direction

Longitudinal bracing by means of horizontal truss with steel X-bracing

Horizontal wind girder at collar beam level

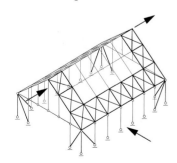

U-shaped truss in the plane of the roof

Achieving structural equilibrium for uplift wind forces by way of anchors

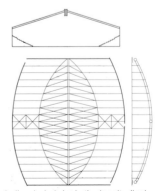

Parabolic wind girder in the longitudinal direction

Longitudinal bracing by means of horizontal truss with timber X-bracing

Longitudinal wind girder with steel X-bracing

Longitudinal wind girder with timber X-bracing, continuous purlins for horizontal forces from gymnastic apparatus

Horizontal girder with timber diagonals

Horizontal girder with steel X-bracing

Transverse girders
The girders must be able to accommodate resultant loads as a result of unavoidable manufacturing and erection inaccuracies. They must also provide lateral restraint to and prevent buckling of the primary loadbearing system.

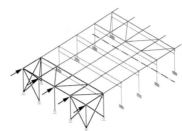
Transverse wind and stability girder as a truss with rising diagonals

On flat roofs the bracing loads are transferred to the columns or the wind girders in the walls by way of trusses in the plane of the roof. The stability girder should be designed for a lateral load q_s when required to restrain the top flanges of slender solid-web beams:

For lattice beams:

$$q_s = \frac{m \cdot N_{girder}}{30 \cdot l}$$

For solid-web beams:

$$q_s = \frac{m \cdot M_{max}}{350 \cdot l \cdot h}$$

The full wind load is to be superimposed on the lateral load q_s for spans > 40 m.
The deformations of the girder should be limited to

$$f \leq l/1000$$

The spacing of the girders should not normally exceed 25 m. However, larger spacings are possible if a more accurate analysis is performed and certain constructional measures are incorporated, e.g. tension-resistant connections for purlins in the longitudinal direction. The elasticity of the fixings must be considered in the analysis of deformations for long spans.

Wind girder variations

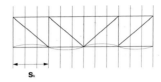
with long buckling length

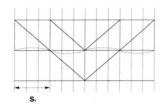
with enhanced stiffness

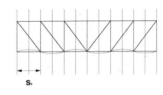
with reduced buckling length

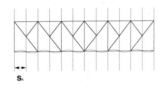
with short buckling length

with inherent stiffness of primary load-bearing system

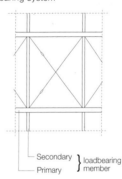
Secondary ⎫ loadbearing
Primary   ⎭ member

Adjustable steel X-bracing

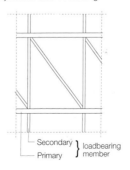
Secondary ⎫ loadbearing
Primary   ⎭ member

Timber diagonals

Beams supported on two columns

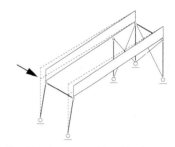
without bracing on one side, without lateral restraint elements

with bracing in the walls

with bracing in the walls and forked supports

stable and braced in all directions

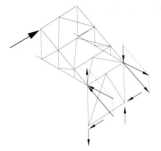

Structural equilibrium for a wind girder in the wall and the (sloping) plane of the roof

Cantilever girders
On steep roofs it is difficult to accommodate the resultant loads at the ridge. Here, the engineer's analytical model can assume a cantilever because it is easy to deal with the forces at the supports for the girder. The structural behaviour has been proved in full-scale tests. Many different arrangements of cantilever girder are possible because the stiffness can be increased significantly through the use of stepping, propping, guying or coupling several bays together.

Cantilever girder variations

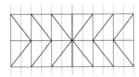

K-bracing over two bays

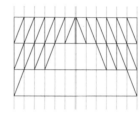

Stepped diagonal bracing

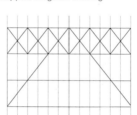

Propped X-bracing

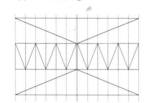

Guyed diagonal bracing

Cantilevers

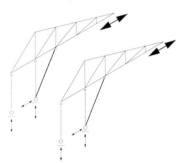

without bracing and restraint

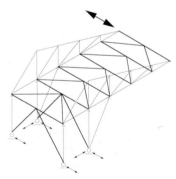

with compression-resistant guying, with horizontal restraint

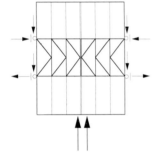

Cantilever girder on plan

Wind girder of squared sections in the plane of the roof

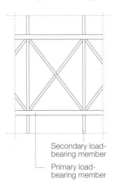

Secondary load-bearing member
Primary load-bearing member

St Andrew's cross

with compression-resistant guying, with horizontal restraint, girder in plane of wall and bottom chord

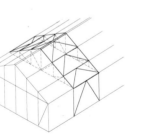

Cantilever K-braced girder

X-bracing of planks

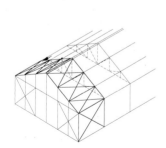

Cantilever X-braced girder in gable bay and walls

Girder in the plane of the roof for bracing and providing restraint to the top chord of the roof truss, purlin frame for providing restraint to the bottom chord against uplift wind forces

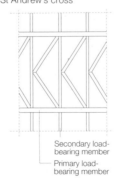

Secondary load-bearing member
Primary load-bearing member

K-bracing

with compression-resistant guying, with horizontal restraint, girder in plane of wall and bottom chord, and restraint to top chord

Girder with X-bracing over two bays

Arch with girders in all bays

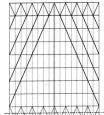

Stepped transverse girder

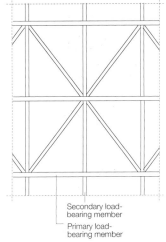

Detail of steel tie with turnbuckle

Transverse girder variations

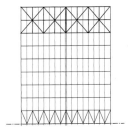

propped

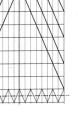

stepped

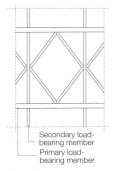

Secondary load-
bearing member
Primary load-
bearing member

Diamond bracing

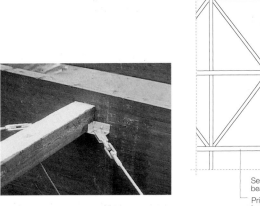

Secondary load-
bearing member
Primary load-
bearing member

Diamond bracing over two bays

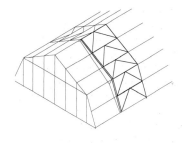

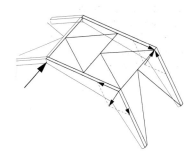

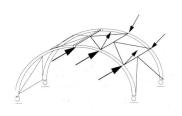

Cranked systems
Due to the geometry of the primary
loadbearing structure, considerable forces from the girders ensue
at the changes of direction for
frames and arches. These forces
can be critical for the design of the
primary loadbearing system. It is
advisable to check the entire structure for long spans, because the
rough calculations lead to high
member and node forces in the
girders, which result in expensive
joints. An approach based on a
cantilever truss is sufficient for
shorter spans.

Three-pin frames

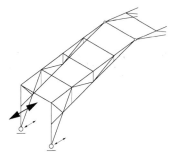

without bracing,
without restraint

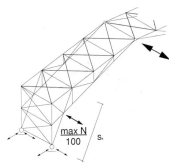

with girder in plane of wall

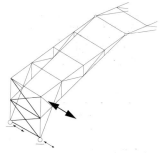

$$\frac{max\ N}{100} \quad s_k$$

with girder in plane of wall and roof

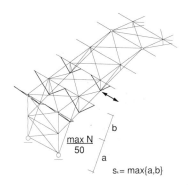

$$\frac{max\ N}{50}$$

$s_k = max\{a,b\}$

with girder in plane of wall and roof and
restraint to compression chord near
corner of frame

Bracing elements, e.g. for roofs

butt-jointed as diagonal decking

with gaps and chamfers as diagonal decking

offset, nailed boards

tongue and groove

double tongue and groove
(F30 profile, DIN 4102)

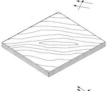

Laminated veneer lumber (LVL)

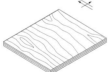

Particleboard, no chamfer

Particleboard with tongue and groove

Plasterboard, fibre-reinforced plaster-board

Trapezoidal profile metal sheeting

Roof and floor plates

made from one layer of boards and planks

A roof decking made from indivi-dual boards fixed with one or two nails has only a low stiffening effect. Chords in compression on roof trusses spanning up to 12.5 m, pitch of trusses < 1.25 m, can be braced by boards, provided the construction recommendations of DIN 1052 are observed. Construc-tional measures, e.g. diagonal decking in one or two directions, can achieve sufficient stiffness to accommodate external loads, e.g. wind. A detailed investigation with analytical models similar to trusses must be carried out. Care must be taken to ensure that the diagonal forces are properly transferred. Planks that are sufficiently wide and nailed rigidly to the chords or flanges produce a Vierendeel-type system. Taking into account the elasticity of the fixings, a girder resisting horizontal deflection on spans up to 30 m is possible. The horizontal deflection should be limited to 1/3000 of the span, the vertical deflection of the boards or planks to 1/400.

made from more than one layer of boards and planks

Extra layers of decking can be used to increase the stiffness of roof and floor plates. The combi-nation of boards and wood-based products to form a shear-resistant diaphragm is another inexpensive variation. The stiffness can be analysed using models similar to solid-web beams.

Care should be taken with the fix-ings, i.e. sufficient nails at the appropriate pitches, and the spac-ing of the joints between boards if continuous, finger-jointed boards are not available.

Standard roof decking

Orthogonal roof decking with rigid nailed connections

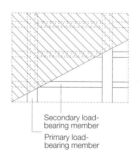

Secondary load-bearing member
Primary load-bearing member

Diagonal decking

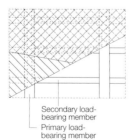

Secondary load-bearing member
Primary load-bearing member

Diagonal decking in both directions

Planks acting as a stiffening girder

Roof truss braced by means of diagonal decking

Roof construction braced by means of diagonal decking

Arch braced by lattice beams in turn braced by diagonal decking

Suspended roof braced by diagonal planking

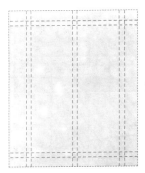

Roof and floor panel

glued, nailed or screwed on one side

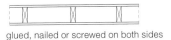

glued, nailed or screwed on both sides

Reinforced floor panel

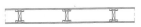

Box section for long spans

Trapezoidal profile metal sheeting

Trapezoidal profile metal sheeting with concrete floor

Timber-concrete composite floor

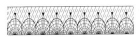

Timber-concrete composite floor with halved logs

Roof plates made from wood-based products

Plates made from wood-based products must be structurally analysed – as an approximation by means of equivalent systems similar to beams in bending consisting of elastically connected cross-sectional components. The design of the joints and the nailing is important here in order to achieve a connection to the primary load-bearing system (e.g. purlin, rafter, top flange of beam, top chord of truss, etc.) that is capable of transferring the forces. As a secondary element we distinguish between stiffened wood panels and ribs, or rather with symmetric and asymmetric planking to one or both sides, in all cases with a static loadbearing function. The width of the plate sharing the load must be verified, taking into account the elasticity of the fixings in the composite cross-section.

Special attention should be paid to the vapour diffusion behaviour and to preventing saturation, also during the construction phase.

A check should be performed to ensure that deflection in the plane of the plate does not exceed span/1000.

The stiffness of the plate can be increased by forming the planking into box sections parallel to the primary loadbearing system, on purlins or directly as a secondary loadbearing system. Stresses in the structural planking must be considered as well.

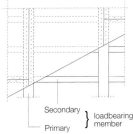

Shear-resistant panels,
e.g. chipboard, plywood, boarding, laminated veneer lumber

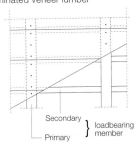

Aerated concrete panels

Roof and floor plates made from composite materials

Primary and secondary loadbearing systems can also be designed to act as diaphragms and used as floor and roof plates. Trapezoidal profile metal sheeting with appropriate fixings or in conjunction with a concrete floor are just two examples. The creation of the composite action between a plate and timber ribs must be analysed separately. The combination of timber ribs, decking and a structural concrete topping results in a high-strength plate but also good resistance to vibration. In addition, such timber-concrete composite construction can prove economic when trying to meet fire protection and sound insulation requirements in the refurbishment of existing buildings, but also for new multi-storey buildings. Special attention should be paid to the long-term behaviour of the composite construction.

Floor element made from parallel-grain plywood

Box elements made from solid-web beams and plywood

Particleboard as bracing to roof beams

Continuous frames

without bracing, without restraint

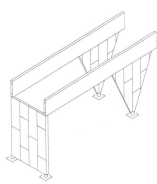

with supporting leg and girder in plane of wall

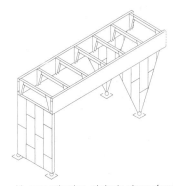

with supporting leg, girder in plane of wall and purlin frames

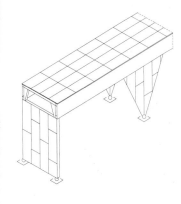

with supporting leg, girder in plane of wall, purlin frames and roof plate, stable and braced in all directions

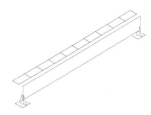

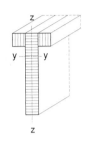

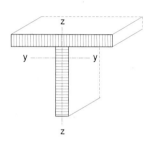

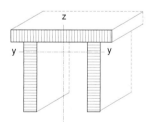

T- and I-sections of glued laminated timber

Stability created by form and geometry

due to the inherent stiffness of the primary loadbearing system in section

Primary loadbearing systems can make use of triangular and circular forms as well as T- and I-sections to gain enhanced stiffness about the y-axis and thus brace themselves against buckling and overturning. Such arrangements result in three-dimensional trusses, which must be checked for buckling in both x- and y-directions, and where the bending stresses must be superimposed on the buckling stresses. The elasticity of the fixings in multiple cross-sections must also be checked.

The overturning of solid-web beams need not be analysed for a slenderness ratio H/B < 4 and when stability at the supports is ensured by means of a forked arrangement (e.g. web cleats).

A simplified buckling analysis to DIN 1052 can be performed for a slenderness ratio ≤ 10, although this results in larger dimensions than an accurate analysis would give. An analysis according to DIN 4114 is recommended for box sections.

Buckling can also be prevented with constructional measures, e.g. by varying the wall thickness, by using laminated veneer lumber or veneer plywood to create a profile, or by adding additional stiffeners.

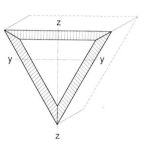

Folded plate beam

Triangular-section beam

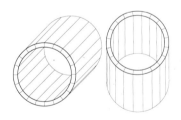

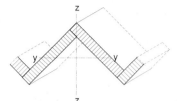

Folded plate – stable due to its geometry

Folded plate roof made from glued laminated timber beams

Radial folded plate roof with trusses

Curved sawtooth roof in shear-resistant design

Filtering tank for chemically aggressive wastewater

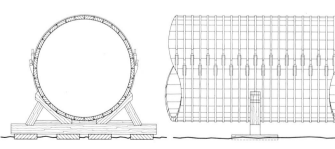

Circular sections for pipes and silos, with steel tension straps

Silo construction with pretensioning

Fish-belly trusses with steel tie

Trussed arrangement with K-braced purlin

Bottom chord of frame braced with steel ties

Inherent stability of the primary load-bearing system in elevation

Trussed arrangements
Trussed systems are characterised by their great variety.
On long spans lateral restraint in the form of props or guys must be provided to the cranked tension member if the form and constructional measures are inadequate. Another possibility is to restrain the post at the upper chord or the transverse purlins. If the upper chord is cranked and there is thus a sufficient distance between the axis of the chord and the level of the supports, further stability measures are unnecessary.
A permanent camber of l/200 for the upper chord under full load may be sufficient.

Linear members, frames and arches
The stability, or rather the load-carrying capacity of linear members, frames and arches can be affected by many constructional measures and depends on the accuracy of workmanship.
Besides preventing buckling at truss level, i.e. overturning of the upper chord, the frame corner deflecting inwards and at risk of buckling must be checked. For simplicity, the additional moment due to an equivalent load of H = N/100 should be allowed for in the frame corner unless a more accurate analysis is performed.
The equivalent member method to DIN 1052, but also – very advantageously – a second order elastic analysis, can be employed for assessing deflection, i.e. buckling, at truss level. Internal forces and deformations are determined here with the loads factored by γ_1 and γ_2. The unwanted eccentricity and the elasticity of the fixings is assumed according to DIN 1052.

Buckling of tension chord in trussed beams

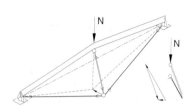

Restraint by inherent resilience

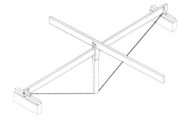

by fixity at supports

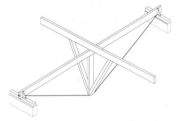

by kneebraces

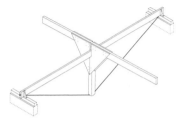

by purlin frame

Measures to prevent buckling of a three-pin frame with solid web-sections

by cross-section width

by purlins and diagonal bracing

by cross-section width and eaves purlin

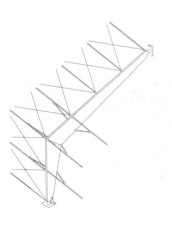

by purlins, diagonal bracing and knee-braces to the purlins at the corner

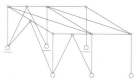

Structural system triangulated
on plan and in elevation

*due to the geometry of the primary
loadbearing system on plan*
The geometry of the primary loadbearing system on plan can be
chosen to produce horizontal shear-
resistant trusses. With high stiffnesses these are in a position to
carry wind loads, seismic loads etc.
The vertical loads should be superimposed on the internal forces due
to horizontal loads.
Special attention should be paid to
bracing the primary systems. The
forces occurring in the truss and at
the various joints must be assessed
accurately.

*due to the geometry of the primary
loadbearing system in three dimensions*
The simplest way of avoiding stability bracing is to design a primary
loadbearing system that is stable
in three dimensions. Only the stability of the individual members
need be analysed, plus the stability of the overall system. This leads
to complex three-dimensional systems.

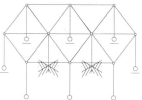

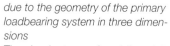

Triangulation, 60° grid,
fixed-based columns

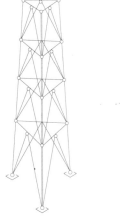

Tower comprising three trusses

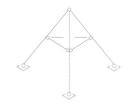

Three-legged trestle

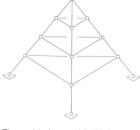

with collar beams

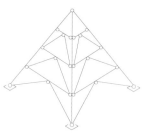

Three-sided pyramid with linear members

Beam grid, braced by way of triangulation
and triangulated purlins

Triangulated secondary loadbearing
structure for bracing the main loadbearing
members

Pyramid, stable in three dimensions

Truncated pyramid, stable in three
dimensions

Four-legged frame, stable in three
dimensions

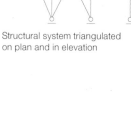

Form stable in three dimensions

Radio mast consisting of four trusses

with K-bracing

Ribbed dome with one ring, dia. = 60 m

Linear member dome with one ring,
dia. = 90 m

Linear member dome with multiple nodes,
dia. = 130 m

Stability due to three-dimensional structural behaviour

Plane and space frames

If we look at the overall structural effect of primary, secondary and bracing systems, almost all timber structures become a three-dimensional framework. It is therefore realistic to determine the load-carrying capacities or internal forces by considering the structure as a complete loadbearing system, and employing non-linear methods of calculation. Here, the engineer can take load safety factors and initial deformations in the construction.

The advantage of structures with a high degree of structural indeterminacy and in which the elasticity of the fixings plays a major role is, principally, their ability to redistribute the loads. The overall behaviour thereby approximates to the load-carrying capacities (modulus of elasticity, slip modulus, ultimate strength) calculated using average static values. Components or parts of the structure subjected to

maximum stresses achieve more favourable values than would be the case when carrying out calculations for individual components using the permissible stresses given by probability. The optimisation criterion for space frames and shells is the cost of the fixings required to stiffen the entire construction sufficiently, for asymmetric loading cases as well. Their elasticity requires special attention.

Vibration behaviour, ductility and seismic resistance

The elasticity of fixings has the advantage that systems sensitive to vibration exhibit a high degree of damping. In addition, the elasticity of the fixings rules out brittle fracture behaviour without prior deformation. For structures in earthquake regions with low dead loads, i.e. a low oscillating mass, the elasticity of the fixings gives excellent damping behaviour.

Remaining stable for centuries in the worst earthquakes zone thanks to ductility

Loading test for determining parameters for the deflection and vibration behaviour of a structure

Windmills – example and challenge for the engineer from the 19th century

Outlook

The economic efficiency, serviceability and reliability of timber structures cannot be the outcome of structural calculations alone. In trying to find an optimum construction it is principally questions relating to choice of material, type of connection and the sensible combination of individual loadbearing systems that have to be answered. These deliberations together with the structural calculations are within the remit of structural engineering.

In timber engineering, if realistic assumptions are made for the stability analysis and if the task of quality assurance is given appropriate, serious attention, we can build

structures with a high level of workmanship that are economical and competitive, and also retain their value.

There is still a large pent-up demand for a compendium of experiences, tests and calculations on models that will enable the most realistic analysis of the reliability of a timber structure. We can only make progress with increased efforts in education, research, development and planning.

Wind turbine project with timber mast as a challenge for the engineer in the 21st century

Part 5   Built examples: structures

Julius Natterer, Wolfgang Winter

The following examples represent a selection of timber structures built in recent years. However, a few older projects featuring particular engineering or architectural aspects have also been included. The order is arranged according to the type of loadbearing system, starting with columns and proceeding through beams, systems of linear members, frames, arches, grids and folded plates, and concluding with stressed-skin structures and space frames. At the end there are several examples that illustrate the use of timber in extremely heavily loaded but also extremely lightweight and highly efficient structures.

The left column on the left-hand page of each double page shows the system with a number of variations, the right column on the right-hand page variations on the system together with loading assumptions and, underneath, the deformations under load. The central column on each page contains an actual example as built. The inner columns either side of the spine show standard details suitable for that loadbearing system. It was not always possible to achieve a direct correlation between the standard details and the loadbearing systems. Many can be used in several, different loadbearing systems. Most of the system drawings indicate the load-carrying capacities, or rather the possible spans, to enable comparison.

The project information and drawings were taken from the documents made available to us by the respective project team.

The size of each structure as built can be seen from the dimensions given for each project, and the possible size of each system is given in the system columns.

Project		Page	Type of construction
1	Offices, Châlons-sur-Marne, F	142	Columns
2	Youth village, Cieux, Haute-Vienne, F	143	
3	Offices, Munich, D	144	
4	Japanese Pavilion, Sevilla, E	145	
5	Indoor riding arena, Garnzell, D	146	
6	Grandstand, Neufahrn, D	147	
7	Sagastäg bridge, Schiers, CH	148	Propped beams
8	Faculty of Architecture, Lyon, F	149	
9	Footbridge over River Alb, D	150	
10	Footbridge over River Aare, Innertkirchen, CH	151	
11	Refectory, Munich TU, Weihenstephan, D	152	
12	Motorway service area building, Niederurnen, CH	153	
13	Bus terminal, Vaduz, FL	154	Simply supported beams
14	Factory building, Bobingen, D	155	
15	Forestry depot, Castrisch, CH	156	
16	Palafitte Hotel, Monruz, CH	157	
17	Warehouses, Payerne and Sion, CH	158	
18	Church, Adelschlag near Eichstätt, D	159	
19	Weiherhof sports centre, Karlsruhe, D	160	
20	Hangar, Locarno, CH	161	
21	Kindergarten, Erdweg, D	162	
22	Ice rink, Grefrath, D	163	
23	Multipurpose hall, Westerheim, D	164	
24	Sports centre, Eching, D	165	
25	Kindergarten, Munich, D	166	
26	Bridge over River Neckar, Remseck, D	167	
27	Traversina Steg bridge, Viamala, CH	168	
28	Haus des Gastes, Bad Wörishofen, D	169	
29	Multipurpose hall, primary school, Bornheim, D	170	
30	Gymnasium, secondary school, Vaterstetten, D	171	
31	Leisure pool, Frankfurt, D	172	
32	Cattle market hall – Bündner Arena, Cazis, CH	173	
33	Salt store, Lausanne, CH	174	
34	Trade fair halls, Nuremberg, D	175	
35	Assembly building, Noréaz, CH	176	Continuous beams
36	Bridge, Martigny, CH	177	
37	Bridge, Vallorbe, CH	178	
38	Factory building, Bad Münder, D	179	
39	Bridge over River Simme, Wimmis, CH	180	
40	Footbridge, Singen, D	181	
41	Residential complex, Munich, D	182	
42	Oslo Airport, Gardermoen, N	183	
43	Ice rink, Surrey, CAN	184	Beams with pinned splices
44	Jägermeister factory building, Kamenz, D	185	
45	Olympic velodrome, Munich, D	186	Cantilever beams
46	Roof over spectator seating, Waldau Stadium, Stuttgart, D	187	
47	St Blasius' Church, Schallstadt, D	188	Pinned beams
48	Indoor riding arena, Schwaiganger, D	189	
49	Ice rink, Deggendorf, D	190	
50	Ice rink, St Ulrich, I	191	

Projekt	Page	Type of construction
51 Parish hall, Munich, D	192	
52 Chihiro art gallery, Azumino, J	193	
53 St Martin's Church, Ingolstadt, D	194	
54 Church centre, Eckenhaid, D	195	
55 Sports centre, Roanne, F	196	Single-pin frames
56 Ice rink, Verbier, CH	197	
57 Tennis centre, Ulm, D	198	Two-pin frames
58 Sports centre, Künzelsau, D	199	
59 Warehouse, Weihenstephan, D	200	Three-pin frames
60 Haithabu Viking Museum, Schleswig, D	201	
61 Indoor riding arena, Munich-Riem, D	202	
62 Gymnasium, Donauwörth, D	203	
63 St Ignatius' Church, Munich-Kleinhadern, D	204	
64 Coal blending plant, Rekingen, CH	205	
65 Ice rink, Davos, CH	206	
66 Bridge for heavy vehicles, Ravine, CH	207	Frames
67 Bridge over River Emme, Signau, CH	208	Two-pin arches
68 Tennis centre, Bezau, Vorarlberg, A	209	
69 City hall, Gersfeld, D	210	
70 Olympic indoor sports stadium, Hamar, N	211	
71 School hall, Wohlen, Aargau, CH	212	Three-pin arches
72 Ice rinklstres, F	213	
73 Pavilion, Stia, Arezzo, I	214	
74 Ice rink, Schaffhausen, CH	215	
75 Warehouse, Walsum, D	216	
76 Sports stadium – Izumo Dome, Izumo, J	217	
77 School, Hooke Park Forest, UK	218	Suspended structures
78 Church, Rouen, F	219	
79 Sports stadium, Dijon, F	220	
80 Depot forecourt, Hohenems, D	221	
81 Restaurant, Chaux, CH	222	Plates and slabs
82 Holiday home, Chino, J	223	
83 Youth camp, Bavarian Forest National Park, D	224	
84 Assembly hall, Mendrisio, CH	225	
85 School for special needs children, Garbsen, D	226	
86 Church, Schneverdingen, D	227	
87 House and school, Triesenberg, FL	228	
88 House, Claerns, CH	230	
89 School, Wilpoldsried, D	231	
90 Post office, Munich-Perlach, D	232	Beam grids
91 Petrol and service station, Lechwiesen, D	233	
92 Law school, Starnberg, D	234	
93 Community centre, Ötlingen, D	235	

Project	Page	Type of construction
94 Large canteen, Volkach am Main, D	236	Lattice beam grids
95 Multipurpose hall, Lüterkofen, CH	237	
96 Sports centre, Nuremberg, D	238	
97 Sunshading, Riyadh, Saudi Arabia	239	
98 Lakeside centre, Arbon, CH	240	
99 Chapel of rest, Reutlingen, D	241	Space frames
100 Ledersteg bridge, Amberg, D	242	Folded plates
101 Pavilion for Hartwald Clinic, Zwesten, D	243	
102 Service station, La Dôle, CH	244	Barrel vaults
103 Gallery, trade fair grounds, Frankfurt, D	245	Lattice barrel vaults
104 Churches in "Zollinger" construction, Cologne and Leverkusen, D	246	
105 Tuscany thermal springs, Bad Sulza, D	247	Ribbed shells
106 Indoor riding arena, Berlin, D	248	Ribbed barrel vaults
107 Gymnasium, Arlesheim, CH	249	
108 Sports centre, Oulo, FIN	250	Lattice domes
109 Trade fair hall, Brussels, B	251	
110 Office and house, Hirituka City, Kanagawa, J	252	
111 Kindergarten, Triessen, FL	253	
112 School of Timber Expertise, Nantes, F	254	
113 Swimming pool, Saint Quentin en Yvelines, F	255	
114 Multipurpose hall, Mannheim, D	256	
115 Exhibition pavilion, Nara, J	257	
116 Leisure pool, Freiburg, D	258	Hyperbolic paraboloid shells
117 Multipurpose hall, Leuk, CH	259	
118 EXPO roof, Hannover, D	260	
119 Manufacturing pavilion, Bad Münder, D	262	Suspended shells
120 Pavilion, Dortmund, D	263	
121 Recycling facility, Vienna, A	264	
122 Brine baths, Bad Dürrheim, D	265	
123 Campanile, Eichstetten, D	266	Towers
124 Viewing platform, Lausanne, CH	267	
125 Viewing platform, Venne, D	268	
126 Transmitter mast, Ismaning, D	269	
127 Log bridge centering, Mülmisch viaduct, D	270	Constructions for heavy loads
128 Glider	271	Lightweight structures

Columns

Pinned-end column

Storey-height column with pinned intermediate prop

Transition to storey-height frame, partially restrained intermediate prop

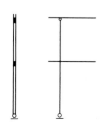

1 · Offices

Châlons-sur-Marne, F; 1989

Architect: R. Schweitzer, Paris

Structural engineer: Robert Loudon, Paris
Consultants: Natterer Bois-Consult, Etoy, CH

The one- and two-storey flat-roof buildings house the administration facilities of the Ministry of Agriculture. The two main buildings are built on a 4 x 8 m rectangular grid formed by log columns and composite beams. The I-section composite beams consisting of squared timber sections and steel channels are connected to the log columns in pairs at each intersection by steel brackets. The log columns are hence left freestanding in front of the facade. The upper floors are in composite construction. The concrete slab on permanent formwork is connected to the timber beams via shear connectors so that the tension forces can be transferred from the timber members. Horizontal forces are resisted by shear walls, which were supplied as prefabricated wood panel elements, and the masonry/concrete components.

⌑ Techniques et Architecture 4/86 (competition)

1 Log column, 250 mm dia.	4 Channel section
2 Composite beam	5 Metal bracket
3 Steel plate	6 Steel circular hollow section, 100 mm dia.

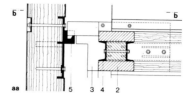

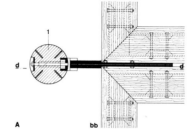

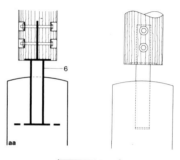

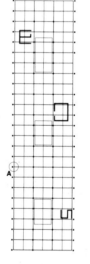

Column base details

Solid timber with height-adjustable pinned base

Solid timber on pinned base

Solid timber on pinned base

Glued laminated timber, pinned in x-direction, partially restrained in y-direction, with sliding fixing

Battened columns

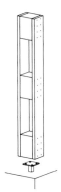

with pinned base and intermediate timber spacer blocks

with pinned base and connecting boards

Laced columns

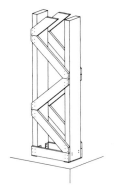

Pinned or restrained, with nailed diagonals

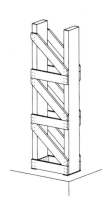

Pinned or restrained, laced and battened

2 · Youth village

Cieux, Haute-Vienne, F: 1985

Architect: R. Schweitzer, Paris

Structural engineers: R. Weisrock S.A., Saulcy-sur-Meurthe, F

This holiday village for young people is formed by a single-storey modular timber-frame construction. Two-part timber pinned-end columns carry the vertical loads of the timber floor and the flat roof. The main beams of glued laminated timber span either one or two bays and are positioned at 90° to the facade. Edge beams between the columns complete the rectangular grid. The I-section roof purlins are formed by separate box beams, which are connected top and bottom by means of wood fibreboard. Horizontal loads are resisted by shear walls and the masonry/concrete components.

📖 Techniques et Architecture 4/86

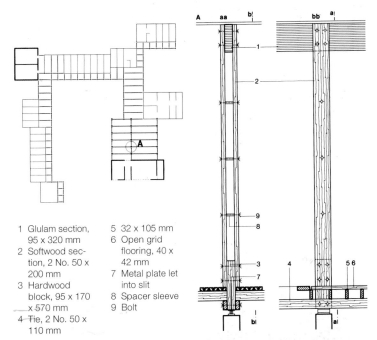

1 Glulam section, 95 x 320 mm
2 Softwood section, 2 No. 50 x 200 mm
3 Hardwood block, 95 x 170 x 570 mm
4 Tie, 2 No. 50 x 110 mm
5 32 x 105 mm
6 Open grid flooring, 40 x 42 mm
7 Metal plate let into slit
8 Spacer sleeve
9 Bolt

Pinned-end column and member with horizontal intermediate prop

buckling length $s_k = l$

slenderness ratio $\lambda = \dfrac{s_k}{l}$

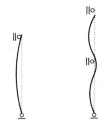

Loading: vertical point load P
uniformly distributed horizontal load q

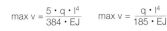

Deformations:

$$\max v = \frac{5 \cdot q \cdot l^4}{384 \cdot EJ} \qquad \max v = \frac{q \cdot l^4}{185 \cdot EJ}$$

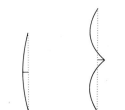

Moments:

$$\max M = \frac{q \cdot l^2}{8} \qquad \max M = \frac{q \cdot l^2}{14,22}$$

$$\min M = \frac{q \cdot l^2}{8}$$

Shear forces:

$$\max V = q \cdot \frac{l}{2} \qquad \max V = \frac{5}{8} \cdot q \cdot l$$

Axial forces: N = P

Vertical trusses

with pinned ends and pretensioning

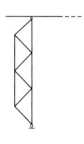

with pinned ends and diagonals

with fixed base, horizontal members
and diagonals

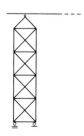

with fixed base, horizontal members
and X-bracing

3 · Offices

Munich, D; 1978

Architects and modular system:
Rouge E. Fahr, A. Fahr-Deistler, Planung
Fahr + Partner PFP, Munich

Structural engineers: Natterer und Dittrich
Planungsgesellschaft, Munich

A one-storey timber-frame construction
containing offices covers the car parking
area measuring 14 x 30 m. Timber cruciform-section columns are placed along
the outer walls at a spacing of 4.8 m.
They are penetrated by continuous glued
laminated timber longitudinal edge beams
carrying the floor construction. The latter
consists of glued laminated timber beams
at 1.8 m centres plus 40 mm double
tongue and groove boards. The roof construction is based on the same grid and
designed to support a further floor at a
later date. The entire loadbearing structure complies with fire resistance class
F90-B. Horizontal loads in the longitudinal
and transverse directions are resisted by
steel diagonal bracing in the walls.

Bauwelt 27/80, Detail 3/84 and
Atlas flache Dächer, 1992, see also
p. 308

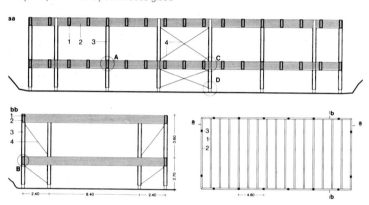

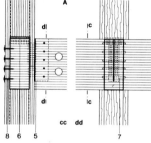

1 Glulam main
  beam, 240 x
  630 mm
2 Glulam edge
  beam, 240 x
  630 mm
3 Cruciform-
  section column,
  240 x 240 or
  360 x 360 mm
4 Wind bracing
5 Connecting pl.

6 Perforated plate
7 Dowel
8 Wood screw
9 Round steel
  bar, 24 mm dia.
10 2 No. bolts
11 Concrete-filled
  steel circular
  hollow section
12 Shear connector
13 4 No. steel stiff.,
  20 mm thk

Beam-column junctions

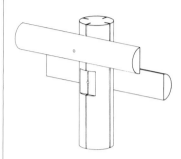

with close tolerance and
clamping bolts

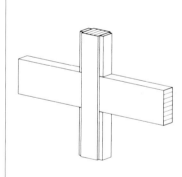

on corbels

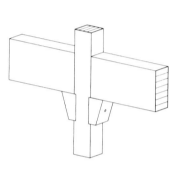

on the timber side plates

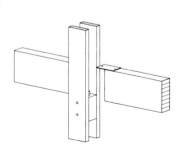

on timber spacer block

Beam-column junctions

with nailed support bracket

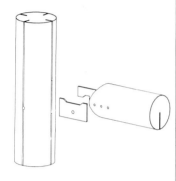

with hooks

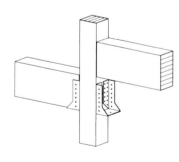

on steel beam hangers

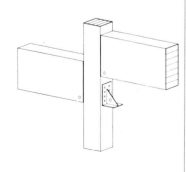

on steel angles

4 · Japanese Pavilion

Seville, E; 1992

Architect: T. Ando, Osaka, J

Structural engineers: Ingeniera Obra Civil, Seville

The roof of this pavilion for Expo 92 in Seville rests on 10 "supporting trees". At the top of each of the four-part columns there is an oversized flared head made from glued laminated timber sections measuring 265 x 265 mm. These are stacked on each other and cantilever further and further out from the column to form a sort of canopy. The flared heads of the 10 columns meet at roof level where they carry a grid of steel sections. These in turn support a translucent roof covering secured with shear-resistant fixings.

📖 Detail 4/92

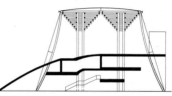

60.00

40.00

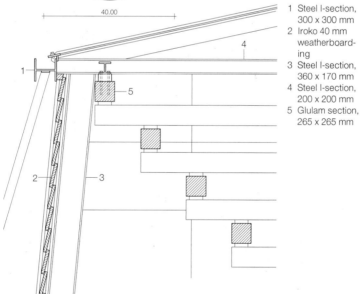

1 Steel I-section, 300 x 300 mm
2 Iroko 40 mm weatherboarding
3 Steel I-section, 360 x 170 mm
4 Steel I-section, 200 x 200 mm
5 Glulam section, 265 x 265 mm

Column restrained at the top

Loading:
vertical point load P
uniformly distributed horizontal load q

Deformations: $\max v = \dfrac{q \cdot l^4}{184{,}6 \, EJ}$

mM

Moments: $\min M = -\dfrac{q \cdot l^2}{8}$

$\max M = \dfrac{q \cdot l^2}{14{,}22}$

Shear forces: $\max V = \dfrac{5}{8} \cdot q \cdot l$

Axial forces $N = P$

Fixed-based columns

with restrained base

with prop

as asymmetrical trestle

as symmetrical trestle

as crossing raking columns

5 · Indoor riding arena

Garnzell, D; 1988

Architect: K. Hitzler, Munich, D

Structural engineer: K. Neumaier, Landshut, D

An indoor riding arena in pole construction with trussed pole roof beams. It is characteristic of this system that the column bases are cast into concrete directly in the ground to provide full restraint at the base; this ensures stability in the transverse direction. Each beam is made of two poles and has a slung truss arrangement on both sides of the ridge, comprising a central post and pairs of round steel ties. These are placed on a 5.18 m grid and span 16.4 m. The central posts are connected to the purlins via kneebraces, which thus provide lateral restraint to the posts. The squared section purlins in turn support the rafters. The roof construction comprises timber decking with counter battens and concrete roof tiles. Stability in the longitudinal direction is ensured by diagonal bracing.

📖 Informationsdienst Holz:
Zweckbauten für die Landwirtschaft

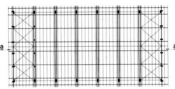

1 Column, 2 No. 300 mm dia.
2 Main roof beam, 2 No. 220 mm dia.
3 Purlin, 180 x 220 mm

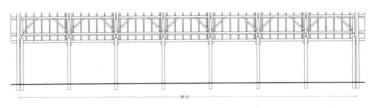

aa

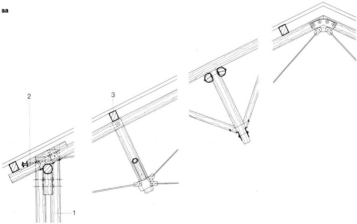

Column fixity details

cast into concrete

with timber side plates

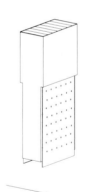

with nailed metal plates

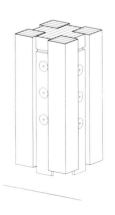

with dowelled timber plates

Column fixity details

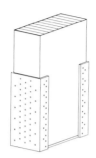

with nailed metal sections

with dowelled gusset plate let into slit

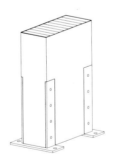

with dowelled external steel straps

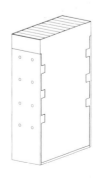

connected with steel flat dowels

6 · Grandstand

Neufahrn, D; 1987

Architects: Büro Vier, Dietersheim

Structural engineers: Natterer und Dittrich Planungsgesellschaft, Munich

A cantilever pole construction forms the roof to this grandstand. Each column on the 5 m grid comprises four poles. The cantilever is tied back by two back-to-back steel T-sections, which can also handle compressive forces.

The roof cantilevering to both sides is supported by pairs of propped pole beams that fan out from the columns at an angle. The squared-section purlins are designed as cantilevers supporting central beams. The two-part ridge purlin is connected to the columns via pole kneebraces to form a vertical wind girder in the longitudinal direction. The roof is braced by the diagonal arrangement of the main beams. Transverse stability is via the three-pin frame formed by the main beams in conjunction with the columns and tying-back.

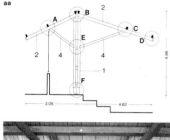

aa

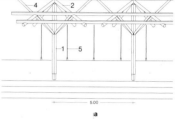

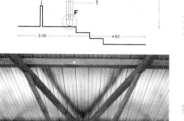

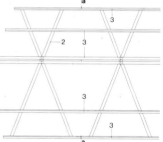

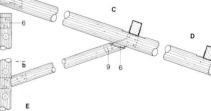

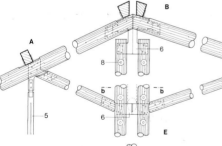

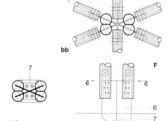

bb

cc

1 Column, 4 No. 140 mm dia.
2 Roof beam, 180 mm dia.
3 Purlins, 80 x 160 mm, 100 x 160 mm, 120 x 160 mm
4 Kneebrace, 120 mm dia.
5 Cruciform section, 2 No. TB 35
6 Metal plate let into slits, 6 mm thk
7 Metal plate, 15 mm thk
8 M12 bolt
9 Dowel, 12 mm dia.

Structures

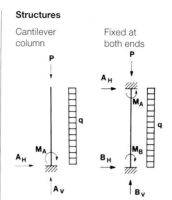

Cantilever column

Fixed at both ends

$$s_k = 2 \cdot l \qquad s_k = 0.5 \cdot l$$

Loading:
vertical point load P
uniformly distributed horizontal load q

Deformations:

$$\max v = -\frac{q \cdot l^4}{8\,EJ} \qquad \max v = -\frac{q \cdot l^4}{384\,EJ}$$

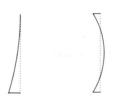

Moments:

$$\max M = \frac{q \cdot l^2}{24}$$

$$\min M = \frac{q \cdot l^2}{2} \qquad \min M = -\frac{q \cdot l^2}{12}$$

Shear forces:

$$\max V = q \cdot l \qquad \max V = q \cdot \frac{l}{2}$$

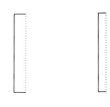

Axial forces: N = P

Propped beams

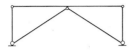

with two props

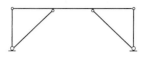

with two props

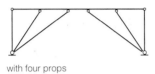

with four props

Kneebraced beams as continuous systems

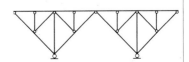

7 · Sagastäg bridge

Schiers, CH; 1991

Structural engineers: Walter Bieler AG, Bonaduz, CH

This 37 m long x 3.6 m wide road bridge is supported by strut frames. The struts carry one longitudinal beam on each of the outer sides of the bridge and a pair of beams in the middle. The struts form a "W" in section and are given lateral restraint by a laminated veneer lumber deck. The tapered cross-sectional form of the bridge means that there are only two bridge bearings on each side – this saved on foundation costs. The loadbearing construction is protected against driving rain and incident solar radiation on both sides with an open cladding of weather-resistant larch wood. The rainproof road deck protects the underlying construction.

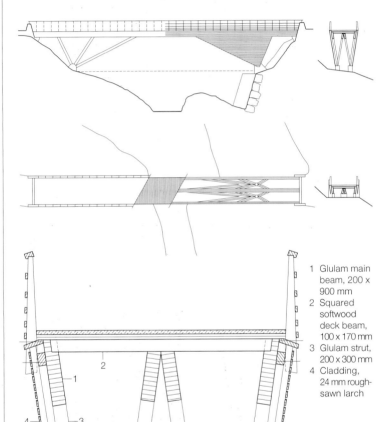

1 Glulam main beam, 200 x 900 mm
2 Squared softwood deck beam, 100 x 170 mm
3 Glulam strut, 200 x 300 mm
4 Cladding, 24 mm rough-sawn larch

Prop connections

with oblique dado joint

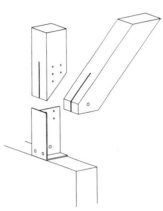

with steel plate let into slits

with T-section

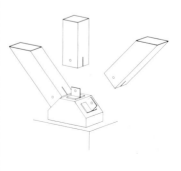

with T-sections let into slits

Prop connections

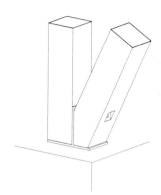

with T-section

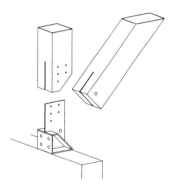

with steel plate let into slits plus end plate

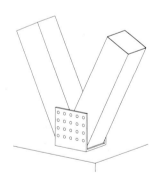

with nailed end plate

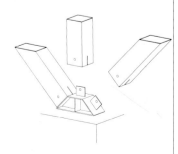

with steel plates let into slits

8 · Faculty of Architecture

Lyon, F; 1987

Architects: Jourda, Perraudin & Partner, Lyon

Structural engineers: M. Francis, P. Rice, J. Ritchie, Paris

Roof over the studio in the top story of the School of Architecture. Main beams of glued laminated timber, 200 x 200 mm, span over two identical parallel wings and a central glass-covered aisle. The top chord, 10.50 m long, is propped by two diagonals at mid-span and trussed on both sides to help carry the loads of the mezzanine floors. The floors in turn provide lateral restraint to the diagonals to prevent buckling. The prefabricated roof elements, 3.45 x 5.15 m, comprise foam-filled plywood boxes with a PVC covering. An articulated linear member provides the bracing in the transverse direction, while stability in the longitudinal direction is provided by the plate action of the roof elements and steel diagonals in the plane of the vertical columns.

Detail 5/88; Architects' Journal 11/88

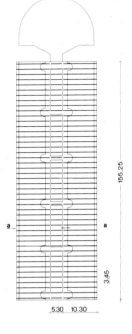

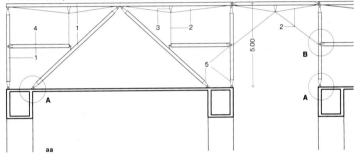

aa

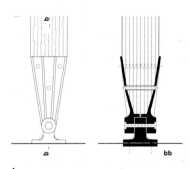

A

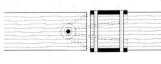

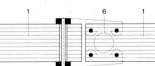

B

1 Main beams, columns, diagonals, 200 x 200 mm glulam sections
2 Steel ties, 20 mm dia.
3 Cast steel post
4 Mezzanine floor
5 Cast steel connectors
6 Rainwater downpipe

Propped beam

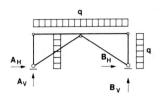

Loading: uniformly distributed horizontal and vertical loads

Deformations

Moment diagram: the top chord can be analysed as a two-span beam with an elastic intermediate support

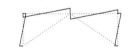

Shear forces

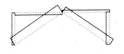

Axial forces

Trussed beams

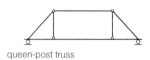

queen-post truss

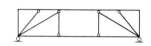

multiple trussing arrangement

elevated multiple overlapping trussing arrangement

Combined propped and trussed beam arrangements

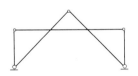

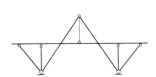

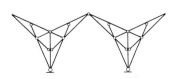

9 · Footbridge over River Alb

D; 1905/1977

Architect: H. Walder

Refurbishment works: R. Arndt, J. Vogeley

Structural engineer: F. Wenzel, Karlsruhe, D

This timber bridge built in 1905 was dismantled, refurbished and re-erected at a new location following refurbishment. The longitudinal beams were replaced, the joints strengthened and the roof construc-tion renewed. The two main beams are actually formed as queen-post trusses, with struts, straining beam, hangers and main beams. Loadbearing members in the transverse direction are twin 70 x 200 mm planks. There are horizontal wind girders below the footway and at roof level. The support reactions of the upper girder are carried by a two-pin frame. The roof covering is carried on rafters.

📖 Bauen mit Holz 8/77

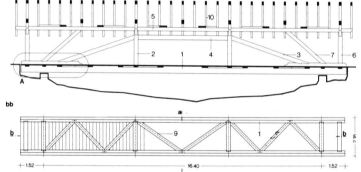

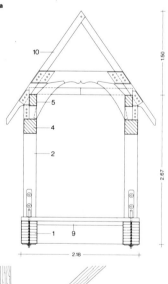

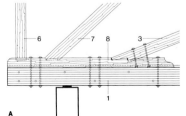

1 Main beam,
 2 No. 150 x 400 mm
2 Hanger, 240 x 240 mm
3 Diagonal strut, 240 x 240 mm
4 Straining beam, 240 x 240 mm
5 Eaves purlin, 140 x 200 mm
6 Leg of frame, 240 x 240 mm
7 Diagonal strut, 140 x 200 mm
8 Sole plate, 240 x 220 mm
9 K-bracing, 70 x 200 mm
10 Rafter, 100 x 120 mm

Kneebrace junctions

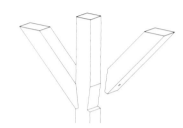

with oblique dado joint

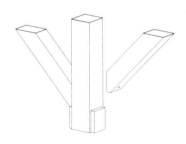

on cleat

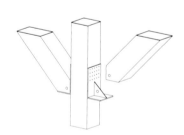

with steel angle let into slit

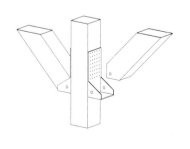

with steel hanger

Kneebrace junctions

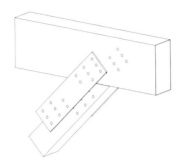

with fish-plates

with oblique dado joint

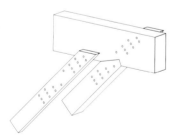

with timber fish-plates and oblique dado joint

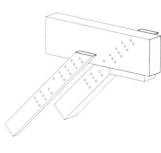

with timber fish-plates and block

10 · Footbridge over River Aare

Innertkirchen, CH; 1997

Architects: H. Banholzer AG, Innertkirchen, CH

Structural engineers: D. Banholzer AG, Innertkirchen, CH; H. Banholzer, Lucerne, CH

The 30 m long footway is suspended from four box-section struts forming a shallow pyramid. The bottom chord is subjected to tension from normal loads and compression from wind loads. Lateral horizontal forces are transferred to the bridge abutments via X-bracing, which also provides lateral restraint to the main beams. The bridge deck is carried on transverse steel beams.

The – on plan – "concave" form of the four struts, measuring 350 x 350 mm at the ends and 550 x 550 mm at the middle, optimises the relationship between dead loads and buckling stability for the compressive stresses that arise.

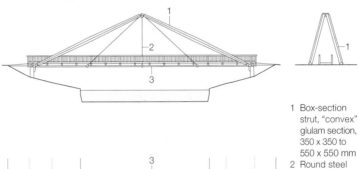

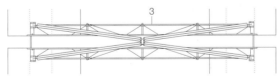

1 Box-section strut, "convex" glulam section, 350 x 350 to 550 x 550 mm
2 Round steel hangers, 27 mm dia.
3 Steel square hollow section bottom chord, 120 x 120 mm

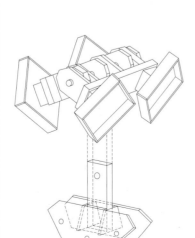

Simple trussed beam

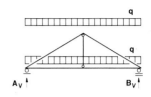

Loading:
vertical uniformly distributed load on top and bottom chords

Deformations

Moments

Shear forces

Axial forces

Strut frames

V-form

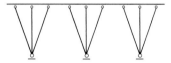

V-form plus posts

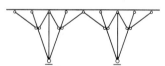

kneebraced strut frame

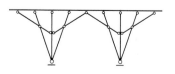

combined strut frame and truss

11 · Refectory

Munich Technical University,
Weihenstephan, D; 1980

Architects: University Building Department; P. Burlanek, H. Geierstanger

Structural engineers: Natterer und
Dittrich Planungsgesellschaft, Munich

The roof over the university refectory is a
beam-grid structure supported on open
flared column heads. The primary beams
spanning up to 7.20 m and following the
slope of the roof form a 2.40 x 2.40 m
square grid together with the secondary
beams. The loads from the beams are
transferred to the concrete columns on a
7.20 x 7.20 m grid via the timber struts
forming the column heads, which along
the facades carry the cantilevering roof
overhang. These column heads consist of
central four-part vertical members and up
to four two-part kneebraces. The connection to the beam is a symmetrical double-
shear arrangement with nail plates and
hinge pins. The facade elements are positioned between the columns. Overall stability is provided by the frame action in
both directions. Rafters at 800 mm centres on the secondary beams carry the
roof decking and roof covering.

📖 Bauen mit Holz 12/81

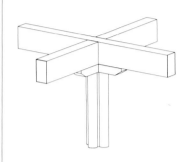

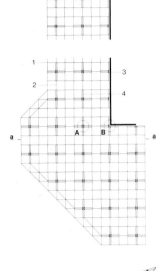

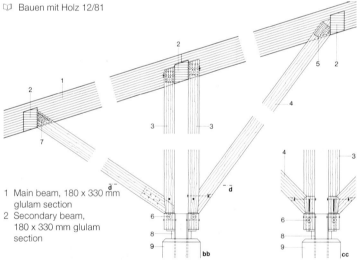

1 Main beam, 180 x 330 mm
   glulam section
2 Secondary beam,
   180 x 330 mm glulam
   section

3 Column, 140 x 140 mm
4 Kneebrace,
   2 No. 140 x 180 mm
5 Nail plate
6 Pin
7 Pin, 27 mm dia.
8 Steel support
9 Concrete column

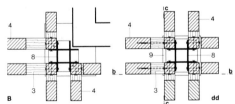

Three-dimensional junctions

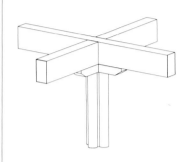

Post connection with spreader plates at
support

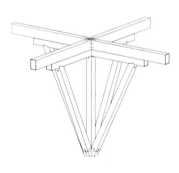

Multiple struts with spreader plates and
oblique dado joints

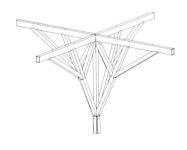

Kneebraced multiple struts

Three-dimensional base details

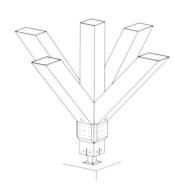

with cleats

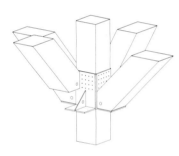

with steel angles let into slits

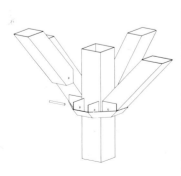

connected to steel stanchion with steel shoe

12 · Motorway service area building

Niederurnen, CH; 1986

Architects: J. Zweifel + W. Leins, Glarus, CH; H. Brunner, Mollis, CH

Structural engineers: Natterer Bois-Consult, Etoy, CH

This roof covering 1400 m² is designed for a snow load of 2.5 kN/m² and is supported on fixed-base concrete columns. Squared sections, 160 x 160 mm, were used exclusively for the exposed timber construction. Two types of three-dimensional pyramids and propped beam geometries derived from them form the primary loadbearing system. The horizontal purlins are positioned every 3.60 m on this three-dimensional frame. The pyramids were prefabricated on the ground. The ties are in two parts and are connected to the central nodes via nail plates. Special nails are driven into the gusset plates without pre-drilling. Horizontal loads are transferred directly into the concrete columns.

Schweizer Holzbau 11/86

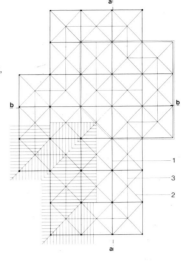

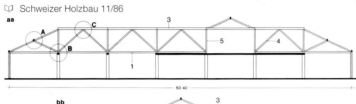

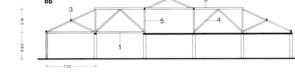

1 Bottom chord, 160 x 100 mm + 2 No. 80 x 200 mm
2 Strut to pyramid, 160 x 160 mm
3 Purlin, 160 x 260 mm
4 Strut, 160 x 160 mm
5 Column, 2 No. 120 x 240 mm + 2 No. 40 x 160 mm

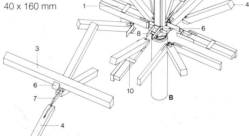

6 Hardwood block, 11 cm thk
7 Plywood gusset, 24 mm thk
8 Steel hanger
9 Metal plate, 10 mm thk
10 Perforated metal strap, 2 mm thk

Strut frame

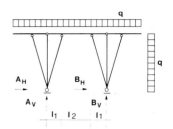

Loading:
uniformly distributed vertical and horizontal loads

Deformations

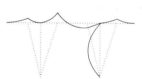

Moments

The posts are subjected to bending under asymmetric loading.

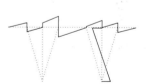

Shear forces

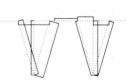

Axial forces

Systems and beam forms

As purlins of squared timber sections
a = 0.5–2.0 m
l = 1–7 m
Spacing of purlins depends on roof construction, loading etc.

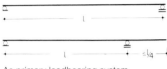

As primary loadbearing system
a = 5–7 m

with glued webs, l = 7–30 m

nailed, glued   h = l/8 to l/14
flanges or webs

glued laminated timber: l = l/10 to l/20

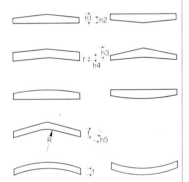

Various beam elevations
(sizes for glued laminated timber)

h1 = l/14 – l/18

h2 = l/18 – l/22

h3 = l/14 – l/18   ∡ = 6° – 15°

h4 = l/30 – l/50   R ≥ 6 m

h5 = l/14 – l/18   f ≤ l/5 – l/10

13 · Bus terminal

Vaduz, FL; 1998

Architects: Hartmann und Eberle Architektur AG, Vaduz, FL

Structural engineers: Frommlet Zimmerei und Ingenieur Holzbau AG, Schaan, FL

The roof of this bus terminal is supported on ten circular hollow section steel columns cast into the concrete foundations to provide full fixity. Separate, planed spruce planks were threaded onto steel circular hollow sections at 5 m centres, with alternate planks facing in opposite directions. Four further aluminium tubes between the main grid lines hold the individual planks in position and prevent them buckling under load. The construction was pre-assembled in the factory and transported to the site "folded". After being "unfolded" onto the columns, the roof was covered with translucent polycarbonate corrugated sheeting. The closely spaced supporting structure provides shading from the sun while still allowing light to penetrate.

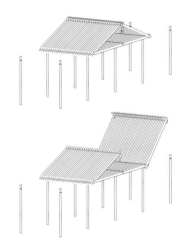

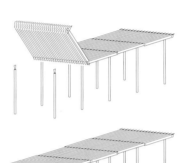

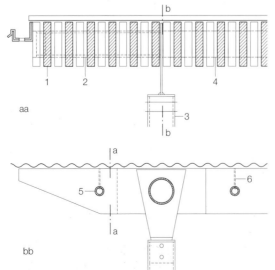

aa

bb

1 Planed spruce planks, 240 x 40 mm
2 Circular hollow steel section at cantilevers, 139.7 dia. x 4 mm
3 Steel column, 152.4 dia. x 12.5 mm
4 Round steel section as main beam, 139.7 mm dia.
5 Aluminium tube, 50 mm dia.
6 Fixing screws

Beam-column junctions with lateral restraint

Log with angular groove

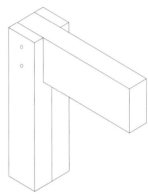

Two-part column, notched in the middle

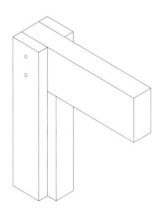

Three-part column

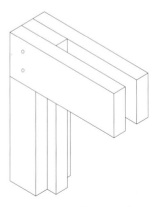

Three-part column with two-part beam

Primary-secondary beam junctions

with ledger strip (nailed, screwed, glued) and nail plate providing tension resistance

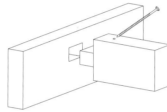

with tenon and screw providing tension resistance

with drop-in tenon and screw providing tension resistance

with special screws

14 · Factory building

Bobingen, D; 1999

Architect: F. Nagler, Munich, D

Structural engineers: Merz Kaufmann und Partner, Dornbirn, A

This two-bay production building with a travelling overhead crane in each bay measures 43 x 76 m on plan. The building derives its identity from its cladding of translucent polycarbonate twin-web panels. The four-part glued laminated timber columns at 6 m centres act like vertical Vierendeel girders. The comparatively large width of the columns and their restraint at the base via steel plates provides bracing in the transverse direction. The taller chords of the outer columns carry the roof construction, the lower inner chords the crane rails. Bracing in the longitudinal direction is provided by steel diagonals in the facades plus the crane rails, and roof decking made from 3-ply core plywood.

Detail 3/2001

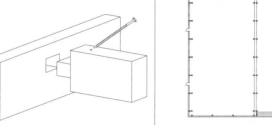

1 Column, pair of 2 No. 120 x 400 mm glulam sections, 40 mm 3-ply core plywood web between pairs of sections
2 Glulam cladding rail, 60 x 280 mm, spruce
3 Translucent polycarbonate twin-web panels, 40 x 500 mm x full height of bldg
4 Steel rod, 12 mm dia.
5 Glulam roof beam, 120 x 920 mm, spruce
6 Glulam edge beam, 160 x 480 mm, spruce
7 Crane rail
8 Nail plate with reinforced holes
9 Pin, 60 mm dia.
10 Galvanised steel support, cast into foundation

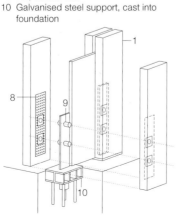

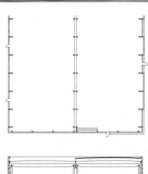

Simply-supported beam, structure

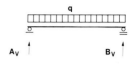

Loading:
uniformly distributed vertical load

Deformations:

$$\max v = \frac{5 \cdot q \cdot l^4}{384\, E \cdot J}$$

Moments: $\max M = \dfrac{q \cdot l^2}{8}$

Shear forces: $\max V = \dfrac{q \cdot l}{2}$

Axial forces: $N = 0$

Simply-supported beam with cantilevers

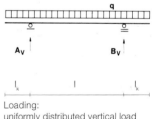

Loading:
uniformly distributed vertical load

$$A_v = B_v = q\left(l_k + \frac{l}{2}\right)$$

Deformations

Moments:

$$M_k = -\, q\, \frac{l_k^2}{2}$$

$$M_F = \frac{q \cdot l^2}{8} - \frac{q \cdot l_k^2}{2}$$

Shear forces:
Axial forces = 0

Systems and beam forms

Simply-supported beam with camber:
s ≥ l/200

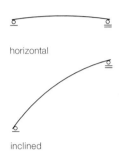

horizontal

inclined

Loadbearing systems for solid-web beams and trusses, simplified for clarity

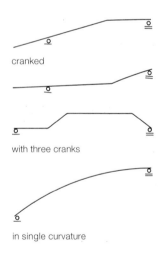

cranked

with three cranks

in single curvature

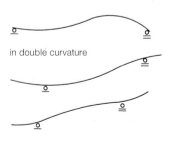

in double curvature

in triple curvature

15 · Forestry depot

Castrisch, CH; 1995

Architects: Gerstlauer und Mohne AG, Chur, CH

Structural engineers: Walter Bieler AG, Bonaduz, CH

The entire structure of this garage consists exclusively of squared timber sections of

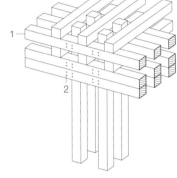

aa

bb

1 Squared softwood section, 120 x 120 mm
2 Nailing, 4 No. 8.5 x 300 mm, predrilled

the same size – 120 x 120 mm – nailed together. Heavier loads are simply carried by using more members. The uniform size has economic advantages: optimum utilisation of the log without kiln drying, and air-dried sawn timber of better quality. The two-part columns and beams are easy to fit together at right angles. This assembly principle functions owing to the large number of contact faces. Double-shear connections help to accommodate large forces with simple means.

Timber beam-concrete column junctions

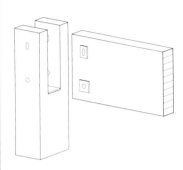

with forked support

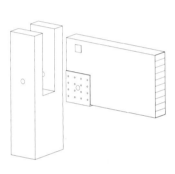

with forked support and pinned joint

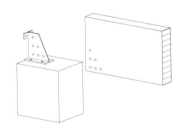

with steel bracket let into slit

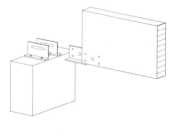

with sliding bearing

Beam forms

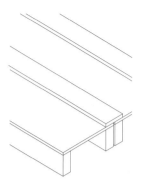

T-beams with LVL top flange

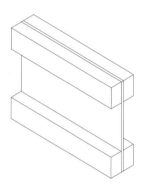

I-beam with web of plywood, LVL, OSB etc.

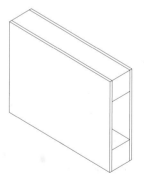

Box beam with webs of plywood, LVL, OSB etc.

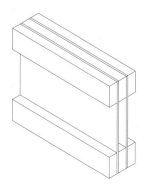

Twin-web I-beam

16 · Palafitte Hotel

Monruz, CH; 2002

Architect: K. Hofmann, Lausanne, CH

Structural engineers: Natterer Bois-Consult, Etoy, CH

This reception building for a 5-star hotel was conceived against the backdrop of Expo 02 in Switzerland. The building is divided into entrance area, coffee bar and dining area.
The engineers at BCN S.A. used a timber-glass composite loadbearing system developed from the IBOIS-EPFL system for the roof structure over entrance area and coffee bar. The span of 6 m is achieved with beams in bending consisting of a vertical pane of glass with a timber frame bonded to both sides. The roof

construction designed for a load of 240 kg/m² is supported on these beams positioned every 3.86 m. The great transparency of the timber-glass composite construction gives the impression of a very lightweight loadbearing structure because only the slender timber sections are visible, and the high-level windows on all sides also help to give the impression of a roof "floating" above the walls.

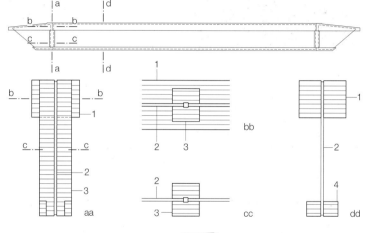

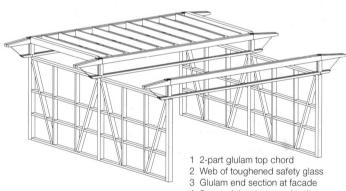

1 2-part glulam top chord
2 Web of toughened safety glass
3 Glulam end section at facade
4 2-part glulam bottom chord

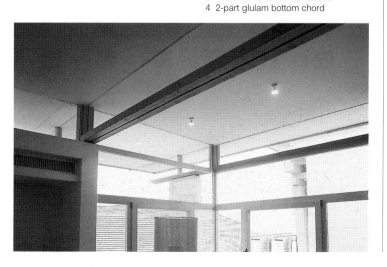

Curved simply-supported beams with and without cantilevers

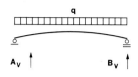

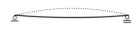

Loading:
uniformly distributed vertical load

Deformations:

$$\max v = \frac{5 \cdot q \cdot l^4}{384 \cdot E \cdot J}$$

Moments:

$$\max M = \frac{q \cdot l^2}{8}$$

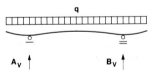

Shear forces

Axial forces

Loading:
uniformly distributed vertical load

Deformations

Moments

Shear forces

Axial forces

Tied triangular frames

with post

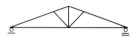

with post and struts

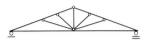

with multiple struts

as transition to arch with multiple struts

Symmetrical trusses

a = 4–10 m   ∡ 12–30°

h = l/10

l = 7.5–30 m

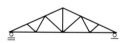

with rising and falling diagonals

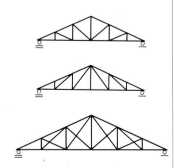

with diamond bracing

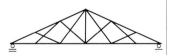

with posts plus rising and falling diagonals

17 · Warehouses

Payerne and Sion, CH; 1987

Architects: H. and L. Meier, Sion; Lausanne Building Department, CH

Structural engineers: Bois Consult Natterer, Etoy, CH

Warehouses made from solid timber which can be opened for the full width and height of the eaves side and with a clear spacing of 6.00 m between columns. The primary loadbearing system consists of four trusses spanning 16.00 m on a 6.20 m grid. The trusses are replaced by columns at the gable ends. The span of the ridge purlin is halved by propping at mid-span. At the same time, these props provide lateral restraint to the bottom chord of the truss when in compression due to wind suction. The roof is braced by a wind girder in the plane of the roof, with a cantilever section to resist the forces from the eaves facade that can be opened.

Impulsprogramm Holz, CH, 1990

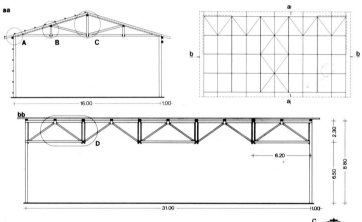

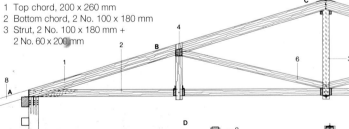

1 Top chord, 200 x 260 mm
2 Bottom chord, 2 No. 100 x 180 mm
3 Strut, 2 No. 100 x 180 mm +
   2 No. 60 x 200 mm

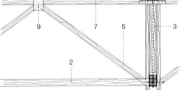

4 Strut, 2 No.
   100 x 180 mm +
   180 x 200 mm
5 Diagonal,
   120 x 180 mm
6 Diagonal,
   160 x 200 mm
7 Purlin,
   180 x 180 mm

8 Rafter,
   180 x 200 mm
9 Timber connector plates,
   60 mm

Ridge junctions

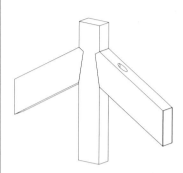

with oblique dado joint for simple hanger

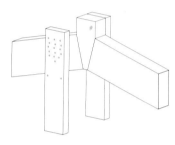

with spacer block and two-part post

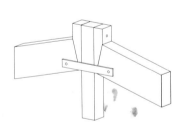

with hardwood wedges

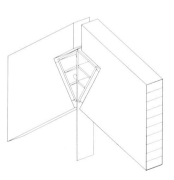

with steel connector

Ridge junctions

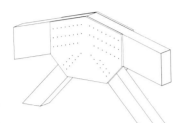

Nailed plywood gussets or punched metal plate fasteners

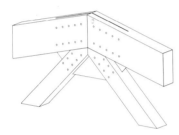

Nailed sheet metal, plywood or LVL gusset let into sawn slits

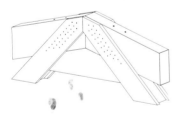

Three-part diagonals nailed to top chord, hardwood block screwed on

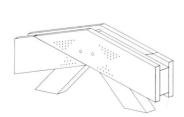

Nailed halving joint

18 · Church

Adelschlag, D; 1974

Architects: K.-J. Schattner, H. Pollak, Eichstätt, D

Structural engineer: K. Stepan, Munich

A rectangular nave covered by a duopitch roof. A total of 15 trusses at 2.00 m centres span 14.60 m. They are supported on pinned-end columns positioned approx. 1.00 m outside the facade. The solid walls, plus a vertical wind girder below the ridge, wind girders in the plane of the roof and diagonals of round steel bars between the columns along the facade all provide stability. The joints in the timber construction are carpentry-style oblique dado and halving joints.

📖 Küttinger: Holzbau-Konstruktionen, Munich, 1984; Baumeister 6/76; Bauwelt 6/81

1. Truss
2. Wind girder
3. Column, 2 No. 80 x 200 mm
4. Bottom chord, 40 x 160 mm
5. Diagonal, 2 No. 60 x 200 mm
6. Top chord, 2 No. 60 x 200 mm
7. Vertical, 100 x 120 mm (3 No. 40 x 100 mm)
8. Purlin, 120 x 120 mm, 120 x 200 mm
9. Longitudinal wind girder
10. Purlin, 100 x 100 mm
11. Steel plate
12. Timber spacer
13. Round steel bar, 12 mm dia.

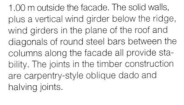

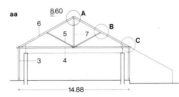

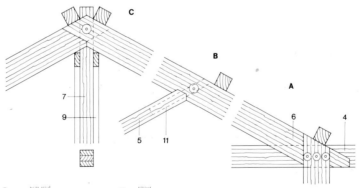

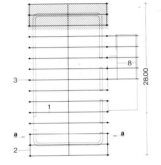

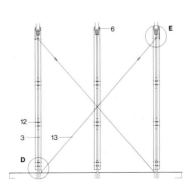

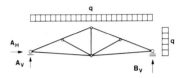

Loading: uniformly distributed horizontal and vertical loads

Deformations

Moment

$$\text{max. } M = \frac{q \cdot l_1^2}{10}$$

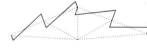

Shear forces

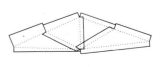

Axial forces

Further trusses

with clerestory windows on one side

with raised bottom chord and clerestory windows

with lantern light along length of roof

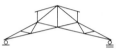

as monitor roof (for lighting and ventilation) with raised bottom chord

Duopitch roof trusses with raised eaves

a = 4–10 m

h ≥ l/12

l = 7.5–35 m
∢ = 3–8°

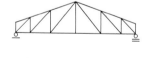

a = 4–10 m

h = l/6 to l/8

l = 20–50 m

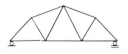

Mansard roof truss

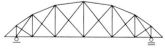

Arch truss

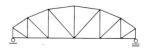

Arch truss with raised eaves

19 · Weiherhof sports centre

Karlsruhe, D; 1981

Architects: Kuhlmann, Biro-Biro, Karlsruhe

Structural engineers: Natterer und Dittrich Planungsgesellschaft, Munich

A truss construction with raised glazed sections to allow daylight into the interior of this sports centre. The main Warren girders spanning 28.8 m are supported on reinforced concrete columns spaced 7.50 m apart. The chords are formed from twin glued laminated timber sections dowelled together. The diagonals in compression are also glued laminated timber sections, but the (rising) diagonals in tension are steel rods. The compressive forces are transferred by way of direct contact via end plates, the tensile forces via steel parts in order to brace themselves against the compression members via end plates. The various forces in the chords are transferred via nailed connections. Struts at 3.60 m centres perpendicular to the axis of the girder provide lateral restraint to the chords, support the raised roof sections and act as intermediate supports for the suspended purlins. The secondary load-bearing members are suspended continuous purlins made from glued laminated timber. At the quarter-points of the main trusses these are made into a complete truss so as to connect the main girders and thus create torsion-resistant pairs. Horizontal X-bracing of steel flats above the timber decking between the main girders provides stability at roof level. The horizontal forces are transferred to the supports via timber struts. The fixed-base reinforced concrete columns carry the forces down to the foundations.

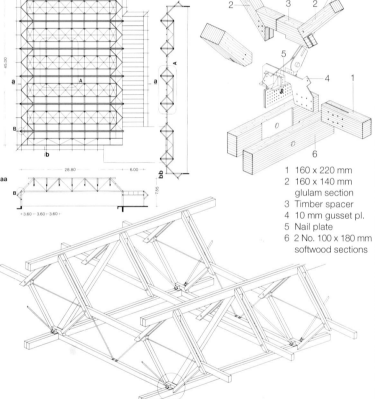

1 160 x 220 mm
2 160 x 140 mm
   glulam section
3 Timber spacer
4 10 mm gusset pl.
5 Nail plate
6 2 No. 100 x 180 mm
   softwood sections

Forms of truss construction

Three-part diagonals nailed to chords

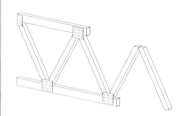

Punched metal plate fasteners

Greim system

Bonded-in dowels with sheet metal connectors

Truss joints at mid-span with post and two diagonals

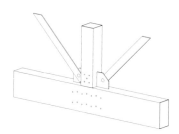

Gusset plate let into slits with steel flat diagonals

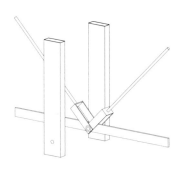

Two-part bottom chord with nailed gusset plates

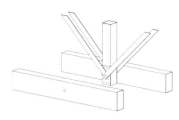

Steel flat tie and steel diagonals with steel lugs

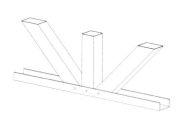

Channel tie with hinge pins

20 · Hangar

Locarno, CH; 1996

Architects: F. Giacomazzi & Assoziati Architetti, Locarno, CH

Structural engineers: Pini & Assoziati Ingegneria, Lugano, CH

This small aircraft hangar measuring 25 x 40 m on plan can be opened along the full length of one longer side. A sturdy lattice beam over the opening carries the loads from the individual roof trusses to the outer, steel columns. Throughout the structure, a visual distinction is always made between tension and compression members. All members in compression, e.g. top chord and diagonals, are fabricated from glued laminated timber, while steel is used for tension members, e.g. the bottom chord and vertical hangers. Oblique dado joints are used for the timber connections subjected to compression. The bottom chord of the lattice beam is made from a welded steel section with abutments for the compression members, while all other tensile forces are carried by slender round steel bars.

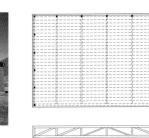

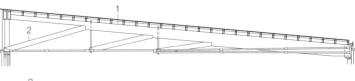

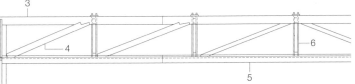

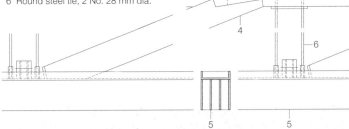

1 Glulam top chord, 297–891 x 200 mm
2 Glulam strut, 330 x 200 mm
3 Glulam top chord, 2 No. 530 x 200 mm
4 Glulam strut, 2 No. 363 x 200 mm
5 Welded steel bottom chord, 400 x 510 mm
6 Round steel tie, 2 No. 28 mm dia.

Structure

Duopitch truss with raised eaves

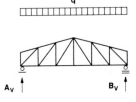

Loading:
uniformly distributed vertical load

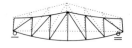

Deformations:

Approximation to DIN 1052 tab. 9:

$$f = \sum \frac{N_i \cdot \overline{N_i}}{E_i \cdot A_i} \cdot l_i$$

where
N_i member force due to external loads
$\overline{N_i}$ member force due to a virtual load "1" applied at the point of the desired deflection
E_i modulus of elasticity
A_i area of cross-section
l_i length of member

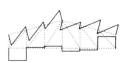

Moments

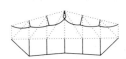

Shear forces

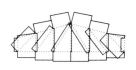

Axial forces

Simply supported plane frames

for monopitch roof
a = 4–10 m

$h_m \geq l/10$

l = 7.5–20 m
∡ = 3–8°

for monopitch roof with raised eaves
a = 4–10 m

$h_m \geq l/12$

l = 7.5–35 m
∡ = 12–30°

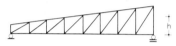

with parallel chords (lattice beams)

slope of top chord 0–4°

as secondary beam:
a = 0.8–1.25 m

h = l/8 to l/12

l = 5–15 m

as primary beam:
a = 2.5–6 m

h = l/10 to l/14

l = 5–25 m

possible with glued laminated timber:
a = 2.5–6 m

h = l/120 to l/15

l = 20–80 m

as diamond girder:
a = 2.5–6 m

h = l/10 to l/14

l = 20–50 m

with rising and falling diagonals matching
purlin spacing

with rising and falling diagonals matching
purlin spacing plus posts at supports

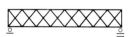

as simple diamond girder

21 · Kindergarten

Erdweg, D; 1975

Architects: O. Steidle + Partner, Munich

Structural engineer: J. Natterer, Munich

This building has a flat roof and a facade set back from the edge of the roof. There are three rows of timber columns, 156 x 156 mm, on an 8.40 m grid; spanning between these are lattice beams 700 mm deep at 2.40 m centres. The top and bottom chords are both in two parts; the diagonals and posts are made from steel circular hollow sections with crimped ends. Two single-sided steel connectors form the connection between the two-part chords. The lattice beams carry 42 mm decking spanning 2.40 m. The horizontal bracing is by means of peripheral girders at roof level and diagonal steel circular hollow sections in the outer rows of columns, plus bracing of squared timber sections along the central row of columns.

⊓ Detail 5/77, plate

1 Column, 156 x
  156 mm
2 Lattice beam
3 Horizontal wind
  girder (Gang-Nail
  system)
4 Squared timber
  sections as verti-
  cal bracing
5 Warm deck roof

  construction,
  glulam top and
  bottom chords,
  2 No. 70 x 150 mm
6 Top girder
7 Diagonals and
  posts, 38 dia. x
  2.5 mm circular
  hollow sections
8 Connector,
  80 mm dia.

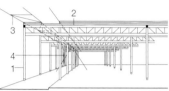

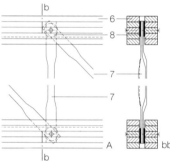

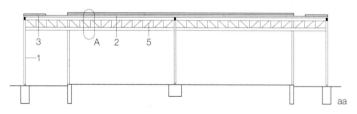

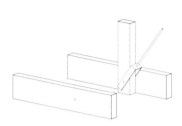

Two-part bottom chord, tie with
forked connector

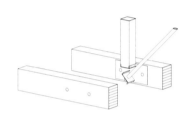

Adjustable steel diagonal

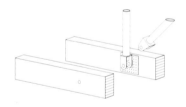

Diagonal and post made from steel
circular hollow sections, with nail plate
and hinge pin

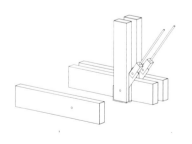

Two-part post and twin diagonals,
three-part bottom chord

Truss nodes with rising and falling diagonals

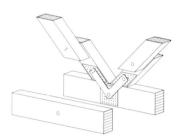

with nail plates and hinge pins

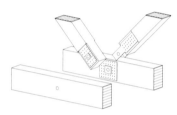

with nail plates and hinge pins, twin bottom chord

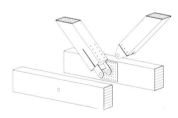

with steel connectors on steel plates let into slits

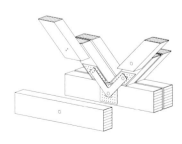

with three-part members

22 · Ice rink

Grefrath, D; 1970

Architect: L. Limmer, Düsseldorf, D

Structural engineers: Timber contractor
Consultant: J. Natterer

The primary loadbearing system for this large roof covering an area 61.20 x 66.50 m consists of four lattice beams at 13.20 m centres spanning almost 60 m. The top and

bottom chords are each in three pieces, the diagonals in two and in the form of I-sections. As a result of the low structural height of just 4.10 m, forces of up to 740 kN can occur in the diagonal members at mid-span, and up to 2350 kN in the chords. Such high member forces created problems at the pinned joints between diagonals and chords. The connection uses nail plates and hinge pins.

📖 Bauen und Wohnen 6/74;
Bauen mit Holz 8/71, p. 382

1 Lattice beam
2 Purlin, 120 x 750 mm
3 Wind girder
4 Glulam top chord, 2 No. 120 x 840 + 170 x 840 mm
5 Bottom chord, 2 No. 85 x 810 + 170 x 810 mm
6 Timber spacer
7 Diagonal, 2 No. 120 or 136 x 80–340 mm deep
8 Nail plates with reinforcing plates welded on
9 42 mm dia. pin in 108 mm dia. sleeve
10 Battens for roof covering
11 Horizontal wind girder, 115 x 80 mm

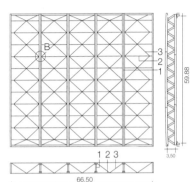

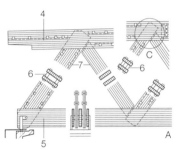

A Lattice beam support

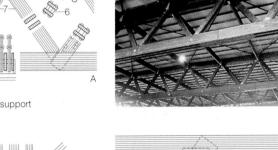

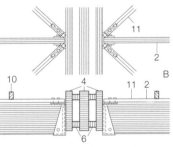

B Connection of purlin and wind girder to top cord
C Top chord node

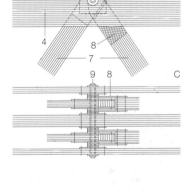

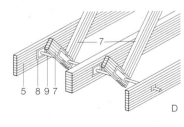

D Connection of diagonals to bottom chord

Structure

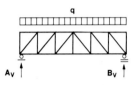

Loading:
uniformly distributed vertical load

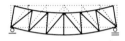

Deformation

Approximation to DIN 1052 tab. 9:

$$f = \frac{5}{384} \cdot \frac{q \cdot l^4}{E \cdot J}$$

where
$J = \Sigma A_i \cdot a_i^2$

l span
E modulus of elasticity
A_i cross-sectional area of chords
a_i distance of centre of gravity of chord from centre of gravity of structure

Moments in top chord under uniformly distributed load

Shear forces in top chord

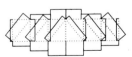

Approximation to DIN 1052 tab. 9:

Diagonals: $N = \dfrac{q \cdot l}{2 \cdot \sin \alpha}$

Chord forces: $N = \dfrac{q \cdot l^2}{8 \cdot h}$

Simply-supported lattice beams

Parallel-chord trusses

with posts plus diagonals in compression
(Howe girder)

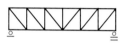

with posts plus diagonals in tension
(Pratt girder)

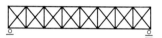

with posts and X-bracing

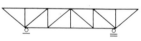

with cantilevers

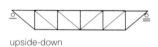

upside-down

with intermediate posts for purlins

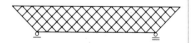

as mesh with cantilevers

23 · Multipurpose hall

Westerheim, D; 1981–84

Architect: D. Juranek, Ludwigsburg, D

Structural engineer: P. Häussermann,
Stuttgart, D

This building comprises cranked lattice
beams in the Greim system to span over a
21 x 36 m hall for sports and other events.
The lattice beams are positioned every
6 m and span 24 m. On one side they rest
on a concrete wall, and are supported by
fixed-base circular concrete columns on
the other. The top chord together with the
transverse diagonals forms the framing to
the glazed rooflights. The 920 mm deep
lattice beam secondary members are
joined to the nodes of the primary beams
using the Greim system. At the gable ends
the secondary members are supported by
cruciform-section columns. The transverse bracing is via the roof girders in the
gable bays, the trussed timber columns
and the concrete wall. All the other wood
joints employ pins and metal plates let
into slits. Continuous purlins carry the roof
decking between the areas of glazing.

📖 Bauen mit Holz 5/83

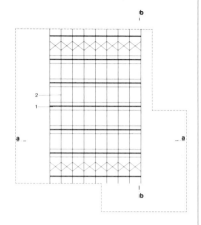

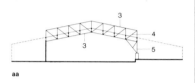

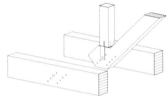

aa

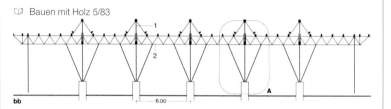

bb   6.00

1 Primary load-
  bearing member
2 Secondary load-
  bearing member
3 Top and bottom
  chords, 240 x
  200 mm
4 160 x 200 mm
5 Strut, 280 x
  200 mm
6 Column, 160 x
  200 mm
7 Top chord and
  diagonals, 120 x
  120 mm
8 Bottom chord,
  120 x 160 mm
9 M24 bolt
10 Geka dowel
  (double-sided tooth-
  plate connector)

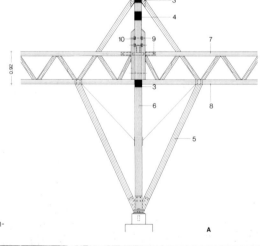

Truss nodes

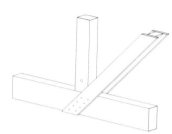

Three-part diagonal, vertical strut
nailed to bottom chord, with Simplex
connector

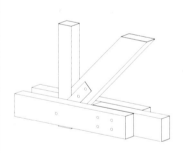

Direct-contact joint for vertical strut

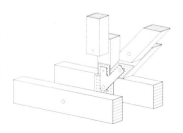

Direct-contact joint for vertical strut

Nail plates and fish-plates for hinge
pin-wood load transfer

Truss nodes

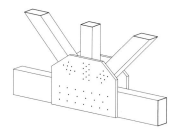

Nailed sheet metal, plywood or LVL
gusset plate

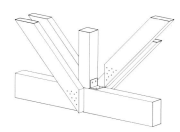

Nailed diagonals

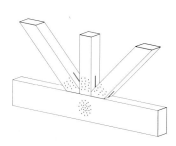

Nails through metal plate, or dowels in
predrilled plate let into slits

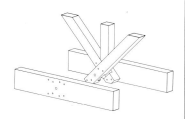

Diagonals with halving joints, plus
hinge pin

24 · Sports centre

Eching, D; 1984

Architects: Wagner, Wanner, Falterer,
Dietersheim, D

Structural engineers: Natterer und Dittrich
Planungsgesellschaft, Munich

A lattice beam construction spanning over
a 30 x 45 m three-part sports hall. Lattice
beams – two-part glulam chords and single glulam diagonals – form the primary
loadbearing system spanning across the
width of the building. The support reactions from each pair are carried back to
the concrete columns by four raking struts.
Peripheral lattice beams cantilever out
and guarantee the overall stability. The
secondary loadbearing members of glued
laminated timber are continuous over the
length of the building above the top
chords and are propped by kneebraces
from the bottom chords. Solid timber purlins consisting of cantilever sections supporting central sections carry the roof
decking, which acts as a stiffening diaphragm.

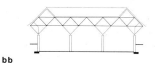

aa

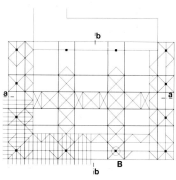

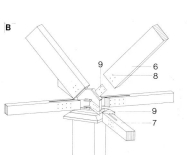

B

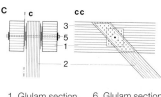

A

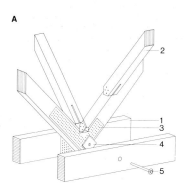

C

1 Glulam section,
  200 x 360 mm
2 Glulam section,
  160 x 160 mm
3 Nail plate
4 Reinforcing plate
5 Pin
6 Glulam section,
  240 x 400 mm
7 Glulam section,
  200 x 200 mm
8 Dowel
9 Metal plate let
  into slits

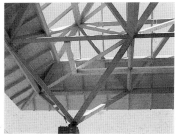

**Structure – lattice beam with
cantilevers**

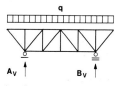

Loading:
uniformly distributed vertical load

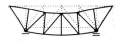

Deformations:

Approximation to DIN 1052 tab. 9:

$$f = \Sigma \, \frac{N_i \cdot N_i}{E_i \cdot A_s} \cdot I_i$$

where
N_i member force due to external loads
N_i member force due to a virtual load
    "1" applied at the point of the
    desired deflection
E_i modulus of elasticity
A_i area of cross-section
I_i length of member

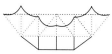

Moments

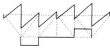

Shear forces

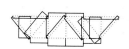

Axial forces

Simply-supported beams with three-dimensional arrangement

with posts plus falling diagonals in tension

with posts plus rising diagonals in compression

with posts and X-bracing

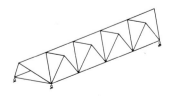

25 · Kindergarten

Munich, D; 1987

Architect: M. Karpf, Taufkirchen, D

Structural engineers: Natterer und Dittrich Planungsgesellschaft, Munich

The duopitch roof construction over this kindergarten was realised using various systems while maintaining the roof profile and the desired clear open space below. A collar roof was chosen for the area without an intermediate ceiling. A timber girder at the level of the collar beams is restrained by the gable walls. Timber girders in the plane of the roof near the ridge create a three-dimensional framework that carries the horizontal and vertical loads between the gable walls.
A simple couple roof forms the roof construction in the area with an intermediate ceiling. Here, the ceiling resists the horizontal loads. The rafters are strengthened locally by ties to create a structure with imperfect collar beams. The connections make use of close tolerance bolts plus steel parts let into slits. The 28 mm timber decking provides stiffening in the plane of the roof.

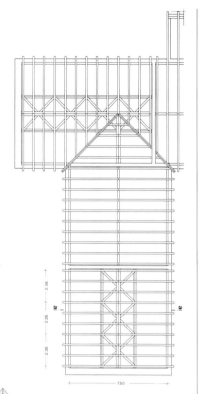

1 Softwood rafter, 120 x 160 mm
2 Glulam ridge purlin, 220 x 220 mm
3 Glulam section, 180 x 220 mm
4 Glulam strut, 140 x 140 mm
5 Spacer rafter, 80 x 160 mm
6 8 mm metal plate let into slits
7 5 mm nail plate
8 12 mm dia. dowel

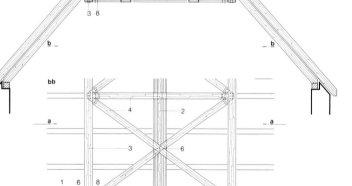

One-piece diagonals, connection with nail plates, shear-plate connector and bolt

Multi-part diagonals, connection as above, oblique dado joint for strut

Multi-part diagonals, connection as above

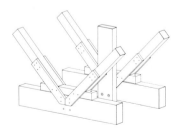

Post fixed to bottom chord with split-ring connectors and bolts, diagonals fixed to spreader blocks with timber fish-plates

Supports for lattice beams

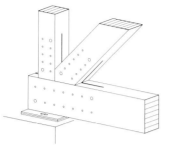

with steel plate let into slits and dowelled

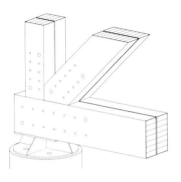

with two-part members and dowelled steel plate in between

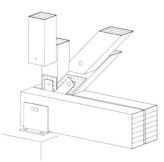

with two-part members, nail plate in between and hinge pin

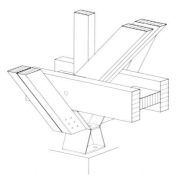

with multi-part chord in three-dimensional arrangement

26 · Bridge over River Neckar

Remseck, D; 1988-89

Architects and structural engineers: E. Milbrandt, D. Sengler, Stuttgart, D

A three-dimensional framework spanning 80 m for pedestrians and cyclists. The three interconnected trusses form an equilateral triangle in section, with a base length of 6.40 m at the abutments and 7.56 m at mid-span. The bottom chords in double curvature and the top chord each consist of two-part glued laminated timber sections with a tapering cross-section of varying depth. These members are spliced twice within their full length – dowels and steel plates let into slits form the splice joints. The bottom framework acts as a horizontal wind girder and carries the longitudinal members supporting the bridge deck. Three horizontal glulam beams positioned adjacent to each other, waterproofing layers, transverse members and pine wood planks form the 3 m wide footway and cycle track. The bridge is covered with overlapping panes of glass fixed to glulam rafters.

📖 Bauen mit Holz 12/88; Glasforum 3/89

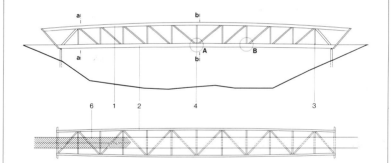

1 Top chord
2 Bottom chord
3 Glulam strut, 240 x 300 mm
4 Glulam strut, 300 x 300 mm
5 Roller bearing
6 Bridge deck
7 Metal plate let into slits
8 Steel dowel, 20 mm dia., and close tolerance bolt, 20 mm dia.

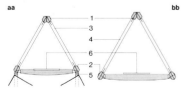

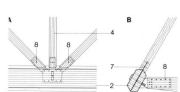

Structure – lattice beam with rising and falling diagonals

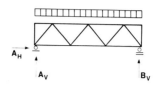

Loading:
uniformly distributed vertical load

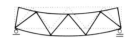

Deformations

Moments

Shear forces

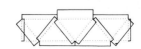

Axial forces

Section

Trussed beams

with one post

with two posts and beam in bending
under asymmetric loading

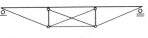

with two posts and X-bracing

as fish-belly beam unsuitable for
asymmetric loads

Trussed beam

a = 3h

h = l/15 to l/20

l = 8–80 m

27 · Traversina Steg bridge

Viamala, CH; 1996

Structural engineers: Branger, Conzett &
Partner, Chur, CH

The exposed position of this bridge called
for a lightweight construction that could
be flown to the site by helicopter; this limited the total weight to 4.3 tonnes. The
bridge consists of two elements that were
able to be transported separately: the parabolic three-chord timber truss, on which all
components in tension were replaced by
steel cables or steel rods, and the two
spandrel beams of 3-ply core plywood.
These prevent torsional movement of the
bridge and were connected to the H-shaped
posts to which the bridge deck is also fixed.
A horizontal diaphragm of glued laminated
timber was attached above the compression chord. The bridge was unfortunately
destroyed in 1999 by a rockfall.

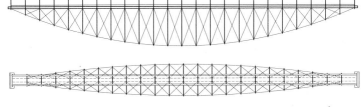

1 Handrail, planed larch,
  40 x 160 mm
2 Spandrel beam, rigid
  3-ply core plywood,
  26 mm Douglas fir
3 Spandrel beam posts, rough-
  sawn larch, 80 x 100 mm
4 Straining plate, 120 x 445 mm
  glulam larch section with
  weatherproof glue
5 Diagonal strut, rough-sawn
  larch, 4 No. 30 x 80 mm
6 Wind girder, galvanised
  round steel bar, 8 mm dia.
7 Transverse member linking
  bottom chords, larch,
  80 x 100 mm
8 Bottom chord, stainless
  steel cable, 24 mm dia.
9 Rocker bearing with
  30 mm dia. steel pins

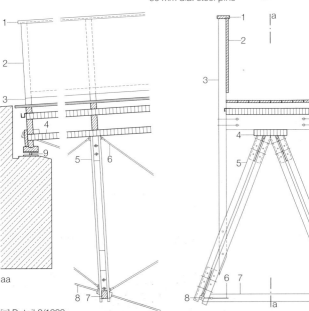

aa

◫ Detail 8/1999

Beam-trussing junction

with steel plate on end grain

with steel angle let into slit and braced
against end grain

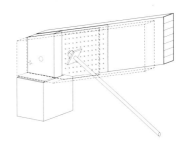

by means of plate welded to nail plate

with hinge pin and reinforced nail plate

Beam-trussing junction

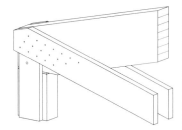

with two-part board trussing

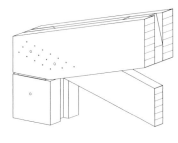

with one-piece glued laminated timber trussing, two-part chord with timber spacers

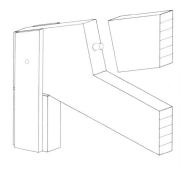

with block

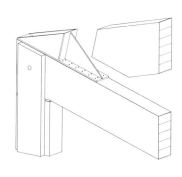

with hinge pin

28 · Haus des Gastes

Bad Wörishofen, D; 1983

Architects: Atelier 4, Gräfeling, D

Structural engineers: Natterer und Dittrich Planungsgesellschaft, Munich

Glass roof over lightwell with beams supported on trussed V-supports. The span varies between 6.7 and 12.5 m. The V-struts of glulam round sections are connected to the glulam top chord by means of tenons. The trussing is by way of round steel bars. Glulam beams on glulam round sections form the peripheral edge support. Lateral restraint to the trussing arrangement is by means of arch-type ties anchored at the corners of the gable walls. The pinned-end columns more than 7 m high are connected to the adjacent concrete walls via steel anchors in order to achieve a horizontal fixing.

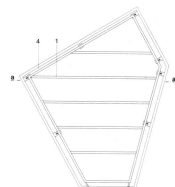

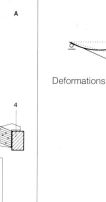

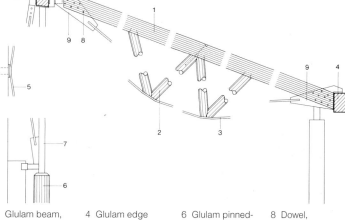

1 Glulam beam, 180 x 240 mm	4 Glulam edge beam, 180 x 240 mm	6 Glulam pinned-end column, 250 mm dia.	8 Dowel, 18 mm dia.
2 Glulam V-strut, 150 mm dia.	5 Tie, 24 mm dia. steel rod	7 Steel circular hollow section	9 10 mm metal plate
3 Trussing, 24 mm dia. steel bar			

Trussed beam

Loading:
uniformly distributed vertical load

Deformations

Moments

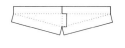

Shear forces

Axial forces

Trussed beams with tie in timber or steel

inclined, with strut perpendicular to beam

inclined, with strut vertical

inclined, with multiple struts

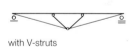

with V-struts

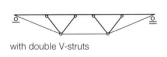

with double V-struts

with double V-struts and cambered beam

29 · Multipurpose hall in a primary school

Bornheim, D; 1998

Architects: Heuer + Faust Architekten, Aachen, D

Structural engineers: Ing.-Gem. Führer-Kosch-Stein, Aachen, D

The roof structure to this hall for sports and other events is formed by a truss with a top chord consisting of a laminated veneer lumber (LVL) board 69 mm thick and 1.50 m wide. This is trussed with a steel cable tie and steel circular hollow sections as struts. The width of the top chord in conjunction with the V-shaped strut arrangement means that lateral support to prevent buckling of the member is unnecessary.
The continuous layer of trapezoidal profile steel sheeting positioned above the top chord carries the roof covering.

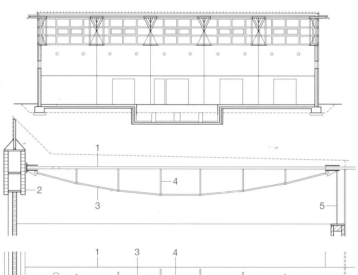

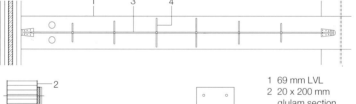

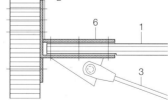

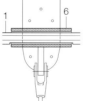

1 69 mm LVL
2 20 x 200 mm glulam section
3 Steel cable, 20 mm dia.
4 V-shaped strut arrangement, 42 mm dia.
5 Steel column, 70 mm dia.
6 20 mm steel plate welded to nail pl.

Post-trussing junction

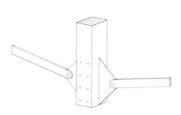

dowelled plate and ties connected via pins

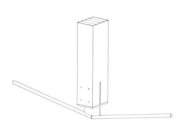

dowelled web plate welded to ties

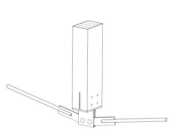

dowelled web plate and ties connected via pins

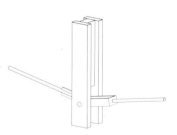

three-part strut with hinge pin or dowel

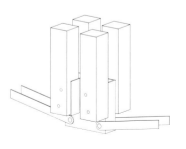

four-part strut with steel connector

V-struts-trussing junction

dowelled plate and ties connected via pins

dowelled plate and ties connected via pins

dowelled web plate welded to ties

dowelled web plate at 90° to grain of struts

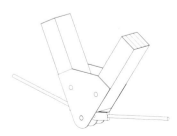

external steel gusset plates with steel dowels

30 · Gymnasium in a secondary school

Vaterstetten, D; 1983

Architect: H. Caspari, Munich

Structural engineer: D. Herrschmann, Munich

An almost square two-part gymnasium with a 30.8 m three-dimensional truss in the middle. The top chord consists of two inclined glued laminated timber beams, the bottom chord a spread steel tie arrangement with glulam transverse members and parabolic ties. The loads are transferred to pinned-end columns. Horizontal transverse beams on both sides every 2.80 m are suspended from this primary loadbearing framework. They carry the purlins, squared timber sections and timber decking. The roof level is stiffened by diagonal boarding and a wind girder between the bottom chords of the main truss. A timber girder braces the raised part of the roof. Horizontal forces are resisted by the concrete walls at the north and south ends.

📖 architektur postgradual 4/85

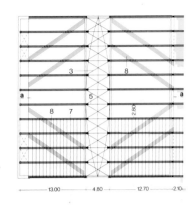

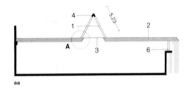

aa

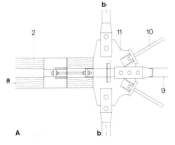

aa

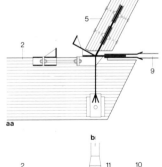

A

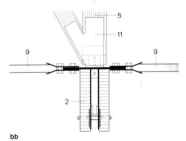

bb

1 Truss
2 Transverse beam, 2 No. 120 x 700 mm
3 Steel tie
4 Top chord, 2 No. 280 x 620 mm
5 Post, 280 x 280 mm
6 Column, 280 x 280 mm, 280 x 320 mm
7 Purlins
8 Diagonal boarding for stability
9 Steel circular hollow section, 89 mm dia.
10 Round steel bar, 35 mm dia.
11 20 mm gusset pl.

Trussed simply-supported beam with V-struts

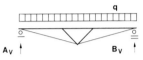

Loading: uniformly distributed vertical load

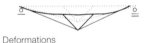

Deformations

Moments

Shear forces

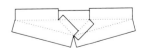

Axial forces

Examples of structural geometries

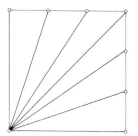

Square on plan

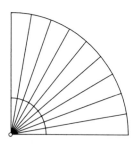

Quarter-circle on plan

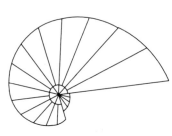

Helical arrangement on plan

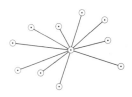

Variable edge conditions

31 · Leisure pool

Frankfurt am Main, D; 1979–82

Architects: Fischer, Glaser, Kretschmer, Fleft, Frankfurt am Main

Structural engineer: W. Prüfer, Butzbach-Ebersgöns, D

The roof over this swimming pool covers an area of 8450 m² using a diagonal column grid with 27.22 m side length. The main loadbearing members between the concrete columns are fish-belly type three-dimensional trusses with curved, glued chords. The tension ribs of glued laminated timber running diagonally and the roof decking (50 mm planks with double tongue and groove) in the direction of the compression arch form a hyperbolic paraboloid in double curvature. The ribs in the end bays are designed as beams in bending, and the edge beams are subjected to bending and torsion. Overall stability is provided by the plate action of the roof decking and by the fixed-base concrete columns. The roof covering of special fireproofing material, untreated glass fleece and PVC sheeting is laid on the decking. The main loadbearing members were assembled at the factory and lifted into position on site with a crane.

   📖 Bauen mit Holz 2/82

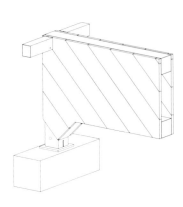

1 Primary load-bearing member	5 Top chord, 2 No. 260 x 600 mm
2 Secondary loadbearing member	6 Bottom chord, h = 580–1000 mm
3 Edge beam	7 Timber post
4 Tension ribs	

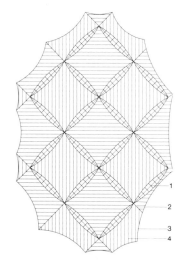

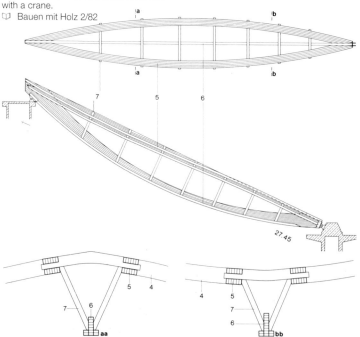

Beam bearing on wall

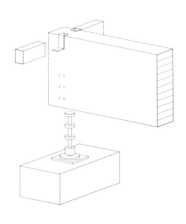

raised

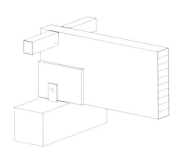

with nail plate or plywood strengthening at support

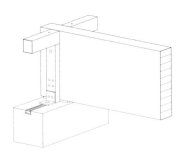

with strengthening at support and fixed to sliding rail

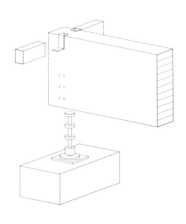

with bonded-in rod on turned support

Central support details

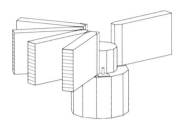

on concrete column, held in position by steel shear connectors

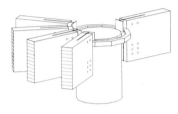

steel ring with peripheral bracket, beams hung on bracket via end plate on dowelled web plate let into slit

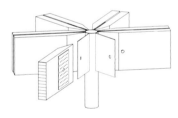

steel circular hollow section with web plates welded on, hinge pin connection

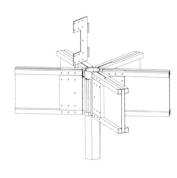

steel tube with rails welded on and beams hung on rails

32 · Cattle market hall, Bündner Arena

Cazis, CH; 1998

Architect: H. Marugg, Thusis, CH

Structural engineers: Walter Bieler AG, Bonaduz, CH

The oval plan shape of the Bündner Arena is spanned by fish-belly trusses radiating around a central point. The top and bottom chords are each in two parts linked via a central "hub". The steel component at the top chord is designed as a ring in compression, and the one at the bottom chord as a star-shaped ring in tension. A steel circular hollow section, 219 mm dia., acts as an axially loaded strut joining the two steel parts together. The round diagonal steel ties in the individual bays of the fish-belly trusses can accommodate uplift wind forces.

The outer columns are held in place by the stiff roof plate of the surrounding flat roof. Further bracing is thus unnecessary and there are clerestory windows around the entire circumference.

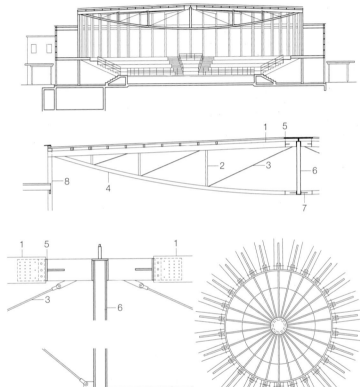

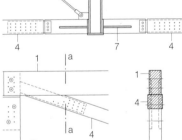

1 Glulam top chord, 330 x 120 mm
2 Glulam strut, 120 x 120 mm
3 Round steel bar, 20 mm dia.
4 Glulam bottom chord, 168 x 180 mm
5 Steel ring in compression, 15 mm thk
6 Steel circular hollow section, 219.5 mm dia.
7 Central steel ring in tension, 10 mm thk
8 Glulam column, 220 x 220 mm

Combination of corbel and simply supported beam

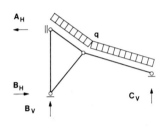

Loading:
uniformly distributed load

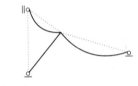

Deformations

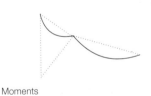

Moments

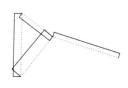

Shear forces

Axial forces

Beam grids produced by shear-resistant connections between simply supported beams

over triangular plan shape

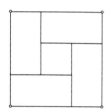

over square plan shape

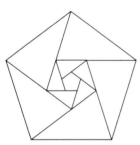

over pentagonal plan shape

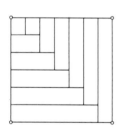

staggered arrangement

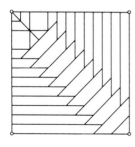

double staggered arrangement

33 · Salt store

Lausanne, CH; 1989

Architects: Atelier Gamma Architectore, Lausanne

Structural engineers: Natterer Bois-Consult, Etoy, CH

This 11-sided salt store is 26 m wide, with reinforced concrete side walls. The primary loadbearing system is a beam grid consisting of 11 glulam beams 13.5 m long, supported on the concrete wall and the neighbouring beam. The inner nodes take the form of hinged splices because they need only transfer shear forces. Squared timber purlins parallel to the side walls form the secondary loadbearing system. The roof covering is of waterproof sheeting bonded to 30 mm decking. There is a glazed rooflight in the centre of the building fabricated from squared timber sections.

📖 Bauen mit Holz 11/89

1	220 x 650–1500 mm		fitted into slit
2	100 x 200 mm or	6	Dowels
	120 x 240 mm	7	120 x 180 mm
3	40 x 120 mm	8	120 x 160 mm
4	Sprocket or bearing	9	16 mm ply-
	timber in oak		wood plate
5	Angled steel I-sec-	10	19 mm fish-
	tion, 12 mm thk.,		plate

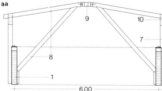

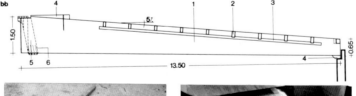

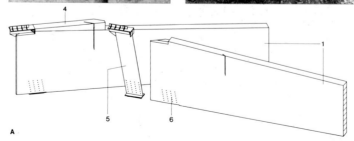

A

Primary-secondary beam junctions

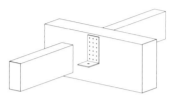

concealed nailed angle

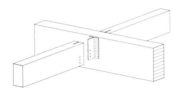

T-section let into slit, nailed to primary beam, dowelled to secondary beam

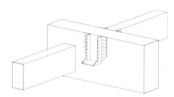

with hanger having fixing legs facing outwards

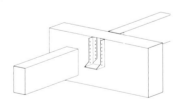

with hanger having fixing legs facing inwards

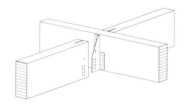

with metal anchor let into slit and dowelled

Primary-secondary beam junctions, load transfer via top edge of beam

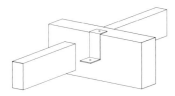

Z-hanger

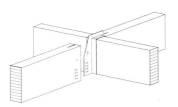

metal anchor let into slits and dowelled

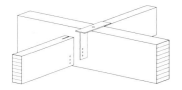

metal anchor let into slits and dowelled, for essentially symmetrical loads

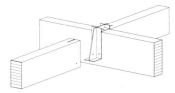

hanger with web plate let into slits

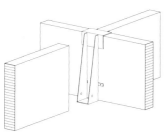

U-shaped hanger

34 · Trade fair halls

Nuremberg, D; 1974

Architects: Plan GmbH, Munich

Structural engineers: J. Natterer and K. März, Munich

Total floor area covered: 60 480 m². The plan shape of the 10 partly interconnected halls is made up of 168 equilateral triangles with a side length of 28.80 m. The roof structure is a statically determinate system of beams with main beams of 180 x 1900 mm spanning 28.10 m, plus secondary beams measuring 120 x 1140 mm and 140 x 700 mm suspended from the main beams. The mesh of 140 x 250 mm purlins is raised above the main beams on 160 x 160 mm posts to provide space for the building services. The purlins carry trapezoidal profile metal sheeting and a warm deck roof. Horizontal bracing is provided by the triangulated system of primary and secondary beams plus the mesh of purlins, all supported on fixed-base reinforced concrete columns. The problem of transferring horizontal forces of up to 120 kN and vertical forces up to 132 kN at the supports has been solved by transferring the horizontal forces to the reinforced concrete column via a nail plate, vertical forces via a screw bonded into the glued laminated timber primary beam. This arrangement obviates the need for any corbels on the column and enables it to be kept very slender. The triangular roof surfaces, including the purlins, were pre-assembled on the ground before being lifted into position on the reinforced concrete columns with a mobile crane.

Zentralblatt für Industriebau 5/74, p. 160; DBZ 6/75, p. 149

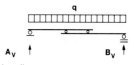

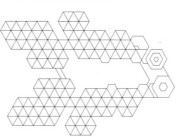

1 Primary beam,
  2 No. 180 x 1900 mm
2 Secondary beam,
  120 x 1140 mm
3 Secondary beam,
  120 x 400 mm
4 Purlin, 140 x 250 mm
5 Post, 160 x 160 mm

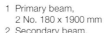

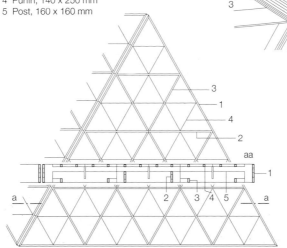

Beam grid system

Loading:
uniformly distributed vertical load

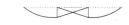

Deformations

Moments

Shear forces

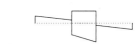

Axial forces: N = 0

Continuous beams and cantilever beams carrying central beam section

made from squared timber sections

a = 0.5–1.5 m
l = 4–8 m

Spliced squared timber sections

a = 0.5–1.5 m
h = l/12 to l/20
l = 4–10 m

made from glued laminated timber

a = 2–6 m
h₁ = l/24
h₂ = l/16
l = 10–30 m
slope of haunch ≤ 1:8

35 · Assembly building

Noréaz, CH; 1982

Architects: Annouk and Jaques Python

Structural engineers: Natterer Bois-Consult, Etoy, CH

In the longitudinal direction there is a continuous, dowelled, gently cambered compound section consisting of three 160 x 160 mm squared timber sections. These are supported at several points and form the primary loadbearing system for the roof. The loads from the ridge purlin and the crane are carried by a cantilever tie arrangement, which is connected by short intermediate posts in the plane of the roof and horizontally at the eaves. Two-part posts create forked supports for the purlins. The bracing elements are arranged so as not to be damaged during lifting and loading operations. The large overhanging eaves designed as cantilevers provide protection against rain and help to blend the building into its surroundings.

📖 Holz bulletin bois/Lignum, No. 13, 1985

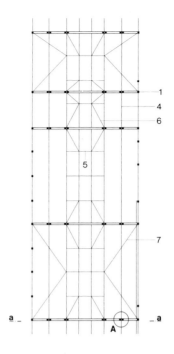

aa

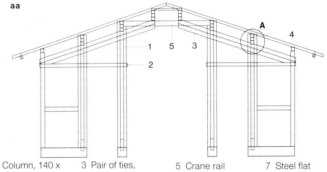

1 Column, 140 x 140 mm structural timber
2 Pair of ties, 2 No. 140 x 200 mm structural timber
3 Pair of ties, 2 No. 140 x 200 mm structural timber
4 Purlin, 3 No. 140 x 200 mm structural timber
5 Crane rail beam, 180 x 240 mm structural timber
6 Diagonal, 100 x 100 mm structural timber
7 Steel flat
8 2 No. Bulldog connectors, 95 mm dia. with bolt (double-sided toothed-plate connectors)

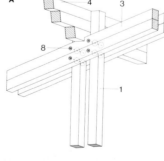

Shear-resistant beam splices

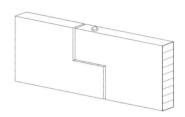

Notched and reinforced with plywood

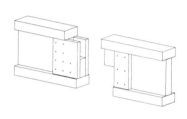

I-beam with notched web reinforced with plywood

Two-part sheet metal shoe

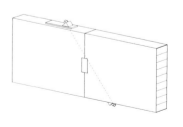

with threaded bar fitted diagonally plus elastomeric bearing

Shear-resistant beam splices

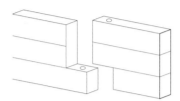

Dowelled beam, with notch and close tolerance bolt

with steel I-section and no eccentricity

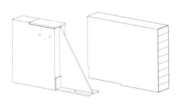

Angled steel I-section

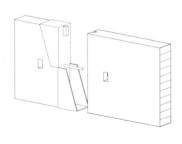

Sheet steel shoe with tension connection

36 · Bridge

Martigny, CH; 1983

Structural engineers: Natterer Bois Consult, Etoy, CH, with the Technical Department of the Pioneer Bataillon 10

This bridge over the River Dranse for pedestrians and cyclists is also approved for forestry vehicles up to 5 tonnes. The clear span of 28 m is formed by two cantilever edge beams cable-stayed from the pylons, and a central section supported between the beam ends. The main beams comprise five larch sections joined with dowels. The bridge is braced against wind by the transverse members mounted underneath and the larch bridge deck nailed to them. The bridge was erected using the Swiss Army's lightweight engineering plant. No wood preservative was applied to the larch beams but they are prevented from rotting by the favourable weather conditions.

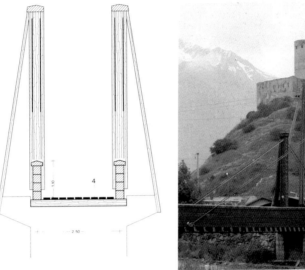

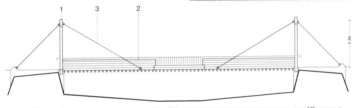

1 Pylon
2 Compound beam
3 Titanium-steel cable stay
4 Bridge deck, 60 mm planks

Two-span beam

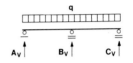

Loading:
uniformly distributed vertical load

Deformations:

$$\max v = q \cdot \frac{l^4}{186,6} \cdot E \cdot J$$

Moments:

$$\min M = -q \cdot \frac{l^2}{8}$$

$$\max M = q \cdot \frac{l^2}{14,22}$$

Shear forces:

$$\max V = \frac{5}{8} \cdot q \cdot l$$

Axial forces: N = 0

Cable-stayed bridges

Cable-stayed bridge with single pylon tied back to end support

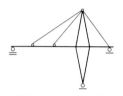

Cable-stayed pinned beams with triangulated pylon

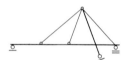

Cable-stayed bridge with single, raking pylon

A-frame pylon as three-legged trestle

Cable-stayed bridge tied back to intermediate support

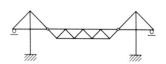

Cable-stayed bridge with central lattice beam

37 · Bridge

Vallorbe, CH; 1989

Structural engineers: Natterer Bois-Consult, Etoy, CH, in collaboration with Vaud Motorway Department

Owing to the steep slope, this footbridge over a trunk road was made in two parts: a 35 m long access ramp parallel to the road and the 24 m bridge. Five simply supported bridge deck units make up the loadbearing system and these are suspended on cables from a raking H-shaped pylon. The pylon itself is braced in the transverse direction by two St Andrew's crosses – one above and one below the deck. The deck has X-bracing below the footway.

The loadbearing structure is assembled from pressure-impregnated fir logs. The longitudinal beams for the bridge deck are made from edge-sawn logs dowelled together. Larch wood planks are used for the bridge deck. Threaded steel reinforcing bars were used for the cable stays and all wind bracing members.

📖 Journal de la construction 21/87

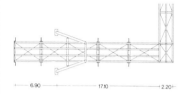

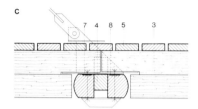

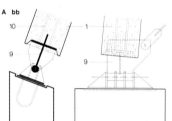

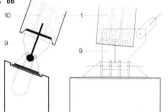

1 Log, 360 mm dia.
2 Log, 300 mm dia.
3 Log, 2 No. 240 mm dia.
4 Squared section, 120 x 140–280 mm
5 Bridge deck, 60 x 200 mm
6 Threaded tie
7 Steel bracket, 5 mm thk
8 Toothed-plate connector
9 Metal plate let into slits, 15 mm thk
10 Bonded-in threaded bar

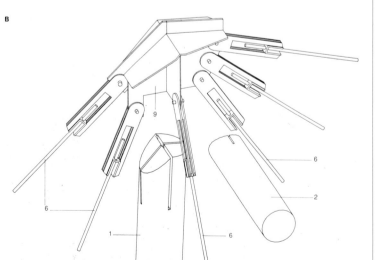

Cable connection details

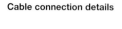

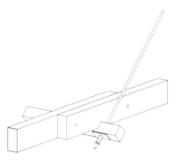

to transverse deck beam

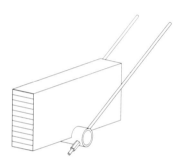

to steel circular hollow section transverse deck beam

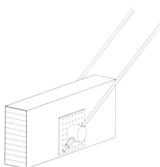

to longitudinal beam via hinge pin

to longitudinal beam via block

Cable support point details

with saddle

with saddle

with web plate

with web plate

38 · Factory building

Bad Münder, D; 1992

Architects: Thomas Herzog, Munich, with Bernd Steigerwald, Haag, von Ohlen, Rüffer und Partner

Structural engineers: Sailer und Stepan, Munich

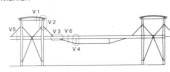

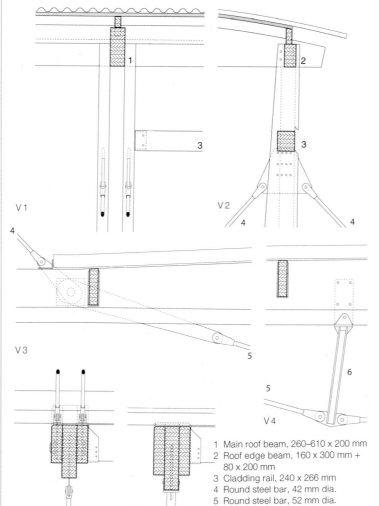

V 1

V 2

V 3

V 4

V 5   5

V 6   6

H-frames 5.40 m wide spaced 30 m apart, with the roofs to the production bays suspended in between. The trussed beams are integrated into the longitudinal bracing. The primary loadbearing structure is of glued laminated timber with tapering columns, F30 fire resistance rating, on a 6.60 m grid. The structural depth of the trussed beams is 1500 mm. Ties made from steel grade St 52 have a 40 kN pretension at the ends. Forces are transferred at the joints by way of dowels and metal plates let into slits. Transition to round bars from cast steel forked heads with a right-left thread. The roof plate is formed by glued panels, 2.7 x 6.6 m, with a covering of plywood reinforced by timber ribs.

1 Main roof beam, 260–610 x 200 mm
2 Roof edge beam, 160 x 300 mm + 80 x 200 mm
3 Cladding rail, 240 x 266 mm
4 Round steel bar, 42 mm dia.
5 Round steel bar, 52 mm dia.
6 HEA 120 steel section

Cable-stayed bridge with central trussed beam

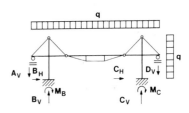

Loading:
uniformly distributed vertical and horizontal loads

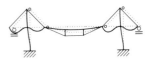

Deformations

Moments

Shear forces

Axial forces

Uniform distribution of maximum moments due to a favourable ratio between spans

Shorter end spans

Cantilever at both ends

39 · Bridge over River Simme

Wimmis, CH; 1989

Structural engineers: Natterer Bois-Consult, Etoy, CH; Gärtl AG, Ütendorf

This is a bridge for pedestrians and cyclists over the Simme valley. At the middle the bridge stands 24 m above the bed of the river. The primary loadbearing system for the bridge consists of two parallel-chord lattice beams continuous over three spans of 27, 54 and 27 m. The bridge deck of planks has transverse beams at 6.75 m centres and spliced purlins. The horizontal girder for bracing the bridge is formed by the bottom chords of the main beams, the transverse deck beams and round steel diagonals. The top chords and the roof are braced with rigid frames at a spacing of 6.75 m. Nail plates and pins form the connections. Large compressive forces from the diagonals are transferred to the chords via nailed "oblique dado" brackets. The roof covering is made from flat metal sheet with a central continuous plastic rooflight.

📖 Impulsprogramm Holz, CH, 1990; Schweizer Holzbau 5/89

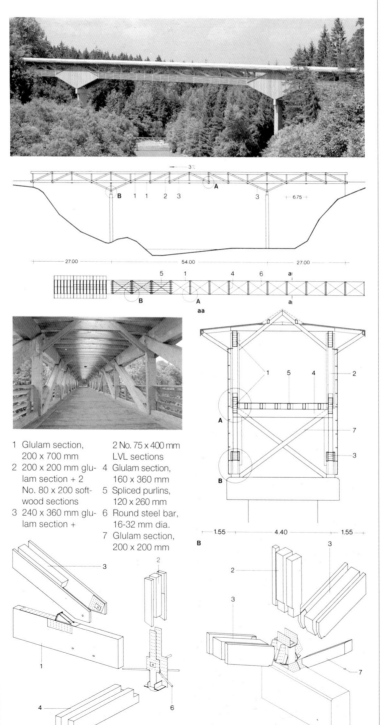

1 Glulam section,
   200 x 700 mm
2 200 x 200 mm glu-
   lam section + 2
   No. 80 x 200 soft-
   wood sections
3 240 x 360 mm glu-
   lam section +
2 No. 75 x 400 mm
   LVL sections
4 Glulam section,
   160 x 360 mm
5 Spliced purlins,
   120 x 260 mm
6 Round steel bar,
   16-32 mm dia.
7 Glulam section,
   200 x 200 mm

Continuous beam with varying beam depth

made from spliced squared timber sections
a = 0.5–1.5 m
h = l/16 to l/20
l = 4–8 m

made from glued laminated timber
a = 2–6 m
h = l/18 to l/22
l = 10–30 m
slope of haunch ≥ 1:8

as lattice beam
a = 2–5 m
h = l/16 to l/18
l = 10–80 m

Continuous beam-column junction

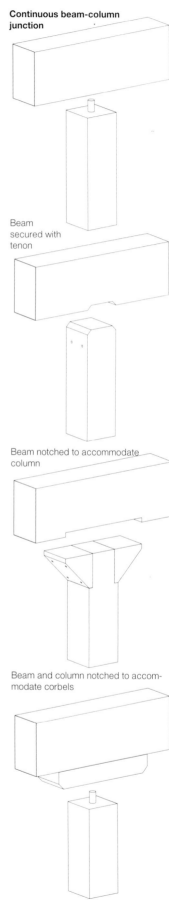

Beam secured with tenon

Beam notched to accommodate column

Beam and column notched to accommodate corbels

with hardwood spreader

Rigid continuous beam-column junction

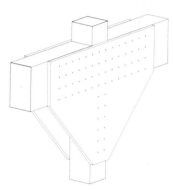

butt-jointed with nailed plywood gussets

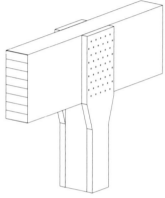

with forked arrangement at head of column

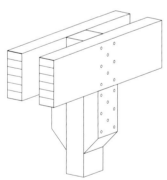

twin beams supported on cleats

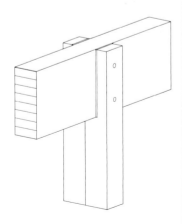

two-part column notched to accommodate beam

40 · Footbridge

Singen, D; 2000

Architect: J. Usleber, Weinheim, D

Structural engineer: Thomas Relling, Singen, D

This covered footbridge consists of two parallel lattice beams with a 150 mm camber designed as two-span beams with a cantilever at one end. Two H-shaped steel frames form the intermediate supports and a concrete foundation supports the bridge on higher ground at one end. The bridge was pre-assembled, delivered in two halves and lifted into position with a crane.

The external cladding of Douglas fir weatherboarding protects the underlying structure.

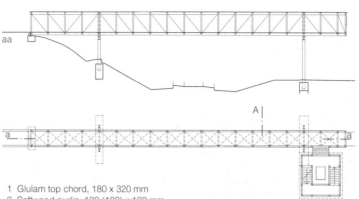

1 Glulam top chord, 180 x 320 mm
2 Softwood purlin, 120 (180) x 180 mm
3 Wood louvres, 40 x 120 mm Douglas fir
4 Wire mesh screen
5 Handrail, galvanised steel circular hollow section, 48.3 dia. x 3.2 mm
6 Glulam bottom chord, 180 x 360 mm
7 Softwood transverse beam, 140 x 200 mm
8 Softwood longitudinal beam, 100 x 130 mm
9 Bridge deck, 40 x 160 mm grooved planks
10 HEB 340 steel column
11 HEB 400 steel column

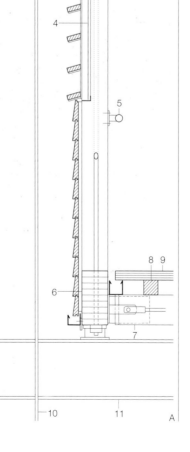

Two-span beam with cantilevers

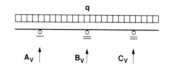

Loading:
uniformly distributed vertical load

Deformations

Moments: min M $= - \dfrac{q \cdot l^2}{12}$

max M $= \dfrac{q \cdot l^2}{24}$

Shear forces: max V $= q \cdot \dfrac{l}{2}$

Axial forces: N = 0

Continuous systems

Inclined continuous beam

Inclined and cranked continuous beam

for duopitch roof

for valley roof

Continuous plane frames

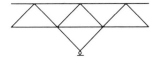

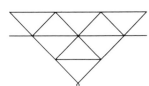

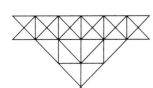

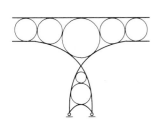

41 · Residential complex

Munich, D; 1982

Architects: T. Herzog, B. Schilling, Munich

Structural engineers: Natterer und Dittrich
Planungsgesellschaft, Munich

A peripheral sole plate of hot-dip galvanised rolled steel sections fixed to the reinforced concrete basement allows adjustment. The timber frame is built off this with
columns at 3 m centres in the longitudinal
direction; floor joists with 40 mm particleboard decking, which also acts as a horizontal diaphragm bracing the construction.
The horizontal forces are carried via diagonals into the walls. Primary and secondary
beams are joined at the same level with
welded steel connectors. All loadbearing
sections are of glued laminated timber.
The depth of the lattice beam with inner facade at bottom chord and roof construction
derived from greenhouse systems on the
top chord are used for through-ventilation.

📖 Werk, Bauen und Wohnen 5/83;
Die andere Tradition, Munich, 1984

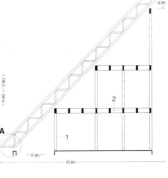

1 Column, 150 x 150 mm	5 Channel section, 100 mm
2 Beams, 90 x 300 mm, 110 x 300 mm, 150 x 300 mm	6 Steel square hollow section, 40 x 40 x 4 mm
3 Glulam section, 2 No. 50 x 100 mm	7 M12 bolt
	8 Nail plate
	9 16 mm dia. tube
4 Glulam section, 50 x 70 mm	10 M10 threaded pin

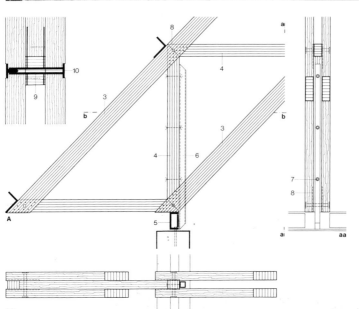

bb

Rigid continuous beam splices over supports

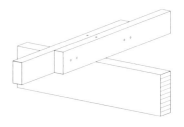

Spliced round-section purlins with
dowels

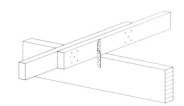

Spliced squared-section purlins nailed
to main beam using sheet metal framing anchor

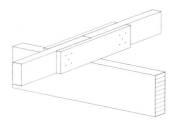

Spliced squared-section purlins
screwed to main beam

Squared-section purlins with nailed
splice plates

Rigid splices for straight and curved beams

Box beam reinforced for tension, with external splice plates

Cranked box beam with metal plates let into slits and nailed

Metal plate let into slits, with rings of dowels

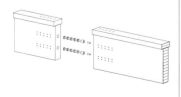

with bonded-in rods

42 · Oslo Airport

Gardermoen, N; 1993–98

Architects: AviaPlan Architects, Oslo, N

Structural engineer: C. Wise, Ove Arup & Partners, London, UK

The roof over the departure hall at Oslo Airport is carried on large, curving, two-span lattice beams with a cantilever at both ends. These timber lattice beams are covered completely with plywood on both sides. Together with the parabolic bottom chord of glued laminated timber, a section through the beam resembles a section through an aircraft wing. The beams are always positioned in pairs and joined to either side of the Y-shaped column head arrangement. Timber lattice beams are suspended between these primary loadbearing members.

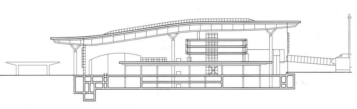

1 Glulam top chord, 700 x 500 mm
2 Diagonal
3 Glulam bottom chord, 560 x 880 mm
4 Steel column head
5 Reinforced concrete column, 1500 mm dia.
6 Plywood side
7 Timber lattice beam

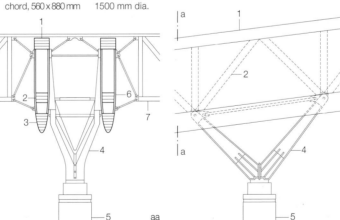

aa

Inclined continuous beam

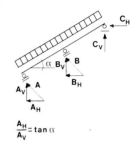

$$\frac{A_H}{A_V} = \tan \alpha$$

Loading:
uniformly distributed load

Deformations

Moments

Shear forces

Axial forces

Beams with pinned splices

with one splice

with two splices and supporting trestle

with central beam

with central truss

with central lattice beam

with trussed central beam

43 · Ice rink

Surrey, CAN; 1990

Architects: L. Trubka Ass., Vancouver, CAN

Structural engineers:
Conception: Natterer Bois Consult, Etoy, CH
Realisation: K. Merz, K. Lau, Vancouver, CAN

Project engineers: Choukalos, Woodburn, McKenzie, Maranda Ltd, Vancouver, CAN

A system of struts made from parallel strand lumber (PSL) with the acknowledged simple compression connections. A frame with two hinges and triangular trusses suspended in between. Continuous sections at the hinges simplify the connection detail and also accommodate asymmetric wind and snow loads.

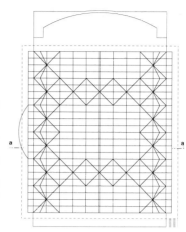

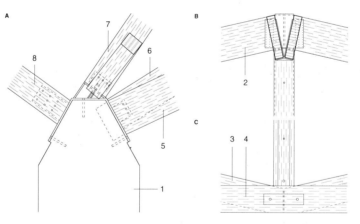

aa

1. Reinforced concrete column, 1120 x 450 mm
2. PSL beam, 222 x 355 mm
3. PSL strut, 222 x 286 mm
4. PSL beam, 2 No. 133 x 286 mm
5. PSL strut, 2 No. 178 x 406 mm
6. PSL strut, 222 x 356 mm
7. PSL strut, 222 x 286 mm
8. PSL strut, 222 x 286 mm

Continuous beam-column junction

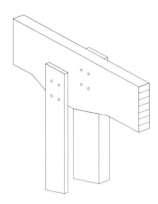

Three-part column, haunched beam

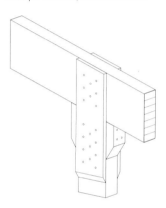

with fish-plates and cleats

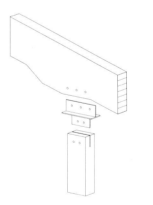

Haunched beam and support reinforced with steel insert

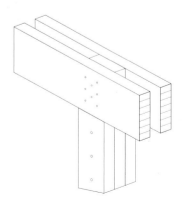

Twin beams and three-part column

Supports for continuous beams

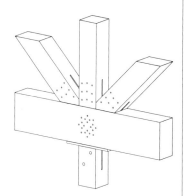

Dowelled metal plate let into slits, plus end plate

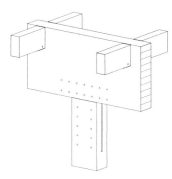

with fixity provided by dowelled steel plate

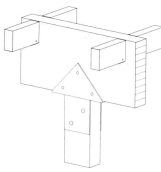

with exposed steel shoe

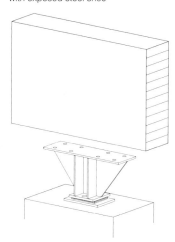

Bearing for heavy loads

44 · Jägermeister factory building

Kamenz, D; 1993-95

Architects: Pook Leiska Partner, Braunschweig, D

Structural engineer: W. Kling, Penzberg, D

Two beams and a central trestle construction form the roof structure over the two bays of this factory building, which is 54 m wide. The two beams are trussed underneath to match the shape of the bending moment diagram. The two-part top chord in glued laminated timber is trussed with two steel cables tensioned over the one-piece props. The outer columns are also in two parts so that the beams simply rest on top. A trestle construction with an accessible upper floor forms the central support. Steel girders in the plane of the roof and in the facade brace the entire construction in all directions.

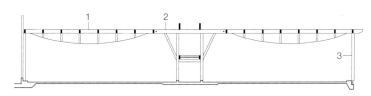

1 Glulam trussed beam,
  2 No. 200 x 600 mm
2 Glulam central beam,
  3 No. 200 x 600 mm
3 Glulam column, 2 No. 160 x 400 mm
4 Glulam secondary beam,
  200 x 600 mm
5 Glulam spacer, 600 x 40 mm,
  glued to top chord
6 Glulam spacer, 600 x 80 mm
7 Hinge pin, steel circular hollow
  section, 193.7 mm dia.

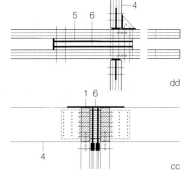

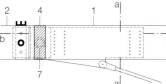

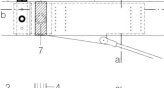

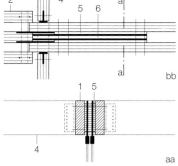

Beam with pinned splices

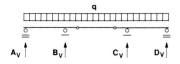

Loading:
uniformly distributed vertical load

Deformations

Moments

Shear forces

Axial forces: N = 0

Systems

Vertical fixity   Horizontal fixity

Vertical fixity   Horizontal fixity
via lever arm   via lever arm

Fixity provided by propping

a = 3–8 m
h = l/5 to l/10
l = 5–30 m

Plane frames

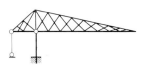

as solid-web or box beam

a = 5–10 m
h = l/5 to l/10
l = 10–30 m

as truss
l = 10–30 m

a = 6–12 m
h = l/4 to l/6
l = 10–50 m

Plane frames with rigid corner

a = 3–6 m
h = l/5 to l/10
l = 5–20 m

45 · Olympic velodrome

Munich, D; 1972

Architects: Dahms, Grube, Harden, Kaiser und Laskowski, Braunschweig, D

Structural engineering consultants: Natterer Bois-Consult, Etoy, CH

The roof over seating for 4700 spectators and the track of the velodrome built for the 1972 Olympic Games. A total of 56 frames at approx. 6 m centres supported at different levels and cantilevering out between 11 and 24 m encompass the whole track. Every frame consists of one top and one bottom member. The bottom member carries the load of the seating and is supported by a reinforced concrete ring beam. The top member forms the roof. Both top and bottom members consist of 160–230 mm wide twin beams that are 1400–2200 mm deep at the point of fixity and 600 mm deep at the end of the cantilever. Each pair of members is joined by a three-part strut and by a hinge in tension at the rearward cantilever to form a frame corner. The hinge consists of steel boxes and adjustable ties. The forces are transferred to the timber by way of nail plates and pins. The strut is also connected by means of nail plates and pins in order to achieve a true hinge and adjustability of the cantilever. Wind loads and bracing to the roof surface is by way of 100 mm web plates up to 2400 mm deep between the frames in the vicinity of the strut, and by a girder of steel circular hollow sections near the cantilever.

Detail 4/1972

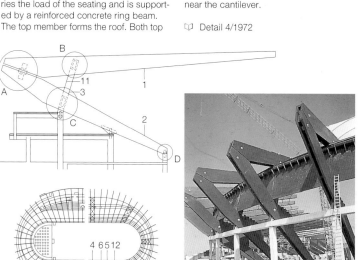

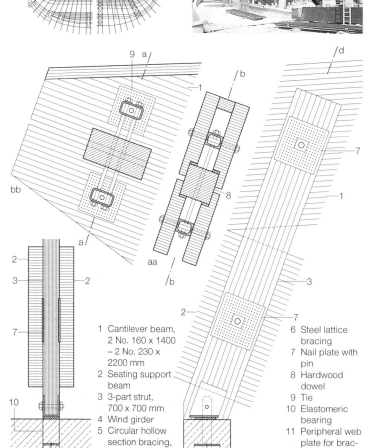

1 Cantilever beam,
  2 No. 160 x 1400
  – 2 No. 230 x
  2200 mm
2 Seating support
  beam
3 3-part strut,
  700 x 700 mm
4 Wind girder
5 Circular hollow
  section bracing,
  76–168 mm dia.

6 Steel lattice
  bracing
7 Nail plate with
  pin
8 Hardwood
  dowel
9 Tie
10 Elastomeric
  bearing
11 Peripheral web
  plate for bracing purposes

Secondary loadbearing systems as bracing

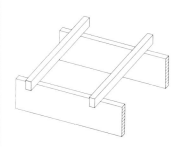

Additional lateral restraint required when secondary beams simply supported on main beams

Diagonal secondary members provide lateral restraint

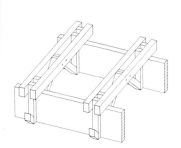

K-braced purlins provide lateral restraint

Inverted K-braced purlins provide lateral restraint and space for a trough gutter

Secondary loadbearing systems as bracing

46 · Roof over spectator seating, Waldau Stadium

Stuttgart, D; 1998

Architects: Herrmann + Bosch, Stuttgart, D

Structural engineers: Pfefferkorn und Partner, Stuttgart, D

The (in section) wing-shaped laminated veneer lumber (LVL) roof construction is supported by a system of steel tension and compression members. The axial forces from dead loads and wind are transferred into the reinforced concrete beams beneath the seating and into the foundation.

The top and bottom chords of the "wing" each consist of a prefabricated LVL board 17 m long x 1.80 m wide. Between the boards there is a framework of individual glued laminated timber ribs whose size matches the bending moment diagram. All the timber sections therefore have identical degrees of utilisation in structural terms, resulting in a very slim roof structure.

Cantilever beam

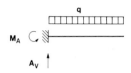

Loading:
uniformly distributed vertical load

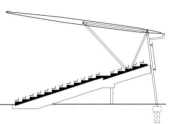

1 Glulam rib, 70 mm thk
2 Longitudinal steel beam
3 27 mm LVL
4 Cover strip over joint between boards
5 Glulam rib at joint between boards, 14 mm thk
6 LVL section

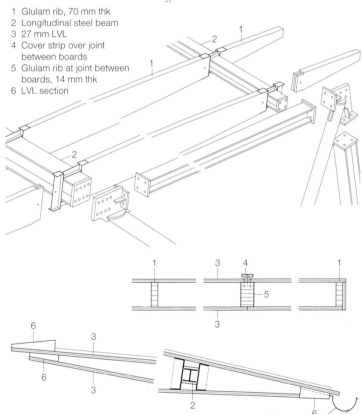

Deformations:

$$v = q \cdot \frac{l^4}{8} \cdot E \cdot J$$

Moments:

$$\min M = - q \cdot \frac{l^2}{2}$$

Shear forces:

$$\max V = q \cdot l$$

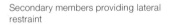
Diagonal secondary members between I-beams

Secondary members providing lateral restraint

K-braced purlins between I-beams

Axial forces: N = 0

Three-pin frames
without tie, solid cross-sections

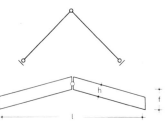

a = 5–8 m
h = l/30 to l/50
l = 15–30 m
f ≥ l/3

with trussed members

with tie, solid cross-sections

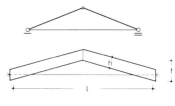

a = 5–8 m
h = l/30 to l/50
l = 15–50 m
f ≥ l/6

with tie cranked downwards

with raised, crossing ties

47 · St Blasius' Church

Schallstadt, D; 1994

Architects: Archbishopric Building
Department, Freiburg, D

Structural engineer: K. Liermann,
Freiburg, D

The roof to the body of the church consists of several Polonceau trusses, with
the glulam top chord being trussed three
times. The struts are softwood while the
tensile forces are resisted by a steel trussing arrangement. The remaining horizontal
thrust is resisted by a reinforced concrete
ring beam. The rafters were pre-assembled
in pairs and lifted onto the ring beam. The
individual roof frames are joined together
by a ridge purlin and braced in the longitudinal direction by the rafters at the ends
of the building.

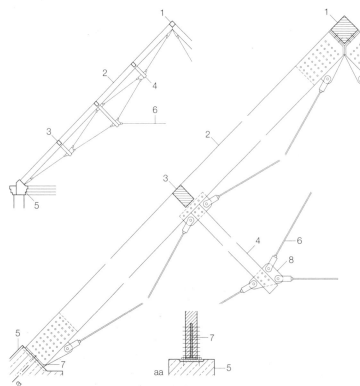

1 Softwood ridge purlin, 260 x 260 mm
2 Glulam top chord, 160 x 360 mm
3 Softwood purlin, 160 x 260 mm
4 Softwood strut, 160 x 160 mm

5 Reinforced concrete ring beam
6 Tie, 36 mm dia. threaded steel bar
7 Abutment, 25 mm welded steel plate
8 Gusset plate, 25 mm thk

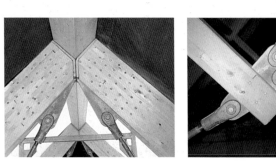

Supports for pinned members

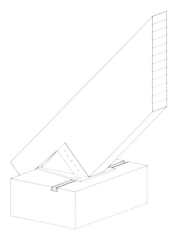

with steel bracket and rail for
adjustment

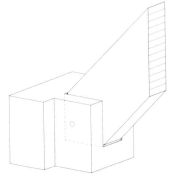

in concrete pocket with elastomeric
bearing

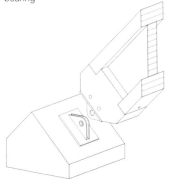

with end plate and hinge pin

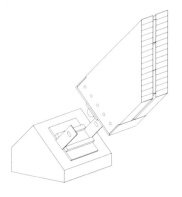

with rocker bearing and steel lugs
both sides

Pinned ridge joints

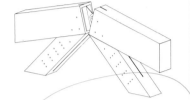

with steel plate let into slits plus hinge pin

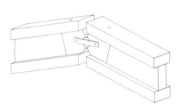

with hardwood block and steel plates on both sides

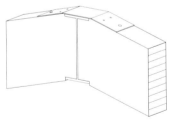

with members notched to accommodate I-section plus top plate to resist tension

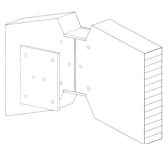

with members notched to accommodate I-section plus side plates to resist tension

48 · Indoor riding arena

Schwaiganger, D; 1979

Architects: M. Eberl, H. Weippert, Munich

Structural engineers: Natterer und Dittrich Planungsgesellschaft, Munich

A three-pin triangular frame spanning 27.5 m carries the roof over this indoor riding arena. The top chords in the form of pairs of glued laminated timber sections are trussed by round steel ties. They meet the timber struts at a steel gusset and continue as a single steel member up to the ridge joint. Pairs of timber struts link these nodes in the longitudinal direction. The roof frames are propped against the fixed-base reinforced concrete columns every 5 m. Spliced purlins of solid timber carry the roof decking in between. Wind girders for longitudinal stability are provided in three bays. The main frames guarantee stability in the transverse direction. Horizontal loads are carried via the concrete columns down to the foundations.

aa

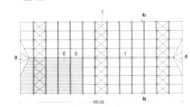

bb

1 2 No. 160 x 900 mm glulam sections
2 2 No. 160 x 160 mm glulam sections
3 200 x 200 mm glulam section
4 Steel tie
5 Glulam spliced purlin, 180 x 180 mm
6 Softwood spliced purlin, 140 x 180 mm
7 Wind girder of round steel bars

Three-pin frame

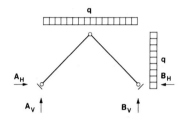

Loading:
uniformly distributed vertical and horizontal loads

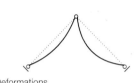

Deformations

Moments

Shear forces

Axial forces

189

Three-pin plane frames
as trusses

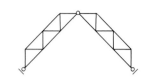

a = 5–8 m
h = l/15 to l/25
l = 15–50 m

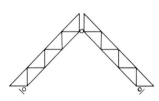

Three-pin plane frames without tie

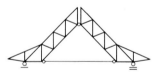

Change in pitch

Symmetrical arrangement with raised
eaves

Asymmetrical arrangement

49 · Ice rink

Deggendorf, D; 1973

Architects: Deggendorf Building Department

Structural engineers: Natterer Bois-Consult, Etoy, CH

A roof over an existing ice rink: in the transverse direction three-pin frames with ties spanning 48 m at 8.5 m centres. The two-part beams are not equal in length and one beam is cranked to match the existing building. The steel ties are slightly inclined and painted with a fire-retardant intumescent paint.

The braced purlins, 160 x 260 mm at 2.5 m centres, carry 19 mm plywood decking with nailed ribs. This construction produces an effective folded plate structure which distributes the overturning and wind loads in the longitudinal direction over several fixed-base reinforced concrete columns. It also enables good water run-off and "softens" the appearance of the 2250 mm deep main beams.

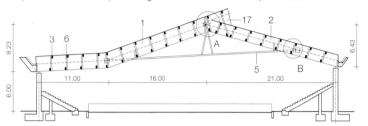

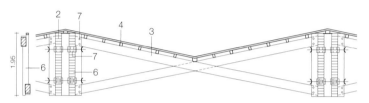

1 Main beam, 2 No. 220 x 2250 mm
2 Main beam, 2 No. 220 x 1950 mm
3 Purlin, 160 x 260 mm
4 19 mm plywood with 100 x 100 mm
  and 60 x 100 mm ribs
5 Twin round steel ties

6 Timber connecting blocks for
  braced purlins, 160 x 200 mm
7 65 mm dia. connectors
8 Reinforced nail plate
9 Disc spring washer
10 70 mm dia. hinge pin
11 Timber spacer,
   200 (220) x 250 mm
12 Steel plate let into slits, with
   shear connector
13 Dormer beam,
   2 No. 200 x 850 mm

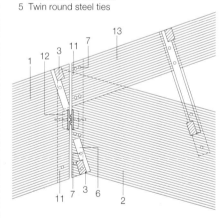

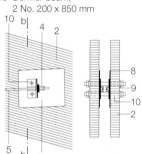

A

B

bb

plate let into slit in beam

stirrup fixed to sides of hanger, height-adjustable

stirrup fixed to sides of hanger

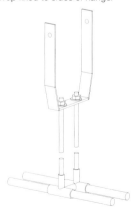

height-adjustable stirrup

Adjustable tie connections

Tensioning ring with nuts

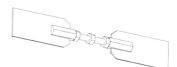

Turnbuckle with opposing threads

Threaded bar with opposing threads,
nuts and locknut

with tensioning socket and locknuts

with opposing threads, adjustable

50 · Ice rink

St Ulrich, I; 1980

Architects: I. Zimperlich, Garmisch, D;
F. Trafojer, Bozen, I

Structural engineers: K. Malknecht, H.
Meinhardt, Vöcklamarkt, A

Three-pin tied lattice beams span in the
transverse direction over the ice rink,
which measures 60.5 x 81 m. These are
supported every 12 m, sometimes on
pinned-end columns, sometimes on
rigid supports. The three-part chords are connected to the diagonals via dowels in multiple shear, oblique dado joints or finger
joints. Pieces are glued to the ends of
some members in order to strengthen
them and accommodate the connections.
The purlins are staggered from bay to bay
by the depth of the beam and are propped
at mid-span between the top chords.
They are also braced by girders in the
plane of the roof in order to provide stability for the main beams. The lower roof surface is carried by trussed secondary
beams. The main roof beams were erected in pairs at one end of the building and
slid into position on rails.

📖 Holzkurier 81/21; Bauen mit Holz 10/81

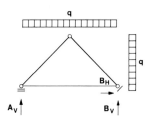

aa

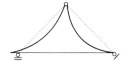

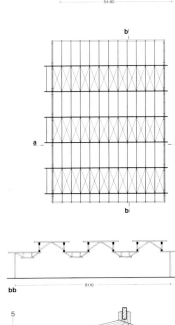

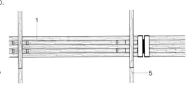

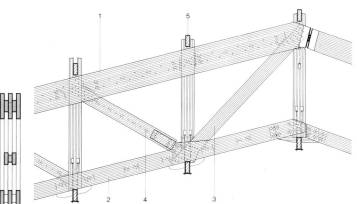

1 Glulam top
   chord, 3 No.
   160 x 1000 mm;
   spacers, 2 No.
   160 x 450 mm
2 Glulam bottom
   chord, 3 No.
   160 x 600 mm

3 Glulam tie, 2 No.
   160 x 500 mm
4 Glulam strut, 2
   No. 160 x 500
   mm; spacers,
   160 x 350 mm
5 Glulam section,
   180 x 350 mm

Three-pin frame with tie

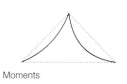

Loading: uniformly distributed vertical
and horizontal loads

Deformations

Moments

Shear forces

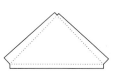

Axial forces

Three-pin frames with raised tie (collar)

fabricated from solid sections

fabricated from cranked solid sections

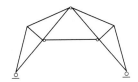

resolved into separate members

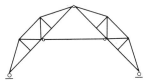

as parabolic plane frame

Three-pin frames in three dimensions

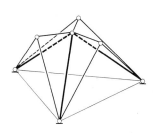

Symmetrical arrangement

51 · Parish hall

Munich, D; 1976

Architects: Riemerschmid, Burger, Schützenhuber, Munich

Structural engineers: Natterer und Dittrich Planungsgesellschaft, Munich

Collar beams in a radial arrangement meet off-centre above this octagonal parish hall. The hip beams, in pairs, run from the four corners to the apex, where they are joined together with dowels via a steel fish-plate to form a rigid connection. The four steel connecting plates are welded to a steel tube from which the collar beams are suspended on a ring nut. Glued laminated timber plates form the connection between hip beams and collar beams. The elastomeric bearings on the fixed-base concrete columns can move with respect to the fixed points. Rings of vertical purlins carry the roof decking of 45 mm planks. These are connected to the hip beams by way of metal plates let into slits and dowels. All beams are fabricated from glued laminated timber. Overall stability is guaranteed by the collar beams. Horizontal loads are transferred to the concrete substructure at the fixed points.

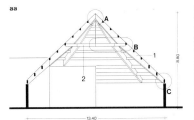

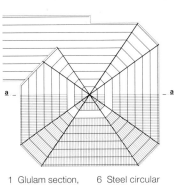

1 Glulam section, 140 x 400–800 mm
2 Glulam section, 140 x 270 mm
3 Glulam section, 120 x 550 mm
4 Glulam section, 120 x 300 mm
5 Glulam plate, 100 x 250 mm
6 Steel circular hollow section, 76 mm dia.
7 Round steel bar, 30 mm dia.
8 Channel section, 80 mm
9 Gusset plate, 15 mm thk
10 M16 bolt
11 Dowel, 14 mm dia.

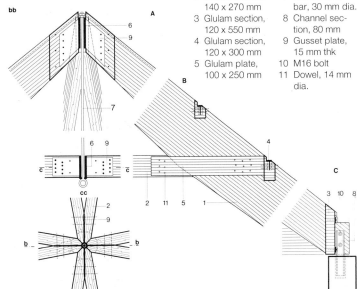

Collar connections

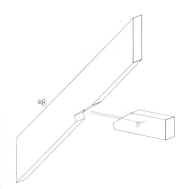

with oblique dado joint and "Simplex connector"

with twin members nailed or dowelled

with oblique dado joint and nailed fish-plates

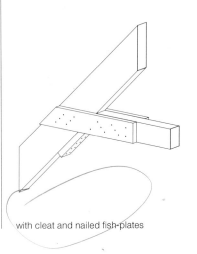

with cleat and nailed fish-plates

Collar connections

with twin members and hinge pin

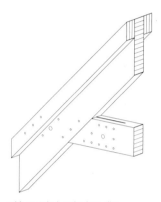

with metal plate let into slits

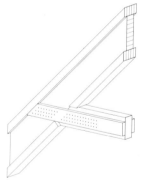

with fish-plates and oblique dado joint

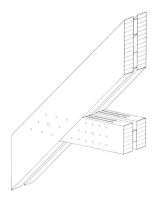

with several metal plates let into slits

52 · Chihiro art gallery

Azumino, J; 1995

Architects: Hiroshi Naito Architect & Associates, Tokyo, J

Structural engineers: Structural Design Group, Tokyo, J

In order to keep the external appearance of this museum as compact is possible, the roof was subdivided into a number of duopitch sections. Solid larch wood was used for the rafters. The curved glued laminated timber collar beams carry the ridge purlin and help to brace the roof. The roof construction does not use any visible metal parts.

1 Roof make-up:
  standing seam metal sheet
  waterproofing
  12 mm roof decking
  50 mm insulation
  45 x 50 mm battens
  vapour barrier
  30 mm larch decking
2 Larch rafter, 90 x 120 mm
3 Larch glulam collar beam, 50 x 60 mm
4 Larch glulam purlin, 120 x 277 mm

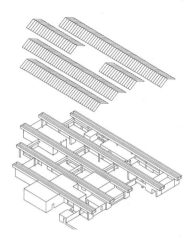

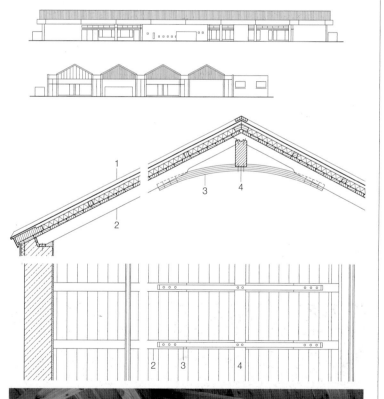

Pinned collar system

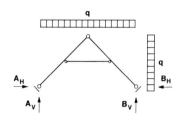

Loading:
uniformly distributed vertical and horizontal loads

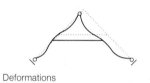

Deformations

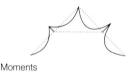

Moments

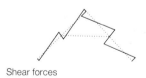

Shear forces

Axial forces

Three-pin frames with raised tie (collar)

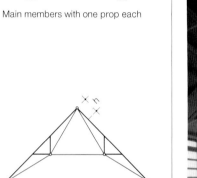

Main members with one prop each

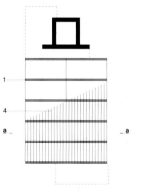

Main members with two props each

Main members with three props each

Four-pin frame

a = 5–8 m

$h = \frac{l}{20}$ to $\frac{l}{35}$

l = 15–50 m

53 · St Martin's Church

Ingolstadt, D; 1979–81

Architects: A. Hempel, F. Brand, Munich

Structural engineers: Sailer + Stepan, Munich

A symmetrical 45° pitched roof spans the 20 m wide nave of this church. The glued laminated timber two-part main rafters at 5.0 m centres form a three-pin frame trussed with steel struts and ties. The roof structure is supported on fixed-base rein-forced concrete columns that accommo-date wind loads in the longitudinal and transverse directions. Continuous solid timber purlins and 36 mm tongue and groove timber diagonal decking form the secondary loadbearing system. The roof structure is braced by the plate effect of the decking. The steel nodes are restrained in the longitudinal direction by a round steel bar fastened to the gable walls. The cold deck roof construction has clay roof-ing tiles on counter battens.

☐ Baumeister 10/82;
Bauen mit Holz 6/84

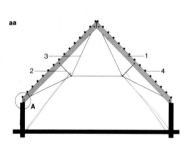

1 Glulam main
   rafter, 2 No.
   200 x 600 mm
2 Steel strut
3 Steel tie

4 Purlin,
   200 x 200 mm
5 Fixing for tie
6 Articulated
   bearing

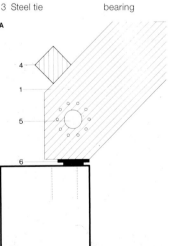

Tie-ridge connection

as simple suspension with welded T-section

with bearing plate and welded web, ties connected with fish-plates

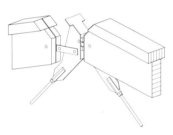

with bearing plate and connecting web, ties fabricated from threaded steel bars

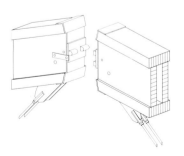

comprising steel bracket with connecting web and rocker nibs, ties in pairs

Post-trussing connection in three dimensions

Metal plate let into slits, with web plate and screwed connections

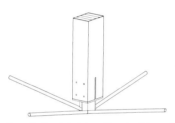

Dowelled metal plate, with web plate and welded ties

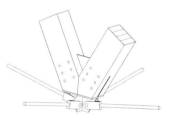

V-posts, metal plate let into slits, with web plate

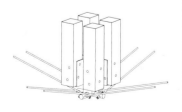

Four separate posts, ties made from threaded reinforcing bars

54 · Church centre

Eckerhaid, D; 1988

Architect: H.-J. Zeitler, Munich

Structural engineers: Natterer und Dittrich Planungsgesellschaft, Munich

The roof structure to this church centre is formed by four intersecting duopitch roofs surmounted by a pyramid roof at the centre. The pyramid roof, with timber columns at the corners, covers a square area of 8.5 x 8.5 m. Trussed glued laminated timber beams are used for the hips. The horizontal connection between the nodes means that the "elevated columns" are braced. Column bracing in three dimensions is via prestressed tendons that connect the column bases to the trussing arrangement. The edge beams of glued laminated timber act as a peripheral tie for this three-dimensional and as two-span beams carrying the rafters. All joints use steel gusset plates let into slits and fixed with dowels. The rafters run parallel to the pitch of the roof and are formed as profiled timber beams.

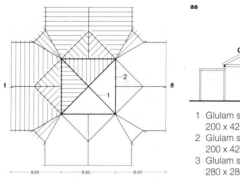

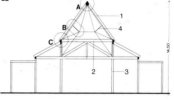

1 Glulam section, 200 x 420 mm
2 Glulam section, 200 x 420 mm
3 Glulam section, 280 x 280 mm
4 Strut, 120 x 120 mm
5 Round steel bar, 20 mm dia.
6 Gusset plate, 8 mm thk
7 Metal plate, 10 mm thk
8 Dowel, 12 mm dia.
9 M24 bolt

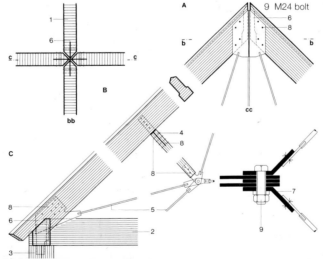

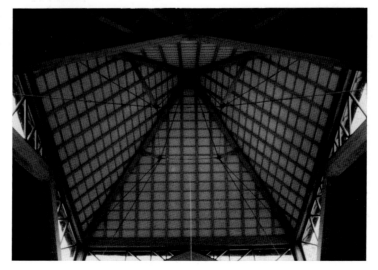

Three-pin frame with trussed members

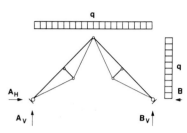

Loading:
uniformly distributed vertical and horizontal loads

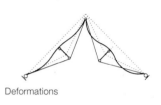

Deformations

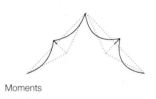

Moments

Shear forces

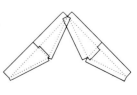

Axial forces

Solid-web sections

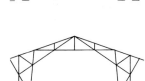

Resolved into separate members

55 · Sports centre

Roanne, F; 1988

Architect: Hiatus, Roanne, F

Structural engineers: M. Flach, R. Weisrock S.A., Saulcy-sur-Meurthe, F

This grandstand and roof construction for a sports centre with seating for 3000 spectators consists of symmetrical frames supported at different levels with a hinge at the ridge. The bottom two-part glued laminated timber members carry a terraced arrangement of intermediate timber members carrying the loads of the seating; the

upper, one-piece, member forms the roof beam. These two members are joined together with a ring of dowels. The lower section of each one-piece strut is strengthened against buckling. The grandstand terracing is made from prefabricated reinforced concrete units. Transverse stability is by means of steel diagonals and struts between the bottom beams. Simply-supported glulam purlins carry the roof covering of trapezoidal profile metal sheeting. Bracing in the plane of the roof is by diagonal glulam members. Horizontal forces in the longitudinal direction are transferred to the foundations by diagonal steel circular hollow sections.

1 160 x 940– 1750 mm
2 2 No. 140 x 1210 mm
3 Glulam strut, 160 x 730 mm
4 Glulam purlin, 80 x 350 mm
5 Glulam wind girder, 110 x 220 mm
6 160 x 250 mm glulam sec.
7 Round steel bar, 27 mm dia.
8 Steel circular hollow section, 140 mm dia.
9 Steel bracket
10 Dowel, 24 mm dia.
11 M24 bolt
12 M20 bolt
13 110 x 260 mm glulam section

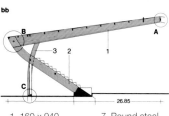

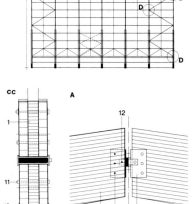

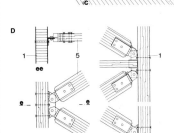

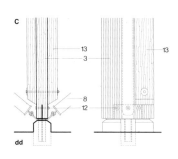

Rigid frame corner with one-piece solid cross-section

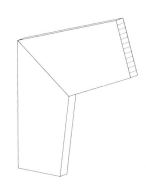

with finger joint

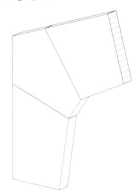

with two finger joints

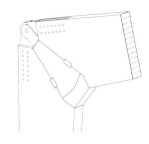

with metal plate let into slits for tension, hardwood block for compression

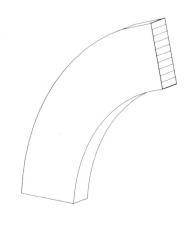

curved corner

Tension perpendicular to the grain at the ridge in curved beams

Cover piece not bonded to beam

Web plate as reinforcement

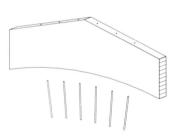

Tension perpendicular to grain resisted by bonded-in threaded bars

Finger joint with pretensioned threaded bar and disc spring washer

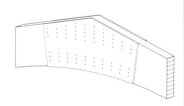

Particleboard, plywood or laminated veneer lumber attached by means of nail-pressure gluing

56 · Ice rink

Verbier, CH; 1983

Architect: A. Zufferey, Sierre, CH

Structural engineers: Natterer Bois-Consult, Etoy, CH

Primary loadbearing system for the roof of statically indeterminate frames designed for a uniformly distributed snow load of approx. 8 kN/m². The construction can be continued as continuous frames for roofing over the adjacent outdoor sports areas. Steel flats are used to tie back the frame. The main struts in the frame were designed for 400 t compression. Tension connections employ nailed metal plates and pins; forces are transferred by direct contact at the main compression nodes with a glued beech plywood block. The secondary beams spanning 10 m are designed as strut frames which, as the depth of the roof construction varies, are formed using identical geometrical principles.

📖 Schweizerische Holzzeitung 23/85; Schweizer Holzbau 9/85

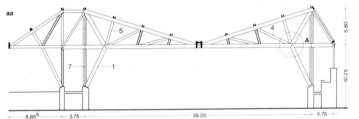

1 5 No. 200 x 600 mm
2 3 No. 200 x 600 mm
3 2 No. 200 x 600 mm
4 3 No. 200 x 360 mm
5 200 x 400 mm
6 3 No. 200 x 620 mm
7 200 x 600 mm + 2 No. 200 x 270 mm
8 2 No. 120 x 260 mm + 120 x 160 mm
9 27 mm plywood block
10 Plywood block
11 Metal plate, 8 mm thk
12 Dowel, 20 mm dia.

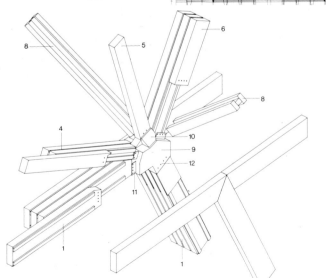

Single-pin frame

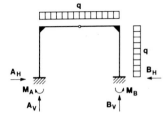

Loading:
uniformly distributed vertical and horizontal loads

Deformations

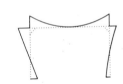

Moments

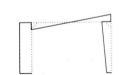

Shear forces

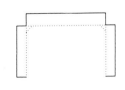

Axial forces

System variations for increasing loads

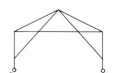

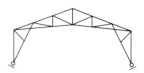

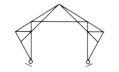

a = 5–8 m

h = l/10 – l/15

l = 15–50 m

57 · Tennis centre

Ulm, D; 1972

Architect: Reuter, Ulm

Structural engineers: J. Natterer and K. März, Munich

Multi-court tennis centre covering a total area of 70 x 31 m. The two-pin frames transverse to the building consist of one-piece beams, 160 x 1440 mm, and legs resolved as separate members. The central section of the raking leg (strut), 160 x 800 mm, is joined to the roof beam by means of an oblique dado joint, and the vertical leg (tie), 2 No. 100 x 280 mm, by means of 115 mm dia. metal connectors near the top of the roof beam. Along the length of the building trapezoidal profile metal sheeting spans the 5 m between the frames. Wind bracing and lateral restraint is provided by trapezoidal profile metal sheeting and steel flat diagonals connected to the adjacent masonry/concrete structures.

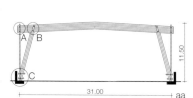

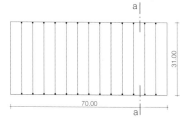

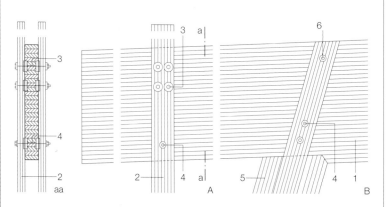

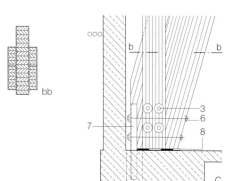

1 Roof beam, 160 x 1440 mm
2 Tie, 2 No. 100 x 280 mm
3 Pairs of connectors, 115 mm dia.
4 16 mm dia. bolt in elongated hole
5 Strut, 160 x 800 mm, with 100 x 280 mm plates
6 16 mm dia. pin
7 200 mm steel channel section to resist horizontal thrust
8 Bitumen felt

Base details for frames resolved into separate members

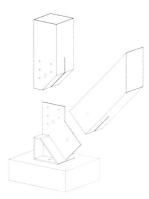

Steel plate let into slits, connected with steel dowels

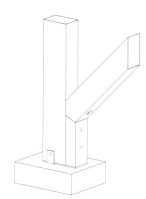

with cleat and cast-in base plate

with hardwood block and T-sections

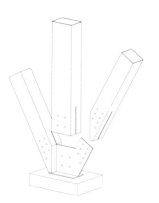

with steel plate let into slits for securing members in position and for resisting uplift loads

Base details for legs of frames resolved into separate members

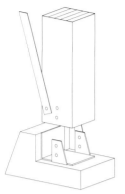

with cast-in base plate, screwed tie

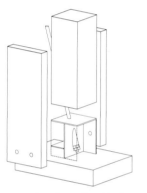

on steel section, adjustable tie

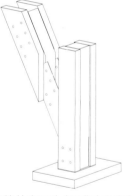

with U-shaped, dowelled steel plate fitted between members

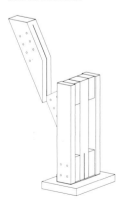

with dowelled steel plate let into slits

58 · Sports centre

Künzelsau, D; 1999

Architects: G. D'Inka + Scheible, Fellbach, D

Structural engineer: E. Schwarz, Künzelsau, D

The structure supporting the roof over this sports centre was designed as a two-pin frame. The top and bottom chords of the timber lattice beams spanning the full width of the building are in pairs with the diagonals fitted between them. A solid web of laminated veneer lumber (LVL) enabled rigid frame corners to be created above the two V-form columns. There are two further lattice beams between each of the main beams, which transfer their loads into longitudinal ridge and eaves beams.

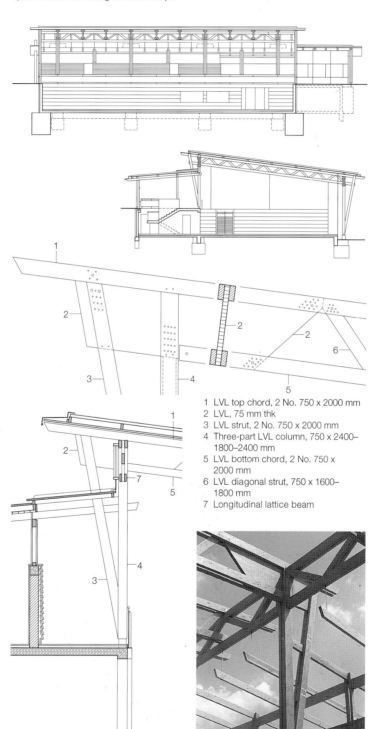

1 LVL top chord, 2 No. 750 x 2000 mm
2 LVL, 75 mm thk
3 LVL strut, 2 No. 750 x 2000 mm
4 Three-part LVL column, 750 x 2400–1800–2400 mm
5 LVL bottom chord, 2 No. 750 x 2000 mm
6 LVL diagonal strut, 750 x 1600–1800 mm
7 Longitudinal lattice beam

Two-pin frame

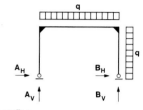

Loading:
uniformly distributed vertical and horizontal loads

Deformations

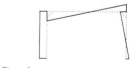

Moments

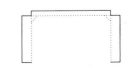

Shear forces

Axial forces

Three-pin frames

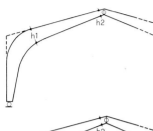

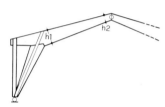

Glued laminated timber
a = 5–10 m
h_1 = l/20 to l/40
h_2 = l/30 to l/60
l = 10–50 m

Box sections or I-sections

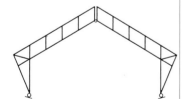

Continuous frames

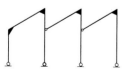

Sawtooth roof

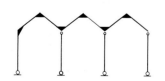

Multi-bay duopitch roof

59 · Warehouse

Weihenstephan, D; 1988

Architects: Weihenstephan Building Department; H. Geierstanger

Structural engineers: Lintl & Siebenson, Munich

A timber-frame construction with a tie forms the primary loadbearing system for this warehouse. Daylight enters the building through a continuous strip of glazing at the ridge. Long overhanging eaves give protection to agricultural vehicles and trailers underneath. The rafters and columns use I-sections with solid webs made from wood-based products. Transverse stability is ensured by the frame with its fixed-base columns. The tie is placed low to clear the suspended walkway and must thus penetrate the main columns so as to be joined to the cantilevering eaves. The connections employ reinforced nail plates, which transfer the forces to a pin/steel fish-plate connection. Steel diagonals provide lateral restraint to the webs and reduce the buckling length of the rafters. T-shaped glued laminated timber purlins support the roof covering of wood-based boards. Horizontal loads in the longitudinal direction are resisted by St Andrew's crosses in the facade.

Roof covering omitted for clarity

1 Rafter, 240 x 900 mm
2 I-section column, 320 x 420 mm
3 Glulam purlin, 140 x 240 mm + 80 x 120 mm

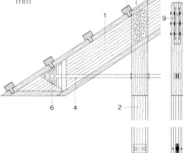

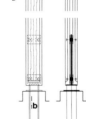

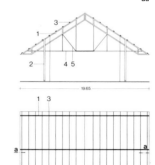

4 Tie
5 Tie
6 Nail plate
7 Steel fish-plate
8 16 mm dia. pin
9 Timber spacer

Rigid frame corners

with gusset plates let into slits

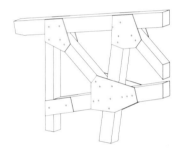

with gusset plates nailed to sides of members

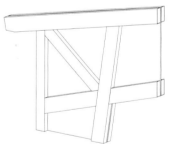

Solid-web beam, glued, nailed or nail-pressure glued

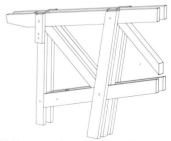

Multi-part members with pins and shear-plate/split-ring or toothed-plate connectors

Rigid frame corners with multi-part members

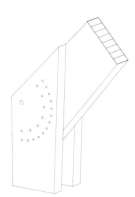

with dowels arranged in an arc

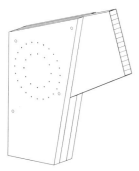

with ring of dowels

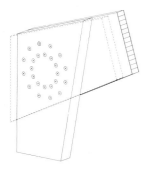

with ring of shear-plate/split-ring connectors

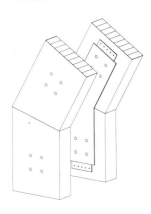

with pins

60 · Haithabu Viking Museum

Schleswig, D; 1982-83

Architects: Central Planning Office, Kiel, D

Structural engineer: H. Mohn, Kiel, D

A three-pin frame made from glued laminated timber sections, 250 x 500 mm and 250 x 550 mm, positioned every 1.20 m, span 10.80 m and 12.96 m, height to ridge 6.20 m and 7.50 m. Finger-jointed frame corners and central section. Hinged ridge connection: HEB 200 steel section with steel plates both sides. Column base: steel support with central web, anchored in foundation by way of welded HEB 100 section. The glued laminated timber beam, 250 x 700 mm, along the ridge is non-loadbearing. Reinforced concrete gable walls provide the necessary stability. Prefabricated timber elements are fitted between the loadbearing timber frame members.

📖 Bauen mit Holz 10/84

1 Three-pin frame
2 Ridge beam
3 Reinforced concrete gable wall
4 Finger-jointed frame corner
5 HEB 200
6 Steel support with central web
7 12 mm dia. dowel
8 M16 threaded bar
9 HEB 100
10 Steel plate both sides

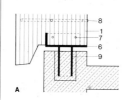

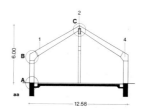

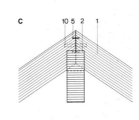

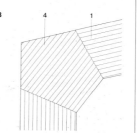

Three-pin frame with tie

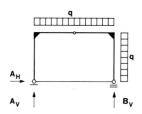

Loading:
uniformly distributed vertical and horizontal loads

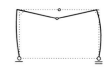

Deformations

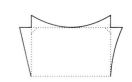

Moments

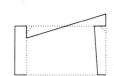

Shear forces

Axial forces

Plane frame systems

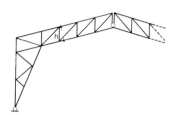

Truss frames
a = 7–10 m
h = l/ to l/18
l = 15–50 m

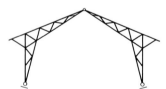

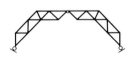

61 · Indoor riding arena

Munich-Riem, D; 1974

Architects: G. and I. Küttinger, Munich

Structural engineer: J. Natterer, Munich

Three-pin trusses span in the transverse direction. The parallel top and bottom chords are each in two parts, the diagonals and posts just single members. Connections are by way of steel plates let into slits (Borg system). Tension leg in one piece, compression leg two pieces. The purlins span 7.0 m in the longitudinal direction but are propped from the bottom chord of the main roof beams. Horizontal wind loads and the horizontal thrust from the purlin props are resisted by pressure-impregnated logs at the gables. To reduce the buckling length of the main beams, additional bracing is required in the plane of the roof and half-trusses around the frame's tension members.

📖 Detail 2/76; Bauen mit Holz 11/76, p. 519

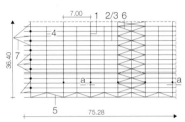

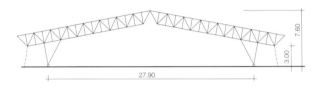

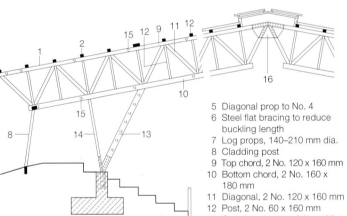

1 Frame
2 Purlin, 120 x 140 mm
3 Props to purlins
4 Strut for propping purlins in y-direction

5 Diagonal prop to No. 4
6 Steel flat bracing to reduce buckling length
7 Log props, 140–210 mm dia.
8 Cladding post
9 Top chord, 2 No. 120 x 160 mm
10 Bottom chord, 2 No. 160 x 180 mm
11 Diagonal, 2 No. 120 x 160 mm
12 Post, 2 No. 60 x 160 mm
13 Compression leg, 2 No. 160 x 220 mm
14 Tension leg, 2 No. 100 x 160 mm
15 50 mm dia. dowel
16 Plywood

Tie connection at end of beam

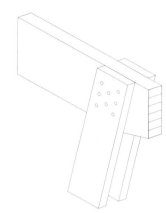

Pair of ties

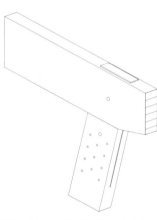

Metal plate let into slit, with end plate and dowels

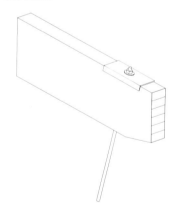

as a round steel bar with end plate

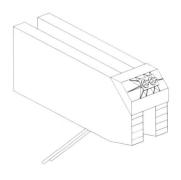

Two-part beam and ties fitted in between

Frame legs resolved into separate members

One-part column with steel flat ties

Three-part column with round steel bar tie

Three-part column with round steel bar tie

Two-part beam, three-part column and single timber tie

62 · Gymnasium

Donauwörth, D; 1984–85

Architects: E. Wachter and F. Meier, Munich

Structural engineers: Natterer und Dittrich Planungsgesellschaft, Munich

Three-pin frames in a radial arrangement. The hinge at the ridge is roughly at the third-point. The shorter side of the frame has a structural depth of 2.00 m, with the top chord in the plane of the roof. The longer side is 2.60 m deep and the top chord forms the hip of the raised glazed rooflights. Chords, posts and diagonals are fabricated from 260 mm wide glulam sections connected at the nodes by two metal plates let into slits and dowelled. The secondary beams connect the posts of the lattice beams in the longitudinal direction of the building. Kneebraces and struts to the glazed lantern lights reduce the span of the secondary beams and provide lateral restraint to the chords of the main beams. Rafters following the slope of the roof support the roof decking. Stability in the transverse direction is by way of the three-pin frames, and in the longitudinal direction via the roof plate effect and vertical girders between the facade columns.

aa

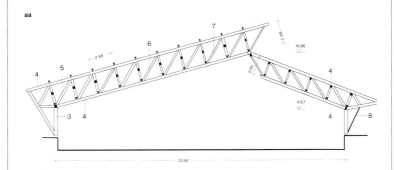

bb

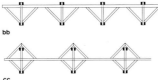

cc

1 Primary beam
2 Secondary beam
3 Column, 400 x 280 mm
4 260 x 280 mm
5 260 x 260 mm
6 200 x 260 mm
7 160 x 260 mm
8 Round steel bar, grade St 52, 2 No. 76 mm dia.

Three-pin frame with duopitch roof beam

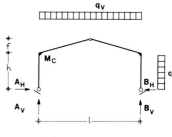

$$A_v = B_v = \frac{q_v \, l}{2}$$

$$A_H = B_H = \frac{1}{8} \, \frac{q \, l^2}{(h + f)}$$

Loading:
uniformly distributed vertical and horizontal loads

Deformations

Moments:

$$M_c = - \frac{q_v \, l^2 \cdot h}{8 \, (h + f)}$$

Shear forces

Axial forces

Polygonal frames

Solid-web members, supports at different levels

Solid-web members, symmetrical

Lattice beams, symmetrical

Radial arrangements

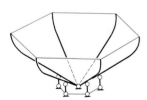

with tie at top

with central column

63 · St Ignatius' Church

Munich-Kleinhadern, D; 1974–79

Architects: J. Wiedemann, F. Christen, V. Westermayer, Munich

Structural engineer: C. Michael, Munich

A radial arrangement of three-pin frames forms the freestanding roof construction of this 12-sided church measuring 22 m across. The legs – subjected to bending – are made from two 300 mm dia poles. These are joined to the twin glued laminated timber rafters by pole struts on both sides. K-bracing, also made from poles, stabilises the columns in the transverse direction. The apex is formed by a steel ring of IPE sections plus steel circular hollow sections. The rings of solid timber purlins carry a radial arrangement of rafters with secondary rafters connected to the sides. The roof decking is laid with alternate open and closed joints for sound insulation purposes. Overall stability is by way of the three-dimensional action of the frame.

📖 Detail 1/83; Küttinger: Holzbau-Konstruktionen, Munich, 1984

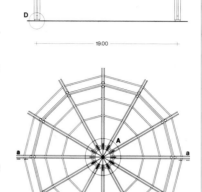

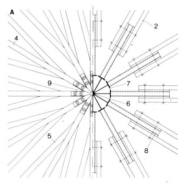

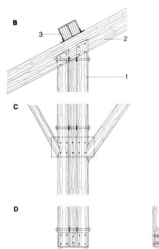

1 Column, 2 No. 300 mm poles
2 Pairs of glulam rafters, 2 No. 100 x 300 mm
3 Purlin, 250 x 350 mm
4 Main rafter
5 Secondary rafter
6 Round steel bar, 100 mm dia.
7 IPE 500
8 Steel rectangular hollow section, 220 x 120 x 10 mm
9 Steel flat, 370 x 60 x 8 mm

Rigid joint in two-pin frame, solid sections

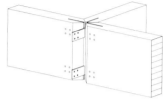

Vertical steel plates in star arrangement fitted to steel circular hollow section, let into slits and dowelled

Tension carried by dowelled metal plates, compression by concrete filling to joint, shear by shear connectors

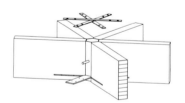

Detail as above but compression carried by LVL core

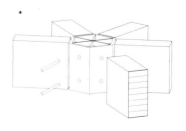

Steel node and bonded-in threaded bars

Hinged joint in three-pin frame

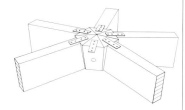

Hardwood core with bonded-in threaded bars

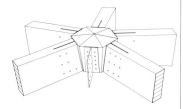

Hardwood core and T-sections let into slits

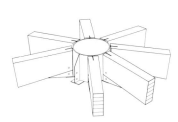

Steel ring with web and bearing plates

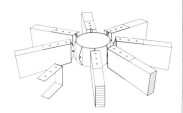

Steel ring with vertical lugs and the U-shaped straps screwed on

64 · Coal blending plant

Rekingen, CH; 1980

Structural engineer: G. Kämpf, Rupperswil

An industrial building with an external diameter of 68 m and a total height of 23 m. The hips between the roof sections at a pitch of 12° are formed by three-pin frames – I-section glued laminated timber beams connected to a concrete-filled steel apex and propped by a multi-part glulam ring beam. The hips between the roof sections at a pitch of 45° act as frames supported at different levels. The hip beams are again glued laminated timber I-sections and are propped against the ring beam. The intermediate glulam beams are simply supported between pinned-end columns and the ring beam. The solid timber purlins are designed as continuous over two bays generally, but as simply-supported in the shallow-pitch central roof section. These carry the fibre-cement roof covering. Every second bay includes diagonal bracing to stiffen the roof construction, brace the main beams and provide stability for asymmetric loads.

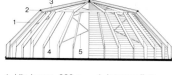

1 Hip beam, 220 x 120–160 mm
2 Glulam ring beam, 240 x 550 mm + 240 x 200 mm
3 Hip beam, 220 x 120 mm
4 Intermediate beam, 220 x 1000 mm
5 Bracing, 160 x 160 mm

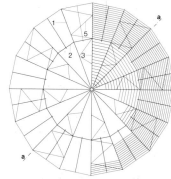

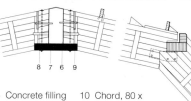

6 Concrete filling to void
7 Steel node, 180 mm thk
8 Groove to insert hardwood
9 Steel plate, 30 x 200 x 20 mm
10 Chord, 80 x 150 mm
11 Purlin, 200 x 100 mm
12 Strengthening to frame corner

Three-pin frame as polygon frame

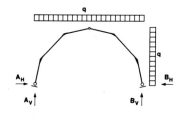

Loading:
uniformly distributed vertical and horizontal loads

Deformations

Moments

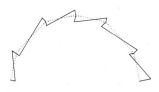

Shear forces

Axial forces

Solid-web systems

Radial-symmetrical arrangements

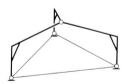

Symmetrical arrangement

Cumulative arrangement of radial frames

65 · Ice rink

Davos, CH; 1979

Architects: Krähenbühl, Davos, CH

Structural engineer: W. Bieler, Chur, CH

Three-dimensional three-pin arch system over an ice rink with seating for 7500. The diagonal valley beams – pairs of glued laminated timber sections – spanning 76.6 m, together with the gable and ridge beams, form the primary loadbearing system. Arches radiate from the bottom of each valley to the ridge beams. Glulam transverse members provide lateral restraint. The purlins are solid timber, and the decking of 40 mm diagonal planking, in addition to carrying the roof covering, also resists wind and buckling forces. Assembly sequence: erection of valley beams and gable beams joined together by the ridge beams.

    Lignum offprint; C. v. Büren: Form und Funktion, Basel/Boston/Stuttgart, 1985

1 Valley beam,
   2 No. 200 x
   1950 mm
2 Ridge beam,
   200 x 1910 mm
3 Intermediate
   beams, 2 No.
   140 x 1350 mm
   to 2 No. 160 x
   1680 mm
4 Purlin

5 Steel plate,
   30–40 mm
6 60 mm dia. pin
7 20 mm dia. pin
8 20 mm dia.
   dowel

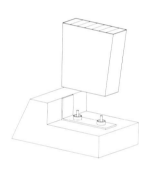

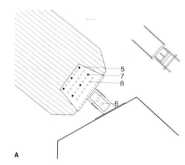

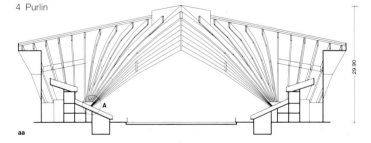

Frame base detail

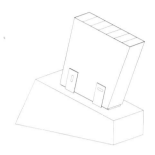

with cast-in steel lugs

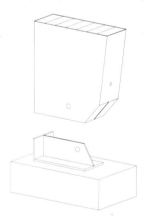

with split-ring connectors in end grain

with steel base plate let into slit

with concrete abutment and steel angles

Frame base detail

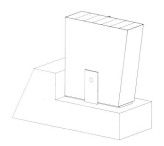

with concrete abutment and steel lugs

with steel base plate let into slit

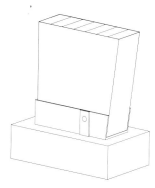

with channel section

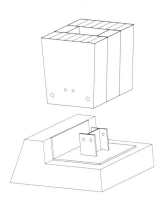

with I-section for box-section leg

66 · Bridge for heavy vehicles

Ravine, CH; 1989

Structural engineers: P. Buchs & J.-L. Plumey, Porrentruy; Natterer Bois-Consult, Etoy, CH

The brief called for the bridge to be able to carry agricultural equipment and timber transporters. Imposed load assumptions: uniformly distributed load of 2.5 kN/m^2, 2 x 60 kN point loads or a load train of 6 x 60 kN (roughly equivalent to SLW 30, DIN 1072); snow load: 1.04 kN/m^2 over 8 m roof width, plus braking and accelerating forces. The aim was to achieve a low number of joints and hence a low cost for the connectors. This led to a frame being chosen for the main loadbearing system. The horizontal forces are transferred via the rigid frame into the nodes of the main system top chord.

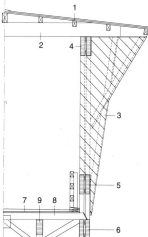

1 Softwood purlin, 100 x 160 mm
2 Glulam roof beam, 300 x 360 mm
3 Softwood frame, 140 x 140 mm, with diagonal cladding
4 Glulam frame element, 2 No. 120 x 430 mm
5 Glulam diagonal tie, 2 No. 120 x 360 mm
6 Glulam bottom chord, 2 No. 120 x 500 mm
7 33 mm planking
8 Transverse glulam deck beam, 180 x 180 mm, with steel flat trussing
9 Longitudinal glulam beam, 180 x 400 mm

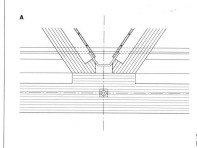

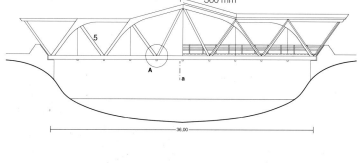

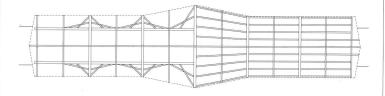

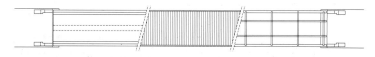

Continuous frame

Loading:
uniformly distributed vertical and horizontal loads

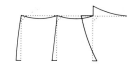
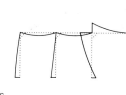

Deformations

Moments

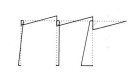

Shear forces

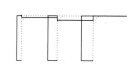

Axial forces

System variations

Double-T, box and solid-web sections of glued laminated timber

a = 5–10 m

h = l/35 – l/50

l = 30–100 m

h = l/6 – l/10

Circular arc

Asymmetric arch

Propped arch

Supported on A-frames with cellular infill

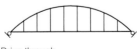

Lever arm providing fixity at centre of arch

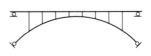

Cross-sections resolved into individual members, plus tie

Arches for bridges

Drive-through

Drive-over

67 · Bridge over River Emme

Signau, CH; 1988

Architects: Cantonal Building Department, Burgdorf, CH

Structural engineer: H. Vogel, Bern

This covered timber bridge with two fully passable carriageways uses a pair of two-part glued laminated timber arches spanning 43.40 m between concrete abutments. The bridge is suspended every 5 m on round steel bars carrying the glulam transverse deck beams. The deck itself is formed by 220 mm deep edge-glued timber laminations pretensioned perpendicular to the grain and anchored back to edge beams of glued laminated timber (beech). A waterproof plastic sheet is laid on the timber and then a continuous 60 mm thk wearing course. Wind forces are resisted by the bridge deck and the upper wind girder, which also provides lateral restraint to the main arches. The portal frame of glued laminated timber with glued plywood corners transfers forces from the upper girder to the supports. The roof is made of squared timber sections. The old wooden bridge with a pier in the middle of the river can be seen in the background in the photograph below.

  Schweizerische Holzzeitung 34/88; Schweizer Holzbau 11/88

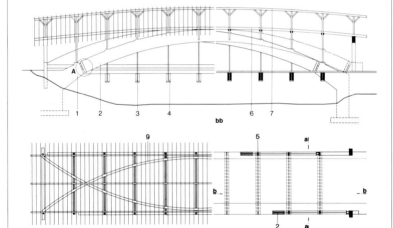

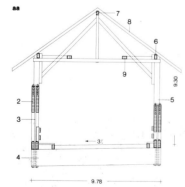

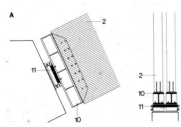

1	Concrete abutment		purlin, 180 x
2	Glulam arch, 2 No.		350 mm
	220 x 1900 mm	7	Ridge beam,
3	Hanger, 19 mm		180 x 280 mm
	dia. steel bar	8	Rafter, 100 x
4	Transverse glulam		180 mm
	deck beam, 2 No.	9	Glulam wind
	280 x 1200 mm		girder, 350 x
5	Glulam post, 400		200 mm
	x 200 mm	10	IPB 260
6	Glulam eaves	11	Neoprene pad

Arch base detail

Solid-web member with reinforced end and cast-in side lugs

Cellular member with reinforced end and cast-in side lugs

Glued laminated timber member on elastomeric bearing

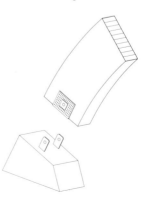

with nail plates and hinge pin

Arch base detail

with end plate and hinge pin

with end plate and transverse stiffeners

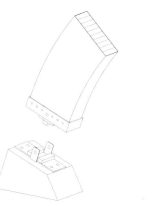

with end plate and rocker bearing, lateral restraint by means of cast-in lugs

with steel part for two-part arch member and heavy loads

68 · Tennis centre

Bezau, Vorarlberg, A; 1989

Architect: L. Kaufmann, Dornbirn, A

Structural engineer: Holzbauwerk Kaufmann, Bezau, A

The flat roof over this pair of tennis courts is raised clear of the main arches on struts in a V-formation. Three two-pin arches span over each court in the longitudinal direction and are supported 2.5 m above the floor on reinforced concrete abutments. Between the two courts there is a pair of inclined lattice beams carrying a walkway and, above it, a central continuous strip of glazing. The chords and posts are of glued laminated timber, the rising diagonals prestressing tendons. There is a support at mid-span formed by a pair of V-shaped columns. The continuous purlins perpendicular to the arches are supported every 4.5 m by timber V-struts. Transverse timber members join each pair of purlins at the support points so as to resist the horizontal component of the inclined strut. The building is braced in the longitudinal direction by the wind girders between the arches.

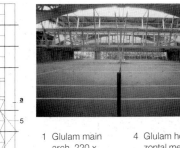

1 Glulam main arch, 220 x 1080 mm
2 Glulam V-struts, 140 x 140 mm
3 Glulam purlin, 140 x 250 mm
4 Glulam horizontal member, 140 x 140 mm
5 Wind girder
6 Top chord, bottom chord, walkway

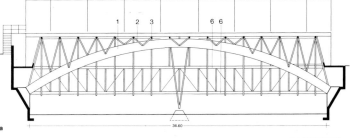

aa

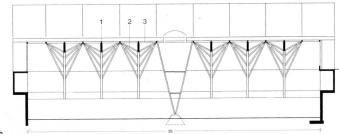

bb

Two-pin arch

Loading: uniformly distributed vertical load

$$A_V = B_V = \frac{q \cdot l}{2}$$

$$A_H = B_H = \frac{q \cdot l^2}{8\,f}$$

Deformations

Moments

Shear forces

Axial forces

Lattice beam systems

Lattice beam of glued laminated timber

a = 5–10 m

h = l/20 to l/40

l = 50–120 m

f = l/5 to l/8

Cellular crescent
lattice beam

with diagonals in compression
(Howe girder)

with diagonals in tension
(Pratt girder)

with X-bracing

69 · City hall

Gersfeld, D; 1987–88

Architects: Architektengemeinschaft
F. Füller

Structural engineer: R. Schnabel

This structure, originally an indoor riding arena, was built in 1907 and is protected by a preservation order. It was designed as a nailed laminated timber construction. The faithful reconstruction takes into account the current regulations and makes use of bonded glued laminated timber. A pretensioned steel tie connects the springing points of the two-pin lattice arches in order to counteract the horizontal thrust. Kneebraced secondary beams run the length of the building and provide lateral restraint to the arches. These are raised up on pairs of posts so as to produce the mansard roof form. The rafters carry timber decking, which provides a stiffening plate at roof level. Horizontal loads are transferred via the masonry walls into the foundations.

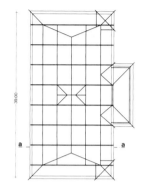

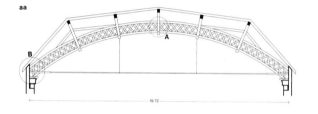

aa

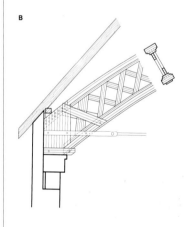

B

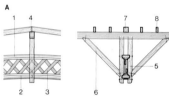

A

1 Glulam top chord, 160 x 150 mm
2 Glulam bottom chord, 160 x 150 mm
3 Diagonal, 50 x 100 mm
4 Glulam secondary beam, 180 x 240 mm
5 Pairs of softwood posts, 2 No. 160 x 180 mm
6 Softwood kneebrace, 160 x 180 mm
7 Rafter, 180 x 180 mm
8 Rafter, 80 x 180 mm

Rigid erection splices

Notched, with bonded-in
threaded bars

Scarf joint and fish-plates

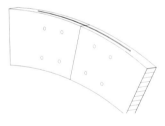

Metal plate let into slits
and dowelled

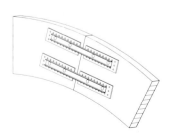

Nail plates with channel-section
fish-plates and pins

Purlin/I-section beam junction, also suitable for arches

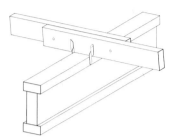

with metal framing anchors for shallow roof pitches

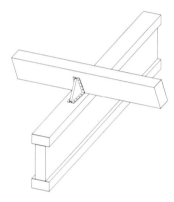

with stiffened angle

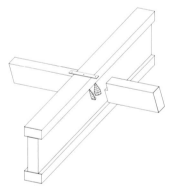

with joist hangers plus fish-plate for tension

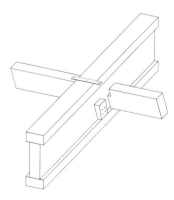

with cleats plus fish-plate for tension

70 · Olympic indoor sports stadium

Hamar, N; 1992

Architects and structural engineers: N. Torp, Biong & Biong, Oslo, N

The structural system for this 260 m long stadium covering 22 000 m² comprises two-pin frames with a rigid connection at the apex and hinges at the reinforced concrete abutments. Individual, 4 m deep lattice arches of different lengths span the hall. The maximum rise of these arches is 35 m, the maximum span 96 m. The glued laminated timber purlins support the roof covering of self-supporting corrugated steel sheets, thermal insulation and two layers of roofing felt. The shell form, purlins and large longitudinal beam provide the necessary stability. The structure is designed for a snow load of 2.5 kN/m².

▢ Detail 3/94

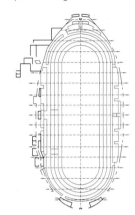

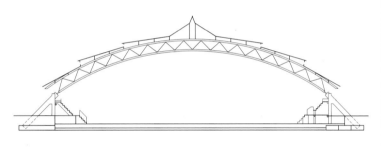

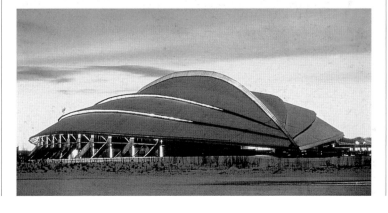

Two-pin arch

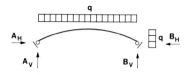

Loading:
uniformly distributed vertical and horizontal loads

Deformations

Moments

Shear forces

Axial forces

System variations

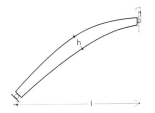

a = 4–6 m

h = l/30 to l/50
l = 30–100 m
f = l/5 to l/7

Basic form
line of thrust for uniformly distributed load
2nd order parabola

Hyperbolic arch with extensions

Asymmetrical arrangement for
supports at different levels

Continuous arch system

71 · School hall

Wohlen, Aargau, CH; 1987

Architects: Burkhard, Meyer, Steiger,
Baden, CH

Structural engineer: S. Calatrava, Zürich

A folded plate structure in spherical curvature spans over this multipurpose hall
measuring 15.65 x 20.04 m. Each of the
10 box elements was prefabricated off
site and consists of a T-section glued laminated timber bottom chord, an L-section
top chord, made in two parts to facilitate
erection, and the folded plates, which are
resolved into struts. These are connected
to the chords with concealed hexagon-
head wood screws and dowels. As the
size of the cross-section increases in the
longitudinal axis, additional threaded bars
are required for bracing near the support.
At the level of the top chord glued laminated timber longitudinal beams, counter
battens and roof decking form the framework for the insulated, ventilated roof construction. The arches gain lateral support
from the folded plate action and the plate
effect of the roof decking.

Schweizer Holzzeitung 47/88;
Bauen mit Holz 11/88

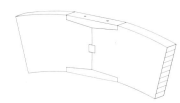

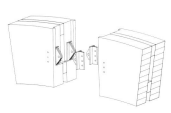

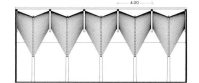

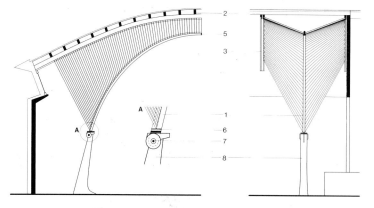

1 Elliptical three-pin arch	3 Two-part trans-verse arch		7 Hinge pin
2 Longitudinal beam	4 Struts		8 Concrete plinth
	5 Hinge		
	6 Steel plate		

Detail at apex

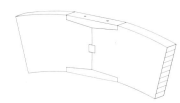

Shear forces transferred by hardwood
key, position secured by plates fitted top
and bottom

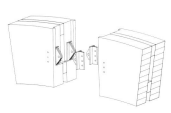

T-sections with webs let into slits,
plus plates and hinge pins

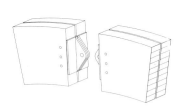

Dowelled steel plate with end plate,
webs and hinge pin

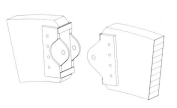

Side plates and hinge pin

Detail at apex

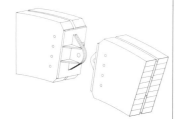

Dowelled steel plate with end plate,
stiffened web and hinge pin

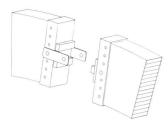

End plate with rocker nibs,
held in position by side lugs

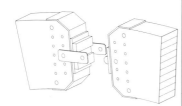

Stiffened end plate with rocker nibs,
held in position by side lugs

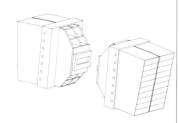

Detail for two-part members carrying
heavy loads

72 · Ice rink

Istres, F; 1981

Architects: Jaussaud & Vallières, Istres, F

Structural engineer: R. Weisrock S.A.,
Saulcy-sur-Meurthe, F

Two three-pin arches each of twin 1600 mm
deep glued laminated timber sections
span 59.2 m over this ice rink. Glulam
transverse beams between the arches,
together with a timber decking, provide
the lateral restraint. Simply-supported
secondary beams at 4.10 m centres are
supported on props on the arches and
create a continuous strip of glazing at the
level of the beams. These are carried on
concrete wall elements in the facade. The
secondary beams are braced by glulam
diagonals and steel circular hollow sections. The solid timber purlins carry the
roof decking. Overall stability in the longitudinal direction is provided by the main
arches, in the transverse direction by the
concrete columns around the periphery.

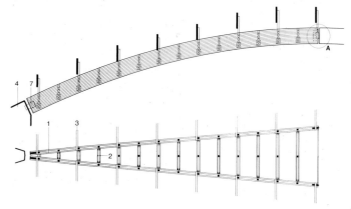

1	Pair of glulam main arches, 110 x 1600 mm	4	Concrete wall
		5	20 mm dia. pin
2	Glulam trans- verse beam,	6	26 mm dia. pin
		7	Steel bracket
3	Glulam secon- dary beam, 160 x 1260– 1600 mm	8	Steel plate, 4 mm thk
	110 x 500 mm	9	200 mm chan- nel section
		10	Glulam spacer, 160 x 200 mm

Three-pin arch

Loading:
uniformly distributed vertical load

Deformations

Moments

Shear forces

Axial forces

Variations in plan shape

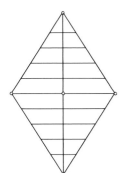

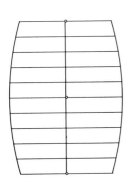

Primary loadbearing system longitudinal, secondary loadbearing system transverse

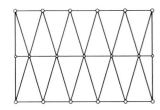

Crossed arrangement

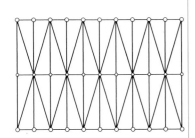

Combined arrangement

73 · Pavilion

Stia, Arezzo, I; 1984

Architects: Lucernario

Structural engineers: Studio Technico Cenci Otsuka

This pavilion at a thermal spa complex has a roof of two symmetrical ribbed shells with pin supports at three positions.

Both segments are bordered by three-pin segmental arches of glued laminated timber. The apex hinges are linked by curved secondary beams. The segmental arch glulam purlins run parallel and carry a timber decking. Both shell segments are joined together rigidly by glulam segmental arches. Overall stability is provided by the triangulation of linking the edge beams. The roof decking and the purlins brace the primary loadbearing system.

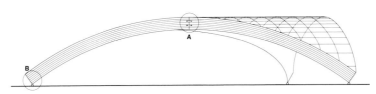

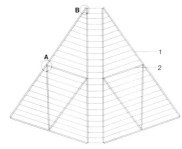

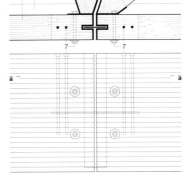

1 Glulam edge beam, 200 x 750–950 mm
2 Glulam purlin, 200 x 810 mm
3 Purlin-apex hinge connection
4 Counter batten
5 Pin joint at base, 8 mm steel bracket
6 Steel bracket
7 24 mm dia. bolt
8 Concrete plinth

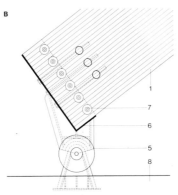

Lateral restraint to main beam

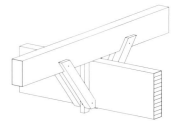

Pair of kneebraces on both sides plus posts

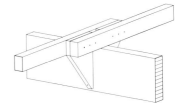

Web plates between spliced purlins

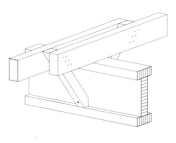

Kneebraces between spliced purlins

Lateral restraint to main beam

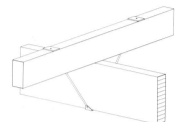

Kneebraces of round steel bars with threaded ends and anchor plates

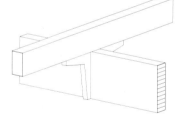

Finger-jointed timber frame

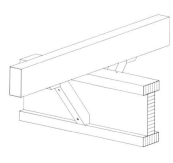

Kneebraces and thrust blocks

74 · Ice rink

Schaffhausen, CH; 1987

Architects: Schaffhausen Building Department

Structural engineers: Plüss & Mayer, Lucerne

The primary loadbearing system consists of six crossing glued laminated timber members in the form of asymmetric three-pin arches, plus steel X-bracing and two gable arches. The ties run horizontally from the higher support to a point part way up the opposite arch. Twin, gently curving beams resist the tensile and compressive forces in the longitudinal direction of the building and also provide lateral restraint to the gable arches. These are connected to the apex hinge of the main arches by means of single-sided toothed-plate connectors. Due to their crossing arrangement, the arches brace each other. Lateral restraint is provided by steel struts and diagonals. The roof covering is a membrane laid on steel circular hollow sections fixed to the arches and tied back to the supports. This ensures that uplift wind forces are transferred directly from the membrane into the supports.

📖 Schweizer Holzbau 11/87

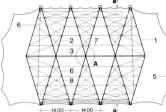

1 Gable arch
2 Glulam arch, 200 x 1333 mm
3 Ridge beam, 15 mm thk
4 Loadbearing node made from channel sections
5 Membrane
6 Tie, 2 No. 32 mm dia.
7 Steel circular hollow section, 220 mm dia.
8 Steel cable, 15 mm dia.
9 Toothed-plate connector, 117 mm dia.
10 Steel plate
11 Hinge pin

A

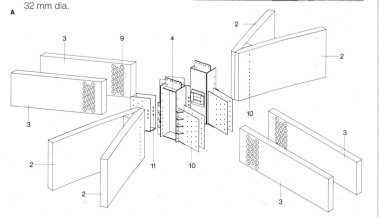

Three-pin arch

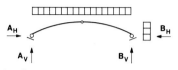

Loading:
uniformly distributed vertical and horizontal loads

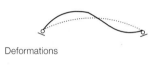

Deformations

Moments

Shear forces

Axial forces

Variations on basic arrangement

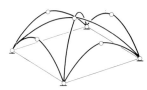

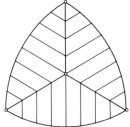

Primary loadbearing system triangular on plan

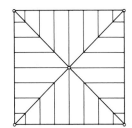

Primary loadbearing system diagonal on plan

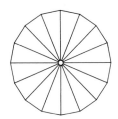

without props around periphery

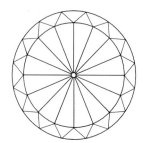

with props around periphery

75 · Warehouse

Walsum, D; 1987

Structural engineers: Brüninghoff Building Department, Heiden, D

A dome for a warehouse with a point load at the apex due to a conveyor belt. Eight three-pin arches spanning 94.60 m; 200 mm wide glued laminated timber with depth varying from 1400 to 2260 mm, with on-site splice. Apex ring assembled on site, direct-contact joints filled with epoxy resin. Lateral restraint provided by knee-braces on one side. Simply supported glulam purlins with a maximum span of 18.40 m. Intermediate support at mid-span to accommodate the loads at roof level, which are carried to the supports around the circumference by means of diagonals. Solid timber bracing in four bays and around the apex. Overall stability ensured by the three-dimensional arrangement of the arches as well as the roof bracing. Roof covering of sheet aluminium.

📖 Informationsdienst Holz: Wirtschaftsbauten aus Holz

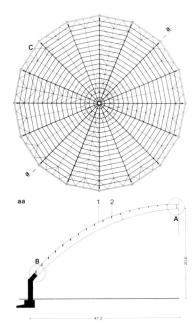

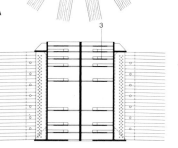

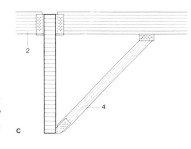

1 Glulam main arch, 200 x 1400–2260 mm
2 Glulam purlin, 80–160 x 160–700 mm
3 Steel apex ring, 1.6 m dia.

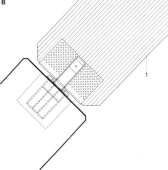

Shear-resistant connection between main and secondary beams

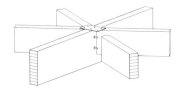

with shear-plate/split-ring connectors, bonded-in threaded bars and fish-plate for tension

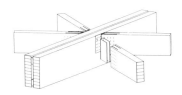

with nails through U-shaped metal plate screwed to steel plate

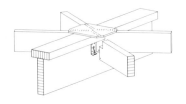

with stiffened angle and nailed plate for tension

Apex detail for crossed arrangement

Central steel node with rocker nibs and end plates let into slits

Central steel node with stiffeners, welded webs and hinge pins, load transferred to timber via end plate

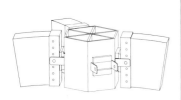

Central steel node with stiffeners, load transferred to end plate via rocker nib

76 · Sports stadium – Izumo Dome

Izumo, J; 1992

Architects: Kajima Design, Tokyo, J; Shigeru Ban, Arata Yoshida

Structural engineers: Kajima Design + Masao Saito, Tokyo, J

This 49 m high dome spans an area 140 m in diameter. The 36 arches positioned every 10° have a radius of 84 m and are supported on a ring in compression at the apex. Every arch is actually a pair of members, and each member consists of four straight and three cranked pieces joined together. The arches are interconnected by V-shaped struts and pretensioned cables. Four internal annular cables brace the dome structure against buckling under asymmetric loads. Each timber arch is supported on a 4 m high reinforced concrete column. At support level there is a steel ring in tension to accommodate the shear forces from the dome construction so that the columns only have to carry vertical loads.

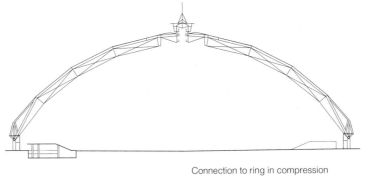

Connection to ring in compression

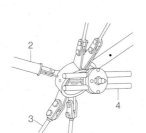

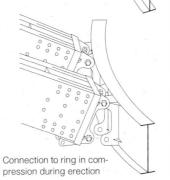

1 Glulam arch, 2 No. 2730 x 9140 mm
2 Stut, 140 mm dia. steel CHS
3 Diagonal tie, 36 mm dia. round steel bar
4 Tension ring, 2 No. 70 mm dia. steel cables

Connection to ring in compression during erection

Trussed three-pin arch

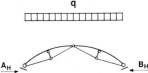

Loading:
uniformly distributed vertical load

Deformations

Moments

Shear forces

Axial forces

Solid sections

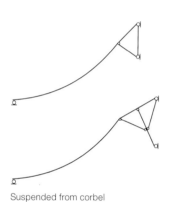

Basic form: catenary for dead loads

Suspended from corbel

Suspended from fixed-based column

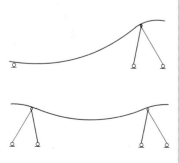

Suspended from trestle

77 · School

Hooke Park Forest, UK; 1985

Architects: P. Ahrends, R. Burton, P. Koralek, London
Consultant: Frei Otto, Stuttgart

Structural engineer: E. Happold, Berlin

This school consists of several variously shaped structures built with timber poles. In order to exploit the very high tensile strength of these round sections, the slender timber members were suspended. The connections utilise threaded steel pins bonded into the end grain with an epoxy resin/cellulose fibres mixture. Pole ends are wrapped in a fibrous tape to prevent splintering. The first building was erected using four interconnected A-frames. The ridge cable connected to each apex carries the suspended rafters. The facade frames – leaning outwards – and the eaves members form the edge support, which is connected to the opposing facade at every column by a long strut. Boards laid horizontally carry an insulated, flexible waterproof covering. Horizontal loads are resisted by the three-dimensional ridge frame and the bracing in the facades.

📖 Detail 6/87; Non-conventional Structures, London, 1987

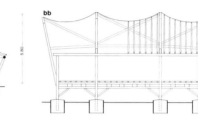

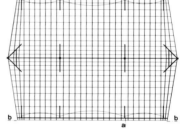

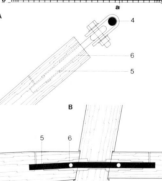

1 A-frame, 200–
   400 mm dia.
2 Strut, 200–
   250 mm dia.
3 Rafter, 150–
   200 mm dia.
4 Cable, 25 mm dia.

5 Threaded bar,
   25 mm dia.
6 Epoxy resin
   reinforced
   with cellulose
   fibres

Hinged joint between tension rib and main beam

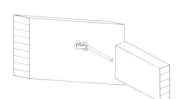

with bonded-in eyebolt

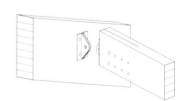

with T-section let into slit,
plus eyebolt

with metal plate let into slit,
plus hinge pin

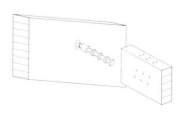

with bonded-in anchor

Support for suspended arch member

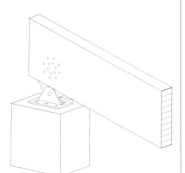

with metal plate let into slit, plus hinge pin

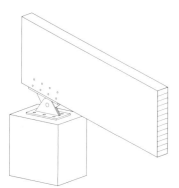

with metal plate let into slit, bearing plate and hinge pin

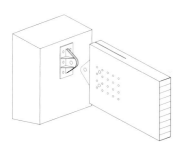

eccentric shear connection with pin

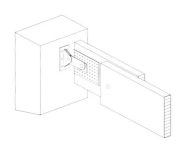

with two-part cross-section and concealed hinge pin connection

78 · Church

Rouen, F; 1979

Architect: L. Arretche, Paris

Structural engineers: U.B.E., Dreux

Concrete facade columns and a steel truss form the primary loadbearing system for this church. The suspended ribs of glued laminated timber span between the steel hollow section edge beams and form hyperbolic-paraboloid roof shells. A layer of planks – left exposed on the underside – perpendicular to the ribs braces and stiffens the ribs. The forces at the edges are transferred to the under-lying construction by steel beams.

📖 Informationsdienst Holz: Holzbauten in Frankreich

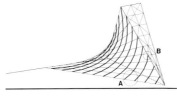

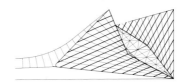

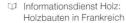

A

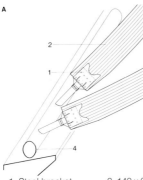

B

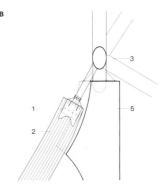

1	Steel bracket, 6 mm thk	2	140 x 600 mm glulam section	4	Steel circular hollow section, 320 mm dia.	5	Reinforced concrete column
		3	Steel beam				

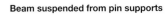
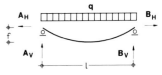

Loading:
uniformly distributed vertical load

$$A_V = B_V = \frac{q \cdot l}{2}$$

$$A_H = B_H = \frac{q \cdot l^2}{8 \cdot f}$$

Deformations

Moments

Shear forces

Axial forces

Sections resolved as individual members

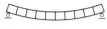

Vierendeel girder

Cellular beam

Lattice beam with diagonals in compression (Howe girder)

Lattice beam with X-bracing

Mesh girder

Options for suspended beams

79 · Sports stadium

Dijon, F; 1976

Architect: J. F. Devaliere, Dijon

Structural engineers: R. Weisrock S.A., Saulcy-sur-Meurthe, F

This sports stadium measures 72.5 x 70.6 m and has space for 4000 spectators. The suspended roof employs glued laminated timber members, 160 x 1500 mm, at 6.75 m centres, which are subjected to bending and tension and joined to the concrete columns via a hinge. Transport, restrictions required a splice at mid-span. The

connection to the outer steel fish-plates is via shear-plate connectors made from an aluminium alloy. In order to overcome the elasticity of the connections, the holes were subsequently pressure-grouted. Lateral restraint on both sides is provided by timber struts. Glulam purlins at 2.53 m centres carry the trapezoidal profile metal sheeting with thermal insulation and waterproofing. Rooftop heating is provided to help prevent accumulations of snow. The wind girders of timber diagonals spread out towards the support according to the law of constant force.

📖 Le Moniteur 4/78;
Bauen mit Holz 1/83

1 Glulam main beam, 160 x 1500 mm
2 Glulam purlin, 110 x 330 mm
3 Strut, 50 x 150 mm

aa   70.00

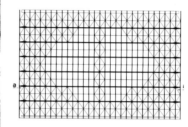

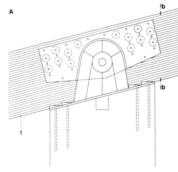

A

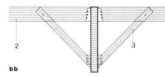

1   2   3

bb

Rigid tension connections

with finger joint

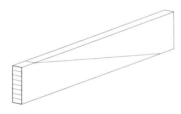

with scarf joint

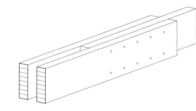

dowelled or screwed

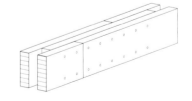

Twin beam with offset joints and dowelled central splice plate

Tension connections

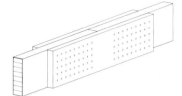

Rectangular cross-section with nailed splice plates of steel, plywood, LVL

Steel plate let into slits and dowelled

Steel plate nailed on top and bottom secured against tension perpendicular to grain, and shear forces transferred via hardwood key

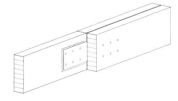

Twin beam with internal nail plate and hinge pin plus dowelled steel plate and hinge pin

80 · Depot forecourt

Hohenems, A; 1999

Architect: Reinhard Drexel, Hohenems, A

Structural engineers: Merz, Kaufmann und Partner, Dornbirn, A; Ingenieurbüro Moosbrugger, Dornbirn, A

This suspended roof over the depot forecourt is connected to the adjoining masonry construction via a horizontal lattice beam on pinned supports. The opposing support consists of a steel trestle. The curving roof surface is made up of individual timber panels, each measuring 18 x 1.80 m. The loadbearing layer is 39 mm laminated veneer board that is loaded in tension in the longitudinal direction. A filling of loose chippings in the panels counteracts the considerable wind uplift forces. In order to achieve the ideal catenary curvature matching the force diagram, the covering of OSB panels was only loosely screwed in place at the factory and the shear-resistant nailed connections completed after erection, thus achieving the necessary rigidity.

📖 Detail 5/2001

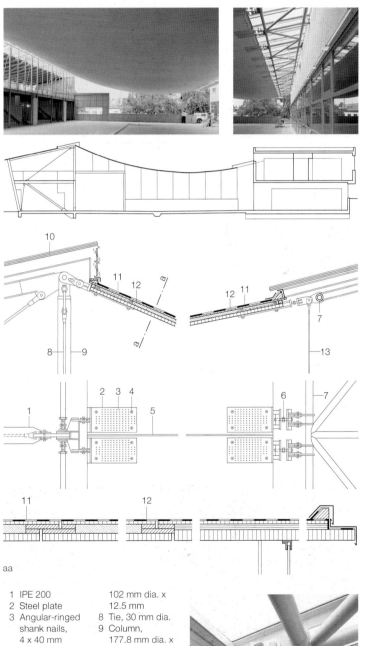

aa

1	IPE 200	102 mm dia. x
2	Steel plate	12.5 mm
3	Angular-ringed	8 Tie, 30 mm dia.
	shank nails,	9 Column,
	4 x 40 mm	177.8 mm dia. x
4	Close tolerance	16 mm
	bolt, 12 mm dia.	10 Rooflight
5	Joint between	11 2-layer mineral-
	panels	faced bitumen
6	Threaded bar,	felt
	36 mm dia.	12 Timber panel,
7	Bottom chord of	1.8 x 18 m
	lattice beam,	13 Tie, 16 mm dia.

Suspended beam with asymmetric loading

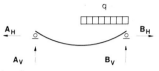

Loading:
uniformly distributed vertical load

Deformations

Moments

Shear forces

Axial forces

Shear wall in log construction

81 · Restaurant

Chaux, CH; 2002

Architect: Germain Peiry, Renens

Structural engineers: Moix ingénieur conseil Sàrl, Monthey
Consultants: Natterer Bois-Consult, Etoy, CH

This restaurant was built in a region in Valais where heavy snowfalls are common, so the structure has to cope with snow loads of 1000 kg/m^2. All the timber used was felled locally and worked using the traditional crafts of log preparation. In order to avoid excessive compression perpendicular to the grain in the continuous beams, the loads from the upper columns were transferred via a height-adjustable threaded bar with steel bearing plates fitted both sides.

Corner joints in log construction

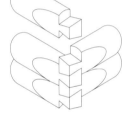

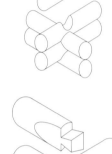

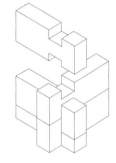

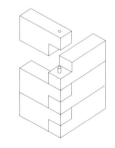

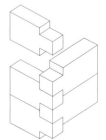

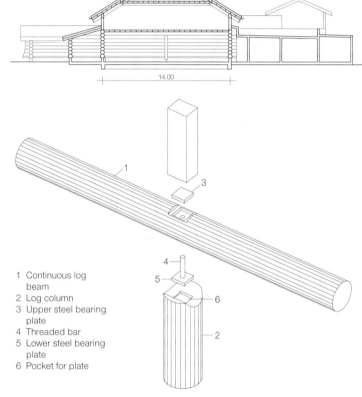

14.00

1 Continuous log
  beam
2 Log column
3 Upper steel bearing
  plate
4 Threaded bar
5 Lower steel bearing
  plate
6 Pocket for plate

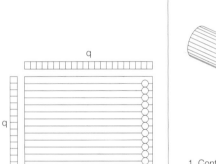

q

q

with surcharge, notched corner joints

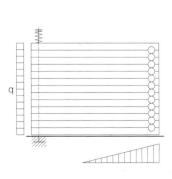

q

without surcharge, with tension anchor,
notched corner joints

Horizontal log wall variations
nailed, dowelled, screwed

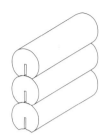

Profiled logs
with relieving groove

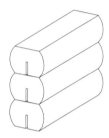

Edge-sawn logs with
relieving groove

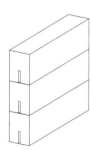

Squared logs with
relieving groove

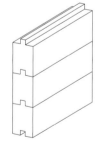

Squared logs with tongue
and groove joints

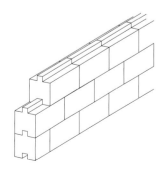

Timber blocks horizontal

82 · Holiday home

Chino, J; 1983

Architect: Masamitsu Nagashina, Tokyo, J

This holiday home is built from vertical logs joined together with separate keys

fitted into grooves. In the areas without further inner lining the edge-sawn logs have two flat faces. The other walls consist of edge-sawn logs with three flat faces plus an inner lining of plywood, which braces the building.

📖 Jutaku Kenchiku 7/83

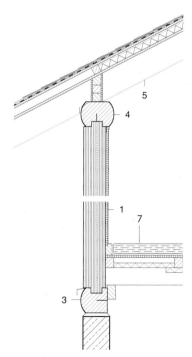

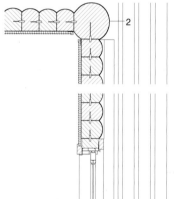

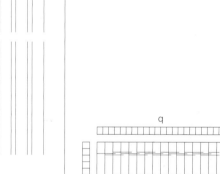

1 External wall: 130 mm
   fabric covering
   12 mm plywood
   135 mm edge-sawn logs with three faces, relieving groove and key
2 210 mm corner column

3 180 mm sole plate
4 180 mm eaves purlin
5 180 mm log rafter
6 Sliding door: aluminium sections, logs
7 *Tatami* (standardised) floor mats

Shear wall in stave construction

with surcharge, nailed,
dowelled, screwed

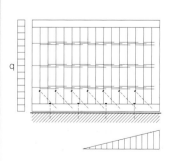

without surcharge, with sole plate and wall plate, tension connections, nailed, dowelled, screwed

Shear wall using edge-glued elements

Loading

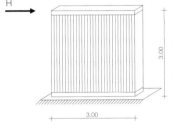

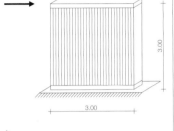

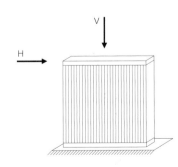

with sole plate and wall plate, nailed, dowelled, screwed

83 · Youth camp

Bavarian Forest National Park, D; 1999

Architect: Passau Building Department

Structural engineers: IEZ Natterer, Saulburg

This building provides facilities and offices for a youth camp in the Bavarian Forest National Park. The softwood available locally was used – fabricated and assembled with the help of the forestry workers and local carpentry shops. The external walls consist of vertical squared sections joined together with dowels, external thermal insulation and timber cladding. Wedges were driven into the joints between individual, straight wall elements to produce the curving plan shape. The building is braced via the internal walls with their diagonal planking. There are plants on the roof, which is designed for high snow loads.

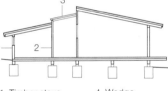

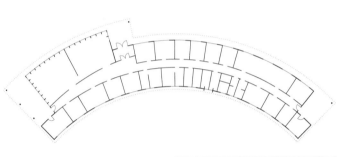

1 Timber stave wall with thermal insulation
2 Timber stave wall
3 Rooflight
4 Wedge
5 Softwood squared sections, joined with dowels

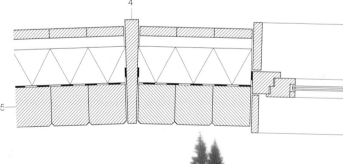

Profiled logs with relieving groove

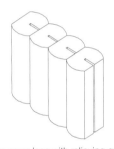

Edge-sawn logs with relieving groove

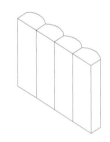

Edge-sawn halved logs

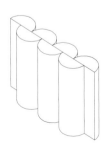

Halved logs

Stave wall variations using sawn timber sections

Squared logs with relieving groove

Split-heart squared logs with tongue and groove joints

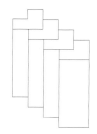

Profiled quartered squared logs

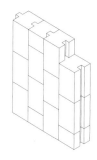

Timber blocks vertical

84 · Assembly hall

Mendrisio, CH; 1997

Architects: M. Botta, A. Galfetti, Lugano, CH

Structural engineers: Natterer Bois-Consult, Etoy, CH

This temporary assembly hall for the "Universita Della Svizzera Italiana" seats 540 and is intended to last about five years. The building complex comprises nailed edge-glued elements. The double-leaf external wall has a loadbearing inner leaf of vertical edge-glued elements and an outer leaf of ventilated edge-glued Douglas fir, which can withstand the rigours of the weather without wood preservative. No additional thermal insulation was required owing to the thick timber sections, and the kraft paper covering the entire surface in the cavity guarantees the airtightness. The edge-glued elements of the roof construction span max. 12.5 m and are strengthened with glued laminated timber ribs, which are supported on the facade and a row of columns.

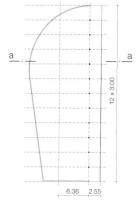

1 Nailed truss
2 Edge-glued floor element
3 Sole plate on nailed truss, curved
4 Edge-glued wall element
5 External cladding of Douglas fir
6 Strengthening ribs
7 Hardboard
8 Waterproofing
9 Airtight barrier of kraft paper

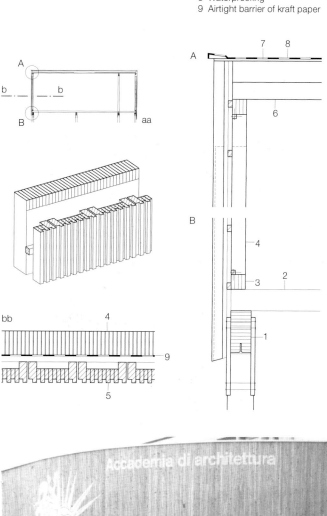

Edge connection for wall of edge-glued elements

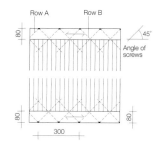

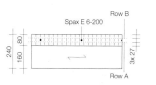

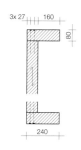

[-element for accommodating thermal insulation, screwed

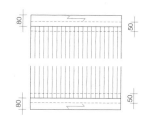

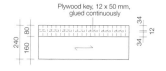

Plywood key, 12 x 50 mm, glued continuously

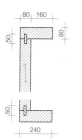

[-element for accommodating thermal insulation, with continuous keys

Floor plate using edge-glued elements

Loading

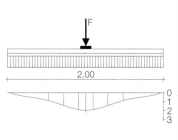

Load distribution of point load without floor finishes

Load distribution of point load with floor finishes (wood-based boards and impact sound insulation)

85 · School for special needs children

Garbsen, D; 2002

Architects: Despang Architekten, Hannover, D

Structural engineers: Ingenieurgemein-schaft Lieberum und Steckstor, Hannover, D

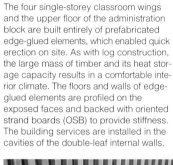

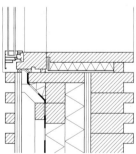

Facade, vertical section

The four single-storey classroom wings and the upper floor of the administration block are built entirely of prefabricated edge-glued elements, which enabled quick erection on site. As with log construction, the large mass of timber and its heat storage capacity results in a comfortable interior climate. The floors and walls of edge-glued elements are profiled on the exposed faces and backed with oriented strand boards (OSB) to provide stiffness. The building services are installed in the cavities of the double-leaf internal walls.

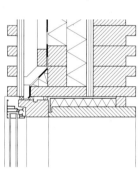

Facade, horizontal section

Variations for edge-glued elements

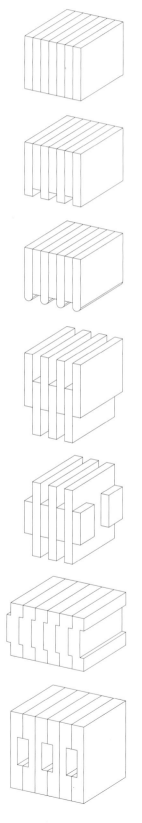

Variations for edge-glued elements

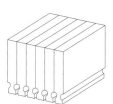

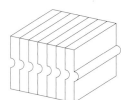

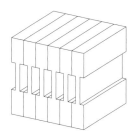

86 · Church

Schneverdingen, D; 1999

Architect: Tabery, Bremervörde, D

Structural engineers: IEZ Natterer, Wiesenfelden, D

A double-leaf facade of edge-glued elements surrounds the approx. 14 x 14 m church. The rear face of the inner, load-bearing leaf of pine wood boards was covered with 10 mm OSB, which serves to brace the entire church. These boards also provide an airtight barrier. Oak wood was used for the edge-glued elements of the outer leaf. The individual elements were fixed in such a way that they can accommodate shrinkage and swelling. The primary loadbearing system of the roof forms a three-dimensional frame of squared sections with additional trussing in the transverse direction. The frame spans the whole church, and carries the bell-tower and the edge-glued roof elements.

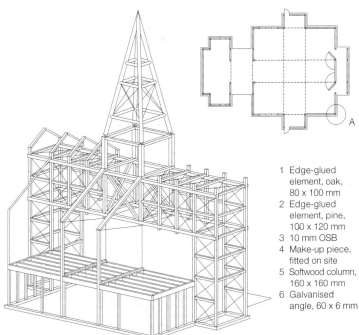

A

1 Edge-glued element, oak, 80 x 100 mm
2 Edge-glued element, pine, 100 x 120 mm
3 10 mm OSB
4 Make-up piece, fitted on site
5 Softwood column, 160 x 160 mm
6 Galvanised angle, 60 x 6 mm

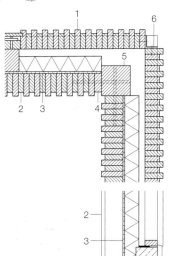

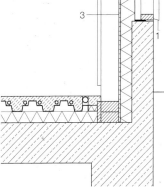

Loadbearing behaviour of edge-glued element

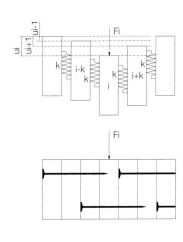

Bending strength [MPa]

n	X_{mov}	$X_{5\%n}$	%
1	80	55	100
2	80	62	113
3	80	66	119
4	80	67	123

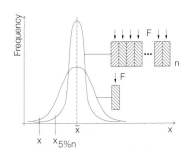

Improvement of 5% fractile

$$X_{5\%,n} = \bar{X} - \frac{1.645 \cdot s}{\sqrt{n}}$$

Solid and composite methods of construction

Ratio of dead loads to span plus acoustic attenuation behaviour

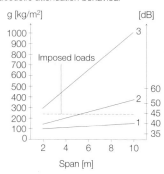

1   Floor of edge-glued elements

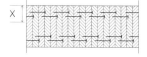

2   Timber-concrete composite floor

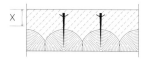

3   Reinforced concrete floor

x = compression zone

87 · House and school

Triesenberg, FL; 1994

Architect: H. Ospelt, Triesen, with Marcus Freund

Structural engineers: Natterer Bois-Consult, Etoy, CH

The floors of the classroom wings employ edge-glued elements throughout for the timber-concrete composite construction. A glued laminated timber upstand beam in the plane of the facade carries the loads from the floors to the columns. The roof to the classroom wings, and the floors, walls and roof of the house were built with edge-glued elements. A special feature in the house is the glued laminated beech beams flush with the floors and with sloping supports. These enabled the forces from the floors to be transferred into the columns directly without any further means.

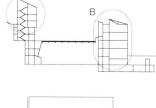

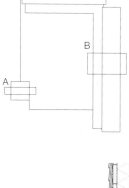

Solid timber-concrete composite floors

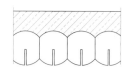

comprising edge-sawn logs with two flat faces and relieving groove

comprising edge-sawn logs with three flat faces and relieving groove

comprising edge-sawn logs with three flat faces and relieving groove

comprising squared sections, with relieving groove

with edge-glued elements

with edge-glued elements supported on bottom flange of steel beam

Timber joist floors with concrete topping

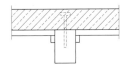

with squared sections and ledger strips to support permanent timber board formwork

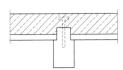

with notched squared timber to support permanent timber board formwork

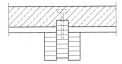

with glued laminated timber laid up in blocks, dowelled, screwed

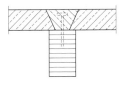

with glued laminated timber and precast concrete slabs, with joint subsequently grouted

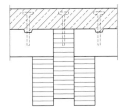

with multi-part glued laminated timber section laid up in blocks, dowelled, screwed

with glued laminated timber elements laid up in blocks

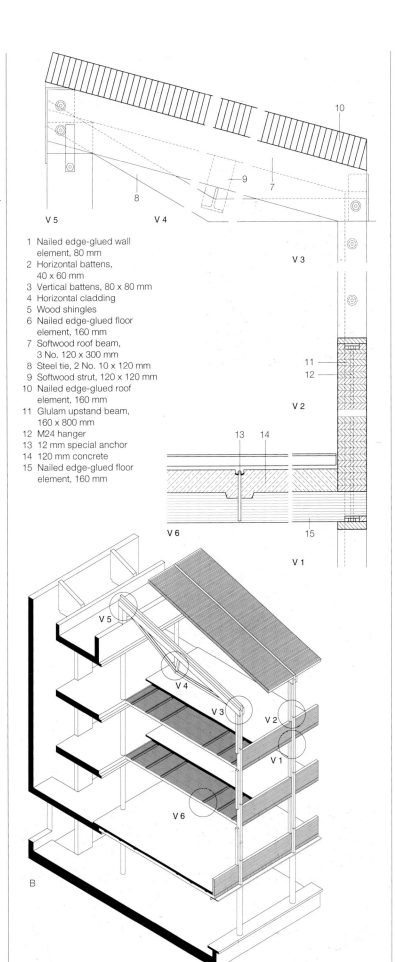

1 Nailed edge-glued wall element, 80 mm
2 Horizontal battens, 40 x 60 mm
3 Vertical battens, 80 x 80 mm
4 Horizontal cladding
5 Wood shingles
6 Nailed edge-glued floor element, 160 mm
7 Softwood roof beam, 3 No. 120 x 300 mm
8 Steel tie, 2 No. 10 x 120 mm
9 Softwood strut, 120 x 120 mm
10 Nailed edge-glued roof element, 160 mm
11 Glulam upstand beam, 160 x 800 mm
12 M24 hanger
13 12 mm special anchor
14 120 mm concrete
15 Nailed edge-glued floor element, 160 mm

Timber-concrete composite floor with shear connectors

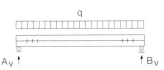

Loading:
uniformly distributed vertical load

Deformations

$$\text{Moments: max } M = \frac{q \cdot l^2}{8}$$

$$\text{Shear forces: max } V = \frac{q \cdot l}{2}$$

Axel forces: N = 0

Timber-concrete composite floor with pocket and tension anchor

88 · House

Clarens, CH; 1992

Architect: Gilles Bellmann, Clarens, CH

Structural engineers: Natterer Bois-Consult, Etoy, CH

In order to achieve flexibility in the use of the layout, the upper floor spans the full width of 7.25 m. For financial reasons the garage roof uses halved logs, the walls are of nailed edge-glued elements (80 mm wide side boards), the south facade and the roof employ squared timber sections, the exposed ground floor is a timber-concrete composite construction, with glulam sections laid flat, and the upper floor is glued laminated timber. This choice of wall and floor types rendered very slender sections possible. The timber-concrete composite construction has bonded-in, adjustable dowels. Prefabrication meant that the work on site took just one week.

Timber-concrete composite construction
Longitudinal section

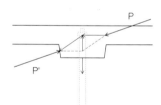

Anchor: threaded bar bonded in at pocket, subsequent adjustment possible

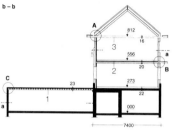

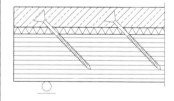

No connection
screed without any connectors

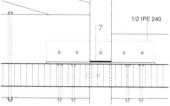

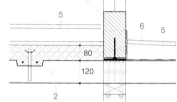

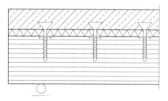

High elasticity connection
with vertical screws and toothed-plate connectors

1 Timber-concrete composite floor
2 Timber-concrete composite floor with glulam sections
3 Glued laminated timber floor

4 Column, 120 x 120 mm
5 Cement screed
6 Tiles
7 Elastomeric bearing

Force diagram:
The approximately horizontal shear forces are essentially transferred to the end grain face in the pocket. The anchor is only loaded in tension, not in shear.

Low elasticity connection
with sloping screws

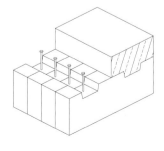

System make-up

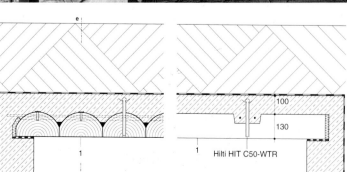

Hilti HIT C50-WTR

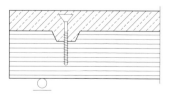

Ideal connection
with pretensioned anchors in pocket

Timber-concrete composite construction
Transverse section

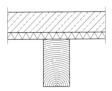

No connection
screed without any connectors

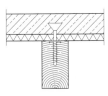

High elasticity connection
with vertical screws and toothed-plate connectors

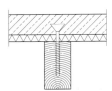

Low elasticity connection
with sloping screws

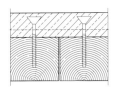

Ideal connection
with pretensioned anchors
in pockets

89 · School

Wilpoldsried, D; 1995

Architect: Zwerch, Kempten, D

Structural engineers: Natterer Bois-Consult, Etoy, CH

A two-storey extension measuring 16.8 x 24 m on plan was added to this school. A timber-concrete composite construction – edge-glued elements plus concrete topping – was used for the floors.
The roof consists of two offset pitched beams spanning 8.2 m. All the loadbearing and non-loadbearing walls are constructed of edge-glued elements, and all the elements required to act as bracing are backed with plywood covering. The floor panels act as a stiff plate and direct their loads into the loadbearing walls.

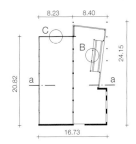

1 Timber-concrete composite floor (180 mm timber, 120 mm concrete)
2 Edge-glued element with plywood backing
3 Log column
4 Nailed beam
5 M16 threaded bar
6 Steel angle, 200 x 90 x 5 mm
7 Edge member connection with key
8 Parallam beam

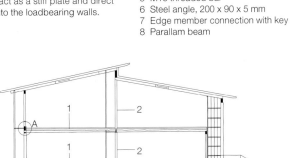

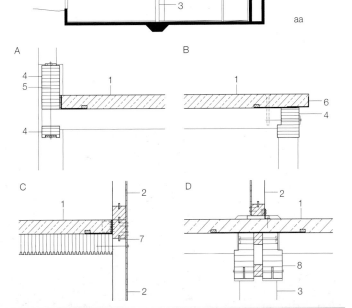

Timber-concrete composite construction
Deflection and stresses

for an upper floor spanning 6.0 m

Dead loading : g = 2.0 kN/m²
Imposed loading: q = 2.0 kN/m²

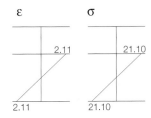

No connection
screed without any connectors

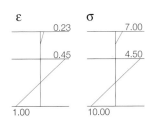

High elasticity connection
with vertical screws and toothed-plate connectors

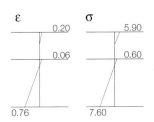

Low elasticity connection
with sloping screws

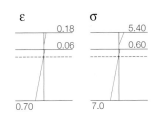

Ideal connection
with pretensioned anchors in pocket

Beam grid systems

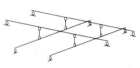

Beams crossing but no joint

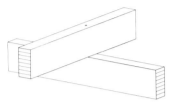

with halving joint

Squared sections:
a = 0.60 – 1.20 m

h = l/20 – l/30

l = 6–2 m

Glued laminated timber
with steel nodes:
a = 2.40–7.20 m

h = l/16 – l/30

l = 12–24 m

232

90 · Post office

Munich-Perlach, D; 1979–81

Architect: Regional Postal Directorate, Munich

Structural engineers: Natterer und Dittrich Planungsgesellschaft, Munich

A double-layer beam grid of glued laminated timber elements forms the flat roof over a building, with lightwell, measuring 33 x 44 m overall on plan.
The square 1.35 m grid forms a beam grid spanning up to 10.80 m, with beams 140 x 180 mm. They cantilever out around

the perimeter to ensure good weather protection for the wood-and-glass facade. Some columns are in glued laminated timber with a cruciform cross-section, others are built as fixed-base reinforced concrete columns. The layout is essentially matched to the uses of the different parts of the building. Tongue and groove boarding on the upper layer of beams carries the warm deck roof construction. Steel flat bracing at roof level distributes the horizontal forces to the fixed-base reinforced concrete columns.

◫ Küttinger: Holzbau-Konstruktionen, Munich, 1984

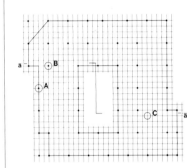

aa

bb

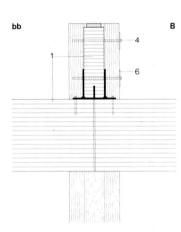

C

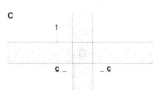

A

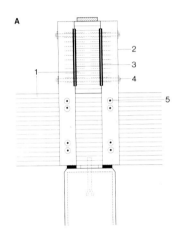

cc

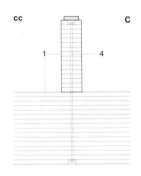

B

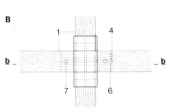

1 160 x 480 mm   4 Bolt
   glulam section   5 Dowel
2 Four-part column   6 Washer
   115 x 135 mm   7 Steel sleeve,
3 Nail plate   25 mm dia.

90° beam grid joints

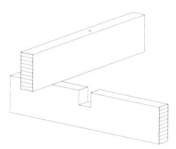

Beams crossing

with notch in one member

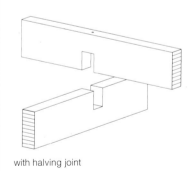

with halving joint

using edge-glued members

Rigid 60° beam grid joints

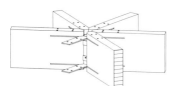

Horizontal metal plates in star arrangement let into slits in beams and dowelled

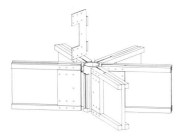

Steel tube with rails welded on and beams hung on rails

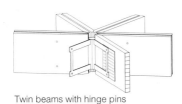

Twin beams with hinge pins

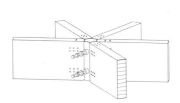

Steel tube with threaded bars or dowels bonded in

91 · Petrol and service station

Lechwiesen, D; 1995

Architects: Herzog + Partner, Thomas Herzog, Hanns Jörg Schrade, with Arthur Schankula, Munich

Structural engineers: Sailer und Stepan, Munich; Wolfgang Winter, Vienna

A petrol and service station with canopy, covered passageway, restaurant and service section. The detail shows the loadbearing construction of the roof to the restaurant, which is supported on steel columns on a 7.50 x 4.50 m grid. The sizes of the individual layers of the timber beam grid decrease from bottom to top. Steel bars above the fourth beam grid layer raise the roof clear and create the slope. All the exposed parts of the beam grid are made from nailed solid spruce planks. The longitudinal joints are formed as hinged splices. The wind forces are resisted by the reinforced concrete service segment, to which the beam grid is connected via steel fins.

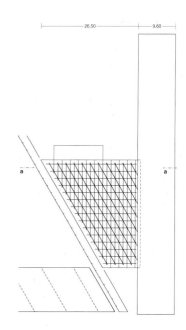

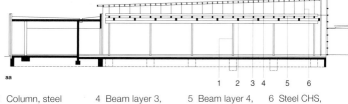

aa

1 2 3 4   5   6

1 Column, steel circular hollow section, 101.6 mm dia. x 5 mm
2 Beam layer 1, 4 No. 40 x 280 mm softwood sections
3 Beam layer 2, 4 No. 40 x 280 mm softwood sections
4 Beam layer 3, 4 No. 40 x 220 mm softwood sections
5 Beam layer 4, 4 No. 40 x 220 mm softwood sections
6 Steel CHS, 30 dia. x 10 mm
7 15 mm 3-ply core plywood planking
8 Softwood rafter, 2 No. 60 x 200 mm
9 200 mm insulation
10 30 mm planking

7 8 9 10

1   6 5 4 3 2

Orthogonal beam grid simply supported on all sides

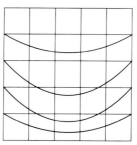

Principal moments in M_x direction, M_y similar

$$\max M_x = q \cdot \frac{l^2}{16}$$

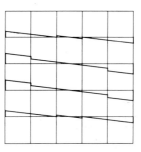

Principal shear forces in Q_x direction, Q_y similar

Characteristics:
· moments with the same sign, + or -
· moments greater than in diagonal grid
· partly less favourable stress distribution than in diagonal grid

Applications:
· rectangular or orthogonal plan shapes with ratio of sides max. 1:1.3

Support arrangements

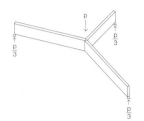

Triangular grid

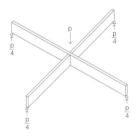

Square grid

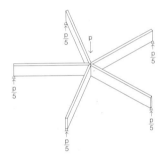

Pentagonal grid

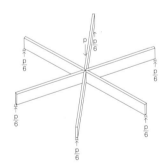

Hexagonal grid

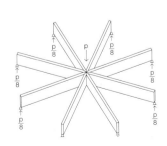

Octagonal grid

92 · Law school

Starnberg, D; 1978

Architects: State Building Department, Munich

Structural engineers: Natterer und Dittrich Planungsgesellschaft, Munich

This single-storey flat-roof pavilion measuring 15 x 15 m on plan consists of a table-like frame with a beam grid. The corner columns are rigidly connected to the eaves beams by steel parts let into slits and dowelled, thereby accommodating the horizontal forces in both directions. The beam grid comprising 140 x 600 mm glulam elements is supported on timber pinned-end columns along the four facades. The individual, 2.10 m long elements are rigidly connected at the intersections with two cruciform steel plates. The direction in which the secondary beams span changes by 90° from bay to bay in order to load the main beams evenly in both directions. The 19 mm roof decking is positioned at the right-angles to the secondary beams. Steel flats join the corner columns diagonally in order to brace the roof level.

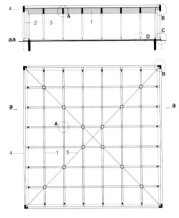

1 Beam, 140 x 600 mm
2 Corner column, 3 No. 140 x 640 mm
3 Pinned-end col. 140 x 140 mm
4 Edge beam, 180 x 650 mm
5 Steel flat diagonal bracing
6 Steel parts, 6, 10 and 12 mm
7 Round steel bar, 30 mm dia.
8 Dowel, 14 mm dia.
9 120 x 100 mm softwood section
10 Steel CHS, 44.5 dia. x 4 mm

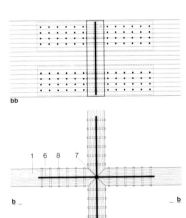

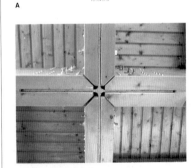

Beam grid connections with compound sections

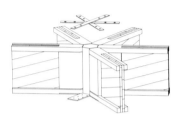

Kämpf solid-web beams with strengthened end dowelled to metal section

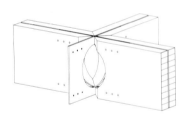

Twin beams with vertical metal plates and cut-out for building services

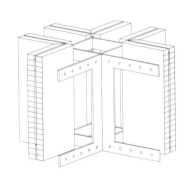

Star of steel plates for multi-part beams and as opening for services, with nail plates and hinge pins

Supports for beam grids

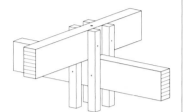

Four-part column, connection by way of dowels, or two shear-plate or single-sided toothed-plate connectors

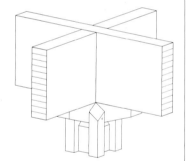

Five-part column, with hardwood block to strengthen support

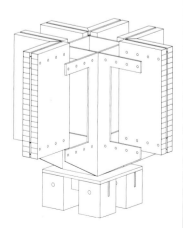

Four-part column with bearing plate and web plates let into slits to secure beams in position

93 · Community centre

Ötlingen, D; 1978-79

Architects: Kammerer + Belz + Partner, Stuttgart, D

Structural engineers: Natterer und Dittrich Planungsgesellschaft, Munich, D

A beam grid on timber columns forms the roof over this community centre. The columns at the intersections of the 3.5 m square grid are either four-part 120 x 120 mm or one-part 210 x 210 mm (with relieving groove) glued laminated timber sections. The beam grid itself consists of 3.5 m long twin 100 x 900 mm glulam elements with rigid connections at the intersections. This arrangement enables the roof to span up to 14 m between columns. The connections are formed by steel plates nailed to the insides of the beams, which are then connected by pins and a steel cross. Solid timber purlins spanning in different directions in adjacent bays carry the 24 mm roof decking. The building is braced by steel X-bracing in the plane of the roof, vertical bracing in the walls in both directions.

📖 Informationsdienst Holz:
Dokumentation Holzbauten in Baden-Württemberg

1 Glulam main beam, 2 No. 100 x 900 mm
2 Purlin, 100 x 160 mm
3 Glulam column,
4 No. 120 x 120 mm
4 Glulam column, 210 x 210 mm
5 Nail plate, 5 mm thk
6 Connecting cross, 14 mm
7 Close tolerance bolt, 27 mm dia.
8 3 x 4 toothed-plate connectors,
85 mm dia.
9 Split-ring connector, 80 mm dia.

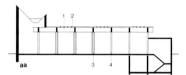

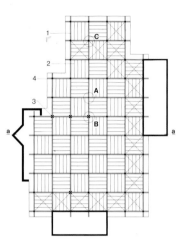

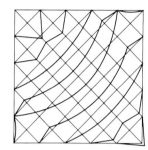

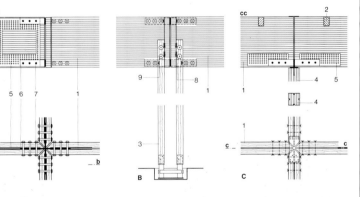

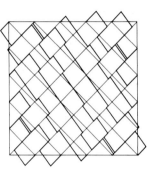

Principal moments at edge

$$\max M = q \cdot \frac{l^2}{14{,}2}$$

Principal shear forces at edge

Characteristics:
· even stress distribution
· uneven bending strains (negative and positive moments)
· reduction of maximum moment at mid-span
· better stiffness compared to orthogonal grids and linear systems

Support arrangements

At the corners of the frame, columns restrained at grid level or in foundation

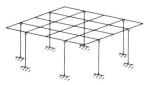

At the intersections of the beam grid frame, columns restrained at grid level or in foundation

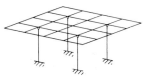

At the intersections of the beam grid, with peripheral cantilever, columns restrained at grid level or in foundation

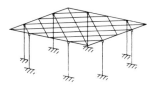

Similar for diagonal beam grid, columns restrained at grid level or in foundation

94 · Large canteen

Volkach am Main, D; 1984

Architects: Würzburg Tax Office, Building Department

Structural engineers: Bertsche, Packenbach, Hübner, Würzburg, D

A grid of glulam lattice beams over the canteen at an army barracks. Top chords, posts and diagonals on a 2.40 m square grid, beam depth 2100 mm. The bottom chords follow the diagonals of the basic grid. Fixed-base reinforced concrete columns are placed every 4.80 m to support the grid. The ends of the beams cantilever 2.40 m beyond the facade on all sides. The connections along the facade have a central steel bar to which steel plates are welded; the plates are let into slits in the timber members, dowelled and secured with bolts. Overall stability is provided by means of the intersecting beam grid and the restraint at the column bases. Timber planks 50 mm thick carry the warm deck covered with chippings.

📖 Bauen mit Holz 1/86

1 Top chords, 220 x 200 mm, 180 x 200 mm
2 Diagonals, 180 x 180 mm, 160 x 160 mm

5 Metal plate, 15 mm thk
6 Dowels and clamping bolts, 14, 18, 20 mm dia.

3 Bottom chord, 160 x 160 mm
4 Round bar, 50 mm dia.

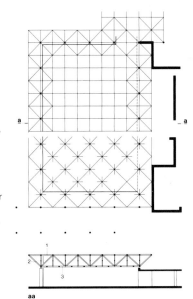

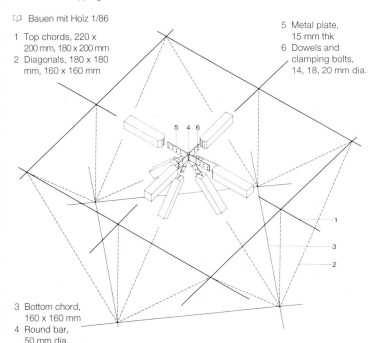

Nodes for lattice beam grid

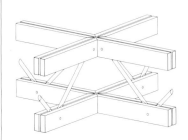

Top and bottom chords in same planes, metal cross connectors, steel diagonals

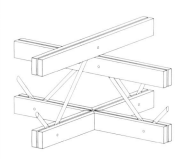

Bottom chords in same plane, top chords stacked, different structural depths for unequal spans

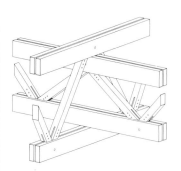

Interlaced lattice beams with different structural depths, over rectangular plan

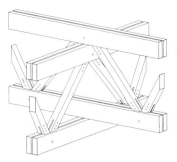

Top and bottom chords stacked, same structural depth

Three-dimensional nodes

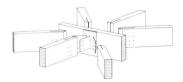

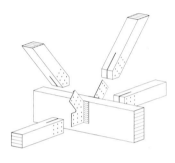

Six incoming members in one plane

Four incoming members at right angles
and diagonal to main member

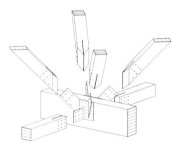

Six incoming members at right angles
and diagonal to main member

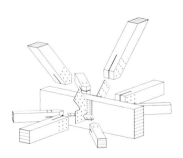

Eight incoming members joined to main
member

95 · Multipurpose hall

Lüterkofen, CH; 1993

Architect: A. Schlup, Solothurn, CH

Structural engineers: Natterer Bois-
Consult, Etoy, CH

The entire roof construction is supported
on columns. The primary loadbearing system is formed by 10 lattice beams spaced
4 m apart; these beams span 16 m
between columns. The secondary loadbearing system is also formed by lattice
beams at 4 m centres, at right-angles to
the main system. Primary loadbearing
system: glued laminated timber top
chord, graded oak, spruce/fir diagonals,
100 x 100 mm; the sections are turned
through 45°; steel bottom chord. Nailed
edge-glued elements cover this entire
system and form a roof plate to brace the
building.

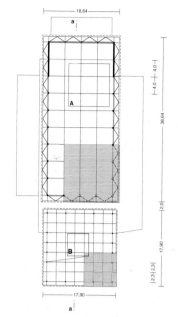

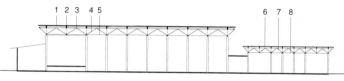

aa

1 100 mm edge-
   glued element
2 Glulam main
   beam, hall, 180
   x 380 mm
3 Softwood

secondary
beam, hall, 160
x 180 mm
4 Softwood diag-
   onal, 100 x
   100 mm

5 Steel tie,
   28 mm thk
6 Softwood
   beam, foyer,
   160 x 240 mm

7 Softwood dia-
   gonal, 100 x
   100 mm
8 Steel tie,
   25 mm thk

A

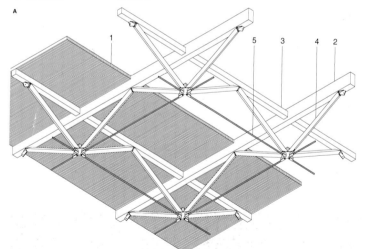

B

**Secondary systems
for even distribution of loads
to primary beam grid**

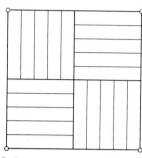

Purlins ∡ = 90°

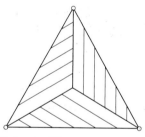

Purlins ∡ = 60°

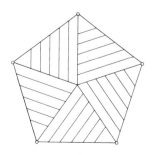

Purlins ∡ = 72°

**Support variations
for lattice beam grids**

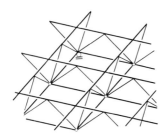

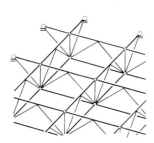

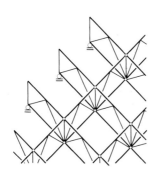

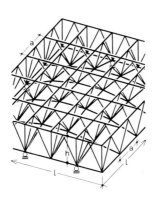

a = 1.20–12.0 m

h = l/8 – l/16

l = 8 –60 m

96 · Sports centre

Nuremberg, D; 1980

Architects: State Building Department,
Nuremberg

Structural engineers: Natterer und Dittrich
Planungsgesellschaft, Munich

A grid of lattice beams in both directions
covers the general sports and judo areas
plus the swimming pool. The main beams
at 90° to each other form a 4.80 m square
grid. The lattice beams are 2050 mm
deep and consist of twin glued laminated
timber chords and one-piece glued laminated timber diagonals. The members are
joined at the nodes by dowels and steel
plates let into slits. The transverse beams
are positioned 180 mm lower than the longitudinal beams so that the chords can
continue uninterrupted. The lattice beams
are either straight supported on glulam
pinned-end columns or cranked, depending on the clear space required and the
roof form. The purlins together with the
diagonal timber planking (30 mm) form a
rigid roof plate. Overall stability is provided by the main beams designed to act as
frames, and the vertical bracing between
the timber columns.

◻ Detail 4/82

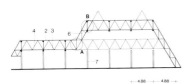

aa

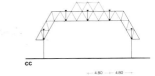

cc

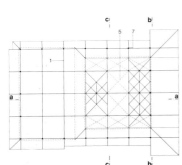

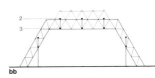

bb

1 Main beam	5 Steel round bar
2 Glulam top	bracing
chord, 2 No.	6 Glulam vertical
160 x 180 mm	post, 2 No. 90
3 Glulam bottom	x 200 mm
chord, 2 No.	7 Pinned-end
140 x 180 mm	column
4 Glulam diago-	8 12 mm dia.
nal, 160 x	dowel
160 mm	9 M16 bolt

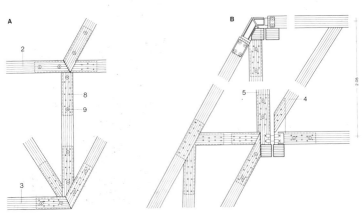

**Concealed connections
(fire/corrosion protection) for
secondary loadbearing systems**

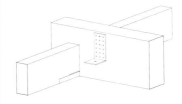

Angle, nailed

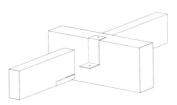

Z-hanger, nailed

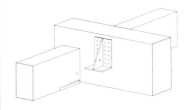

Stiffened angle

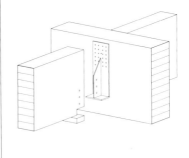

Stiffened angle nailed to main beam

Supports for secondary loadbearing systems, with strengthening for tension perpendicular to grain at secondary-main beam junction

Bonded-in threaded bar or wood screw

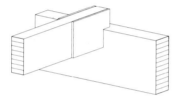

Glued side plates

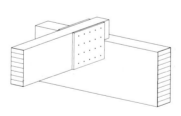

Strengthening plates nailed or glued and nailed

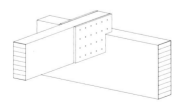

Strengthening plate nailed or glued and nailed, also increases width of bearing

97 · Sunshading

Riyadh, Saudi Arabia; 1986

Architects: High Executive Committee of the Kingdom of Saudi Arabia

Structural engineer: M. Speich, Hannover, D

Sunshading covering a total of 1500 m² for the internal courtyards of four mosques. A space frame of glued laminated timber members (four laminations; species: iroko) with a high degree of static indeterminacy. Top and bottom chords are continuous over 6 m, with halving joint intersections, on a 1.20 m square grid but offset on plan by 0.60 m in x- and y-directions. Four diagonals arranged symmetrically about the chord intersections. Depth of system: 600 mm. Diagonals are connected via steel brackets and close tolerance bolts to halved Mero nodes. These and the continuous chords are connected – depending on load – with one close tolerance bolt or a steel cross and close tolerance bolt (near the supports). Shading provided by timber frames fitted into the bays at the level of the top or bottom chord.

📖 Bauen mit Holz 2/87

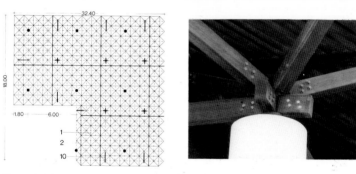

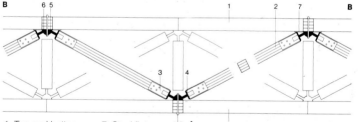

1 Top and bottom chord, 50 x 80 mm
2 Strut, 60 x 68 mm
3 Steel plate, 128 x 60 x 4 mm
4 End plate, 60 x 44 x 6 mm
5 Mero node, 60 x 54 mm
6 Washer
7 Steel flat, 50 x 6 mm
8 Hexagonal socket, 19 x 13 mm
9 Pin

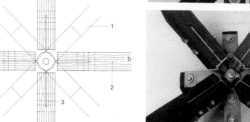

Loadbearing behaviour of three-dimensional lattice beams

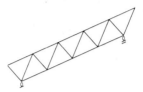

Weak in torsion:
loadbearing structure is only stiff in the plane of the girder, very weak perpendicular to it

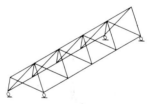

Weak in torsion owing to lack of diagonals in plane of bottom chords:
only the nodes of the upper chord can accommodate external actions

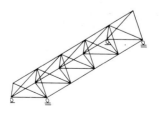

Torsionally rigid due to diagonals and transverse members in all three planes:
all nodes can accommodate external actions

Support variations for orthogonal beam grids

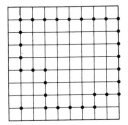

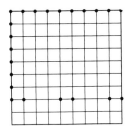

Some unsupported edges

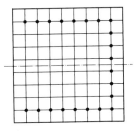

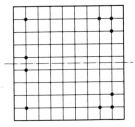

Symmetrical about one axis

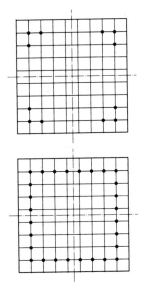

Symmetrical about both axes

98 · Lakeside centre

Arbon, CH; 1984

Architect: P. Haas, Arbon, CH

Structural engineers: Ing.-Büro Wälli AG, Arbon, Rorschach, CH

Multipurpose hall for a leisure facility on the banks of Lake Constance. The roof structure is designed as a space frame and divided into two loadbearing bays measuring 27 x 30 m and 27 x 15 m by an integral steel transfer structure. The size of the structural mesh is 3 m x 2.5 m. Steel columns support the roof structure. Reinforced concrete walls at ground and basement level ensure the overall stability of the building. The cross-section and the species of wood (spruce or beech) of the individual members vary with the load. The members are connected by cast parts and steel spheres with internal threading. The roof structure supports a warm deck with chippings.

📖 C. v. Büren: Neuer Holzbau in der Schweiz; Schweizer Holzbau 7/85; Werk, Bauen + Wohnen 12/85; DBZ 10/86; Space Design 1/87

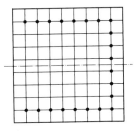

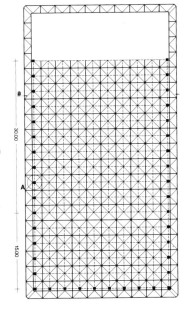

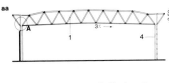

1 Frame members, 110 x 110 to 170 x 170 mm
2 Steel sphere with internal threading
3 Cast part
4 Steel column
5 Hexagonal bar with thread
6 Facade column
7 Facade beam

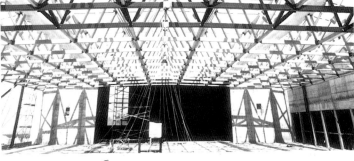

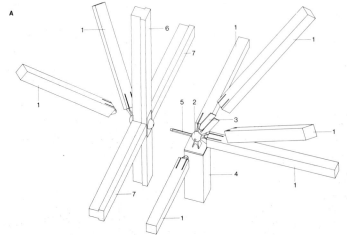

Space frame connections

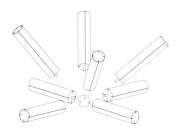

Bonded-in threaded bars and metal sphere

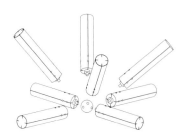

Tubes in slits, radial dowelling and metal sphere (Mero system)

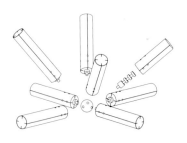

Metal sphere with grouted-in dowels or threaded bars

Space frame connections

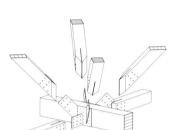

Continuous chord and
steel plates let into slits

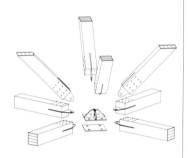

Steel plates let into slits, base plate
rotated through 90°, diagonals 45°

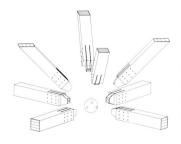

Dowelled cast iron connectors and
metal sphere

99 · Chapel of rest

Reutlingen, D; 1986–87

Architect: W. Riehle, Reutlingen

Structural engineer: N. Nebgen, Reutlingen

Timber frames in both directions for a
pyramid roof square on plan (15.60 x
15.60 m). Four intersecting trapezoidal
main beams form a three-dimensional
frame of 120 x 120 mm members connected via Mero nodes. Forces

transferred via steel tubes let into the
timber and dowelled. Glulam pinned-end
columns carry the vertical loads. The hip
beams and the intermediate rafters are
raised at the nodes of the top chord and
connected to the glulam eaves purlins.
Horizontal forces are transferred to the
fixed-base concrete facade columns.
Roof construction: bullnose double-lap
tiling, battens, counter battens and tongue
and groove boarding.

Detail 6/87

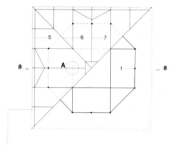

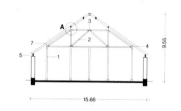

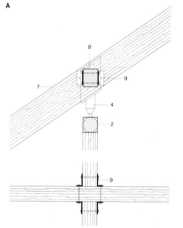

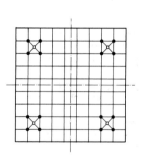

1 Column, 180 x
180 mm
2 Frame member
3 Mero node
4 Rafter support
bracket
5 Glulam purlin,
120 x 220 mm
6 Glulam hip beam,

160 x 240 mm
7 Glulam inter-
mediate rafter,
120 x 220 mm
8 Glulam trans-
verse member,
120 x 140 mm
9 Angle, 106 x
56 x 6 mm

**Support variations
for orthogonal beam grids**

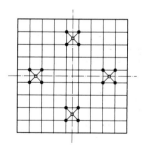

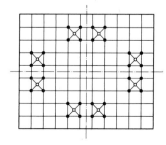

Four-point bearing per column
for maximum shear forces

Folded plate variations

in solid-web or box construction

as truss

as frame

as arch

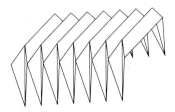

as framework

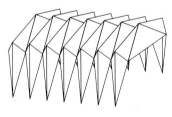

as folded plate to be designed for:

f ≥ l/8; ∡ ≥ 30°

for Kämpf solid-web beams, glued laminated timber or plywood with transverse ribs as compound section for transverse bending

d ≥ h/20 – h/30

for truss

d ≥ l/4 – l/6

100 · Ledersteg bridge

Amberg, D; 1978

Architects: Amberg Building Department

Structural engineers: Natterer und Dittrich Planungsgesellschaft, Munich

A folded plate forms the primary structural system in this covered footbridge spanning 24 m. Two glued laminated timber plates form the duopitch roof, from which the bridge deck is suspended. Transverse frames with legs resolved into separate members direct the vertical loads into the roof and transfer the horizontal forces into the lower bracing girder. The frame over the end supports transfers the loads from the folded plate into the foundations. The bridge deck consists of 60 mm planks on continuous longitudinal beams supported on transverse beams every 2.2 m. The edge beams of glued laminated timber together with the timber diagonals form the horizontal girder. Bracing in the longitudinal direction is by way of the frame action which results from the connection between the roof plate and the legs over the supports.

📖 F. Leonhard: Brücken, Stuttgart, 1981

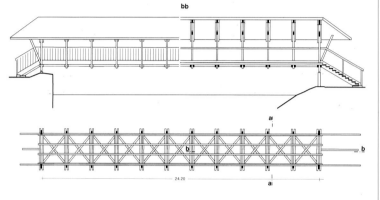

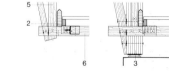

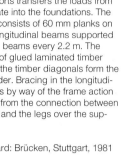

1 170 x 2950 mm glulam section
2 100 x 360 mm
3 140 x 360 mm glulam section
4 2 No. 120 x 200 mm softwood sections
5 120 x 180 mm soft-
6 2 No. 120 x 200 mm softwood sec.

Make-up of plates

Cement-bonded chipboard/OSB

Laminated veneer lumber (LVL) board

Plywood

At least three layers of boards glued together, with grain of adjacent boards at right angles

as edge-glued element

Make-up of ribbed plates for folded-plate structures

as T-section with webs, flanges and plywood

as box section with plywood and timber spacers

as box section with double plywood web

as T-section with squared sections and diagonal boards

as T-section with diagonal boards

101 · Pavilion for Hartwald Clinic

Zwesten, D; 1977

Architect: A. Frank, Building Department, W. Wicker KG

Structural engineers: Natterer und Dittrich Planungsgesellschaft, Munich

A multipurpose hall on a hexagonal plan measuring 32 m across and covered by a radial folded plate construction. Roof plates resolved into triangular trusses, with 140 x 240 mm and 180 x 240 mm glulam sections. A glulam tension ring resists the horizontal thrust due to the vertical loads. Forces from horizontal loads are transferred into concrete walls. Steel columns arranged in pairs in the centre of the facade carry the roof. Connections use plates let into slits and steel brackets, fixed with concealed nailing or dowels. There is a glulam node at the apex. The exposed roof decking above the trusses carries the warm deck roof construction. Bracing at roof level is by way of the trusses.

▢ Bauen mit Holz 8/78

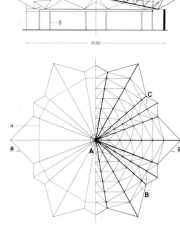

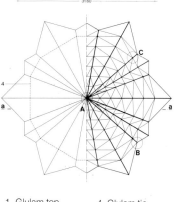

1 Glulam top chord, 180 x 240 mm
2 Glulam bottom chord, 2 No. 140 x 240 mm
3 Glulam diagonal, 140 x 240 mm
4 Glulam tie, 200 x 240 mm
5 Steel circular hollow section column, 216 mm dia.

A

B

C

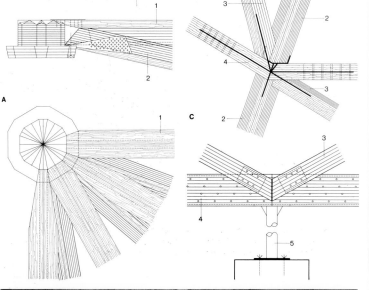

Possible deformations

under a symmetric loading due to snow and wind. Design simplified according to beam theory, sloping surfaces as T-beams, with rigid corners as continuous system.

▢ Hölzerne Dachflächentragwerke, in: *Holzbau-Taschenbuch*, Berlin, 1988

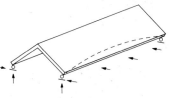

Buckling of one plate

Buckling of both plates

Displacement of bottom edge

Change to angle of fold

Bracing against critical deformation of outer edge

as a result of a uniformly distributed load on one side

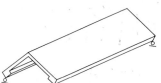

Edge stiffening in plane of plate

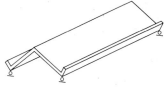

Edge stiffening in plane of plate

Edge beam perpendicular to plane of plate

Edge beam as horizontal prop

Barrel vaults

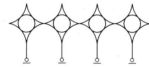

Silos: cone, truncated cone and cylinder

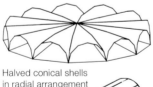

Groined vault

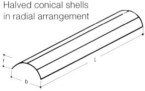

Halved conical shells
in radial arrangement

b < l/5   long barrel vault f ≤ b/2

b > l/5   short barrel vault f ≥ b/2

l = 5–35 m

102 · Service station

La Dôle, CH; 1992

Architect: Vincent Mangeat, Nyon, CH

Structural engineers: Natterer Bois-
Consult, Etoy, CH, und Wolfgang Winter,
Biel, E

Mountain-top service station with living
quarters and ancillary rooms for a radar
installation. Difficult conditions due to the
altitude of 1670 m and the extremely
windy conditions, no access roads and a
very restricted erection time. The structure
consists of nine units each weighing 3.7 t
and measuring 3 x 6.5 x 4 m, and modules forming a link to an existing building.

The elements were prefabricated and pre-
assembled in the factory, then taken on a
low-loader to the foot of the mountain,
from where they were lifted by helicopter
up to the site. Every 3 m wide unit consists of solid timber ribs connected with
special screws. The multi-layer wall to the
units comprises curved, bonded wood-
based boards: two layers of 6 mm OSB
and three layers of 1.2 mm hardboard, in
alternate layers. Attached to the outside
are counter battens and battens for the
sheet aluminium cladding. The form of
these cylindrical shells together with the
shear strength of the double-leaf, rigid
construction provides the necessary overall stability. The timber shell and timber
floor were fixed to a concrete frame.

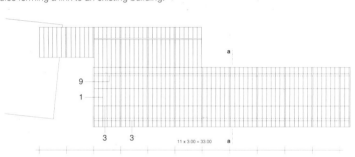

1 Softwood rib,
   60 x 200 mm
2 Curved cladding of bonded
   wood-based boards
3 Timber block
4 Counter battens,
   2 No. 20 x 40 mm
5 Softwood battens,
   30 x 60 mm
6 Special screw
7 2 mm sheet aluminium
8 Temporary bracing
9 Concrete frame

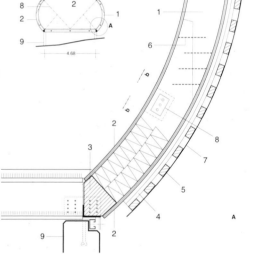

Plywood and LVL forms

Half cylinder

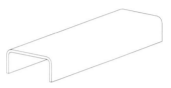

Narrow rectangular form

Wide rectangular form

Multiple-curvature shell

Chair shape

Ribbed slabs

Squared section ribs with plywood on one side, nailed or nail-pressure glued

with plywood on both sides, nailed or glued

Squared section grid, notched joints, curved in one direction, with planking to one side

with planking to both sides, in single curvature

103 · Gallery, trade fair grounds

Frankfurt am Main, D; 1983

Architect: O. M. Ungers, Frankfurt/Main, D

Structural engineers: S. Polónyi, H. Fink, Cologne, D

This 120 m long lattice barrel vault with a semicircular cross-section forms the roof over a gallery linking two trade fair halls, but does not add extra load to their foundations. The steel arch portals form the supports and also brace the barrel vault, which is resolved into transverse glulam arches, 250 x 670 mm, longitudinal glulam beams, 230 x 410 mm, and round

steel bar diagonals. The joints are designed in such a way that the arches, purlins and diagonals intersect in one plane. The main sections of the longitudinal beams pass through openings sawn in the arches, diagonals threaded through the intersections. Forces are transferred between timber and diagonals by direct contact via a steel cable, steel angle sections and steel cover plates. The connection to the steel portal frame is via welded steel crosses and steel fish-plates. Cranked steel glazing bars support the patent glazing.

Bauen mit Holz 7/83;
Die Bautechnik 11/83;
Glasforum 1/84; Detail 2/85

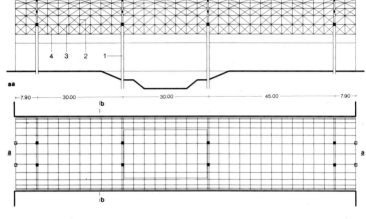

aa

|←7.90→| 30.00 | 30.00 | 45.00 | 7.90 |

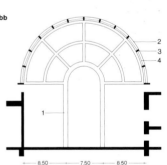

bb

1 Steel portal frame
2 Glulam arch, 250 x 660 mm
3 Glulam longitudinal beam, 230 x 410 mm + 2 No. 230 x 130 mm
4 Steel tie
5 Bearing plate, 25 mm thk
6 Corner angle, 15 mm thk
7 M24 bolt
8 Pin, 42 mm dia.

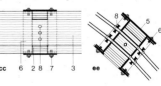

cc   6 2 8 7   3   ee

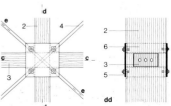

dd

Internal forces in longitudinal direction

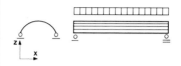

$n_x(x)$

$n_{xp}(x)$

Internal forces in longitudinal direction of shell for linear stress distribution (theory of bending)

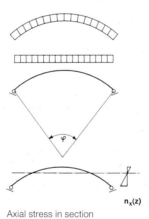

$n_x(z)$

Axial stress in section

$n_{x\varphi}(z)$

Shear forces at support

$n_x(z)$

Transverse bending due to uniformly distributed load

Hölzerne Dachflächentragwerke, in: Holzbau-Taschenbuch, Berlin, 1988

Structural variations

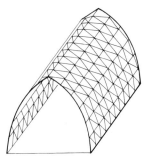

Pointed arch

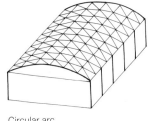

Circular arc

Parabolic arc

104 · Churches in "Zollinger" construction

Cologne/Leverkusen, D; 1957/67

Architects: J. Lehmbrock, K. Schulting, Düsseldorf, D

Structural engineers: P. Schweiger, Munich, D

The roofs to the St Albert Magnus Church in Leverkusen and the Church of the Transfiguration in Cologne comprise shells with timber ribs in a diamond-shaped layout. The junctions between the ribs in this method of construction – devised by Zollinger, a city building surveyor, in the 1920s – are arranged offset so as to connect each pair of ribs with the same bolt or nail. In one case the ribbed shell has a ridge beam, in the other an intersecting ridge and hip beams, which, in the form of a three- or two-pin arch, support the shell. Edge forces are transferred to a concrete beam on the external walls. The roof decking braces the timber ribs.

aa

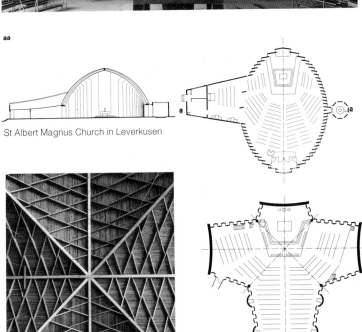

St Albert Magnus Church in Leverkusen

Church of the Transfiguration in Cologne

Junctions between ribs in diamond arrangement

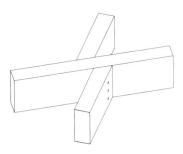

"Zollinger" construction with offset ribs screwed or nailed through the diagonal

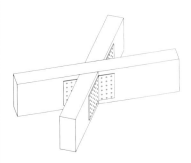

with bent steel plates, nailed

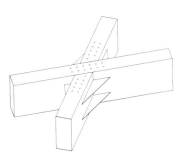

with horizontal steel plates let into slits and nailed

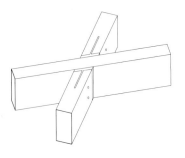

T-sections, let into slits and dowelled

Mesh member-perimeter beam junction

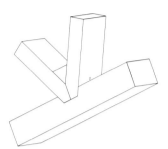

fitted into notch in perimeter beam, fixed with wedge and bolts

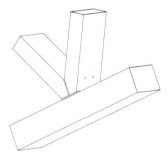

dowelled T-section

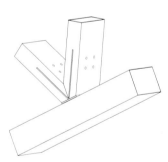

K-shaped steel plate, let into slits and dowelled

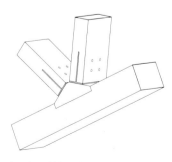

hardwood block in notch, T-sections let into slits

105 · Tuscany thermal springs

Bad Sulza, D; 1999

Architects: Ollertz & Ollertz, Fulda, D

Structural engineers: Trabert und Partner, Geisa, D

This free-form timber ribbed shell was developed using a computer program to simulate the form of a suspended cable net. The final computer model is inverted, the cables in tension are replaced by struts in compression, and the intermediate surfaces are braced, producing a shell essentially in compression. It can then be built with the corresponding slenderness. The shell itself was assembled from individual members but with the number of steel connectors kept to an absolute minimum to reduce the risk of corrosion. Every member has different dimensions, but this presented no problems to the automated fabrication system. The compressive forces resulting from the shell form are carried on the edge beams in double curvature.

Ribs: 160 x approx. 240 mm

Mesh size: approx. 160 x 160 mm

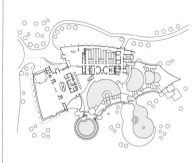

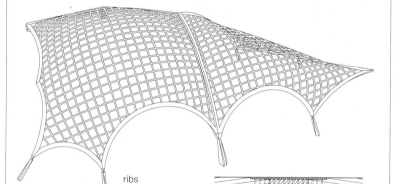

ribs
160 x approx.
240 mm

mesh, approx.
1600 x 1600 mm

aa

a   a

Fixed-base arch

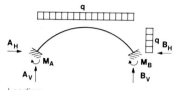

Loading:
uniformly distributed vertical and horizontal loads

Deformations

Moments

Shear forces

Axial forces

Load-carrying behaviour of barrel-vault meshes

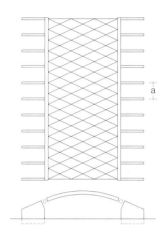

with regular supports
a = 1.2–2 m

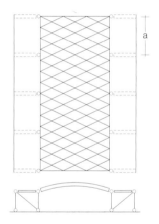

Horizontal edge beam with discrete supports
a = 4-6 m

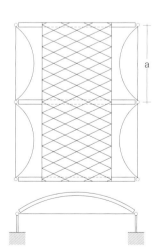

Edge beam integrated in ribbed shell, with tie, fixed-base columns
a = 12–25 m

106 · Indoor riding arena

Berlin, D; 1997

Architects: Sasse & Frode, Berlin, D

Structural engineers: Natterer Bois-Consult, Etoy, CH

This indoor riding arena measures 35 x 45 m on plan. Apart from a section of 20 x 40 m, the construction includes 28 horse stalls, a restaurant area and offices.

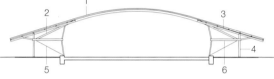

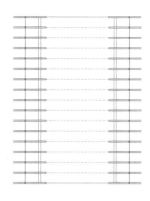

The roof consists of a glued timber ribbed shell spanning 20 m and supported every 5.5 m on log trestles. These carry both the vertical and horizontal loads down to the foundations, whereby the horizontal forces from the shell are taken by the steel edge beams spanning between the columns. Longitudinal bracing is by means of the roof decking attached to the ribs, while stability in the transverse direction is provided by frames.

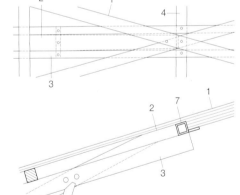

1   Glued softwood timber rib, 6 No. 30 x 150 mm
2   Log, 240 mm dia.
3   Halved log, 2 No. 240 mm dia.
4   Log column, 240 mm dia.
5   Tie, 50 mm dia. round steel bar
6   Pair of softwood ties, 2 No. 100 x 200 mm
7   Steel square hollow section, 150 x 150 x 10 mm

Vertical perimeter beam

Two-part glued laminated timber, with laminations on edge, screwed to shell

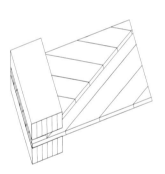

Two-part glued laminated timber, with laminations vertical, glued to shell

One-part glued laminated timber, with laminations vertical, screwed to shell

Perimeter beam perpendicular to shell

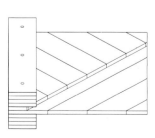

Two-part glued laminated timber, with laminations on edge, glued to shell

Two-part glued laminated timber, with laminations horizontal, glued to shell

Two-part glued laminated timber, with laminations horizontal, screwed to shell

107 · Gymnasium

Arlesheim, CH; 1997

Architects: R. Meuli Architekt, Minusio; May Architekten AG, Neuenegg, CH

Structural engineers: Natterer Bois-Consult, Etoy, CH

This shallow barrel vault formed by a timber ribbed shell over the three sections of this gymnasium covers a total area of 54 x 35 m. Two superimposed ribbed structures support the roof. The upper, straight, ribs carry most of the loads, the lower, diagonal and exposed, ribs act as longitudinal bracing. Both sets of ribs transfer the horizontal forces resulting from the roof form to the arches in the plane of the roof and the eaves beams.

The arches that divide the gymnasium into three parts can be used to support gymnastic apparatus and their ties resist the horizontal forces due to the shell construction.

1   200 x 600 mm glulam section
2   30 mm 3-ply board
3   200 x 600 mm glulam arch
4   160 x 600 mm glulam section
5   Straight rib, 45 x 120 mm
6   30 mm roof decking
7   Diagonal rib, 45 x 120 mm

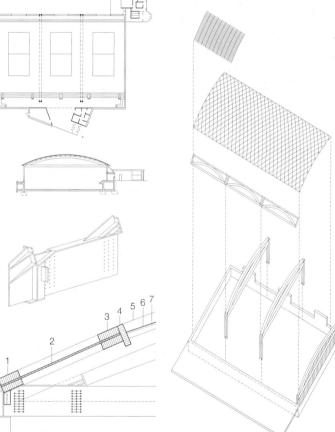

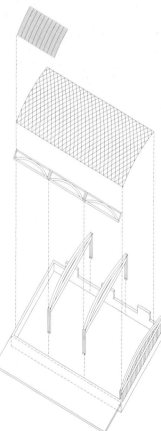

Pinned-base arch

Asymmetric load (e.g. snow)

Dead loads plus constant load (e.g. snow)

Support reactions

Arch shell with perimeter beam and horizontal tie

Classification of ribbed domes

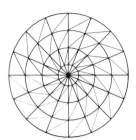

Radial ribs, trapezoidal bays
with diagonals

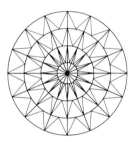

Radial ribs, trapezoidal bays
with K-bracing

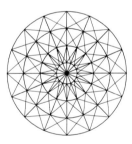

Radial ribs, trapezoidal bays
with X-bracing

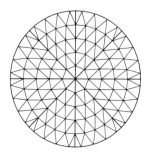

Radial ribs, battens in bays

108 · Sports centre

Oulu, FIN; 1986

Architect: Risto Harju, Oulu, FIN

Structural engineer: Pekka Heikkilä, Oulu,
FIN

This circular sports centre has an internal
diameter of 115 m and a height of 25 m.
This results in a radius of about 90 m for
the spherical dome, which is based on
the hexagonal principle. The primary
loadbearing construction consists of laminated veneer lumber beams. Timber-con-
crete-steel composite joints are used
throughout. The steel plates at the ends of
the two-part beams are in the form of nail
plates to both sides and were attached
prior to gluing. After being bolted to the
central node, the whole node was filled
with a low-slump concrete mix to attain
fire resistance class F30.

1 Laminated veneer lumber beam, two
   parts, glued, FSH 148, 204 x 700 mm
2 Nail plates to both sides
3 Central steel node element
4 M20 high-strength bolt
5 Filling of low-slump concrete

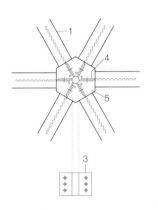

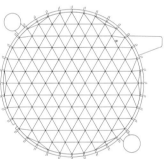

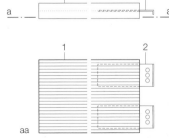

Lattice dome nodes

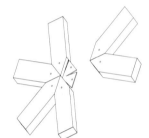

Flat plate let into slits in ribs and
dowelled

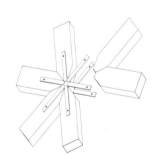

Steel tube with metal straps top
and bottom in star arrangement

Web plates let into slits, with hinge

Lattice dome nodes

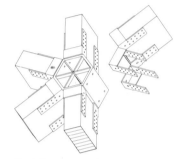

Steel straps screwed to stiffened steel node

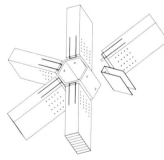

U-shaped nail plate webs screwed to steel node

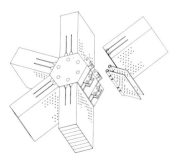

Hardwood block with web plates let into slits, with connecting pins (Blumer system)

109 · Trade fair hall

Brussels, B; 1988

Architect: J. v. Pottelsberghe de la Potterie

Structural engineers: A. v. Wetter, Brussels, Dr Waldner AG, and Blumer AG, Herisau, CH

This exhibition hall at the Brussels trade fair is 74 m wide x 141 m long, and takes the form of a cylindrical barrel vault mesh with hipped gable roofs. Each main arch is made up of a number of rigid-jointed straight glued laminated timber members, each about 13.5 m long. Diagonal ribs fixed at the nodes complement the meridians to form a mesh of flat triangular segments. The nodes are fabricated from octagonal glulam blocks with steel plates, which guarantee both fixity and a high fire resistance. The timber construction is supported on reinforced concrete abutments approx. 6 m high. The roof elements – prefabricated plates comprising timber frame and insulated chipboards – are self-supporting.

📖 Bauen mit Holz 2/89; db 4/89; Schweizer Holzzeitung 1/89

1 16 mm dia. round steel bar
2 Sleeve welded to steel plate
3 12 mm steel plate
4 Pin

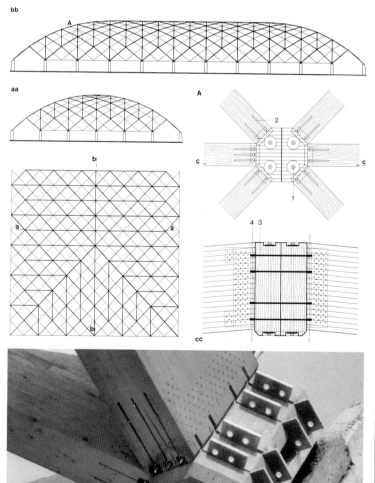

Frames

h ≈ l/75

Ribs

h ≈ l/7100

Trusses

h ≈ l/200

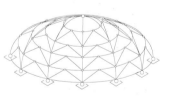

Ribbed shell

h ≈ l/300

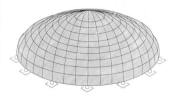

Geometrically assembled lattice dome forms

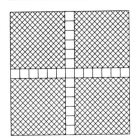

Plan

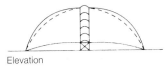

Elevation

spanned diagonally over a square between perimeter arches, with central glazing strip in both directions

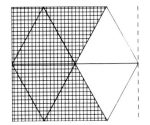

Plan

Elevation

Section

orthogonally spanned perimeter arches arranged between the diagonals

110 · Office and house

Hirituka City, Kanagawa, J; 1988

Architect: Shinji Yoshino, Tokyo, J

Structural engineers: TIS & Partner

During construction the timber lattice shell – in double curvature and without intermediate columns – supported the formwork for casting the five concrete shells that form the curving roof. In the finished condition it remains as an exposed element without any loadbearing function. The timber ribs were assembled on the ground in a 500 mm square mesh. This comprises two layers of boards bolted together at the intersections, plus timber spacers. After lifting into position they were joined to the timber edge members in their final position. The excess rib lengths were cut back to suit at the edges. The shell was cast after attaching the permanent formwork and fixing the reinforcement.

📖 Space Design 1/89

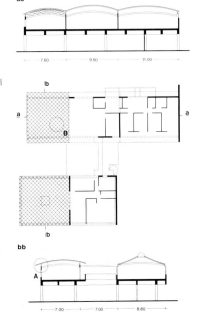

aa

bb

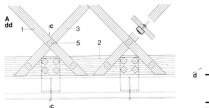

A
dd

cc

1 70 × 35 mm glulam section
2 2 No. 170 × 15 mm
3 Glulam timber spacer, 70 × 35 mm
4 250 mm I-section
5 M10 bolt
6 Concrete shell

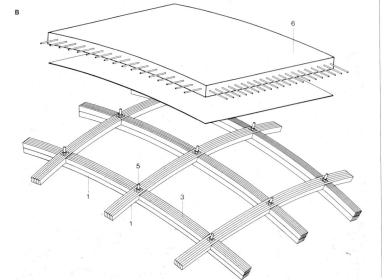

Timber ribbed shells of glued laminated timber and layers of boards

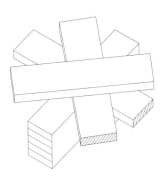

Main rib with three layers of boards

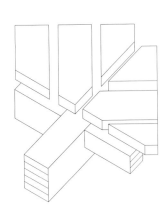

Main rib with annular rib and one layer of diagonal boards

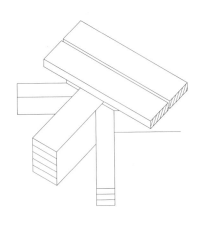

Main rib with diagonal ribs and one layer of boards

Make-up of lattice shells

Two layers of orthogonal ribs, with diagonal boarding

Two layers of orthogonal ribs, with diagonal boarding in two directions

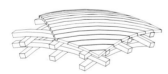

Four layers of orthogonal ribs, with diagonal boarding

Grid of edge-glued elements, orthogonal, with timber spacers

111 · Kindergarten

Triesen, FL; 1998

Architects: Effeff AG, Triesen, FL

Structural engineers: Natterer Bois-Consult, Etoy, CH

A dome consisting of a mesh of board ribs bolted together spans over this kindergarten. Built on a square plan measuring 17 x 17 m, the dome is carried by steel perimeter arches supported only at the four corners. The spacing of the ribs running diagonally between the corners was reduced so that these carry 50% of the loads directly to the foundations. The perimeter arches and the roof decking laid with gaps provide the shell with the necessary three-dimensional stability – especially important under asymmetric loading. Thanks to the perimeter arches there is no horizontal thrust at the foundations.

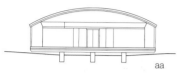

aa

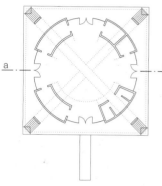

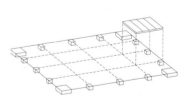

1 Pretensioned glass fibre-reinforced roof membrane; pretension: 1.5 kN/m
2 Spacer, 27 mm dia. plastic sleeve
3 120 mm transparent thermal insulation
4 Polyethylene vapour barrier
5 Roof decking, 27 x 120 mm, laid with 60 mm gaps
6 Diagonal loadbearing ribs each of 4 No. 27 x 160 mm boards bolted together
7 Perimeter beam, IPE 270

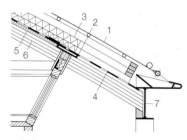

Measures to reduce the risk of punching at nodes

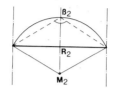

Reducing the radii of spherical segments: $R_2 < R_1$
Reducing the angle of contingence: $\beta_1 < \beta_2$

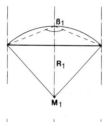

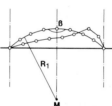

Rigid nodes enable moments to be accommodated

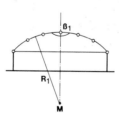

Reducing the angle of contingence: $\beta_2 < \beta_1$ by displacing nodes to the 2nd spherical surface

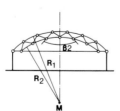

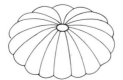

Domes assembled from several highly curved segments (1), which reduce the risk of node punching (after Klöppel)

Surface ratios of spherical segments and equal radius for geodetic and great-circle meshes

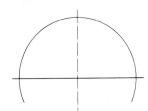

Surface area 100% $\frac{h}{r} = 1$

Area covered 100%

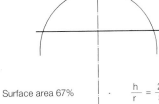

Surface area 67% $\frac{h}{r} = \frac{2}{3}$

Area covered 89%

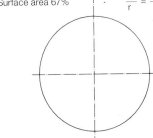

Surface area 50% $\frac{h}{r} = \frac{1}{2}$

Area covered 75%

112 · School of Timber Expertise

Nantes, F; 1995

Architect: J.-P. Logerai, Anger, F

Structural engineers: ICS Bois, M. Flach, J. Natterer, Peisey-Nancroix, F

Log columns carry an orthogonal, square layer of main beams. Arranged on this is a diagonal grid of squared sections within which a circular ribbed dome with edge-glued elements is constructed. The horizontal forces from the dome are resisted by a glued laminated timber ring. The vertical loads from the dome are carried by timber columns which also form the load-bearing structure for the truncated cone. Its timber cladding braces the structure against wind forces.

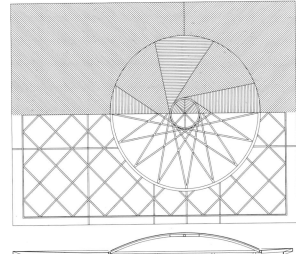

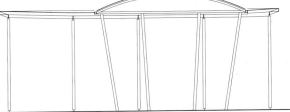

1 Glulam outer ring, 210 x 212 mm
2 Dome support beam, 136 x 168 mm
   edge-glued elements
3 Softwood "spoke", 112 x 201 mm

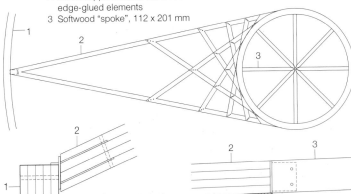

Dome supports

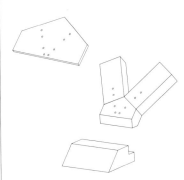

with hardwood block and gusset

with hardwood block and plate let into slits fixed to channel section

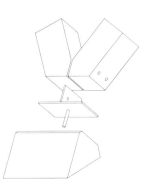

on T-section with cast-in pin

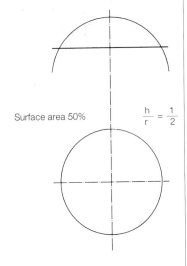

Dome supports

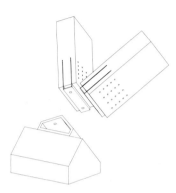

Channel sections let into slits and bolted to steel bearing, filled with epoxy resin

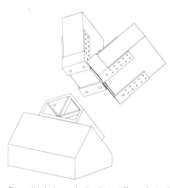

Dowelled shoes bolted to stiffened steel bearing

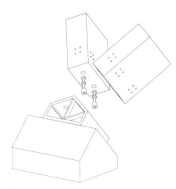

Bonded-in dowels
and stiffened steel bearing

113 · Swimming pool

Saint Quentin en Yvelines, F; 1997

Architects: M. Carduner & Partner, Paris, F

Structural engineers: ICS Bois, M. Flach, J. Natterer, Peisey-Nancroix, F

The roof to the restaurant, changing rooms and plant rooms of this swimming pool complex is a torus-shaped 225° circular segment with a diameter of 54 m. This timber shell is supported on reinforced concrete columns around the perimeter and a central pedestal in the middle, also in reinforced concrete. Around the edge there is a horizontal, curving glued laminated timber beam, acting as a ring in tension. BVD bonded anchors were used for the on-site joints subjected to tension. The loadbearing elements of the ribbed dome are arranged along geodetic lines in order to avoid curvature about two axes. They are glued in the flat outer area owing to the high bending stresses, merely nailed in the middle section of the shell. A layer of planks on edge covers the ribs. These were curved on site and bolted together and to the ribs. The cross-section of the planks varies depending on span and radius of curvature.

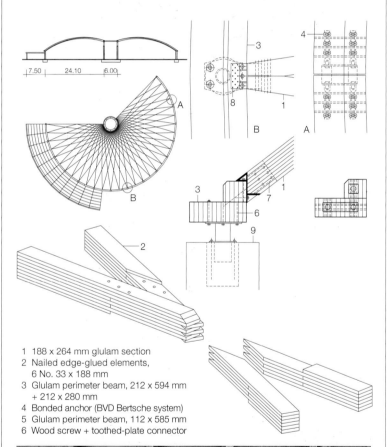

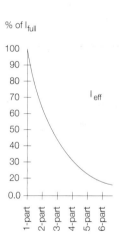

1 188 x 264 mm glulam section
2 Nailed edge-glued elements,
   6 No. 33 x 188 mm
3 Glulam perimeter beam, 212 x 594 mm
   + 212 x 280 mm
4 Bonded anchor (BVD Bertsche system)
5 Glulam perimeter beam, 112 x 585 mm
6 Wood screw + toothed-plate connector

Load-carrying behaviour of mesh dome

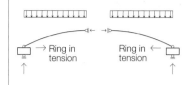

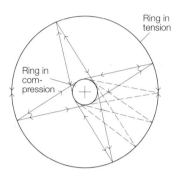

Stiffness of ribs:
The ribs consist of several layers of boards nailed together. This creates an elastically connected compound section, which achieves only a fraction of the stiffness of a homogeneous section (e.g. glued) depending on number of individual parts and span.

Two-way-spanning edge-glued domes

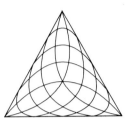

over triangular plan

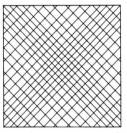

over square plan with spacing of ribs gradually decreasing towards diagonals, and vertical perimeter arches

over square plan with perimeter arches inclined towards centre of dome

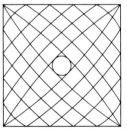

as great-circle mesh with vertical perimeter arches

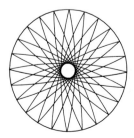

as great-circle mesh with horizontal ring in compression at apex and ring in tension at springing point

114 · Multipurpose hall

Mannheim, D; 1975

Architects: C. Mutschler und Partner, Mannheim; F. Otto und Partner, Warmborn, D

Structural engineers: Ove Arup & Partners, London, GB

A shell-type lattice grid covering an area of 4700 m². It spans up to 60 m as a three-dimensional curved grid of individual members. When flat, the 50 x 50 mm battens in two, three or four layers form a regular orthogonal 500 x 500 mm mesh. Lifting the mesh to form a curved shell causes the squares to become diamonds

with angles from 70° to 110°. The force transfer at the nodes is by friction between the timber members, plus pins and up to three disc spring washers, which ensure the frictional resistance. The shape of the shell is chosen so that only compressive forces occur under a uniformly distributed vertical load. The asymmetric snow and horizontal wind loads critical for the design of the structure are resisted by the rigidity of the multi-layer grid of battens and by the tension cables running diagonally across the diamonds.

Baumeister 8/75, p. 702;
The Structural Engineer 3/75, p. 99;
Holzbau 6/75, p. 162

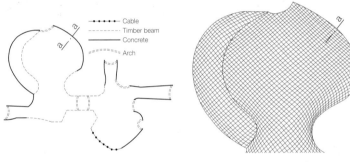

Cable
Timber beam
Concrete
Arch

1 Finger-jointed squared sections, 50 x 50 mm
2 8 mm dia. pin
3 55 mm dia. washer
4 35 mm dia. disc spring washer
5 Spacer
6 Nailing strip
7 Roof covering
8 Elongated hole
11 Plywood edge board
12 Support bracket made from steel section

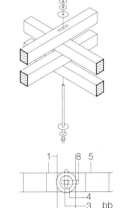

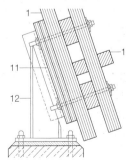

Node details

with bolt

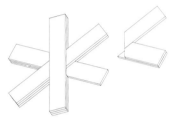

alternately continuous edge-glued elements bolted, nailed or nail-pressure glued, with timber spacers

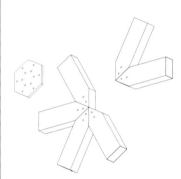

nailed plywood or steel plate

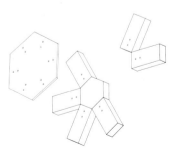

with hardwood plywood or concrete block and nailed plates

Ribbed shells in edge-glued construction

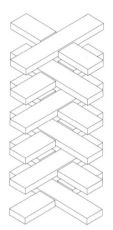

Edge-glued mesh made from individual boards screwed continuously to form a rigid ribbed shell

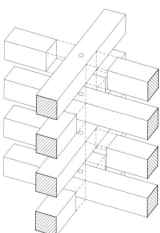

Lattice grid made from squared sections joined with pins

115 · Exhibition pavilion

Nara, J; 1987

Architect: Masahito Kibayasni, Kikutake & Ass.

Structural engineers: Maeno, Wada, Nagase, Hisatoku

Two exhibition pavilions and an information centre are each roofed over by a grid of battens curving in three dimensions. Form-finding was carried out by means of suspended wire models, which were subsequently computed and analysed as a mathematical model. The bending stresses due to the pre-bending of the 40 x 70 mm battens are limited by keeping to a minimum radius. The form was established such that only membrane stresses occur under dead loads. The battens are at 500 mm centres in four intersecting layers. Timber spacers ensure local rigidity. Plate action is enhanced by steel diagonals. The shell was assembled from 4 m wide, prefabricated curved individual elements. Connections utilise pins and steel plates. A 3 m high peripheral reinforced concrete wall forms the substructure. The roof covering is a membrane.

📖 Space Design 1/89

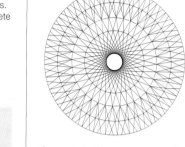

Nara Pavillon
62.5 m

Theme Pavillon
104.5 m

Information Centre
39.5 m

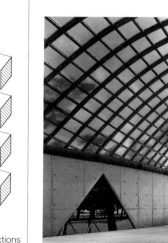

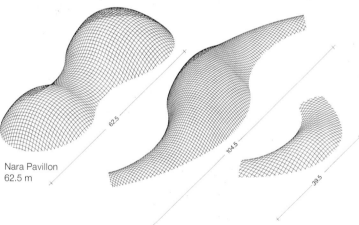

Edge-glued dome, deformations

Geometry on plan

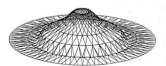

Perspective view of geometry

Distribution of wind pressure coefficients

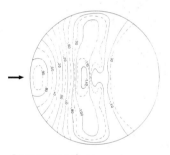

Deformation due to dead loads and snow

Deformation due to dead load, snow and wind

📖 Diploma thesis at Lausanne University and Ruhr University, Bochum, 1990

Hyperbolic paraboloid shells

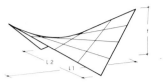

for $l_1 = l_2$ edge beam

$$h = b = \frac{l}{60} \text{ to } \frac{l}{80}$$

l = 14–60 m
(2–3 or 4–5 layers of boards × 21 m)
finger-jointed throughout

Combined hyperbolic paraboloid shells

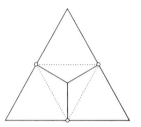

Cantilever shells supported at three points, plus ties

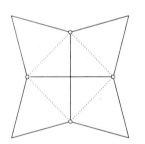

Cantilever shells supported at four points, plus ties

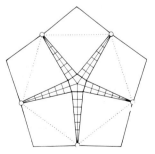

Cantilever shells with strips of roof glazing, supported at five points, plus ties

116 · Leisure pool

Freiburg, D; 1981–83

Architect: H. D. Hecker, Freiburg

Structural engineer: M. Scherberger, Freiburg

A sequence of 10 hyperbolic paraboloid shells forms the roof over this swimming pool. Each shell segment rests on four reinforced concrete columns placed in two rows 21 m apart. The segments cantilever out at the facade and the high points at mid-span are supported by trussed struts.

The three layers of 22 mm diagonal boarding on the shell segment enable each one to act as a shear-resistant secondary loadbearing system. The edge members are two-part, twisted, glued laminated sections. The joints between the segments are used to admit daylight and for ventilation. Overall stability is guaranteed by the shell segments acting as plates. Continuity results from the trussing and the fixed-base columns. Roof covering of PVC coating on polyurethane foam insulation. The shell segments were built on the ground adjacent to the site and lifted into place with a crane.
📖 Bauen mit Holz 12/86

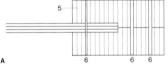

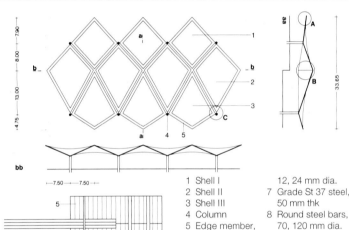

1 Shell I
2 Shell II
3 Shell III
4 Column
5 Edge member,
   2 No. 200 x
   700 mm
6 Dowels,

   12, 24 mm dia.
7 Grade St 37 steel,
   50 mm thk
8 Round steel bars,
   70, 120 mm dia.
9 Gusset plate,
   20 mm thk
10 Geka dowel

Make-up of hyperbolic paraboloid shells

Round-section edge members and ribs, with diagonal layers of boards

Two diagonal layers of boards with nail-pressure glued two-part edge member

Three diagonal layers of boards

Twisted glued laminated timber edge members and ribs

Corner details for hyperbolic paraboloid shells

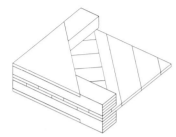

Two diagonal layers of boards with two-part edge member, glued corner reinforcement

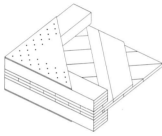

Plywood or steel corner reinforcement, nailed

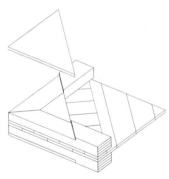

Edge member notched to accommodate plate, plus glued timber fillet

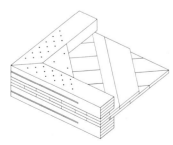

Plates let into slits, plus dowelled hardwood fillet

117 · Multipurpose hall

Leuk, CH; 1986

Architects: H. and P. Wenger, Brig, CH

Structural engineer: H. Gasser, Lungern, CH

This hexagonal multipurpose hall is covered by a timber shell of six identical hyperbolic paraboloid segments. The 260 m² roof is supported at the six low points. Each segment was produced on a jig using two diagonal layers of 24 mm boards and edge members of glued laminated timber. The parallel boards were curved and laid without open joints. The boards were glued together and to the edge members using resorcinol resin, with pressure applied by nails or screws. The finished segments were lifted into place by crane and joined together. The underside has been left exposed, while the topside is insulated and covered with a synthetic roofing felt.

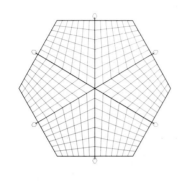

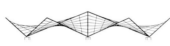

1 Glulam main beam,
   120 x 350 mm
2 Glulam edge beam,
   2 No. 80 x 120 mm
3 24 mm decking
4 Metal bracket

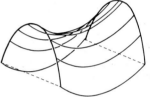

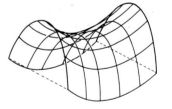

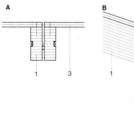

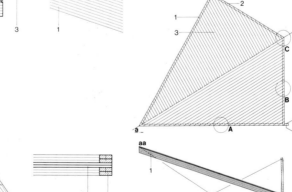

Generation of a hyperbolic paraboloid

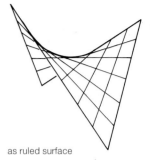

as ruled surface

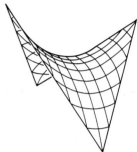

as translational surface

as a group of identical parabolas suspended between two vertical parabolas

as a group of identical, vertical parabolas suspended from a parabola

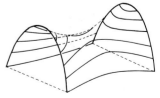

with all vertical sections as parabolas

with all horizontal sections as hyperbolas

259

Subassemblies

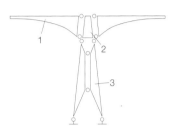

1 Cantilever bracket
2 Steel pedestal
3 Tower

Vibration behaviour

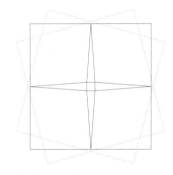

Oscillations due to torsion
f = 0.45 Hz

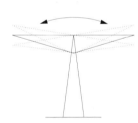

Oscillations due to rocking motion
f = 1.23 Hz

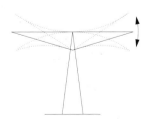

Oscillations due to butterfly effect
f = 1.93 Hz

118 · Expo roof

Hannover, D; 2000

Architect: T. Herzog + Partner, Munich

Structural engineers: IEZ Natterer GmbH,
Wiesenfelden, D; Peter Bertsche, Pracken-
bach, D; Ingenieurbüro ks, Martin
Kessel, Dirk Gnutzmann, Hildesheim, D

Each individual canopy consists of several subassemblies: four shell segments,

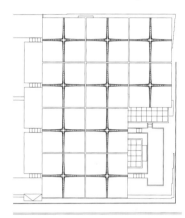

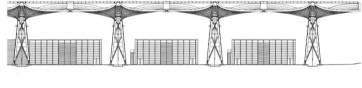

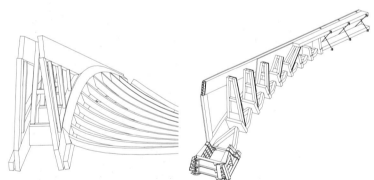

four cantilever brackets, a central steel
truncated pyramid pedestal and the
tower. The shell segments, measuring
19 x 19 m, are built as ribs of edge-glued
members intersecting at 90° and covered
with a translucent synthetic membrane.
The vertical distance between high points
and low point is 6 m. Each segment carries the loads – through the shell effect
but also through bending – from dead
loads (37 t), wind and snow to the edge
beams.

The cantilever brackets take the loads
from the edge beams (transferred at the
tip) and from the shell (transferred continuously along the bottom chord). The bottom chord of the cantilever bracket follows the curvature of the edge of the shell
and is connected to the top chord in the
outer third. The depth of each cantilever
bracket increases towards the centre of
the canopy in line with the stresses and
strains.

The four cantilever brackets are supported on the central steel pedestal, which
directs all the forces from the roof area
into the tower.

All the horizontal and vertical loads are
transferred to the foundations via the
tower, which consists of four interconnected log columns and triangular bracing
fins. The connection between the central
pedestal and the tops of the four columns
is a hinge so that only axial and shear
forces are transferred. The bracing fins

Make-up of timber lattice shells using edge-glued construction

from membrane to rigid grid depending on stiffness of connections

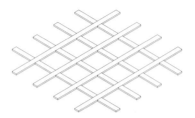

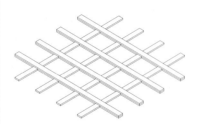

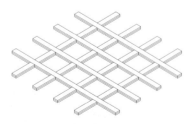

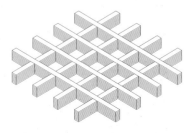

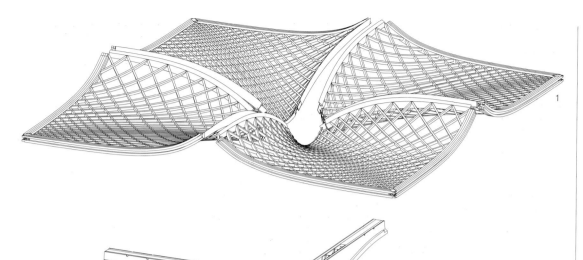

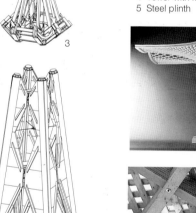

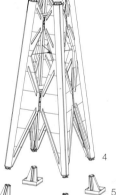

resist the entire horizontal loads due to wind and any forces due to unintentional out-of-plumb effects.

The support reactions are transferred to the foundations via steel plinths. The foundations for each tower consist of four 1200 mm dia. bored piles, 10–15 m long, linked by a reinforced concrete pilecap. Wind tunnel tests were very important during the development of the loadbearing structure. Unfavourable snow load distributions arose on the individual canopies due to the effects of the wind. In addition, it was discovered that side winds caused a severe additional downward load. The uplift due to wind suction was negligible.

📖 Müller: *Laminated Timber Construction*, Birkhäuser, 2000, p. 171

1 Lattice shells
2 Cantilever bracket
3 Steel pedestal
4 Tower with four solid timber legs
5 Steel plinth

100 %	100 %
100 %	100 %

full

75 %	95 %
75 %	95 %

shifted by
side wind

30 %	100%
60 %	30 %

shifted by
diagonal wind

+0,8	+1,20
+0,5	+0,75

Aerodynamic behaviour
(pressure coefficients) max. V

Combined hyperbolic paraboloid shells

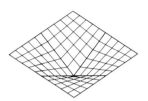

Valley folds fall to a common low point

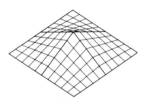

Hip folds rise to a common high point

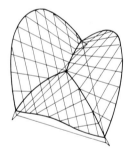

Three intersecting, identical hyperbolic saddle surfaces with inclined outer hyperbolic arches as edge members

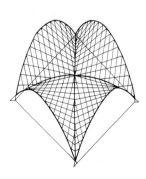

Four identical, radially arranged hyperbolic paraboloid surfaces with vertical outer parabolic arches

119 · Manufacturing pavilion

Bad Münder, D; 1987

Architects: Frei Otto and Planungsgruppe Gesternig, Bremen, D

Structural engineers: M. Speich, F.-J. Hinkes, Hannover, D

Two flat three-pin frames at an angle to the vertical and joined together with transverse tension members are positioned on one axis of symmetry. The fixed-base perimeter columns support an eaves

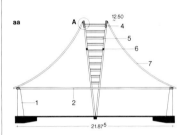

aa

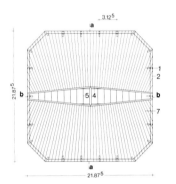

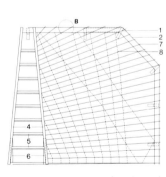

B

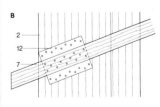

A

purlin right around the building. Ribs suspended between the three-pin frames and the horizontal eaves purlin carry the roof decking of tongue and groove boards. The ribs have a uniform radius of curvature of 20 m and form, as a saddle surface, a free membrane form between straight edge members. Ties positioned at 90° to the suspended ribs prevent the three-pin frames deflecting sideways under asymmetric loads.

📖 Bauen mit Holz 12/86; Müller: *Laminated Timber Construction*, Birkhäuser, 2000, p. 153

1 Perimeter column, 20 x 500–1000 mm
2 Glulam eaves purlin, 210 x 450 mm
3 Strut, 200 x 300 mm
4 Three-pin glulam frame, 200 x 650–450 mm
5 Transverse member, 100 x 350 mm
6 Collar, 200 x 300 mm
7 Suspended rib, 65 x 93 mm
8 Diagonal brace, 2 x 60 mm
9 80 mm dia. Geka single-sided connector
10 Pin
11 Dowel
12 BMF perforated plate
13 Steel plate

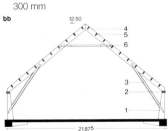

bb

Suspension details

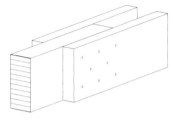

Connected with dowels on both sides

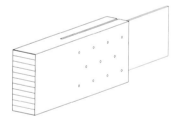

Metal plate let into slit

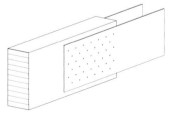

Metal plates nailed to both sides

Supports for hyperbolic paraboloid shells

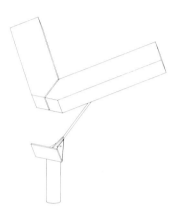

on a steel column, with tie for resisting horizontal forces

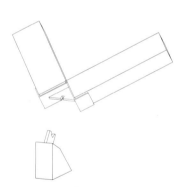

on a concrete abutment, with rocker bearing

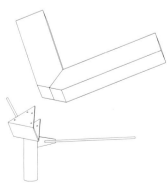

on a steel column, with ties forming a ring anchor

120 · Pavilion

Dortmund, D; 1969

Structural engineer: G. Scholz, Munich

Consultants: Natterer Bois Consult, Etoy, CH

Pavilion for German's national gardening exhibition held in Dortmund in 1969.
A suspended shell similar to a diamond on plan. The edge members of glued laminated timber, 2 No. 180 mm deep x 1400 mm wide, twisted and in double curvature,

span between the high and low points. The high points are propped by raking columns and have one or two guy cables. The main loadbearing members are the ribs, 200 x 200 mm at 1.5 m centres, spanning up to 65 m in concave form between the high points and the edge members. The edge members carry the tensile forces from the suspended ribs with opposing convex curvature into three layers of boards laid at an angle of 45° to each other and fixed with shear-resistant nailing. The suspended shell was pretensioned by cables to increase the buckling resistance.

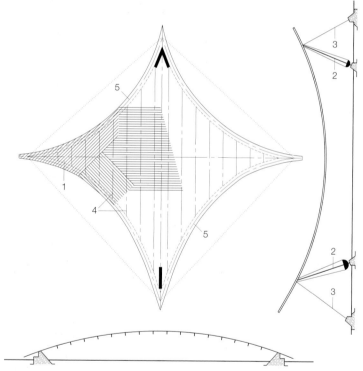

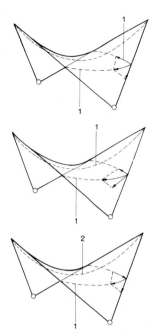

1 Suspended rib, 200 x 240 mm
2 Cruciform leg (with opposing tapers) in compression, 280 x 500–2500 mm + 280 x 500–1600 mm
3 Tensioning cable, 91 or 217 individual wires, 7 mm dia., as parallel-lay wire rope
4 Layers of boards, 1 No. 24 mm and 2 No. 16 mm
5 Edge member, 360 x 1400 mm, twisted and in double curvature

Loadbearing behaviour of hyperbolic paraboloid shells

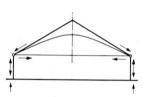

Subjected to a uniformly distributed load, the forces combine at the edge to form resultant forces in the direction of the edge.

1 Tension arc
2 Compression arc

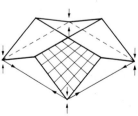

Horizontal forces from the saddle surface can be resisted by ties between the support points.

Suitable combinations of several saddle surfaces enable the ties to be placed in the external walls.

$$H = X_y \cdot \frac{l}{n} \cdot \frac{l^2}{8f}$$

$$V = X_x \cdot q \; \frac{l}{n} \cdot \frac{l}{2}$$

X_x, X_y = load component factors

l = distance between opposing high or low points of shell measured on projection

Generation of a form in double curvature through rotation

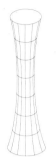

Paraboloid of revolution, with circle and parabola having identical radii about an axis of rotation

Translational paraboloid, with circle and straight lines

Generated from circle segments, sine-wave lines, parabolas or hyperbolas about an axis of rotation

Torus segments of geometrically definable forms

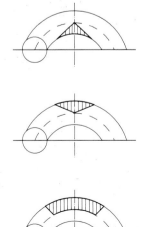

121 · Recycling facility

Vienna, A; 1981

Architect: L. M. Lang, Vienna

Structural engineers: Natterer und Dittrich Planungsgesellschaft, Munich

Tent-like suspended roof construction, 170.6 m dia., for a waste processing plant. The shape of the 48 radial suspended ribs was chosen so that only tensile forces occur under symmetrical loading. Asymmetric loads are distributed over the roof surface by the annular purlins and subject the ribs to bending. The addition of bracing around the perimeter and a layer of diagonal boards turn the mesh formed by the ribs and the purlins into a stable shear-resistant structure, providing bracing to the ribs and a shell effect. The central 67 m tall reinforced concrete cylinder is restrained at the base and carries part of the wind loading as well as the symmetrical erection loads. The 11 m tall perimeter supports are constructed as triangular reinforced concrete walls on pad foundations. These can accommodate the anchorage forces of the ribs without significant deformation.

　Küttinger: *Holzbau-Konstruktionen*, Munich, 1984; Müller: *Laminated Timber Construction*, Birkhäuser, 2000, p. 162

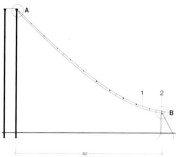

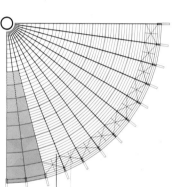

1	Suspended glulam rib, 200 x 800– 1100 mm	2	Annular glulam purlin, 120 x 390 mm	4	Hinge pin, 90 mm dia.	7	Web
				5	Nail plate	8	Gutter
		3	Steel ring	6	Base plate	9	120 x 390 mm glulam section

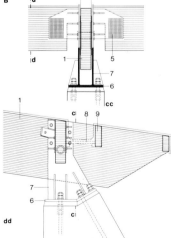

Connection between suspended rib and edge member or support

Twin tie with round steel bar shear connector and nail plate strengthening

Beam with steel tie connected via nail plates and hinge pin

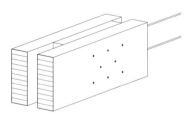

Two-part rib and steel flat connected via dowelled timber spacer with steel end plate

Connection between suspended rib and central pylon

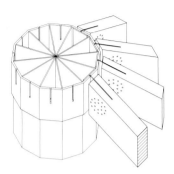

with T-section let into slit in timber and slotted into support ring

with steel plate between two-part rib, with ring of dowels

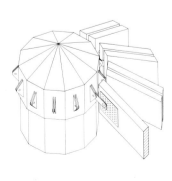

with nail plates and pins

122 · Brine baths

Bad Dürrheim, D; 1987

Architects: Geier & Geier, Stuttgart

Structural engineers: Wenzel, Frese, Pörtner, Haller, Barthel, Karlsruhe; Linkwitz, Preuss, Stuttgart (form study)

A suspended shell of timber ribs spans between five "tree columns" and the perimeter arches over this 1500 m² leisure complex. After specifying the edge conditions, the shape of the shell was determined such that the loads could essentially be carried as membrane stresses. The meridian and annular glulam ribs, twisted and in double curvature, interlock at the nodes. They were manufactured in the form generated by the computer model and follow – approximately – the principal stress trajectories. Two layers of diagonal timber boarding give the shell its high shear strength. The connections to the "tree columns" and the perimeter arches are via inclined glulam arches positioned tangentially to the surface of the shell. The "tree columns" constructed from glulam segments can be lifted by jacks. Connection between edge members and facade columns is by way of cast ball-and-socket joints. The roof covering is PVC.

📖 Detail 6/87; Bauen mit Holz 5/87; DRZ 11/88; Gutdeutsch: *Building in Wood*, Birkhäuser, 1996, p. 44

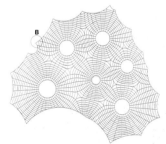

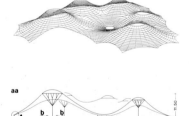

aa

1 120 x 240 mm glulam section
2 300 x 160 x 30 mm glulam section
3 Cast aluminium column head
4 140 x 120 mm glulam section
5 205 x 200 mm glulam section
6 120 x 120 mm glulam section
7 Dowel, 18 x 270 mm
8 Plywood
9 Corner support

bb

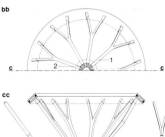

cc

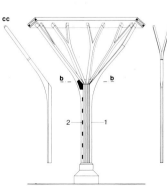

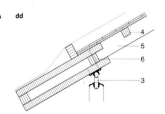

A dd

B

Shells of revolution

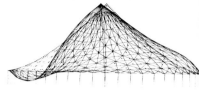

Deformations due to wind and asymmetric snow loads (deformations exaggerated for clarity)

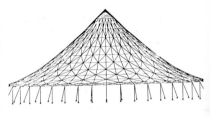

Computer model of system

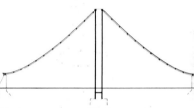

Section

Radial system with compression system

Radial system with rings in compression for bracing the shell against asymmetric loads, plus guyed suspended arches as perimeter beams

Tower system variations

comprising straight members with restraint due to support at three points

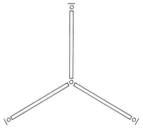

comprising glued laminated timber members

123 · Campanile

Eichstetten, D; 1977

Design and structural engineering:
W. Hirzle, Umkirch

This freestanding campanile for a chapel of rest consists of two V-shaped frames, one upside-down. These two frames are connected at the level of the bells to avoid bending moments. A triangular frame joins the tips of the two main frames and, together with the purlins, forms a pitched roof surface. This three-legged trestle is stabilised by axial forces. The buckling length of the members is reduced by the connection at the intersection. The legs are founded on concrete pad foundations.

📖 Bauen mit Holz 3/78

1 Conical glulam leg,
  180–400 x 180 mm
2 Pins and dowels,
  12 mm dia.
3 Split-ring connec-
  tor, 65 mm dia.
4 Motor platform

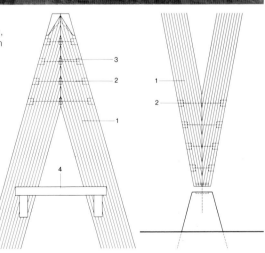

Connection of round steel wind girder diagonals to primary loadbearing system

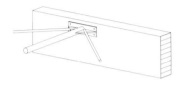

Wind girder comprising steel circular hollow sections and round steel bar diagonals

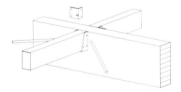

Timber wind girder on joist hangers, round steel bar diagonals threaded

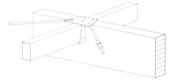

Timber wind girder on joist hangers, round steel bars or steel flats with turn-buckles

Connection of flat steel wind girder diagonals to primary loadbearing system

Timber wind girder on angles, diagonal ties screwed

Timber wind girder on Z-hangers, diagonals screwed to opposing support section

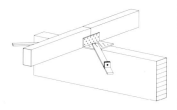

Timber wind girder connected to main beam via angled nail plates, steel flat diagonals with tension screws

124 · Viewing platform

Lausanne, CH; 2003

Architects: City of Lausanne, B. Bolli, R. Mohr, Lausanne, CH

Structural engineers: Natterer Bois Consult, Etoy, CH

This 36 m tower has a viewing and observation platform at a height of 30 m. There are also intermediate platforms at 9 m and 20 m. The diameter of this circular tower tapers from 12 m at the bottom to 6 m below the main platform. Arranged regularly around the circumference are 24 half-round columns forming the outer supports for a double-helix staircase, with two completely independent routes to the top. In the middle the steps of solid Douglas fir, 200 x 400 mm, are threaded over a metal spindle. Edge-glued elements make up the main viewing platform and the two intermediate platforms.

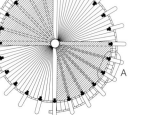

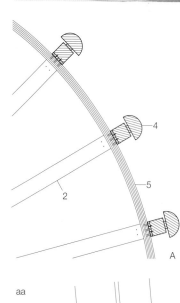

aa

bb

1 Intermediate platform, 200 mm edge-glued element
2 Platform beam, 200 x 200 mm Douglas fir
3 Step, 400 x 200 mm
4 Column, compound section, 350 mm dia. half-round + 200 x 200 mm square section Douglas fir
5 Curved glulam edge beam, 100 x 200 mm

Space frames

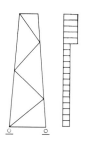

Loading:
uniformly distributed horizontal loads

Deformations

Axial forces

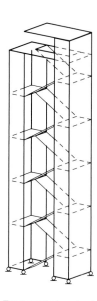

Tower made from two U-shaped loadbearing sections, with stairs, restrained via four supports for each section

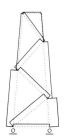

Space frame variations

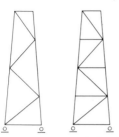

with diagonals in both directions,
with and without horizontal members

with horizontal members,
plus diagonals in one direction

with horizontal members
and X-bracing

with diamond or K-bracing

125 · Viewing platform

Venne, D; 1976

Architects: Osnabrück Building Department

Structural engineers: W. Seifert,
F. Schneider, Bramsche, D

A square viewing platform 18 m high.
Four columns, each of two dowelled solid
timber sections, with an erection splice at
half height. K-bracing and transverse
members at every level brace the structure. The impregnated larch wood and
connections with galvanised and plastic-coated nail plates let into slits (Greim
system) provide protection against the
weather. The staircase is positioned diagonally across the tower. The joists of the
intermediate landings (with screwed oak
planks) stiffen the structure on plan. The
corner columns are anchored with dowelled steel sections cast into the concrete
foundations. Overall stability is through
the frame action.

☐ Bauen mit Holz 5/77

1 Column, 2 No.
   180 x 180 mm
2 Transverse
   member,
   180 x 140 mm
3 K-bracing,
   180 x 160 mm
4 Steel plate,
   100 x 7 mm
5 Toothed-plate
   connector,
   95 mm dia.
6 4 No. plates
7 Bolt

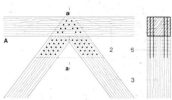

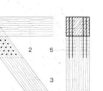

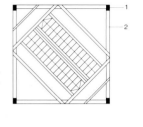

dd

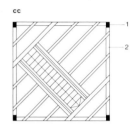

cc

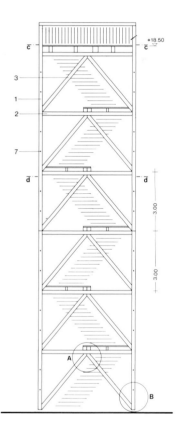

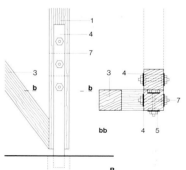

**Connection details for bracing
members in primary loadbearing
systems of timber**

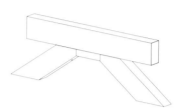

with rectangular straining block
and wood screws

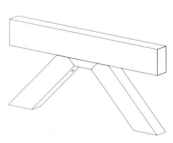

with trapezoidal hardwood straining
block and wood screws

with nailed angle plates

Connection details for bracing members in primary loadbearing systems of timber

with spit-ring connectors and bolts

with gusset plate let into slits and dowelled

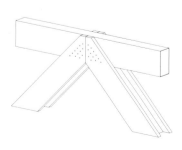

with three-part nailed diagonals

126 · Transmitter mast

Ismaning, D; 1932/46

Structural engineers: Kübler (timber engineering), Stuttgart, D

This transmitter mast belonging to Bavarian Radio was demolished in 1983 as it threatened to collapse. The upper part 115 m tall measured 20 m wide at the base and 2 m at the top, and was originally erected in 1932 as a tower in its own right. It was later made taller by adding a 39 m high substructure and by extending the tip to reach a total height of 165 m.

A

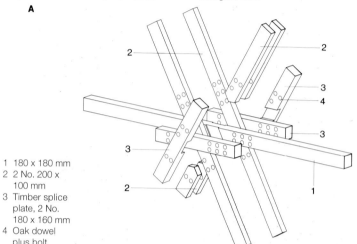

1 180 x 180 mm
2 2 No. 200 x 100 mm
3 Timber splice plate, 2 No. 180 x 160 mm
4 Oak dowel plus bolt

154.00

39.00

A

This was a truss construction that used the Kübler system. American pitch pine wood was used to provide a high rotting resistance. The largest individual section was 140 x 240 mm. Kübler dowelled connections with bronze bolts were used throughout. Owing to the high cost of refurbishment, which was largely due to the enhanced requirements of current building regulations, the mast was demolished in 1983 – stability according to DIN 1052 had never been proved.

☐ Bauen mit Holz 8/82; C. v. Büren: *Form und Funktion*, Basel/Boston/Stuttgart, 1985

Wind load assumptions (preliminary calculations)

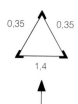

Wind perpendicular
c = 2.1

Wind diagonal
c = 2.1

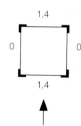

Wind perpendicular
c = 2.8

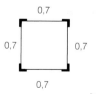

Wind diagonal
c = 3.08

$W = c \cdot q \cdot F$
where
F = surface area of one wall
W = wind load
c = pressure coefficient

Centering variations

in fan form

in fan form

in tower form

as arch of boards, Cruciani system

127 · Log bridge centering

Mülmisch viaduct, D; 1985–88

Architects: Central Railways Building Department, MBS project group, Frankfurt am Main

Structural engineers: Harries + Kinkel GmbH, Neu-Isenburg, Holzbau Rinn, Heuchelheim

As a change from cantilevering with temporary guying, the construction of the A-frame for this railway viaduct made use of timber centering on which the concrete box section was cast symmetrically. The 100 m long, 60 m high and just 7 m wide temporary structure was stabilised by guys on both sides, with the prestressed steel cables converging at two anchorage points on sheet piling. Log trestles and columns together with steel diagonals form the basic element for the three-storey bottom section. Log struts support the purlins carrying the formwork. These are connected to the main beams of squared timber sections by way of timber shims and oblique dado joints. Nailed steel straps form a mesh of tension diagonals to give a frame effect in both directions. Vertical and horizontal jacks permit deformations to be compensated for and the centering to be lowered.

  Bauingenieur 64/89;
  Bauen mit Holz 11/88

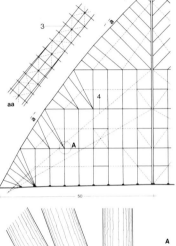

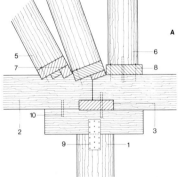

1 Log column, 270–400 mm dia.
2 Main beam, 260 x 360 mm
3 Transverse beam, 70 x 280 mm
4 Steel tie, 60 x 2 mm
5 Raking log strut, 250 mm dia.
6 Vertical log strut, 250 mm dia.
7 Timber shim
8 Wood screw, 12 x 200 mm
9 Nail plate
10 Dowel

Erection of centre

Tower of logs and squared sections

Multiple diamond lattice trusses of squared timber sections

Bracing the structure

Erection

Wright standard type A

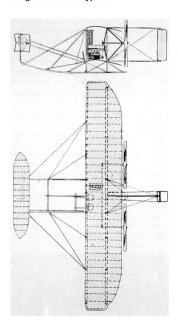

Orville's flight to Berlin

Light aircraft

Section through wing

128 · Glider

Designers: A. Markwalder, Räterschen, CH; H. Berchthold, Mänikon, CH

A glider with a span of 17 m and 23 kg/m^2 lift. Proportions of materials used: timber 70%, plastics 20%, miscellaneous metals 10%. Parts of the fuselage and the leading edge of the wing are made from laminated veneer lumber (LVL). The latter consists of seven layers of 3 mm okoume, bonded with resorcinol resin, formed into a tapering shell in double curvature. The low weight of the wood compared to polyester added an extra 2 kg/m^2 lift. The use of LVL overcomes the problems of cracks in polyester wings due to bending stresses. Such cracks are detrimental to the aerodynamics.

Spruce Goose
span: 97.5 m
overall length: 66.7 m
overall height: 24.2 m
flying speed at 5000 ft: 370 km/h
max. speed on water: 355 km/h

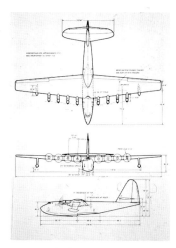

Aircraft fuselage during assembly

Stiffening rings

Wing

Maiden flight on 2 November 1947

Howard Hughes and his "flying boat", Barton Charles, USA, 1982

Part 6   Built examples: facades

The diversity of the modern age

Thomas Herzog

Similarly to the colour plates at the beginning of this book, the following, second collection of colour plates again concentrates on effects with an aesthetic significance, taking examples of buildings from recent decades. The enormous differences bring home the diversity of today's possibilities when the aim is to allow wood to become the memorable characteristic in architectural projects fit for the future.

The construction of many of the structures shown in the photographs is briefly described and illustrated in the subsequent section covering current buildings.

1
2 | 3
    | 4

Plate 16

1 Chapel of rest, Budapest, Hungary
   (architects: Imre Makovecz and Gabor Mezei), 1975
2 Campsite building, Nagykállo, Hungary
   (architects: Deszö Erkler and Imre Makovecz), 1988
3 Arts centre (Vigado), Szibetvar, Hungary
   (architect: Imre Makovecz), 1985
4 Sárospatak school, Hungary
   (architect: Imre Makovecz)

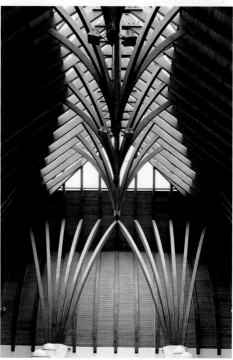

Plate 17

1–4 Caplutta Sogn Benedetg ("Chapel of St Benedict"),
Sumvitg, Grisons, Switzerland
(architect: Peter Zumthor), 1988

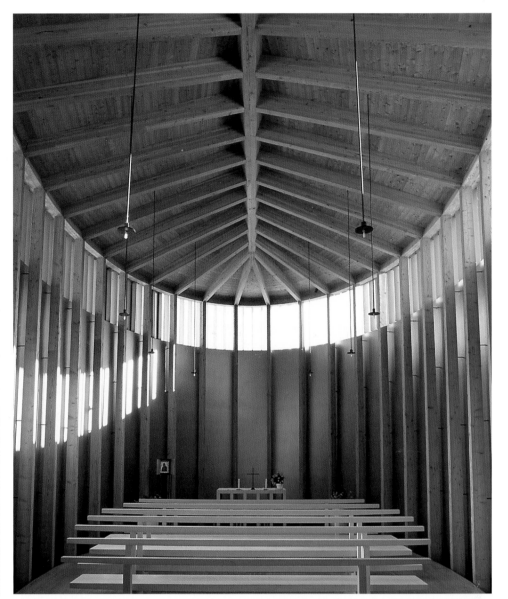

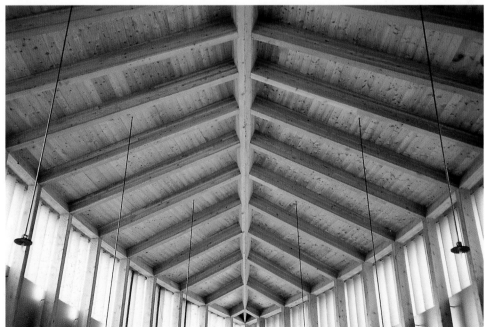

1 |2|
  |3|

Plate 18

1 Terrace houses, Paris, France
    (architect: Roland Schweitzer, with A. Levandowsky),
    1979–83
2 Youth village, Cieux, Haute Vienne, France
    (architect: Roland Schweitzer), 1970
3 Chapel of the Technical University, Otaniemi, Finland
    (architects: Heikki and Kaija Sirèn), 1957

Plate 19

1 Sea Ranch, California, USA
   (architects: MLTW / Moore, Lyndon, Turnbull &
   Whitaker), 1965
2 Holiday home, Fuji-Yoshida, Japan
   (architect: Kazunari Sakamoto), 2001
3 Gallery, Munich, Germany
   (architects: Herzog & DeMeuron and J. P. Meier
   Scupin), 1992
4 Private house, Ito, Japan
   (architects: Motoyoshi Itagaki and Hiromi Sugimoto),
   1997

1 | 4
2 | 5
3 |

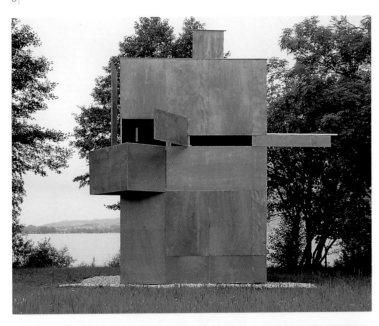 

Plate 20

1, 4 "Gucklhupf", Innerschwand, Mondsee, Austria
       (architect: Hans Peter Wörndl), 1993
2, 5 Holiday home, Vallemaggia, Switzerland
       (architect: Roberto Briccola), 1998
3   Holiday home, Lake Ossiach, Carinthia, Austria
       (architect: Manfred Kovatsch), 1977

Plate 21

1   Semi-detached houses, Allensbach, Germany
     (Schaudt Architekten), 1996
2   Multistorey apartment block, Innsbruck, Austria
     (architects: Kathan, Schranz, Strolz), 1996
3   Training school for forestry workers, Lyss, Switzerland
     (architects: Itten und Brechbühl), 1997

1 |
---|---
2 | 4
3 |

Plate 22

1, 4 Home for the elderly, Neuenbürg, Germany
(architects: Mahler, Günster, Fuchs), 1996
2, 3 Swiss pavilion, Expo 2000, Hannover, Germany
(architect: Peter Zumthor), 2000

Plate 23

1, 3   Residential complex, Munich, Germany
       (architects: Thomas Herzog, Bernhard Schilling),
       1982
2, 4, 5 Detached house, Regensburg, Germany
       (architect: Thomas Herzog), 1978

Plate 24 (facing page)

6, 9   Semi-detached houses, Pullach, Germany
       (architects: Thomas Herzog, Michael Volz, with
       Michael Streib), 1989
7, 8   Youth education centre, Windberg, Germany
       (architects: Thomas Herzog, with Peter Bonfig),
       1989

6 | 8
7 | 9

1|2

Plate 25

1, 2 Further education academy, Herne,
Germany
(architects: Jourda et Perraudin,
with Hegger, Hegger, Schleiff
Architekten), 1999

| 3 |
1	4
	5
2	6

Plate 26

1, 3, 4, 5   Demountable pavilion for non-permanent exhibitions (architects: Renzo Piano Building Workshop), 1984
2, 6   Faculty of architecture, Lyon, France (architects: Jourda et Perraudin), 1987

$\frac{1}{2}$

Plate 28 (facing page)

3, 6, 7 Arts centre, Noumea,
New Caledonia
(architects: Renzo
Piano Building Work-
shop), 1997
4, 5 Botanical museum,
Koski, Japan
(architects: Hiroshi
Naito & Ass.), 2001

Plate 29

1   Semi-detached houses, Munich-Solln, Germany
     (architect: Werner Bäuerle), 1999
2, 3 University building, Utrecht, Netherlands
     (mecanoo Architekten), 1996
4   Holiday home with studio, Vejby, Denmark
     (architects: Henning Larsens Tegnestue A/S), 2000

Plate 30 (facing page)

5, 6 Multistorey car park, Heilbronn, Germany
     (architects: Mahler, Günster, Fuchs), 1998
7, 9 Sports stadium, Odate, Japan
     (architects: Toyo Ito & Associates), 1997

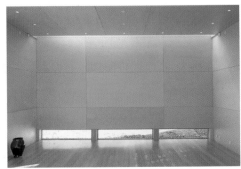

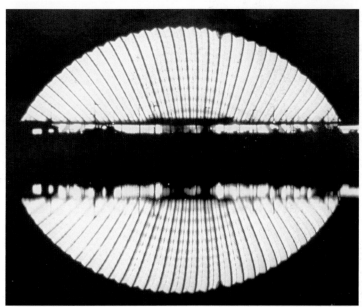

Facades – built examples in detail

Plate 31 (facing page)

10, 11   Extension to criminal courts,
         Bordeaux, France
         (architects: Richard Rogers
         Partnership), 1992–98
12   Ice rink, Munich, Germany
         (architects: Kurt Ackermann und
         Partner), 1983

Thomas Herzog and Michael Volz

The following examples are a selection of various facade constructions built in recent years. A number of older examples have also been included owing to their particular characteristics. The examples are arranged in order of increasing technical complexity, transparency and lightness of construction. All are listed in a table on pp. 290–91, distinguished according to their main features. The pages covering the construction of each project deal with the structural geometry, arrangement of the various layers and all significant joints and details. The horizontal sections have been placed between the vertical sections to lend clarity to the relationships between the various sections. They are separated by horizontal lines. Axonometric views have been included for some projects because they help to establish the arrangement of individual components. Not all building geometries are easy to capture in a simple two-dimensional drawing.

To ease orientation, the building envelopes are shown in the form of small-scale schematic plans and sections on which the large-scale details are marked. This is also intended to illustrate the components adjoining the facade details, from which, for example, the way in which the timber is protected can be derived during the design. The correctness of the construction in terms of building technology and building science aspects was an important criterion for selection. Nevertheless, some questions will always remain unanswered. The influence of the boundary conditions that, for example, help to determine the structure of a facade, is just too great. The reader is therefore reminded that the projects are examples – not prescriptions. In every new building project the architect and the engineer must first clarify the boundary conditions. All the details correspond to the drawings provided by the respective project team. Identifiable weaknesses have been pointed out. The project and material designations have been taken from the documents made available to us.

All detail sections are drawn at a scale of 1:20.

Structures:
1 Solid timber sections
2 Edge-glued elements
3 Cross-laminated timber
4 Box-frame and panel construction
5 Post-and-beam construction
6 Timber-frame construction
Wood plus other materials:
7 with masonry
8 with concrete/reinforced concrete
9 with steel
10 Roof constructions

Project	Structure no.	Page
1 • "Gucklhupf", Innerschwand, Mondsee, A	6	292
2 • Sea Ranch, California, USA	1	293
3 • Private house, Brasília, BR	6	294
4 • Holiday home, Chino, J	1	295
5 • Temporary café, Helsinki, FIN	2	296
6 • Temporary arts centre, Munich-Neuperlach	2	297
7 • Private house, Höhen Neundorf, D	6	298
8 • School hall, St Peter, CH	6	299
9 • "Silo house", Lukasöd, D	1	300
10 • Holiday home, Vallemaggia, CH	5	301
11 • Private house, Darien, Connecticut, USA	4	302
12 • Detached house, Bensberg, D	4	303
13 • Housing and studios, Paris, F	4	304
14 • House and studio, Deisslingen, D	4	305
15 • Media centre, Küsnacht, CH	4	306
16 • Laboratories and offices, Würzburg, D	4	307
17 • Offices, Munich, D	6	308
18 • Holiday home, Breitbrunn, D	4	309
19 • Private house, Sunvitg, CH	4	310
20 • Radio transmission station, Brauneck, D	6	311
21 • Semi-detached houses, Ebenhausen, D	6	312
22 • Youth conference centre, Michelrieth, D	6	313
23 • Garden retreat, Meckenbeuren, D	6	314
24 • Three houses on hillside, Brugg, CH	4	315
25 • Parish hall, Ebersberg, D	6	316
26 • Private house, Stuttgart, D	4	317
27 • Cemetery, Eching, D	6	318
28 • Terrace houses, Eching, D	6	319
29 • Semi-detached houses, Munich-Solln, D	6	320
30 • Studio house, Darmstadt, D	7	321
31 • Private house, Aachen, D	6	322
32 • Private house, Brest, F	6	323
33 • "Green" houses, Berlin, D	6	324
34 • School, Dischingen, D	6	325
35 • Private house, Regensburg-Kumpfmühl, D	6	326

Characteristics (● = applies)

Make-up
- single layer: 3, 4
- multi-layer without air cavity: 1, 2, 4, 6, 9, 15, 16, 17, 29, 31
- multi-layer with outer air cavity: 5, 6, 10, 11, 13, 14, 20, 21, 23, 32, 33, 34, 35
- multi-layer with inner cavity: 11, 12, 20, 21, 24
- multi-layer with services duct: 12, 30
- sliding/folding shutters: 4, 18, 19, 27
- double-leaf: —

Position of facade relative to structure
- structure and facade combined: 4, 5, 9, 12, 14
- within the structure: 1, 3, 6, 7, 10, 12, 14, 16, 20, and further
- changing position: —
- outside the structure: 2, 9, 18, 19

Outer layer
- shingles: 18, 19
- staggered planks: 21, 22, 27
- weatherboarding: 26, 35
- profiled boards: 2, 8, 9, 10, 11, 12, 13, 14, 26, 29, 31, 33, 35
- boards: 1, 5, 6, 16, 17, 18, 24, 25, 28, 34
- with open joints: 5, 16, 25, 28

Direction of outer layer
- vertical: 2, 3, 4, 9, 11, 12, 13, 14, 18, 19, 26, 33
- horizontal: 8, 10, 14, 16, 25, 26, 29, 31, 33, 34, 35
- diagonal: 27

Inner layer
- profiled boards: 2, 7, 8, 23, 25, 29, 35
- boards: 1, 4, 6, 10, 13, 14, 20, 24, 27, 29, 33, 34, 35

Column cross-section
- round: 3, 4
- square, rectangular: 1, 2, 3, 6, 7, 10, 13, 15, 16, 20, 21, 23 and further, 35
- compound: 5, 7, 13, 16, 20, 21
- with grooves: 3, 4, 9, 28, 31
- with rebates: 5, 17

Beam cross-section
- round: 3
- square, rectangular: 1, 2, 3, 6, 7, 13 and further
- compound: 2, 5
- with grooves: 4
- with rebates: 26, 27

prefabricated elements: 3, 4, 5, 10, 15, 17, 23, 25, 27, 29, 31, 33, 35

Architects (by project number)
1 Hans Peter Wörndl, Vienna
2 MLTW, Berkeley
3 Jose Zanine Caldas, Brasília
4 Masamitsu Nagashina, Tokyo
5 Niko Sirola, Helsinki
6 Florian Nagler, Munich
7 Heinz Bienefeld, Swisttal-Ollheim
8 Conradin Clavuot, Chur
9 Eberhard Stauß, Munich
10 Roberto Briccola, Giubiasco
11 Richard Meier, New York
12 Wolfgang Döring, Düsseldorf
13 Roland Schweitzer, Paris
14 M. Bächle, K. Meid-Bächle, Constance
15 M.-C. Bétrix & E. Consolascio, Erlenbach
16 Michael Volz, Frankfurt
17 Planung Fahr + Partner PFP, Munich
18 R. + R. Then Bergh, Munich
19 Valentin Bearth & Andrea Deplazes, Chur
20 Karin Maurer and OPD, Munich
21 Elmar and Sigrid Dittmann, Munich
22 Theodor Hugues, Munich
23 Jauss und Gaupp, Friedrichshafen
24 Ruedi Dietiker, Beat Klaus, Roland Keller, Brugg
25 Georg and Ingrid Küttinger, Munich
26 Schlude Ströhle, Stuttgart
27 Sampo Widmann, Stephan Romero, Munich
28 Reinhold Tobey, Munich
29 Werner Bäuerle, Constance
30 Ute Schauer, Franz Vollhard, Darmstadt
31 Erich Schneider-Wessling, Cologne
32 Roland Schweitzer, Paris
33 Otto Steidle, Munich
34 Klaus Mahler and Jürgen Schäfer, Stuttgart
35 Thomas Herzog, Munich

	36	37	38	39	40	41	42	43	44	45	46	47	48	49	50	51	52	53	54	55	56	57	58	59	60	61	62	63	64	65	66	67	68	69	70	71	Category
Building	Youth education centre, Windberg, D	Private house, Waldmohr, D	Semi-detached houses, Pullach, D	Clubhouse, sports facility, Eclubens, CH	Pavilion, Langnau am Albis, CH	Private house, Cambridge, UK	Residential complex, Munich-Perlach, D	Further education academy, Herne, D	Youth village, Cieux, Haute Vienne, F	Holiday home, Fuji-Yoshida, J	Private house, Brunswick, D	Modular house, Bad Iburg, D	House and studio, Tsukuba, J	Private house, Gmund am Tegernsee, D	Private house, Glonn-Haslach, D	Private house, Allensbach, D	Forestry station, Turbenthal, CH	Local government offices, Starnberg, D	Home for the elderly, Neuenbürg, D	Gallery, Munich, D	University building, Wiesbaden, D	Multistorey building, Innsbruck, A	Training school for forestry workers, Lyss, CH	Residential complex, Regensburg, D	Multistorey car park, Heilbronn, D	Mixed office and residential block, D	High-rise block, Hannover, D	Factory building, Gelting, D	Sports centre, Bretigny, F	Factory building, Reuthe, A	Factory building, Bad Münder, D	Exhibition pavilion, various locations	Sports stadium, Odate, J	Holiday home, Göd, H	Forest culture house, Visegrad, H	Admin. building, observ. tower, Miskolc, H	
(no. of storeys)	7/8	6	6	6	6	6	6	6	6	6	6	7/8	6	9	9	8	8	8	8	8	8	8	8	8	8	8	8	8	9	6	9	10	10	10	10	10	
single layer				•					•					•									•									•					**Make-up**
multi-layer without air cavity				•	•							•				•				•								•		•		•					
multi-layer with outer air cavity	•	•	•	•			•			•	•	•			•	•				•		•	•	•		•		•	•	•						•	
multi-layer with inner air cavity																			•																		
multi-layer with services duct																		•			•																
sliding/folding shutters						•				•	•		•																								
double-leaf													•														•										
structure and facade combined																																•					**Position of facade relative to structure**
within the structure	•	•		•	•					•	•	•		•	•		•	•		•		•		•		•		•		•			•	•	•	•	
changing position							•	•																													
outside the structure			•						•									•		•		•	•	•	•												
shingles																																				•	**Outer layer**
staggered planks													•																								
weatherboarding	•						•										•			•					•					•		•					
profiled boards		•	•								•				•	•							•	•				•		•	•						
boards			•		•	•					•								•			•						•	•								
with open joints													•			•							•	•													
vertical							•		•			•				•						•						•	•	•							**Direction of outer layer**
horizontal	•	•	•		•	•					•				•	•		•				•						•		•				•	•	•	
diagonal																																					
profiled boards		•										•				•						•															**Inner layer**
boards	•				•												•					•						•	•	•							
round													•					•		•							•	•					•	•		**Column cross-section**
square, rectangular	•	•	•		•		•		•	•	•						•	•		•		•			•		•			•	•					•	
compound		•	•																•																		
with grooves																			•																		
with rebates					•														•																		
round																																		•			**Beam cross-section**
square, rectangular	•	•			•		•			•	•						•	•		•		•			•		•			•	•					•	
compound									•																			•			•						
with grooves		•																																			
with rebates																																					
prefabricated elements				•						•				•			•			•		•	•								•	•					
page	327	328	330	332	333	334	335	336	337	338	339	340	341	342	343	344	345	346	347	348	349	350	351	352	353	354	355	356	357	358	359	360	361	362	363	364	**page**
Architect	Thomas Herzog, Munich	Thomas Herzog, Michael Volz, Munich	Thomas Herzog, Michael Volz, Munich	Atelier Cube, Lausanne	Marianne Burkhalter, Christian Sumi, Zurich	Marcial Echenique, Cambridge	Doris and Ralph Thut, Munich	Jouda et Perraudin, Paris	Roland Schweitzer, Paris	Kazunari Sakamoto, Architectural Laboratory, Tokyo	Schulitz + Partner, Brunswick	Eberhard Stauß, Munich	Naito Architects & Ass., Tokyo	Hans Busso von Busse, Munich	Werner und Grete Wirsing, Munich	Schaudt Architekten, Constance	Marianne Burkhalter, Christian Sumi, Zurich	Auer + Weber, Munich/Stuttgart	Mahler Günster Fuchs, Stuttgart	J. Herzog, P. de Meuron, Basel	Mahler Günster Fuchs, Stuttgart	A. Kathan, M. Schranz, E. Strolz, Innsbruck	Itten und Brechbühl, Bern	Fink und Jocher, Munich	Mahler Günster Fuchs, Stuttgart	Alexander Reichel, Munich	Thomas Herzog + Partner, Munich	Beck-Enz-Yelin, Munich	Patrick Berger, Paris	H. Kaufmann, Schwarzach	Thomas Herzog, Munich	Renzo Piano Building Workshop, Genua	Toyo Ito & Associates, Tokyo	Imre Makovecz, Budapest	Imre Makovecz, Budapest	Benö Taba, Miskolc	

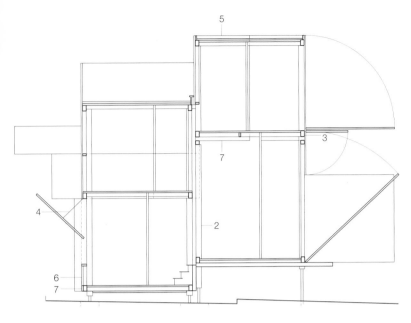

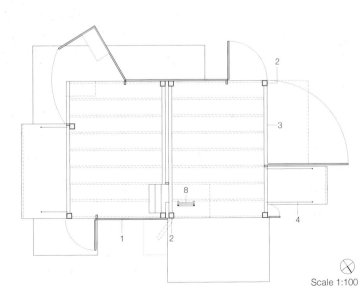

Scale 1:100

1 · "Gucklhupf"

Innerschwand am Mondsee, A; 1993

Architect: Hans Peter Wörndl, Vienna

Werk, Bauen und Wohnen 5/98
A + U, 332/1998
Architectural Record, 4/99
Techniques et Architecture, 441/1999

· Timber-frame construction
· 3 individual components,
  L×B×H 1× 4/3/6 m, 2× 4/3/3 m joined
  together to form two boxes
· Construction period: 3 months

1 External wall panel, 35mm:
   6 mm okoume plywood, red, waterproof glue, 3 coats of extra-clear boat
   varnish
   8 mm plywood
   building paper/airtight barrier
   20 x 30 mm spruce battens with
   20 mm insulation between
   6 mm okoume plywood, red,
   2 coats of extra-clear boat lacquer
2 Column, 120 x 120 mm spruce
3 Beam, 60 x 120 mm spruce
4 Cable/rope with winch for variability
   by means of turning, folding, pivoting,
   pulling; silver anodized aluminium
5 Roof: gravel, waterproofing, thermal
   insulation, plywood
6 Glazing
7 Aluminium section
8 Steel steps

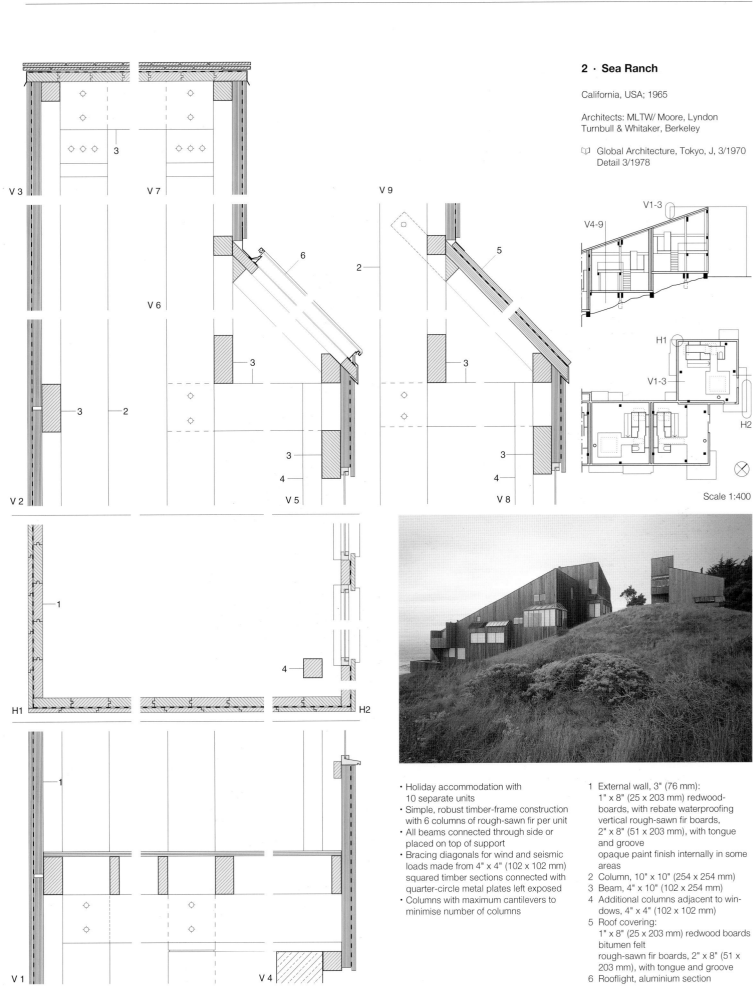

2 · Sea Ranch

California, USA; 1965

Architects: MLTW/ Moore, Lyndon
Turnbull & Whitaker, Berkeley

Global Architecture, Tokyo, J, 3/1970
Detail 3/1978

V 3

V 7

V 9

V1-3

V4-9

6

5

2

V 6

3

3

3

3

2

3

3

4

3

4

V 2

V 5

V 8

H1

V1-3

H2

Scale 1:400

1

1

4

H1

H2

1

1

V 1

V 4

· Holiday accommodation with
10 separate units
· Simple, robust timber-frame construction
with 6 columns of rough-sawn fir per unit
· All beams connected through side or
placed on top of support
· Bracing diagonals for wind and seismic
loads made from 4" x 4" (102 x 102 mm)
squared timber sections connected with
quarter-circle metal plates left exposed
· Columns with maximum cantilevers to
minimise number of columns

1 External wall, 3" (76 mm):
1" x 8" (25 x 203 mm) redwood-
boards, with rebate waterproofing
vertical rough-sawn fir boards,
2" x 8" (51 x 203 mm), with tongue
and groove
opaque paint finish internally in some
areas
2 Column, 10" x 10" (254 x 254 mm)
3 Beam, 4" x 10" (102 x 254 mm)
4 Additional columns adjacent to windows, 4" x 4" (102 x 102 mm)
5 Roof covering:
1" x 8" (25 x 203 mm) redwood boards
bitumen felt
rough-sawn fir boards, 2" x 8" (51 x
203 mm), with tongue and groove
6 Rooflight, aluminium section

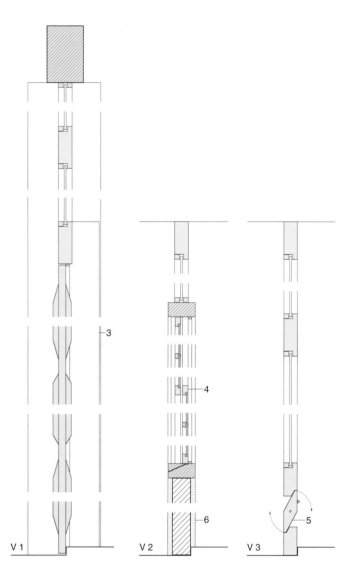

3

4

5

6

V 1   V 2   V 3

3 · Private house

Brasilia, BR; 1975

Architect: Jose Zanine Caldas, Brasilia

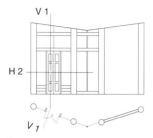

V 1
H 2
V 1

Part-elevation, upper floor

V 2   V 3
H 1
V 2   V 3

Part-elevation, ground floor   Scale 1:250

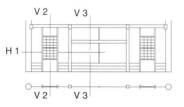

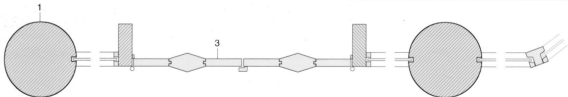

1

3

H 2

4   2

H 1

Zanine, Sentir e Fazer,
Rio de Janeiro, 1988

- Octagonal plan shape with star-shaped roof
- Permanent ventilation at base of facade (region with hot, humid climate)
- Cedar wood doors and windows

1 Log column, 400 mm dia.
2 Column, 200 x 200 mm
3 Solid wood doors
4 Sash window
5 Pivoting louvre
6 Masonry with plaster inside, rendering outside

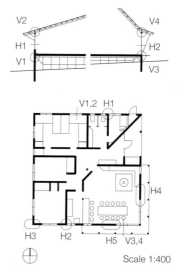

4 · Holiday home

Chino, J; 1983

Architect: Masamitsu Nagashina, Tokyo
Assistant: H. Seki

📖 Jutaku Kenchiku 7/1983

Scale 1:400

- Grid: 900 mm
- Module: 90 mm
- Timber walls left exposed externally and partly internally, made from poles left round on one or two sides

1 External wall, 130 mm:
   135 mm poles, sawn on 3 sides,
   with relieving groove and key
   12 mm plywood
   fabric covering
2 Corner column, 210 mm
3 Sole plate, 180 mm

4 Eaves purlin, 180 mm
5 Pole rafters, 180 mm
6 Sliding door, aluminium sections
7 Sliding shutters of poles sawn on
   3 sides
8 Tatami (standardised) floor mats

V 2

V 4

H 3

H 1

H 4

H 2

H 5

V 1

V 3

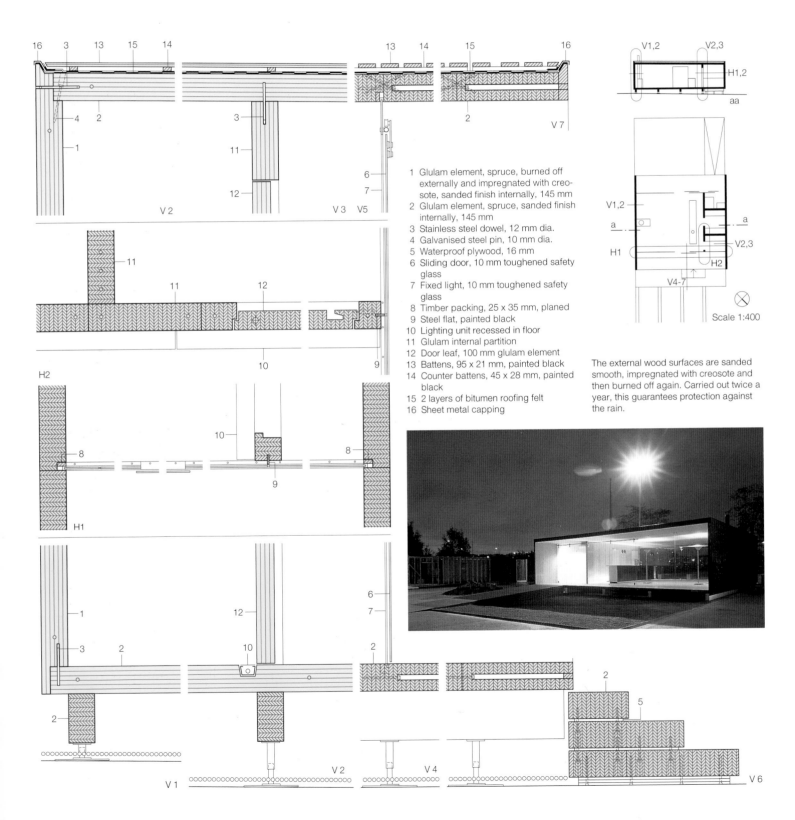

1 Glulam element, spruce, burned off
   externally and impregnated with creosote, sanded finish internally, 145 mm
2 Glulam element, spruce, sanded finish
   internally, 145 mm
3 Stainless steel dowel, 12 mm dia.
4 Galvanised steel pin, 10 mm dia.
5 Waterproof plywood, 16 mm
6 Sliding door, 10 mm toughened safety
   glass
7 Fixed light, 10 mm toughened safety
   glass
8 Timber packing, 25 x 35 mm, planed
9 Steel flat, painted black
10 Lighting unit recessed in floor
11 Glulam internal partition
12 Door leaf, 100 mm glulam element
13 Battens, 95 x 21 mm, painted black
14 Counter battens, 45 x 28 mm, painted
   black
15 2 layers of bitumen roofing felt
16 Sheet metal capping

Scale 1:400

The external wood surfaces are sanded
smooth, impregnated with creosote and
then burned off again. Carried out twice a
year, this guarantees protection against
the rain.

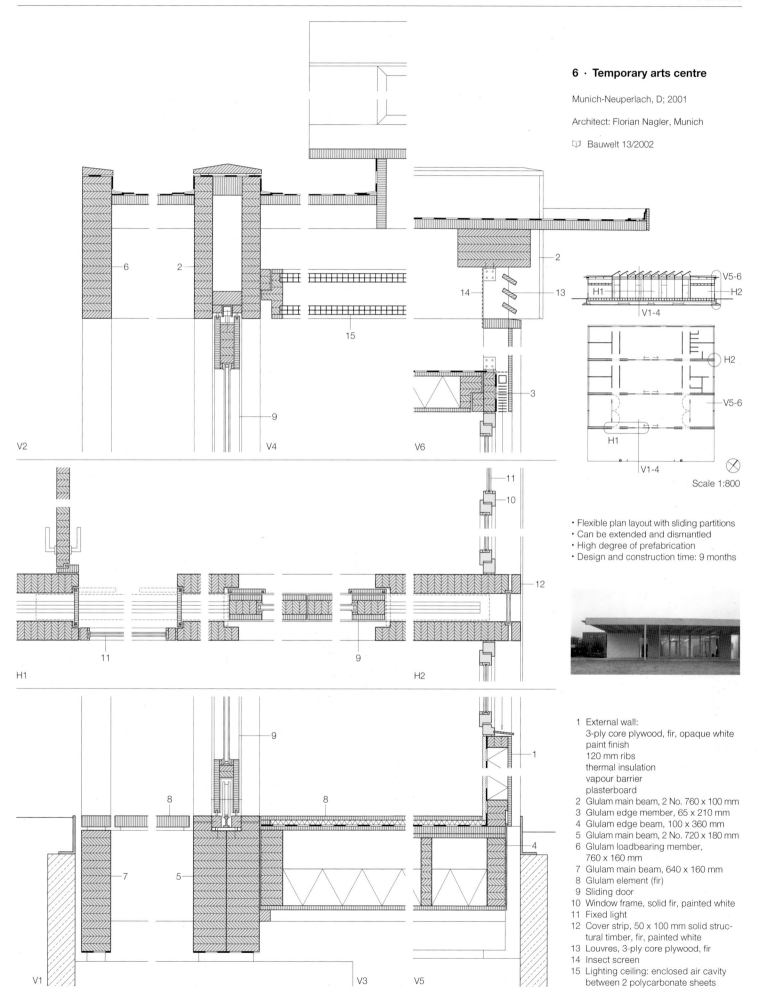

6 · Temporary arts centre

Munich-Neuperlach, D; 2001

Architect: Florian Nagler, Munich

  Bauwelt 13/2002

V5-6
H1   H2
V1-4

H2

V5-6

V1-4

Scale 1:800

· Flexible plan layout with sliding partitions
· Can be extended and dismantled
· High degree of prefabrication
· Design and construction time: 9 months

1 External wall:
   3-ply core plywood, fir, opaque white
   paint finish
   120 mm ribs
   thermal insulation
   vapour barrier
   plasterboard
2 Glulam main beam, 2 No. 760 x 100 mm
3 Glulam edge member, 65 x 210 mm
4 Glulam edge beam, 100 x 360 mm
5 Glulam main beam, 2 No. 720 x 180 mm
6 Glulam loadbearing member,
   760 x 160 mm
7 Glulam main beam, 640 x 160 mm
8 Glulam element (fir)
9 Sliding door
10 Window frame, solid fir, painted white
11 Fixed light
12 Cover strip, 50 x 100 mm solid structural timber, fir, painted white
13 Louvres, 3-ply core plywood, fir
14 Insect screen
15 Lighting ceiling: enclosed air cavity
   between 2 polycarbonate sheets

V2   V4   V6

H1   H2

V1   V3   V5

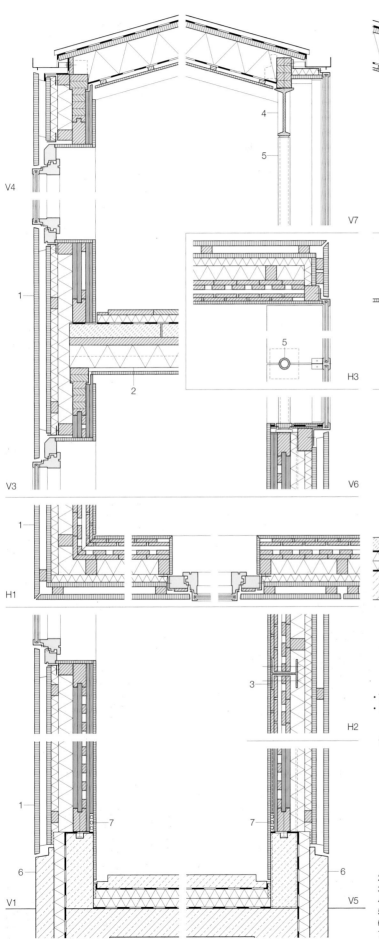

7 · Private house

Hohen Neuendorf, D; 1997

Architects:
Heinz Bienefeld, Nikolaus Bienefeld,
Swisttal-Ollheim

📖 Baumeister 1/1998

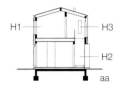

Scale 1:400

- Timber block panel construction
- High degree of prefabrication

1 External wall
   27 mm laminated veneer lumber
   (Kerto Q), fir
   40 x 60 mm battens/ventilation layer
   24 mm bitumen-impregnated wood
   fibre insulating board
   40 x 60 mm battens/insulation
   80 x 60 mm battens/insulation
   110 mm timber block panel wall
   element
   3-ply core plywood, fir/spruce,
   opaque white paint finish
2 Beam, 240 x 120 mm
3 Steel beam
4 Steel beam, slotted
5 Steel circular hollow section column
6 Concrete plinth
7 Heating pipes

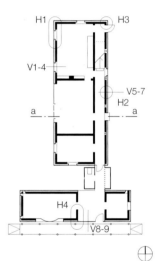

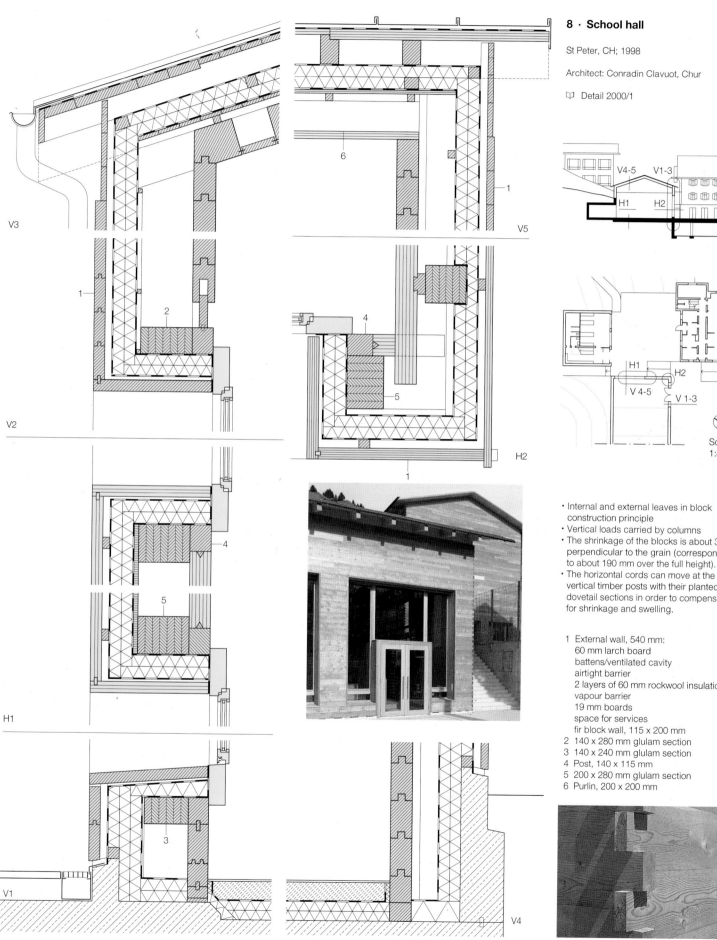

8 · School hall

St Peter, CH; 1998

Architect: Conradin Clavuot, Chur

📖 Detail 2000/1

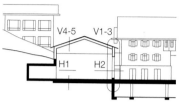

Scale
1:800

- Internal and external leaves in block construction principle
- Vertical loads carried by columns
- The shrinkage of the blocks is about 3% perpendicular to the grain (corresponds to about 190 mm over the full height).
- The horizontal cords can move at the vertical timber posts with their planted dovetail sections in order to compensate for shrinkage and swelling.

1　External wall, 540 mm:
　　60 mm larch board
　　battens/ventilated cavity
　　airtight barrier
　　2 layers of 60 mm rockwool insulation
　　vapour barrier
　　19 mm boards
　　space for services
　　fir block wall, 115 x 200 mm
2　140 x 280 mm glulam section
3　140 x 240 mm glulam section
4　Post, 140 x 115 mm
5　200 x 280 mm glulam section
6　Purlin, 200 x 200 mm

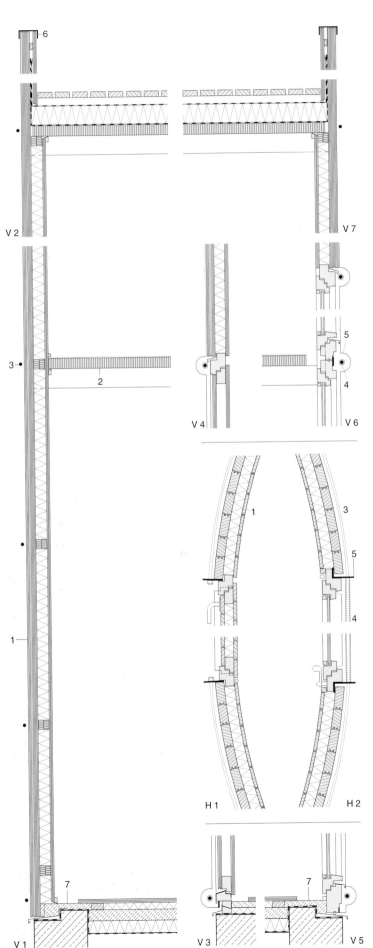

9 · "Silo house"

Lukasöd, D; 1988

Architect: Eberhard Stauss, Munich
Assistant: A. Leibelt

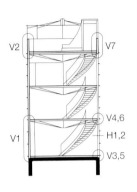

Scale 1:300

📖 Detail 4/1989
space design 1/1989

· Converted from a standard animal feed
  silo
· Compressive forces around window
  openings resisted by steel angle frame
  and steel circular hollow section struts
· Building system for housing, offices,
  leisure facilities
· Registered design

1 External wall, 168 mm:
  50 mm silo planks, with double tongue
  and groove
  100 mm insulation
  18 mm tongue and groove boarding
2 Plywood
3 Steel tie, 16 mm dia.
4 Steel strut
5 Window frame of steel angles
6 Channel section, 115 x 55 x 4 mm
7 Screed

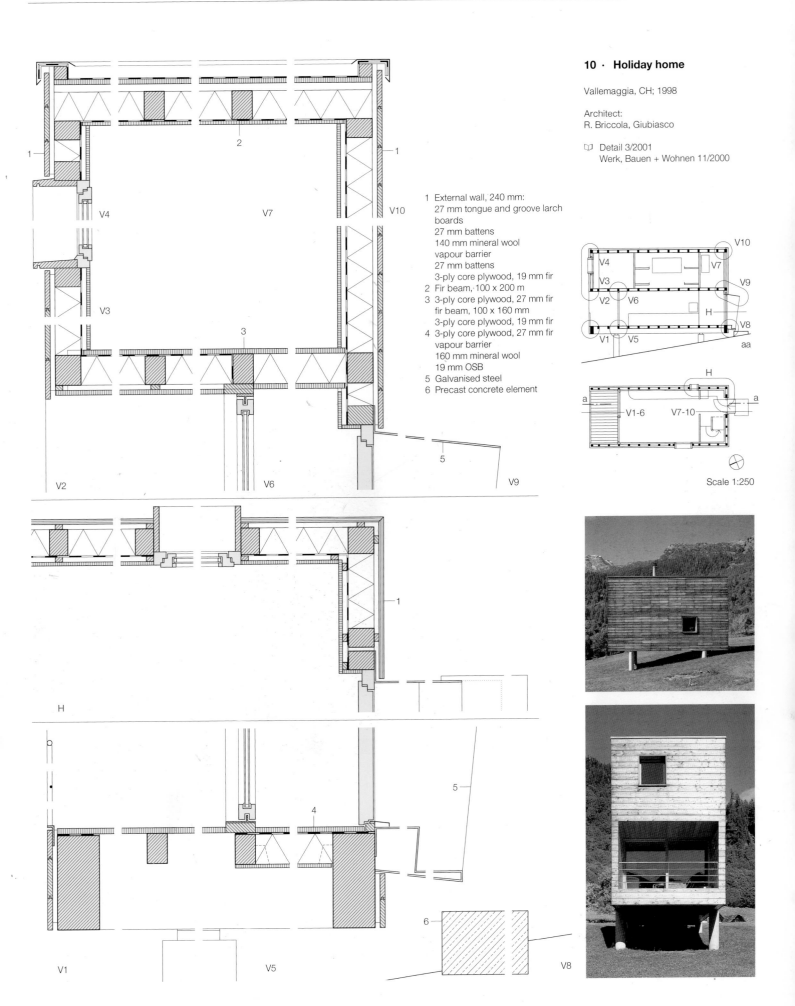

10 · Holiday home

Vallemaggia, CH; 1998

Architect:
R. Briccola, Giubiasco

Detail 3/2001
Werk, Bauen + Wohnen 11/2000

1 External wall, 240 mm:
  27 mm tongue and groove larch
  boards
  27 mm battens
  140 mm mineral wool
  vapour barrier
  27 mm battens
  3-ply core plywood, 19 mm fir
2 Fir beam, 100 x 200 m
3 3-ply core plywood, 27 mm fir
  fir beam, 100 x 160 mm
  3-ply core plywood, 19 mm fir
4 3-ply core plywood, 27 mm fir
  vapour barrier
  160 mm mineral wool
  19 mm OSB
5 Galvanised steel
6 Precast concrete element

Scale 1:250

301

V 5
10
11

V 7
1

V 4

V 6
9

V 3
1

V 11
7

V 18
8

V 10

V 2

V 14

V 17

11 · Private house

Darien, Connecticut, USA; 1967

Architect: Richard Meier, New York

Global Architecture, Tokyo; J 22/1973

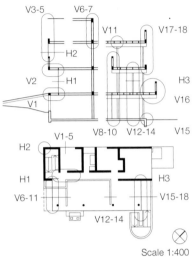

V3-5   V6-7
V11   V17-18
H2
V2   H1   H3
V1   V16
V1-5
V8-10   V12-14   V15

H2
V1-5
H1   H3
V6-11   V15-18
V12-14

Scale 1:400

· Platform construction
· Utilises standardised timber sections
· All exposed timber and metal parts
  painted white, apart from floorboards

H 2
2
5

H 1

6

H 3
1

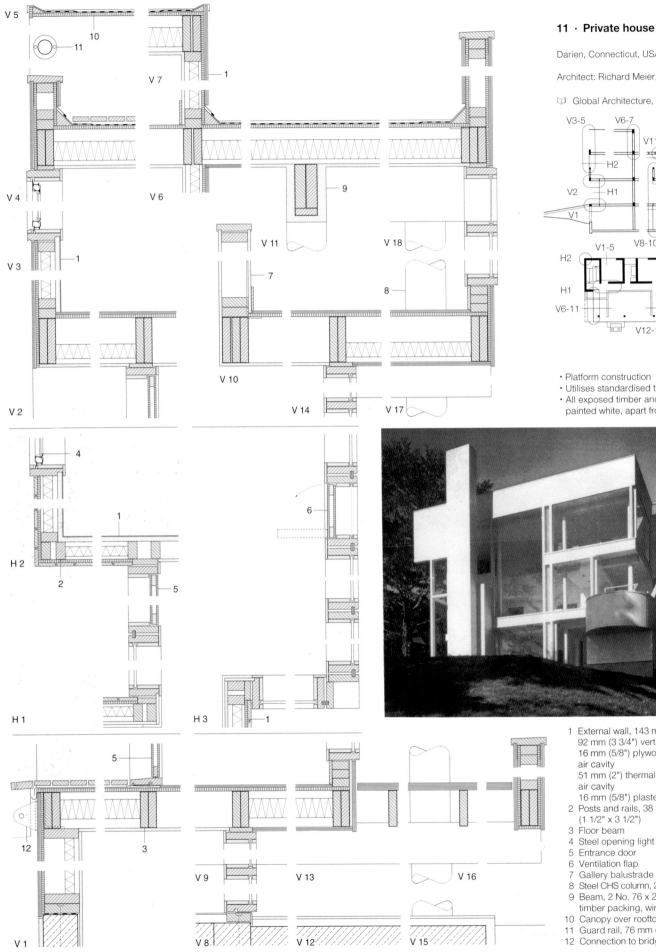

5

12
3

V 9   V 13   V 16

V 1

V 8   V 12   V 15

1 External wall, 143 mm (5 5/8"):
   92 mm (3 3/4") vertical t&g boards
   16 mm (5/8") plywood
   air cavity
   51 mm (2") thermal insulation
   air cavity
   16 mm (5/8") plasterboard
2 Posts and rails, 38 x 89 mm
   (1 1/2" x 3 1/2")
3 Floor beam
4 Steel opening light
5 Entrance door
6 Ventilation flap
7 Gallery balustrade
8 Steel CHS column, 219 mm dia. (8 5/8")
9 Beam, 2 No. 76 x 254 mm (3" x 10"),
   timber packing, wire mesh, plaster
10 Canopy over rooftop terrace
11 Guard rail, 76 mm dia. (3") steel CHS
12 Connection to bridge

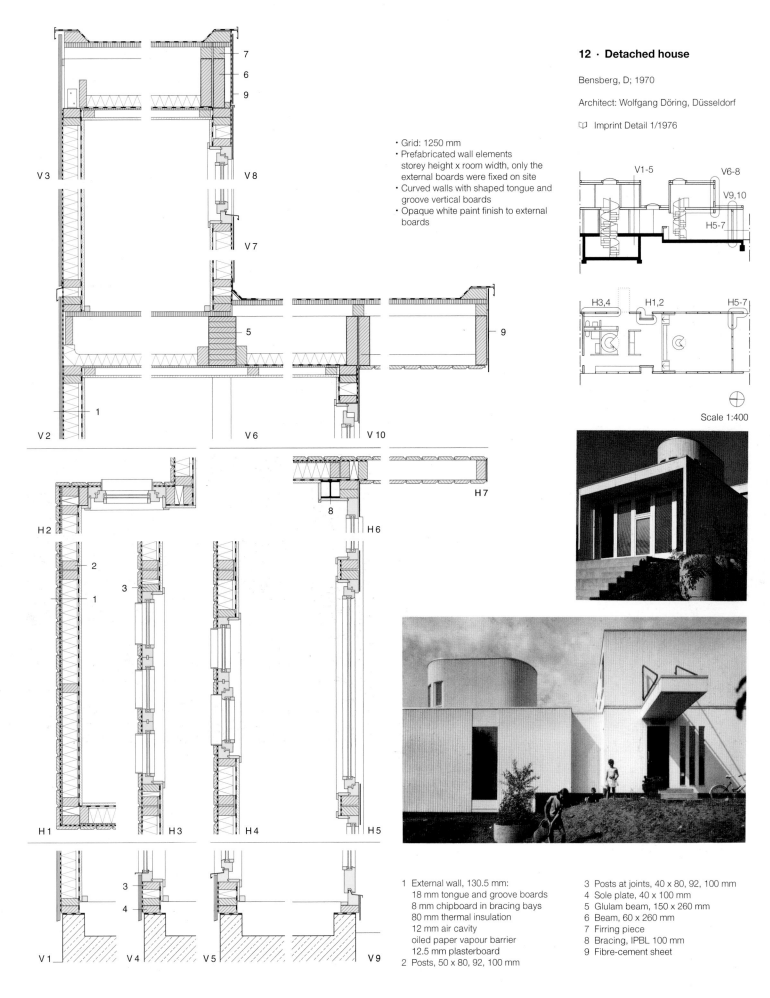

V 3

V 8

7

6

9

V 7

5

9

V 2

1

V 6

V 10

H 2

8

H 6

H 7

2

1

3

H 1

H 3

H 4

H 5

3

4

V 1

V 4

V 5

V 9

12 · Detached house

Bensberg, D; 1970

Architect: Wolfgang Döring, Düsseldorf

📖 Imprint Detail 1/1976

- Grid: 1250 mm
- Prefabricated wall elements
  storey height x room width, only the
  external boards were fixed on site
- Curved walls with shaped tongue and
  groove vertical boards
- Opaque white paint finish to external
  boards

V1-5   V6-8

V9,10

H5-7

H3,4   H1,2   H5-7

Scale 1:400

1 External wall, 130.5 mm:
     18 mm tongue and groove boards
     8 mm chipboard in bracing bays
     80 mm thermal insulation
     12 mm air cavity
     oiled paper vapour barrier
     12.5 mm plasterboard
2 Posts, 50 x 80, 92, 100 mm

3 Posts at joints, 40 x 80, 92, 100 mm
4 Sole plate, 40 x 100 mm
5 Glulam beam, 150 x 260 mm
6 Beam, 60 x 260 mm
7 Firring piece
8 Bracing, IPBL 100 mm
9 Fibre-cement sheet

Paris, F; 1979–1983

Architect: Roland Schweitzer, Paris
Assistant: A. Levandowsky

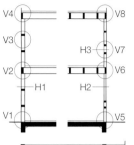

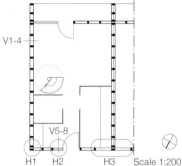

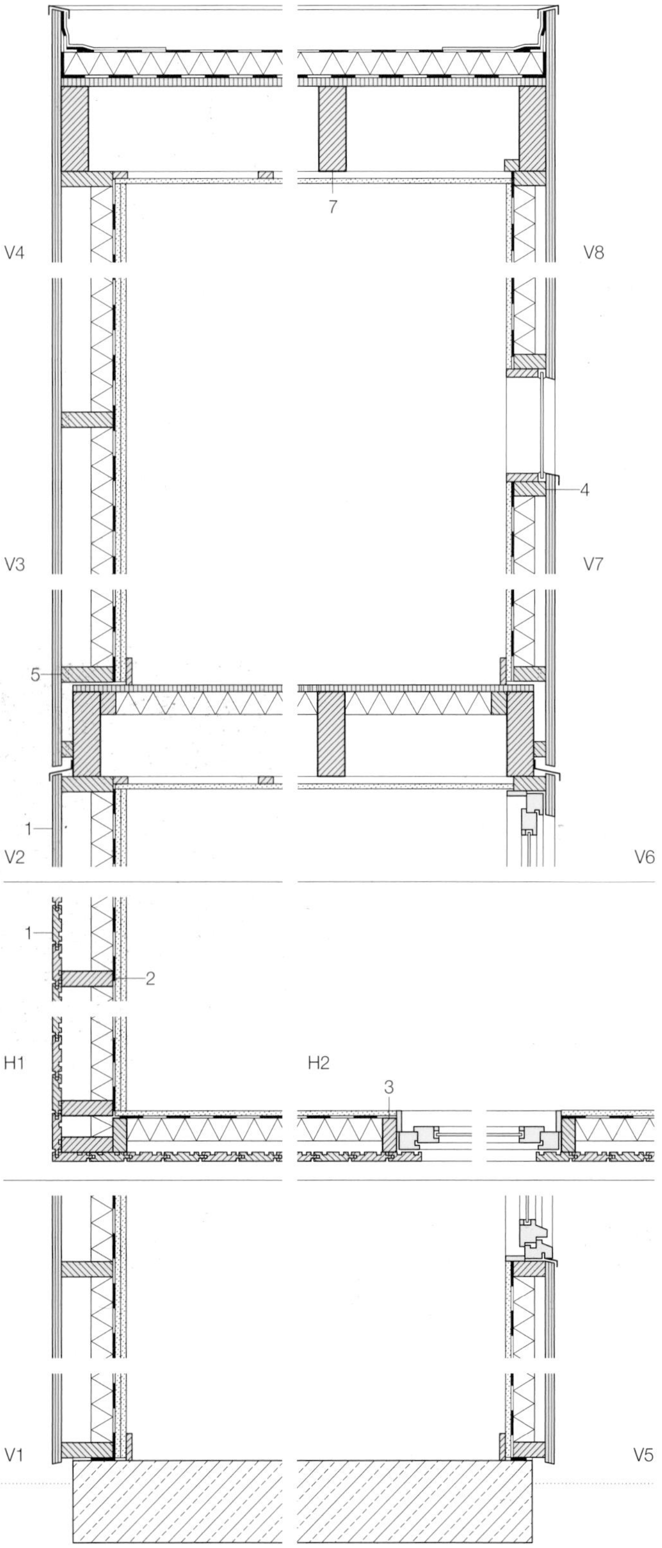

Scale 1:200

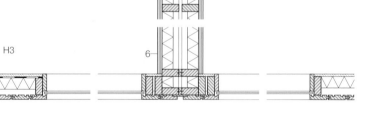

· Grid: 600 mm
· Loadbearing posts in transverse and
  party walls, 600 mm grid
· Red glaze finish to external boards
· Very low building costs

1 External wall, 128 mm and 197 mm:
  25 mm vertical tongue and groove
  boards
  vertical air cavity, 30 or 82 mm
  60 mm thermal insulation
  plasterboard, 13 mm and
  2 No. 15 mm
2 Post, 38 x 142 mm
3 Post, 38 x 90 mm
4 Rail, 38 x 90 mm
5 10 mm dia. holes at 150 mm centres
  for equalising vapour pressure and
  for drainage
6 Party wall
7 Edge and floor beam, 75 x 225 mm

V2

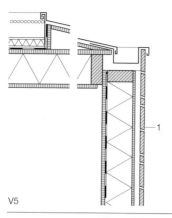

V5

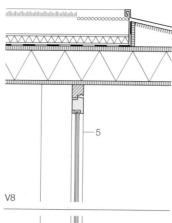

V8

14 · House and studio

Deisslingen, D; 1998

Architects: Linie 4, Constance
M. Bächle, K. Meid-Bächle

db das buch, DVA Verlag 2001

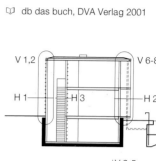

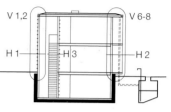

Scale 1:400

1 External wall, 245 mm:
  22 mm untreated Douglas fir plain-
  edge boards
  30 mm framing/ventilated cavity
  13 mm bitumen-impregnated softboard
  glulam timber-frame construction,
  160 x 60 mm, with 160 mm mineral
  fibre insulation between
  vapour barrier/airtight barrier
  3-ply core plywood, 19 mm fir, painted
  white
2 160 x 60 mm glulam section, painted
  white
3 Glulam rafter, 140 x 60 mm
4 30 mm fascia board
5 Wood-glass facade, larch, waxed and
  oiled
6 Double glazing, 24 mm satin finish
7 Opening light
8 Grid of plain-edge boards, 40 mm
  untreated Douglas fir
9 Galvanised steel

V4

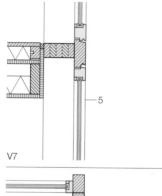

V7

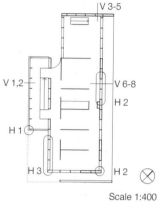

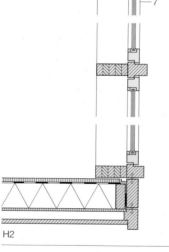

H2

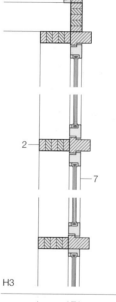

H3

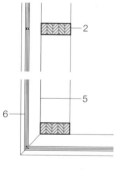

H1

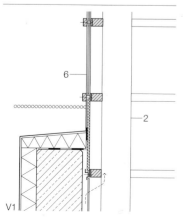

V1

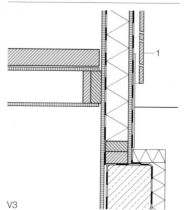

V3

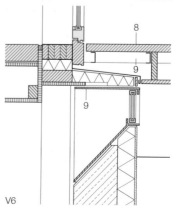

V6

· Column grid: 1.075 m
· Timber-frame construction
· High degree of prefabrication

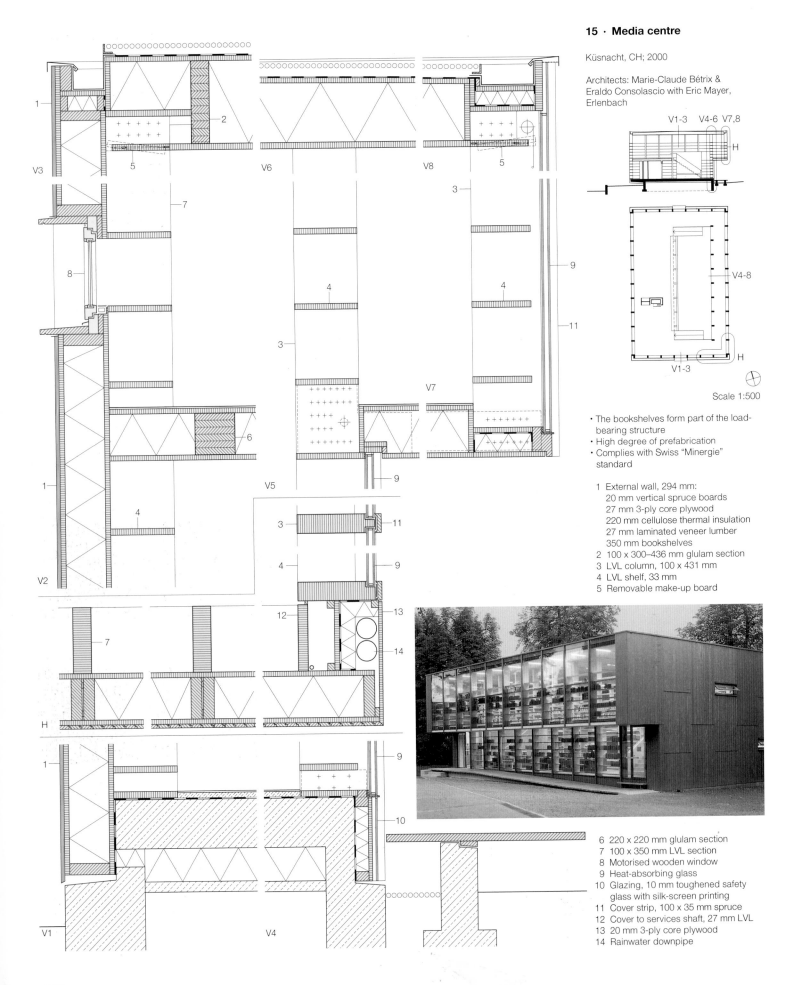

15 · Media centre

Küsnacht, CH; 2000

Architects: Marie-Claude Bétrix &
Eraldo Consolascio with Eric Mayer,
Erlenbach

Scale 1:500

- The bookshelves form part of the loadbearing structure
- High degree of prefabrication
- Complies with Swiss "Minergie"
  standard

1 External wall, 294 mm:
   20 mm vertical spruce boards
   27 mm 3-ply core plywood
   220 mm cellulose thermal insulation
   27 mm laminated veneer lumber
   350 mm bookshelves
2 100 x 300–436 mm glulam section
3 LVL column, 100 x 431 mm
4 LVL shelf, 33 mm
5 Removable make-up board

6 220 x 220 mm glulam section
7 100 x 350 mm LVL section
8 Motorised wooden window
9 Heat-absorbing glass
10 Glazing, 10 mm toughened safety
   glass with silk-screen printing
11 Cover strip, 100 x 35 mm spruce
12 Cover to services shaft, 27 mm LVL
13 20 mm 3-ply core plywood
14 Rainwater downpipe

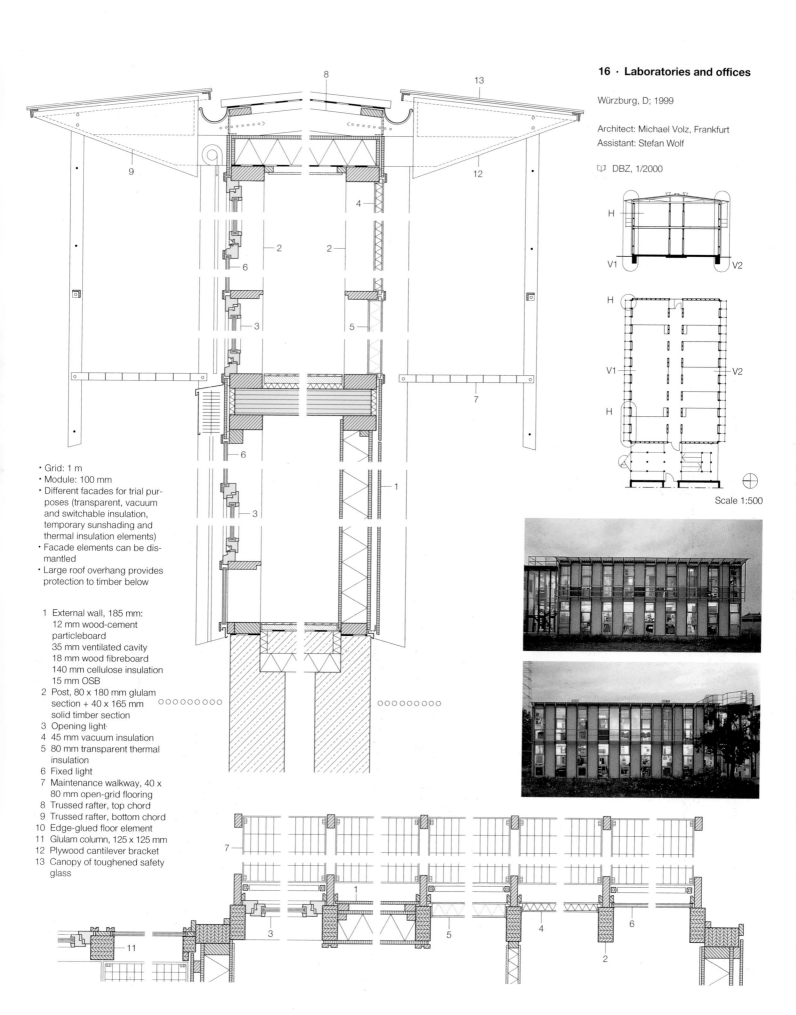

Würzburg, D; 1999

Architect: Michael Volz, Frankfurt
Assistant: Stefan Wolf

DBZ, 1/2000

Scale 1:500

· Grid: 1 m
· Module: 100 mm
· Different facades for trial purposes (transparent, vacuum
  and switchable insulation,
  temporary sunshading and
  thermal insulation elements)
· Facade elements can be dismantled
· Large roof overhang provides
  protection to timber below

1 External wall, 185 mm:
   12 mm wood-cement
   particleboard
   35 mm ventilated cavity
   18 mm wood fibreboard
   140 mm cellulose insulation
   15 mm OSB
2 Post, 80 x 180 mm glulam
   section + 40 x 165 mm
   solid timber section
3 Opening light·
4 45 mm vacuum insulation
5 80 mm transparent thermal
   insulation
6 Fixed light
7 Maintenance walkway, 40 x
   80 mm open-grid flooring
8 Trussed rafter, top chord
9 Trussed rafter, bottom chord
10 Edge-glued floor element
11 Glulam column, 125 x 125 mm
12 Plywood cantilever bracket
13 Canopy of toughened safety
   glass

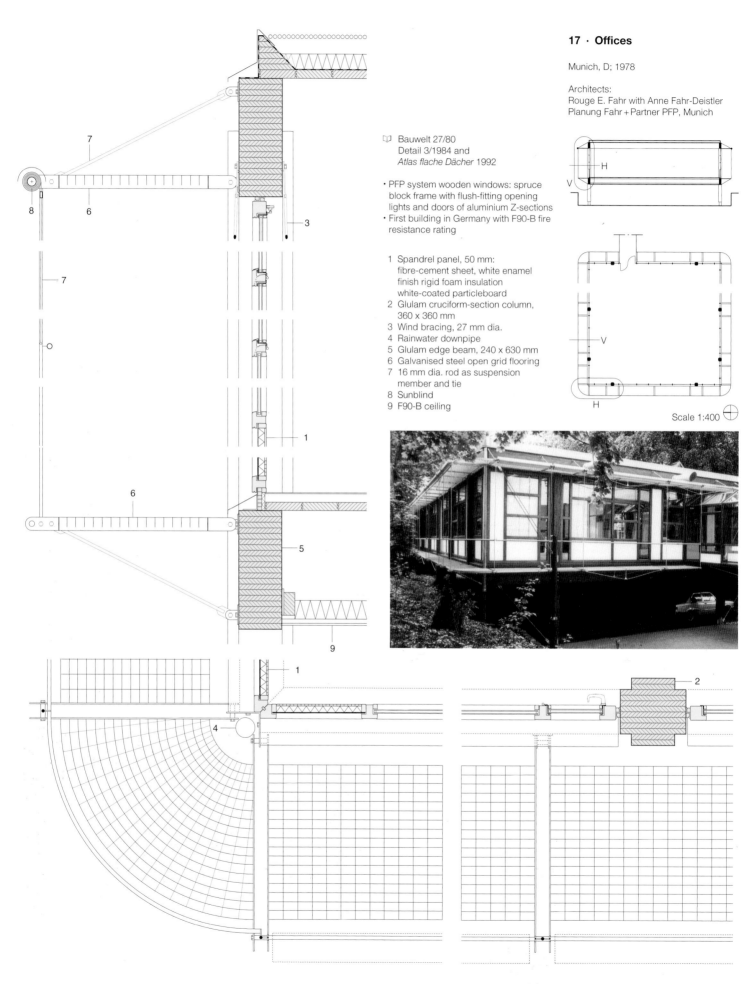

Munich, D; 1978

Architects:
Rouge E. Fahr with Anne Fahr-Deistler
Planung Fahr + Partner PFP, Munich

Bauwelt 27/80
Detail 3/1984 and
Atlas flache Dächer 1992

- PFP system wooden windows: spruce block frame with flush-fitting opening lights and doors of aluminium Z-sections
- First building in Germany with F90-B fire resistance rating

1　Spandrel panel, 50 mm:
　　fibre-cement sheet, white enamel finish rigid foam insulation white-coated particleboard
2　Glulam cruciform-section column, 360 x 360 mm
3　Wind bracing, 27 mm dia.
4　Rainwater downpipe
5　Glulam edge beam, 240 x 630 mm
6　Galvanised steel open grid flooring
7　16 mm dia. rod as suspension member and tie
8　Sunblind
9　F90-B ceiling

Scale 1:400

18 · Holiday home

Breitbrunn, D; 1987

Architects: R. + R. Then Bergh, Munich

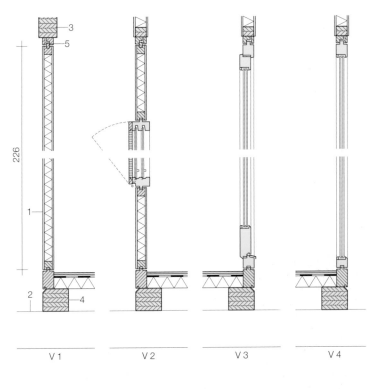

226

1

2

V 1 V 2 V 3 V 4

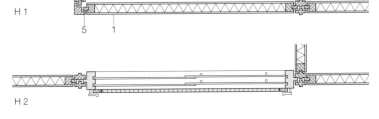

H 1

5 1

H 2

H 3

H 4

6 113 6

· Separate loadbearing structure and
building envelope
· Grid for wall elements: 1130 + 60 mm
· Movable wall elements

1 External wall, 60 mm
   sandwich element, 3 mm fibre-cement
   sheets both sides, white finish
   54 mm thermal insulation core
2 Main beam
3 Roof beam
4 140 x 120 mm sole plate
5 Joint cover strips

H3,4 H1,2

V3,4 V1,2

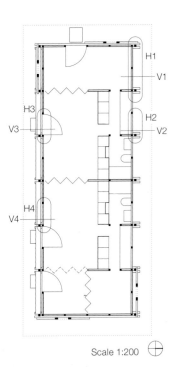

H1

V1

H3

V3

H2

V2

H4

V4

Scale 1:200

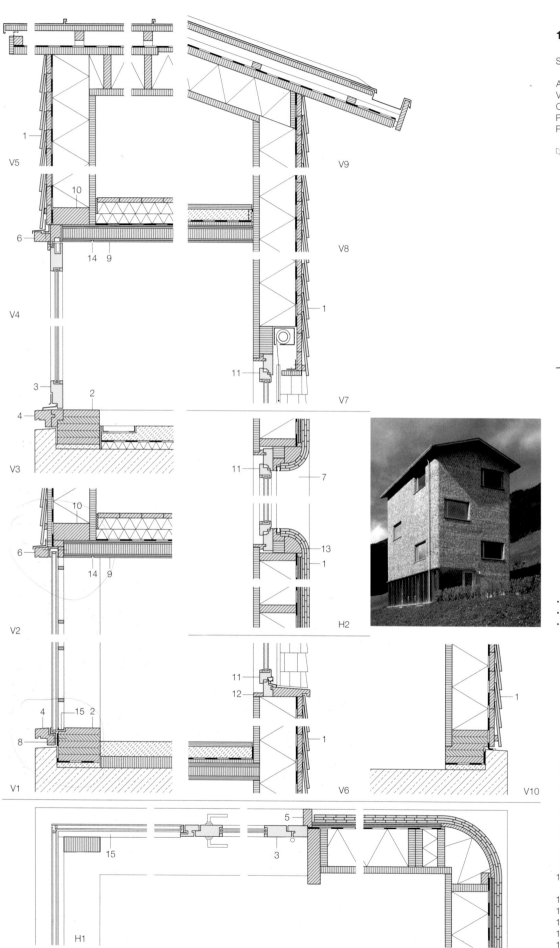

Sumvitg, CH; 1998

Architects:
Valentin Bearth und Andrea Deplazes,
Chur
Partner: Daniel Ladner
Project manager: Bettina Werner

▢ Detail 1/2000

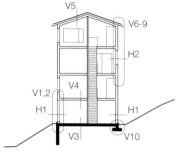

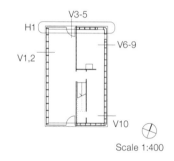

Scale 1:400

· Panel construction
· High degree of prefabrication
· Construction time: 12 months

1 External wall, 302 mm:
 300 x 40 mm larch shingles
 27 mm butt-jointed horizontal boards
 airtight barrier
 40 x 200 mm timber ribs with 200 mm
 mineral wool insulation between
 35 mm 3-ply core plywood
2 Glulam sole plate, 190 x 213 mm
3 Larch door frame
4 Larch weatherboard fitted into door
 frame
5 Squared timber section, 50 x 103 mm
 larch
6 Larch transom, 50 x 82 mm
7 Larch lintel board, 20 mm, removable
8 Hot-dip galvanised steel section
9 3-ply core plywood ceiling, 90 mm
10 Window lintel, glued to 3-ply core
 plywood, 100 x 200 mm
11 Larch window frame
12 Spruce window sill, 20 mm, painted
13 Quarter-round fillet, 91 mm spruce
14 Slot for curtain rail
15 Steel water bar

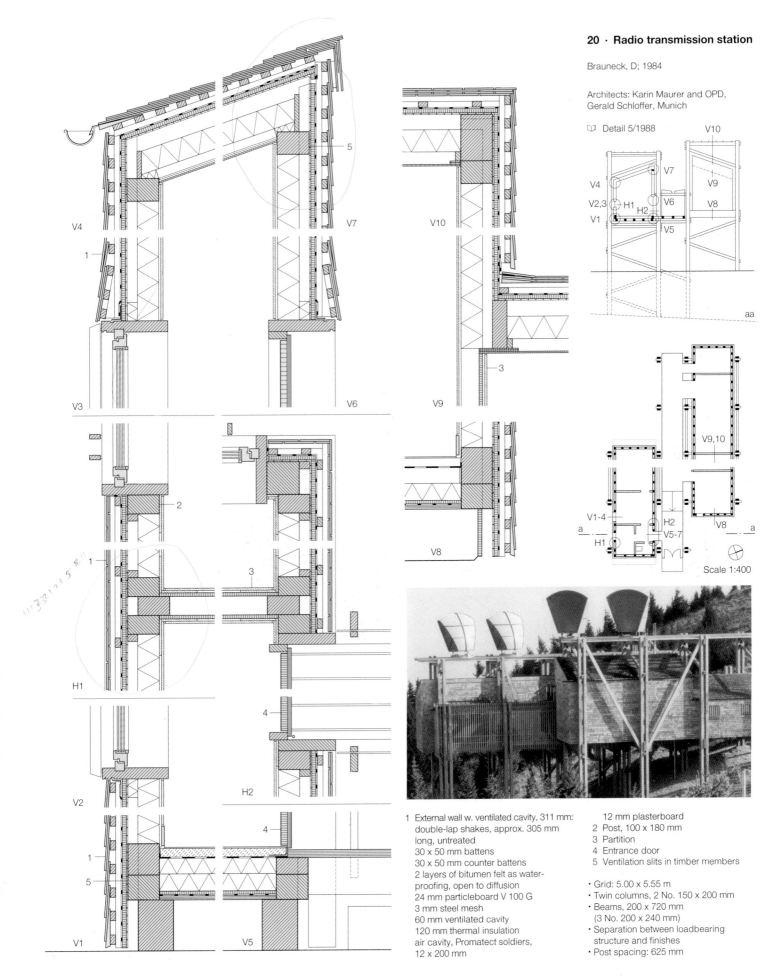

Brauneck, D; 1984

Architects: Karin Maurer and OPD,
Gerald Schloffer, Munich

Detail 5/1988

aa

Scale 1:400

1 External wall w. ventilated cavity, 311 mm:
  double-lap shakes, approx. 305 mm
  long, untreated
  30 x 50 mm battens
  30 x 50 mm counter battens
  2 layers of bitumen felt as waterproofing, open to diffusion
  24 mm particleboard V 100 G
  3 mm steel mesh
  60 mm ventilated cavity
  120 mm thermal insulation
  air cavity, Promatect soldiers,
  12 x 200 mm

  12 mm plasterboard
2 Post, 100 x 180 mm
3 Partition
4 Entrance door
5 Ventilation slits in timber members

· Grid: 5.00 x 5.55 m
· Twin columns, 2 No. 150 x 200 mm
· Beams, 200 x 720 mm
  (3 No. 200 x 240 mm)
· Separation between loadbearing
  structure and finishes
· Post spacing: 625 mm

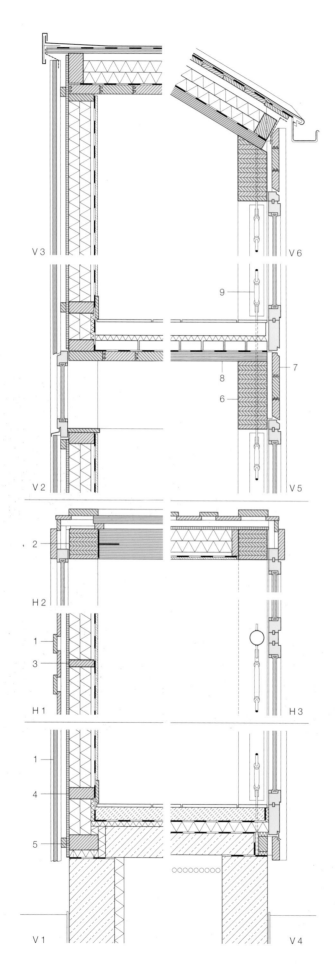

V 3

9

V 6

V 2

V 5

8

7

6

2

H 2

1

3

H 1

H 3

1

4

5

V 1

V 4

21 · Semi-detached houses

Ebenhausen, D; 1983–1984

Architects:
Elmar und Sigrid Dittmann, Munich

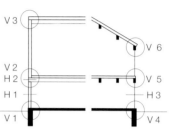

V 3

V 6

V 2
H 2

V 5
H 1

H 3

V 1

V 4

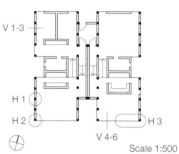

V 1-3

H 1

H 2

H 3

V 4-6

Scale 1:500

📖 Sack/Rautert: *Einfache Paradiese*,
Stuttgart 1985

· Grid: 1500 mm
· Masonry core
· Untreated external cladding
· Low-cost construction
· High degree of self-build

1 External wall w. ventilated cavity, 232 mm:
  21 x 100 mm outer boards
  21 x 140 mm inner boards
  ventilated cavity, 30 x 50 mm battens
  15 mm wood-cement particleboard
  2 layers of 60 mm thermal insulation
  12.5 mm air cavity
  vapour barrier
  12.5 mm plasterboard

2 Glulam column, 160 x 160 mm
3 Post, 40 x 145 mm
4 Rail, 60 x 145 mm
5 Sole plate, 80 x 160 mm
6 Glulam edge beam, 160 x 360 mm
7 Cladding to beam
8 50 mm double tongue and groove
  planks
9 Wind bracing

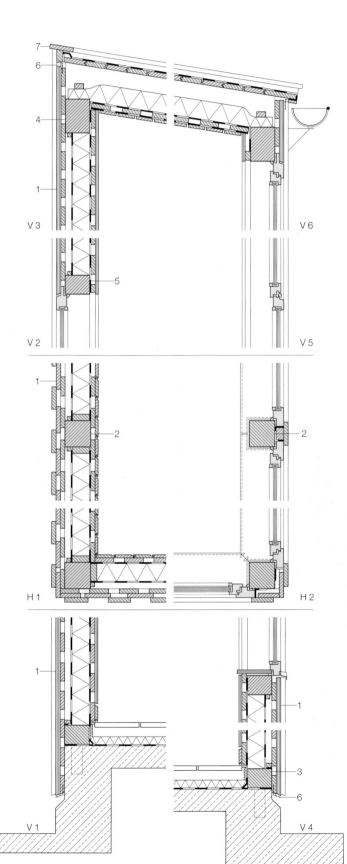

22 · Youth conference centre

Michelrieth, D; 1983–1984

Architect: Theodor Hugues, Munich
Assistants: H. Hugues, M. Ludwig

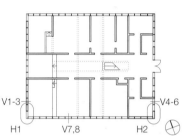

📖 Detail 1/1985

- Grid: 900 mm
- Braced by diagonal boarding
- Grid width of boarding: 225 mm
- Loadbearing structure and facade in spruce

Scale 1:500

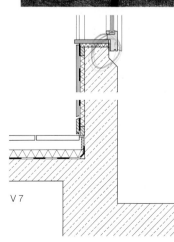

1 External wall w. ventilated cavity, 252 mm:
   staggered planks, 21 x 140 and 21 x
   120 mm, green, pressure-impregnated
   24 mm diagonal boarding laid with gaps
   40 mm air cavity
   airtight barrier, open to diffusion and
   water-repellent
   100 mm thermal insulation
   vapour barrier
   24 mm diagonal boarding laid with gaps
   16 mm untreated vertical tongue and
   groove boards
2 Column, 140 x 140 mm
3 Sole plate, 100 x 140 mm
4 Purlin, 140 x 180 mm
5 Trimmer, 140 x 100 mm
6 Perforated metal plate as insect screen
7 Timber capping, 24 x 120 mm

23 · Garden retreat

Meckenbeuren, D; 1994

Architects:
Jauss und Gaupp, Friedrichshafen

Detail 4/1996
DB 9/1995

· Flexible plan layout with movable room
dividers
· External walls of prefabricated
timber stud elements

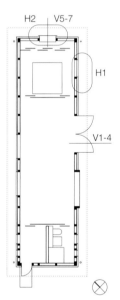

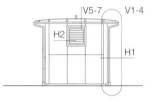

Scale 1:250

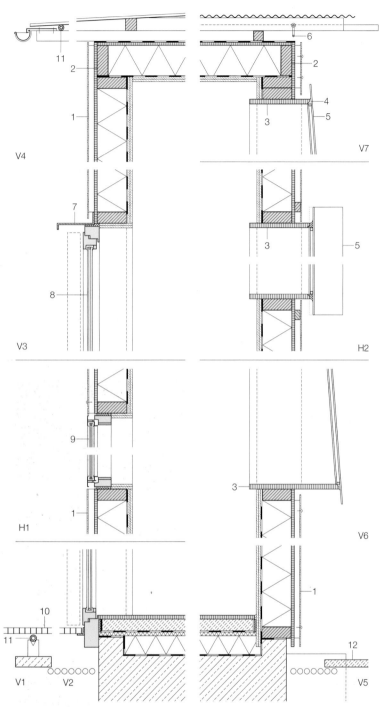

1 External wall, 250 mm:
  fibre-cement sheets, glaze finish
  vertical battens, ventilated cavity
  16 mm chipboard
  160 x 60 mm timber studs with
  160 mm thermal insulation between
  vapour barrier
  2 No. 12.5 mm plasterboard
2 Beam, 160 x 60 mm
3 3-ply core plywood

4 Silicone bedding
5 Wired double glazing
6 Stainless steel tension cable
7 Bent sheet aluminium, painted black
8 Double glazing to door leaves
9 Top-hung opening light
10 Open-grid flooring
11 Galvanised steel tube
12 Concrete paving flags

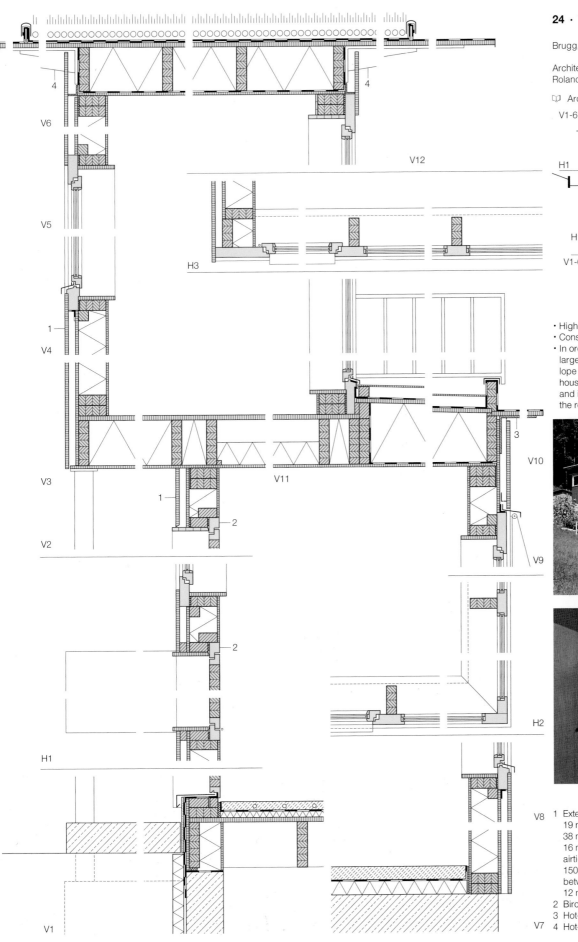

V6

V12

V5

H3

V4

1

V3

V11

1

2

V2

H1

V10

3

V9

2

H2

V8

V1

V7

24 · Three houses on hillside

Brugg, CH; 1994

Architects: Ruedi Dietiker, Beat Klaus, Roland Keller; Brugg; CH

Archithese, 5/1995

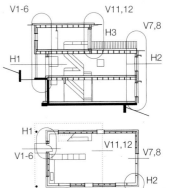

V1-6   V11,12   V7,8

H3

H1   H2

H1

V11,12

V1-6   V7,8

H2

Scale 1:400

- High degree of prefabrication
- Construction time: 8 months
- In order to exploit the advantages of large-scale production, the outer envelope and main construction of all three houses are identical but the partitions and internal fittings are designed to suit the requirements of the occupants.

1 External wall w. ventilated cavity, 235 mm:
   19 mm pine Batipin plywood, painted
   38 mm ventilated cavity
   16 mm wood fibreboard as
   airtight barrier
   150 mm cellulose fibre insulation
   between 55 x 150 mm loadbearing ribs
   12 mm birch plywood
2 Birch door frame
3 Hot-dip galvanised steel angle
4 Hot-dip galvanised steel bracket

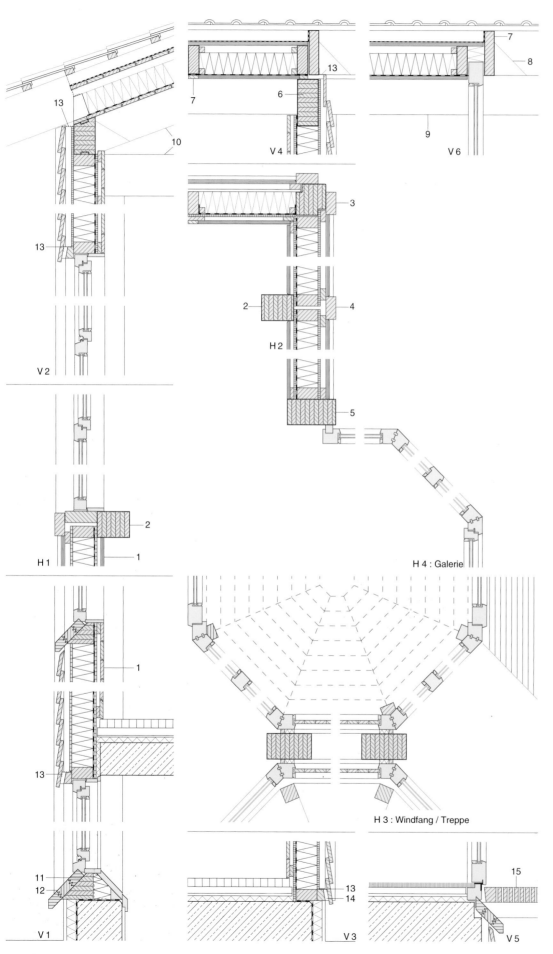

V 4

V 6

V 2

H 2

H 1

H 4 : Galerie

H 3 : Windfang / Treppe

V 1

V 3

V 5

25 · Parish hall

Ebersberg, D; 1985

Architects: Georg and Ingrid Küttinger,
with Tilo Röder, Andreas Heene, Munich

📖 Detail 1/1988

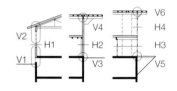

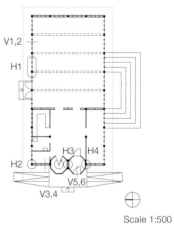

Scale 1:500

- Wall and roof elements 250 mm wide
- Posts and rafters at 625 mm centres

1 External wall with ventilated cavity,
   254 mm:
   20 x 140 mm weatherboarding
   ventilated air cavity, 30 x 60 mm battens
   30 mm particleboard V 100 G
   120 mm thermal insulation
   vapour barrier
   13 mm chipboard V 100 G
   air cavity, 20 x 60 mm battens
   18 mm horizontal t&g boards
2 Glulam column, 140 x 180 mm
3 Glulam corner column, 168 x 168 mm
4 Cover board, 55 x 140 mm
5 Glulam column, 140 x 340-218 mm
6 Glulam edge beam, 120 x 250 mm
7 Rafters, 60 x 160 and 55 x 242 mm
8 Lateral restraint
9 Glulam purlin, 140 x 250 mm
10 Glulam chords to roof truss,
   140 x 220 mm
11 Glulam fillet, 50 mm
12 Sill, glued oak, vertical annual rings
13 Copper insect screen
14 Fresh air inlet, 20 x 100 mm at 200 mm
   centres
15 Timber open-grid bridge

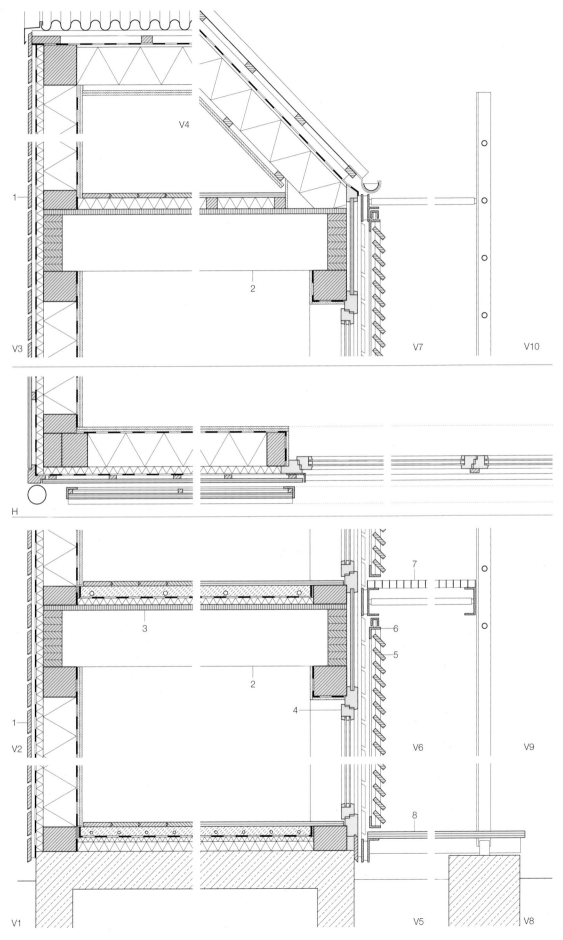

26 · Private house

Stuttgart, D; 1997

Architects: Schlude Ströhle, Stuttgart

DBZ 4/1999
Baumeister 1/1999

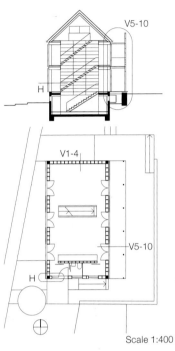

Scale 1:400

· Low-energy building with high degree of prefabrication
· Erection time: 3 days

1 External wall, 280 mm:
   20 mm Douglas fir boards
   20 mm counter battens
   airtight barrier, open to diffusion
   40 mm softboard
   180 mm mineral fibre insulating board
   180 mm frame construction,
   impregnated with borate
   0.2 mm vapour barrier
   2 No. 10 mm plasterboard
2 Glulam beam, 60 x 300 mm
3 Laminated veneer lumber (Kerto)
4 Larch window frame
5 Larch sliding shutter
6 Galvanised steel frame
7 Galvanised steel construction
8 Timber grid

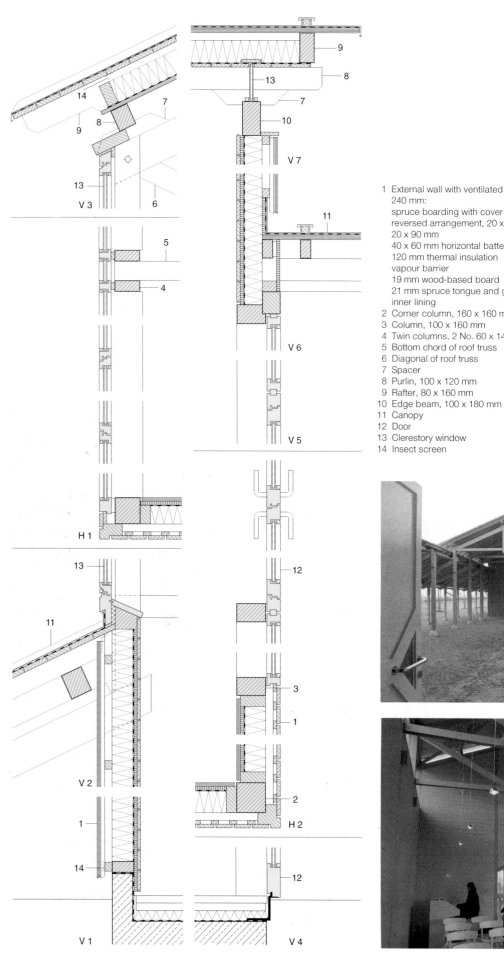

Eching, D; 1985

Architects: Sampo Widmann
and Stephan Romero, Munich
Assistant: H. Huber

Baumeister 4/1987
Informationsdienst Holz 22

1 External wall with ventilated cavity,
   240 mm:
   spruce boarding with cover strips in
   reversed arrangement, 20 x 40 and
   20 x 90 mm
   40 x 60 mm horizontal battens
   120 mm thermal insulation
   vapour barrier
   19 mm wood-based board
   21 mm spruce tongue and groove
   inner lining
2 Corner column, 160 x 160 mm
3 Column, 100 x 160 mm
4 Twin columns, 2 No. 60 x 140 mm
5 Bottom chord of roof truss
6 Diagonal of roof truss
7 Spacer
8 Purlin, 100 x 120 mm
9 Rafter, 80 x 160 mm
10 Edge beam, 100 x 180 mm
11 Canopy
12 Door
13 Clerestory window
14 Insect screen

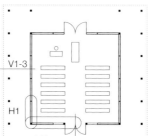
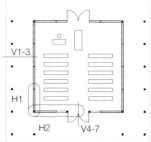

Scale 1:400

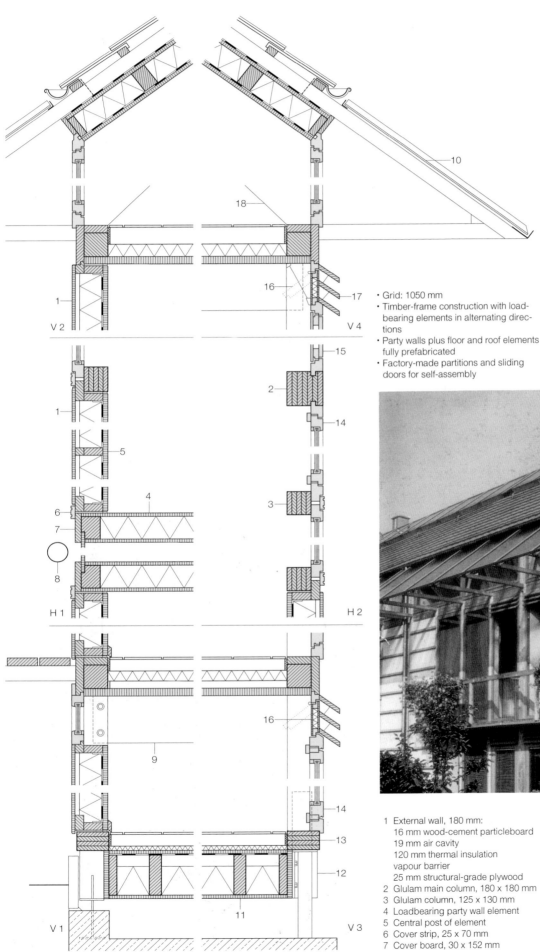

28 · Terrace houses

Eching, D; 1988

Architect: Reinhold Tobey, Munich
Assistants: M. Streib, W. Dilcher-Tobey

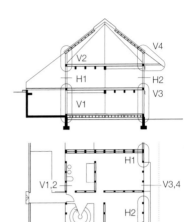

- Grid: 1050 mm
- Timber-frame construction with load-bearing elements in alternating directions
- Party walls plus floor and roof elements fully prefabricated
- Factory-made partitions and sliding doors for self-assembly

Scale 1:400

1 External wall, 180 mm:
    16 mm wood-cement particleboard
    19 mm air cavity
    120 mm thermal insulation
    vapour barrier
    25 mm structural-grade plywood
2 Glulam main column, 180 x 180 mm
3 Glulam column, 125 x 130 mm
4 Loadbearing party wall element
5 Central post of element
6 Cover strip, 25 x 70 mm
7 Cover board, 30 x 152 mm

8 Rainwater downpipe
9 Glulam main column, 180 x 300 mm
10 Wired glass on 80 x 80 mm softwood section
11 Timber panel element
12 Steel circular hollow section, fin, end plate
13 Glulam sole plate, 100 x 160 mm
14 Centre-pivot window
15 Door leaf
16 Ventilation flap
17 Wooden louvres

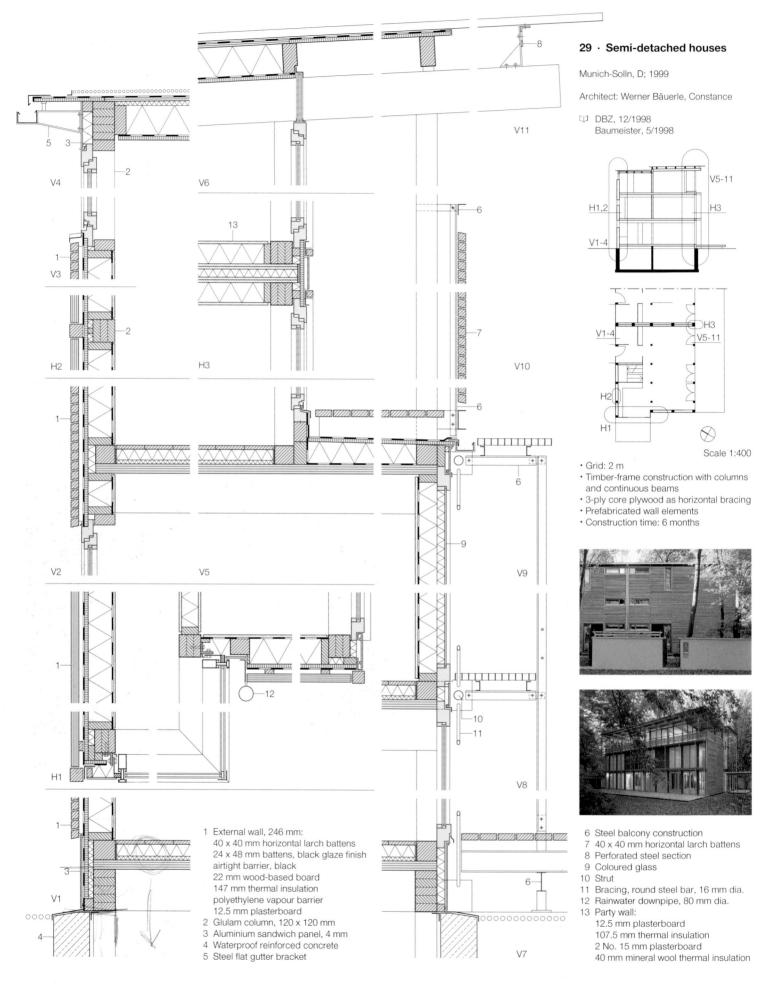

29 · Semi-detached houses

Munich-Solln, D; 1999

Architect: Werner Bäuerle, Constance

DBZ, 12/1998
Baumeister, 5/1998

V5-11

H1,2   H3

V1-4

V1-4   H3
                       V5-11

H2

H1

Scale 1:400

· Grid: 2 m
· Timber-frame construction with columns and continuous beams
· 3-ply core plywood as horizontal bracing
· Prefabricated wall elements
· Construction time: 6 months

V4

V6

V11

V3

V6

V10

V2

V5

V9

H2

H3

1 External wall, 246 mm:
  40 x 40 mm horizontal larch battens
  24 x 48 mm battens, black glaze finish
  airtight barrier, black
  22 mm wood-based board
  147 mm thermal insulation
  polyethylene vapour barrier
  12.5 mm plasterboard
2 Glulam column, 120 x 120 mm
3 Aluminium sandwich panel, 4 mm
4 Waterproof reinforced concrete
5 Steel flat gutter bracket

6 Steel balcony construction
7 40 x 40 mm horizontal larch battens
8 Perforated steel section
9 Coloured glass
10 Strut
11 Bracing, round steel bar, 16 mm dia.
12 Rainwater downpipe, 80 mm dia.
13 Party wall:
  12.5 mm plasterboard
  107.5 mm thermal insulation
  2 No. 15 mm plasterboard
  40 mm mineral wool thermal insulation

V1

V8

V7

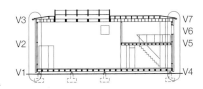

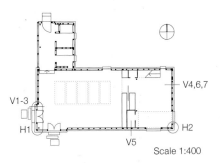

Scale 1:400

- Timber box-frame construction with panels of rendered lightweight cob units
- High degree of prefabrication

1 Wall construction, 290 mm:
30 mm lightweight mineral rendering
lightweight reed boards with splatter-dash finish, 2 No. 50 mm
18 mm plywood
120 mm lightweight cob units LLS 0.7 in loam mortar between 60 x 120 mm softwood posts
triangular fillets
electric cables
15 mm fibre-reinforced loam under-coat
glass-fibre fabric
5 mm slaked lime final coat
2 Solid-web wood-based beam, 302 mm deep
3 Oak frame with heat-absorbing glass
4 Softwood beam, 100 x 180 mm
5 Parallelstrand lumber, 160 x 241 mm

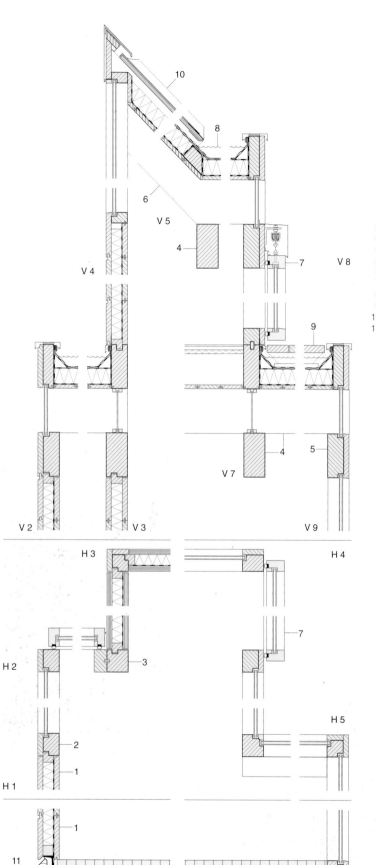

31 · Private house

Aachen, D; 1976–1980

Architects: Erich Schneider-Wessling with Ilse Walter, Helmut Brinkhaus, Cologne

Bauen mit Holz 3/1983

1 External wall, 120 mm:
   30 x 233 mm diagonal boarding outside
   60 mm mineral fibre thermal insulation
   polyethylene vapour barrier
   30 x 233 mm diagonal boarding inside
2 Column, 90 x 120 mm
3 Corner column, 120 x 120 mm
4 Beams, 120 x 233 mm
5 Edge beam, 90 x 233 mm
6 Rafter, 120 x 165 mm
7 Sliding door
8 Warm deck construction, flooded
9 Timber grid, 40 x 120 mm
10 Cold deck construction
11 Engineering bricks in mortar bed,
   52 x 52 x 240 mm

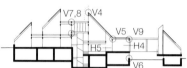

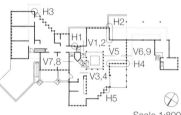

Scale 1:800

• Grid: 1250 x 1250 mm
• Vertical module: 700 mm
   (700 ÷ 3 = 233 mm)
• Spacing of columns and beams: 6.25 m
• Connections on member axes
• All exposed timber members in larch

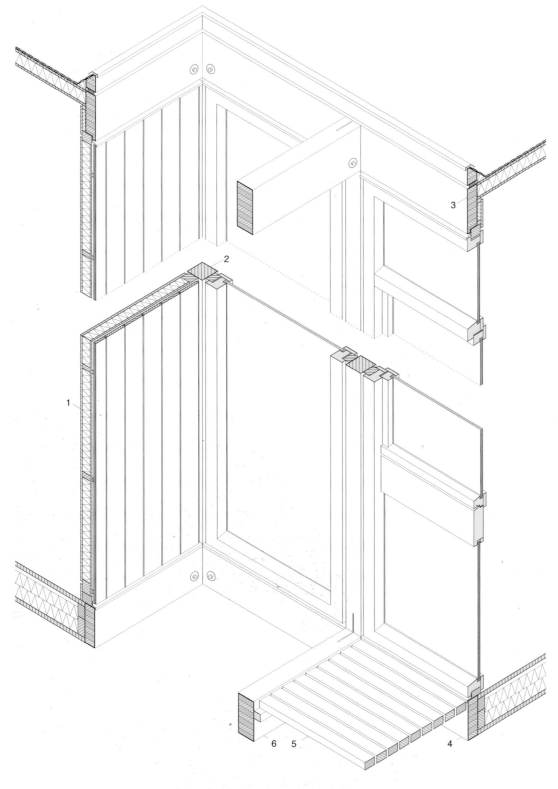

32 · Private house

Brest, F; 1983

Architect: Roland Schweitzer, Paris
Assistant: P. Jean

Techniques et Architecture,
Paris 4–5/1986

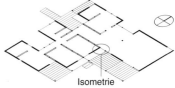

Isometrie

- Grid: 2700 + 100 mm (square)
- Studs, secondary beams for fitting-out:
  900 mm grid
- All exposed timber members in tropical
  hardwood

1 External wall, 104 mm:
   20 mm vertical boarding outside
   air cavity, horizontal 10 mm battens
   12 mm particleboard
   50 mm thermal insulation
   12 mm boarding or chipboard
2 Column, 100 x 100 mm
3 Glulam edge beam, 65 x 240 mm
4 Glulam edge beam, 70 x 210 mm
5 Timber grid
6 Beam, 100 x 120 mm

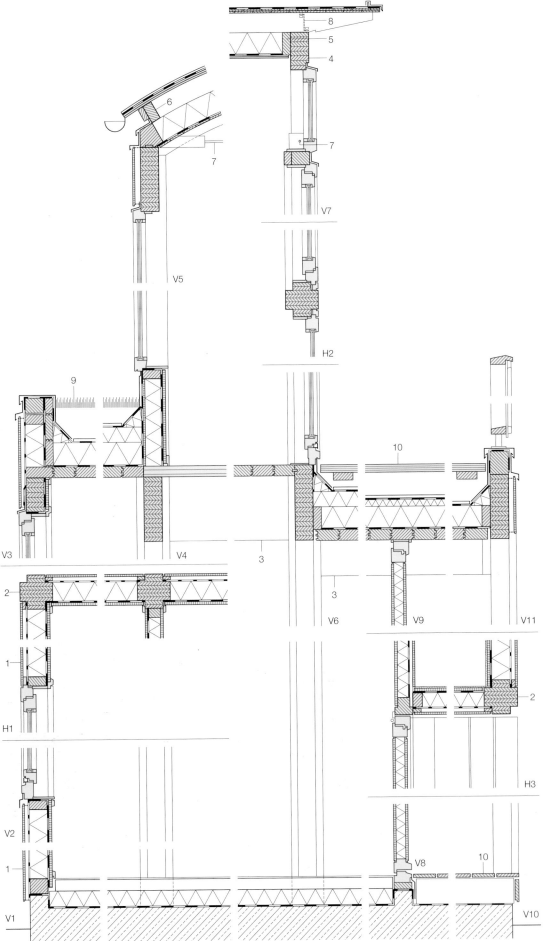

Berlin, D; 1985

Architect: Otto Steidle
with Hans Kohl, Munich

📕 Detail 4/1985

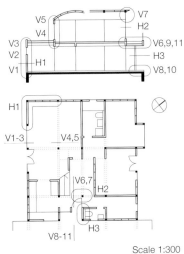

Scale 1:300

- Timber-frame construction, F30 fire resistance
- Grid: 1.975 and 2.600 m
- Vertical module: 300 mm

1 External wall w. ventilated cavity, 155 mm:
  12 x 330 mm wood-cement particle-board, 300 mm cover width
  27 mm ventilated air cavity
  2 layers of bitumen felt
  50 x 100 mm studs at 625 mm centres
  100 mm thermal insulation
  0.2 mm polyethylene sheet
  16 mm particleboard V 20
2 Glulam cruciform-section column, 180 x 180 mm
3 Beams, 100 x 180, 200, 340, 400 mm
4 Glulam arch, 100 x 200 mm
5 Glulam intermediate frame, 60 x 120 mm
6 Purlin, 60 x 100 mm
7 Tie bar, 10 mm dia.
8 Perforated sheet metal as insect screen
9 Rooftop planting
10 Timber grid (entrance, terrace)

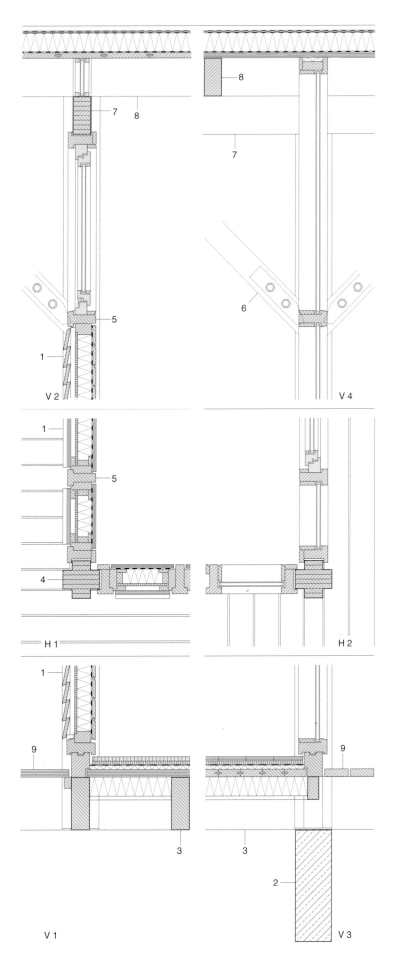

V 2

V 1

H 1

V 4

H 2

V 3

34 · School

Dischingen, D; 1979–1980

Architects: Klaus Mahler and
Jürgen Schäfer, Stuttgart

☐ Detail 2/1983

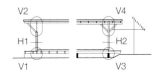

Scale 1:1500

- Grid: 8.64 x 8.64 m
- Post spacing: 1.08 m
- Wind bracing by means of particleboard
  and pairs of kneebraces
- Roof overhang: 1.89 m
- External sunshade of permanent
  wooden louvres

1 Ext. wall with ventilated cavity, 171 mm:
  18 mm weatherboarding on profiled
  strip
  24 mm air cavity
  13 mm chipboard
  2 layers of 40 mm thermal insulation
  vapour barrier
  18 mm tongue and groove boarding
2 Reinforced concrete ground beam,

  200 x 600 mm
3 Beam, 100 x 280 mm
4 Glulam cruciform-section column,
  200 x 200 mm
5 Posts and rails, 80 x 160 mm
6 Kneebraces, 2 No. 50 x 130 mm
7 Glulam main beam, 100 x 200 mm
8 Beam, 100 x 200 mm
9 Walkway planks, 40 x 130 mm

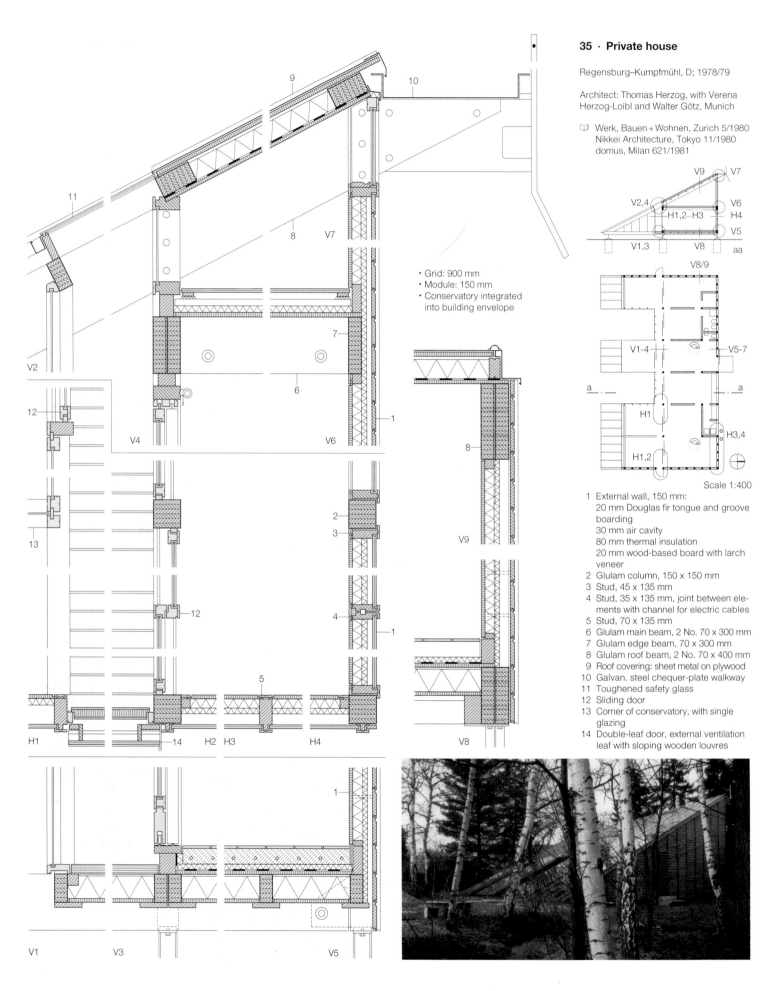

35 · Private house

Regensburg–Kumpfmühl, D; 1978/79

Architect: Thomas Herzog, with Verena Herzog-Loibl and Walter Götz, Munich

Werk, Bauen + Wohnen, Zurich 5/1980
Nikkei Architecture, Tokyo 11/1980
domus, Milan 621/1981

Scale 1:400

- Grid: 900 mm
- Module: 150 mm
- Conservatory integrated into building envelope

1 External wall, 150 mm:
   20 mm Douglas fir tongue and groove boarding
   30 mm air cavity
   80 mm thermal insulation
   20 mm wood-based board with larch veneer
2 Glulam column, 150 x 150 mm
3 Stud, 45 x 135 mm
4 Stud, 35 x 135 mm, joint between elements with channel for electric cables
5 Stud, 70 x 135 mm
6 Glulam main beam, 2 No. 70 x 300 mm
7 Glulam edge beam, 70 x 300 mm
8 Glulam roof beam, 2 No. 70 x 400 mm
9 Roof covering: sheet metal on plywood
10 Galvan. steel chequer-plate walkway
11 Toughened safety glass
12 Sliding door
13 Corner of conservatory, with single glazing
14 Double-leaf door, external ventilation leaf with sloping wooden louvres

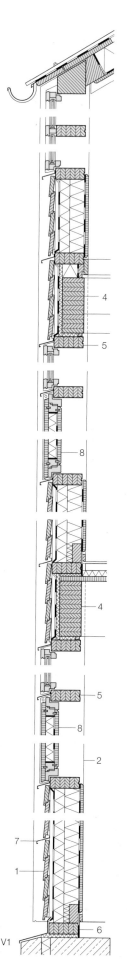

36 · Youth education centre

Windberg, D; 1990

Architect: Thomas Herzog, with Peter Bonfig and Walter Götz, Munich

📖 DBZ, 1/1991
Techniques et Architecture, Paris 398/1991
World Architecture, London 27/1994

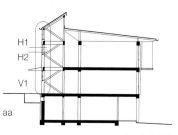

aa

Scale 1:400

- Module: 150 mm
- Larch weatherboarding, clear glaze finish
- Z-sections at regular intervals as rain protection
- Length of building: 70 m

1 External wall, 197 mm:
   22 x 137 mm larch weatherboarding
   20 mm air cavity
   perforated "breathing" foil
   140 mm thermal insulation
   polyethylene vapour barrier
   15 mm plywood
2 Glulam column, 150 x 175 mm
3 Glulam post, 70 x 175 mm
4 Glulam beam, 120 x 300 mm
5 Glulam rail, 60 x 160 mm
6 Glulam sole plate, 60 x 160 mm
7 Aluminium Z-sections at 450 mm centres
8 Ventilation flap

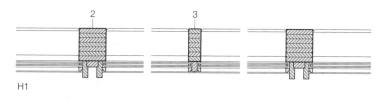

H1

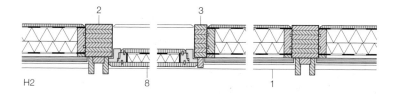

H2   8   1

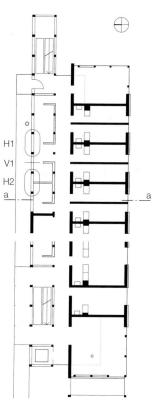

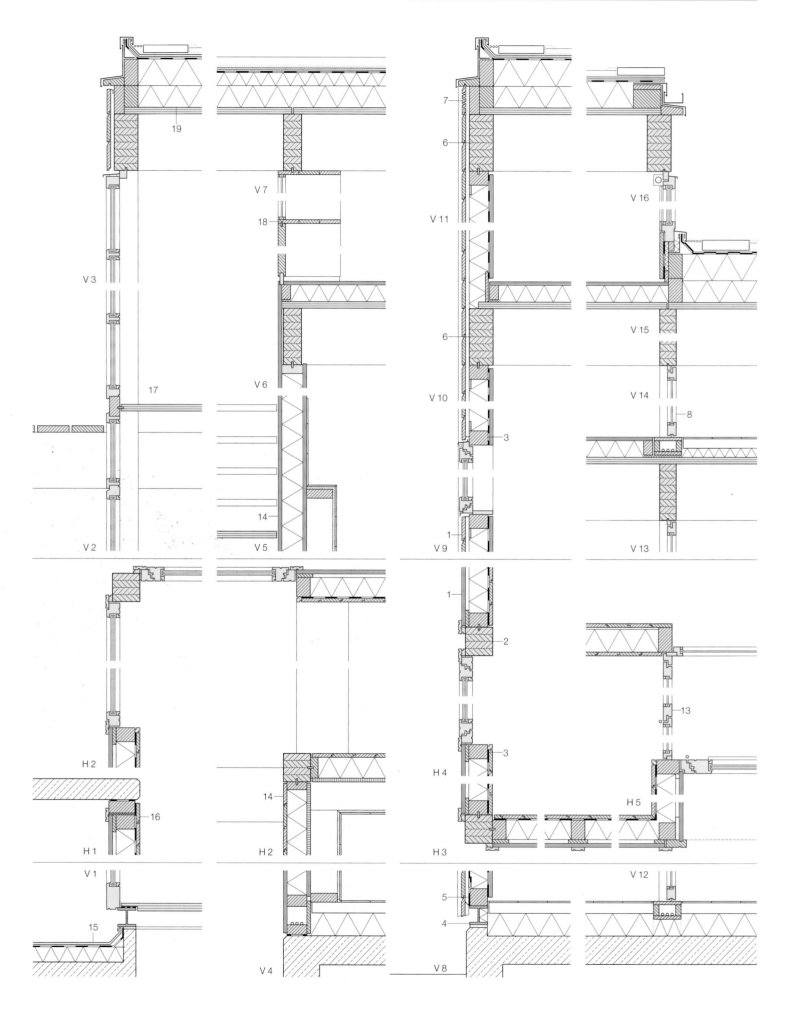

37 · Private house

Waldmohr, D; 1982–84

Architects: Thomas Herzog,
Michael Volz, Munich

📖 World Architecture, London 27/1994

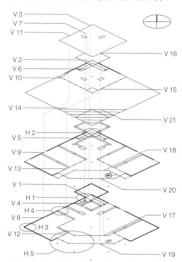

19

9

11

12

V 21

V 18   10   V 20

10

H 5

V 17

V 19

4

· Module: 150 mm
· Grid: 1.050 m; column bays: 3.150 m
· Square on plan: 1.275 x 1.275 m
· Diagonal facade faces south
· Storey height: 2.700 m
· Generous areas of glazing on south
  side, with conservatory

· Essentially solid, insulated facades
  facing northwest and northeast
· Temperature gradient on plan: warmer
  rooms are buffered by rooms at lower
  temperatures

1 External wall with ventilated cavity,
   169 mm:
   24 x 70 mm cover strips
   19 x 150 mm larch boards
   20 mm vertical battens
   ventilated cavity
   110 mm thermal insulation
   vapour barrier
   19 x 150 mm vertical tongue and
   groove larch boards
2 Glulam column, 150 x 150 mm
3 Posts and rails, 75 x 110 mm
4 Sole plate, steel section
5 Timber sole plate, 90 x 110 mm
6 Glulam facade beam, 130 x 300 mm
7 Elongated holes for cavity ventilation

8 Glazed internal door, with duct in
   threshold for services
9 Gallery balustrade
10 Sliding door to conservatory
11 Double glazing with internal roller
   blind
12 Strengthening transom
13 Glazed internal wall
14 Internal wall with duct at base for
   services
15 Roof over basement
16 Junction with basement
17 Stair landing and balcony
18 Shelves
19 Foam glass

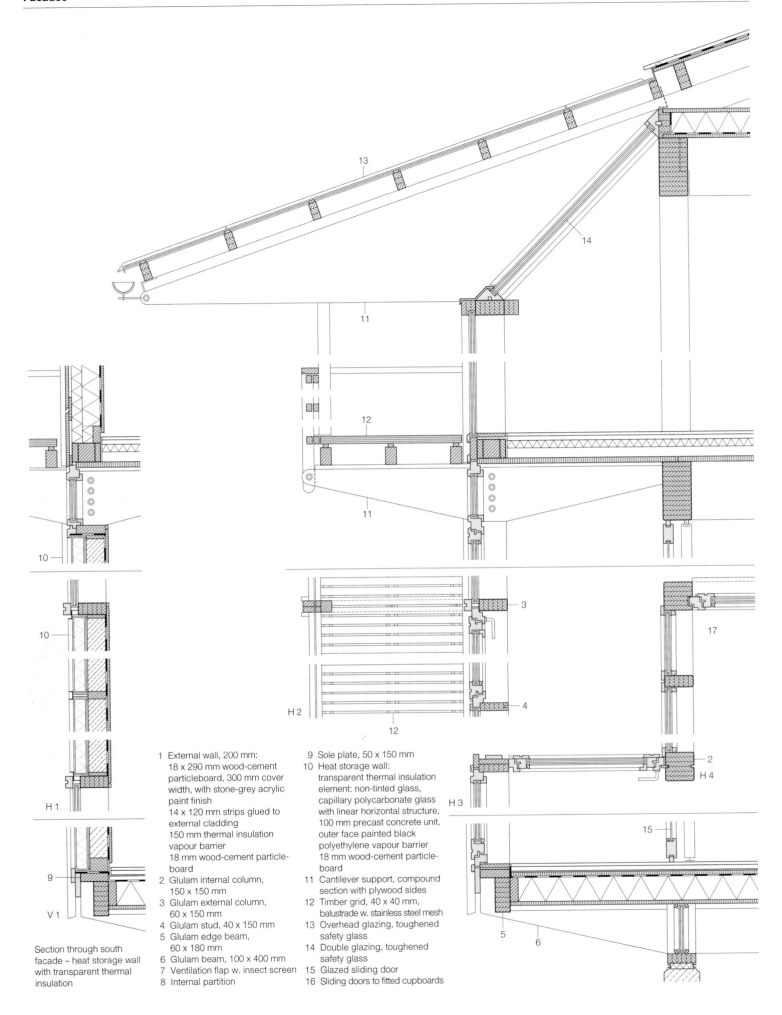

13

14

11

10

11

12

12

10

H 2

H 1

9

V 1

3

4

12

17

2

H 4

H 3

15

5

6

1 External wall, 200 mm:
   18 x 290 mm wood-cement
   particleboard, 300 mm cover
   width, with stone-grey acrylic
   paint finish
   14 x 120 mm strips glued to
   external cladding
   150 mm thermal insulation
   vapour barrier
   18 mm wood-cement particleboard
2 Glulam internal column,
   150 x 150 mm
3 Glulam external column,
   60 x 150 mm
4 Glulam stud, 40 x 150 mm
5 Glulam edge beam,
   60 x 180 mm
6 Glulam beam, 100 x 400 mm
7 Ventilation flap w. insect screen
8 Internal partition

9 Sole plate, 50 x 150 mm
10 Heat storage wall:
   transparent thermal insulation
   element: non-tinted glass,
   capillary polycarbonate glass
   with linear horizontal structure,
   100 mm precast concrete unit,
   outer face painted black
   polyethylene vapour barrier
   18 mm wood-cement particleboard
11 Cantilever support, compound
   section with plywood sides
12 Timber grid, 40 x 40 mm,
   balustrade w. stainless steel mesh
13 Overhead glazing, toughened
   safety glass
14 Double glazing, toughened
   safety glass
15 Glazed sliding door
16 Sliding doors to fitted cupboards

Section through south
facade – heat storage wall
with transparent thermal
insulation

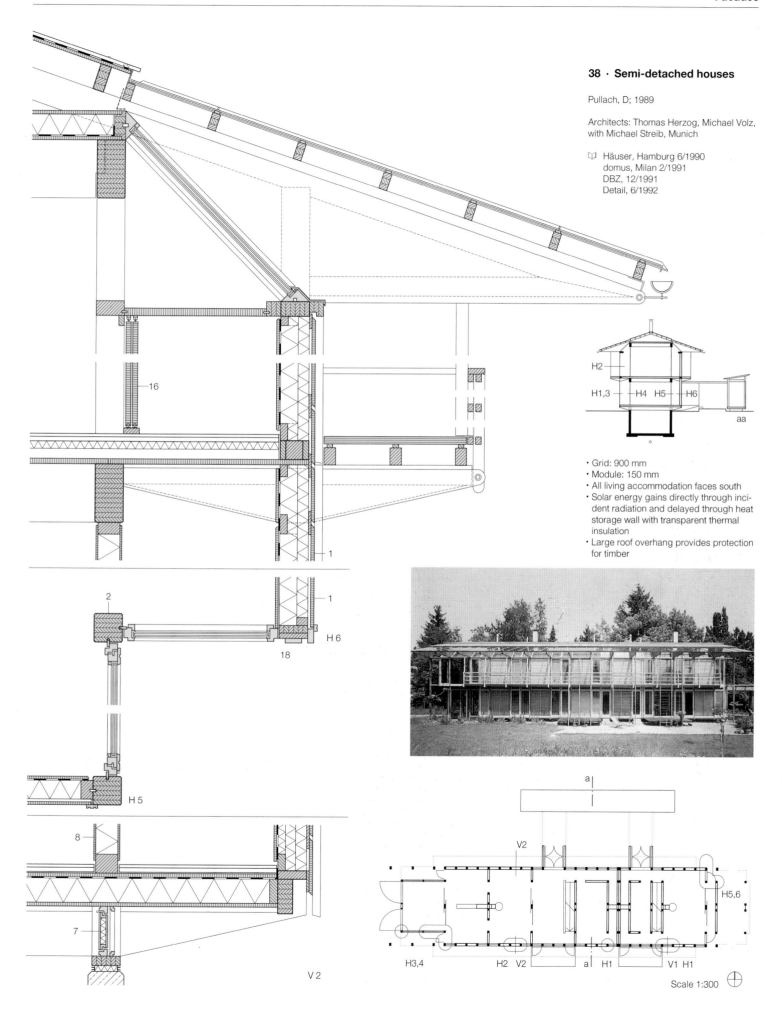

38 · Semi-detached houses

Pullach, D; 1989

Architects: Thomas Herzog, Michael Volz,
with Michael Streib, Munich

📖 Häuser, Hamburg 6/1990
domus, Milan 2/1991
DBZ, 12/1991
Detail, 6/1992

- Grid: 900 mm
- Module: 150 mm
- All living accommodation faces south
- Solar energy gains directly through incident radiation and delayed through heat storage wall with transparent thermal insulation
- Large roof overhang provides protection for timber

Scale 1:300

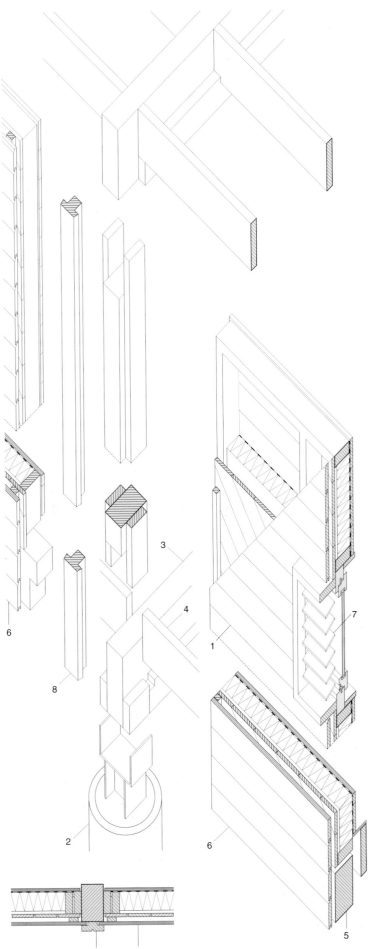

Ecublens, CH; 1984

Architects: Atelier Cube, Lausanne
Guy & Marc Collomb, Patrick Vogel

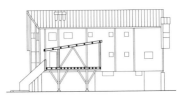

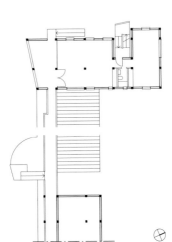

📖 Werk, Bauen und Wohnen 9/1985

· Loadbearing construction and fitting-out in spruce, external stairs and floor to open gallery in larch
· Facade components up to 2 storeys high are prefabricated from external cladding, diagonal boards, posts and rails
· Insulation, vapour barrier and inner lining added on site
· Building braced by diagonal boarding

Scale 1:500

1 External wall, 186 mm:
   22 mm tongue and groove external cladding
   ventilated cavity, 40 mm pressure-impregnated vertical battens
   22 mm diagonal boarding
   80 mm thermal insulation
   vapour barrier
   22 mm untreated, rough-sawn

horizontal inner lining
2 Concrete column
3 Glulam main beam
4 Secondary beam
5 Facade beam, 120 x 240 mm
6 Facade component, prefabricated, inner lining added on site
7 Matt-finish glass louvres, movable
8 Cover strip

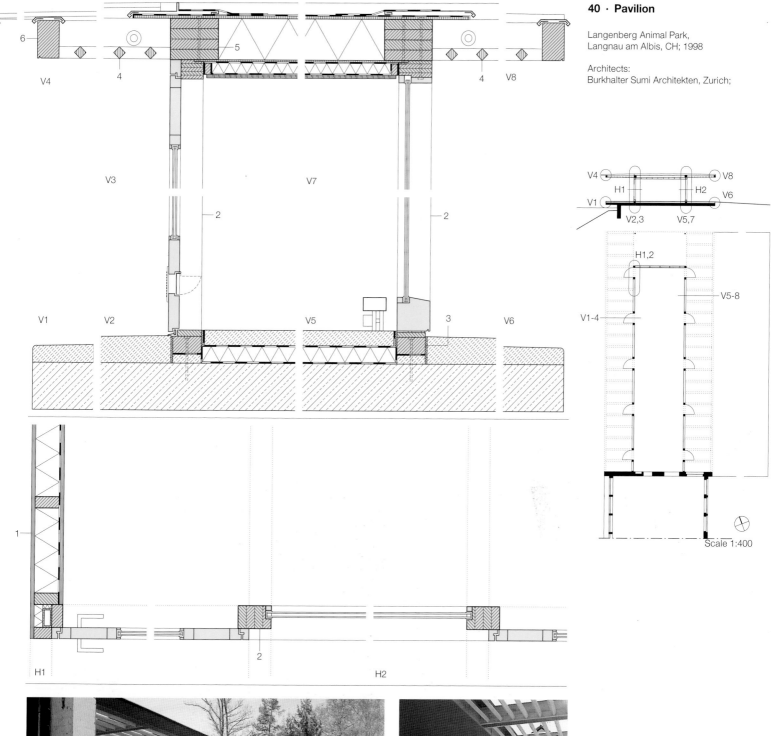

V4   4   5   4   V8

V3   V7

V1   V2   V5   V6

2   2

3

H1   H2

2

40 · Pavilion

Langenberg Animal Park,
Langnau am Albis, CH; 1998

Architects:
Burkhalter Sumi Architekten, Zurich;

V4   V8
H1   H2   V6
V1
V2,3   V5,7

H1,2
V5-8
V1-4

Scale 1:400

1 Wall construction, 180 mm:
   20 mm 3-ply core plywood
   timber posts dowelled to concrete slab
   with rockwool thermal insulation between
   vapour barrier
   20 mm 3-ply core plywood
   joint with key between panels, painted
2 Glulam frame construction with glass
   infill panels, painted
3 Timber sole plate for wall elements
   anchored to concrete with steel bar
   10 dia. x 280 mm
4 Larch louvres, 45 x 45 mm, untreated
5 Glulam beam, 260 x 220 mm
6 Softwood edge beam, 120 x 200 mm

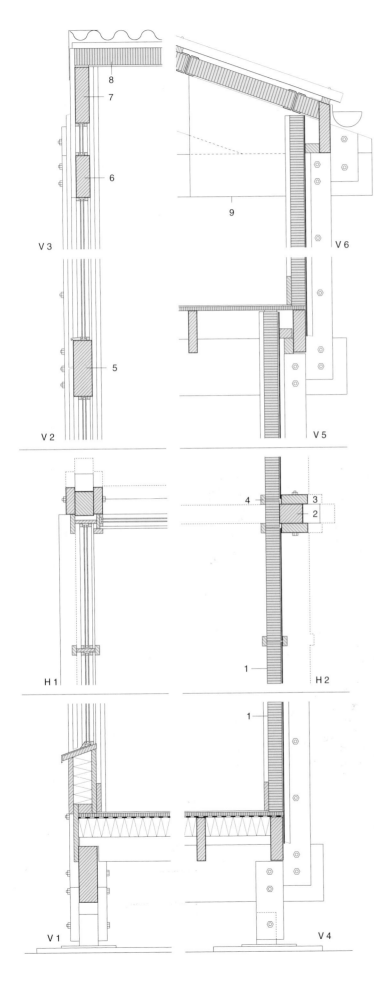

V 3

8
7

6

V 6

9

V 2

5

V 5

H 1

4
3
2

H 2

1

V 1

1

V 4

41 · Private house

Cambridge, UK; 1974

Architect: Marcial Echenique, Cambridge

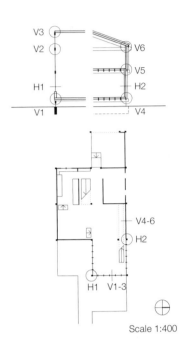

Scale 1:400

📖 Architectural Review 4/1974
Baumeister 1/1978

· Grid: 3.81 x 3.81 m
· Fitting-out grid: 600 mm
· Hemlock used throughout
· Standard sizes for wood-wool slabs and
  fibre-cement sheets, windows and doors
· Took 1 year to plan, 3 months to build
· Low-cost development
· Partly without any protection for the
  timber

1 External wall, 79 mm (3 1/8"):
   3 mm (1/8") fibre-cement sheets,
   enamelled
   76 mm (3") wood-wool slabs
2 Column, 102 x 127 mm (4" x 5")
3 Pair of ties, 2 No. 51 x 152 mm (2" x 6")
4 Cover strip, 25 x 50 mm (1" x 2")
5 Beam, 102 x 305 mm (4" x 12")
6 Frame member, 76 x 229 mm (3" x 9")
7 Beam, 102 x 305 mm (4" x 12")
8 Wood-wool slabs with [-section edging
9 Plywood gusset

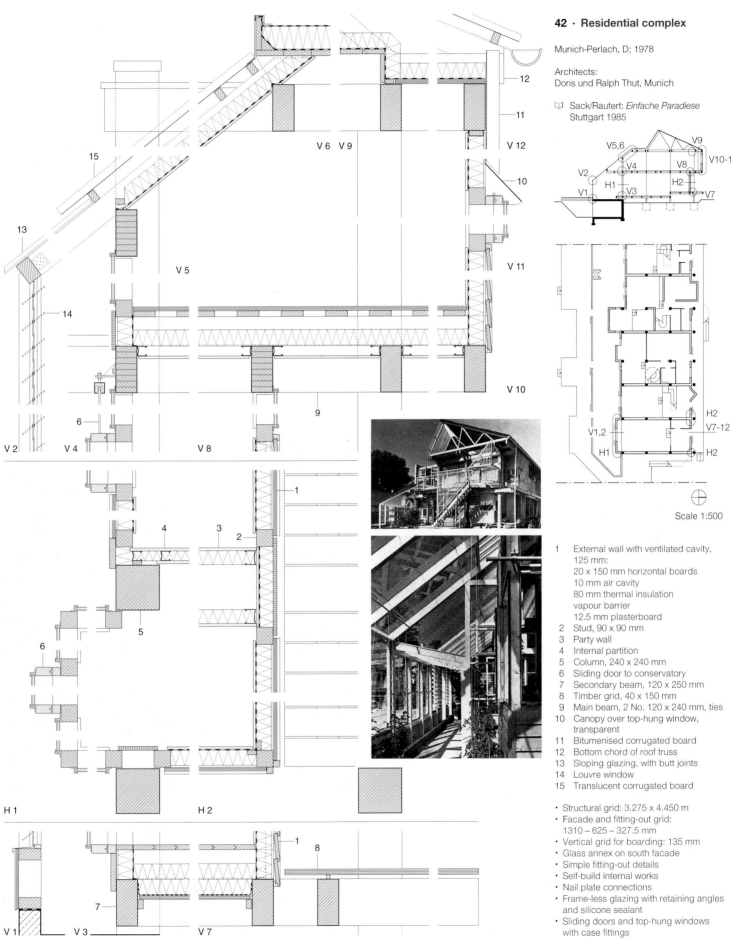

Munich-Perlach, D; 1978

Architects:
Doris und Ralph Thut, Munich

Sack/Rautert: *Einfache Paradiese*
Stuttgart 1985

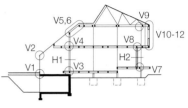

Scale 1:500

1 External wall with ventilated cavity,
125 mm:
20 x 150 mm horizontal boards
10 mm air cavity
80 mm thermal insulation
vapour barrier
12.5 mm plasterboard
2 Stud, 90 x 90 mm
3 Party wall
4 Internal partition
5 Column, 240 x 240 mm
6 Sliding door to conservatory
7 Secondary beam, 120 x 250 mm
8 Timber grid, 40 x 150 mm
9 Main beam, 2 No. 120 x 240 mm, ties
10 Canopy over top-hung window,
transparent
11 Bitumenised corrugated board
12 Bottom chord of roof truss
13 Sloping glazing, with butt joints
14 Louvre window
15 Translucent corrugated board

· Structural grid: 3.275 x 4.450 m
· Facade and fitting-out grid:
1310 – 625 – 327.5 mm
· Vertical grid for boarding: 135 mm
· Glass annex on south facade
· Simple fitting-out details
· Self-build internal works
· Nail plate connections
· Frame-less glazing with retaining angles
and silicone sealant
· Sliding doors and top-hung windows
with case fittings

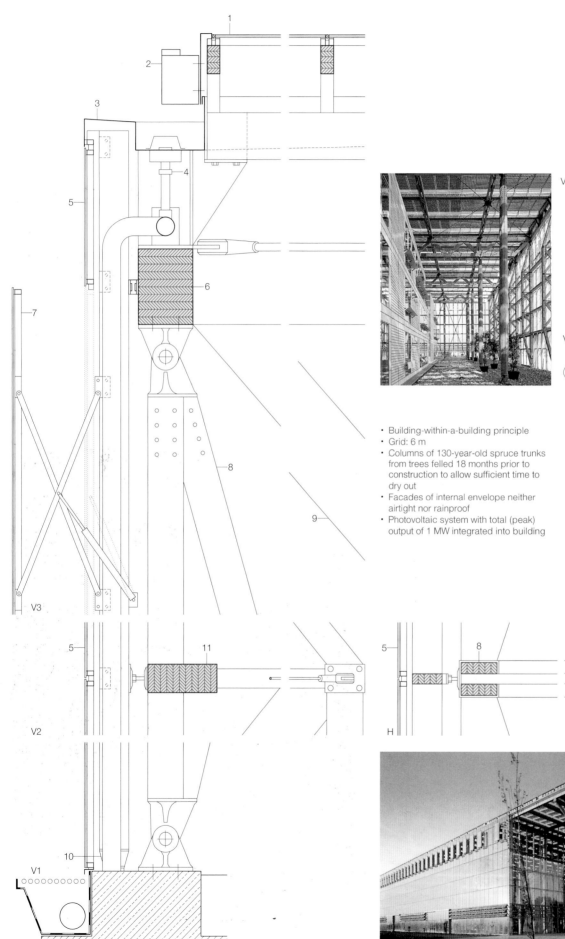

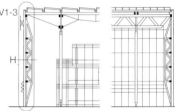

43 · Further education academy

Herne, D; 1999

Architects: Jourda et Perraudin, Paris
mit Hegger Hegger Schleiff Architekten,
Kassel

Detail 3/1999
Architektur aktuell 235

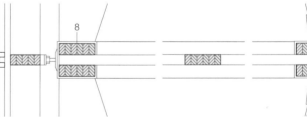

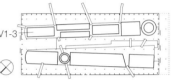

Scale 1:500

Scale 1:4500

- Building-within-a-building principle
- Grid: 6 m
- Columns of 130-year-old spruce trunks from trees felled 18 months prior to construction to allow sufficient time to dry out
- Facades of internal envelope neither airtight nor rainproof
- Photovoltaic system with total (peak) output of 1 MW integrated into building

1 Overhead glazing, laminated safety glass
6 mm heat-treated extra-clear glass
photovoltaic cells in casting resin, 2 mm
8 mm heat-treated glass
2 Power inverter
3 Galvanised steel gutter
4 Rainwater fast-drain system
5 Single glazing to facade:
structural sealant glazing on glulam facade posts, 160 x 60 mm
6 Glulam edge beam, 300 x 400 mm
7 Opening light
8 Timber lattice beam facade post
9 Timber roof frame
10 Steel base to facade post
11 Glulam facade rail

44 · Youth village

Cieux, Haute Vienne, F; 1985

Architect: Roland Schweitzer, Paris
Assistant: C. Peyret

Techniques et Architecture,
Paris 4–5/1986

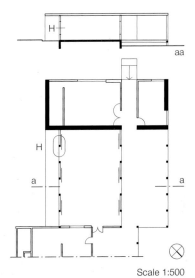

Scale 1:500

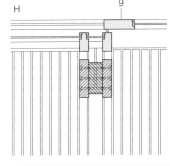

Section through dining hall
· Structural grid: 2.10 m
· Prefabricated wall and floor element

1 Steel channel sections,
2 No. 65 x 42 mm
2 Beam, 2 No. 50 x 110 mm

3 Grid support beam, 32 x 105 mm
4 Batten, 40 x 40 mm
5 Sole plate, 45 x 42 mm
6 Hardwood section, 95 x 200 mm
7 Sliding door
8 Twin column, 2 No. 50 x 200 mm
9 Glulam beam, 95 x 320 mm

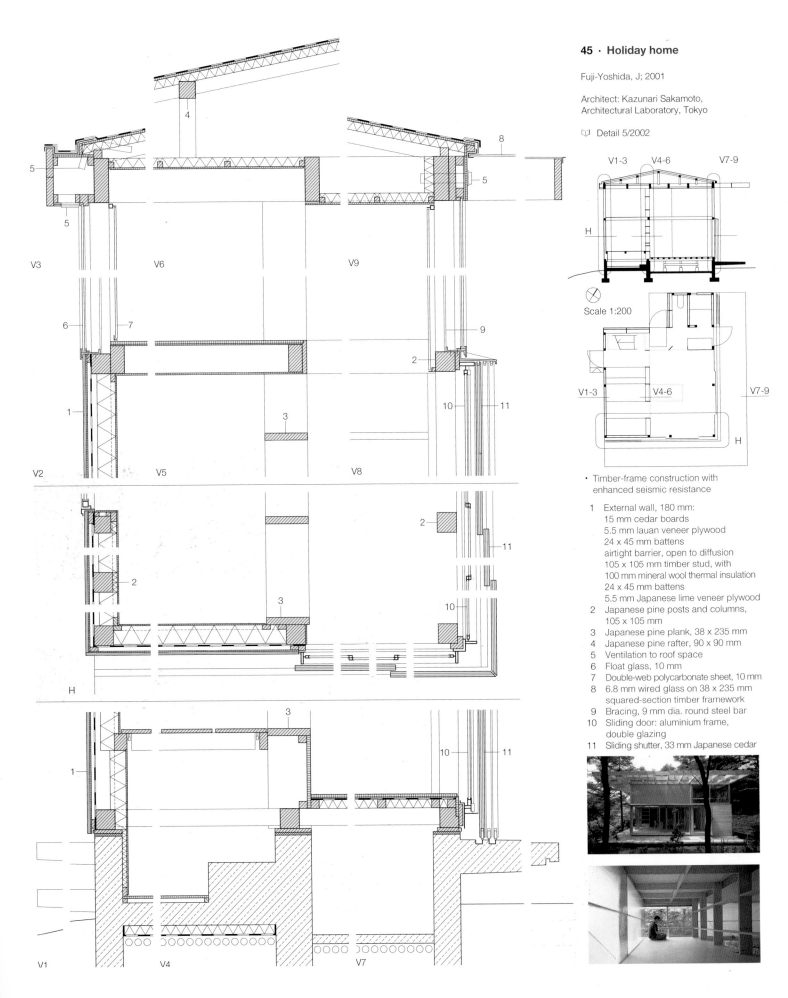

45 · Holiday home

Fuji-Yoshida, J; 2001

Architect: Kazunari Sakamoto,
Architectural Laboratory, Tokyo

Detail 5/2002

V1-3   V4-6   V7-9

H

Scale 1:200

V1-3   V4-6   V7-9

H

- Timber-frame construction with
  enhanced seismic resistance

1   External wall, 180 mm:
     15 mm cedar boards
     5.5 mm lauan veneer plywood
     24 x 45 mm battens
     airtight barrier, open to diffusion
     105 x 105 mm timber stud, with
     100 mm mineral wool thermal insulation
     24 x 45 mm battens
     5.5 mm Japanese lime veneer plywood
2   Japanese pine posts and columns,
     105 x 105 mm
3   Japanese pine plank, 38 x 235 mm
4   Japanese pine rafter, 90 x 90 mm
5   Ventilation to roof space
6   Float glass, 10 mm
7   Double-web polycarbonate sheet, 10 mm
8   6.8 mm wired glass on 38 x 235 mm
     squared-section timber framework
9   Bracing, 9 mm dia. round steel bar
10 Sliding door: aluminium frame,
     double glazing
11 Sliding shutter, 33 mm Japanese cedar

V3   V6   V9

V2   V5   V8

H

V1   V4   V7

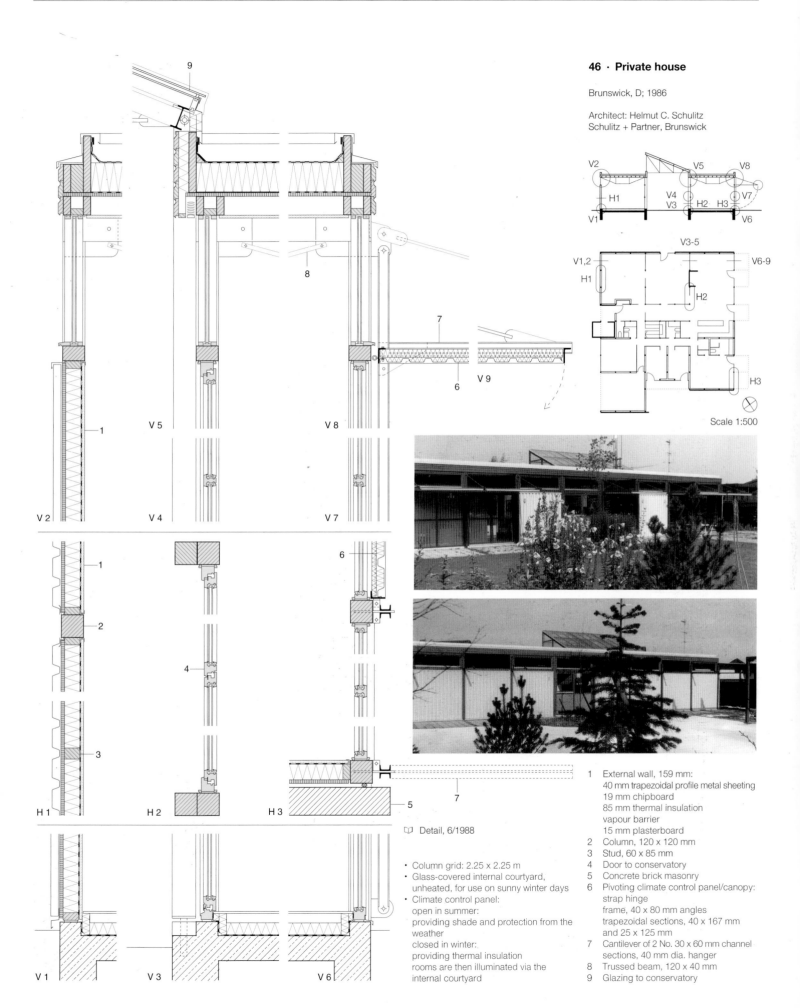

Brunswick, D; 1986

Architect: Helmut C. Schulitz
Schulitz + Partner, Brunswick

V3-5

V1,2   V6-9

H1

H2

H3

Scale 1:500

V 5   V 8

V 9

6

7

V 2   V 4   V 7

6

1

2

4

5

7

H 1   H 2   H 3

📖 Detail, 6/1988

· Column grid: 2.25 x 2.25 m
· Glass-covered internal courtyard, unheated, for use on sunny winter days
· Climate control panel:
  open in summer:
  providing shade and protection from the weather
  closed in winter:
  providing thermal insulation
  rooms are then illuminated via the internal courtyard

V 1   V 3   V 6

1   External wall, 159 mm:
    40 mm trapezoidal profile metal sheeting
    19 mm chipboard
    85 mm thermal insulation
    vapour barrier
    15 mm plasterboard
2   Column, 120 x 120 mm
3   Stud, 60 x 85 mm
4   Door to conservatory
5   Concrete brick masonry
6   Pivoting climate control panel/canopy:
    strap hinge
    frame, 40 x 80 mm angles
    trapezoidal sections, 40 x 167 mm
    and 25 x 125 mm
7   Cantilever of 2 No. 30 x 60 mm channel
    sections, 40 mm dia. hanger
8   Trussed beam, 120 x 40 mm
9   Glazing to conservatory

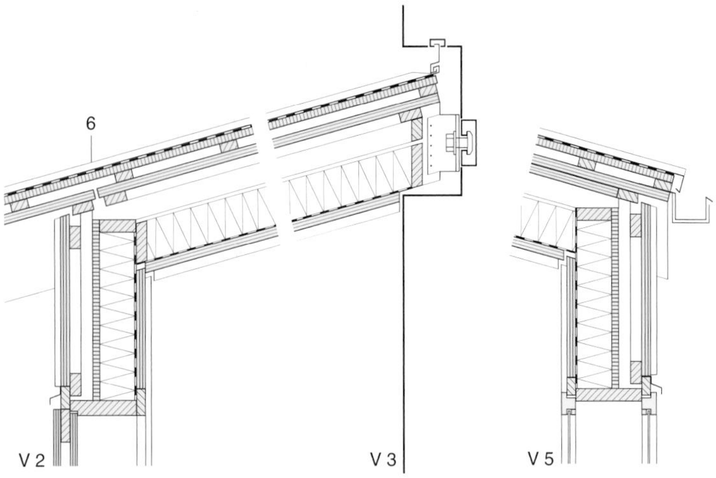

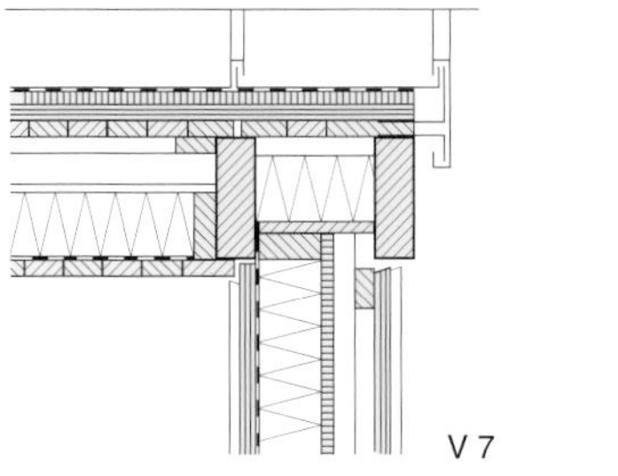

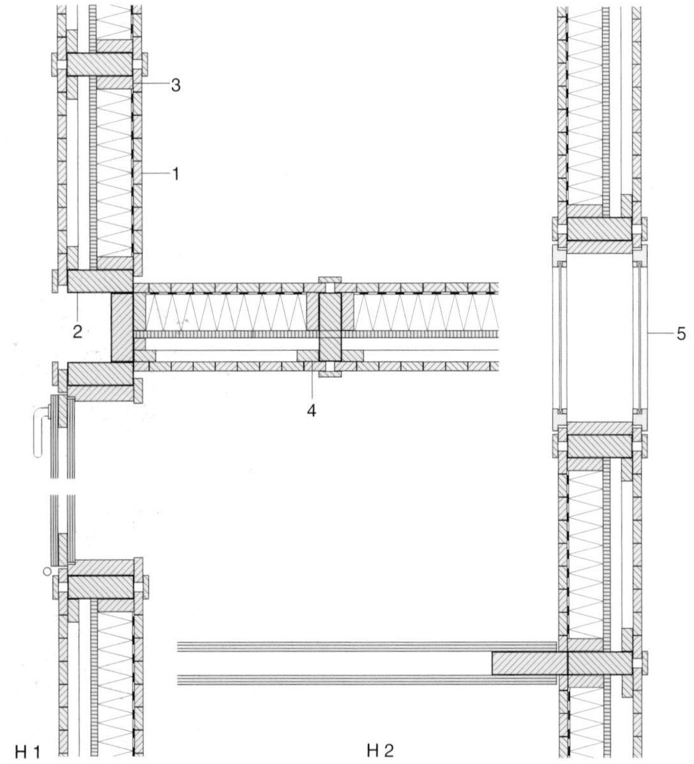

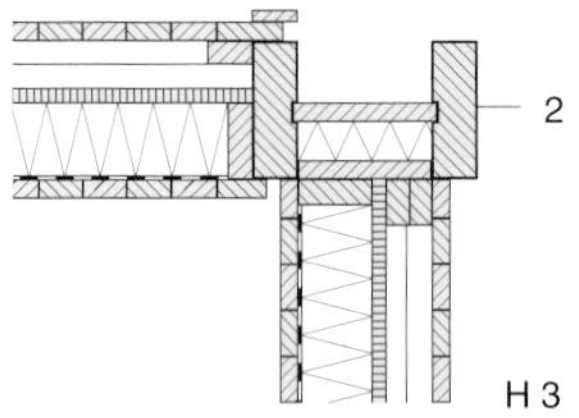

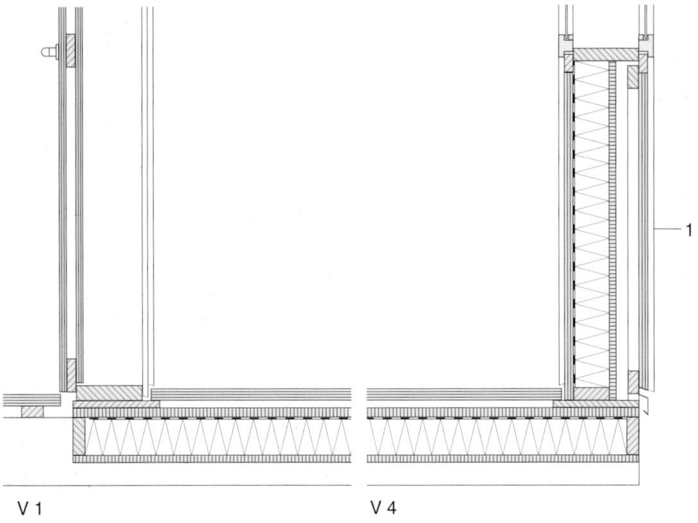

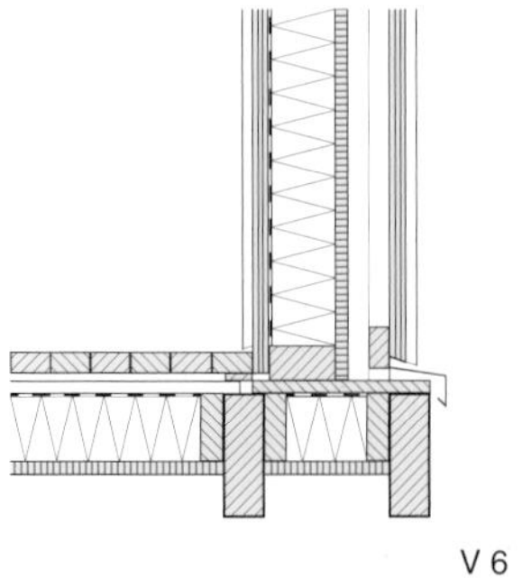

V 2

V 3

V 5

V 7

6

3

1

2

4

5

2

H 3

H 1

H 2

V 1

V 4

1

V 6

47 · Modular house

Bad Iburg, D; 1989

Architect: Eberhard Stauss, Munich
Assistant: U. Wangler

Detail 1/1989

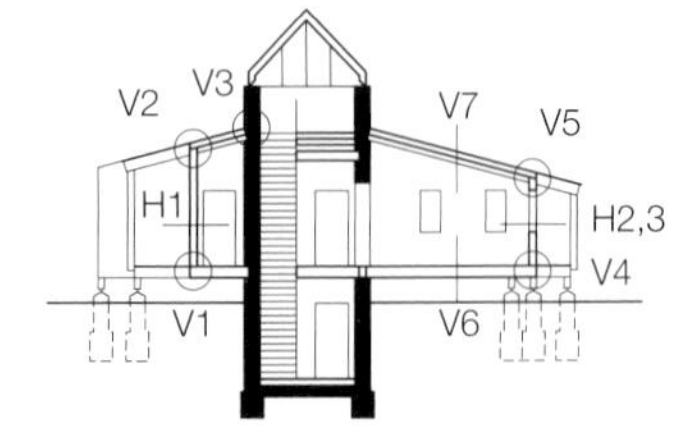

V2 V3 V7 V5

H1 H2,3

V4

V1 V6

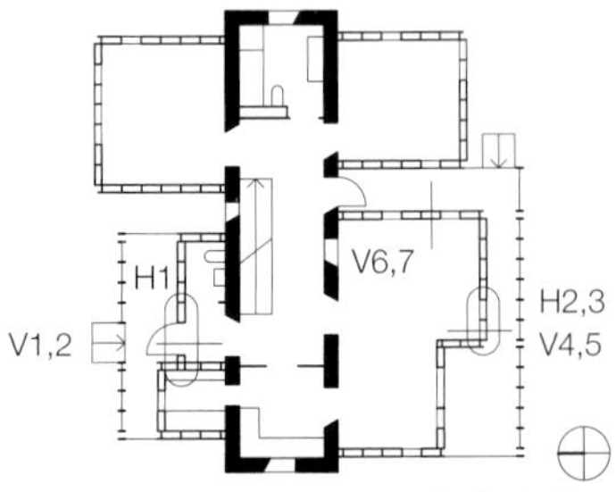

H1 V6,7

V1,2 H2,3

V4,5

Scale 1:400

· Timber-frame grid: 600 mm
· Combination of masonry/concrete and
  lightweight timber constructions
· Casement windows
· Facades, floors and roof of
  prefabricated elements

1 External wall/vertical air cavity, 197 mm:
   24 x 60 mm tongue and groove boarding
   30 mm air cavity
   19 mm particleboard
   100 mm thermal insulation
   vapour barrier
   24 x 60 mm tongue and groove boarding
2 Column, 180 x 60 mm
3 Stud, 100 x 30 mm
4 Batten, 60 x 30 mm
5 Casement window
6 Standing seam sheet metal roof covering

48 · House and studio

Tsukuba, J; 1994

Architects: Naito Architects & Ass., Tokyo
Hiroshi Naito, Tatsuo Yoshida

📖 Detail 4/1996

aa

Scale 1:400

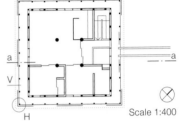

1   External wall, 140 mm:
    12 mm cedar boards with cover strips
    airtight barrier
    105 mm thermal insulation
    6 mm plywood
2   Fixed light
3   Glazed sliding element to inner wall
4   Sliding element at front of balcony
5   Balustrade of 3 mm dia. stainless steel
    cables
6   Japanese pine column, 105 x 105 mm

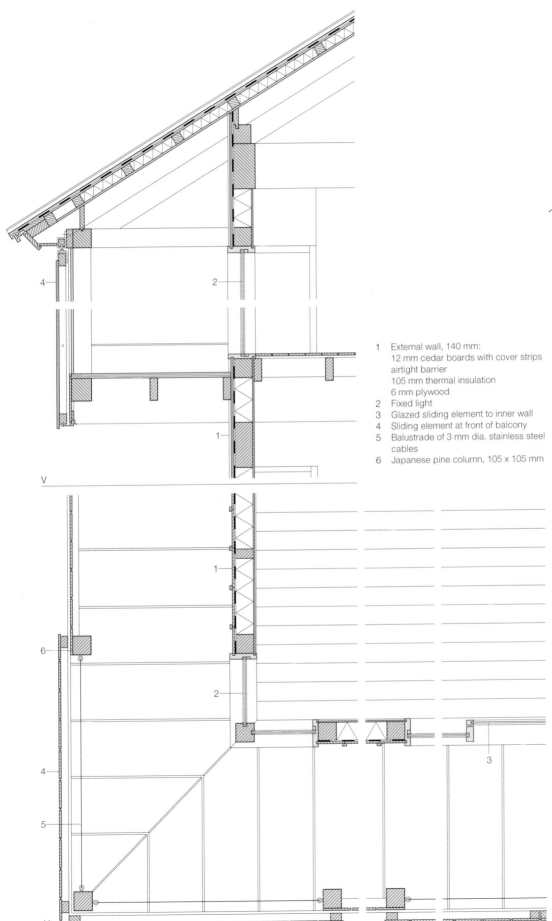

341

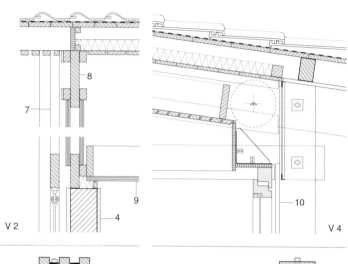

V 2

7

8

9

4

V 4

10

H 1

3

4

4

5

H 2

4

3

4

10

2

V 1

4

V 3

6

Gmund am Tegernsee, D; 1960

Architect:
Hans Busso von Busse, Munich
Assistant: B. von Busse

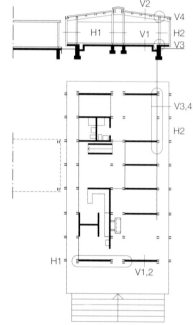

V2
V4
H2
H1
V1
V3

V3,4

H2

H1

V1,2

Scale 1:400

· Grid: 1.25 m
· Column spacing: 2.50 m in longitudinal direction, 3.75 m in transverse direction
· Columns of oak sections in 2 or 3 parts depending on load
· Window frames of Styrian red larch

1 3-part column at gable,
  3 No. 60 x 200 mm oak sections +
  2 No. 140 mm steel channels
2 2-part column in bay, 60 x 200 mm
3 Wind girders in end bays
4 Masonry with rendering outside,
  plaster inside
5 Entrance door
6 Heating duct with convectors
7 Strut, 50 x 180 mm
8 Glued beam, 50 x 260 mm
9 Suspended ceiling
10 Track for roller shutter

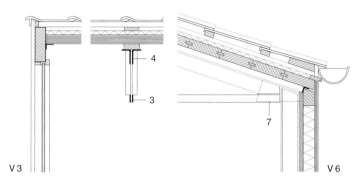

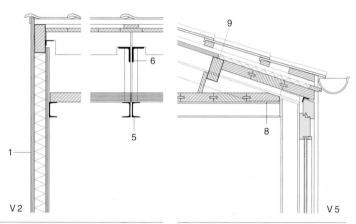

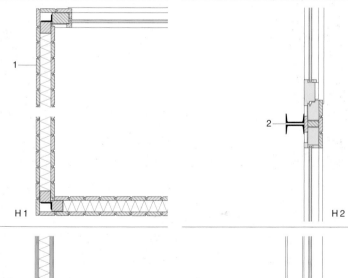

50 · Private house

Glonn-Haslach, D; 1963

Architects:
Werner and Grete Wirsing, Munich

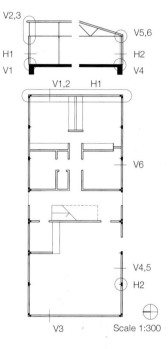

- Loadbearing structure of rolled steel sections
- Grid for columns and trusses: 2.50 m
- Facade grid: 1.25 m
- Prefabricated wall, window and glazed door panels of larch

1 External wall, 100 mm:
   120 x 84 mm outer boards
   60 mm thermal insulation
   20 x 84 mm tongue and groove inner boards
2 Column, 2 No. 100 mm channels
3 Steel flat bottom chord, 2 No. 5 x 40 mm
4 Top chord, 2 No. 50 x 80 x 5 mm angles
5 Bottom chord, 2 No. 80 mm channels
6 Top chord, 2 No. 80 x 65 x 8 mm angles
7 Gusset plate
8 50 mm boarding
9 Beam, 60 x 120 mm

Scale 1:300

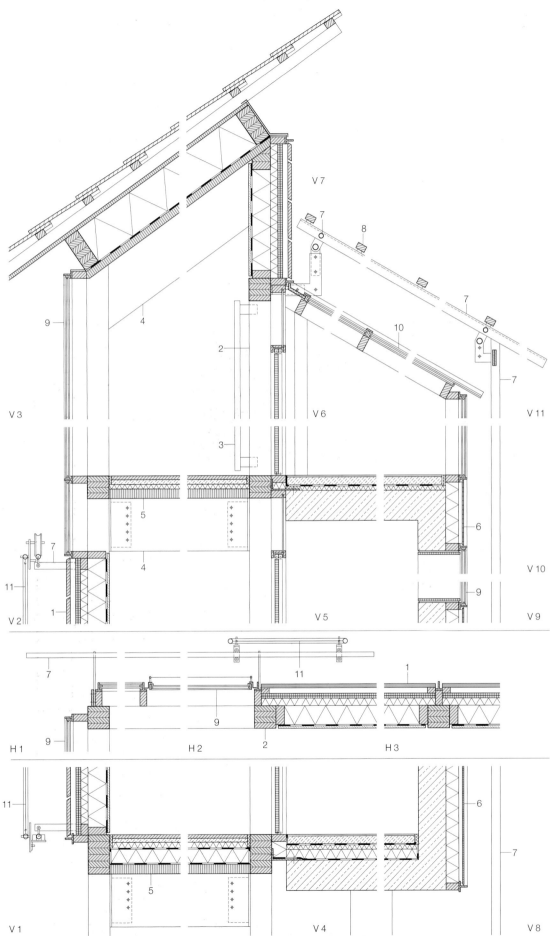

V 7

V 3

V 6

V 11

V 10

V 9

V 5

V 2

9

4

2

3

5

4

1

7

11

7

8

7

10

7

6

9

H 1

H 2

H 3

7

9

9

11

1

9

2

V 1

V 4

V 8

11

5

6

7

51 · Private house

Allensbach, D; 1996

Architects:
Schaudt Architects, Constance
Helmut Hagmüller

Detail 1/2000

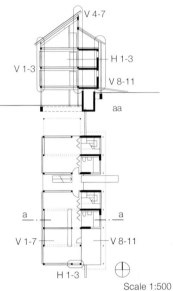

V 4-7

V 1-3

H 1-3

V 8-11

aa

a

a

V 1-7

V 8-11

H 1-3

Scale 1:500

· Timber-frame construction
· Column grid: 2.4 x 5.0 m

1   External wall/ventilated cavity, 240 mm:
    20 mm untreated red cedar boarding
    40 x 60 mm battens
    2 No. 13 mm porous wood fibreboard
    40 mm rigid foam thermal insulation
    100 mm mineral wool thermal insulation
    0.4 mm polyethylene vapour barrier
    12.5 mm plasterboard
2   Continuous column, F30 fire resistance
3   Structural strengthening to column
    (galvanised steel circular hollow
    section, 31.8 dia. x 2.6 mm)
4   Glulam floor and roof beams,
    120 x 280 mm
5   Floor plate for stability: 50 mm
    plywood, or wind girder of round steel
    bars, 106 mm dia.
6   Wall construction, ancillary rooms:
    8 mm particleboard
    20 mm air cavity
    70 mm mineral wool thermal insulation
    50 mm reinforced concrete wal
7   Galvanised steel frame
8   Larch batten, 50 x 28 mm
9   Heat-absorbing glass
10 Heat-absorbing laminated safety glass
11 Sliding fabric sunshade

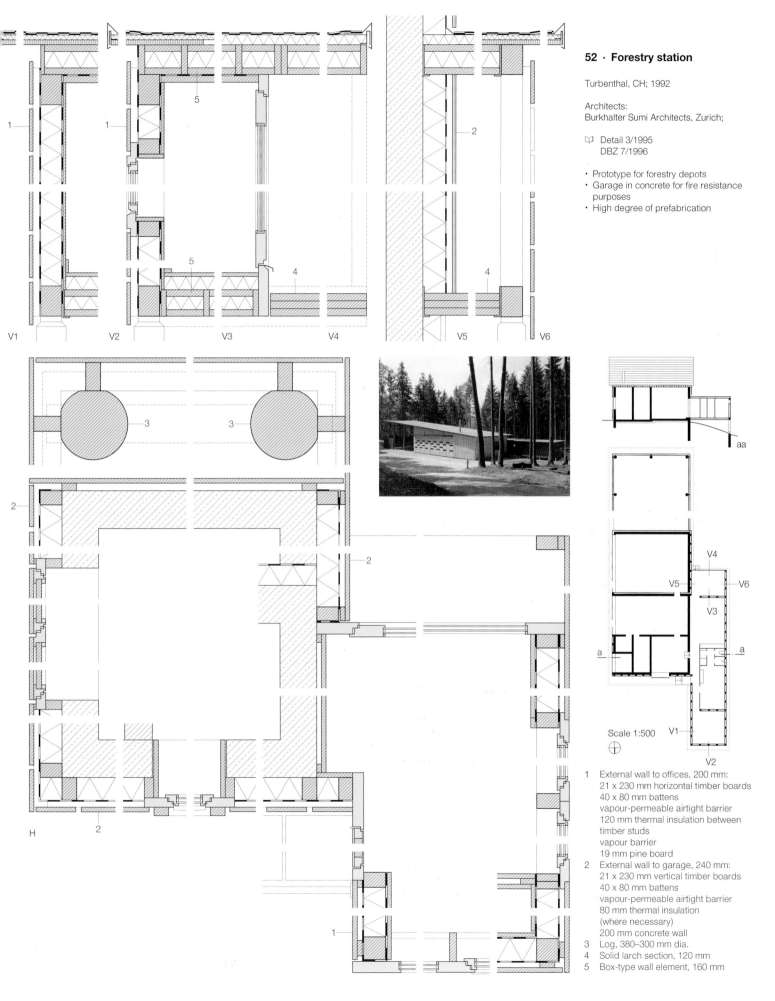

V1 · V2 · V3 · V4 · V5 · V6

H

52 · Forestry station

Turbenthal, CH; 1992

Architects:
Burkhalter Sumi Architects, Zurich;

Detail 3/1995
DBZ 7/1996

· Prototype for forestry depots
· Garage in concrete for fire resistance
 purposes
· High degree of prefabrication

Scale 1:500

1 External wall to offices, 200 mm:
 21 x 230 mm horizontal timber boards
 40 x 80 mm battens
 vapour-permeable airtight barrier
 120 mm thermal insulation between
 timber studs
 vapour barrier
 19 mm pine board
2 External wall to garage, 240 mm:
 21 x 230 mm vertical timber boards
 40 x 80 mm battens
 vapour-permeable airtight barrier
 80 mm thermal insulation
 (where necessary)
 200 mm concrete wall
3 Log, 380–300 mm dia.
4 Solid larch section, 120 mm
5 Box-type wall element, 160 mm

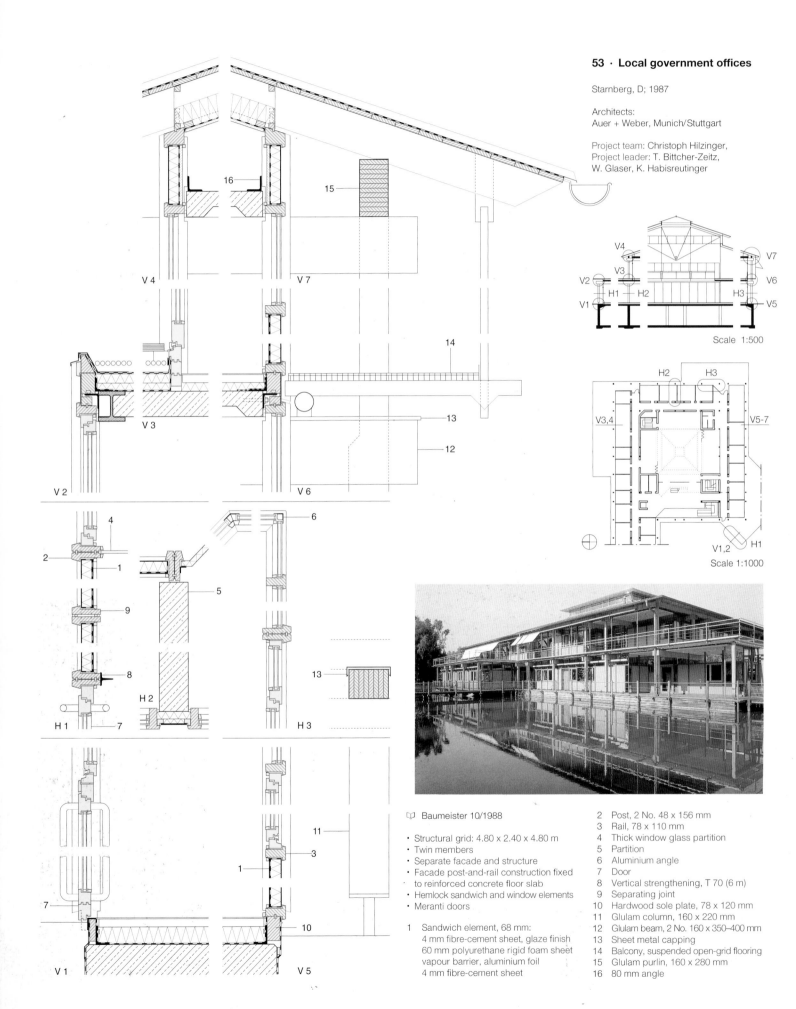

53 · Local government offices

Starnberg, D; 1987

Architects:
Auer + Weber, Munich/Stuttgart

Project team: Christoph Hilzinger,
Project leader: T. Bittcher-Zeitz,
W. Glaser, K. Habisreutinger

Scale 1:500

Scale 1:1000

Baumeister 10/1988

· Structural grid: 4.80 x 2.40 x 4.80 m
· Twin members
· Separate facade and structure
· Facade post-and-rail construction fixed
  to reinforced concrete floor slab
· Hemlock sandwich and window elements
· Meranti doors

1   Sandwich element, 68 mm:
    4 mm fibre-cement sheet, glaze finish
    60 mm polyurethane rigid foam sheet
    vapour barrier, aluminium foil
    4 mm fibre-cement sheet

2   Post, 2 No. 48 x 156 mm
3   Rail, 78 x 110 mm
4   Thick window glass partition
5   Partition
6   Aluminium angle
7   Door
8   Vertical strengthening, T 70 (6 m)
9   Separating joint
10 Hardwood sole plate, 78 x 120 mm
11 Glulam column, 160 x 220 mm
12 Glulam beam, 2 No. 160 x 350–400 mm
13 Sheet metal capping
14 Balcony, suspended open-grid flooring
15 Glulam purlin, 160 x 280 mm
16 80 mm angle

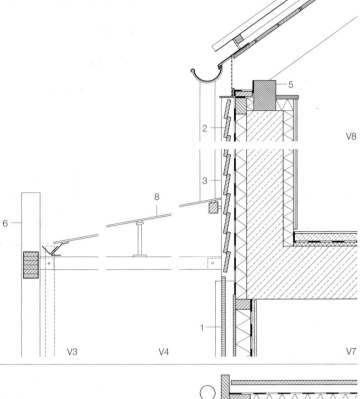

54 · Home for the elderly

Neuenbürg, D; 1996

Architects:
Mahler Günster Fuchs, Stuttgart

Detail 5/1996
Bauwelt 5/1997

1 External wall, 182 mm timber facade:
2 No. 21 mm natural Douglas fir
weatherboarding, planed
22 mm framing/ventilated cavity
Percalor sheet
13 mm chipboard with waterproof glue
80 mm mineral fibre between timber
vapour barrier
2 No. 12.5 mm plasterboard
2 External wall, timber boarding on
concrete wall:
No. 21 mm natural Douglas fir,
weatherboarding, planed
19 mm larch multi-ply board
22 mm framing/ventilated cavity
vapour barrier
60 mm mineral fibre between timber
framing
concrete wall
mineral fibreboard
12.5 mm plasterboard
3 Weatherboarding broken up by
vertical strips
4 Wooden sliding shutters, 3-ply core
plywood, Douglas fir
5 Purlin, 120 x 180 mm
6 Glulam column, 100 x 100 mm
7 Floorboards, 105 x 40 mm
8 Roof over walkway
9 Door to storage room

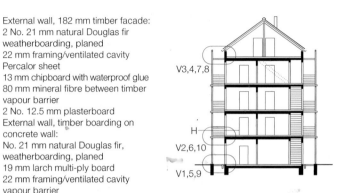

V3,4,7,8
V2,6,10
V1,5,9

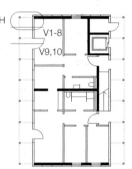

V1-8
V9,10

Scale 1:400

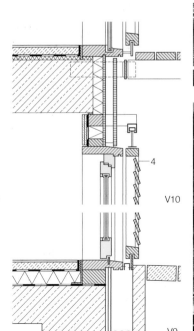

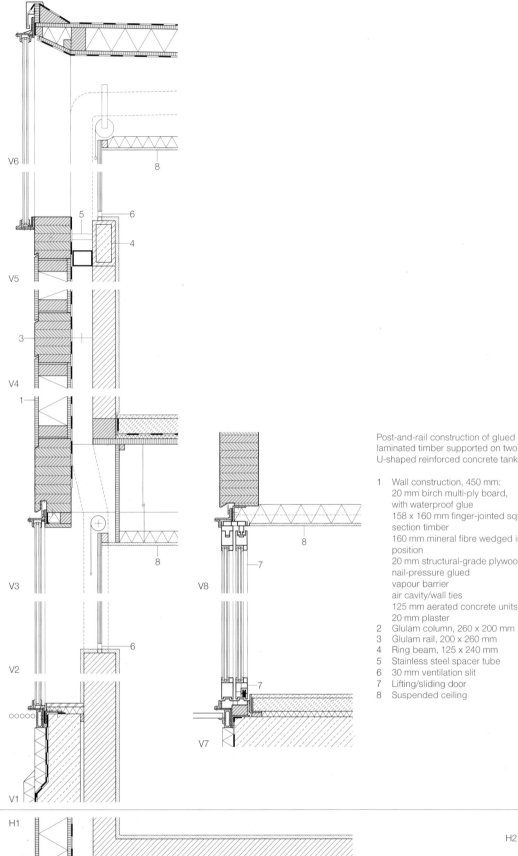

V6

V5

V4

V3

V2

V1

V8

V7

H1

H2

55 · Gallery

Munich, D; 1992

Architects:
Jaques Herzog, Pierre de Meuron, Basel
Josef Peter Meier-Scupin, Munich

Bauwelt 5/1993
El Croquis 60/1993
Werk, Bauen + Wohnen 1–2/1994

V1-6 H2
H1

V1-6
H1 H2
V7-8

Scale 1:800

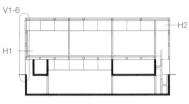

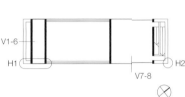

Post-and-rail construction of glued laminated timber supported on two U-shaped reinforced concrete tanks

1 Wall construction, 450 mm:
   20 mm birch multi-ply board, with waterproof glue
   158 x 160 mm finger-jointed squared section timber
   160 mm mineral fibre wedged in position
   20 mm structural-grade plywood, nail-pressure glued
   vapour barrier
   air cavity/wall ties
   125 mm aerated concrete units
   20 mm plaster
2 Glulam column, 260 x 200 mm
3 Glulam rail, 200 x 260 mm
4 Ring beam, 125 x 240 mm
5 Stainless steel spacer tube
6 30 mm ventilation slit
7 Lifting/sliding door
8 Suspended ceiling

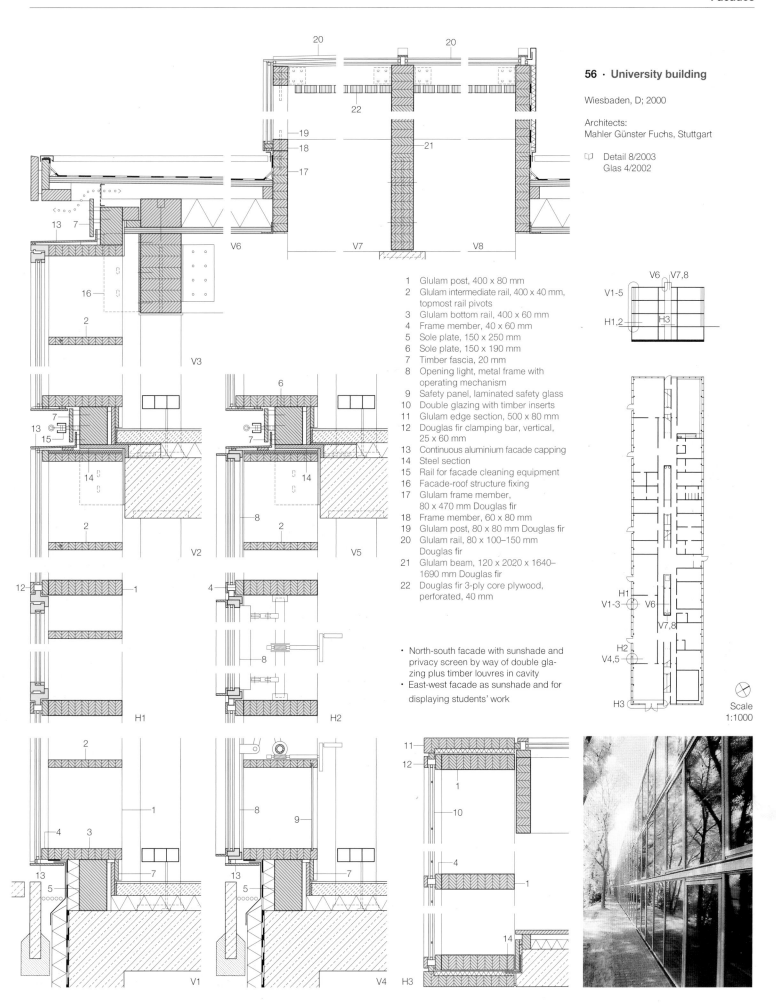

56 · University building

Wiesbaden, D; 2000

Architects:
Mahler Günster Fuchs, Stuttgart

Detail 8/2003
Glas 4/2002

1 Glulam post, 400 x 80 mm
2 Glulam intermediate rail, 400 x 40 mm, topmost rail pivots
3 Glulam bottom rail, 400 x 60 mm
4 Frame member, 40 x 60 mm
5 Sole plate, 150 x 250 mm
6 Sole plate, 150 x 190 mm
7 Timber fascia, 20 mm
8 Opening light, metal frame with operating mechanism
9 Safety panel, laminated safety glass
10 Double glazing with timber inserts
11 Glulam edge section, 500 x 80 mm
12 Douglas fir clamping bar, vertical, 25 x 60 mm
13 Continuous aluminium facade capping
14 Steel section
15 Rail for facade cleaning equipment
16 Facade-roof structure fixing
17 Glulam frame member, 80 x 470 mm Douglas fir
18 Frame member, 60 x 80 mm
19 Glulam post, 80 x 80 mm Douglas fir
20 Glulam rail, 80 x 100–150 mm Douglas fir
21 Glulam beam, 120 x 2020 x 1640–1690 mm Douglas fir
22 Douglas fir 3-ply core plywood, perforated, 40 mm

• North-south facade with sunshade and privacy screen by way of double glazing plus timber louvres in cavity
• East-west facade as sunshade and for displaying students' work

Scale
1:1000

349

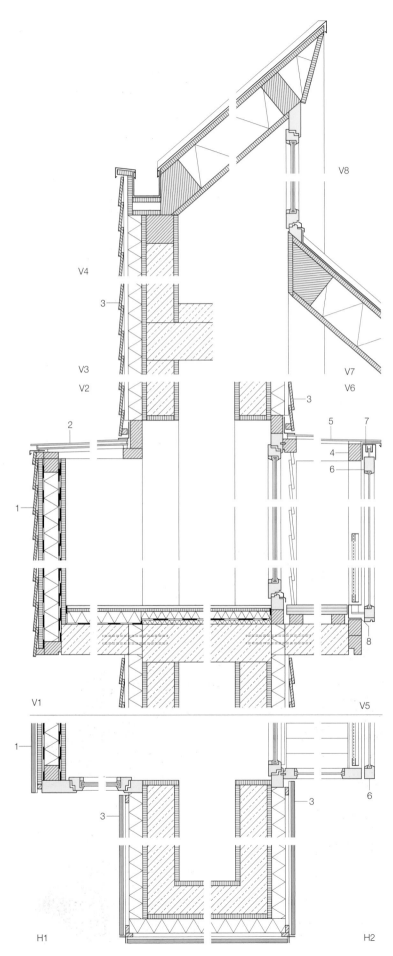

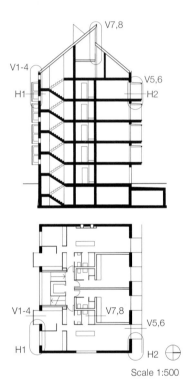

Innsbruck, A; 1996

Architects:
A. Kathan, M. Schranz, E. Strolz,
Innsbruck
Assistants: H. Hofer, C. Hrdlovics,
F. Reiter, S. Schwarzmann

Detail 7/1997

Scale 1:500

• Wall boarding – including battens,
  insulation and windows – serves as
  permanent formwork for concrete with
  recycled aggregate
• High degree of prefabrication
• Construction time: 11 months

1 External wall, bay:
   15 x 150 mm oak weatherboarding
   25 mm chipboard with edging
   5.5 mm sound insulation foil
   70 mm rockwool between timber
   frame members
   5.5 mm sound insulation foil
   vapour barrier
   chipboard, with skim plaster coat
   ready for painting
2 Double glazing, 10 + 6 mm toughened
   safety glass, glued to wooden frame
3 External wall:
   15 x 150 mm oak weatherboarding,
   16.7 mm headlap
   20 x 40 mm vertical battens
   horizontal counter battens with 80 mm
   rockwool between
   25 mm chipboard
   150 mm reinforced concrete
   25 mm chipboard, with skim plaster
   coat ready for painting
4 Timber frame construction, 68 x 90 mm
5 Single glazing, 6 + 6 mm laminated
   safety glass glued to wooden frame
6 Single-glazed sliding window:
   61 x 90 mm wooden frame
   6 mm toughened safety glass
7 Galvanised suspension track
8 Guide track

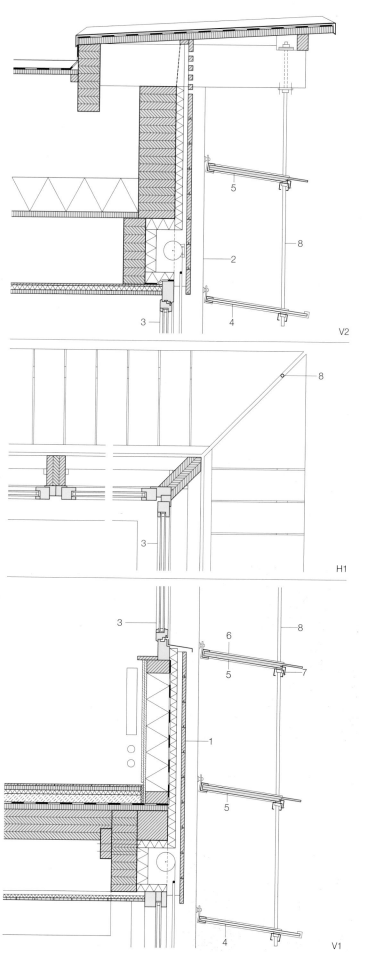

5

8

2

3 · · · · · · 4

V2

8

3

H1

3

6

5

7

5

1

5

4

V1

Lyss, CH; 1997

Architects: I+B, Itten und Brechbühl, Bern

Detail 7/1997; DBZ 10/1997

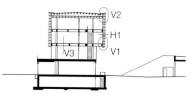

V2
H1
V3
V1

- Silver fir debarked columns, 550–350 mm dia.
- The larch louvres act as a sunshade and protect the facade from the weather; they are conceived as easily replaceable wear parts.

1 External wall, 210 mm:
   24 mm larch boarding
   24 mm ventilated cavity
   40 mm wood fibre insulating board airtight barrier
   40 mm wood fibre insulating board
   120 mm thermal insulation
   2 No. 12.5 mm plasterboard
2 Glulam post, 100 x 160 mm larch
3 Double glazing in wooden frame
4 Toughened safety glass, 10 mm, acid-embossed finish
5 24 mm larch board
6 Steel flat
7 Steel section
8 Round steel bar, 16 mm dia.
9 Floor element:
   3-ply core plywood on 150 mm dia. logs
10 Services

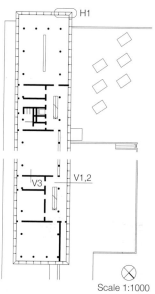

H1

V3

V1,2

Scale 1:1000

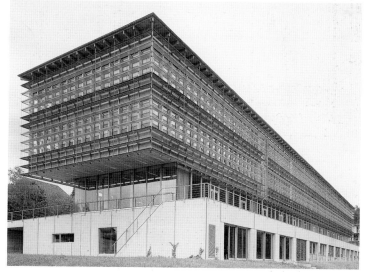

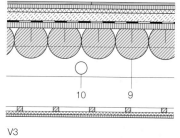

10   9

V3

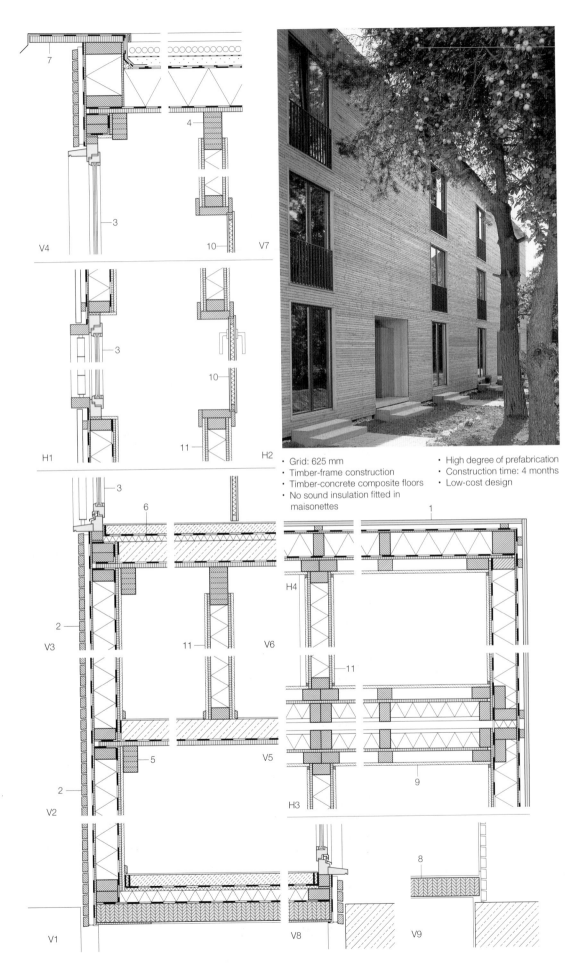

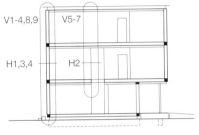

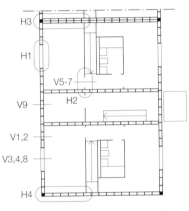

59 · Residential complex

Regensburg, D; 1996

Architects: Dietrich Fink,
Thomas Jocher, Munich

Detail 1/1997

Scale 1:300

- Grid: 625 mm
- Timber-frame construction
- Timber-concrete composite floors
- No sound insulation fitted in maisonettes

- High degree of prefabrication
- Construction time: 4 months
- Low-cost design

1 Loadbearing external wall:
  48 x 24 mm Larch external boarding on battens
  airtight barrier
  oriented strand board
  60 x 120 mm timber studs with mineral fibre thermal insulation between
  polyethylene vapour barrier
  oriented strand board
  80 x 60 mm strengthening to studs
  15 mm plasterboard
2 Non-loadbearing external wall
3 Glazed door with double glazing
4 Glulam floor joist, 80 x 160 mm
5 Glulam floor joist, 80 x 140 mm
6 Timber-concrete composite floor:
  120 mm in situ reinforced concrete
  0.2 mm polyethylene separating layer
  25 mm maritime pine plywood
  80 x 140 mm glulam floor joist
7 3-ply core plywood with metal facing
8 100 mm glulam floor on glulam beam
9 Party wall, F30-B fire resistance:
  15 mm plasterboard
  60 x 80 mm strengthening to studs
  13 mm chipboard
  60 x 100 mm timber studs
  80 mm mineral wool thermal insulation
  40 mm air cavity
10 Wooden internal door
11 Plasterboard partition

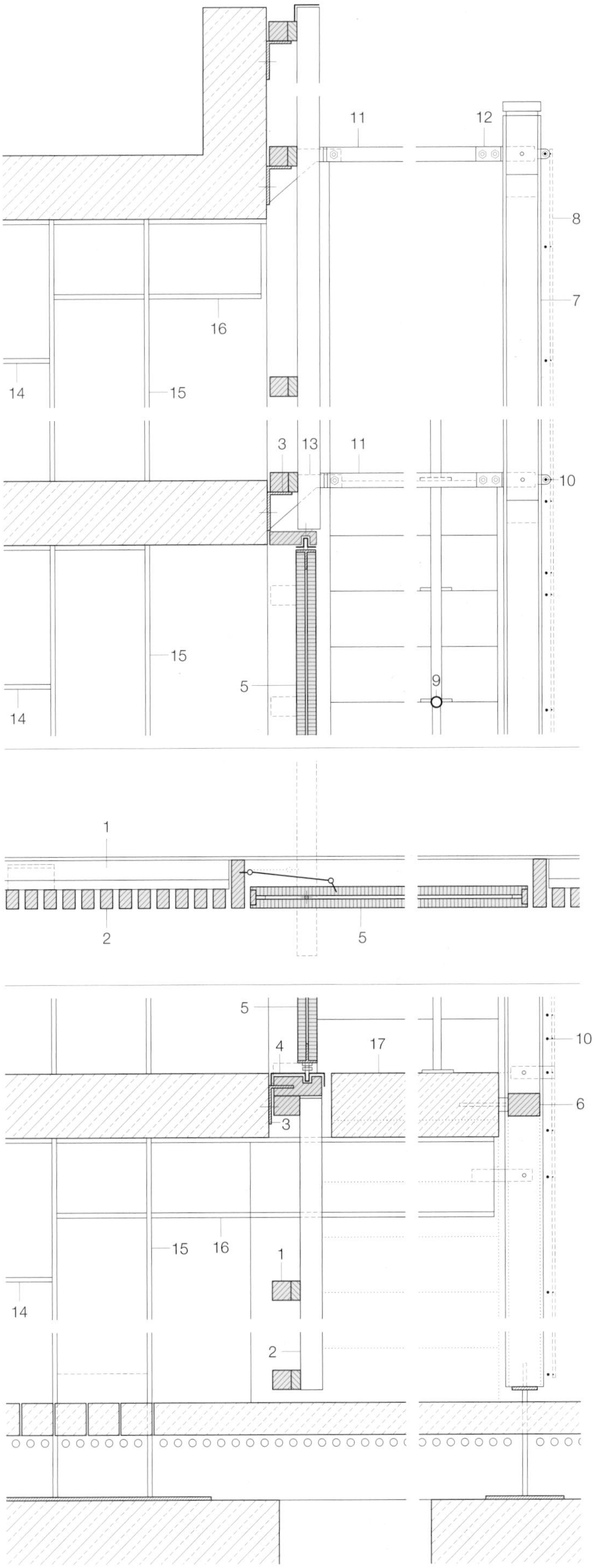

Heilbronn, D; 1998

Architects: Mahler, Günster, Fuchs; Stuttgart

📖 Detail 2/2000

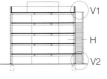

Scale 1:1000

The louvre facade aids the natural lighting and ventilation of this structure.

1 Battens, Douglas fir
   60 x 60 mm + 30 x 60 mm
2 Facade framing, 40 x 60 mm,
   untreated Douglas fir
3 Fixing for timber facade
   steel angle, 120 x 80 x 12 mm
4 Sole plate, sheet metal water bar
5 Pivoting door, 2 x 28 mm leaf
   3-ply core plywood, veneered
6 Squared section to close gap,
   70 x 100 mm Douglas fir,
   fixed with wooden dowels,
   40 mm dia. steel
7 Glulam facade column
   120 mm dia. Douglas fir
8 Hot-dip galvanised wire mesh
9 Handrail, galvanised steel circular
10 Stainless steel tension cable
11 Strut, galvanised steel circular
   hollow section
12 Steel flat in slit tube
13 Steel flat bracket
14 Steel flat bracket
15 Steel column
16 Steel bracket
17 Precast concrete stair

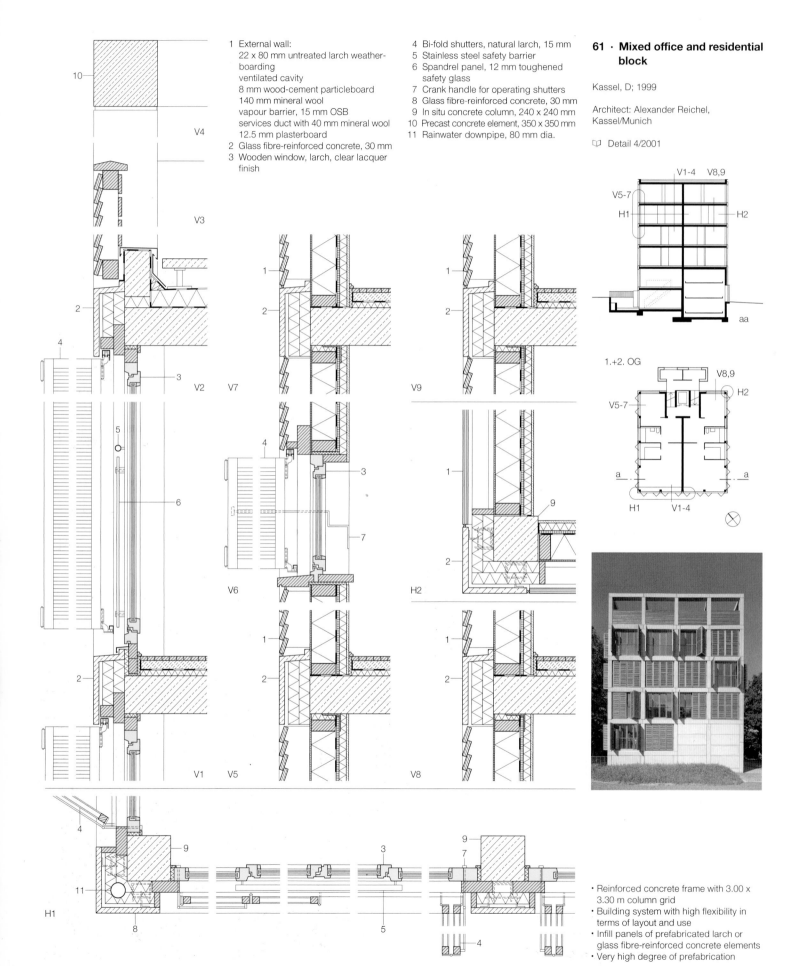

1 External wall:
22 x 80 mm untreated larch weather-boarding
ventilated cavity
8 mm wood-cement particleboard
140 mm mineral wool
vapour barrier, 15 mm OSB
services duct with 40 mm mineral wool
12.5 mm plasterboard
2 Glass fibre-reinforced concrete, 30 mm
3 Wooden window, larch, clear lacquer finish

4 Bi-fold shutters, natural larch, 15 mm
5 Stainless steel safety barrier
6 Spandrel panel, 12 mm toughened safety glass
7 Crank handle for operating shutters
8 Glass fibre-reinforced concrete, 30 mm
9 In situ concrete column, 240 x 240 mm
10 Precast concrete element, 350 x 350 mm
11 Rainwater downpipe, 80 mm dia.

61 · Mixed office and residential block

Kassel, D; 1999

Architect: Alexander Reichel, Kassel/Munich

Detail 4/2001

V1-4 V8,9
V5-7
H1   H2
aa

1.+2. OG
V8,9
V5-7   H2
a   a
H1 V1-4

· Reinforced concrete frame with 3.00 x 3.30 m column grid
· Building system with high flexibility in terms of layout and use
· Infill panels of prefabricated larch or glass fibre-reinforced concrete elements
· Very high degree of prefabrication

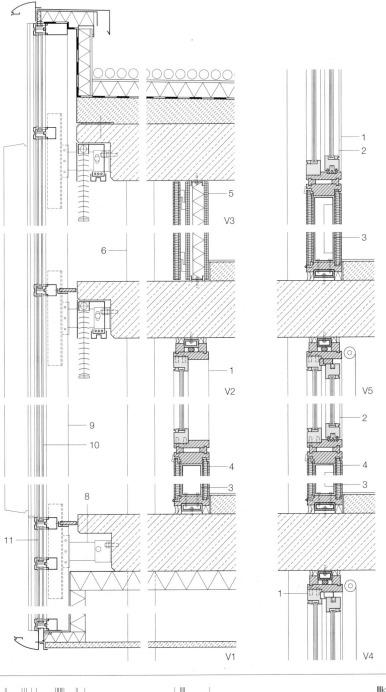

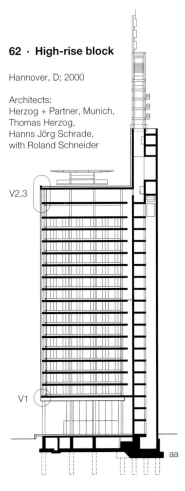

62 · High-rise block

Hannover, D; 2000

Architects:
Herzog + Partner, Munich,
Thomas Herzog,
Hanns Jörg Schrade,
with Roland Schneider

▢ Detail 3/2000

· Double-leaf facade, horizontally continuous
· Natural ventilation by way of
  storey-height sliding windows
  in inner leaf of timber facade

1 Timber facade element,
   hemlock, high-build coating
2 Sliding window
3 Mechanical ventilation, duct
   beneath window with air
   outlet
4 Hemlock veneer on ply-
   wood, 35 mm
5 Plant floor only: veneer plywood cladding to plasterboard wall
6 Reinforced concrete column,
   500 mm dia.
7 Hot-dip galvanised steel
   angle
8 Cast aluminium facade
   fixing bracket
9 Facade post with fixing slot
10 Glazing to steel facade,
   8/16/8 mm, extra-clear glass
11 Glazing to steel facade,
   8/16/8 mm, outer pane with
   white printing
12 Aluminium ventilation element
13 Louvres as weather protection
14 Ventilation duct with glass
   louvres

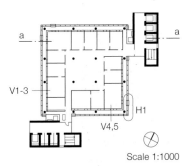

Scale 1:1000

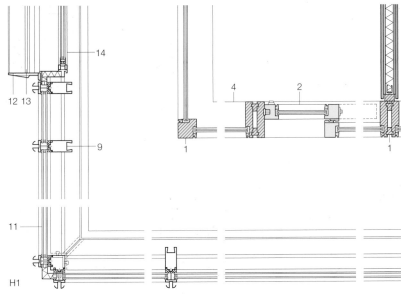

355

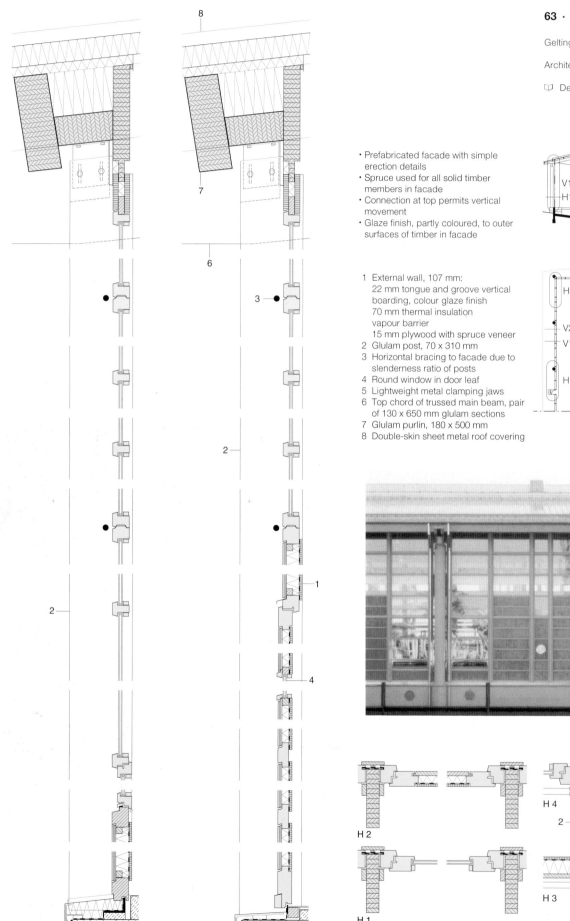

Gelting, D; 1986

Architects: Beck-Enz-Yelin, Munich

📖 Deutsche Bauzeitung 7/1989

- Prefabricated facade with simple erection details
- Spruce used for all solid timber members in facade
- Connection at top permits vertical movement
- Glaze finish, partly coloured, to outer surfaces of timber in facade

1 External wall, 107 mm:
  22 mm tongue and groove vertical boarding, colour glaze finish
  70 mm thermal insulation
  vapour barrier
  15 mm plywood with spruce veneer
2 Glulam post, 70 x 310 mm
3 Horizontal bracing to facade due to slenderness ratio of posts
4 Round window in door leaf
5 Lightweight metal clamping jaws
6 Top chord of trussed main beam, pair of 130 x 650 mm glulam sections
7 Glulam purlin, 180 x 500 mm
8 Double-skin sheet metal roof covering

Scale 1:800

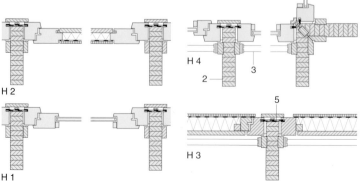

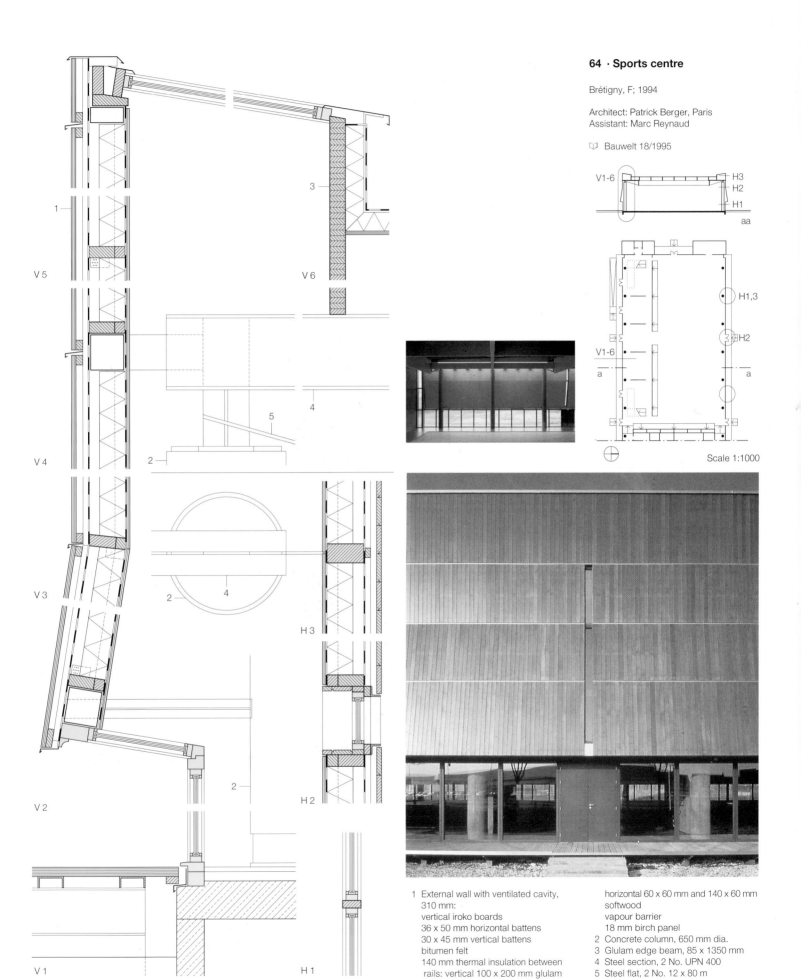

64 · Sports centre

Brétigny, F; 1994

Architect: Patrick Berger, Paris
Assistant: Marc Reynaud

Bauwelt 18/1995

Scale 1:1000

1 External wall with ventilated cavity,
  310 mm:
  vertical iroko boards
  36 x 50 mm horizontal battens
  30 x 45 mm vertical battens
  bitumen felt
  140 mm thermal insulation between
  rails: vertical 100 x 200 mm glulam

horizontal 60 x 60 mm and 140 x 60 mm
softwood
vapour barrier
18 mm birch panel
2 Concrete column, 650 mm dia.
3 Glulam edge beam, 85 x 1350 mm
4 Steel section, 2 No. UPN 400
5 Steel flat, 2 No. 12 x 80 m

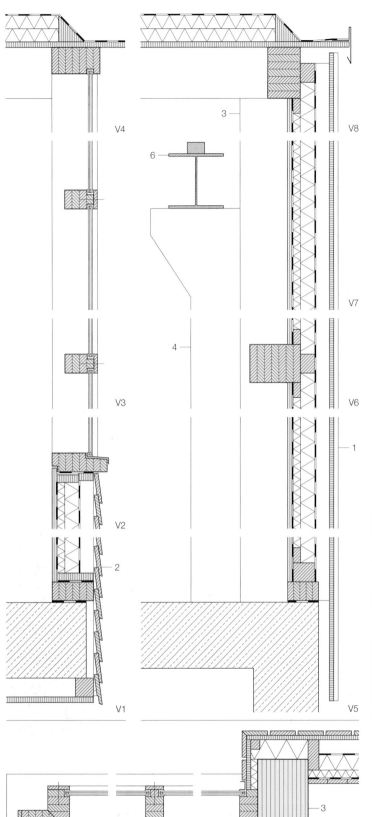

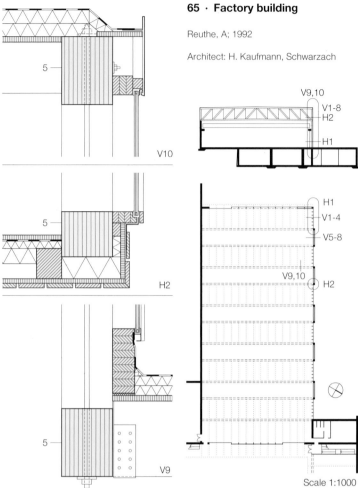

Scale 1:1000

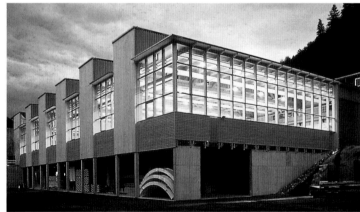

Baumeister, 10/1995
A + D, 4/1995

· Facade grid: 6 m
· Floor area (30 x 60 m) without inter-
  vening columns, with 2 overhead cranes
  each of 6.3 t carrying capacity
· Columns of Parallam Canadian parallel
  strand lumber
· Raised roof sections comprising
  2 Parallam lattice beams enable slim
  overall design

1 External wall:
   24 mm vertical boards
   25 mm 3-ply core plywood
   80 mm ventilated cavity
   airtight barrier
   insulation, 40 + 80 mm
   vapour barrier
   non-woven fabric, black
   30 mm vertical boards
2 Weatherboarding
3 Parallam column, 280 x 400 mm
4 Crane rail support column with
   corbel, 280 x 280 mm Parallam
5 Parallam lattice beam
6 Crane rail support beam
7 Steel support for crane rail

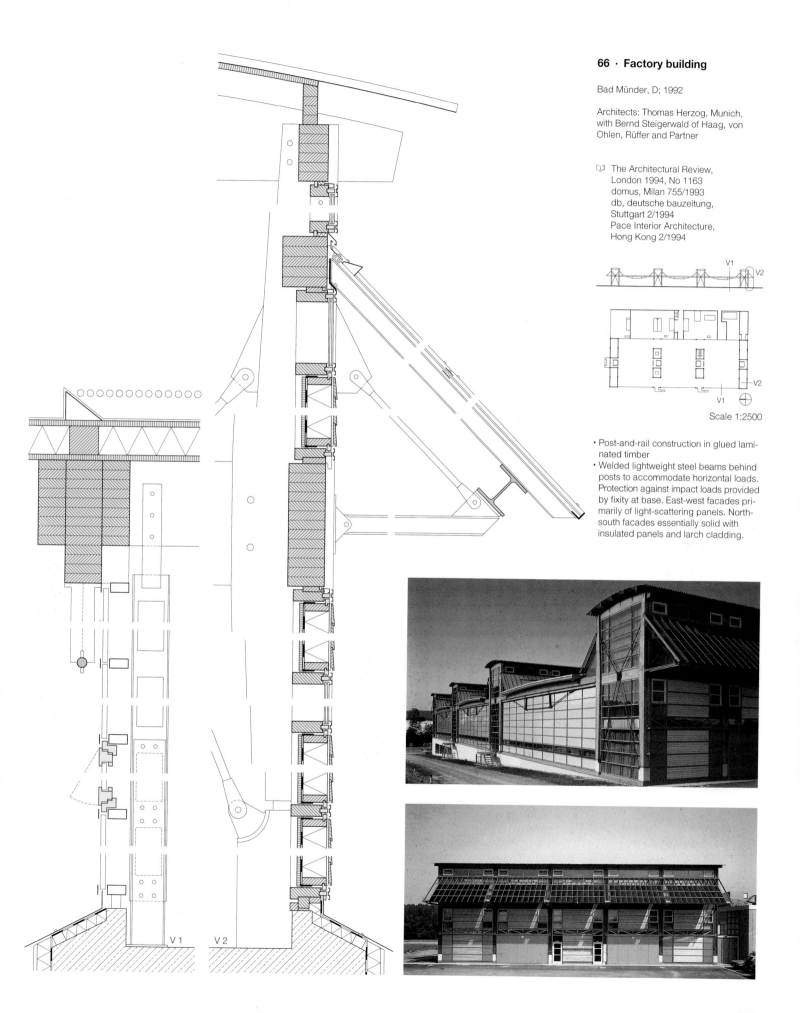

66 · Factory building

Bad Münder, D; 1992

Architects: Thomas Herzog, Munich, with Bernd Steigerwald of Haag, von Ohlen, Rüffer and Partner

The Architectural Review, London 1994, No 1163
domus, Milan 755/1993
db, deutsche bauzeitung, Stuttgart 2/1994
Pace Interior Architecture, Hong Kong 2/1994

Scale 1:2500

- Post-and-rail construction in glued laminated timber
- Welded lightweight steel beams behind posts to accommodate horizontal loads. Protection against impact loads provided by fixity at base. East-west facades primarily of light-scattering panels. North-south facades essentially solid with insulated panels and larch cladding.

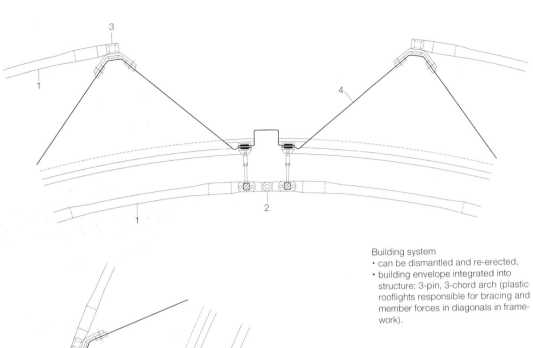

67 · Exhibition pavilion

Various locations, 1982–1984

Architect: Renzo Piano
Building Workshop, Genoa

Progressive Architecture 2/1988;
A + U, 3/1989

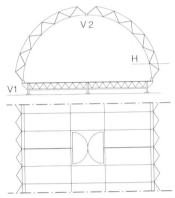

Scale 1:300

Building system
· can be dismantled and re-erected,
· building envelope integrated into
structure: 3-pin, 3-chord arch (plastic
rooflights responsible for bracing and
member forces in diagonals in framework).

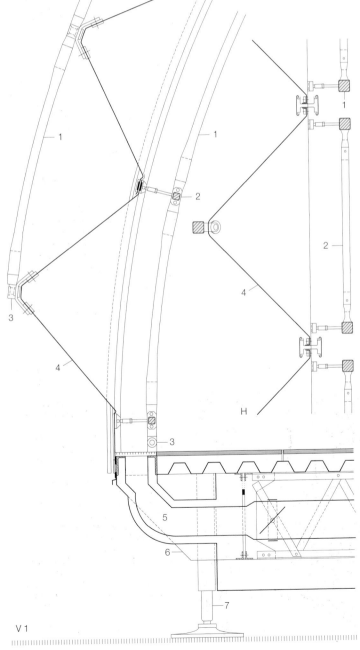

1 Top and bottom chords, 60 x 60 mm,
  glued
2 System rail, 40 x 40 mm, glued
3 Cast aluminium fixings, glued to timber
4 Polycarbonate pyramid (sunshading

by means of perforated sheet aluminium fitted internally)
5 Air duct
6 Fin
7 Height-adjustable foot

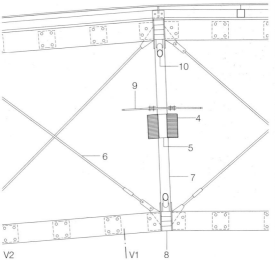

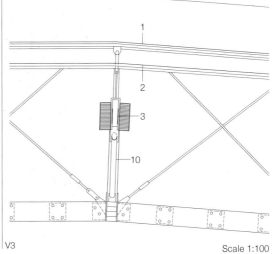

V1

V2

V3

Scale 1:100

68 · Sports stadium

Odate, J; 1997

Architects:
Toyo Ito & Associates, Tokyo

Detail 6/1998

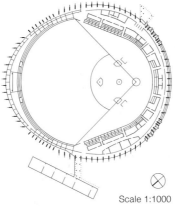

Scale 1:1000

- Construction grid: 6 x 6 m
- Asymmetric dome on inclined, elevated reinforced concrete ring beam
  (L x W x H = 178 x 157 x 42 m)
- Primary timber construction comprises pairs of crossing glued laminated timber members (indigenous softwood: akita cedar)
- Steel parts for bracing and connections
- Translucent envelope of welded Teflon sheets

1 Outer Teflon membrane
2 Inner Teflon membrane, both clamped between aluminium strips and tensioned with steel cables
3 Steel plate for connecting tubular steel diagonals and resisting membrane tension force
4 Pair of glulam members, akita cedar, size to match force diagram
5 218 mm timber spacer between pairs of members,
6 Vertical bracing, round steel bars, various diameters
7 Vertical member, 200 x 300 x 9 mm steel hollow section
8 Connector, welded steel flats with steel plates bolted to sides for connecting No. 4 above
9 Horizontal bracing, 25 dia. x 1 mm steel circular hollow section
10 Diagonals in plane of pairs of members, 139.8 dia. x 5 mm steel circular hollow section, plates welded into slits at ends
11 Steel flat ring welded to No. 7 above for connecting horizontal bracing

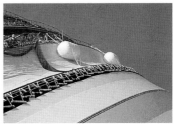

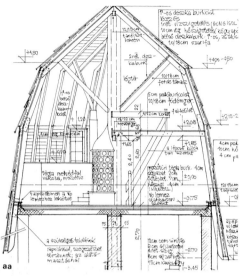

aa

bb

69 · Holiday home

Göd, H; 1986

Architect: Imre Makovecz, Budapest

- Loadbearing construction: oak;
  columns: oak logs
- Plinth: clay brickwork
- Roof covering:
  "Granica" timber roof covering of
  recycled board offcuts of different
  lengths

- Construction of solid facade:
  "Granica" timber covering
  battens
  moisture-control barrier
  100 mm thermal insulation
  spruce boards
  100 x 180 mm oak rafters
- Windows:
  spruce, stained, double glazing

Architektuur-Instituut catalogue,
Rotterdam, 1989; "Häuser" 1/88

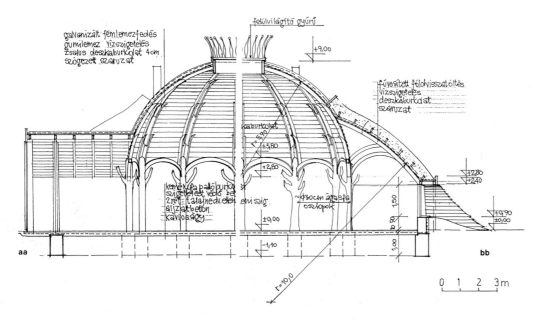

galvanizált fémlemezfedés
gumilemez vízszigetelés
zsalus deszkaburkolat 4 cm
szögezett szaruzat

felülvilágító gyűrű

+9,00

fúvosított fölolvisszatöltés
vízszigetelés
deszkaburkolat
szaruzat

aa

bb

0 1 2 3m

70 · Forest culture house

Visegrad, H; 1986

Architect: Imre Makovecz, Budapest

Architektuur-Instituut catalogue, Rotterdam, 1989; "Häuser" 1/88

- Loadbearing construction: oak
- Columns: oak logs, approx. 300 mm dia., door leaves imitate eagle wings
- Natural ventilation:
  through rooflight, r = 1290 x 600 x 150 mm, and through dormer-like window openings

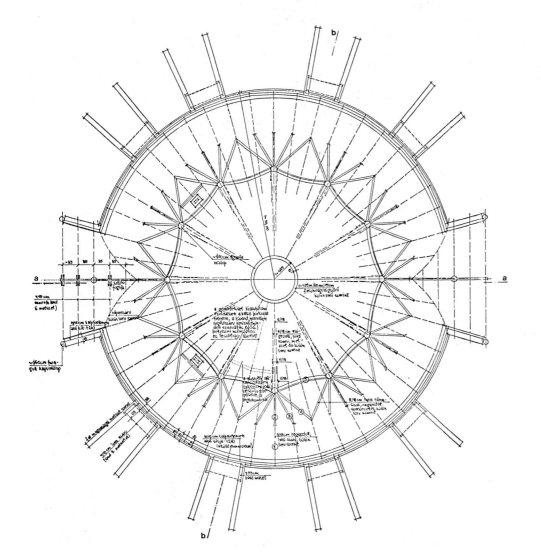

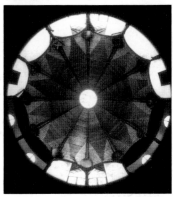

- Roof construction:
  galvanised metal sheets
  moisture-control barrier
  thermal insulation
  inner lining of spruce weatherboarding
  rafters
- Construction up of solid facade/roof:
  planting
  moisture-control barrier
  weatherboarding
- Windows:
  spruce
  double glazing

363

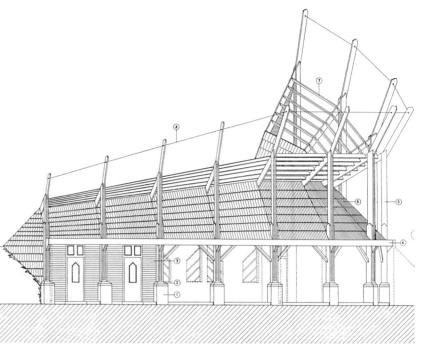

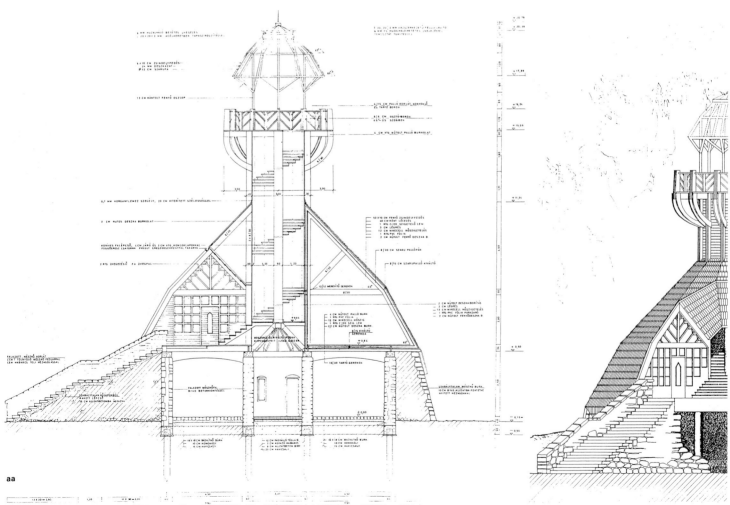

aa

71 · Administration building, observation tower and museum

Bük National Park near Miskolc, H; 1985

Architect: Benö Taba, Miskolc

· Loadbearing construction: spruce
· Roof construction:
  500 x 100 mm spruce shingles
  battens
  foil
  30 mm cavity
  120 mm thermal insulation
  PVC foil
  20 mm spruce boards
· Wall construction, tower:
  20 mm timber boards
  30 mm cavity
  120 mm thermal insulation
  PVC foil
  spruce boards
· Plinth:
  calcium-silicate brickwork with concrete
  core

A   Structural drawing of dome
B   Structural drawing of observation level

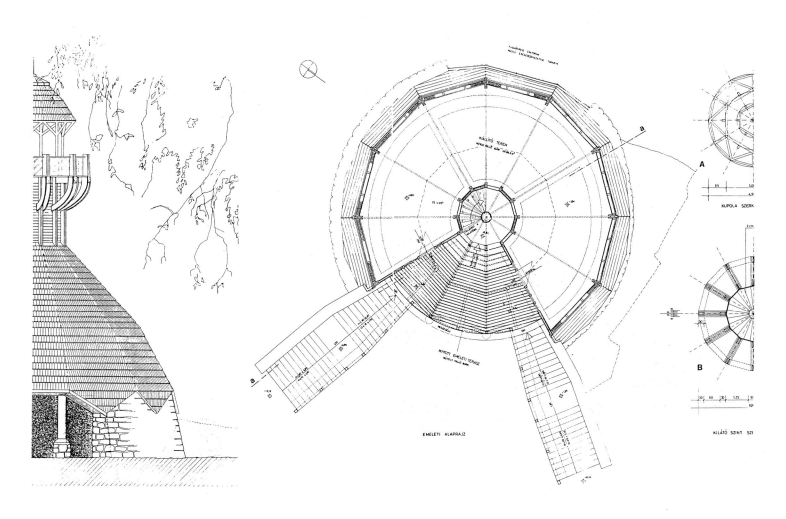

Bibliography

Bibliography

Affentranger, C.: Neue Holzarchitektur in Skandinavien. (1997)

Bairstow, J.E.N.: Practical & Decorative Woodworking Joints (1987); Bauern-häuser aus Oberbayern und angrenzen-den Gebieten Tirols. (1981)

Bauer-Böckler, H.-P.: Holzhäuser attraktiv und individuell, Blottner Verlag

Baulicher Holzschutz: Informationsheft für Baufachleute, steir. Agrarverlag, (1997)

Baus, Siegele: Holzfassaden; db das buch. Vol. 17, dva, (2000)

Becker, G.: Tragkonstruktionen des Hochbaues – Planen – Entwerfen – Berechnen – Part 1: Konstruktionsgrund-lagen. Düsseldorf (1983) – Part 2: Trag-werkselemente und Tragwerksformen. Düsseldorf (1987)

Beispiele moderner Holzarchitektur. Fachverlag Holz

Bertolino, F.: Vérification à la Ruine des Barres comprimées et flechies en bois suisse, research report FN 2005-5.308, EPF Lausannes/IBOIS. Lausanne (1988) (unpublished)

Beuth - Kommentar; Holzbauwerke. Beuth Verlag

Binding G.: Kleine Kunstgeschichte des deutschen Fachwerkbaus. 3. Aufl. (1984)

Biologischer Holzschutz: Literaturstudie. Landwirtschaftsverlag, (1998)

Blaser, W.: Fantasie in Holz. (1986)

Blaser, W.: Bauernhaus der Schweiz. (1983)

Blaser, W. : Schweizer Holzbrücken – Ponts de bois en Suisse – Wooden bridges in Switzerland. Basel (1982)

Brücken aus Holz, Konstruieren – Berechnen – Ausführen. Fachverlag Holz

Büren von, C., (ed.): Neuer Holzbau in der Schweiz: Mit Tradition und Erfahrung zu neuen Gestaltungen in Holz. Zurich (1985)

Büren von, C.,: Funktion und Form im Ingenieur-Holzbau. (1985)

Büttner, O., Hampe, E.: Bauwerk, Trag-werk, Tragstruktur. Stuttgart (1977)

Cerliani, Baggenstos: Holzplattenbau. Baufachverlag Lignum

Cerliani, Baggenstos: Sperrholzarchitek-tur. Baufachverlag Lignum

Chemie in Hobby und Beruf. dtv, Munich

Constantin, U.: Der Holzbau. Reprint Verlag, Leipzig

Cziesielski, E., Friedmann, M.: Holzbau. Osnabrück (1988)

Davies, R.M. (ed.): Space Structures: a study of methods and developments in three dimensional construction resulting from the International Conference on Space Structures. University of Surrey, Sept. 1966. Oxford (1967)

Die Energiesparverordnung im Holzbau.

Die Holzkonstruktionen. Holzbau und Holzkonstruktion. Reprint Verlag, Leipzig

Die klima-aktive Fassade. Koch, (1999)

Die Stellung der Biomasse im Vergleich zu ... Landwirtschaftsverlag, Münster (1995)

Dröge, G., Stoy, K.-H.: Grundzüge des neuzeitlichen Holzbaus. Munich (1981)

Dworschak, Wenke: Holzwohnhäuser. Intern. Projekte. Verlag für Bauwesen

Ehlbeck, J., Steck, G. (ed.): Ingenieurholzbau in Forschung und Praxis. Karlsruhe (1982)

Engel, H.: Tragsysteme – Structure Systems, 4th ed., Stuttgart (1967) European Communities – Commission (ed.), report prepared by: Crubilé, P., Ehlbeck, J., Brünninghoff, H., Larsen, H. J., Sunley, J.: EUR 9887 – Eurocode 5 – Common unified rules for timber structures. Luxembourg (1988)

Franz, G. (ed.): Betonkalender. verschie-dene Jahrgänge, Berlin

Gattnar, A., Trysna, F.: Hölzerne Dach- und Hallenbauten. 7th ed. Berlin (1961)

Glahn, H.: Baustatik in der Praxis des konstruktiven Ingenieurbaus: Hinweise zur Wahl zweckmäßiger statischer Systeme. Berlin (1987)

Göggel, M.: Bemessung im Holzbau. 2. ed. Wiesbaden (1981)

Götz, K.-H., Hoor, D., Möhler, K., Natterer, J.: Construire en bois. Lausanne, Edition en langue française, 1st ed. (1983), 2nd ed. (1987)

Götz, K.-H., Hoor, D., Möhler, K., Natterer, J : Holzbau-Atlas. Institut für internationale Architektur-Dokumentation, 1st ed. Munich (1978)

Götz, K.-H., Hoor, D., Möhler, K., Natterer, J.: Timber Design & Con-struction. Source-book. New York, London, Sydney, Toronto, USA and English Edition (1989)

Gollwitzer, G.: Bäume, Bilder und Texte aus drei Jahrtausenden. Herrsching (1980)

Graubner, W.: Holzverbindungen: Gegen-überstellung japanischer und europä-ischer Lösungen. 2nd ed. Stuttgart (1987)

Grundzüge des Holzbaus. (2 vol. Holz-tragwerke und Holzbauten), Ernst und Sohn (1999)

Guggenbühl, P.: Unsere einheimischen Nutzhölzer. (1986)

Gunzenhauser v.,C.: Baukonstruktionen in Holz. Manuscript, (1997)

Gutdeutsch, G.: Building in Wood – Construction and Details, Birkhäuser (1996)

Halasz von, R. (ed.): Holzbau-Taschenbuch. 7th ed. Berlin (1974)

Halasz von, R., Scheer, C. (ed.): Holzbau-Taschenbuch vol. no. 2: DIN 1052 und Erläuterungen – Formeln – Tabellen – Nomogramme. 8th ed. Berlin (1984)

Hansemann, W.: Effektlacke für Holz und Holzwerkstoffe. DVA, (2000)

Hansen, H.J. (ed.): Holzbaukunst. Gerhard Stalling Verlag, Oldenburg-Hamburg (1969)

Herzog, T., Natterer, J.: Gebäudehüllen aus Glas und Holz. (1984)

Herzog, T., Natterer, J. (ed.): Gebäude-hüllen aus Glas und Holz: Maßnahmen zur energiebewussten Erweiterung von Wohn-häusern. Lausanne (1984)

Hindermann, F.: Sag ich's Euch, geliebte Bäume.

Historischer Holzschutz. Ökobuch (1990)

HOAI – Scale of fees for architects and engineers, Wiesbaden

Holz und Anstrich: Umwelt- und Gesund-heitsfragen. expert Verlag, (1996)

Holzbau im dritten Jahrtausend. Fach-verlag Holz

Holzbau: Wände, Decken, Dächer. Teubner Verlag, (1998)

Holzbaukalender. Bruder Verlag, Karlsruhe

Holzbausysteme. dva, (2000)

Holzfacetten: Begegnungen mit dem Schönen. DRW Verlag, (1999)

Holzlexikon, vol. 1 A–M , vol. 2 N–Z, DRW-Verlag (ed.), 3rd ed. Stuttgart (1989)

Holzschutz ohne Gift? Ökobuch

Holzschutz ohne Menschenschaden. Unionsverlag, (1991)

Holzschutz: ein Handbuch für Baufach-leute. Fachbuchverlag, (1988)

Holzschutz: Informationen für Bauherren, Architekten + Ingenieure. Sächs. Staats-ministerium

Holzschutzpraxis. Ergänzungsband (Handbuch in Tabellen). Bauverlag

Hugues, Th., Steiger, L., Weber, J.: Timber Construction. DETAIL Practice, Birkhäuser, Basel (2004)

Issel, H.: Holzbau umfassend den Fachwerk-, Block-, Ständer- und Stahlbau und deren zeitgemäße Wiederverwendung. (1985)

Kempe, K.: Dokumentation Holzschäd-linge. Verlag für Bauwesen, Berlin (1999)

Kleinen, M., Lewitzki, W., Musso., F.: Holzbaudetails: Baukonstruktionen, Bauphysik, Kosten, Beispiele. Dusseldorf (1989)

Klöckner, K.: Alte Fachwerkbauten: Geschichte einer Skelettbauweise. 2. ed. Munich (1981)

Klöckner, K.: Der Blockbau, Massiv-bauweise in Holz. Stuttgart (1982)

Konstruktiver Holzschutz: Bauen mit Holz ohne Chemie. Werner Verlag, (1996)

Kordina, K., Meyer-Ottens, C.: Holz Brandschutz Handbuch. Munich (1983)

Krenov, J.: Worker in Wood. (1981)

Küttinger, G.: Holzbaukonstruktionen: Dachtragwerke – Hallen – Brücken. Munich (1984)

Lachner, C.: Geschichte der Holzbau-kunst in Deutschland. (1983)

Lachner, C.: Die Holzbaukunst. Reprint Verlag Leipzig

Landsberg, H., Pinkau, S.: Holzsysteme für den Hochbau. Kohlhammer Verlag, (1999)

Lehmann, H.-A., Stolze, B. J.: Ingenieur-holzbau. 6th ed. Stuttgart (1975)

Leiße, B.: Holz natürlich behandeln. C.F. Müller Verlag

Leiße, B.: Holz natürlich schützen. Schäden vermeiden, Werte erhalten. C.F. Müller Verlag

Leiße, B.: Holzschutzmittel im Einsatz. Bauverlag

Lips-Ambs, F.-J.: Holzbau heute. DRW Verlag, (1999)

Mainichi, F.: Japanisches Schreinerwerk-zeug. (1983)

Mayer, V.: Holzkirchen; Neuentdeckte Baukultur in Böhmen, Mähren, Schlesien und der Slowakei. (1986)

Mehrgeschossiger Holzbau in Österreich. pro: Holz Steiermark

Mehrgeschossiger Holzhausbau. Ott Verlag, (1997)

Meilach, D.Z.: Kunst in Holz; Dinge, Möbel, Objekte. (1987)

Merkblattreihe Holzarten. Fachverlag Holz

Mönk, W.: Bauen und Sanieren mit Holz. (1987)

Mönk, W.: Holzbau. Bemessung u. Konstruktion. Verlag für Bauwesen

Mönk, W.: Holzbau: Grundlagen für die Bemessung. 3rd ed. Berlin (1961)

Moderner Holzbau in der Steiermark. Akademische Druck- und Verlagsanstalt

Nakahara, Y.: Japanese Joinery; A handbook for joiners and carpenters. (1983)

Natterer, J., Kessel. M.H.: Theoretische und experimentelle Untersuchungen zur seitlichen Stabilisierung von Biegeträgern, research report KFWFNo. 1075, EPF Lausanne/IBOIS (unpublished). Lausanne (1985)

Natürlicher Holzschutz: wirksamer Schutz auch ohne Gift. Michaels Verlag

Niemeyer, P.: Werterhaltung Holz. VDE Berlin

Norberg-Schulz, C., Suzuki, M.: Holzhäuser in Europa. 2nd ed. (1989)

Odate, T.: Japanese Woodworking Tools: Their traditions, spirit and use. (1984)

Otto, F.: Form und Konstruktion. Stuttgart (1976)

Otto, F.: Natürliche Konstruktionen. Stuttgart (1982)

Otto, F.: Spannweiten: Ideen und Versuche zum Leichtbau. Berlin (1965)

Pahl, G., Beitz, W.: Konstruktionslehre: Handbuch für Studium und Praxis. Berlin (1977)

Paläste und Gehöfte im Grasland von Kamerun. K. Krämer Verlag

Phleps, H.: Der Blockbau. Bruderverlag Karlsruhe (1942/1981)

Phleps, H.: Allemannische Holzbaukunst.

Pierer, H.: Holzbau Handbuch. (2000)

Pierer, H.: Holzbau in der Steiermark. Springer, Vienna, New York

Pierer, H.: Holzbau in Vorarlberg. Springer, Vienna, New York

Pracht, K.: Holzbau-Systeme. (1984)

Prix Lignum: die Auszeichnung für Bauten und Fassaden mit Holz. Lignum Baufachverlag, (2000)

Proceedings of the 1st International Timber Construction Symposium, Fachverlag Holz

Reiners, H.: Bauen mit Holz. Die besten Einfamilienhäuser. Callwey Verlag

Rodenacker, W.G.: Methodisches Konstruieren. 2nd ed. Berlin (1976)

Roth, K.: Konstruieren mit Konstruktionskatalogen. Berlin (1982)

Ruske, W.: Holzarchitektur im Detail. Kissingen (1986)

Ruske, W.: Holzskelettbau. (1980)

Sattlberger, H.: Das Holzhaus als dritte Haut. Michaels Verlag, (1995)

Scheer, von Halasz: Holzbau 1/2. Springer Verlag, Heidelberg

Scheer, Muszala: Der Holzbau. Material, Konstruktion, Detail. A. Koch Verlag

Schunck, E., Oster, H. J., Barthel, R., Kießl, K.: Dachatlas: Geneigte Dächer. Institut für internationale Architektur-Dokumentation, 4th ed. Munich (2003)

Seike, K.: The Art of Japanese Joinery. 10. Aufl. (1986)

Sell, J.: Eigenschaften und Kenngrößen von Holzarten. Baufachverlag AG, Zürich Dietikon (1989)

Sell, J.: Eigenschaften und Kenngrößen von Holzarten. Baufachverlag Lignum

Stungo, N.: Neue Holzarchitektur. dva

Swoboda, O.: Holzbaukunst in Österreich. (1998)

Teiji, I.: Alte Bauernhäuser in Japan. (1984)

The Woodbook. Taschen-Verlag, Cologne (2002)

The Woodworker's Handbook. The London College of Furniture. (1987)

Und du begleitest mich. Wie Bäume und Hölzer dem Menschen nutzen. Thoma Verlag, (1999)

Wachsmann: Holzausbau, Technik, Gestaltung. Baufachverlag Lignum

Wagenführ, R.: Anatomie des Holzes. Fachbuchverlag, Leipzig (1999)

Wagenführ, R.: Holzatlas. Fachbuchverlag im Carl Hanser Verlag, Leipzig (2000)

Waldfacetten: Begegnungen mit dem Wald. DRW Verlag, (1998)

Werner, P.: Das Bundwerk: Eine alte Zimmermannstechnik. Konstruktion – Gestaltung – Ornamentik. Stuttgart (1988)

Wesser, R.: Der Holzbau. Reprint Verlag, Leipzig

Widmer, C.: 35 Holzmuster; Nach drei Hauptgruppen geordnet: Nadelhölzer, Laubhölzer, exotische Laubhölzer. 18. ed.

Willeitner, H., Schwab, E. (ed.): Holz-Außenverschalung im Hochbau. Verlagsanstalt Alexander Koch, Stuttgart (1981)

Wohnungen in Holzbauweise; Wohnmodelle in Bayern. Karl Krämer Verlag, Stuttgart + Zurich

Wood Conference 98/99, Fachverlag Holz

Wood Conference: Mensch-Holz-Umwelt, Fachverlag Holz

Standards

Deutsches Institut für Normung e.V. 10772 Berlin

DIN 1052 part 1: Structural use of timber; design and construction

DIN 1052 part 2: Structural use of timber; mechanically fastened joints

DIN 1052 part 3: Structural use of timber; buildings in timber frame construction; design and construction

DIN 1055 part 1: Actions on structures; densities and weights of building materials, structural elements and stored materials

DIN 1055 part 3: Actions on structures; self-weight and imposed load in building

DIN 1055 part 4: Design loads for buildings; imposed loads; wind loads on structures unsusceptible to vibration

DIN 1072: Road bridges and footbridges; design loads

DIN 1074: Wooden bridges

DIN 4074 part 1: Strength grading of coniferous wood; coniferous sawn timber

DIN 4074 part 2: Building timber for wood building components; quality conditions for building logs (softwood)

DIN 18334: Contract procedures for building works – Part C: General technical specifications for building works; carpentry and timber construction work

DIN 68140: Wood finger-jointing

DIN 68141: Wood adhesive s – determination of properties of use of wood adhesives for loadbearing timber structures

DIN 68800 part 1: Protection of timber used in buildings; general specifications

DIN 68800 part 2: Protection of timber; preventive constructional measures in buildings

DIN 68800 part 3: Protection of timber; preventive chemical protection

DIN 68800 part 4: Wood preservation; measures for the eradication of fungi and insects

DIN 68800 part 5: Protection of timber used in buildings; preventive chemical protection for wood-based materials

Articles in trade journals

Informationsdienst Holz. Entwicklungsgemeinschaft Holzbau (EGH) in the Deutsche Gesellschaft für Holzforschung (DGfH), Munich (pub.) in collaboration with the Bund Deutscher Zimmermeister in the ZDB, Bonn, and Arbeitsgemeinschaft Holz e.V., Düsseldorf

• Erneuerung von Fachwerkbauten, 11/78

• Entwurfsüberlegungen bei Holzbauten, 11/79

• Statische Werte für Vollholz, Brettschichtholz und Holzwerkstoffe – Dachbauteile und Anschlüsse – Sporthallendetails – Stützen und Wandbauteile, 12/79

• Auflagerpunkte – Unterspannte Träger – Sonderbauweisen – Dachscheiben, Dachverbände – Trägerroste – Räumliche Stabwerke, 1982

• Vorbemessungen (Binder – Stützen – Rahmen) part 1, 2/85

• Ausgeklinkte Träger – Fachwerke – Knotenpunkte – Kastenträger – Sheddächer, 2/85

• Ausschreibungsbeispiele Zimmerer- und Holzbauarbeiten, 5/85

• Bemessungshilfen, Knoten, Anschlüsse, part 3, 9/85

• Sparrenpfetten – Biegeträger – Stützen – Rahmen – Verbände – Gelenke, part 2, 12/85

• Queranschlüsse – Fachwerk F30 – Montagestöße – Balkenschuhe – Hirnholzdübelverbände – Voutenträger, part 5, 12/85

• Bemessungshilfen, Knoten, Anschlüsse part 2, 6/86

• Fachwerkbinder – Berechnung, Konstruktion, 6/86

• Der unterspannte Balken, 9/86

• Beurteilungskriterien für Rissbildung bei Bauholz im konstruktiven Holzbau, 11/87

• Bau-Furniersperrholz aus Buche, 1988

• Überdachung mit großen Spannweiten, 1/88

• Brücken – Planung, Konstruktion, Berechnung, 11/88

• Zimmermannsmäßige Verbindungen, 11/88

• Zweckbauten für die Landwirtschaft, 11/88

• Mehrzweckhallen, 12/91

• Feuerhemmende Holzbauteile (F30-B), 5/94

• Bemessung nach Eurocode 5-1-1, 5/95

• Baulicher Holzschutz, 9/97

• Verbände und Abstützungen, 11/97

• Grundlagen des Schallschutzes, 10/98

• Schalldämmende Holzbalken- und Brettstapeldecken, 5/99

• Holzbauzeichnungen, 12/99

• Konstruktive Vollholzprodukte, 6/00

• Lärmschutzwände, 12/00

• Grundlagen des Brandschutzes, 12/01

EPF Lausanne, Chair of Timber Engineering (IBOIS), Prof. J. Natterer (ed.): Chronological list of publications 1979–88/89 (unpublished). Lausanne (1989)

Holzbau – Statik – Aktuell. Informationen zur Berechnung von Holzkonstruktionen. Arbeitsgemeinschaft Holz e.V.(ed.), Dusseldorf, part 1–8

Brüninghoff, H., Schmidt, K.: Verbände und Abstützungen: genauere Nachweise – allgemeine Informationen, in: Informationsdienst Holz, 11/97

Cziesielski, E., Wagner, C.: Dachscheiben aus Spanplatten, in: bauen mit holz 1–2/79

Cziesielski, E.: Stabilität von Holzhäusern unter Horizontalbelastung, in: bauen mit holz 7/82

Duddeck, H.: Die Ingenieuraufgaben, die Realität in ein Berechnungsmodell zu übersetzen, in: Die Bautechnik 7/83

Gerold, W.: Durchbiegungsnachweis und Konstruktion von Aussteifungsverbänden, in: bauen mit holz 6/86

Gerold, W.: Zur Frage der Beanspruchung von stabilisierenden Verbänden und Trägern, in: Stahlbau 32, pp. 278–281, (1963)

Gliese, R.: Sanieren von Brettschichtträgern mit Epoxidharz, in: bauen mit holz 7/80

Gravert, F.W. et al.: Checkliste für die Grundlagenermittlung in der Tragwerks-Planung, Beratende Ingenieure 7–8/84

Heimershoff, B.: Probleme der Stabilitäts-theorie und Spannungstheorie II. Ordnung im Holzbau, in: Holzbau – Statik – Aktuell. Informationen zur Berechnung von Holz-konstruktionen, Arbeitsgemeinschaft Holz e.V. (ed.), part 9, 3/87

Henrici, D.: Zur Bemessung windausstei-fender hölzener Wandscheiben, in: bauen mit holz 12/84

Kessel, M.H. et al.: Zur Sicherung eines Dreigelenkrahmens gegen Kippen, in: Bauingenieur 59, pp. 189–327, (1989)

Kessel, M.H., Sandoz, J.L.: Zur Effizienz der Festigkeitsorientierung von Fichten-kantholz: Einfluß der Klassengrenzen der Sortierparameter, in: Holz als Roh- und Werkstoff 47, pp. 323–327, (1989)

Kessel, M.H., Sandoz, J.L.: Zur Effizienz der Festigkeitsorientierung von Fichten-kantholz: Vergleich europäischer Normen, in: Holz als Roh- und Werkstoff 47, pp. 278–284, (1989)

Lange, R.-P.: Der Standsicherheitsnach-weis von Anlehnhäusern, in: bauen mit holz 7/86

Natterer, J. et.al.: Praxisbezogene Theorie-anwendung im Holzbau, in Ehlbeck, J., Steck, G. (ed.): Ingenieurholzbau in For-schung und Praxis, Karlsruhe (1986)

Natterer, J., Sandoz, J.L.: Mechanische Eigenschaften der Schweizer Fichte, in: Schweizerische Holzzeitung Holz 3/88

Natterer, J., Winter, W.: Gedanken zum methodischen Konstruieren im Holzbau, in: Der Architekt 2/81

Natterer, J.: Verbundkonstruktionen im Holzbau – Entwicklungen und Tendenzen. 14th Austro-German-Swiss Wood Con-ference, Interlaken, CH

Sandoz, J.L.: Grading of construction tim-ber by ultrasound, in: Wood Science and Technology 23, S. 95–108, (1989)

Steinmetz, D.: Die Aussteifung von Holz-häusern am Beispiel des Holzrahmen-baus, in bauen mit holz 12/88

Gerd Hauser
Thermal performance of buildungs

Standards

DIN 4108 part 2: Thermal protection and energy economy in buildings; minimum requirements for thermal insulation

DIN 4108 supplement 2: Thermal insula-tion and energy economy in buildings – thermal bridges – examples for planning and performance

DIN 4108 part 6: Thermal protection and energy economy in buildings; calculation of annual heat and energy use

DIN 4108 part 7: Thermal insulation and energy economy of buildings; airtightness of building, requirements, recommenda-tions and examples for planning and per-formance)

DIN V 4701 part 10 (pre-standard): Energy efficiency of heating and ventilation systems in building; heating, domestic hot water, ventilation

DIN EN 13829: Thermal performance of buildings – determination of air permeabil-ity of buildings – fan pressurisation method

DIN EN ISO 6946: Building components – thermal resistance and thermal transmit-tance – calculation method

DIN EN ISO 7345: Thermal insulation – physical quantities and definitions

DIN EN ISO 10211 part 2: Thermal bridges in building construction – calculation of heat flows and surface temperatures – linear thermal bridges

Bibliography

Arbeitsgemeinschaft kommunaler Ver-sorgungsunternehmen zur Förderung rationeller, sparsamer und umweltscho-nender Energieverwendung und rationel-ler Wasserverwendung: Niedrigenergie-haus. Cologne

Arbeitsgemeinschaft für zeitgemäßes Bauen e.V.: Ökologisches Bauen No. 183 (1989), No. 186 (1990), No. 187 (1991)

Bansal, N. K., Hauser, G. and Minke, G.: Passive Building Design. A Handbook of Natural Climatic Control; Elsevier Science B.V., Amsterdam, London, New York, Tokyo (1994)

Borsch-Laaks, R.: Holzbauwände für das Passivhaus, ein wärmetechnischer Sys-temvergleich. die neue quadriga, Verlag Kastner, Wolnzach (5/2001)

Borsch-Laaks, R., Köhnke, E.U., Winter, S.: Durchblick erwünscht, die Optimierung des Fensteranschlusses. die neue qua-driga, Verlag Kastner, Wolnzach (3/2001)

Borsch-Laaks, R., Winter, S., Bodenplatten in Holzbauweise. Condetti-Detail. die neue quadriga, Verlag Kastner, Wolnzach (5/2001)

Boy, E.: Transparente Wärmedämmung im Praxistest – Zwischenergebnisse aus einer zweijährigen Untersuchungsperiode. Bauphysik 11 (1989), issue 2, pp. 93–99

Byberg, M. R., Djurtoft, R. G. and Saxhof, B.: 6 Low-energy houses in Hjortekaer; Laboratory for Thermal Insulation, Den-mark Technical University, report No. 83, (May 1979)

Das energieautarke Solarhaus. Fraunhofer Institute for Solar Energy Systems, (1992)

Dimensionierung von Lüftungsanlagen. Proceedings vol. 17, AKKP, Darmstadt (1999)

Erhorn, H. und Reiß, J.: Niedrigenergie-häuser Heldenheim. Isoliertechnik (1992), issue 6, pp. 26–42

Feist, W.: Passive Häuser. Research report of the Wohnen und Umwelt Institute, Darmstadt (1992)

Feist, W., Peper, S., von Oesen, M.: Klimaneutrale Passivhaus-Reihenhaus-siedlung in Hannover-Kronsberg. CEPHEUS project information

Feist, Klien: Das Niedrigenergiehaus. C. F. Müller Verlag, Karlsruhe (1989)

Feist, W.: Passivhaus, Sommerklima, Studie. Darmstadt (1998)

Fenster für das Passivhaus. Proceedings vol. 14, AKKP, Darmstadt (1998)

Geiger, B.: Energiebedarfsdeckung im Niedrigenergiehaus. VDEW congress "Integrierte Haustechnik im Niedrigener-giehaus", on 14 April 1994 in Bad Seege-berg

Gertis, K.: Außenwände mit transparenten Wärmedämmstoffen. Bauphysik 9 (1987), issue 5, pp. 213–217

G + H ISOVER: Das Niedrigenergiehaus – Wohnmodelle der Zukunft realisieren. Ludwigshafen (1992)

Gruber, E., Erhorn, H. and Reichert, J.: Solarhäuser Landstuhl; Verlag TÜV Rhein-land (1989)

Hauptberatungsstelle für Elektrizitäts-anwendung-HEA: Handbuch Niedrig-energiehaus. Frankfurt (1993)

Hauser, G.: Beeinflussung des Innen-klimas durch Außenwände und durch Wintergärten. Bauphysik 9 (1987), issue 5, pp. 155–162; Glaswelt 41 (1988), issue 10, pp. 12–16, issue 11, pp. 52–56

Hauser, G. and Hausladen, G.: Energie-kennzahl zur Beschreibung des Heiz-energieverbrauchs von Gebäuden; pub.: Gesellschaft für Rationelle Energiever-wendung e.V. (1994)

Hauser, G. and Maas, A.: Energiespar-verordnung 2002 (EnEV – Energy Economy Act); Kalksandstein-Informationen GmbH + Co. KG, Hannover (Jan 2002)

Hauser, G.: Holz-Glaskonstruktionen. Report of the Timber Engineering Devel-opment Group in the Deutsche Gesell-schaft für Holzforschung, (Sept 1986)

Hauser, G. and Otto, F.: Niedrigenergiehäuser – bauphysikalische Entwurfsgrundlagen. holzbau handbuch, series 1, part 3, instalment 2, Timber Engineering Development Group in the DGfH e.V., Munich (1997)

Hauser, G., Otto, F.: Niedrigenergie-häuser. holzbau handbuch, series 1, part 3, instalment 3, Informationsdienst Holz, DGfH, Munich (March 1995)

Hauser, G. and Stiegel H.: Pauschalierte Erfassung der Wirkung von Wärme-brücken. Bauphysik 17 (1995), issue 3, pp. 65–68

Hauser, G.: Passive Sonnenenergienut-zung durch Fenster, Außenwände und temporäre Wärmeschutzmaßnahmen – Eine einfache Methode zur Quantifizie-rung durch k-Werte. HLH 34 (1983), issue 3, pp. 111–112, issue 4, pp. 144–153, issue 5, pp. 200–204, issue 6, pp. 259–265

Hauser, G.: Tragende Außenwände als Wärmespeicher unter Verwendung einer hochwertigen durchlässigen Wärme-dämmung: Report of the RKW congress "Passive Solararchitektur". Berlin (1982)

Hauser, G. and Stiegel, H.: Wärme-brücken-Atlas für den Mauerwerksbau. Bauverlag Wiesbaden (1996)

Hauser, G. and Stiegel, H.: Wärme-brücken-Atlas für den Holzbau. Bau-verlag, Wiesbaden (1992)

Hauser, G., Stiegel, H. and Haupt, W.: Wärmebrückenkatalog auf CD-ROM. Ingenieurbüro Hauser, Baunatal (1998)

Hauser, G., Schulze, H. and Stiegel, H.: Wärmetechnische Optimierung von Anschlussdetails bei Niedrigenergie-häusern und Erarbeitung von Standard-lösungen. IRB-Verlag, Stuttgart (1996)

Hauser, G. and Kempkes, C.: Wasser-durchströmte Bauteile zur Raumkondition-ierung. From: Bauphysik, Berichte aus Forschung und Praxis, commemorative volume on 60th birthday of Karl Gertis. Ed.: G. Hauser, IRB-Verlag Stuttgart (1998), pp. 87–110; Ges.-Ing. 120 (1999), issue 3, pp. 126–135; TAB 32 (2001), issue 6, pp. 49–56

Hauser, G., Stiegel, H.: Wärmebrücken, Informationsdienst Holz, holzbau handbuch, series 3, part 2, instalment 6, DGFH, Munich (Oct 1997)

Hauser, G. and Maas A.: Auswirkungen von Fugen und Fehlstellen in Dampf-sperren und Wärmedämmschichten. Aachen Building Experts Congress 1991. Bauverlag Wiesbaden (1991), pp. 88–95; DBZ 40 (1992), issue 1, pp. 97–100

Hausladen, G. and Springl, P.: Heizung und Lüftung im Niedrigenergiehaus. Research report for Federal Ministry for Regional Planning, Building and Urban Development, Kirchheim (1993)

Haustechnik im Passivhaus, proceedings vol. 6. AKKP, Darmstadt (1997)

Horn, Gerrit: Vergleich energieeffizienter Holzbausysteme: Wärmebrücken, Luft-dichtheitskonzepte, Kosten. Proceedings of the 3rd Passive House Congress, 1999. Bregenz and Darmstadt (1999)

I B K congress: Das Niedrigenergiehaus heute und morgen. Darmstadt (14. and 15. Nov. 1990)

I B K congress: Der neue Wärmeschutz – Niedrigenergiehäuser in der Praxis. Darm-stadt (2 and 3 Dec 1992).

Kast, W.: Gebäude ohne Heizwärme-verbrauch? Gesundheits-Ingenieur 112 (1991), issue 5, pp. 268–271

Kaufmann, B., Schnieders, J., Pfluger, R.: Passivhaus-Fenster. Proceedings of the 6th European Passive House Conference. Basel (2002), p. 289

Kehl, D., Borsch-Laaks, R.: Wärmebrücken im Holzrahmenbau. die neue quadriga, Verlag Kastner, Wolnzach (6/2000)

Klose. G.-R.: Niedrigenergiehäuser als künftiger Standard. DBZ (1992), issue 6, pp. 883–893

Luftdichte Projektierung von Passiv-häusern. CEPHEUS project information No. 7, 4th ed., Darmstadt (2002)

Lutz, P., Jenisch, R., Klopfer, H., Frey-muth, H. and Krampf, L.: Lehrbuch der Bauphysik. Teubner, Stuttgart (1985)

Maas, A., Hauser, G. and Höttges, K.: Die Energieeinsparverordnung. Bau-physik 24, (2002), issue 1, pp. 26–38; wksb 47 (2002), issue 48, pp. 15–25

Maas, A., Dönch, M. and Winkler, S.: Luftdichtheit von Wohngebäuden in Niedrigenergiebauweise. DBZ (1999), issue 1, pp. 79–82

Möhl, Hauser, Müller: Baulicher Wärmeschutz, Feuchteschutz und Energieverbrauch. Expert-Verlag,

Kontakt & Studium, Bauwesen, vol. 131, Grafenau (1984).

Nill, R.: Niedrigenergiehaus als Regelfall? DAB (1991), issue 12, pp. 1987–1993

Passivhaus Holzbau Teams. die neue quadriga, Verlag Kastner, Wolnzach (1/2001)

Passivhaus Versorgungstechnik. Proceedings vol. 20, AKKP, Darmstadt (2000)

PESAG: Das Niedrigenergiehaus. Essen (1993))

Pflüger, A. und Stahl, W.: Das Energie-einsparpotential der transparenten Wärmedämmung. Glaswelt (1986), issue 9, pp. 151–158

Pflüger, R., Feist, W.: Kostengünstiger Passivhaus-Geschosswohnungsbau in Kassel-Marbachshöhe. Messtechnische Untersuchung und Auswertung. CEPHEUS project information No. 15, Darmstadt (2001)

Schnieders, J.: Passivhausfenster. Passive House Congress, Kassel (March 2000)

SIA 180 (Swiss standard): Thermal insulation and moisture-control measures in buildings; appendix

Esslingen Technical Academy: course of study "Low-energy buildings" (9 Nov 1992); VDEW "Heizungssysteme im Vergleich". Frankfurt (March 1993)

Legislation on energy-saving thermal insulation and energy-saving systems in buildings (Energieeinsparverordnung – EnEV, Energy Economy Act, 16 Nov 2001. Federal Gazette part I, No. 59, 21 Nov 2001)

Voss, K., Braun, P. O. and Schmid, J.: Transparente Wärmedämmung, Materialien, Systemtechnik und Anwendung. Bauphysik 13, (1991), issue 6, pp. 217–224

Voss. K., Stahl, W. and Goetzberger, A.: Das energieautarke Solarhaus. Bauphysik 15, (1993), issue 1, pp. 10–14

Wärmebrückenfreies Konstruieren, proceedings vol. 16, AKKP, 2nd ed., Darmstadt

Ytong: Das Niedrigenergiehaus. Munich (1993)

Zeller, J.: Luftdichtheit von Wohngebäuden, Messung, Bewertung, Ausführungsdetails. Pub.: RWE, Essen, ebök, Tübingen; copies obtainable from Fachverband Luftdichtheit im Bauwesen e.V., Kassel (www.flib.de)

Gerd Wegener, Bernhard Zimmer
Building with wood is building for the future

Burschel, P., Huss, J.: Grundriss des Waldbaus – Ein Leitfaden für Studium und Praxis. Parey-Verlag, Hamburg (1987)

FAO, Food and Agriculture. Org. of the United Nations, Rome (2001)

Frühwald, A., Pohlmann, C.M., Wegener, G.: Holz – Rohstoff der Zukunft. Informationsdienst Holz. Pub.: DGfH, Munich,

and Holzabsatzfonds (public body), Bonn (2001)

Speckels, L.G.: Ökologischer Vergleich verschiedener Verwertungs- und Entsorgungswege und Entsorgungswege für Altholz. Dissertation, Faculty of Biology, Hamburg University (2001)

Wegener, G., Windeisen, E., Zimmer, B., Frühwald, A.: Agenda 21 – Wald und Holz in Städten und Gemeinden. Pub.: DGfH, Munich, and Holzabsatzfonds (public body), Bonn (2000)

Wegener, G., Zimmer, B., Frühwald, A., Scharai-Rad, M.: Ökobilanzen Holz. Fakten lesen, verstehen, handeln. Informationsdienst Holz. Pub.: DGfH, Munich (1997)

Wegener, G., Zimmer B.: Holz als Rohstoff. In: Der Deutsche Wald – Der Bürger im Staat 51. (2001), issue 1, pp. 67–72

Michael Volz
Protecting wood

Standards

DIN 4108: Thermal protection and energy economy in buildings

DIN 4108 part 2: Minimum requirements for thermal insulation

DIN 4108 part 3: Protection against moisture subject to climate conditions; requirements and directions for design and construction

DIN 4108 part 4: Characteristic values relating to thermal insulation and protection against moisture

DIN 4108 part 5: Methods of calculation

DIN 4108 part 7: Airtightness of building, requirements, recommendations and examples for planning and performance

DIN 68364: Characteristic values for wood species; strength, elasticity, resistance

DIN 68800 part 2: Protection of timber; preventive constructional measures in buildings

DIN 68800 part 3: Protection of timber; preventive chemical protection

DIN EN 350 part 2: Durability of wood and wood-based products – natural durability of solid wood – guide to the natural durability and treatability of selected wood species of importance in Europe

DIN EN 460: Durability of wood and wood-based products – natural durability of solid wood – guide to the durability requirements for wood to be used in hazard classes

Bibliography

Bellmann, H, et al.: Beuth-Kommentar "Holzschutz - Eine ausführliche Erläuterung zu DIN 68 800-3", Beuth-Verlag, (1992)

Gockel, H.: Konstruktiver Holzschutz: Bauen mit Holz ohne Chemie. Beuth, Berlin; Werner, Düsseldorf (1996)

Grünzweig + Hartmann AG: Dämmstoffanordnung, Volldämmung nach DIN 4108. EGH wood information publication, (1997)

Leiße, B.: Holzbauteile richtig geschützt. Bernhard DRW-Verlag, (2002)

Lewitzki, W., Schulze, H.: Holzschutz; Bauliche Empfehlungen. EGH wood information publication, (1997)

Schulze, H.: Baulicher Holzschutz. EGH wood information publication, (1991, 1997, 2001)

Schulze, H.: Holzbau – Wände, Decken, Dächer – Konstruktion, Bauphysik, Holzschutz. Teubner-Verlag, (1996)

Schulze, H.: Dampfsperren in Holzaußenbauteilen – Erfordernis und Risiko. Bauphysik. issue 6, (1996)

Schulze, H.: Holzhäuser, eine Entscheidung für Generationen; Aussagen zur Lebensdauer. EGH wood information publication, (1991)

Schulze, H.: Nachträglicher Dachgeschossausbau. EGH wood information publication, (1992)

Schulze, H.: Warum diffusionsoffene Unterspannbahnen? wksb – Zeitschrift für Wärmeschutz – Kälteschutz – Schallschutz – Brandschutz, issue 33, (1993)

Schulze, H.: Vorschläge zur Reduzierung des chemischen Holzschutzes in Wohngebäuden. Holz als Roh- und Werkstoff. (1989), pp. 373-381

Schulze, H.: Geneigte Dächer ohne chemischen Holzschutz auch ohne Dampfsperre? bauen mit holz, (1992), pp. 646–659

Schulze, H.: Decken unter nicht ausgebauten Dachgeschossen. bauen mit holz, (1993), pp. 26–30

Schulze, H.: Naßbereiche in Bädern. EGH wood information publication, (1987, 2000)

Willeitner, H.: Holz-Aussenverwendung im Hochbau: Beanspruchungsverhältnisse, geeignete Holzarten, richtige Konstruktion, wirksamer Schutz, einschlägige Vorschriften. Stuttgart (1981)

Subject index

A-weighted sound level → 68
acoustic bridge → 69, 70, 139
adhesive-bonded particleboard → 44, 45
Africa → 26, 36
Agenda 21 → 47
air change rate → 64–66
air drying → 38
airborne sound → 68–70
airtight barrier → 62, 66, 227, 292, 299, 305, 310, 313, 315, 317, 320, 358
airtightness → 62, 64, 66, 70, 91, 225
aluminium → 118, 154, 216, 220, 223, 244, 265, 292, 293, 295, 308, 314, 355, 360, 361
anchor → 95, 114–117, 123, 174, 175, 182, 215, 218, 222, 229, 230, 255, 263
anchor bolt → 77, 123
anisotropy → 32, 105
annual ring → 55, 58, 59, 98, 316
annular-ringed shank nail → 110, 114
arch → 97, 115, 128, 158, 169, 172, 206, 208, 209, 211–217, 219, 242, 245–247, 249, 251, 270, 324, 360
arris knot → 58, 59
articulated system → 102
as-built drawing → 91
assembly → 72, 75, 87, 90, 97, 101, 115, 156, 225, 271, 319
Austria → 10, 12, 21, 277, 278
axial force → 87, 187, 266

Balloon-frame construction → 53
balsa → 32
bamboo → 10, 26
bark pocket → 32
barrel vault → 29, 141, 244–246, 249, 251
base detail → 20, 142, 153, 206–209
basic services → 91
batten → 39, 56, 214
battened column → 124, 143
beam grid → 79, 141, 174, 232–241
beam hanger → 145
beam-column junction → 180, 184
bearing → 98, 108, 109, 113, 115, 123, 156, 167, 168, 172, 174, 176, 186, 188, 194, 205, 208, 209, 219, 222, 230, 235, 239, 241, 255, 263
bearing pressure → 108, 113, 123
bearing stress → 115
beech → 31, 36, 41–46, 57, 73, 82, 122, 197, 208, 228, 240
behaviour in fire → 42, 71
bending moment → 81, 102, 106, 185, 187, 266
bending strength → 57, 92, 94
bending stress → 57, 87, 92, 136, 255, 257, 271
Beta method → 95
bill of quantities → 94
biomass → 48
bitumen-impregnated wood fibre insulating board → 298
blockboard → 30, 43
blue stain → 34–36, 56–59
board → 30, 39, 41–46, 49, 51, 56, 59, 63, 73, 79, 95, 104, 169, 170, 187, 221, 229, 242, 249, 253, 256, 298, 299, 305, 307, 310, 316–320, 324, 326, 362

boarding → 39, 50, 51, 70, 122, 135, 171, 232, 241, 253, 258, 265, 300, 313, 318, 322, 323, 325, 326, 332, 356
bolt → 113, 117, 147, 164, 166, 167, 176, 177, 182, 192, 195–198, 214, 221, 235, 238, 239, 245, 246, 250, 252, 256, 269
bonded-in rod → 95, 123, 172, 183
bottom chord → 79, 115, 117, 119, 120, 128, 132, 151, 157–168, 171, 173, 180–183, 187, 191, 199, 202, 207, 209, 210, 212, 236–239, 243, 260, 307, 360
bow → 58, 59
box section → 102, 104, 119, 124, 135, 136, 243, 270
boxed-heart conversion → 55
bracing → 38, 39, 42–46, 53, 55, 63, 75, 79, 85–87, 91, 93, 101, 122, 125–133, 135, 135–139, 144, 146, 149, 151, 155, 158, 160, 162, 164, 166, 168, 173, 175, 176, 178–180, 182, 186, 187, 195, 198, 202, 204, 205, 210, 212, 215, 216, 218, 220, 231, 232, 234, 235, 238, 242, 244, 248–250, 260, 264, 265, 268, 269, 303, 308, 312, 320, 325, 356, 360, 361
bridge → 22, 29, 39, 61, 65, 66, 84, 87, 123, 128, 139–141, 148–151, 167, 168, 177–181, 207, 208, 242, 270, 302, 316
brittle failure → 106
brittle fracture → 139
buckling → 87, 93, 101, 112, 114, 124, 125, 128, 129, 131, 136, 137, 143, 149, 151, 154, 170, 196, 200, 202, 206, 217, 263, 266
buckling length → 125, 131
building class → 54, 72
building code → 68, 69, 71–73, 78, 86, 92
building envelope → 60, 64–66, 79, 84, 85, 87, 91, 289, 309, 326, 360
building materials class → 38, 42, 44–46, 71
building services → 64, 65, 68, 70, 78, 94, 175, 226, 234

CAD → 77, 84, 85
callusing → 93
camber → 51, 137, 156, 181
cambium → 31
cantilever → 78, 114, 132, 133, 145, 147, 158, 165, 176, 177, 181, 183, 186, 232, 234, 236, 258, 260, 307
carbon dioxide → 30, 47, 48, 49
cast-in channel → 77, 123
cedar → 35, 41, 62, 361
cell cavity → 32
cell wall → 30, 32, 33, 47
cellular beam → 105
cellulose → 31, 32, 45, 46, 63, 218, 306, 307, 315
cement fibreboard → 30, 46
cement-bonded particleboard → 44
centering → 141, 270
chamfer → 38, 134
chemical wood preservative → 38, 39, 42
China → 15, 26, 27
chipboard → 73, 77, 105, 135, 242, 303, 314, 316, 323, 325
church → 16, 188, 194, 195, 204, 219, 227

cladding → 20, 39, 42, 61, 73, 148, 155, 181, 207, 224, 225, 229, 244, 254, 312, 330, 332, 355, 359
close tolerance bolt → 116, 221, 235
collar → 130, 138, 166, 192–194
column → 20, 28, 50, 52, 53, 90, 95, 98, 101–104, 109, 115, 123, 124, 127, 140, 142–147, 152, 154, 156, 169, 170, 172, 173, 175, 180, 181, 183–185, 195, 199, 200, 203, 204, 217–219, 222, 223, 227, 231, 232, 234–236, 238, 240, 241, 243, 248, 262, 263, 265, 270, 294, 295, 298, 302, 306–308, 312, 316, 318–320, 322, 324–327, 329, 330, 332, 354–358
compound section → 29, 77, 95–99, 106, 156, 176, 234, 242, 255, 267, 330
compression wood → 32, 39, 59
concrete → 64, 66–69, 73, 75, 94, 95, 97, 99, 101, 108, 114, 115, 123, 127, 135, 142, 143, 146, 152–154, 156, 160, 164, 165, 169, 171–175, 181–184, 186–190, 192, 194, 196, 198, 201, 204–209, 211, 213, 217, 219, 220, 228–233, 236, 240, 241, 243, 244, 246, 250, 255–258, 261, 263, 264, 266, 268, 270, 290, 301, 320, 325, 330, 333, 354, 355, 361, 365
condensation → 60–63
connector → 63, 77, 83, 106–108, 111, 114, 115, 117–119, 122, 144, 158, 162, 164, 166, 170, 178, 189, 190, 192, 215, 235, 255, 262, 264, 266, 268
construction moisture → 74, 127
continuous beam → 129, 181–183, 185, 222, 320
continuous purlin → 92, 130, 160, 209
conversion → 28, 38, 39, 49, 55, 65
converted timber → 47
corbel → 173, 218, 358
core → 30, 34, 35, 42, 43, 59, 155, 168, 204, 205, 233, 297, 298, 301, 305, 306, 309, 310, 312, 314, 320, 333, 358, 365
core plywood → 42, 155, 168, 233
corrosion → 63, 93, 115, 238, 247
cramp → 108
cranked system → 77, 133
creosote → 296
cross-laminated timber → 39, 51, 53, 77, 104, 290
cruciform → 98, 101, 144, 164, 232, 234, 308, 324, 325
cubic extent index → 78
cup → 58
curved beam → 102, 183, 197
cutting class → 56

Damage → 31–33, 39, 55, 56, 58, 59, 61, 63, 65, 73, 77, 94, 95
dead load → 78, 86, 139, 151, 187, 218, 228, 257, 260
debarking → 38
decking → 39, 43, 63, 80, 134, 135, 146, 152, 155, 160, 162, 164–166, 171, 172, 174, 182, 189, 190, 192–194, 203, 204, 206, 210, 212–214, 234, 235, 243, 246, 248, 249, 253, 259, 262
deep beam → 82, 87
deflection → 86, 87, 92, 106, 134, 135, 137, 139, 161, 165

deformation behaviour → 33, 43, 106, 109, 116, 129
diagonal → 39, 77, 80, 112, 118, 119, 126, 127, 130, 132, 134, 137, 144, 146, 147, 162–164, 171–173, 194, 196, 199, 205–207, 216, 224, 233, 234, 236–238, 243, 246, 249, 252–254, 258, 259, 261, 264, 265, 267, 269, 291, 313, 322, 332
diagonal boarding → 171
diagonal bracing → 132, 137, 144, 146, 205, 234
diagonal planking → 127, 134, 206, 224
disc spring washer → 197, 256
discoloration → 32, 39, 55, 59, 63
distortion → 39, 55, 59, 61
dome → 29, 139, 216, 217, 250–257, 361, 365
door → 65, 126, 223, 295–297, 302, 310–315, 322, 326, 329, 330, 356, 363
Douglas fir → 34, 38–44, 56, 58, 62, 100, 168, 181, 225, 267, 305, 317, 326
dowel → 83, 95, 111, 116, 117, 164, 166, 167, 170, 186, 201, 202, 206, 238, 258, 269, 296
dowelled beam → 97
drying → 12, 31, 33, 38–40, 49, 54, 55, 58, 61, 63, 96, 98, 156
duo beam → 40

Early wood → 31, 32, 34–37
eccentricity → 87, 106, 108, 137, 177
economic efficiency → 76, 79, 84, 85, 91, 95, 104, 106, 139
edge beam → 60, 87, 144, 155, 169, 172, 177, 179, 195, 208, 214, 219, 242, 247, 248, 258–260, 267, 297, 308, 312, 316, 323, 326, 330, 333, 357
edge member → 102, 252, 258, 259, 262–265, 297
edge-glued element → 224–231, 237, 242, 253–256, 267
edge-sawn log → 50, 82, 96, 223, 228
ekki → 39, 62
end grain → 32, 61, 91, 119, 122, 168, 206, 218, 230
end plate → 149, 160, 173, 185, 188, 202, 209, 212, 213, 217, 264, 319
energy → 30, 33, 47–49, 54, 64–67, 70, 74, 78, 317, 331
Energy Economy Act → 54, 64, 65
energy requirement → 47, 49, 64, 65, 67
environment → 24, 27, 47–49, 76
equilibrium moisture content → 33, 55, 100, 120
erection → 54, 55, 74, 75, 86–88, 90–93, 95, 97, 106, 122, 124, 131, 206, 210, 212, 217, 221, 226, 244, 264, 268, 356
eucalyptus → 31, 45, 46
Eurocode 5 → 77, 93
Europe → 8, 24, 28, 29, 31, 34–38
external wall → 42, 44, 46, 61, 63, 66–68, 71, 93, 224, 225, 246, 263

Fabrication → 61, 75, 76, 84–90, 93, 95, 106, 108, 110, 113, 115, 117, 124, 247
fabrication drawing → 84, 85, 89, 93, 110
facade → 20, 52, 53, 66, 67, 91, 125, 142, 143, 152, 157–159, 162, 185, 200,

203, 213, 218, 219, 225, 227, 230, 232, 236, 241, 243, 258, 265, 289–291, 294, 305, 313, 329, 330, 356, 362, 363
facing leaf → 46, 63
factor of safety → 106
factory → 49, 74, 93, 100, 105, 106, 113, 117, 119, 121, 140, 154, 172, 185, 221, 244
fastener → 113
felting → 41, 45, 46
fibreboard → 45, 46, 49, 73, 143, 307, 315
final drying → 98
finger joint → 39, 40, 51, 56, 90, 92, 93, 100, 103, 104, 120, 191, 196, 220
Finland → 11, 12, 20, 275
fir → 31, 34, 38–46, 56, 58, 62, 100, 168, 178, 181, 225, 237, 267, 293, 297–299, 301, 305, 317, 326
fire compartmentation → 72, 73
fire protection → 33, 71, 72, 73, 77, 78, 80, 82, 83, 90, 91, 95, 115, 135
fire resistance → 42, 71–73, 91, 95, 108, 115, 144, 179, 250, 251, 308, 324
fire resistance class → 91, 144, 250
firring piece → 303
fishplate → 108
fissure → 56, 59
fixed-base column → 79, 124, 200, 248, 258
fixing → 70, 122, 142, 169, 174, 252, 355
flame-retardant treatment → 43
flange → 121, 124, 135, 157, 228
flanking transmission → 69, 70
floor covering → 34, 35, 37, 43, 48, 60
floor joist → 95, 182
floor space index → 78
flooring → 36, 43, 49, 71, 143, 308, 314
folded plate → 103, 129, 136, 140, 190, 212, 242, 243
forest → 47–49, 76
formwork → 39, 44, 90, 95, 97, 142, 229, 252, 270
foundation → 24, 38, 76, 78, 88, 92, 94, 130, 148, 155, 181, 187, 201, 234, 236
four-piece beam → 40, 55, 56
frame → 17, 20, 28, 38, 39, 51, 53, 56, 60, 68, 70, 72, 75, 80, 81, 83, 86, 94, 98, 102, 103, 109, 115, 117, 120, 125–128, 130, 132, 133, 137, 138, 142–144, 147, 150, 152, 153, 157, 178, 180, 182, 184, 186, 189, 191, 192, 194, 200–205, 207, 208, 215, 218, 227, 234, 236, 239, 242, 244, 245, 251, 262, 266, 268, 270, 290, 292, 293, 297, 300, 305, 308, 310, 315, 317, 319, 320, 321, 324, 333, 354
France → 16, 21, 29, 50, 275, 283, 289
fungal attack → 34, 36, 93
furniture → 8, 34, 36, 37, 49, 73

Gable → 21, 130, 132, 158, 164, 166, 169, 194, 201, 206, 215, 251
general arrangement drawing → 88
glued joint → 99, 100, 120, 121
glued laminated timber → 30, 40, 38, 41, 43, 49, 50, 55–58, 71, 73, 77, 82, 83, 85, 90, 92, 93, 100–104, 109, 115, 119, 120, 124, 126, 128, 136, 143, 145, 149, 154, 155, 160, 161, 162, 165, 167–169, 171, 172, 175, 176, 179, 180, 182, 183, 185, 187, 189, 192–196, 200, 201, 204–206, 208–216, 219, 220, 225, 228–230, 232, 235, 237–239, 242, 245, 248, 249, 251–255, 258, 259, 262, 263, 264, 267, 296, 299, 305, 307, 356, 357, 361
grade → 39, 41, 55, 57, 88, 92, 93, 107, 179, 203, 319
grading → 32, 33, 38–40, 55–59, 82, 86, 92, 93, 100
grain → 20, 32, 34, 36, 37, 39, 40, 42, 43, 56, 58, 59, 61, 87, 91, 93, 98, 100, 102, 104, 106, 108, 109, 118, 119, 120,

123, 135, 168, 171, 197, 206, 208, 218, 221, 222, 230, 239, 242, 299
grain orientation → 34, 36
Greece → 25
greenhouse effect → 49
Greim system → 112, 160, 164
growth ring → 31, 32, 36, 37, 39, 93
gusset → 105, 112, 117, 147, 153, 159–161, 165, 171, 189, 195, 200, 254, 269
gusset plate → 112, 147, 153, 161, 165, 171, 195, 200, 269
guy → 75, 91, 125, 132, 178, 179, 263, 265, 270
gypsum → 44, 46
gypsum-bonded particleboard → 44, 45

Half-round section → 105
halved log → 40, 50, 82, 90, 96, 97, 135, 224, 230
halving joint → 108, 159, 165, 232, 239
hanger → 150, 153, 158, 174, 175, 190, 229, 238
hardboard → 244
hardwood → 29, 30, 38, 39, 57, 73, 106, 108, 109, 116, 118, 120, 158, 159, 180, 189, 196, 198, 205, 212, 221
haunch → 176, 180
heart shake → 56
heartwood → 31, 34–37, 62, 96
heat capacity → 64, 67
helical-threaded shank nail → 110
high-build coating → 355
hinge pin → 83, 113, 152, 161, 163, 165, 167–170, 173, 178, 188, 189, 190, 193, 208–210, 212, 213, 217, 219, 221, 233, 234, 264
hip → 192, 203, 205, 241, 246
horizontal force → 128, 131, 151, 160, 175, 182, 207, 232, 234, 242, 248, 249, 254, 263
horizontal load → 81, 124, 138, 143, 145, 147, 153, 166, 179, 189, 191, 193, 195, 197, 199, 201, 203, 205, 207, 211, 215, 243, 247, 248, 261, 267, 359
house → 16, 17, 25, 26, 28, 64, 66, 67, 99, 130, 141, 142, 228, 252, 276, 280, 290, 291, 294, 298, 300, 302, 303, 310, 317, 321, 322, 323, 326, 329, 363
humidity → 33, 62, 93, 100
HWS class → 42–44, 46
hyperbolic-paraboloid shell → 129

Ice rink → 84, 140, 141, 163, 184, 190, 191, 197, 206, 213, 215, 289
impact sound → 46, 68, 69, 91, 226
imposed load → 78, 88, 91, 124
infestation → 39, 56, 59, 63
infrastructure → 78
inner bark → 31, 56
insect attack → 34, 36, 43, 44, 62, 93
interior climate → 33, 47, 90, 100, 115, 120, 226
internal forces → 86, 87, 124, 138, 139
internal wall → 224, 226, 329
Italy → 8, 20, 22, 25, 29

Japan → 10, 14, 15, 20, 22, 25, 27, 276, 284, 286

Kerto → 42, 104, 298, 317
kiln drying → 38, 39, 49, 55, 156
kneebrace → 115, 210
knot → 56, 58, 59

Laced column → 124, 143
laminated veneer board → 221
laminated veneer lumber → 42, 49, 82, 92, 95, 104–106, 109, 121, 126, 128, 135, 136, 148, 170, 187, 197, 199, 250, 271, 298, 306
laminboard → 30, 43

larch → 31, 34, 38–41, 62, 82, 100, 148, 168, 177, 193, 268, 299, 301, 305, 310, 320, 322, 326, 327, 329, 332, 354, 359
late wood → 31, 32, 34, 35
lateral restraint → 117, 128, 129, 131, 137, 146, 148, 149, 151, 154, 158, 160, 186, 187, 198, 200, 203, 206, 208–210, 213, 215
lattice beam → 121, 129, 131, 134, 160, 161–165, 167, 178, 180–184, 191, 199, 203, 209–211, 221, 236–239, 358
lattice girder → 71, 87, 111, 112
lattice-type purlin → 77, 129
laying up in blocks → 102
life cycle assessment → 48, 49
lignin → 31, 32, 41
lignum vitae → 32
lime → 31, 321
linear member → 38, 41, 50, 83, 87, 103, 104, 137–140, 148–151, 188–195
lining → 42, 223, 318, 332, 363
log → 28, 50, 96–98, 127, 142, 156, 222, 223, 226, 248, 260, 270
log beam → 50, 222
log column → 50, 142, 222, 231, 248, 254, 260, 270, 294
louvres → 181, 319, 325, 326, 333, 355
low-energy building → 54, 64–66, 317
low-strength wood → 40, 96

Machine grading → 32, 55, 57
machining → 38
masonry → 64, 65, 67–69, 94, 108, 114, 115, 127, 142, 143, 198, 210, 221, 290
mast → 8, 12, 28, 125, 138, 139, 141, 269
medium board → 45
medium density fibreboard → 45, 49
melamine resin → 56, 120
Mero node → 239, 241
modulus of elasticity → 55, 92–94, 139, 161, 163, 165
moisture content → 32–34, 36, 38–40, 42, 55, 58, 60, 61, 63, 90–93, 99, 100, 106, 108, 109, 120
moment → 81, 82, 96, 97, 101, 102, 124, 137, 185, 187, 235
moment of inertia → 81, 82, 97, 101, 124
moulding → 105
multiple shear → 83, 107, 111, 191
multistorey structure → 75, 76

Nail plate → 113, 122, 152, 153, 155, 162, 163, 166–168, 172, 175, 186, 190, 200, 208, 221, 234, 250, 251, 264–268
nailing → 110–114, 135, 243, 263
nail-pressure gluing → 95, 99, 101, 102, 120, 197
non-destructive testing → 92, 94
notch → 28, 95, 100, 177, 232, 247

Oak → 28, 32, 37, 39, 44, 57, 62, 71, 82, 174, 227, 237, 268, 316, 362, 363
oblique dado joint → 108, 109, 148, 150–152, 158, 166, 191–193, 198, 270
offices → 144, 224, 248, 291, 300, 307
open joint → 51, 60, 61, 259, 290, 291
open planking → 51
orientation → 34, 36, 66, 78, 289
oriented strand board → 30, 44, 49, 104, 120
outer bark → 31
out-of-plumb effect → 124, 125, 261
oven-dry density → 32, 73, 92, 93
oven-dry method → 93
overturning → 81, 87, 93, 124, 136, 190

Panel → 38, 44–46, 66, 75, 77, 102, 104, 121, 122, 127, 135, 142, 221, 290, 292, 298, 308, 319, 320, 354, 357
paper → 10, 46–48, 225, 292, 303
parallel strand lumber → 104, 184, 358

parallel-grain plywood → 135
partial restraint → 87, 124
particleboard → 49, 128, 182, 308, 311, 312, 316, 319, 323–325, 330, 354
partition → 296, 330
party wall → 304, 319
pavilion → 21, 141, 145, 214, 234, 257, 262, 279, 283, 291, 360
phenol-resorcinol resin → 56
pine → 31, 34, 35, 82, 100, 167, 227, 269, 315
pinned joint → 83, 113, 115, 156, 163
pinned-end column → 101, 142, 143, 159, 169, 171, 191, 205, 234, 238, 241
pith → 31, 32
plain-edge boards → 305
plane frame → 81, 87, 162, 182, 186, 190, 192, 202
planing → 100, 105
plank → 98
planking → 127, 134, 135, 206, 207, 224, 233, 238, 245
plasterboard → 134, 297, 302–304, 311, 312, 314, 317, 320, 354, 355
plastic → 8, 90, 95, 105, 180, 208, 253, 268, 360
plate → 9–23, 77, 83, 95, 103–106, 112, 113, 117–119, 127, 129, 135, 136, 142–144, 147–150, 152, 153, 155, 159, 162, 164–176, 178, 179, 182, 183, 185, 186, 188–190, 192–203, 205, 207, 209, 210–213, 215, 216–226, 230–232, 235–239, 241–243, 245, 247, 250, 251, 254–256, 258, 259, 262, 264, 265, 268, 269, 270, 273–288, 295, 303, 309, 310, 312, 313, 319, 326, 327, 329, 330, 333, 361
platform construction → 53, 302
plywood → 30, 34–36, 82, 90, 95, 106, 108, 109, 117, 120, 117, 128, 135, 136, 149, 155, 157, 159, 165, 168, 172, 174, 176, 179, 181, 183, 190, 197, 208, 221, 223, 231, 233, 242, 243, 245, 256, 292, 295, 298, 301–306, 310, 314, 315, 319–321, 326, 327, 330, 333, 355, 356, 358
pockets drawing → 88
pole construction → 96, 146, 147
pool → 79, 140, 141, 172, 238, 255, 258
porous wood fibre insulating board → 45, 46
post-and-beam construction → 125
post-and-rail construction → 53
precamber → 97, 103
predrilled hole → 112, 116, 117, 123
predrilling → 111, 112, 153
prefabricated → 29, 74, 75, 106, 121, 142, 149, 153, 187, 196, 212, 226, 244, 251, 257, 290, 291, 314, 319, 332, 354
prefabrication → 74, 75, 297, 298, 305, 306, 310, 315, 317, 321, 354
primary beam → 52, 121, 152, 162, 164, 174, 175, 237
primary structural system → 79, 80, 85, 86, 103, 124, 242
profiled section → 41, 82, 96, 98, 99, 102, 104, 120
progress chart → 91
prop → 108, 109, 125, 132, 142, 143, 146, 149, 150, 153, 158, 165, 186, 189, 191, 194, 202, 205, 243, 263
proportion of knots → 55, 59
punched metal plate fastener → 39, 77, 113, 160
purlin → 97, 108, 114, 128, 132, 135, 137, 147, 150, 158, 162, 163, 166, 176, 181, 188, 189, 193, 196, 200, 202, 207, 209, 214, 216, 220, 223, 241, 262, 264, 295, 316, 356
purlin frame → 77, 128, 132, 135, 137

Quality assurance → 38, 139
quality control → 76, 90, 92, 102

quartered log → 40, 50, 98
quartered squared log → 50, 225

Rafter → 102, 135, 166, 193, 194, 204, 223, 233, 241, 305, 307
rate of charring → 73
ray → 31
reactions drawing → 88, 91
recycling → 41, 46, 49, 74, 141, 264
refurbishment → 39, 77, 94, 95, 135, 150, 269
relieving groove → 38, 50, 61, 91, 96, 97–99, 223, 225, 228, 235, 295
resawing → 38
residual strength → 77, 94
resin → 31, 32, 34–37
resin pocket → 32, 39, 55, 57, 93
resorcinol-formaldehyde resin → 100
resultant load → 125, 126, 131, 132
ridge → 26
rigid corner → 103, 186
rigid frame → 180, 199, 207
rigid joint → 83
ring shake → 58
ripewood tree → 31
risk class → 54, 60, 62
robinia → 31
rocker bearing → 168, 188, 209
roller shutter → 67
Rome → 25, 29
roof → 21, 26
rot → 56, 58, 59, 62, 63, 92, 94
rough sawn → 39, 55, 82
round section → 39, 41, 51, 96, 105, 122, 169, 218
round wire nail → 110, 111

Safety factor → 91, 93, 139
sapwood → 31, 34–36, 57, 62
sawing → 39, 41, 50, 51, 105
sawmill → 39, 49, 85, 92
sawn → 34, 35, 38–41, 47, 49, 55–59, 77, 82, 92, 96–100, 112, 148, 156, 159, 168, 178, 223–225, 228, 245, 293, 295, 332
sawn timber → 38, 47, 49, 55, 57, 59, 77, 92, 98–100, 156, 224, 225
scaffold → 39, 77, 122
scarf joint → 42, 92, 108, 220
school → 140, 141, 170, 171, 218, 228, 231, 234, 273, 278, 291
secondary beam → 52, 99, 121, 152, 155, 162, 174, 175, 182–186, 191, 197, 203, 210, 213, 214, 216, 234, 237, 323
secondary structural system → 80, 85
self-tapping connector → 111
shakes → 35, 56, 58, 59, 95, 100, 311
shear → 46, 55, 83, 86, 87, 95, 98, 105–108, 110, 113, 118, 119, 122, 123, 127, 134, 136, 138, 142, 143, 145, 152, 156, 166, 173, 174, 190, 191, 200, 201, 204, 216, 217, 219, 220, 221, 229, 230, 233, 235, 241, 244, 258, 260, 263, 264, 265
shear connector → 108, 142, 173, 190, 204, 229, 264
shear force → 95, 106, 174, 217, 221, 230, 233, 235, 241, 260
shear plane → 107
shear strength → 95, 105, 244, 265
shear wall → 127, 142, 143
shear-plate connector → 118, 166, 220
shell → 79, 103, 105, 129, 211, 214, 244–249, 251–253, 255–260, 263–265, 271
shingles → 35
ship → 12, 28
shrinkage → 32, 34–36, 55, 58–61, 63, 87, 91, 93, 95, 96, 98, 100, 106, 116, 119, 123, 127, 227, 299
side boards → 230
simply-supported beam → 157, 171
single-pin frame → 141, 196, 197
single-storey shed → 63, 73, 76, 91, 98,

121, 125
single-storey structure → 52
slab → 44, 45, 67, 69, 70, 95, 105, 123, 142, 292, 333
slenderness ratio → 87, 136, 143, 356
slip modulus → 106, 139
slope of grain → 39, 58, 59, 93
sloping grain → 32, 87, 92
snow load → 78, 86, 124, 153, 184, 197, 207, 211, 222, 224, 261, 265
soft rot → 62
softboard → 305, 317
softwood → 30, 38–40, 42, 49, 55–58, 100, 148, 156, 160, 180, 188, 210, 224, 233, 234, 242, 248, 319, 321, 357, 361
solar energy → 47–49, 64, 66, 331
sole plate → 53, 150, 182, 223–225, 295, 303, 309–313, 319, 327, 329, 330, 333
solid timber → 30, 32, 33, 39–41, 50, 54–56, 69, 73, 75, 80, 92, 95, 116, 125, 158, 189, 194, 204–206, 213, 244, 261, 268, 307, 356
solid-web beam → 121, 129, 131, 134–136, 156, 234, 242
sound insulation → 45, 46, 68–71, 77, 78, 91, 94, 95, 135, 204, 226
sound pressure level → 68
sound reduction index → 68–70
space frame → 39, 43, 51, 77, 80, 139–141, 239, 241, 267, 268
spandrel panel → 61, 308, 354
special services → 87, 91
spiral grain → 36, 37
splice → 116, 117, 119, 120, 167, 182–184, 216, 220, 221, 268, 269
split-heart conversion → 55
split-ring connector → 95, 119, 122, 166, 206, 216
sports centre → 140, 160, 196, 199, 250
sports stadium → 141, 211, 220
spring → 59, 123, 190, 197, 256
spruce → 31, 32, 35, 38, 42–46, 49, 56, 58, 82, 92, 154, 155, 233, 237, 240, 292, 296, 298, 306, 308, 310, 313, 318, 332, 356, 362, 363, 365
squared log → 50, 51, 61, 98, 99, 225
squared section → 39, 40, 50, 55, 56, 58, 59, 82, 90, 96, 98, 99, 105, 121, 127, 128, 132, 146, 224, 227–229, 243, 254–257, 270
stability → 34–37, 39–41, 46, 51, 75, 76, 79–81, 87, 91, 93, 104, 124, 130, 131, 136–139, 146–149, 151, 152, 159, 160, 165, 171, 172, 189, 191, 192, 196, 200, 201, 204, 205, 211, 213, 214, 216, 236, 238, 240, 244, 248, 253, 258, 268, 269
stairs → 37, 43, 48, 55, 69, 102, 267, 332
standardisation → 74
stave → 28, 223, 224
steel → 29, 71, 73, 75, 81, 83, 89, 90, 93, 107, 109, 112–120, 122, 125, 126, 128, 130, 131, 133, 136, 137, 142, 144, 145–151, 153–156, 158–163, 166–171, 173, 174, 177–182, 184–190, 192, 194–196, 198–222, 228, 232–241, 243, 245–248, 250, 251, 253, 255–261, 263–268, 270, 290, 296, 300–302, 305, 308, 310, 311, 314, 315, 317, 320, 326, 329, 330, 333, 354, 355, 359, 361
stepped oblique dado → 109
stiffness → 77, 81, 95, 104, 106, 126, 131, 132, 134, 136, 226, 235, 255, 260
storage → 31, 32, 36, 54, 61, 75, 90, 93, 115, 226, 330, 331
streaks → 35, 37, 56, 58, 59
stressed-skin structure → 43, 140
strip → 56, 69, 155, 187, 200, 209, 213, 252, 256, 297, 306, 319, 325, 332
structural calculations → 78, 85, 86, 88, 94, 139
structural drawing → 84, 85, 88, 89, 91

structural model → 106
structural system → 76, 77, 79, 81, 83–88, 103, 106, 124, 129, 211, 242
structural veneer lumber → 30, 42
structure-borne sound → 68, 69, 70
strut → 81, 103, 109, 115, 148, 152, 161, 164, 166, 170, 173, 184, 186, 188, 191, 194, 198, 199, 209, 218, 229, 270, 300
strut frame → 81, 148, 152, 153, 197
sunshade → 325
sunshading → 66, 67, 307, 360
support → 20, 32, 79, 86, 99, 115, 122, 144–146, 149, 150, 152, 155, 156, 160, 163, 165, 169, 170, 172, 173, 178, 179, 184–186, 200, 201, 203, 209, 211, 212, 215–218, 220, 221, 229, 235, 236, 240, 241, 245, 246, 249, 254, 261–267, 270, 293, 330, 358
surface finish → 39, 41, 51, 55, 93
swelling → 32, 60, 61, 63, 91, 227, 299
Switzerland → 17, 20–22, 28, 29, 50, 157, 274, 277, 278

Taper → 96
teak → 39, 62
temporary works → 77, 91, 93, 122
tender drawing → 88
tenon → 108, 155, 180
tension connection → 119, 177, 220, 223
tensioning element → 77, 123
tertiary structural system → 80
texture → 34, 36
thermal bridge → 64, 66
thermal insulation → 32, 45–47, 63–68, 72, 77, 79, 80, 90, 91, 94, 211, 220, 224, 225, 253, 297, 302–304, 306, 307, 309, 311–314, 316, 318, 320, 322–327, 329–333, 356, 357, 362, 363, 365
thermal performance → 64–66, 82, 91
thermal transmittance value → 65
three-pin arch → 141, 206, 213–217
three-pin frame → 86, 120, 133, 137, 141, 147, 188–192, 194, 195, 200, 201, 203–206, 262
tie → 29, 86, 103, 133, 137, 161, 162, 170, 171, 176, 178, 188–192, 194, 195, 197–201, 203, 204, 207, 208, 210, 217, 229, 237, 243, 245, 248, 249, 263, 264, 270, 300, 308
timber packing → 302
timber preservative → 35, 100
timber spacer → 143, 144, 243, 252, 253, 256, 264, 361
timber stud element → 314
timber-concrete composite construction → 95, 97, 135, 228, 230, 231
timber-frame construction → 28, 38, 39, 51, 53, 60, 72, 75, 127, 143, 144, 200, 290, 292, 293, 305, 319, 320, 324
tolerance → 77, 116, 117, 144, 166, 167, 177, 221, 235, 239
tongue and groove board → 144, 241, 262, 300, 303, 304, 313, 325, 326
toothed-plate connector → 106, 118, 176, 178, 200, 215, 230, 231, 235, 255
top chord → 132, 135, 149, 157, 159, 161–165, 167, 169–171, 173, 180–183, 185, 188, 189, 191, 199, 203, 207, 210, 212, 236–238, 241, 243, 260, 307
torsion → 87, 106, 160, 172, 239, 260
tower → 125, 227, 260, 261, 267, 270, 291, 365
transparent thermal insulation → 66, 253, 307, 330, 331
transport → 31, 61, 65, 74–76, 86, 88, 90, 91, 93, 100, 103, 106
trapezoidal profile metal sheeting → 127, 175, 196, 198, 220
trio beam → 40, 55
trunk → 30–32, 38, 41, 51, 55, 59, 94, 178
truss → 81, 83, 87, 108, 117, 119, 128–

135, 137, 138, 146, 150, 152, 158, 160, 161, 168, 170, 171, 184, 186, 219, 225, 242, 269, 316, 318
trussed beam → 117, 137, 150, 151, 179, 185
tubular particleboard → 105
turnbuckle → 133
twist → 40, 51, 58, 87, 123
two-pin arch → 141, 208–211, 246
two-pin frame → 141,150, 198, 199, 204, 211
two-span beam → 149, 181, 195

Ultimate strength → 139
ultrasound → 92, 94
underfloor heating → 67
upper chord → 106, 137, 239
USA → 11, 271, 276, 290, 293, 302

Valley → 180, 182, 206
vapour barrier → 62, 193, 253, 297, 299, 301, 303, 305, 312–314, 316–319, 320, 322, 325, 327, 329, 330, 332, 333, 354, 356–358
vapour check → 62
veneer → 30, 34–36, 42, 43, 49, 77, 82, 92, 95, 104–106, 108, 109, 121, 126, 128, 134–136, 148, 170, 187, 197, 199, 221, 242, 250, 271, 298, 306, 317, 326, 355, 356
ventilation → 21, 61, 62, 64–66, 73, 78, 79, 90, 160, 182, 258, 294, 298, 326, 329, 355, 363
vertical → 37, 60, 78, 87, 99, 102, 104, 112, 134, 138, 143, 145, 147, 149, 151–153, 155, 157, 159, 161–167, 169–171, 173, 175, 177, 179, 181, 183, 185, 187, 189, 191–193, 195, 197–199, 201, 203, 205, 207, 209, 211, 213, 215, 217, 219, 221, 223–226, 229, 231, 234, 235, 238, 241–243, 247, 248, 254, 256, 259, 260, 262, 289–291, 293, 299, 302–304, 306, 313, 314, 316, 323, 329, 332, 356, 358
vibration → 68, 91, 95, 135, 139
Vierendeel girder → 155, 220
visual grading → 39, 55, 57–59, 82, 92

Wane → 39, 40, 55, 59
waste → 41, 47, 49, 74, 78, 264
wavy grain → 36
weatherboarding → 41, 51, 60, 145, 181, 290, 291, 310, 316, 325, 327, 354, 363
web → 50, 82, 98, 104, 111, 121, 128–131, 134–137, 155, 157, 170–176, 179, 186, 194–196, 199, 201, 204, 206, 208, 213, 234, 235, 242, 243, 251, 321
welded steel connector → 117, 182
wet process → 41, 45
width of the annual rings → 59
wind bracing → 101, 126, 178
wind girder → 122, 130–132, 147, 150, 158, 159, 162, 163, 167, 171, 196, 208, 209, 220, 266, 267
wind load → 78, 87, 126, 128, 130, 131, 138, 151, 190, 194, 202, 256, 264, 269
window → 49, 56, 65–67, 69, 72, 126, 294, 300, 306, 310, 317–319, 354– 356, 363
wood fibreboard → 45, 46, 73, 143, 307, 315
wood preservative → 38, 39, 42–44, 54, 62, 63, 120, 177, 225
wood screw → 111, 212, 239, 268
wood-based product → 41–43, 47, 48, 60, 61, 63, 70, 71, 92, 95, 109, 120, 127, 134, 135, 200
working drawing → 77, 78, 86, 87, 89, 91
workmanship → 65, 69, 77, 93, 109, 112, 124, 137, 139

Zollinger construction → 141, 246, 297, 298, 301, 306, 310, 314, 320, 333, 358

Index of architects and engineers

Aalto, A. → 12
Ahrends, P. → 218
Amberg Building Department → 242
Ando, T. → 145
Archbishopric Building Department,
   Freiburg → 188
Arndt, R. → 150
Arretche, L. → 219
Arup, O. → 265
Atelier 4 → 169
Atelier Cube → 332
Atelier Gamma Architectore → 174
Auer (+ Weber) → 346
Avia Plan Architects → 183

Bächle, M. → 305
Ban, S. → 217
Banholzer, D. → 151
Banholzer, H. → 151
Barthel, (Wenzel, Frese, Pörtner,
   Haller) → 265
Bäuerle, W. → 286, 320
Bearth, V. → 310
Beck, (Enz, Yelin) → 356
Bellmann, G. → 230
Belz, (Kammerer + Partner) → 235
Berchthold, H. → 271
Berger, P. → 357
Bertsche, (Packenbach, Hübner)
   → 236, 260
Bétrix, M.-C., (Consolascio, E.)
   → 306
Bieler, W. → 148, 156, 173, 206
Bienefeld, H., N. → 298
Biong & Biong, (Torp, N.) → 211
Biro-Biro → 160
Bittcher-Zeitz, T. → 346
Blumer AG → 251
Bonfig, P. → 280
Bosch, (+ Herrmann) → 187
Botta, M. → 225
Branger, (Conzett & Partner) → 168
Brechbühl, (Itten I+B) → 278, 351
Briccola, R. → 277, 301
Brinkhaus, H. → 322
Brüninghoff Building Department → 216
Brunner, H. → 153
Buchs, P., (+ Plumey, J. L.) → 207
Burger, (Riemerschmid, Schützenhuber)
   → 192
Burkhalter, M., (Sumi, C.) → 333, 345
Burkhard, (Meyer, Steiger) → 212
Burlanek, P. → 152
Büro Vier → 147
Burton, R. → 218
Busse, von, H. B., B. → 342

Calatrava, S. → 212
Caldas, J. M. → 294
Cantonal Building Department, Burg-
   dorf → 208
Carduner, M., (+ Partner) → 255
Caspari, H. → 171
Central Planning Office, Kiel → 201
Central railways, Building Department,
   MBS project group → 270
Choukalos, (Woodburn, McKenzie,

Maranda Ltd) → 184
Christen, F. → 204
Clavuot, C. → 299
Collomb, G. M. → 322
Consolascio, E., (Bétrix, M.-C.) → 306
Conzett, (Branger & Partner) → 168

D´Inka, (+ Scheible) → 199
Dahms, (Grube, Harden, Kaiser,
   Laskowski) → 186
Deggendorf Building Department → 190
de Meuron, P., (Herzog, J.) → 276, 348
Department of Federal Building
   Works, Lausanne → 158
Deplazes, A. → 310
Despang Architekten → 226
Devaliere, J. F. →
Dietiker, R., (Klaus, B. + Keller, R.)
   → 315
Dietrich, R. → 22, 352
Dilcher-Tobey, W. → 319
Dittmann, E. and S. → 312
Dittrich, (+ Natterer, Planungs-
   gesellschaft) → 144, 147, 152, 160,
   165, 166, 169, 182, 189, 192, 195,
   203, 232, 234, 235, 238, 242f., 264
Döring, W. → 303
Drexel, R. → 221

Eberl, M. → 189
Eberle, (+ Hartmann) → 154
Echenique, M. → 334
Effeff AG → 253
Enz, (Beck, Yelin) → 356
Erkler, D. → 273

Fahr + Partner PFP → 144, 308
Fahr, R. E. → 144, 308
Fahr-Deistler, A. → 144, 308
Falterer, (Wagner, Wanner) → 165
Faust, (+ Heuer) → 170
Fink, D., (Jocher, T.) → 352
Fink, H. (Polónyi, S.) → 245
Fischer, (Glaser, Kretschmer, Kreft)
   → 172
Flach, M. → 196, 255
Francis, M. → 149
Frank, A. (W. Wicker KG) → 243
Freund, M. (Ospelt, H.) → 228
Frese, (Wenzel, Pörtner, Haller,
   Barthel) → 265
Frode (& Sasse) → 248
Frommlet Zimmerei und
   Ingenieurholzbau AG → 154
Fuchs, (Mahler, Günster) → 279, 286,
   347, 349, 353
Führer, (Kosch, Stein) → 170
Füller, F., (Architektengemeinschaft)
   → 210

Gärtl AG → 180
Galfetti, A. → 225
Gasser, H. → 259
Gaupp, (+ Jauss) → 314
Geier, (+ Geier) → 265
Geierstanger, H., (University Building

Department, Weihenstephan) → 152, 200
Genie Bataillon 10 → 177
Gerstlauer, (+ Mohne) → 156
Giacomazzi, F. (+ Assoziati Architetti)
   → 161
Glaser, (Fischer, Kretschmer, Kreft)
   → 172
Glaser, W. → 346
Gnutzmann, D. (Ingenieurbüro kgs) → 260
Grube, (Dahms, Harden, Kaiser,
   Laskowski) → 186
Günster, (Mahler, Fuchs) → 279, 286,
   347, 349, 353

Haag, (von Ohlen, Rüffer und Partner)
   → 179, 359
Haas, P. → 240
Habisreutinger, K. → 346
Häussermann, P. → 164
Hagmüller, H. → 344
Haller, (Wenzel, Frese, Pörtner, Barthel)
   → 265
Happold, E. → 218
Harden, (Dahms, Grube, Kaiser,
   Laskowski) → 186
Harju, R. → 250
Harries, (+ Kinkel) → 207
Hartmann, (+ Eberle) → 154
Hauser, G. → 64
Hecker, H. D. → 258
Heene, A. → 316
Hegger (Hegger, Schleiff) → 282, 336
Heikkilä, P. → 250
Hempel, A. → 194
Herrmann, (+ Bosch) → 187
Herrschmann, D. → 171
Herzog, J., (de Meuron, P.) → 276, 348
Herzog, T. → 8, 179, 182, 233, 260,
   272, 280, 284, 289, 326f., 329, 331,
   355, 359
Heuer, (+ Faust) → 170
Hiatus → 196
High Executive Committee of the
   Kingdom of Saudi Arabia → 239
Hilzinger, C. → 346
Hinkes, F.-J. → 262
Hirzle, W. → 266
Hisatoku, (Maeno, Wada, Nagase)
   → 257
Hitzler, K. → 146
Hochbauamt Osnabrück → 268
Hofer, H. → 350
Hoffmann, J. → 12
Hofmann, K. → 157
Holzbauwerk Kaufmann → 209
Hrdlovics, C. → 350
Huber, H. → 318
Hübner, (Bertsche, Packenbach)
   → 236ff.
Hugues, T. → 313

ICS Bois → 254f.
IEZ Natterer GmbH → 260
Ingenieria Obra Civil → 145
Itagaki, M. (Sugimoto, H.) → 276
Ito, T. → 286, 361
Itten, (+ Brechbühl, I+B) → 278, 351

Jauss, (+ Gaupp) → 314
Jaussaud, (+ Vallières) → 213
Jean, P. → 323
Jourda, F. → 149, 282f., 336
Juranek, D. → 164

Kaiser, (Dahms, Grube, Harden,
   Laskowski) → 186
Kajima Design (+ Saito, M.) → 217
Kammerer, (+ Belz + Partner) → 235
Kämpf, G. → 205
Kamunen, R. → 12
Karpf, M. → 166
Kathan, A. → 278, 350
Kaufmann, (Merz, Partner) → 155, 221
Kaufmann, H. → 258
Kaufmann, L. → 209
Keller, R. → 315
Kessel, M. (Ingenieurbüro kgs) → 260
Kibayasni, M., (Kikutake & Ass.) → 257
Kikutake & Ass., (Kibayasni, M.) → 257
Kinkel, (+ Harries) → 270
Klaus, B., (Dietiker, R.) → 315
Kling, W. → 185
Kohl, H. → 324
Koralek, P. → 218
Kosch, (Führer, Stein) → 170
Kovatsch, M. → 277
Krähenbühl → 206
Kreft, (Fischer, Glaser, Kretschmer)
   → 172
Kretschmer, (Fischer, Glaser, Kreft)
   → 172
Kübler, Holzbaufirma → 269
Kuhlmann, (Biro-Biro) → 160
Küttinger, G. and I. → 202, 316

Ladner, D. → 310
Lang, L. M. → 264
Larsens, H. → 286
Laskowski, (Dahms, Grube, Harden,
   Kaiser) → 186
Lau, K. → 184
Lauri, J. → 11
Lehmbrock, J. → 246
Leins, W., (+ Zweifel, J.) → 153
Leiska, (Pook, Partner) → 185
Levandowsky, A. → 304
Lieberum, (+ Steckstor, Ingenieurgem.)
   → 226
Liermann, K. → 188
Limmer, J. → 163
Linie 4 → 305
Linkwitz, (Preuss) → 265
Lintl (+ Siebenson) → 200
Logerai, J.-P. → 254
Lourdin, R. → 142
Lucernario → 214
Ludwig, M. → 313
Lyndon, (MLTW / Moore Turnbull,
   Whitaker) → 276, 293

Maeno, (Wada, Nagase, Hisatoku)
   → 257
Mahler, (Günster Fuchs) → 279, 286,
   347, 349, 353
Mahler, K., (+ Schäfer, J.) → 325

Makovecz, I. → 273, 362, 363
Malknecht, K. → 191
Mangeat, V. → 244
Maranda, (Choukalos, Woodburn,
  McKenzie Ltd) → 184
Markwalder, A. → 271
Marugg, H. → 173
Maurer, K. → 311
May, (Menli) → 249
Mayer, (+ Plüss) → 215
Mayer, E. → 306
McKenzie, (Choukalos, Woodburn,
  Maranda Ltd) → 184
mecanoo architekten → 286
Menli, (May) → 249
Meid-Bächle, K. → 305
Meier, (+ Wachter) → 203
Meier, H. and L. → 158
Meier, R. → 302
Meier-Scupin, J. P. → 276
Meinhardt, H. → 191
Merz, (Kaufmann Partner) → 155, 221
Merz, K. (and J. Natterer) → 184
Meyer, (Burkhard, Steiger) → 212
Mezei, G. → 273
Michael, C. → 204
Milbrandt, E. → 167
Mohn, H. → 201
Mohne, (Gerstlauer) → 156
Moix Ingenieur Conseil Sàrl → 222
Moore, (MLTW / Lyndon, Turnbull,
  Whitaker) → 276, 293
Moosbrugger, Ingenieurbüro → 221
Mutschler, C. (+ Partner) → 256

Nagase, (Maeno, Wada, Hisatoku)
  → 257
Nagashina, M. → 223, 295
Nagler, F. → 155, 297
Naito, H. → 193, 284, 341
Natterer Bois-Consult → 142, 153, 157f.,
  174, 176ff., 184, 186, 190, 197, 207,
  222, 225, 228, 230f., 237, 244, 248f.,
  253, 263, 267
Natter +Dittrich, Planungsgesellschaft
  → 144, 147, 152, 160,
  165f., 169, 182, 189, 192, 195, 203,
  232ff., 238, 242f., 264
Natterer J. → 76, 140, 162f., 175, 198,
  202, 254f.,
Nebgen, N. → 241
Neumaier, K. → 146

Ohlen, von, (Haag, Rüffer und Partner)
  → 179, 359
Ollertz (+ Ollertz) → 247
Ospelt, H. (Freund, M.) → 228
Otto, F. → 218, 256, 262

Packenbach, (Bertsche, Hübner) → 236
Palladio, A. → 22
Passau Building Department → 224
Peiry, G. → 222
Perraudin, G. → 149, 282f., 336
Peyret, C. → 337
Pfefferkorn + Partner → 187
Piano, R. Building Workshop
  → 283f., 360
Pini (+ Assoziati Ingegneria) → 161
Plan GmbH → 175
Planungsgruppe Gesternig → 262
Plumey, J. L. (& Buchs, P.) → 207
Plüss (& Mayer) → 215
Pollak, H. → 159
Polónyi, S. (Fink, H.) → 245
Pook, (Leiska, Partner) → 185
Pörtner, (Wenzel, Frese, Haller, Barthel)
  → 265
Pottelsberghe de la Potterie, von, J.
  → 251
Preuss, (Linkwitz) → 265

Prüfer, W. → 172
Python, A. and J. → 176

Regional Postal Directorate, Munich → 232
Reichel, A. → 354
Reiter, F. → 350
Relling, T. → 181
Reuter → 198
Reynaud, M. → 357
Rice, P. → 149
Riehle, W. → 241
Riemerschmid, R. → 12
Riemerschmid, (Burger, Schützenhuber)
  → 192
Rinn Holzbau → 270
Ritchie, J. → 149
Röder, T. → 316
Romero, S. → 318
Rüffer, (Haag, von Ohlen und Partner)
  → 179, 359

Sailer, (Stephan) → 179, 194, 233
Saito, M. (Kajima Design) → 217
Sakamoto, K. → 276, 338
Sasse (+ Frode) → 248
Schäfer, J., (+ Mahler, K.) → 325
Schaffhausen Building Department → 215
Schankula, A. → 233
Schattner, K.-J. → 159
Schaudt Architekten → 278, 344
Schauer, U. → 321
Scheible, (+D´Inka) → 199
Scherberger, M. → 258
Schilling, B. → 182, 280
Schleiff, (Hegger, Hegger) → 282, 336
Schloffer, G. → 311
Schlude, (Ströhle) → 317
Schlup, A. → 237
Schnabel, R. → 210
Schneider, R. → 355
Schneider-Wessling, E. → 322
Schnieder, F. → 268
Scholz, G. → 263
Schrade, H. J. → 233, 355
Schranz, M. → 278, 350
Schulitz, H. C. (+ Partner) → 339
Schulting, K. → 246
Schützenhuber, (Riemerschmid, Burger)
  → 192
Schwarz, E. → 199
Schwarzmann, S. → 350
Schweiger, P. → 246
Schweitzer, R. → 24, 142f., 275, 304,
  323, 337
Seifert, W. → 268
Seki, H. → 295
Sengler, D. → 167
Siebenson, (+ Lintl) → 200
Sirèn, H. und K. → 275
Sirola, N. → 296
Speich, M. → 239, 262
Stainer, J. → 10
State Building Department, Munich → 234
State Building Department, Nuremberg
  → 238
Stauß, E. → 300, 340
Steckstor (+ Lieberum, Ingenieurgem.)
  → 226
Steidle, O. → 162, 324
Steiger, (Burkhard, Meyer) → 212
Steigerwald, B. → 179, 359
Stein, (Führer, Kosch) → 170
Stephan, K. (Sailer) → 179, 194, 233
Streib, M. → 280, 319, 331
Ströhle, (Schlude) → 317
Strolz, E. → 278, 350
Structural Design Group → 193
Studio Technico Cenci Otsuka → 214
Sugimoto, H. (Igataki, M.) → 276
Sumi, C., (Burkhalter, M.) → 333, 345

Taba, B. → 365
Tabery → 227
Then Bergh, R. + R. → 309
Thut, D. und R. → 335
TIS (und Partner) → 252
Tobey, R. → 319
Torp, N. (Biong + Biong) → 211
Trabert, (+ Partner) → 247
Trafojer, F. → 191
Trubka, L. → 184
Turnbull, (MLTW / Moore, Lyndon,
  Whitaker) → 276, 293

U.B.E. → 219
Ungers, O. M. → 245
University Building Department, Weihen-
stephan → 152
Usleber, J. → 181

Valliéres, (+ Jaussaud) → 213
Vaud Motorway Department → 178
Velez, S. → 21
Vogel, H. → 208
Vogel, P. → 332
Vogeley, J. → 150
Volhard, F. → 321
Volz, M. → 31, 60, 280, 289, 307,
  328, 330

Wachter, (+ Meier) → 203
Wada, (Maeno, Nagase, Hisatoku)
  → 257
Wagner, (Wanner, Falterer) → 165
Wagner, G. → 68, 71
Walder, H. → 150
Waldner, Dr., AG → 251
Wälli, Ing. Büro; AG → 240
Walter, I. → 148, 322
Wangler, U. → 340
Wanner, (Wagner, Falterer) → 165
Weber, (+ Auer) → 346
Wegener, G. → 47
Weihenstephan Building Department
  (Geierstanger, H.) → 200
Weippert, H. → 189
Weisrock S.A., R. → 196
Wenger, H. and P. → 259
Wenzel, (Frese, Pörtner, Haller, Barthel)
  → 265
Wenzel, F. → 150
Werner, B. → 310
Westermayer, V. → 204
Wetter, von, A. → 251
Whitaker, (MLTW / Moore, Lyndon,
  Turnbull) → 276, 293
Wicker, W., KG → 243
Widmann, S. → 318
Wiedemann, J. → 204
Wiegand, T. → 55
Winter, W. → 74, 233, 244
Wirkkala, T. → 11
Wirsing, W. and G. → 343
Wise, C. (O. Arup & Partners) → 183
Wolf, S. → 307
Woodburn, (Choukalos, McKenzie,
  Maranda Ltd) → 184
Wörndl, H.-P. → 277, 292
Würzburg Tax Office, Building Department
  → 236

Yelin, (Beck, Enz) → 356
Yoshida, A. → 217
Yoshida, T. → 341
Yoshino, S. → 252

Zeitler, H.-J. → 195
Zeitter, H. → 68, 71
Zimmer, B. → 47
Zimperlich, I. → 191
Zufferey, A. → 197
Zumthor, P. → 274, 279

Zweifel, J., (+ Leins, W.) → 153
Zwerch → 231

Picture credits

Photographs not specifically acknowledged were supplied from the archives of the architects named in the "Index of architects and engineers", or from the archives of the journal DETAIL.

Part 1
Cultural dimensions

Tradition and variety

A Century of Chair Design;
    Verlag Rizzoli, N.Y. (p. 12: 3)
Artec, Helsinki, FIN (p. 12: 1)
Associated Press GmbH,
    Frankfurt/Main, D (p. 23: 10)
Bäckmann, R., Helsinki, FIN (p. 9)
Baumann-Schicht,
    Bad Reichenhall, D (p. 23: 8)
Giraudon, Paris, F (p. 20: 4)
Herzog-Loibl, V., Munich, D (p. 10: 1;
    p. 13: 8, 9; p. 15: 2, 4, 5; p. 16: 4, 5;
    p. 17: 1–3, 5, 6; p. 19: 12; p. 22: 1–3, 5;)
Ishimoto, Y., Tokyo, J (p. 14)
Jordens-Meintker, D.,
    Munich, D (p. 10: 2, 3)
Kaltenbach, F., Munich, D (p. 17: 7;
    p. 20: 3; p. 21: 7)
Luft, G., Felldorf, D (p. 13: 7)
Mani Kupfermann, Zimmerei
    Thusis, CH (p. 23: 9)
Picture archives, Deutsches Museum,
    Munich, D (p. 13: 5)
Picture archives, Munich City
    Museum, D (p. 12: 4)
Pfistermeister, U., Artelshofen, D
    (p. 16: 1, 3)
Presseagentur Novosti,
    Moskau, RUS (p. 16: 2)
Schittich, Ch., Munich, D (p. 15: 3;
    p. 17: 4; p. 20: 2; S .21: 5, 6; p. 23: 7)
Schweitzer, R., Paris, F. (p. 13: 10; p. 15: 1;
    p. 16: 6; p. 18; p. 19: 10, 11, 13–17;
    p. 20: 1; p. 21: 8–10; p. 22: 4)
Träskelin, R., Helsinki, FIN (p. 11; p. 12: 2;
    p. 13: 6)
Tschudi, J., Chur, CH (p. 23: 6)

Wood as a building material –
from the beginnings to the 19th century

p. 24
Traité de l'Art de Bâtir, Jean Rondelet: plate 1

p. 25
after: Die bandkeramische Ansiedlung bei
Köln-Lindenthal, W. Buttler,
W. Halberay: plate 2

after: Kunio Ota, Jômon mémorial,
Utsunomiya: plate 3

Compagnons du Devoir
du Tour de France: plate 4

Traité de l'Art de Bâtir, Jean Rondelet: plate 5

Edifices de Rome moderne,
Paul Letarouilly 1857: plate 6

Etude et reconstitution,
Jean-Pierre Adam: plate 7

Entretien sur l'architecture,
Viollet-le-Duc 1874: plate 8

p. 26
Shelter in Africa ,
Paul Olivier 1971: plate 1, 2, 3

ETH Zürich, Gaudenz Domenig 1980:
plate 4, 5, 6, 7

p. 27
Compagnons du Devoir
du Tour de France: plate 13

Office du Livre de Fribourg,
Teiji Itoh 1983: plate 17

Kura, Teiji Itoh 1973: plate 18

p. 28
Compagnons du Devoir
du Tour de France: plate 1, 2, 3

Documents L.M. Lissenko: plate 4

Der Schweizer Holzstil,
Ernst Gladbach 1897: plate 5, 6

Relevé de
Dominique Chauvelot: plate 7, 8, 9, 10

Le vaisseau de 74 canons,
Jean Boudriot: plate 11, 12, 13

p. 29
Traité de l'art de la charpenterie,
A.R. Emy 1841: plate 1, 2

Traité de l'art de bâtir,
Jean Rondelet: plate 3, 4, 5, 6, 7

after: John Weale 1852: plate 8, 9

Part 2
Fundamentals

Grosser, Dr., Timber Research, Munich
Technical University,D (pp. 34–37)
Heyer, H.-J., Werkstatt für Photographie,
    Stuttgart University, D (p. 38; p. 39
    centre, bottom; p. 40 top, centre;
    p. 42; p. 43 centre, bottom; pp. 44–46)
Michael Wenig AG, D (p. 40 top)
Zeitler, F., Penzberg, D (p. 39 top)

Part 3
Basis for planning

Ege, H., Lucerne, CH (p. 60 centre right)
Eigstler, p., Thun, CH (p. 61 centre)

Part 5
Built examples in detail:
structures

Buchacher Holzleimbau Hermagor, A
    (p. 191)
Eigstler, p., Thun, CH (p. 182)
Halbe, R., Stuttgart, D (p. 183)
Hermagor, A, Buchacher Holzleimbau,
    (p. 193)
Hirschbrunner, U., Aschau, D, (p. 210)
Korn, M. (p. 260)
Krewinkel, H. W., Böblingen, D, (p. 169)
Krupp, B., Freiburg, D (p. 258)
Leenders, P., Niederkrüchten, D (p. 218)
Leiska, H., Hamburg, D (p. 187; p. 203)
Leistner, D., Mainz, D (p. 181; p. 245;
    p. 261 centre, bottom)
Müller-Naumann, p., Munich, D, (p. 158)
Neubert, p., Munich, D, (p. 161; p. 184)
Scheffler, G., Frankfurt a. M., D (p. 174)
Schneider, R., D (p. 261 top)
Shabo, N., Hiroshima, J (p. 219)
Soyland, J. E., Oslo, N (p. 185)
Stahl, H., Cologne, D (p. 172)
Studio Sfriso, Camucia di Cortona, I (p. 216)
Tschudy, J., Chur, CH (p. 170)
Zeitler, F. Penzberg, D (p. 227)

Part 6
Built examples in detail: facades

The diversity of the modern age

Blunck, R., Tübingen, D (p. 277: 3; p. 278: 1)
Busam, F., Architekturphoto, Düsseldorf, D
    (p. 277: 2, 5)
Ege, H., Luzern, CH (p. 278: 3)
Freeman, M., London, UK (p. 276: 1)
Geleta & Geleta, Budapest, H
    (p. 273: 3, 4)
Herzog-Loibl, V., Munich , D (p. 273: 1;
    p. 274: 2, 4)
Hiruta, K., Tokyo, J (p. 285: 4, 5)
Kaltenbach, F., Munich, D (p. 279: 2, 3)
Kamaya, M., Odate, J (p. 287: 7, 8)
Leistner, D., Mainz, D (p. 281, p. 284),
Lindhe, J., Copenhagen, DK (p. 286: 4)
Müller-Naumann, p., Munich, D
    (p. 286: 1)
Ott, P., Graz, A (p. 277: 1, 4)
Richters, Christian, Münster, D (p. 279: 1,
    4; p.286: 2, 3)
Schenkirz, R., Leonberg, D (p. 280)
Schink, H.-C., Leipzig, D (p. 247)
Schlupp, H., Düsseldorf, D (p. 285: 3)
Schranz, M., Aldrans, A (p. 278: 2)
Schweitzer, R., Paris, F. (p. 275: 1,2)
Sessner, P., Munich, D (p. 288: 12)
Shinkenchiku-Sha, Tokyo, J (p. 276: 2, 3;
    p. 285: 6, 7)
Strauß, D., Besigheim, D (p. 287: 5, 6)

Van der Vlugt & Claus, Amsterdam, NL
    (p. 273: 2)
Waki, T., Shokokusha, Tokio, J (p. 287: 9)
Wessely, H., Munich, D (p. 274: 3)
Wimmer, F., Munich, D (p. 276)

Examples of facades

Blunck, R., Tübingen, D (p. 344; p. 317)
Bonfig, P., Munich, D (p. 352)
Busam, F., Architekturphoto,
    Dusseldorf, D (p. 301)
Ege, H., Lucerne, CH (p. 351)
Feiner, R., Malans, CH (p. 299; p. 310)
Freeman, Michael, London, GB (p. 296)
Gardin, G. B., Genua, I (p. 360)
Gonçalves, M., (p. 296)
Helfenstein, Heinrich, Adliswil, CH (p. 345)
Huttunen, Marko, Lahti, FIN (p. 296)
Jantscher, Thomas, Colombier, CH (p. 306)
Kandzia, Chr., Esslingen, D (p. 346)
Korn, Moritz (Artur), Cologne, D (p. 355 left)
Leistner, D., (Artur), Cologne, D (p. 355
right; p. 359)
Lüttge, Th., Ascholding, D (p. 313; p. 318)
Mikio Kamaya, Odate, J (p. 361)
Monthiers, J.-M., Paris, F (p. 357)
Müller-Naumann, Stefan, Munich, D
    (p. 297; p. 320)
Myrzik, Ulrike, Munich, D (p. 314)
Neubert, p., Munich, D (p. 342; p. 343)
Ott, Paul, Graz, A (p. 292)
Richters, Christian, Münster, D (p. 336;
    p. 347; p. 354)
Rodermeier, H., Cologne, D (p. 322)
Roth, Lukas, Cologne, D (p. 298)
Schranz, Martin, Aldrans, A (p. 350)
Shinkenchiku-cha, Tokyo, J (p. 338)
Spitta, W, Zeitlarn, D (p. 326)
Strauß, Dietmar, Besigheim, D (p. 353)
Tohru Waki, Shokoshuka, Tokyo, J,
    (p. 341; p.361 centre top)
Wimmer, Franz, Munich, D (p. 348)